OTHER A TO Z GUIDES FROM
THE SCARECROW PRESS, INC.

The A to Z of
African-American
Television

Kathleen Fearn-Banks

The A to Z Guide Series, No. 49

The Scarecrow Press, Inc.
Lanham, Maryland • Toronto • Plymouth, UK
2009

Published by Scarecrow Press, Inc.
A wholly owned subsidiary of
The Rowman & Littlefield Publishing Group, Inc.
4501 Forbes Boulevard, Suite 200, Lanham, Maryland 20706
http://www.scarecrowpress.com

Estover Road, Plymouth PL6 7PY, United Kingdom

British Library Cataloguing in Publication Information Available

Library of Congress Cataloging-in-Publication Data

The hardback version of this book was cataloged by the Library of Congress as
follows:

Fearn-Banks, Kathleen.
  Historical dictionary of African-American television / Kathleen Fearn-Banks.
    p. cm. — (Historical dictionaries of literature and the arts ; no. 7)
  Includes bibliographical references.
    1. African Americans on television—Dictionaries. 2. African Americans in
  television broadcasting—Biograph—Dictionaries. I. Title. II. Series.
  PN1992.8.A34F43 2006
  791.43'089'96073—dc22   2005016899

ISBN 978-0-8108-6832-8 (pbk. : alk. paper)
ISBN 978-0-8108-6348-4 (ebook)

∞™ The paper used in this publication meets the minimum requirements of
American National Standard for Information Sciences—Permanence of Paper
for Printed Library Materials, ANSI/NISO Z39.48-1992.

Printed in the United States of America

Contents

Editor's Foreword

Looking back, African-American television has come a rather long way in a relatively short time, although every step forward seemed to take forever at the time. In the early days, when the medium was young, this particular branch of it was afflicted by tokenism in every sense. There were only token actors (and not even token producers, directors, and other personnel), there were only token roles in shows with otherwise white casts, and the roles and shows gave a very partial and highly skewed view of the realities of African-American life.

Half a century later, most noticeably, there are thousands of actors—some of them big stars—and similar numbers in every other position in the industry as well as African-American production companies and networks. The roles have spread from domestic to president, including everything in between, and they have become distinctly less stereotyped and more real. And programs that focus on African-American realities look at every possible aspect, whether the indignity of slavery or the trials and tribulations of running a family, and take on every possible genre: comedy and tragedy, home drama and melodrama, pop music and opera, documentaries and news programs, talk shows and sitcoms.

The A to Z of African-American Television provides amazingly broad coverage in various ways. The chronology traces the progress made over the past half century, showing what happened and when. But the introduction gives a feel for just how slow that progress seemed then and how many efforts had to be made to reach the present situation. Inevitably, the most popular section will be the dictionary, which reflects both the work of the pioneers and more recent achievements and shows the profusion of talent that was generated, the actors, singers, dancers, and rest of the cast. Numerous other entries present the programs, not only the long-running series but many specials as well, and these in all the genres just mentioned and more. There are also general entries on occupations, gender, and stereotypes. The appendixes on rankings, ratings, and Emmy Awards will doubtlessly interest many, and the bibliography will help those most interested in locating further reading on specific subjects.

This book was written by Kathleen Fearn-Banks, who has had a rather intriguing career. Initially, she worked for 21 years as a publicist and publicity manager for the NBC-TV network, which produced many of the breakthrough African-American programs, so she knows how the industry operates and has also gotten to know many of the leading figures in it. She still writes occasionally for *Emmy Magazine* and participates in Emmy Award judging panels. But since 1990, she has been a professor at the Department of Communication of the University of Washington in Seattle.

Her specialization is crisis communications, on which she has also written books and articles, and her courses must have been rather special since she was singled out as teacher of the year twice. Now, on top of everything else, she is the principal of The Write Woman Public Relations Agency. This multifaceted career has allowed Professor Fearn-Banks to know African-American television from within, and also to see it more objectively from without and thus be able to convey its story in an informative and also lively manner.

Jon Woronoff
Series Editor

Preface

The A to Z of African-American Television lists in alphabetical order African-American actors and performers with starring, regular, or key roles in nationally aired television series, made-for-television motion pictures, and miniseries. It also lists key productions with African-American casts or African-American themes in all the genres. In the area of news and sports, news anchors and reporters on network broadcasts are listed as well as broadcasts, including documentaries, with African-American themes. The dictionary covers the period spanning from the beginning of national television through early 2005.

We could not possibly list every African-American actor in every show or every broadcast journalist or sportscaster and every production in which they were seen. However, an effort has been made to cover as many of the performing artists and productions as possible in the predetermined length of the volume. It should be noted that the appearance of a black actor or entertainer in any television show was big news in the 1950s and 1960s and was noteworthy in the 1970s. From the 1980s on, the numbers of black actors increased to the point that merely having a black person on the show, either as a regular or a guest star, did not make the show significant in African-American television history.

The actors, entertainers, and broadcast journalists listed are persons of African descent working in U.S. television. No effort has been made to determine citizenship or nationality of persons listed. Similarly, no effort was made to determine whether a performer was partly black; persons listed are widely considered to be black. Though longtime headline entertainer Carol Channing revealed in her 2002 autobiography that she is "part African American," she is not included in the dictionary because she was considered a white entertainer by television casting professionals as well as viewers throughout her stellar career.

The A to Z of African-American Television does not list producers, directors, and other behind-the-camera personnel. This in no way insinuates that they are not important, even crucial, to television programs. However, because of space, a limit had to be made. Some are mentioned in program listings and others in captions of photographs.

Also, we want to emphasize that African Americans are not a monolithic body with identical attitudes, feelings, and opinions. The very show that one person may hate may be the favorite of another. The show that offends one may be groundbreaking, cutting-edge, to another. This division is more extreme in the new millennium than was the case when television was born. Education, age, maturity, socioeconomic status, exposure to the arts and literature, literacy levels, and the disappearance of borders in the so-called black community, and other influences affect each black person's critique of television and television programs. We have attempted to include shows and subjects relevant to the various subgroups of African Americans.

The word "black" is often used to refer to African Americans and African-American shows partly because when there is a space limitation, the term "African American" is too long and partly because the author prefers the term "black" to refer to people of black African descent in contrast to white African Americans.

Each listing of a performer is in bold followed by a list of credits. Each listing of a show is in uppercase and bold, followed by the network abbreviation, the date or dates the show aired, and information about the show.

In the body of the listings, names in bold are listed in alphabetical order in the dictionary. Titles of shows are listed in italics; if they are in boldface, they are listed elsewhere in the dictionary, also in alphabetical order.

In addition, the following subjects are included: African-American audiences; African-American History Month; animation; anthology series; athletes' biopics; biopics; biracial characters; boxing matches on television; broadway plays and musicals; child TV actors/performers who maintained success as adults in show business; courtroom reality series; documentaries; domestic workers in the 1950s; domestic workers in the 1960s; domestic workers in the 1970s; domestic workers in the 1980s; domestic workers in the 1990s; domestic workers' names; drama series; family series; gender and television; historical events dramatized; interracial romances/relationships; jobs in the television industry; long-running series; movie stars whose careers began on TV series; music veejays; music video; news on television; occupations of TV characters; rappers turned TV actors; reality television; series about school life; series with one black supporting actor/performer before 1980; sitcoms; skin color of actors; spin-off series; stereotypes; talk shows; television pioneers; variety series; variety specials.

Acknowledgments

I thank all the actors, producers, directors, and other professionals in the television industry who offered their opinions and memories, particularly Howard Bingham, Diahann Carroll, Bernie Casey, Ivan Dixon, Robert Guillaume, Lynn Hamilton, Temple Hatton, Robert Hooks, Jayne Kennedy-Overton, Joseph Marcell, Denise Nicholas, Juanita Moore, Brock Peters, Kristoff St. John, Justin Schutz, Oz Scott, Jack Smith, Hal Williams, Cal Wilson, and Aldore Collier and his staff in the west coast offices of Johnson Publications.

I appreciate my proofreading family and friends Albert Sampson, Dr. Kayte M. Fearn, Agnes Marsh, and Charlette Hunt, and I am grateful for their memories too. I owe a debt of gratitude to the Academy of Television Arts and Sciences and particularly Sarah Guyton, John Leverence, and Hank Rieger. I thank Brian Robinette at NBC, Aldore Collier at Johnson Publishing Company, Mary Ryan at Wordcrafters Northwest, and Billie J. Green of the Beverly Hills/Hollywood Branch of the NAACP. Randy Lewis and his staff at McDowell's U-Frame-It in Seattle were very helpful in unframing and reframing personal photographs used in the book. Without Jeremy Fearn and Dr. Lou Falk, I would know nothing about the *Star Trek* series. Dr. Marilyn Kern-Foxworth provided important resources. Chas Floyd Johnson and Anne Burford-Johnson were also great resources.

I especially thank doctoral candidate April Peterson, my graduate research assistant at the University of Washington Department of Communication; the department chair, Gerald Baldasty; and the office manager, Nancy Dossman, and her staff. University of Washington Reference Librarian Jessica Albano taught undergraduate research assistants to find information not necessarily on the Internet.

These undergrads in CMU 499 Directed Research, over a two-year period, are also appreciated: Desiree Antoine, Grace Bai, Gemma Barajas,

xv

Lian Chan, Yvonne Chandler, Cherron Davis, Kellen Davison, Christin Evans, Adrian Eyre, Yolanta Femiak, Alex French, Felicia Fuller, Julianne Gallion, Jenny Gregorak, William Haugen, Deborah Henry, Fiona Ho, Kristin Hodges, Brooke Jones, Sarah Keller, Kaylynn Kelley, Joanna Kham, Julie Kim, Wan Hsuan Lee, Adam Lile, Jennifer Liu, Daneille Ludwigsen, Ryan Madayag, Heather Maggio, Tiffany McIntosh, Valerie Moses, Ashley North, Ashley Petty, Isaac Phillips, Andrew Potter, Andrew Ralston, Diana Roe, Sonny Rosenthal, Beth Ruhwedel, Jen Sandburg, Maria Santos, Jamie Scatena, Daniel Schwalbe, Un Sin, Christian St. Jacques, Rochelle Tate, Gena Stallings, Christopher Sylvia, Peter Trueblood, Andrew Waits, Anthony Walters, David Webb, and Jessica Wible.

Acronyms and Abbreviations

A&E   **Arts and Entertainment Channel**. Launched in 1984, A&E, a cable channel, consisted largely of cultural programs, documentaries, and other informational programs. Its *Biography* series was highly rated and featured numerous African-American celebrities.

ABC   **American Broadcasting Company**. The youngest of the "big three" networks began programming as a network in 1948. Its first program with a black star or cast was *The Southernaires*, a black gospel-singing quartet, which had a 15-minute show on Sunday nights at 7:30 beginning September 19, 1948, and ending two months later.

BET   **Black Entertainment Television**. The formerly black-owned cable channel was launched in 1980 and featured programming about black life. Early programming featured black cast movies and musical shorts from the 1930s and 1940s. Later, popular videos were the principal fare. *See listing for* BLACK ENTERTAINMENT TELEVISION.

BIOPICS   **Biographical Pictures**. Dramatized stories of the lives of notable persons.

CBS   **Columbia Broadcasting System** and **CBS, Inc.** One of the original "big three" networks, it began in 1927 in radio broadcasting. Its first program with a black star or cast was *Amos 'n' Andy*, which made its debut in 1951 and continued under fire from black viewers until 1953. The series began on CBS radio with white stars playing the principal black characters.

COM **Comedy Central**, also the **Comedy Channel**. A basic-cable network that started in 1991 with the merger of The Comedy Channel and HA! Its programming began with stand-up comedy routines and sitcom reruns.

CNBC **Consumer News and Business Channel**. This 24-hour basic-cable network launched by NBC in 1989.

CNN **Cable News Network**. Founded by Ted Turner in 1980; shortly thereafter, it broadcast news all over the world by satellite. It changed the face of breaking news and also includes CNN/SI, the sports arm.

CTV **Courtroom Television Network**. Launched in 1991, Court TV carried live high-profile court trials and analyses. It attracted much attendance in 1995 with the O. J. Simpson murder trial. In prime time, it aired documentary or reality series like *Forensics Files* and *The System* as well as crime drama reruns like *NYPD Blue* and *Wiseguy*.

CTW **Children's Television Workshop**. Founded in 1967 to produce *Sesame Street*. The workshop received federal grants and funds from private foundations.

DIS **The Disney Channel**. Cable network founded in 1983 to provide wholesome family programming, primarily but not exclusively for children. Along with cartoons and reruns, among its original programs were *The Famous Jett Jackson* and *That's So Raven*.

DRAMEDY Series that is comedy and drama with actors playing regular roles.

DUM DuMont was almost the third network and began programming in the 1940s, but it had difficulty getting the best stations in each city: NBC and CBS (and eventually ABC) were too strong. The other three had radio networks; DuMont did not. It also had trouble keeping talent; the others would steal successful talent from DuMont. As for series starring blacks, DuMont's musical show *Hazel Scott*, starring the singer/pianist, made its debut as a summer music show on July 3, 1950, and ran for nearly three months. DuMont was off the air by 1955.

ESPN
Entertainment and Sports Programming Network. Founded in 1979, the 24-hour, all-sports cable channel is seen in more than 20 languages all over the world and covers more than 65 sports, including some off-beat sports, like sailboat racing. ESPN had four cable channels. Its success is being challenged by Fox Sports Net and CNN/SI.

FAM
The ABC Family Channel. A cable channel, the Family Channel was launched in 1977 as CBN, the Christian Broadcasting Network, by founder Pat Robertson. Its programming was primarily religious, then it expanded to wholesome family programs, essentially reruns. Its original programming consisted of sitcoms and light-action shows that stressed values and courage. The channel was sold several times and eventually came to be called the ABC Family Channel.

FOX
Fox Broadcasting Company. The fourth network was introduced in 1986 and was owned by Rupert Murdoch and Barry Diller. Murdoch also owned 20th Century Fox Studios; thus, the new network was also named Fox. It started with a limited prime-time schedule and set its goal to appeal to a youthful audience. In 1987, **Arsenio Hall** hosted *The Late Show* on Fox after the departure of Joan Rivers. Fox scheduled its fall premiere shows in August so that viewers would tune out reruns of the other network series and become fans of Fox's new series before the big three launched their new seasons in September.

FSN
Fox Sports Net. A consortium of 22 regional cable sports networks, a competitor to ESPN and CNN/SI.

HBO
Home Box Office. A pay cable channel, it was founded in the early 1970s. It later dominates the TV-movie genre.

LIF
Lifetime. The cable channel was launched in 1984 and offered programs specifically for female viewers. Programming has been varied—original films, talk shows, drama series, game shows, as well as reruns of relevant series. Other subsidiary networks are Lifetime

Movie Network (all films) and Lifetime Real Women (reality programs).

MINISERIES   Literally, a short television series but actually a TV film longer than two hours. Miniseries are usually four or six hours but may be much longer. For example, *Roots* was 12 hours.

MTV   **Music Television.** The cable channel was founded in 1981 and featured, at first, an entire programming schedule of rock music videos. Its marketing campaign echoed the requests of teens ("I want my MTV") and was largely responsible for the increase in subscriptions to cable television. As years passed, the channel departed from all videos to some original programming, most notably *The Real World*, *Beavis and Butt-Head*, the *MTV Video Music Awards*, and the *MTV Movie Awards*. MTV spawned VH-1.

NAACP   Formerly the abbreviation for **National Association for the Advancement of Colored People**, NAACP has become the organization's formal name. The organization was formed in 1910 to battle in courts and other areas of life for the civil rights of black people. The organization is known primarily by its abbreviation since the term "colored people" is not currently politically correct.

NBC   **National Broadcasting Company.** One of the "big three" networks, it was inaugurated in 1926 as the first national network. Originally, its purpose was to sell radios and televisions for its principal owner, RCA. Its first series with a black cast or black star was *The Nat King Cole Show*, which premiered on November 5, 1956, and was kept on the air despite problems with sponsors until December 1957.

NIK   **Nickelodeon.** The cable network, often called Nick, is devoted during the early daytime hours to young children. Late afternoon programming is designed for older kids, and late night Nick at Night features classic sitcoms ostensibly for baby boomers. Nick Too on many cable stations features the same shows as Nick at different times. The network spawned TV Land, a cable channel of reruns of drama and variety series as well as sitcoms.

OXY **Oxygen Network**. Launched in 2000, this women's network was founded to compete with Lifetime offering programs for a female audience. **Oprah Winfrey** was one of the backers and one of her shows, *Oprah after the Show*, was aired.

PBS **Public Broadcasting Service**. Originally called Educational Television, it began in 1952 and became public television after the passage of the Public Broadcasting Act of 1967. It operated without commercials and was funded by federal and state funds as well as grants from foundations, corporations, and individual subscribers. Consequently, productions are often low budget compared to commercial networks. It is respected for quality cultural, informational, news, and educational programs.

SHO **Showtime**. A pay/premium cable channel, it was launched in 1978. In addition to showing feature films, it produces some specials and series. Among its shows were *Jeremiah*, *Linc's*, and *Soul Food*. Also, concerts of stand-up comics are often aired.

SITCOM **Situation comedy**. Half-hour series written to make viewers laugh and featuring actors playing the same characters in each episode. Most sitcoms have a laugh track designed to encourage laughter in the right places.

SPECIAL A one-time airing of a variety show featuring musical acts and/or comedy, dance, and other performances.

SYN **Syndicated**. These television programs are bartered to local stations that may run them according to their own desires. They are generally less expensive than network programs. At one time, syndicated shows ran from 4:30 to 8:00 P.M., just before network hours. However, as more and more local stations and cable stations were born, more programs were needed to fill programming schedules.

TBS   **Turner Broadcasting System.** A basic-cable service that produces news and entertainment around the world.

TNT   **Turner Network Television.** The 24-hour advertiser-supported basic-cable network's programming centers on original films, broadcast premieres, one-hour drama, reruns, and some sports coverage.

TV1   **TV One.** The cable network aimed at black viewers was launched on Martin Luther King's birthday, January 19, 2004. Its programming includes original programming, reruns of black-cast or black-themed sitcoms, drama series, reality programs, and syndicated programs. *See listing for* TV ONE.

UPN   **United Paramount Network.** The cable network was launched in 1995 and was a joint venture of Paramount Studios and Chris-Craft Industries' United Television group. Each controlled half of the network. In 2000, Viacom bought out Chris Craft to gain 100 percent control. Viacom then dropped the United from its name and became officially known as "UPN." UPN is on the air five days a week from 8:00 to 10:00 P.M. Its key launch show was *Star Trek: Voyager*, which led to *Star Trek: Enterprise*. The programming consisted of sitcoms, one-hour dramas, and WWF Wrestling and is geared to adults ages 18 to 34.

USA   **USA Network.** The cable TV network was organized in 1977 as the Madison Square Garden Network and was one of the first national channels to use satellite delivery instead of traditional television broadcasting. The name was changed in 1980. It shows both original and rerun programs, including movies and syndicated television series, and also has some sports coverage. Its hit detective series *Monk* made it one of the major networks.

VH1   **VH1.** A cable channel from parent MTV, it was launched in 1985. Popular programs on VH1 are the musical specials, particularly the Divas, featuring popular female recording artists.

WB **Warner Bros. Television.** A cable channel begun in 1994, it airs original sitcoms and dramas during prime time Sundays through Fridays and children's programs (KidsWB!) on weekday afternoons and Sunday mornings.

Chronology

1923   For the first time, radio programs are aired at the same time in different cities making a network and thereby setting a precedent for television. David Sarnoff, of RCA (Radio Corporation of America), predicted, "I believe that television, which is the technical name for seeing as well as hearing by radio, will come to pass in due course."

1926   RCA inaugurates its subsidiary, NBC, as the first television network.

1927   CBS (Columbia Broadcasting System) is launched by owner William Paley.

1928   A television drama titled *The Queen's Messenger* is broadcast in Schenectady, New York; it was experimental programming to only several hundred.

1935   The Nielsen ratings begin for radio audiences.

1938   Five manufacturers have television sets being sold even though programming is sporadic and lacking in technical quality.

1939   *The Ethel Waters Show*, also an experiment, is broadcast by NBC. It featured dramatic scenes, comedy, and lectures and was probably the first black-cast TV show. Franklin D. Roosevelt, at the New York World's Fair, becomes the first U.S. president to appear on television.

1940   RCA gets permission from the Federal Communications Commission (FCC) to broadcast commercial television and warns viewers that television sets on the market might not meet standards developed in the future.

1942   The advancement of television is halted by World War II.

1946   DuMont, a small network, makes its debut and broadcasts some programs only in New York City during the war. **19 June:** Gillette becomes the first advertiser to sponsor a TV network show, on NBC, when Joe Louis defended his title again Billy Conn.

1947 **20 November:** *Meet The Press*, a former radio public affairs show, makes its debut on NBC and survives into the 21st century.

1948 ABC (American Broadcasting Company) begins programming. **20 June:** *The Toast of the Town* (later called *The Ed Sullivan Show*), a variety series, premieres on CBS and has numerous popular black entertainers over the years. Lena Horne was among the entertainers who made their television debut on this series. **19 September:** *The Southernaires*, a black male gospel quartet, has a show briefly on ABC. The cost of five- to seven-inch television sets ranges from $375 to $500. Fewer than 2 percent of U.S. homes have a television set.

1949 For the first time, television sets are sold through the Sears Roebuck catalog; the price is $149.95. The first Emmy Awards are presented in New York. **13 September:** *Sugar Hill Times*, a musical variety series starring Harry Belafonte (then spelled Bellafonte), Willie Bryant, and Timmie Rogers, runs for a month on CBS.

1950 **3 July:** *The Hazel Scott Show*, starring the black singer/pianist, airs on DuMont for about three months. **3 October:** *Beulah* premieres on ABC with Ethel Waters playing Beulah, the maid. **21 October:** *Life with the Erwins* (later titled *Trouble with Father* and *The Stu Erwin Show*) makes its debut with Willie Best as a regular cast member playing Willie the handyman. **28 October:** *The Jack Benny Show*, also a radio hit, premieres on CBS with Eddie Anderson playing Benny's valet, Rochester. ABC begins children's programming on Saturday mornings. Nearly four million households have television sets; an increase in sales has lowered the price to about $200.

1951 **4 September:** A new coaxial cable carries the first transcontinental U.S. television broadcast. **28 June:** *Amos 'n' Andy*, popular on radio with white actors playing the lead black characters, premieres on CBS with an all-black cast. The NAACP, convening in Atlanta, immediately protests stereotypical depictions.

1952 *Amos 'n' Andy* finishes its first season as the 13th most popular television series on all networks. Louise Beavers replaces Ethel

Waters as the title character on *Beulah*. Child singer Leslie Uggams performs on *Arthur Godfrey's Talent Scouts*. **14 January:** *The Today Show* premieres on NBC. The Republican and Democratic conventions air in their entirety nationally for the first time.

1953 *Amos 'n' Andy* finishes its second season as the 25th most popular television series, but it is canceled because of pressure from the NAACP and other protest groups. Gladys Knight makes her TV debut as a child contestant on *Ted Mack's Amateur Hour*. **20 January:** The inauguration of the president (Dwight Eisenhower) is televised for the first time. **19 March:** The first telecast of the Academy Awards airs. Hattie McDaniel had won the Best Supporting Actress Oscar 13 years before the first telecast. It would be ten years before Sidney Poitier would win for Best Actor. *Make Room for Daddy* (later titled *The Danny Thomas Show*) premieres with Louise Beavers as a regular cast member playing the family maid. *Beulah* is canceled. Eighty percent of network shows are live performances. As television grows in popularity, 25 percent of motion picture theaters are closed.

1955 DuMont perishes. Anthology series air numerous dramas with black actors and casts including *A Man Is Ten Feet Tall* with Sidney Poitier, *The Emperor Jones* with Ossie Davis, and *Toward Tomorrow* and *D.P.*, both with James Edwards. There were not as many the year before or the year after. Amanda Randolph takes the role of the maid on *Make Room for Daddy*. Gloria Lockerman, a 13-year-old Maryland girl spells, "antidisestablishmentarianism" on *The $64,000 Question*. Leontyne Price is the first black performer in a televised opera; she starred in *Tosca*.

1956 **5 November:** *The Nat King Cole Show*, a musical variety series, premieres on NBC. NBC keeps the show on despite the fact that no sponsor would take it and southern affiliate stations would not run it.

1957 **24 September:** News cameras cover the integration of a high school in Little Rock, Arkansas, as President Eisenhower sends in troops to keep peace. *The Nat King Cole Show* is canceled. *American Bandstand* makes its debut from Philadelphia: black recording artists make appearances, but it is much later that black teenagers are chosen to be dancers in the studio.

1958 Investigations show that TV quiz shows have been rigged; some contestants had been given answers, and thereby viewers were misled. About 20 quiz shows are ended.

1959 *Bonanza* on NBC is the first prime-time network series broadcast in color on a regular basis. The Television Information Office is founded to improve the image of television after the quiz show scandals.

1960 Harry Belafonte is the first black to win the Emmy Award. Nearly 46 million households have at least one television set.

1961 FCC chairman Newton Minnow, in a speech to the National Association of Broadcasters, said, "I invite you to sit down in front of your television set when your station goes on the air and stay there without a book, magazine, newspaper, profit-and-loss sheet or rating book to distract you—and keep your eyes glued to that set until the station signs off. I can assure you that you will observe a vast wasteland."

1962 Mal Goode joins ABC as a network news correspondent. **1 October:** Johnny Carson begins hosting *The Tonight Show* from New York (Steve Allen and Jack Paar had hosted previously). Networks start programming documentaries to repair their images after the quiz show scandals; 253 hours of documentaries air.

1963 Bill Matney joins NBC as a network news correspondent. **13 April:** Sidney Poitier is the first black actor to win the Best Actor Oscar (for *Lilies of the Field*) at the Academy Awards telecast. **28 August:** The March on Washington is the top news story. **2 September:** CBS News airs a three-hour program on civil rights. **23 September:** Cicely Tyson is the first black woman with a key role in a drama series; she was Jane in *East Side, West Side*, which ran for a year. **22 November:** The assassination of President John F. Kennedy, the **(24 November)** murder of suspect Lee Harvey Oswald, and the **(25 November)** funeral and burial of the president are the subjects of continuous news coverage, preempting regular programming. An estimated 93 percent of homes were tuned to the burial; televisions were on for an average of 13 hours that day. Many consider the coverage television's finest hour. News coverage strives to top itself by being present for all news events.

1964 Tap dancer Art Duncan joins the cast of *The Lawrence Welk Show*. The drama series *Profiles in Courage*, based on the book by President John F. Kennedy, airs; one episode centers on a black American, Frederick Douglass.

1965 **11–16 August:** The Watts riots in Los Angeles, the first of several big-city riots, are broadcast nationally. **15 September:** *I Spy* premieres with Bill Cosby starring. **17 September:** *Hogan's Heroes* premieres with Ivan Dixon as a regular cast member.

1966 The following series with black cast members make their debut: *Daktari*, *Star Trek*, and *Mission Impossible*. Bill Cosby is the second black person to win the Emmy Award (for *I Spy*). It was the first of four consecutive Emmy wins for Cosby.

1967 **15 January:** The first Super Bowl game is played. The following series with black casts make their debut: *Mannix*, *High Chaparral*, and *Ironside*. President Lyndon B. Johnson signs the Public Broadcasting Act, paving the way for the Corporation for Public Broadcasting. *The Tony Awards* are first telecast nationally; the ceremony was shown to a New York audience as early as 1956 on the DuMont channel.

1968 **4 April:** The Rev. Dr. Martin Luther King Jr. is assassinated in Memphis and is the subject of extensive news coverage all over the world. **9 April:** Harry Belafonte is a guest on the special *Petula*, and many viewers objected strongly by phone when star Petula Clark touches Belafonte's arm. **5 June:** Senator Robert Kennedy, campaigning for the U.S. presidency, is assassinated in Los Angeles. Sports stars Rafer Johnson and Roosevelt Grier are in his entourage and try to aid him. **17 September:** *Julia* premieres on NBC with Diahann Carroll starring, the first sitcom with a black actress in the most important role. **23 September:** Otis Young is the first black actor to star in a TV western (*The Outcasts*). **16 October:** At the Olympic Games in Mexico City, winning sprinters Tommie Smith and John Carlos hold up black-gloved hands in protest to U.S. discriminations. *Black Journal*, a public affairs program, begins on PBS. In this year, there is at least one black actor/performer on network television each night.

1969   **17 September:** *Room 222*, a school drama with an interracial cast, premieres; it wins an Emmy Award for Outstanding New Series. **28 September:** *The Leslie Uggams Show*, a musical variety series, airs for almost three months. **September:** *The Bill Cosby Special* wins the Emmy Award as Outstanding Music or Variety Program. **Fall:** *Sesame Street* premieres.

1970   **21 February:** The Jackson 5 make their television debut on *American Bandstand*. **17 September:** *The Flip Wilson Show* makes its debut on NBC; it is the first successful variety series with a black star. *Black Journal* becomes *Tony Brown's Journal*, named for its host and executive producer. Cigarette advertising on television is banned by Congress. Networks ban cigarettes in their print advertising and publicity. The FCC limits networks to three hours nightly, making a way for syndicated programming.

1971   **12 January:** Norman Lear's *All in the Family* makes its debut with the disclaimer warning that the series "seeks to throw a humorous spotlight on our frailties, prejudices, and concerns. By making them a source of laughter we hope to show—in a mature fashion—just how absurd they are." The show was successful and ended the season as the number one show on all networks. *The Flip Wilson Show* was number two. **14 March:** The Grammy Awards are telecast for the first time. **30 November:** *Brian's Song*, a TV film starring Billy Dee Williams, airs and is a ratings and critical success. The U.S. surgeon general issues the report "Television and Growing Up: The Impact of Televised Violence." *The Electric Company* begins airing. *Soul Train*, a teenage dance program with recording artists, the first nationally syndicated television show sponsored by a black business (Johnson Products, Inc.), begins in Chicago and goes national.

1972   *The Tonight Show with Johnny Carson* moves to Burbank, California. Home Box Office (HBO) begins service.

1973   **February:** The earliest reality surveillance show, *An American Family*—which traced the lives of members of the Loud family of Santa Barbara, California—airs, and viewers watch the family disintegrate.

1974 **January:** Cicely Tyson stars in *The Autobiography of Miss Jane Pittman* and earns two Emmy Awards; the production also earns the Emmy. **1 February:** *Good Times* makes its debut on CBS, the first black-cast sitcom about a family with a mother and father. More Americans get their news from television than newspapers, according to a Roper poll.

1975 **18 January:** *The Jeffersons* makes its debut on CBS; it is the first black-cast sitcom about wealthy people and also the first with an interracial couple. The show becomes the longest-running black-cast sitcom. **11 October:** *Saturday Night Live* premieres with Garrett Morris in the cast. Networks must air programs from 8:00 to 9:00 P.M. for the family hour; only shows without violence and sex can be aired. The first home video-cassette recorder, Sony's Betamax, is introduced at $1,300.

1977 **23–30 January:** The miniseries *Roots* dramatizing Alex Haley's novel about several generations of a black family dating back to slavery airs for 12 hours on eight consecutive nights and reaches an unprecedented audience of 36.3 million households. *TV Guide* is the most popular magazine in the United States with a circulation of 20 million.

1978 Max Robinson cohosts ABC's *World News Tonight* and is the first black network news anchor. On PBS, Charlayne Hunter-Gault joins the two-year-old *MacNeil-Lehrer Report*. TV news cameraman Bob Brown, an African American, is killed in an attack by followers of the Rev. Jim Jones along with Congressman Leo Ryan and others who were investigating the lives of Jones's followers. Most of the religious followers, a large percentage African Americans, were forced to commit suicide.

1979 There are an estimated 79.3 million black-and-white television sets and 71.3 million color sets in use in the United States.

1980 Black Entertainment Network (BET), The Movie Channel, and Cable News Network (CNN) are launched. BET is the first black-owned (Robert L. Johnson) cable television channel. Bernard Shaw is CNN's first news anchor. **6 July:** Pope John Paul advises that television and radio may manipulate the human mind.

1981 Eddie Murphy joins the cast of *Saturday Night Live* after Garrett Morris departs. By the end of this year, two million home videotape recorders are sold. **13 September:** Isabel Sanford is the first black to win the Emmy for Outstanding Lead Actress in a Comedy.

1982 Bryant Gumbel begins hosting *The Today Show.* **10 April:** Eddie Murphy, on *Saturday Night Live*, asks viewers to call in votes on whether "Larry the Lobster" should be boiled alive on network television. More than 426,000 viewers responded to a 900-code number that cost each fifty cents. Larry was not cooked. **Fall:** A strike by pro football players forces networks to find other programming.

1983 Max Robinson resigns from ABC News. **16 May:** *Motown 25: Yesterday, Today and Tomorrow* airs and presents Michael Jackson doing the moonwalk and other Motown stars.

1984 The Arts and Entertainment Channel is launched. The Academy of Television Arts and Sciences Hall of Fame begins honoring individuals for extraordinary contributions to the television industry. **September:** Vanessa Williams, Miss New York, is the first African American to win the Miss America title. **20 September:** *The Cosby Show* debuts and becomes one of the highest-rated sitcoms in television history. It is the only black-cast sitcom to finish a season as the number one show. It was the number one show for five consecutive seasons, 1985–1986, 1986–1987, 1987–1988, 1988–1989, and 1989–1990.

1985 **1 January:** Marvin Gaye's is the first video to be aired on VH1. **22 September:** Robert Guillaume is the first black actor to win the Emmy for Outstanding Lead Actor in a Comedy Series (for *Benson*). *The Cosby Show* is the first black-cast sitcom to win the Emmy for Outstanding Comedy Series.

1986 **8 September:** *The Oprah Winfrey Show* (later titled *Oprah*) makes its debut on syndicated television and becomes the highest-rated daytime talk show in television history. Fox Broadcasting Company is launched. *The Soul Train Awards*, the first awards show honoring black musicians, airs.

1987 **14 September:** The lauded sitcom *Frank's Place* premieres on CBS.

1988 Bryant Gumbel hosts the Summer Olympic Games in Seoul, Korea.

1989 *The Arsenio Hall Show*, the first late night talk series starring a black host, makes its debut.

1990 *In Living Color* premieres with a largely black cast and a black creator-producer, Keenen Ivory Wayans. **14 February:** After more than 27 years, South Africa frees Nelson Mandela from prison and makes news all over the world.

1991 Bill Cosby is inducted into the Academy of Television Arts and Sciences Hall of Fame. Court TV and Comedy Central (aka Comedy Channel) are launched. **3 March:** Rodney King is beaten by officers of the Los Angeles Police Department; police complained that television's repeated airing of the videotaped incident caused a misunderstanding with the public. **6 October:** Controversial congressional hearings are held and televised after U.S. Supreme Court nominee Clarence Thomas is accused of sexual harassment by a former employee, Attorney Anita Hill. **15 October:** The Senate, by a vote of 52 to 48, confirms Clarence Thomas as a U.S. Supreme Court justice.

1992 **29 April:** After four police officers are acquitted of the beating of Rodney King, rioting erupts in Los Angeles.

1993 Oprah Winfrey is inducted into the Academy of Television Arts and Sciences Hall of Fame.

1994 Warner Bros. Television, called the WB, premieres. **11 January:** *The Wayans Brothers* is the WB's first series. **21 March:** Whoopi Goldberg, a previous Oscar winner in the Supporting Actress category, is the first African American to host the Academy Awards telecast. **April:** Nelson Mandela is elected president of South Africa, and the first interracial elections are held there. Also, thousands die in a continuing Rwandan massacre. **17 June:** After a nationally televised "slow auto chase," football star/actor O. J. Simpson is arrested for murdering his wife, Nicole, and her friend Ron Goldman.

1995 The United Paramount Network (UPN) is launched. **3 October:** O. J. Simpson is declared not guilty of murdering his wife and friend after a lengthy televised trial. **16 October:** The Million Man March is held in Washington, D.C.; television estimates several thousand black men attend, but participants say the count was drastically underestimated, as there was no place one could stand and count all the men gathered.

1996 **23 January:** *Moesha* debuts and is UPN's first hit sitcom. **19 July:** Muhammad Ali lights the torch at the opening ceremonies of the Summer Olympics in Atlanta.

1999 **8 January:** A wave of reality shows begins with the immediate popularity of *Who Wants to Be a Millionaire?*

2000 BET is sold to Viacom for nearly $3 billion. Oxygen Network is launched. **31 May:** *Survivor*, a reality show in which contestants are forced to live together on a remote island, makes its debut and begins the craze of reality shows in which one contestant is eliminated by other contestants each week. **June:** *Soul Food*, the TV series based on the film of the same title, airs on Showtime and survives for four years, a record for a black family drama.

2002 **19 March:** Vecepia "Vee" Towery, an African-American office manager from Portland, Oregon, wins *Survivor: Marquesas*.

2003 Ruben Studdard wins *American Idol*.

2004 TV One, a cable network aimed at black viewers, is launched. Fantasia Barrino wins the title on *American Idol*. An African-American couple, Chip and Kim McAllister, take home a million dollars as winners of the reality series *The Amazing Race*.

Introduction

Most African Americans who recall early television will say the first nationwide black-cast TV series they saw was *Amos 'n' Andy*. The controversial situation comedy aired from 1951 to 1953. This was the time when Americans began to buy television "sets." If your family didn't have a DuMont, a Philco, or an RCA, then a friend or a neighbor usually did. And blacks were excited that the TV show had black actors playing the characters; the popular radio show *Amos 'n' Andy* had white actors playing the black characters. The show was hilarious and popular—for a while.

1950s TO 1964

Actually, *Amos 'n' Andy* was not the first black-cast television show. In the fall of 1948, a singing quartet called *The Southernaires* had a 15-minute concert show. According to historian Donald Bogle, this was not even the first. In 1939, there was *The Ethel Waters Show*, a one-time experiment by the NBC radio network to see if television would work. Waters was primarily known for singing the blues, but she was also an actress. At the time, she was starring in a Broadway play titled *Mamba's Daughters*, so the television show featured a scene from the play with Waters and actresses Fredi Washington and Georgette Harvey as well as comedic skits. In 1949, *Sugar Hill Times*, a musical variety series featuring Harry Belafonte and others, aired for a few weeks. *The Hazel Scott Show*, also a 15-minute concert by the singer-pianist, aired briefly in 1950. *Beulah* also began in 1950; the title character, the sensible maid, was black, but the series was actually about an insensible white family.

Nevertheless, it would be difficult to call any of these shows truly national or network series since there were few television sets outside New York City. In 1940, NBC began broadcasting from New York City to Schenectady, still not nationwide but a kind of network. By late 1948, the East Coast states and the Midwest were linked, and Chicago became an important production city. In 1951, a link was completed on the West Coast, making television truly nationwide, and Hollywood became the place to film in the late 1950s. During the 1950s, people in large cities started to purchase black-and-white television sets, often small screens with large cabinets. Soon, television spread even to small cities and rural areas.

So, when television became a national pastime, *Beulah* and *Amos 'n' Andy* were on the air. *Beulah* basically self-destructed when each actress cast in the title role quit the show; it was over in 1953. *Amos 'n' Andy* was killed by the NAACP and other black organizations for perpetuating negative stereotypes of black people and black life. A central character was Kingfish, who was without morals or ethics; he never had a real job and would cheat his best friend out of his last dollar. Andy was Kingfish's best friend, and he was so stupid that he allowed Kingfish to dupe him in each episode. The critics said the characters painted a negative picture of black life and black people. What is entertaining and what is demeaning to black people as a whole? What is laughable, and what should not be laughable? This conflict, especially among African Americans, still exists today.

There were no sustaining black-cast series or series with black stars for many years after that. However, black performers were seen on television during the 1950s and early 1960s in the following ways:

1. Super performers including Sammy Davis Jr., Harry Belafonte, Lena Horne, Dizzy Gillespie, Pearl Bailey, and Cab Calloway appeared in variety series like *The Toast of the Town* (later *The Ed Sullivan Show*). They were headliners in some variety specials, including the following: Marian Anderson on *The Ford 50th Anniversary Show* in 1953, Dorothy Dandridge and Louis Armstrong in the Cole Porter tribute *You're the Top* in 1956, and Nat "King" Cole and Ella Fitzgerald in the patriotic special *I Hear America Singing* in 1955.

2. Actors who had earned respect in legitimate theater had roles in anthology series. These were series which, each week, presented a different drama, often a play like "Blues for a Junk Man" (Dorothy Dan-

dridge and Ivan Dixon), which was a 1962 episode of *Cain's Hundred*; "Winner By Decision" (Harry Belafonte), which was an episode of *General Electric Theater* in 1955; and "A Man Is Ten Feet Tall" (Sidney Poitier), an episode of *Philco Television Playhouse*.

3. Actors were cast members of series starring white actors. In the 1950s, these roles were primarily of domestic workers: Willie Best on *The Stu Erwin Show* (1950–1955), Amanda Randolph on *Make Room for Daddy* (also titled *The Danny Thomas Show*,1953–1965, 1970–1971), and Eddie "Rochester" Anderson on *The Jack Benny Show* (1950–1977). Nick Stewart was an African native on *Ramar of the Jungle* (1952–1954).

In the 1960s, Leslie Uggams was on *Sing Along with Mitch* (1961–1966), and Cicely Tyson was on the drama *East Side, West Side* (1963–1964). These shows were indicators of what was to come, of the types of roles blacks could and would play, and that the black domestic worker was gone or at least changed.

4. There were one-time appearances that are printed indelibly in the memories of African-American viewers during those years. These were events that prompted viewers to call friends on the telephone to say, "There's a Negro on television. Turn it on quick." Appearances other than as African natives on *Ramar of the Jungle* (1952–1954) and *Tarzan* (1966–1969) were worth conversation. Among those events was 13-year-old Gloria Lockerman, who was on the big-money game show *The $64,000 Question* as a spelling expert in 1955. Actress Maidie Norman was cast in an episode of *Dragnet* in 1955. Singer-actress Ethel Waters was interviewed by Edward R. Murrow on *Person to Person* (1954). Occasional black women down on their luck were showered with gifts on *Queen for a Day* (1955–1964).

5. Sports, particularly boxing, was important on early television. Many people who did not have television sets in their homes watched television in bars. Boxers in all weight classes, great or destined to be great, had bouts on television on broadcasts like *Gillette Cavalcade of Sports*, *Boxing from St. Nicholas Arena*, *Boxing for Eastern Parkway*, *Boxing from Jamaica Arena*, and many more. Sugar Ray Robinson and Cassius Clay were among them. In 1960, the Olympic Games had same-day coverage for the first time in its history, even though there was a six-hour delay. Rafer Johnson was the U.S. hero when he won the decathlon.

6. Blacks began to integrate local television news in the 1960s, and some went on to national broadcasts. Among them were Mal Goode on ABC in 1962 and Bill Matney on NBC in 1963.

1965 TO 1979

Television reflected, affected, and was affected by racial problems in the 1960s. When television news brought the horrors of the civil rights struggles into their living rooms, Americans who had not chosen to be aware of the dire necessity of the civil rights struggle could no longer deny it. By 1965, 95 percent of all families in the United States had at least one television. Many of these viewers had seen white faces full of hate when nine black high schoolers integrated an Arkansas school in 1957, when Charlayne Hunter and Hamilton Holmes integrated the University of Georgia in 1961, when James Meredith integrated the University of Mississippi in 1962, and when three civil rights workers were murdered in Mississippi. But these incidents were far less visually dramatic than the newscasts of March 7, 1965, when regular television shows were preempted by newscasts and viewers saw Alabama law officers attack Martin Luther King Jr.'s peaceful demonstrators walking from Selma to Montgomery to push the right to vote. Viewers saw officers on horseback billy-clubbing walkers, clouds of tear gas forcing people to gasp and fall, and children terrorized when police set snarling German shepherds on them. This came to be known as Bloody Sunday, a day that grabbed the nation's attention. President Lyndon Johnson, on a nationwide TV broadcast, denounced the actions and vowed, "We shall overcome," borrowing the lyric of the marchers' own song, and sent in federal troops.

The incident also angered blacks. The Black Power movement began soon after. Beginning with the Watts riot in Los Angeles later in 1965, the big cities erupted with riots and organizations demanding equality by nonviolence or violence sprang into the picture.

Television policymakers—producers, writers, and television executives—were among the growing percentage of Americans who were appalled. Some of them began to plan productions with black actors and performers and scripts about black life. By 1970, it was clearly not just the moral thing to do but also the smart thing to do. Research revealed that black buying power topped $25 billion and that black viewers watched more television than whites, making sponsors realize that they were potential buyers of their products seen in commercials.

Consequently, changes took place in television fare. Shows starring Bill Cosby, Gail Fisher, Diahann Carroll, and Flip Wilson were very popular. Then, and now, a show could not survive on TV airwaves unless the white majority watched it. Therefore, most white viewers liked Cosby and the others. It was difficult to like Cosby and hate all other black people. One had to consider, "If Bill Cosby is okay, then maybe other black people are too." So, television played a role in easing race relations.

In 1965, the espionage drama *I Spy* made its debut with Bill Cosby, then a likable stand-up comedian, playing one of two leads. In that same year, *Hogan's Heroes* premiered with Ivan Dixon as one of the regular cast playing prisoners in a Nazi war camp.

Daktari (with Hari Rhodes), *Star Trek* (with Nichelle Nichols), and *Mission Impossible* (with Greg Morris) began airing in 1966. *Mannix* (with Gail Fisher), *High Chaparral* (with Frank Silvera), and *Ironside* (with Don Mitchell) premiered in 1967. By 1968, television was becoming more colorful in two ways. The three networks were going from black-and-white programs to full color, and there was at least one black entertainer on television every night of the week. In addition to the previously mentioned shows, there were the following: *The Mod Squad* (with Clarence Williams III), *The Outcasts* (with Otis Young), *Land of the Giants* (with Don Marshall), and *Rowan and Martin's Laugh-In* (with Chelsea Brown and black celebrity guest stars). Without doubt, televisions in most black homes were tuned to those shows. The desire of black people to see other black people on television continues into the 21st century (this does not suggest that black people watch only black performers and actors). However, by 1980, there were too many shows with one black actor for casting to be the primary reason for watching a show.

The Flip Wilson Show (1970) was the first hit variety series with a black star. However, the real change was the dawning of the black family sitcom. By then, there were more sitcoms on TV than any other genre. The anthologies were gone except for occasional broadcasts. *Julia* premiered in 1968 with Diahann Carroll as a nurse and single mother and was the first successful series with a female lead. The Norman

Lear/Bud Yorkin sitcoms premiered and were very popular with black as well as mainstream viewers. Many African-American actors, producers, directors, and writers got their careers started on these series. Those comedies were *Sanford and Son* (1972–1977), *Good Times* (1974–1979), and *The Jeffersons* (1975–1985). The latter two were spin-offs of other Lear sitcoms. All but *Good Times* spawned other sitcoms, though none of the spin-offs were particularly successful.

In the area of newscasters, Max Robinson coanchored *ABC's World News Tonight* beginning in 1978. Various reporters were seen on national broadcasts. Some of the important news events relating to black Americans and reported on newscasts during this period were the big-city riots in the mid- and late 1960s, civil rights demonstrations like the March on Washington in 1963, and the 1968 assassination of Martin Luther King Jr.

In sports, highlights were the Olympic Games of 1968 when Tommie Smith and John Carlos held up black-gloved hands in silent protest to discrimination in the United States and numerous Muhammad Ali fights.

1980 TO 1999

The black-cast sitcoms, also including *What's Happening!!* (1976–1979), thrived until the end of the 1970s. They had all ranked in the top 30 shows in the 1970s. By 1980, only *The Jeffersons* was still on the air. In 1978, *Diff'rent Strokes*, a racially integrated family sitcom, premiered and was high in the Nielsen ratings, so networks started integrating shows in hopes of getting both mainstream and black viewers. *Diff'rent Strokes* (1978–1986) and *Webster* (1983–1987) centered on white parents adopting black children; *Gimme a Break* (1981–1987) centered on a black housekeeper/substitute mother to a trio of teenaged white girls whose mother had died. *Benson* (1979–1986) spun off of *Soap* with Robert Guilluame as a butler who became lieutenant governor and gubernatorial candidate; Benson was the only black regular character in the series. In these, the African-American actor was the key player in the series.

Networks believed the black cast sitcom was dead until *The Cosby Show* premiered in 1984 and won the hearts of critics and viewers alike.

It was a middle-class family with kids who behaved like real children in many middle-class families, no matter what race. The family had issues like families everywhere. *The Cosby Show* spawned *A Different World*, about life in a predominantly black college, and following soon was *The Fresh Prince of Bel-Air*, about a black family more wealthy than the Huxtables in *The Cosby Show*. All were successful in the ratings.

The next change in the sitcom came when new commercial networks went national. Fox (1986), the WB (1994), and UPN (1995) were launched with black programs, while the big three networks had few black-cast or primarily black-cast shows. Most sitcoms and drama series on the networks had at least one black actor in the regular cast.

In 1990, the series *In Living Color* was the closest thing to the big variety series of the 1960s and 1970s, though it was primarily comedy sketches with a little music and dancing. *The Flip Wilson Show* and *The Carol Burnett Show* (1967–1979) had been the last of the true variety shows with acts of all kinds and big-name guests; even the Burnett show was primarily comedy sketches with a regular cast. Probably the closest to the old variety series would be the late night shows like *The Arsenio Hall Show* (1989–1994). The closest to the variety specials would be the special cable shows like *Sinbad's Soul Music Festivals* (late 1990s) and *Motown 25* (1983) with various musical acts and revues like *Tina Turner: Live in Rio* (1988) highlighting one performer.

The Oprah Winfrey Show premiered in 1986 and soon dominated the talk show market. *Montel* (Williams) made its debut in 1991.

Bryant Gumbel began hosting *The Today Show* on NBC in 1982, and even more black reporters and correspondents began broadcasting. The conflict leading to the Clarence Thomas Supreme Court confirmation dominated programming in October 1991. The O. J. Simpson murder trial dominated the news in 1994 and 1995, from the slow chase leading to his arrest to his trial, his acquittal, and after.

Another change in programs occurred in the area of "long-form" film productions—movies and miniseries. The networks had been proud during the late 1970s, 1980s, and early 1990s that television could do better than feature films in the area of miniseries. People would not sit through long films in theaters or come back on successive days to see complete productions. *Roots* (1977) and *Backstairs at the White House* (1979) were praised as examples of what television could do best. In addition, the made-for-television movie was often a pilot for a proposed series.

THE NEW MILLENNIUM

Cable television virtually took over the made-for-television movie genre. In the 2003–2004 season, 18 cable networks got 220 prime-time Emmy nominations (125 were for HBO), while the networks got a total of 207 nominations. The networks historically had topped the Emmy nominations, and this difference came about because of TV films, although HBO began to make inroads in episodic series like *The Sopranos*.

At the turn of the century, reality television became the most plentiful type of series. It would be difficult to call the genre "popular" because it was not known whether viewers preferred reality programs or merely looked at what was offered them. The choice was not whether to watch reality shows or some other genre but which reality show to watch. Most reality shows also had one or two African-American participants.

Cedric the Entertainer attempted a variety series, *Cedric the Entertainer Presents*, in 2002. The half-hour had musical and dance production numbers and comedy sketches. It was popular with black viewers but was canceled because it did not get mainstream ratings. *The Wayne Brady Show* (2002–2004) was a talk-variety series syndicated in daytime. *Chappelle's Show*, mostly comedy with a bit of music, was a huge hit on Comedy Central and on DVD; it also won an Emmy nomination in 2004.

Sensational news stories dominated newscasts. Among them were entertainer Michael Jackson accused of child molestation and basketball star Kobe Bryant accused of rape.

LOOKING BACK AND LOOKING FORWARD

It is important to remember when examining television past, present, and future that it is a business first and an art in a very secondary way. Many commercial television producers and executives would like to produce quality programs, but they can do that only if they meet bottom-line demands. It is true that television is a powerful socializing agent. Research has shown that viewers do feel they know groups of people (including nationalities, races, and ethnic groups) as well as individuals based on what they see on television. This aspect of television's power is rarely addressed by decision makers in the television industry. It is doubtful that bodies of persons planning programming on television set out to abuse or harm any group of people. However, their decisions can cause and have caused harm to people because of their insensitivity to the socialization that results from programs.

There have been (and hopefully always will be) industry professionals of all races who struggled to create quality television. There have been professionals of all races who are aware of the discriminatory nature of some viewers and decision makers, yet they still fight for fairness in television programming. All these professionals, including those who tried and were not successful, deserve credit.

The Dictionary

– A –

AARON, HANK. Hammerin' Hank of the Atlanta Braves hit his 715th home run on April 8, 1974, breaking Babe Ruth's record in a game televised from Atlanta's Fulton County Stadium. It was Dodger pitcher Al Downing's pitched ball that Aaron's bat sent out of the ballpark. A few weeks before, he said that he was picking the day and the game in which he would break the record; he was that confident. Though the majority of Americans saluted him, Aaron received numerous death threats from people who were not happy that an African American had broken the Babe's record. Later that year, he had hit 733 home runs. When he was inducted in the Baseball Hall of Fame, 406 out of 425 votes went to him. As the home run king, he made the rounds on television series, including a *Dean Martin Celebrity Roast* and *The Flip Wilson Show*.

ABDUL-JABBAR, KAREEM. The basketball superstar was the subject of the *All-Star Tribute to Kareem Abdul-Jabbar* in 1989. He played himself in *The Hero Who Couldn't Read* in 1984. In 1987 and 1990, he was a member of the casts of a *Star-Spangled Celebration* Fourth of July specials. He had several roles in episodic series, including *Diff'rent Strokes*, and in the "Sports Chat" segment of the sitcom *Good Sports*, appearing as himself in both. He was interviewed too many times to mention on talk shows like *Later with Bob Costas*.

ABERNATHY, DONZALEIGH. Abernathy played Henrietta King in *Don King: Only in America* in 1997.

ABOUT US: THE DIGNITY OF CHILDREN (*ABC, March 29, 1997*). **Oprah Winfrey** hosted this show celebrating children who struggled to survive in a troubled world. Study guides were sent to schools all over the United States by the Children's Dignity Project.

ACADEMY AWARD CEREMONY (*annually, various networks*). **Sidney Poitier** was the first black actor to win the coveted Oscar on television; he won the statuette in 1963 for his starring role in *Lilies of the Field*. It was not until 2002 that black actors again won the top Oscar; **Denzel Washington** won it for *Training Day*, and Halle Berry also won it for *Monster's Ball*. **Whoopi Goldberg** hosted the telecast in 1994. Goldberg had won the supporting actress award in 1991 for *Ghost*.

The ceremony in 2005 was a big event in African-American television because **Jamie Foxx** won the leading actor Oscar for his role in *Ray* and **Morgan Freeman** the supporting actor Oscar for his role in *Million Dollar Baby*. **Chris Rock** was master of ceremonies; **Halle Berry**, Prince, and **Samuel L. Jackson** were presenters. Beyonce sang three of the nominated songs; Sean Combs introduced one of the songs. Goldberg led the tribute to Johnny Carson, who had died a few weeks before the telecast.

ACADEMY AWARD SONGS (*NBC, March 15, 1960*). **Nat "King" Cole** was one of the popular singers performing songs that won the coveted Oscar Award for best song in this one-hour special. Others were The Four Aces, Gogi Grant, Elsa Lancaster, Kay Starr, and Tex Ritter.

ADVENTURES OF MUHAMMAD ALI, THE (*NBC, 1977–1978*). Ali provided the voice for this animated series about a heroic character who traveled the world helping others and battling evildoers.

AESOP'S FABLES (*CBS, October 31, 1971*). **Bill Cosby** starred as Aesop in this half-hour live and animated fantasy story. He was a hip, contemporary Aesop, and the production included children and cartoon animals. The story told was a version of "The Tortoise and the Hare."

AFI SALUTE TO SIDNEY POITIER (*NBC, April 4, 1992*). The American Film Institute started honoring actors, directors, and producers with annual testimonial dinners in 1973. Each honoree received the Life Achievement Award on the show. Praising **Sidney Poitier** was host **Harry Belafonte** and Dan Aykroyd, Kirstie Alley, **Bill Cosby**, Tony Curtis, **Morgan Freeman, Danny Glover, Louis Gossett Jr.**, Lee Grant, **James Earl Jones, Quincy Jones**, Stanley Kramer, Gregory Peck, Rod Steiger, **Denzel Washington**, Richard Widmark, and Shelley Winters.

AFRICAN-AMERICAN AUDIENCES. Media scholars study African-American television audiences in a variety of ways. So far, scholarly studies have not revealed a monolithic African-American audience, the behavior of which can be predicted or directed. African-American audiences watch entertainment television for a variety of reasons and respond to and make use of what is shown in a variety of ways. For example, Gloria E. Abernathy found that African-American soap opera fans, teens through adults, watched soaps because they liked the ongoing multiple story lines and enjoyed seeing specific actors or characters. African-American viewers also watch soap operas to gain insight into mainstream culture, relax and escape, and have something in common to talk about with relatives, coworkers, and friends. Meanwhile, Jeffrey Tyus found that African-American viewers of black-themed situation comedies watch for entertainment and a chance to laugh while preferring realistic settings, situations, or characters they could relate to or learn something from. And Freda Lewis's research found that college-age African-American viewers watch shows out of "an overwhelming fondness for characters of the same race." Lewis's findings are interesting in that they show that African-American college students are continuing to watch African Americans on television just as their parents and grandparents did in the early days of television.

Studies of African-American audiences have also focused on a specific show. In their study of *The Cosby Show*, Jhally and Lewis talked to African-American viewers and white viewers of the hit show to gain insight into "how audiences interpret images and issues of race and class." For African-American viewers, *The Cosby Show* held different meaning than it did for white viewers. Overall, African-American viewers saw the show as "an escape and respite" from the typically negative images offered by television. White viewers, meanwhile, saw the program as evidence of the viability of the American dream because the Huxtables were thought of as upper middle class more than as black. However, these viewers remained suspicious of working-class or poor African Americans on- and off-screen. "They will . . . distinguish between the Huxtables and most other black people, and their welcome is clearly only extended as far as the Huxtables," wrote Jhally and Lewis.

Scholar Robin Means Coleman also studied the African-American audience. In her 1998 work on African-American audiences and situation comedies, she asked African-American viewers to talk about how they saw themselves relative to characters in black situation comedies. Coleman found that viewers identified more with what is perceived as positive aspects such as the middle-class images of family presented through *The Cosby Show* or the independent outlook of the female characters in *Living Single*. Meanwhile, audience members expressed concern that mainstream audiences believed negative images were presented in black situation comedies.

African-American audiences of television news have also been examined. Wood found that African-American audiences combated poor treatment in television news through what she terms Afrocentric talk: critiquing and analyzing the news with other African-American viewers in an effort to protect African-American identity from the easy dichotomy of good and bad presented through television news. On television news, African Americans too often appear as "poor, criminal, drug addicted, and dysfunctional" or exceptional figures such as athletes or entertainment personalities. *See also* RATINGS.

AFRICAN-AMERICAN HISTORY MONTH. From 1926 until 1976, the second week in February was called Negro History Week and was celebrated primarily in schools, especially in the South. During the 1976 U.S. Bicentennial, the celebratory period was expanded to the entire month and became Black History Month. When that was no longer politically correct, the term African-American History Month was used. Historically, the month of February has been the period of the year in which networks and stations air productions about the African-American experience. Some critics of this less-than-30-day celebration, like Rosemary Bray at the *New York Times* (March 3,

1991), say it is because February is the shortest month and the air-waves can swiftly go back to a "predominantly white universe." She said, "I can do without those annual attacks of earnestness." Others, though preferring a yearlong schedule of ethnically diverse program-ming, praise the networks for airing some productions, many of qual-ity and historical significance, during this month. February is also a sweeps period in which advertisers pay particular attention to ratings.

In the 1970s, NBC ran three miniseries with black themes during February: *King* (1978), *Backstairs at the White House* (1979), and *Roots: The Next Generations* (1979). In 1975, there was the *Flip Wilson Special*.

The 1980s saw the PBS documentary *Brown Sugar* (1980), CBS's *Crisis at Central High* (1981), PBS's *Chasing a Rainbow: The Life of Josephine Baker* (1989), PBS's *A Raisin in the Sun* (1989), and the syndicated specials *Diana Ross in Central Park* (1985) and *Dionne Warwick in London* (1988).

In the 1990s, NBC aired *Murder in Mississippi* in 1990, and PBS aired *The Colored Museum* in 1991. In the 21st century, *Freedom Song* aired in 2000, HBO's *Lumumba* and CBS's *The Rosa Parks Story* aired in 2002, and Showtime's *Good Fences* aired in 2003. These mentioned are a scant few of the February fare.

AFRICANS IN AMERICA: AMERICA'S JOURNEY THROUGH SLAVERY (*PBS, October 1998*). Angela Bassett narrated this four-part documentary that traced the history of African Americans from the early colonial era through the Civil War. The focus of the production was blacks who were slaves and their efforts to escape from slavery. Some attention was also given to free blacks during that era. Included were interviews with historians and public figures including Margaret Washington, David Blight, Norrece T. Jones Jr., and Colin Powell. The four episodes were "The Terrible Transformation," "Revolution," "Brotherly Love," and "Judgment Day." Reviewer Peter Kolchin said, "Perhaps the greatest strength of the series lies in its relentless pursuit of two interrelated themes . . . the cruelty and horror of slavery . . . and the callousness displayed by white Americans (including some traditional American heroes)." *See also* DOCU-MENTARIES.

AFTER SHOCK: EARTHQUAKE IN NEW YORK (*CBS, November 14 and 16, 1999*). A four-hour miniseries, this drama starred **Charles S. Dutton** as the mayor of New York City as its citizenry tried to cope with a killer earthquake and its aftermath. Sharon Lawrence was a nervous mother, **Cicely Tyson** was a grandmother, and **Lisa Nicole Carson** was her granddaughter. Tom Skerritt was the police chief.

AIN'T MISBEHAVIN' (*NBC, June 21, 1982*). A hit on Broadway, this musical revue was mounted for television starring **Nell Carter**, whose television career started after she won a Tony Award for this musical. Based on the music of Thomas "Fats" Waller, the production set in a 1930s nightclub also starred **Andre DeShields**, **Ken Page**, **Charlaine Woodard**, and **Armelia McQueen**—all from the original Broadway cast. Carter won an **Emmy Award** for the revue. DeShields was nominated for an Emmy. *See also* BROADWAY PLAYS AND MUSICALS.

AJAYE, FRANKLYN. Comic Ajaye made several appearances on *The Midnight Special* (1974–1976) and on *The Sunday Comics* (1991–1992). He was a regular member of the cast of the 1975 comedy/variety series *Keep on Truckin'*.

ALDRIDGE, DAVID. Aldridge joined ESPN in 1996 after a career in sports reporting for newspapers. At ESPN, as a reporter for the National Basketball Association (NBA), he reported breaking news and feature stories and provided analysis for *SportsCenter*, the network's daily news telecast, as well as for *NBA 2Night*, the daily NBA show. His credits also include substitute hosting ESPN's talk show *Pardon the Interruption* and a column for ESPN.com.

ALEXANDER, ERIKA. Alexander was Pam on *The Cosby Show* from 1990 to 1992 and Maxine Shaw on *Living Single* from 1993 to 1998. She played Cheryl Carter in *Going to Extremes* from 1992 to 1993 and Dee Mulhern on *Street Time* beginning in 2002. She had a key role in television films *Mama Flora's Family* in 1998 and *Common Ground* in 1990.

ALEXANDER, FLEX. Alexander starred as Mark "Flex" Washington in the sitcom *One on One* (2001–) and Ty in *Homeboys in Outer Space* (1996–1997). He played Darnell Wilkes in *Girlfriends* (2000–2001) and Reggie in the 1993 sitcom *Where I Live* and was a regular in the comedy stand-up and sketch series *Uptown Comedy Club* (1992–1994). In 2004, he played super entertainer Michael Jackson in the TV film *Man in the Mirror*.

ALEXANDER, KHANDI. Alexander was Alexx Woods in *CSI Miami* (2002–). She played a key role in the miniseries *The Corner* (2000) and was Catherine Duke in *NewsRadio* (1995–1998). She played the recurring role of Jackie Robbins in *ER* from 1995 to 2001. She was a regular in the 1985 musical variety series *Motown Revue Starring Smokey Robinson*. In TV films, she had roles in *Shameful Secrets* (1993), *To My Daughter with Love* (1994), *Terminal* (1996), and *Partners* (1999).

ALEX HALEY'S QUEEN (*CBS, February 14, 16, and 18, 1993*). In this miniseries, **Halle Berry** starred in the title role as a mulatto woman, an outcast because of her mixed-race heritage who tried to find acceptance and respect. She was the child of a slave woman and a plantation owner, and the story took place through the Civil War into the early 20th century. This film was based on a project on which author Alex Haley was working at the time of his death. **Danny Glover** (as Alec Haley), **Ossie Davis** (as Parson Dick), **Dennis Haysbert** (as Davis), **Tommy Hollis** (as Fred), **Jasmine Guy** (as Easter), **Lonette McKee** (as Alice), **Madge Sinclair** (as Dora), and **Lorraine Toussaint** (as Joyce) also starred. *See also* BIRACIAL CHARACTERS.

ALI: AN AMERICAN HERO (*FOX, August 31, 2000*). This TV film starred David Ramsey as Cassius Clay/Muhammad Ali and centers on the champion's struggle not only with boxing but with racial, social, and political issues as well. The story, told in flashbacks, was his life up to his career-defining 1974 fight with George Foreman. **Clarence Williams III** played Cassius's father, Marcellus; **Joe Morton**, Malcolm X; **Vondie Curtis-Hall**, Drew "Bundini" Brown; and **Antonio Fargas**, Elijah Muhammad. Thomas Carter was executive producer.

ALICE, MARY. Alice played Helen Mayfield in the drama *Just an Old Sweet Song* (1976) and had a key role in *Charlotte Forten's Mission: Experiment in Freedom* (1985). She had a recurring role on *Sanford and Son* as Fred Sanford's niece and a regular role on *A Different World* as Lettie, the dorm mother (1988–1989). She won the **Emmy Award** in 1993 for Outstanding Supporting Actress in a Drama Series for a guest role in *I'll Fly Away*. She starred in the miniseries *Laurel Avenue* (1993) and had a key role in *The Vernon Johns Story* (1994).

ALI, MUHAMMAD. Before he took the name Muhammad Ali, as Cassius Clay he made an appearance on *The Jerry Lewis Show* in 1963 to announce to the world that he would beat Sonny Liston in the upcoming title fight. Both Ali and **Joe Frazier** appeared on *Saturday Night Live with Howard Cosell* on the eve of the "Thrilla in Manila" championship fight. After his predictions came true, Ali made numerous appearances on television as himself. Some of the shows were the following: a **Flip Wilson** special titled *Travels with Flip* in 1975; *The American Parade*, a 1984 magazine show about the triumphs (or tragedies) of Americans; *Into the Night*, a late night interview show; and *Get High on Yourself*, a 1981 public service special on which he and other celebrities spoke out against drug abuse. Ali became an actor when he starred in *Freedom Road*, a two-hour made-for-television film, in 1979. He did voice-overs for the animated series *The Adventures of Muhammad Ali* (1977–1978) and was the voice of Gerry Berger in the animated *Garfield on the Town* in 1983. *See also* MUHAMMAD ALI FIGHTS; KING OF THE WORLD.

ALI, TATYANA M. Ali played Ashley Banks on *Fresh Prince of Bel-Air* (1990–1996).

ALL ABOUT THE ANDERSONS (*WB, 2003*). Comedian **Anthony Anderson** played a struggling actor and single father trying to provide a good environment for his eight-year-old son, Tuga (Damani Roberts), so they move in with his parents, Flo (**Roz Ryan**) and Joe (**John Amos**). To Joe, Anthony had not grown up yet, so he often went to extreme measures to help him mature, give up acting and find a "real" job working in the family beauty salon and barbershop. The series was said to be loosely based on star Anderson's life. *See also* FAMILY SERIES.

ALLEN, BYRON. Host of the syndicated celebrity interview show *Entertainers* since 1994, **Byron Allen** began his show business career at open-mike night at The Comedy Store in Hollywood when he was only 15 years old. He was asked to make an appearance on the late night talk series *The Tonight Show with Johnny Carson* and soon was a member of the regular cast of the series *Real People* from 1979 to 1984. He also made appearances in *Battle of the Network Stars* in 1980, *Hollywood Stars' Screen Tests* in 1984, and *A Salute to Lady Liberty*, also in 1984. In 1988, he was a regular comedian on *Live! Dick Clark Presents*, a series designed to fill airtime until the Writers Guild of America strike was over. Prior to *Entertainers*, he was host of *Jammin*, a weekly music interview show that had primarily black celebrities in 1992–1993, and host of *The Byron Allen Show*, a syndicated late night talk show (1989–1992) that eventually became a show of comedy sketches and appearances by guest comics. As chairman and chief executive officer of CF Entertainment, he syndicates eight different shows, including *Kickin' It with Byron Allen*, *Every Woman*, and *Destination Stardom*. Allen also took his television business to the Web with EntertainmentStudios.com. This site has numerous celebrity interviews, tours of celebrity homes, and also an e-commerce link that permits businesses to access 800 hours of television shows and 1,500 celebrity interviews free of charge. The businesses can earn commissions on products like CDs and memorabilia. Allen said, "Our children are going to think that we are cavemen for letting a few networks decide what shows we watched. They will be able to watch their show of choice whenever they desire. At this site, you get your entertainment needs and your shopping needs." *See also* CHILD ACTORS WHO MAINTAINED SUCCESS AS ADULTS IN SHOW BUSINESS.

ALLEN, DEBBIE. Allen's first series was a 1977 summer series called **3 Girls 3**, a variety series showcasing the multiple talents of Mimi Kennedy, Ellen Foley, and Allen. She played Nan Haley, one of Alex Haley's ancestors, in *Roots: The Next Generations* in 1979. In

1982–1983, she starred in the drama series *Fame* as Lydia Grant, the dance teacher. In 1995, she played a role in the first season of the sitcom *In the House*. In 2003, she starred in, choreographed, and produced the reality talent competition *Fame*. In made-for-television films, Allen played Ebony in *Ebony, Ivory, and Jade*, a 1979 film. She had key roles in *Women of San Quentin* in 1983 and the miniseries *Celebrity* in 1984. She directed *Stompin' at the Savoy* in 1992. In the variety special genre, she hosted *The Debbie Allen Special* in 1989 and was a leading performer in *The Kids from Fame* in 1983. She was a guest on *Emmanuel Lewis: My Very Own Show* in 1987 and *Ben Vereen—His Roots* in 1978. She was in the guest cast of many tributes, celebrations, and salutes, including *It's Black Entertainment* in 1997. In 1982, she was a performer in the *Texaco Star Theater: Opening Night*, a salute to American musical theater. In 1983, Allen participated in the benefit for the Actor's Fund *Parade of Stars*. In 1984, she helped honor Lena Horne in *The Kennedy Center Honors*. In 1985, she helped celebrate *Disneyland's 30th Anniversary*. In 1986, she was in a tribute to the Statue of Liberty in *Liberty Weekend: Opening Ceremonies*. In 1987, Allen participated in Hollywood's 100th birthday, *Happy Birthday, Hollywood* and also Las Vegas' 75th anniversary, *Las Vegas: An All-Star 75th Anniversary*. Also in 1987, she was in *Superstars and Their Moms* and *Our Kids and the Best of Everything*, about celebrity parents talking about rearing children. In 1990, she performed in *Motown 30: What's Going On?*, and she was part of *Sammy Davis Jr.'s 60th Anniversary Celebration*. She was director/producer of *A Different World* for several years.

ALLEN, JONELLE. After a Broadway career, Allen made her way to Hollywood and television. In variety specials, she sang in *Cotton Club '75* and *Opryland U.S.A.*, also in 1975. She played key roles in the television films *Cage without a Key* in 1975, *Vampire* in 1979, and *Brave New World* in 1980. She played Stacey Russell in the short-lived 1985 nighttime soap opera *Berrenger's*, Bessie Freeman in the drama *Palmerstown U.S.A.* (1980–1981), and Grace in the drama *Dr. Quinn, Medicine Woman* (1983–1998).

ALLEN, RAYMOND. Allen had a regular role in the sitcom *The Sanford Arms* (1977) and a recurring role on *Sanford and Son*

(1976–1977); in both he played Woody, Aunt Esther's husband. He played the recurring role of Ned, the Wino, in *Good Times* (1974). Prior to all these productions, he made an appearance in *Wattstax 1973*, a film documentary featuring entertainment that aired on television in 2001.

ALLEY CATS STRIKE! (*DIS, March 18, 2000*). **Tim Reid** and **Daphne Maxwell Reid** starred in this children's program in which four teenagers are outcasts because of their nonconformist attitude and interest in bowling. **Robert Ri'chard** played Todd McLemore, one of the teens.

ALL GOD'S CHILDREN (*ABC, April 28, 1980*). **Ossie Davis**, **Ruby Dee**, and young George Spell played the black family in this two-hour made-for-television movie about the friendship between two families—one white and one black—in a story about forced busing of schoolchildren.

ALL IN THE FAMILY (*CBS, 1971–1992*). Archie Bunker (Carroll O'Connor), as the head of a Queens, New York, blue-collar family, was often called "a lovable bigot." African Americans argue about the term "lovable" but generally agree that the show was funny and handled racial humor sensitively. Archie was always put down for his racist comments even though he was not often aware of the put-downs. He loved to talk, but he didn't know what he was saying. In his own vernacular, he "misconscrewed" the words. At the very least, this sitcom spun off one of the most successful sitcoms about an African-American family, *The Jeffersons*. **Michael Evans** was first introduced as the next-door neighbor who became a friend to Archie's liberal son-in law, Mike (Rob Reiner). Lionel Jefferson took great pleasure in insulting Archie, and the audience was with Lionel. Then, Lionel's mother, Louise (**Isabel Sanford**), became Edith's (Jean Stapleton) friend, and she continued to be foil to Archie. Later, **Sherman Hemsley** was added as Lionel's father, George, and **Mel Stewart** as Lionel's uncle. They were all foil for Archie, and Hemsley was what was then called "a reverse racist." Hemsley, Sanford, and Evans were the core family of the spin-off series. In 1980, the character Edith died, and Archie hired a black housekeeper (**Barbara**

Meek), a relative of the Bunkers' neighbor, Polly Swanson (**Janet MacLachlan**).

In addition, there were several African-American guest stars playing characters to contrast Archie's bigotry. One of the most memorable scenes was on February 19, 1972, when guest **Sammy Davis Jr.** kissed Archie. When posing for a photograph, Sammy asked the photographer to press the shutter at the count of three. On three, Sammy kissed racist Archie's cheek, and the audience roared at his expression of confusion and horror. Creator-producer Norman Lear calls it "the most famous kiss in television history." *TV Guide* said, "Archie's deep-seated prejudice was tested. It made us laugh, but it also made us think." The episode won an **Emmy Award** for directing. After a guest stint on one episode, **Demond Wilson** was cast to star in another Norman Lear/Bud Yorkin series, *Sanford and Son*. *See also* RATINGS; SERIES RANKINGS AND RATINGS (APPENDIX A); SPIN-OFF SERIES.

ALL OF US (*UPN, 2003–*). Promoted widely as being loosely based on the lives of **Will Smith** and his actress-wife, **Jada Pinkett Smith** (who were originally executive producers), this sitcom told the story of Robert James, an entertainment reporter (**Duane Martin**) who tried to keep peace with his wife, Tia (**Elise Neal**), and his former wife, Neesee (LisaRay). Neesee was the mother of Robert's son, Bobby Jr. (Khamani Griffin), an important part of his daily life.

ALL STAR JAZZ (*NBC, December 30, 1957*). This musical program starred Steve Allen and featured **Louis Armstrong, Carmen McRae, Duke Ellington**, Dave Brubeck, Paul Desmond, Woody Herman, Gene Krupa, and Charlie Ventura.

ALL STAR JAZZ (*CBS, November 10, 1958*). This musical show starred **Louis Armstrong, Lionel Hampton**, Les Brown, Gene Krupa, and Jane Morgan.

ALL-STAR SWING FESTIVAL (*NBC, November 29, 1972*). **Count Basie, Duke Ellington, Ella Fitzgerald, Dizzy Gillespie, Lionel Hampton**, Benny Goodman, and Gene Krupa were among the music makers in this one-hour special, which won a Peabody Award.

ALL-STAR TRIBUTE TO KAREEM ABDUL-JABBAR (*NBC,* *May 12, 1989*). This one-hour variety program saluted **Kareem Abdul-Jabbar** as a great basketball player on behalf of the Variety Clubs International Children's Charities. Participating in the tribute were **Gladys Knight, Whoopi Goldberg, Danny Glover, Jackee Harry,** and **Herbie Hancock** as well as Billy Crystal, Angie Dickinson, Bruce Willis, Joan Van Ark, and Martin Mull.

AL ROKER INVESTIGATES (*CTV, 2003– *). **Al Roker,** the weatherman on NBC's *Today Show,* was the anchor and executive producer of this occasional documentary program that, according to the Court TV description, "goes beyond the headlines to examine bias crimes, how police investigate them, and how communities respond to these crimes." *See also* DOCUMENTARIES.

ALVIN AILEY AMERICAN DANCE THEATER: STEPS AHEAD (*PBS, February 8, 1991*). A production of *Great Performances'* Dance in America series, this show offered two works: "For Bird— With Love," Ailey's tribute to saxophonist Charlie Bird, and Ulysses Dove's "Episodes," introduced by Judith Jamison.

ALWAYS OUTNUMBERED (*HBO, March 21, 1998*). In this made-for-television movie, **Laurence Fishburne** starred as Socrates Fortlow, an ex-con with a violent past who tried to make his life better. He had deep moral strength and a finely tuned sense of right and wrong despite his past. This story of hope and redemption also featured **Bill Cobbs, Natalie Cole, Cicely Tyson, Bill Duke,** and **Isaiah Washington.** From the Walter Mosley book, Mosley wrote the teleplay, and Fishburne and Mosley were also executive producers.

AMAZING RACE, THE (*CBS, 2001– *). This reality series, similar to the old-fashioned scavenger hunt, took contestants all over the world. Teams of two people each competed; the two might be a married couple, siblings, parent and child, or friends. All were given a limited amount of money for transportation and any other challenges that might arise. Airfare was paid by the show. The couple that completed their challenges and tasks and returned to the appointed spot first won a million dollars. In 2004, an African-American couple, Chip and Kim

McAllister of Coto de Caza, California, were the winners after traveling 72,000 miles around the world. The McAllisters planned to give a tenth of their prize to their church and pay bills. *The Amazing Race* won the **Emmy Award** in 2004 for Outstanding Reality Competition Series.

AMBUSHED (*HBO, 1998*). This made-for-television film starred **Courtney B. Vance.** The conflict began when a leader of the Ku Klux Klan was murdered and the only witness to the slaughter was the victim's son, who was young and burning with racist hatred. The county's only black cop (Vance) stood accused.

AMBUSH MURDERS, THE (*CBS, January 5, 1982*). This made-for-television film was based on the 1971 case in which an outspoken black activist was accused of murdering two white policemen in Lindero, California. **Dorian Harewood** played the central figure, Ray Ellsworth, who spent more than two years in jail while trials ended in hung juries. The film explored patterns of racism and intimidation. **Alfre Woodard** and **Antonio Fargas** had key roles.

AMEN (*NBC, 1986–1991*). *Amen* was the first successful sitcom about a Christian church. The central characters were the personnel who headed the fictitious First Community Church of Philadelphia. **Sherman Hemsley** was Ernest Frye, the deacon whose father had founded the church many years before. **Clifton Davis** was the Rev. Reuben Gregory, hired by Frye and the church board to lead the flock. **Anna Maria Horsford** played Thelma Frye, Ernest's daughter, who had a crush on the reverend throughout most of the series; during the final season, they were married. **Barbara Montgomery** and **Roz Ryan** were sisters and board members Casietta and Amelia Hetebrink, respectively. **Jester Hairston** portrayed the eldest board member, Rolly Forbes. **Rosetta LeNoire** played Leora, who eventually married Rolly.

During the final years, Elsa Raven as Inga, Tony T. Johnson as Chris, and Bumper Robinson as Clarence were added to the cast. Reality was an important component of the sitcom. Davis, though an actor for many years, was an assistant pastor at a Seventh-Day Adventist church in Loma Linda, California, and had earned bachelor's and master's degrees in theology. Most of the cast members were professional singers with Broadway experience, so when they sang with the church choir (some were from a Los Angeles church), they actually sang. Child minister Rev. William Hudson III, in several episodes, played the 12-year-old pastor Rev. Johnny Tolbert. **Little Richard** was the choir director in the series pilot, but **Franklyn Seales** was cast in the role for the series. Hairston was well known all over the world as a choir director and writer of hymns and other religious songs. Ironically, his most famous song, used in many Christian church hymnals, is titled "Amen" and was sung by **Sidney Poitier** in "Lilies of the Field." He once directed a choir in Russia with more than a thousand singers. During rehearsal for the first episode, he said the producers of the series were unaware of his musical background and that he did not plan to tell them.

AMERICA BEYOND THE COLOR LINE (*PBS, February 2004*). African-American scholar Henry Louis Gates examined in four one-hour presentations the state of life for African Americans in the 35 years after the assassination of Martin Luther King Jr. He sought to discover what had changed socially, politically, and economically. In "South: The Black Belt," he examined the lives of numerous blacks who returned to the South to live after seeking refuge and prosperity in the North and West. **Morgan Freeman** and **Maya Angelou** were interviewed. In "Chicago: Streets of Heaven," Gates looked at the poverty of families living in infamous housing projects, and the **Rev. Jesse Jackson** offered information about his hometown. In "East Coast: Ebony Towers," Gates took a look at the new black power elite—including Colin Powell, Fannie Mae chief executive officer Franklin Raines, hip-hop mogul Russell Simmons, and others—and what this means to the overall progress of black Americans. In "Los Angeles: Black Hollywood," he examined race and the film industry and spoke with **Quincy Jones**, **Samuel Jackson**, **Nia Long**, **Chris Tucker**, and others. *See also* DOCUMENTARIES.

AMERICAN BANDSTAND (*ABC, 1957–1987; SYN, 1987–1988*). This music/dance program with top recording stars was a hit for many years with teenage viewers. It premiered in prime time but, for most of its 31-year-run, was aired weekdays in the afternoons, after school. The show began as a radio program, then went into television in Philadelphia in 1952 hosted by Bob Horn. Then Dick Clark took over in 1956, and it went national; it was the first of its kind. Clark insisted that the show's performers be racially integrated since much of the music popular at that time was performed by black recording artists.

When the show began, there were no black teenagers dancing, but that was not alarming since basically there were no black people on television anyway. However, the show did feature black recording artists, and that made the show hot to black viewers. Johnny Mathis debuted his song "It's Not for Me to Say." **Little Richard**, The Platters, **Fats Domino**, and **Chuck Berry** were frequent guests. **Chubby Checker** was popular on the show and did "The Twist"; Sam Cooke had the women swooning when he sang "You Send Me." The Jackson Five performed "I Want You Back" as well as other songs.

The Supremes made one of their earliest television appearances on the show and even traveled with Clark's traveling bus troupe, the Caravan of Stars. **Little Anthony and the Imperials** also did the bus tours. The entertainers were part of summer tours that began in 1960 and went from Memorial Day to Labor Day. The tours and appearances on the show helped sell records and promoted names.

AMERICAN BANDSTAND'S 50TH . . . A CELEBRATION (*ABC, May 3, 2002*). A host of entertainers, black and white, appeared either live or on film clips on this special celebrating 50 years since *American Bandstand* made its debut in 1952. Among them were **Michael Jackson, Brandy, Stevie Wonder,** The Village People, **Little Richard,** Ray Parker Jr., **Whitney Houston, Janet Jackson, Lenny Kravitz, Patti LaBelle, Donna Summer,** and many others.

AMERICAN IDOL (*FOX, 2002– *). This talent competition for singers in their late teens and early twenties was based on a successful British series, "Pop Idol," which also spawned a version in South Africa and numerous other countries. Each season of the limited series began with massive cattle calls in various cities where hopefuls by the thousands auditioned. The auditions were basically comedy, as dreadful singers who should not sing in their showers tried out and were surprised when they were rejected. Some hopefuls showed at least raw talent and were invited to try out in Los Angeles, where the show was produced. Each week the pool was narrowed until one singer remained, the American Idol. The Idol received a recording contract and enjoyed some fame, though perhaps fleeting. The runners-up, in some seasons, also boosted their careers.

There were four in-studio judges—music producer Simon Cowell (who was with the original British show), music producer and writer **Randy Jackson**, singer-dancer Paula Abdul, and a guest celebrity. Debra Byrd served the series as vocal coach. The judges critiqued each singer, sometimes unmercifully—especially Cowell. However, after 10 to 12 finalists were chosen, the singers were eliminated not by the judges but based on call-in votes from the studio audience. The finalists sang on the Tuesday broadcast. Viewers voted within two hours of the end of the show. The singer getting the least votes was announced on the Wednesday show and was dropped. The finalists were required to sing various kinds of music each week—Motown, disco, country, or music by well-known writers.

In 2002, the African Americans among the 10 finalists were Justin Guarini (who came in second in the competition), Tamyra Gray (fourth), Christina Christian, and Ejay Day. In 2003, **Ruben Studdard** was the winner, the American Idol. Other African-American finalists were **Kimberley Locke**, Trenyce, Rickey Smith, Charles Grigsby, and Corey Clark. In 2004, African-American singer **Fantasia Barrino** was the American Idol.

In South Africa's version in 2002, blacks complained that viewers had to vote by computer or phone and that many black viewers had neither. A white singer won. *See also* REALITY SERIES.

AMERICAN LEGACY (*TV1, 2004*). This half-hour series, which could be called reality programming or documentary, was based on articles in *American Legacy* magazine. Featured were stories of how African Americans helped make the United States a great nation. Some themes included the settling of the West, scientific discoveries, accomplishments of black soldiers in wars, and numerous extraordinary stories of achievements. *See also* DOCUMENTARIES.

AMERICAN MASTERS: JAMES BROWN (*PBS, October 29, 2004*). This profile of entertainer James Brown at 70 years of age showed performances that illustrated why he is nicknamed "the hardest working man in show business." Commenting were **Little Richard**, Dan Aykroyd, and the Rev. Al Sharpton, who said that Brown's hit "releases the scream in all of us." The documentary, with some footage never seen previously, explained how Brown's rhythm-driven music connects soul, gospel, hip-hop, and funk and also delved into his personal life, including his tax problems and other turbulence. *See also* DOCUMENTARIES.

AMERICAN REVOLUTION OF '63 (*NBC, September 2, 1963*). This three-hour documentary centered on the struggle for civil rights. *See also* DOCUMENTARIES.

AMERICAN TRAGEDY (*November 12–15, 2000*). **Ving Rhames** starred in this miniseries about the gradual disintegration of O. J. Simpson's Dream Team during Simpson's murder trial in 1995. The film depicts backstabbing and undermining tactics between the team members.

AMERICA'S BLACK FORUM (*SYN, 1977– *). The show was a national news and opinion show similar to *Meet The Press*. It proclaimed that it is "the only credible weekend news source for African American perspectives on national issues." The show featured debates on critical issues facing African Americans. Guests included President Nelson Mandela, Colin Powell, **Denzel Washington, Oprah Winfrey, Spike Lee**, and former U.S. presidents George Bush and Bill Clinton. The show was under fire in early 2005, when Armstrong Williams, a frequent guest commentator on the show, admitted to accepting funds from President Bush's secretary of education, Rod Paige. In the contract, among other tasks, Williams promised to encourage producers of *America's Black Forum* to periodically address Paige's controversial No Child Left Behind Act.

AMERICA'S DREAM (*HBO, February 24, 1995*). This was three stories centering on black life from 1948 to 1958. "Long Black Song" was based on a short story by Richard Wright; its central character was Silas (**Danny Glover**), an Alabama farmer whose lonely wife, Sarah (Tina Lifford), became romantically attached to a white traveling salesman. In "The Boy Who Painted Christ Black," by John Henrik Clarke, young Aaron (Norman D. Golden II) painted a portrait and gave it to his teacher (**Vanessa Bell Calloway**). Controversy erupted, especially with the principal (**Wesley Snipes**). "The Reunion" by **Maya Angelou** was about a jazz pianist (**Lorraine Toussaint**) who met her childhood nemesis, the daughter of a white couple who employed her parents as servants. **Jasmine Guy, Carl Lumbly**, and **Yolanda King** had roles. Glover was executive producer. **Bill Duke** and Kevin Rodney Sullivan were directors.

AMOS, JOHN. Amos played the recurring role of Gordon Howard on *The Mary Tyler Moore Show* (1970–1973). He was a regular on the short-lived sketch comedy series *The Funny Side* (1971). He started his role as Florida's (**Esther Rolle**) husband on *Maude* (1973–1974) and continued to play James Evans on the sitcom *Good Times* (1974–1976). He played Capt. Dolan on *Hunter* (1984–1985) and Coach Sam on *In the House* (1996–1997). He was the adult Kunta Kinte in *Roots* (1977–1978) and played Ernie Cumberbatch in *The 704 Hauser* (1994). He was the mayor of Washington, D.C., in *The District* (2000–2001). He played the patriarch in the sitcom *All About the Andersons* beginning in 2003. He had key roles in the TV films *Alcatraz: The Whole Story* (1980) and *Cops and Robbers* in 1978 and *Disappearing Acts* in 2000.

AMOS 'N' ANDY (*CBS, 1951–1953*). This, the first all-black cast sitcom, was popular in radio where white actors, producers Freeman Gosden and Charles Correll, played the characters. A four-year search was conducted to find just the right black actors for the television version.

The series was set in Harlem and was centered primarily on the devious schemes of George Stevens (**Tim Moore**), who was known as Kingfish, his title as head of the Mystic Knights of the Sea fraternal lodge. Kingfish's buddy and lodge brother, the easily led, somewhat dim Andy Brown (**Spencer Williams Jr.**), was usually the victim of the schemes. Kingfish's wife, Sapphire (**Ernestine Wade**), and mother-in-law (**Amanda Randolph**) were the loudmouthed voices of reason who threatened him with violence whenever he got out of line. He always did, and they often made their threats good. Amos (**Alvin Childress**) was also a lodge brother who was the series narrator and easily the least objectionable character in the series; he earned a living as a taxi driver, reared his children, had a good relationship with his wife, spoke well, and tried to keep peace among the brothers. Lightning (**Nick Stewart** aka **Nick O'Demus**) was the show's slow-moving, slow-talking, slow-thinking Stepin Fetchit–like character, the janitor at the lodge hall. Algonquin J. Calhoun (**Johnny Lee**) was the local lawyer and lodge member with questionable knowledge of law and even more questionable ethics.

Recurring characters were the following: **Lillian Randolph** (Amanda's sister) as Madame Queen, Andy's overbearing girlfriend; **Jester Hairston** as Sapphire's cousin Leroy; and **Roy Glenn** as various upstanding male characters, particularly Sapphire's employer.

Though proud of the actors' talents in portraying the roles, the National Association for the Advancement of Colored People (NAACP) and other civil rights groups charged that the series promoted negative stereotypes of black Americans. Among the grievances listed by the NAACP were the following:

"'Amos 'n' Andy' on television is worse than on radio because it is a *picture*, a living talking moving picture of Black Americans, not merely a story in words over a radio loudspeaker. Millions of white Americans see this 'Amos 'n' Andy' picture of Black Americans and think the entire race is the same."

The criticism grew among African-American viewers who admitted then that the series was very funny but that it painted an inappropriate picture of black life. During its premiere season, the sitcom finished 13th in a ranking of all series in the Nielsen ratings with a 38.9 rating, meaning that 38.9 percent of all homes with television were tuned to *Amos 'n' Andy*. In the following year, it had slipped to 25th place. The series ended original programming in 1953, although reruns continued for the next 10 years. Videotapes of the series are still available but difficult to find. *See also* STEREOTYPES; WADE, ERNESTINE.

AMOS 'N' ANDY: ANATOMY OF A CONTROVERSY (*PBS, August 23, 1984*). **George Kirby** hosted this one-hour examination of the controversial **Amos 'n' Andy** television series. Cast members were interviewed as well as **Redd Foxx**, the **Rev. Jesse Jackson**, and **Marla Gibbs**. Rare clips from the series were shown.

ANANDA LEWIS SHOW, THE (*SYN, 2001–2002*). This talk/interview show hosted by Ananda Lewis was geared to women 18 to 49 and centered on current issues affecting Americans. Unfortunately, the daily show premiered on September 10, 2001, the day before the terrorist attacks. The show was taped in New York, so a production decision was made that Lewis would take the show into the streets and show viewers what was going on. It did not work. Reviewers said that people preferred looking at actual newscasts. *See also* TALK SHOWS.

. . . AND BEAUTIFUL I (*SYN, September 1969*). These 60-minute specials spotlighted performances of black entertainers. The first starred **Della Reese**, The Blossoms, Jerry Butler, **Redd Foxx**, Little Dion, and Wilson Pickett. Music was by H. B. Barnum. **Cal Wilson** was on the writing team.

. . . AND BEAUTIFUL II (*SYN, September 1970*). The second program of 60-minute specials highlighting black entertainers featured various kinds of music, including jazz, blues, and gospel. Gospel singer **Mahalia Jackson**, when asked to distinguish and compare the three types of music, said, "The blues and spirituals are closely related, but the big difference is that a spiritual has hope, whereas the blues is sad all the way through and stays that way. Another thing about jazz—it makes people happy on the surface, but when it's over, it's through. But a gospel song lasts—it penetrates much deeper and stays with you." The program was a showcase, however, and not a competition of musical genres. In addition to Jackson, the show included **Louis Armstrong, B. B. King**, The Cannonball Adderley Quintet, **Count Basie, Duke Ellington, Billie Holliday**, Nina Simone, and Sly and the Family Stone. *See also* VARIETY SPECIALS.

ANDERSON, ANTHONY. Comic Anthony Anderson starred in the sitcom *All About the Andersons* beginning in 2003.

ANDERSON, CARL, II. Known first as Judas in the 1973 musical film *Jesus Christ Superstar*, Anderson was Baker in the 1979 TV film *Mind over Murder* and King Monroe in the daytime series *Another World* (1997–1998). He died of leukemia four days shy of his 59th birthday in 2004.

ANDERSON, EDDIE "ROCHESTER." Anderson played the character Rochester in *The Jack Benny Show* for 15 years. He appeared on most of the Jack Benny specials after the series. He was Noah in **"The Green Pastures"** on *Hallmark Hall of Fame* in 1957. He made a guest appearance on *Christmas with the Stars* in 1953. In variety specials, he was a guest on *Go* hosted by Ryan O'Neal in 1967 and on *A Tribute to Jack Benny* in 1974. Anderson was born in 1906 and died in 1977.

ANDERSON, MARIAN. Contralto singer Marian Anderson performed in 1953 on *The Ford 50th Anniversary Show* celebrating the anniversary of the Ford Motor Company. In 1954, she made an appearance on *Dateline* (not the newsmagazine), a tribute in music to men and women who had given their lives in the cause of a free press. In 1956, she sang again in *Festival of Music*, a special of concert artists and opera singers. In 1959, she performed songs associated with the month of May in *America Pauses for the Merry Month of May*. That same year, she sang Christmas songs on *Christmas Startime with Leonard Bernstein*. She was one of the first honorees of *The Kennedy Center Honors* in 1978. Anderson lived from 1902 to 1993.

ANDRE WATTS IN CONCERT WITH THE INDIANAPOLIS SYMPHONY ORCHESTRA (*PBS, August 10, 1983*). Pianist Watts was host of this special in which he performed Beethoven's Piano Concerto No. 5 ("The Emperor") and Zoltan Kodaly's "Dances of Galanta."

ANDREWS, TINA. Andrews had regular roles in the drama series *Falcon Crest* in 1983–1984 and *The Contender* in 1980 and the sitcom The Sanford Arms in 1977. She played a key role in *Billy: Portrait of a Street Kid* in 1977. She later became a writer/producer and created and produced the animated series *Sistas in the City*, which began in 2003.

AND STILL I RISE: MAYA ANGELOU (*PBS, February 3, 1985*). This broadcast featured an interview with the author/performer.

ANDY GRIFFITH SHOW, THE. *See* TARKINGTON, ROCKNE.

ANDY WILLIAMS AND THE NBC KIDS (*NBC, December 20, 1985*). The child stars of NBC shows joined Andy Williams in a holiday celebration. Some were **Tempestt Bledsoe, Lisa Bonet, Keshia Knight Pulliam, Malcolm Jamal-Warner** (all from *The Cosby Show*), **Cherie Johnson** from *Punky Brewster*, and **Alfonso Ribeiro** from *Silver Spoons.*

ANGELOU, MAYA. Angelou made numerous appearances on talk and interview shows, especially *Oprah.* She played the role of Nyo Boto in the miniseries *Roots* in 1977. In earlier years, she appeared on both **Richard Pryor** specials in 1977 and 1982. She was interviewed on the PBS special *And Still I Rise* in 1985. The 1979 telefilm was based on her autobiography *I Know Why the Caged Bird Sings*. She recited her poem "On the Pulse of Morning" at the televised inauguration of President Bill Clinton's first term of office on January 20, 1993.

ANGRY VOICES OF WATTS, THE (*NBC, August 16, 1966*). An NBC News special, the program featured black writers and poets presenting their works from the Watts Writers Workshop established by Budd Schulberg in the riot-torn Watts section of Los Angeles.

ANIMATION. Television's animated series and specials did not include African-American characters until the 1970s. During that decade there were the following: *The Harlem Globetrotters* (1970–1973), showing the feats of the celebrated basketball team; *The Jackson Five* (1971–1973), featuring the adventures of characters named for the actual singing family members and using the voices of the Jacksons; *Clerow Wilson and the Miracle of P.S. 14* (1972), a one-time cartoon telling a story from Flip Wilson's childhood in Jersey City, New Jersey; *Kid Power* (1972–1984), based on the newspaper strip titled Wee Pals and featuring a multicultural cast; *Fat Albert and the Cosby Kids* (1972–1984), created by Bill Cosby and centering on his childhood memories in North Philadelphia; and *The Adventures of Muhammad Ali: I Am the Greatest* (1977–1978), featuring Ali's voice in adventure and comedy stories.

Going into the 1980s, there was a group of black teenagers in the segment titled "Rickity Rocket" in *The Plasticman Comedy-Adventure Show* (1979–1980). *The Super Globetrotters* (1979–1980) was a return of the adventures of the Harlem Globetrotters with added super powers.

Then there were the spin-off cartoons. Gary Coleman's TV film *The Kid with the Broken Halo* became an animated series titled *The Gary Coleman Show* (1982–1983). Mr. T, popular in *The A-Team*, was the center of *Mister T* (1983–1986), a story of a gym owner and neighborhood kids who solved mysteries. *The Real Ghostbusters* (1986–1992) was a spin-off of the feature film *Ghostbusters*.

In the 1990s and 2000s, several animated series with multicultural characters and noted black actors providing voices were *Spider-Man* (1995) with **Roscoe Lee Browne** as the mob boss; *South Park* (1997–) about some youngsters mentored by Chef with **Isaac Hayes** providing the voice; *The PJs* (1999–2001), which featured the voices of **Eddie Murphy**; *Little Bill* (1999–) with the voice of **Bill Cosby**; *The Proud Family* (2001–), about a middle-class black family; and *Fatherhood* (2004–) another Cosby offering based on his book of the same title and about the Bindlebeep family.

ANNE RICE'S "THE FEAST OF ALL SAINTS" (*SHO, November 11–12, 2001*). This dramatic miniseries centered on the "free people of color" in 1840s New Orleans. These people lived between the black and white worlds as exemplified by Marcel (**Robert Ri'chard**), a 16-year-old boy with a biracial mother (**Gloria Reuben**) and a white father (Peter Gallagher). Others in the cast were **Jennifer Beals**, **Ossie Davis**, **Ruby Dee**, **Pam Grier**, **Jasmine Guy**, **James Earl Jones**, **Eartha Kitt**, **Ben Vereen**, **Forest Whitaker**, **Victoria Rowell**, **Bianca Lawson**, and **Nicole Lyn**.

ANTHOLOGY SERIES. From the beginning of nationwide television, there were dramatic series featuring serious live and later filmed plays. Each week, there was a different play. There were classics, Broadway plays, and plays from original scripts. Some were low budget with small casts and meager sets. Others had large casts and elaborate sets. Some were half-hour plays and some one hour, and most were named for the commercial sponsors of the series. *The Kraft Television Theatre* was the first, dating back to 1947, and aired regularly until 1958. Others were *Philco Television Playhouse* (1948–1955), *Chevrolet Tele-Theater* (1948–1950), *Studio One* (1948–1958), *Ford Theater* (1949–1957), *Armstrong Circle Theater* (1950–1953), *Lux Video Theater* (1950–1957), *Schlitz Playhouse of Stars* (1951–1959), *General Electric Theater* (1953–1962) with future President Ronald Reagan as host, *U.S. Steel Hour* (1985–1963), and others. Only *Hallmark Hall of Fame* still airs with special dramatic presentations but not on a regular schedule.

Occasionally there were black actors and/or black themes. The year 1955 was a big one for black actors in anthology series. **James Edwards** was in *Alfred Hitchcock Presents* in the "Breakdown" episode. Edwards also had roles in that same year in *DuPont Cavalcade Theater* in the teleplay "Toward Tomorrow" and in *General Electric Theater* in "D.P." **Paul Robeson** played the title role in "The Emperor Jones" in *Kraft Television Theatre*; **Ossie Davis** and **Rex Ingram** were cast in the same production. **Sidney Poitier** played a starring role in **"A Man Is Ten Feet Tall"** on *Philco Television Playhouse*. **Ethel Waters** and **Harry Belafonte** starred in "Winner by Decision" on *General Electric Theater*.

There were black performers making appearances on one-time anthology episodes throughout the airing of such series. For example, the black play **"The Green Pastures"** was a segment of *Hallmark Hall of Fame* in 1957.

ANYA'S BELL (*CBS, October 31, 1999*). Della Reese starred in this made-for-television movie as a lonely blind woman who helped a young boy learn to live with dyslexia. He, in turn, helped her live a better life through using a cane.

A. PHILIP RANDOLPH: FOR JOBS AND FREEDOM (*PBS, 1996*). A. Philip Randolph was the African-American labor leader who led the 1963 **March on Washington**, at which Martin Luther King Jr. delivered his "I Have a Dream" speech. The speech became so well known that later generations assumed that King himself was the leader when actually he was one of several speakers. This documentary restored Randolph to his proper place in history. After being a radical journalist, he helped organize the Brotherhood of Sleeping Car Porters and, after a 12-year battle, won the first national labor agreement for a black union. He had threatened to organize a D.C. protest march as far back as the presidency of Franklin Roosevelt, and that forced Roosevelt to ban segregation in the federal government and defense industries. Similarly, he was instrumental in urging Harry Truman to integrate the military. Then he carried his longtime plan out in 1963 and was successful in placing civil rights on the nation's legislative and moral agenda. This 86-minute production is available on videotape.

APOLLO AT 70: A HOT NIGHT IN HARLEM (*NBC, June 19, 2004***).** This two-hour special celebrated the 70th anniversary of the historic theater "where stars are born and legends are made." Entertainers who could make it at the Apollo were on the way to stardom because the tough audience would boo inferior artists off the stage. The famed Amateur Night began in 1934 and launched the careers of **Ella Fitzgerald, Sarah Vaughn, Ruth Brown,** Wilson Pickett, and others. A form of Amateur Night continued with the TV series *It's Showtime at the Apollo*. Regulars at the Apollo were **Aretha Franklin, Redd Foxx, Nancy Wilson, Flip Wilson, Richard Pryor, Billy Eckstine,** Pigmeat Markham, Moms Mabley, **Dionne Warwick,** and many others. Among the entertainers appearing in the TV special were **Patti LaBelle, Natalie Cole,** Herbie Hancock, **Branford Marsalis, Savion Glover, Denzel Washington,** Donnie McClurkin, Fred Hammond, Yolanda Adams, **Vivica A. Fox,** Ashanti, and others. **Quincy Jones** was consulting producer with Suzanne de Passe as producer. *See also* VARIETY SPECIALS.

APOLLO COMEDY CLUB, THE (*SYN, 1992–1995***).** This one-hour comedy/variety series featured sketch comedy and had a primarily black and Hispanic regular cast of performers as well as guest musical performers and guest stand-up acts. The regulars included Derrick Fox, Ken Jackman, Paula Jai Parker (1992–1993), Yusef Lamont (1992–1993), **Lisa Carson** (1992–1993), Kool Bubba Ice, Deborah Magdalena (1993–1994), Grace Garland (1993–1995), Ronda

Fowler (1994–1995), Karne June Sanchez (1994–1995), and Ilan Kwittken (1994–1995).

APOLLO THEATER HALL OF FAME, THE (*NBC, August 4, 1993*). This two-hour concert honored the alumni of the Apollo Theater in Harlem. **Bill Cosby** was host. Some entertainers were honored posthumously; others were present. Honorees were Sam Cooke, **Ella Fitzgerald, Billie Holliday**, The Ink Spots, **and Richard Pryor**. Performers included the following: Bryan Adams, **B. B. King, Thelma Carpenter, Ray Charles**, Eric Clapton, The Cleftones, **Mark Curry**, Al Green, Buddy Guy, Brian McKnight, **Teddy Pendergrass, Smokey Robinson, Diana Ross**, and Robin Williams.

APPRENTICE, THE (*NBC, 2004– *). This reality series made its debut in 2004 with 16 contestants competing against each other by doing business projects in groups. Each week for 15 episodes, host Donald Trump fired one of them. The contestant left standing after all others were fired would win the opportunity to head one of Trump's companies with a salary of $250,000 a year. In the first season, there were two African-American contestants: Kwame Jackson, a Harvard MBA who had given up a job with the investment firm Goldman Sachs, and Omarosa Manigault-Stallworth, a Howard University graduate student who had worked at the White House on Vice President Al Gore's staff. The contestants were known to TV viewers only by their first names until they were fired. Omarosa was controversial from the beginning, a problem for some of the contestants but a plus for the series' ratings, which were consistently high enough to get a pickup for a second season. She was basically the contestant viewers loved to hate. Kwame lost in the final project when his team member, Omarosa, failed to follow through on an assignment. Trump said he should have fired her; he said he did not realize he could. Instead, he heard Trump's famous line, "You're fired!" Entrepreneur Bill Rancic was hired.

In the second season, African-American Stacie Jones Upchurch, a restaurant owner, was eliminated early in the season in a controversial battle with the white female contestants who decided she was crazy. Kevin Allen, with an MBA from Emory University and a law degree from the University of Chicago, lasted to be in the final four. The third season pitted the college-educated contestants against the street smart. Among the street smart were African-American players Tara and Craig; Verna, an information-technology executive, was among the book smart. Neither finished in the top two. *See also* REALITY TELEVISION.

ARANHA, RAY. Aranha starred as Nick Williams in the sitcom *Married People* (1990–1991) and starred as Mr. Mike in the drama series *The Heights* (1992).

ARETHA FRANKLIN: DUETS (*FOX, May 9, 1993*)**.** Aretha Franklin, the Queen of Soul, sang solos and duets with other great singers. Among them were the following: Elton John, who sang with her "Spirit in the Dark"; Rod Stewart, "People Get Ready"; Bonnie Raitt, "Since You've Been Gone"; **Smokey Robinson**, "Just to See Her"; and Gloria Estefan, "Coming Out of the Dark." Other guests were En Vogue, Candice Bergen, **Whoopi Goldberg**, and **Lena Horne** (many of the guests were seen in cameos).

ARETHA FRANKLIN: GOING HOME (*VH1, February 19, 1995*)**.** This production earned nominations for the NAACP Image Awards and was widely praised for telling Aretha's life story intercut with original performances emanating from the piano in her Detroit living room.

ARETHA FRANKLIN: IN PERFORMANCE AT THE WHITE HOUSE (*PBS, October 12, 1994*)**.** Aretha was the headliner with guest **Lou Rawls**. President Bill and First Lady Hillary Rodham Clinton were the hosts.

ARETHA FRANKLIN: THE QUEEN OF SOUL (*PBS, August 22, 1988*)**.** The Queen of Soul, Aretha Franklin, was the subject of this documentary, which told her life story from singing in her father's church, through foiled personal relationships, and an up-and-down career. A highlight was her singing "Precious Lord" at the funeral of Martin Luther King Jr. and "Spirit in the Dark" with Ray Charles. She sang "Can't Turn You Loose" and other songs. Reviews were critical that her performances were cut short in favor of testimonials from celebrities.

ARMSTRONG, LOUIS. Singer and jazz trumpeter Louis "Satchmo" Armstrong was popular in variety specials and series. He was the mystery guest on the pioneering game show *What's My Line?* twice—in 1954 and 1964. In 1956, he was one of several top entertainers who sang Cole Porter songs in *You're the Top*. Three highlights of his career took place in 1957. Armstrong performed in *Crescendo*, a look at American culture through music. He was one of the entertainers in *The Edsel Show*, a variety show sponsored by the Ford Motor Company to promote the Edsel automobile. The show was tops; the car was a failure. He began a series of appearances on *The Timex All-Star Jazz Show I, II, III, and IV* airing in 1957, 1958, and 1959. The first was billed as "the first sponsored jazz concert" and was sponsored by Timex watches. He was a guest on a Bing Crosby special in 1959 and a Danny Kaye special in 1960. In 1965, he and others who had won Grammy Awards that year performed their winning music in *The Best on Record*. Armstrong made an appearance on *Johnny Carson Presents the Sun City Scandals* in 1970, the same year he and a group of black singers and musicians made up the special *. . . And Beautiful*. In February 1971, he was a guest on a Bing Crosby show and sang "Pennies from Heaven." He died in his sleep in July 1971, just a few months later. He was 71. His songs were used as theme music for numerous TV shows and TV films including *Frank's Place* (1987) and *Family Matters* (1989). He was the subject of a posthumous tribute at the halftime show of Super Bowl VI in 1972.

ARNOLD, TICHINA. Known primarily as Pam in the sitcom *Martin* (1992–1997), Arnold had roles in the daytime dramas *Ryan's Hope* (1987–1989) and *All My Children* (1989–1990). She played Nicole in the series *One on One* (2001–) and Susie in the TV film *Perfect Prey* (1998).

ARSENIO HALL SHOW, THE (*FOX, 1989–1994*). Comedian Hall was host and headliner of this late night talk show, which started with the comedy monologue like other talk shows starring comics and featured conversations with celebrity guests, but the atmosphere was more like a party than a show. There were some musical and comedy performances. His show was able to capture a younger, hipper audience than Johnny Carson, who ruled the late night hours at the time. Hall had no desk in the sitting area and did not have a sidekick like other late night talk show hosts. At stage left, there was the "dog pound," a group of people who cheered with dog-barking sounds. Hall also spoke out for safe sex and was the first talk show host to have Magic Johnson as a guest after he announced he was HIV positive. He was also able to get musical acts that did not appear on other late night series. One of them was then presidential candidate Bill Clinton, who played the saxophone on the June 3, 1992, show. That incident was one of *TV Guide*'s 100 Most Memorable Moments. Hall also had some controversy and negative feedback when he had Nation of Islam leader Louis Farrakhan as a guest.

ARTHUR GODFREY'S TALENT SCOUTS (*CBS, 1948–1958*). On this talent show, hosted by Arthur Godfrey, talent scouts brought their discoveries on the show to perform, and an applause meter would choose the winner of the evening. Singer/actress **Leslie Uggams** appeared on the show in 1952 and went on to a successful career.

A-TEAM, THE (*NBC, 1983–1987*). Veteran actor George Peppard, as Col. John "Hannibal" Smith, had top billing in this popular action adventure series, but relative newcomer **Mr. T** (who had a key role in Sylvester Stallone's *Rocky III*) was the center of the action. His character was Sgt. B. A. Baracus (B. A. formerly stood for Bad Attitude, but viewers understood that it was actually Bad Ass. Censors at the time did not allow such words.) He was big, tough, wore several pounds of gold chains on his neck, and always said, "I pity the fool." Hannibal and B. A. were part of a team of former soldiers from the Vietnam War who, as civilians, were chasing and capturing crooks. B. A. was not only a mighty warrior but also a top mechanic who could build armored vehicles and guns out of old junk pieces. The series was considered at one time to be the most violent series on television, but only one person ever died on-screen. Other deaths were mentioned but not seen.

ATHLETES' BIOPICS. The lives of athletes have been portrayed primarily in inspirational films that say, "You can do this, too." Often the athlete has overcome a disability or utter poverty or a situation in which he or she was the worst player on the grade-school team. In depicting black athletes, there is usually the added drama of having suffered some racial discrimination. These films often air to promote the Olympic Games or during **African-American History Month**. *Brian's Song* (1971 and 2001), the story of how the friendship of football players Brian Piccolo and Gale Sayers (played by **Billy Dee Williams** in 1971 and **Mekhi Phifer** in 2001) thrived despite Piccolo's losing battle with cancer. *It's Good to Be Alive* (1974) was the life of baseball great Roy Campanella, who suffered paralysis. **Paul Winfield** played Campy. *The Jesse Owens Story* was a 1984 dramatization of the four-time medalist who was the star of the 1936 Olympic Games in Berlin. **Dorian Harewood** played Owens, who was snubbed by Adolf Hitler. *Wilma* was the 1977 story of Olympic sprinter Wilma Rudolph, who had polio as a child. She was played by **Shirley Jo Finney. Bernie Casey** played boxing champion Joe Louis in *Ring of Passion* in 1978. *The Tai Babilonia Story* in 1990 related how the famous champion figure skater **Tai Babilonia** had her 1980 Olympic dreams dashed when her partner, Randy Gardner, suffered an injury. Actress Rachel Crawford played Babilonia, but the real skating twosome did the skating sequences. College basketball star Hank Gathers was memorialized in the film *Final Shot: The Hank Gathers Story* in 1992. *Tyson*, in 1994, was the story of world heavyweight champion "Iron" Mike Tyson and mentioned his criminal charges as well as his triumphs. **Michael Jai White** portrayed Tyson. *King of the World*, in 2000, was the story of Cassius Clay in the 1960s with Terrence Howard playing Clay and Steve Harris playing Sonny Liston. *Joe and Max* (2002) was the story of the unlikely friendship between rival boxers Joe Louis (Leonard Roberts) and Max Schmeling of Germany as their two countries were on the brink of war.

ATKINS, ESSENCE. Atkins played Yvette in the sitcom *Smart Guy* (1997–1999) and Dee Dee Thorne in the sitcom *Half & Half* (2002–).

ATKINS, SHARIF. Atkins played Michael Gallant on *ER* in 2002, then he joined the cast of the cop drama *Hawaii* in 2004.

ATLANTA CHILD MURDERS, THE (*CBS, February 10–12, 1985*). In 1980 and 1981, the city of Atlanta was plagued with a killer of its children. Eventually, Wayne Williams (**Calvin Levels**) was convicted of two of 29 murders and implicated in 23 others. The film implied that Williams is innocent, that there was southern injustice. Atlanta officials were reportedly outraged. **Morgan Freeman** narrated the two-part made-for-television movie. **Gloria Foster** also starred as Camile Bell, mother of one of the slain children. Martin Sheen, Rip Torn, and Jason Robards had key roles.

AUTOBIOGRAPHY OF MISS JANE PITTMAN, THE (*CBS, January 31, 1974*). This made-for-television dramatic motion picture was based on the novel by Ernest J. Gaines, whose aunt, Augusteen Jefferson, served as the principal role model for the central character played by **Cicely Tyson**. As Miss Jane Pittman, Tyson aged from 19 to 110. Pittman was a former slave who recounted her life from the Civil War era to the 1960s civil rights struggle. She observed numerous changes in racial equality and social dignity in her lifetime. The highlight of the film and a highlight of Miss Jane's life was her determination to drink from a water fountain reserved for whites only. With 12 nominations, the film won nine **Emmy Awards** including Outstanding Special of 1973–1974. Awards were also won for writing, direction, music, costume design, makeup, and hairstyling. Tyson won two Emmys, one for Outstanding Actress in a Drama and one for Actress of the Year—Special. When she accepted the award, she addressed her parents, who had discouraged her from a Hollywood career. She said, "Mom, this wasn't a den of iniquity after all." Others in the cast included **Odetta** as Big Laura, **Joel Fluellen** as "Unc" Isom, **Josephine Premice** as Madame Gautier, **Rod Perry** as Joe Pittman, and **Thalmus Rasulala** as Ned.

AVERY, JAMES. First recognized as Attorney Philip Banks, Will Smith's uncle in *Fresh Prince of Bel-Air* from 1990 to 1996, Avery also had a role in a 1989–1990 sitcom, *FM*, about a radio station.

Later, he starred as Alonzo Sparks, the head of a law firm, in the sitcom *Sparks* (1996–1998). His credits in made-for-television movies include the following: *Samaritan: The Mitch Snyder Story* in 1986, *Roe vs. Wade* in 1989, *Without Warning: Terror in the Towers* and *Simple Justice* in 1993, *A Friend to Die For* in 1994, and *The Advanced Guard* in 1998.

AVERY, MARGARET. Avery had key roles in the made-for-television film *Louis Armstrong—Chicago Style* in 1976, *Heat Wave* in 1990, and *The Jacksons: An American Dream* in 1992.

– B –

BABATUNDE, OBBA. Babatunde played Rusty Bennett in *All My Children* in 1987. He had a key role in *The Cherokee Kid* in 1996. In 1997, he played a key role in the TV movie *Miss Evers' Boys* and, for his work, was nominated for the **Emmy Award** for Supporting Actor.

BABILONIA, TAI. Champion ice skater Tai Babilonia helped Bob Hope celebrate his 77th birthday in a special in 1980. She performed with her partner Randy Gardner in several Christmas specials: *Christmas Dream* in 1984, *A Crystal Christmas* in 1987, and Disney's *Christmas on Ice* in 1990. *See also* ATHLETES' BIOPICS.

BABY I'M BACK (*CBS, 1978*). This sitcom starred **Demond Wilson** and **Denise Nicholas** and introduced **Kim Fields**. Seven years after he had deserted his wife, Olivia (Nicholas), because he could not take the pressures of being married, Raymond Ellis (Wilson) found that she had declared him dead. He had trouble proving he was alive, but he ended up living in the apartment building where Olivia and their two children (Fields and Tony Holmes) lived and tried to rekindle the romance. Olivia, however, was romantically linked to Col. Dickey (Ed Hall), a Pentagon official. Olivia's mother (**Helen Martin**) also opposed Ray's return.

BACKSTAIRS AT THE WHITE HOUSE (*NBC, January and February 1979*). The nine-hour, four-part miniseries was based on a book by Lillian Rogers Parks and Frances Spatz Leighton about the careers of domestics in the White House. The primary black actors and characters were the following: **Olivia Cole** as the hairdresser and maid, Maggie Rogers; both Tania Johnson and **Leslie Uggams** as seamstress Lillian Rogers; and **Lou Gossett Jr.** as Levi, butler and footman. Both Gossett and Cole were nominated for an **Emmy Award** for their roles.

BADGE OF THE ASSASSIN (*CBS, 1985*). This two-hour dramatic made-for-television movie starred **Yaphet Kotto** and James Woods as New York Detective Cliff Fenton and Assistant District Attorney Robert Tannenbaum, respectively. Based on fact, the film concentrated on the investigation of the ambush killing by a band of black "revolutionaries" of black officer Waverly Jones and white officer Joesph Piagentini. **Larry Riley**, **Pam Grier**, **RaeDawn Chong**, **Kene Holliday**, **Tamu**, and **Akosua Busia** had key roles.

BADU, ERYKAH. The singer performed on the musical special *One Love: The Bob Marley All-Star Tribute* in 1999 and was a popular guest star on variety, talk, and awards shows.

BAILEY, PEARL. Singer/comedienne Pearl Bailey and Mike Douglas hosted the musical special *Mike and Pearl* in 1968. She shared billing in the musical special *Carol Channing and Pearl Bailey on Broadway* in 1969. Other specials guest-starring Bailey were *One More Time* in 1974, many Bob Hope specials in the 1950s and 1960s, and a Bing Crosby special, *Bing! . . . A 50th Anniversary Gala* in 1977. She was host of *A Capitol Fourth*, the Independence Day celebration originating from Washington, D.C., with the National Symphony Orchestra in 1981, 1982, and 1989. Bailey starred as Bernice in a live television version of the stage drama *A Member of the Wedding* in 1982. Then, in 1985, she played a shopping cart lady with magical powers who befriended 15-year-old Cindy in "Cindy Eller: A Modern Fairy Tale," an *ABC Afterschool Special*. She performed at the *50th Presidential Inaugural Gala* and *In Performance at the White House* in 1988. She was very proud of her appearances at the White House during the Ronald Reagan administration and would tell total strangers, "Honey, you know I sang at the White House!" Pearl Bailey was born in 1918 and died in 1990.

BAKER, SHAUN. Baker played Russell Montego on the sitcom *Living Single* (1993–1998), Devo Griffin on the sitcom *The Show* (1996), Quick Williams on the sitcom *V.I.P.* (1998), and Malcolm on the sitcom *Where I Live* (1993).

BANFIELD, BEVER-LEIGH. She played key roles in made-for-television productions like *Roots: The Next Generations* in 1979 and *Benny's Place* in 1982.

BANKS, CAROL TILLERY. She had a key role in the 1978 made-for-television film *Love Is Not Enough* and the 1979 series that was spawned by it : *Harris & Company*. She also had a role in *Brave New World*, a 1980 telefilm.

BANKS, TYRA. Banks hosted and created and was executive producer of the reality television competition show, *America's Top Model* in 2003 and *America's Next Top Model* in 2004. She played Jackie, Will's girlfriend, in the 1993–1994 season of *Fresh Prince of Bel-Air*. In fall 2005, she started hosting her own talk show, *The Tyra Banks Show.*

BARBARA MCNAIR AND DUKE ELLINGTON SPECIAL, THE (*SYN, February 1968*). **Barbara McNair** and **Duke Ellington** made music in an hour of solos and duets.

BARBERSHOP *(Showtime, 2005).* **J. Omar Gooding** starred in this racy sitcom based on the popular film of the same title.

BAREFOOT IN THE PARK (*ABC, 1970–1971*). This sitcom was a black version of the Neil Simon Broadway comedy *Barefoot in the Park* and starred **Scoey Mitchlll** and **Tracy Reed** as newlyweds Paul and Corie Bratter. Corie's interfering mother, Mabel, was played by **Thelma Carpenter**. Honey, the owner of the local pool hall and family friend, was played by **Nipsey Russell**. Many claim that the series was a good depiction of a middle-class black family, something rarely seen on television at the time. Others argue that point. African-American television historian Donald Bogle claimed that "the characters are unbelievable black middle-class figures" as contrasted to the later characters in *The Bill Cosby Show* or *The Cosby Show*, which Bogle termed "realistic." The series died after four months on the air.

BARKLEY, CHARLES. After playing professional basketball for 16 seasons, Barkley joined CNN News Group in 2002 to offer commentary and analysis to news and political stories. He also provided analysis on *Inside the NBA*, the TNT studio show.

BARNES, ERNIE. Artist Barnes's paintings were displayed as the works of J.J. in the sitcom *Good Times* (1976–1979). He also played a key role in the TV film *Don't Look Back* in 1981.

BARNEY MILLER (*ABC, 1975–1982*). Hal Linden, as the captain, was the star of this sitcom about the detectives, other personnel, and people who chanced to be present in the squad room of what seemed to be a rundown Greenwich Village precinct station. However, **Ron Glass** as the African-American, smart-mouthed, funny, flamboyant Detective Ron Harris, who always said whatever was on his mind, was very much a reason for watching the show. The show was racially mixed also with Asian (Jack Soo) and Latino (Gregory Sierra) characters, and there was ethnic humor at first, but most of the race jokes were gone after the first season. *See also* SERIES WITH ONE BLACK SUPPPORTING ACTOR/PERFORMER BEFORE 1980.

BARRINO, FANTASIA. Singer Barrino was winner of *American Idol* in 2004.

BARRY, TOM. Barry played a regular role in the drama series *Cold Case* (2003–).

BASIE, COUNT. As early as 1957, Basie was a guest performer on the *Dinah Shore Special*. He composed the theme for *M Squad*, a 1957–1960 series. In 1960, he contributed to an hour of music and dance hosted by Fred Astaire in *Astaire Time* and a hour of music of the big-band era, *The Swingin' Years*. In 1965, he was one of **Sammy**

Davis's musical friends in *Sammy and His Friends*. In 1967, Basie performed the music of the composer and lyricist in *Rodgers and Hart Today*. In 1968, he was the music director on the special *One More Time*. In 1970, he was one of the black musicians spotlighted in *. . . And Beautiful, II*. In 1972, he was one of the leading jazz musicians in the concert taped at Lincoln Center in New York for *All Star Swing Festival* and in *The Big Band and All That Jazz*. In 1973, Basie, with other singers and musicians, paid tribute to their comrade in *Duke Ellington . . . We Love You Madly*. He helped relate the history of jazz in *The Original Rompin' Stompin' Hot and Heavy, Cool and Groovy All-Star Jazz Show* in 1976. He performed on *Sinatra: The Man and His Music* in 1981, the same year he was an honoree on *The Kennedy Center Honors*. Basie was born in 1904 and died in 1984.

BASSETT, ANGELA. Bassett starred with Corbin Bernsen in *Line of Fire: The Morris Dees Story* in 1991. She starred as Katherine Jackson in *The Jacksons: An American Dream* in 1992 and played the title role in *The Rosa Parks Story*, a made-for-television film in 2002. She narrated the 360-minute, four-part PBS documentary *Africans in America: America's Journey Through Slavery* in 1998.

BATTERED (*NBC, September 6, 1978*). **LeVar Burton** and **Chip Fields** starred in one of three stories about women victims of domestic abuse.

BATTLE, HINTON. Battle had a key role in the 2001 made-for-television film *Child Star: The Shirley Temple Story*.

BATTLE, KATHLEEN. The soprano starred in 1990 in *Kathleen Battle & Jessye Norman Sing Spirituals*. In 1989, she starred in the special *Christmas in Washington*.

BAYOU CLASSIC (*NBC, annually*). This football game, a historic rivalry between black colleges (Grambling State University and Southern University) at the Louisiana Superdome in New Orleans is held on the weekend following Thanksgiving. The battle of the marching bands is as much a draw as the sporting event, as the city is flooded with celebrants.

BEACH, MICHAEL. Beach had a recurring role as Al Boulet, the husband who passed the HIV virus onto his wife (series regular **Gloria Reuben**) on *ER* from 1995 to 1997.

BEAH: A BLACK WOMAN SPEAKS (*HBO, February 2004*). **LisaGay Hamilton** narrated, wrote, and directed this documentary celebrating the life of actress **Beah Richards**. Richards's career spanned 50 years; she was not only an actress but also a human rights and civil rights activist and a poet. The production centers on conversations with Richards. She offered sage advice about the craft of acting as well as insightful observation on living life to the fullest. Footage of her work was included as well as comments from persons—some famous, some not—who knew her well. Richards died in 2000, shortly after receiving the **Emmy Award** for her final role in *The Practice*; Hamilton accepted the award for her. In the final scenes of the 90-minute production, Hamilton presented the award to the ailing Richards, who wanted her ashes spread over a Confederate cemetery; Hamilton complied.

BEALS, JENNIFER. Beals played Justin Madsen Judd in the religious drama *Nothing Sacred* (1997–1998) and Perry Quinn in the short-lived serialized drama *20000 Malibu Road* (1992). In TV films, she had a starring role in *A House Divided* in 2000 and a key role in *Anne Rice's "The Feast of All Saints"* in 2001.

BEARD, STYMIE. The alumnus of the *Our Gang* comedies had a key role in the made-for-television film *It's Good to Be Alive* in 1974. He made several appearances on *Sanford and Son*. Beard was born in 1925 and died of a stroke in 1981.

BEAUVAIS-NILON, GARCELLE. Beauvais (aka Garcelle Beauvais) played Fancy in the sitcom *The Jamie Foxx Show* (1996–2001). Prior to that, she played Cynthia Nichols, a model, in the drama series *Models, Inc.* from 1994 to 1995. In 2005, she began a role in the regular cast of the private investigator drama *Eyes*.

BEAVERS, LOUISE. Beavers, known primarily for the 1939 version of the film *Imitation of Life*, was one of the actresses who played the title role in *Beulah*. In 1955, she joined the cast of *Make Room for*

Daddy as the housekeeper Louise but stayed for only one season. She had roles in *Playhouse 90's* "*The Hostess with the Mostest*" and *Walt Disney Presents* "*Swamp Fox.*" Louise Beavers was born in 1902 and died in 1962. *See also* DOMESTIC WORKERS.

BEING BOBBY BROWN *(Bravo, 2005).* Cameras followed entertainer Bobby Brown as he frolicked through his day-to-day life. The idea was that people would see the "real" Bobby Brown and not the person with the "bad boy" image on whom the news media concentrated. Viewers saw his meetings with family, friends, total strangers, and people in the musical world. High points and low points of the limited-run reality series were his encounters with his famous wife, **Whitney Houston**. They bickered and kissed, had bizarre conversations and kissed, and sometimes just kissed.

BELAFONTE, GINA. A daughter of **Harry Belafonte**, Gina played Carmela Pagan, a police officer, on *The Commish* (1991–1993).

BELAFONTE, HARRY. Belafonte was a guest star on numerous variety series and specials, including *The Nat "King" Cole Show*, *The Ed Sullivan Show*, *The Flip Wilson Show*, and others. He was a regular on the 1949 short-lived musical variety series *Sugar Hill Times* and in 1955 starred with **Ethel Waters** in *Winner by Decision*, a drama on *General Electric Theater*. In 1955, he starred in the CBS special *Three for Tonight* with Marge and Gower Champion. He headlined his own specials, including "Tonight with Belafonte," the *Revlon Revue* special on CBS in 1959, which won him the **Emmy Award** in 1960 for Outstanding Performance in a Variety or Musical Program. He was the first black to win the coveted Emmy. He followed that with a 1960 CBS special, *Belafonte, New York*. He was a guest on the ABC special *Dinah Shore*, a tribute to the Peace Corps in 1965, in *An Evening with Julie Andrews and Harry Belafonte* in 1969, *Harry and Lena* in 1970, and *The Diahann Carroll Show* in 1971. As a dramatic actor, Belafonte starred as Coach Eddie Robinson in the made-for-television film *Grambling's White Tiger* in 1981. *See also* PETULA.

BELAFONTE-HARPER, SHARI. **Harry Belafonte**'s daughter, Belafonte-Harper (aka Shari Belafonte), played Julie Gillette in the drama *Hotel* from 1983 to 1988. She was Laura Wingate in the sci-fi series *Beyond Reality* (1991–1993) and was cohost (1994–1995) of *Lifestyles with Robin Leach and Shari Belafonte*, a spin-off of *Lifestyles of the Rich and Famous*.

BELAFONTE, NEW YORK (*CBS, November 20, 1960*). Host **Harry Belafonte**, in this one-hour special, sang folk songs and duets with guest Gloria Lynne.

BELCON, NATALIE. Belcon played Jenise on *Roc* (1992–1993) and Janise Williams on *Beverly Hills 90210* from 1994 to 1995.

BELLAMY, BILL. Bellamy was the voice of Skeeter in live-action series with a puppet, *Cousin Skeeter* (1998–2000). He played Deaq in the police drama *Fast Lane* (2002–2003) and starred as Jerimiah in the sitcom *Men, Women & Dogs* (2001).

BELL, DARRYL. Bell earned TV fame as Ron Johnson on the sitcom *A Different World* (1987–1993). He also starred as Mo in *Homeboys in Outer Space* (1996–1997). He hosted segments of *Friday Night Videos* (1983–2000) and had a role in the 1995 TV film *Black Scorpion*.

BENJAMIN, PAUL. Benjamin had key roles in *One in a Million: The Ron LeFlore Story* in 1978 and *I Know Why the Caged Bird Sings* in 1979.

BENNY'S PLACE (*ABC, May 31, 1982*). Louis Gossett Jr. played the central character in this two-hour made-for-television film as Benny Moore, the owner of a factory repair shop who was not accepting aging well and found that he had to take on a younger assistant. **Cicely Tyson** played Odessa. **Anna Maria Horsford** played Charmaine. **Pauline Myers** played Miss Atty Carter. The production won the ABC Theater Award for new plays in 1982. Michael Schultz was director.

BENSON (*ABC, 1979–1986*). Robert Guillaume was the star of this sitcom, which was a spin-off of his character, the butler in *Soap*. Benson, the butler, became state budget director and finally lieutenant governor in the course of the series. As the series began, Benson was sent to help Governor James Gatling (James Noble) in his household.

He was the strong and fatherlike figure to Katie (Missy Gold), the governor's daughter. He fought Gretchen (Inga Swenson), the stern German housekeeper. Primarily, he helped the timid, indecisive governor run the state, and that is how he earned the promotions. Guillaume said he wanted kids of all backgrounds to see his characters as real and the success of Benson as possibilities in their own lives. Guillaume, who won the **Emmy Award** for Outstanding Supporting Actor in a Comedy for *Soap* in 1979, won the Emmy for Outstanding (lead) Actor in a Comedy for *Benson* in 1985. *See also* BENSON; DOMESTIC WORKERS; LONG-RUNNING SERIES.

BENTLEY, LAMONT. Bentley played Hakeem in the sitcom *Moesha* (1996–2001) and Rashad in *South Central* (1994). He was killed in a car crash in Los Angeles in 2005.

BEN VEREEN . . . COMIN' AT YA (*NBC, 1975*). Entertainer **Ben Vereen** had won the Tony Award for the Broadway play *Pippin* in 1973 when he starred in this summer musical-variety series. There was music, comedy, and, of course, dance. **Lola Falana** was a regular as well as Liz Torres, Avery Schreiber, and Arte Johnson. In one of the shows, Vereen did a tribute to minstrel performer Bert Williams. Vereen, in an effort to show the abuse Williams and others of his day endured, did the performance in blackface makeup. He also did some "darkie" bits to reflect Williams's performances and ended the act singing "Nobody." Some viewers, black and white, were very vocal about their objections to the act. Vereen felt that people did not look into the content or the meaning of his performance. "A lot of black people felt ashamed but actually we should honor Williams and other black entertainers of his day. They made it possible for me and other black entertainers to do what we do today. In knowing who we were, we learn who we are." *See also* VARIETY SERIES.

BEN VEREEN—HIS ROOTS and also titled **BEN VEREEN: SHOWCASE FOR A MAN OF MANY TALENTS (*ABC, March 2, 1978*).** After starring in the 1977 hit ABC miniseries *Roots*, singer/dancer/actor **Ben Vereen** starred in a variety special on which he is said to have "traced his musical roots." His guests were **Debbie Allen**, **Louis Gossett Jr.**, and Cheryl Ladd. There are conflicting sources about the title of the special. *See also* VARIETY SPECIALS.

BERNARD, ED. Ed Bernard played Tony Baylor in the 1972–1973 series *Cool Million* starring James Farentino. He played Earl in the first two episodes of *That's My Mama* in 1974, and from 1974 to 1978, he was Detective Joe Styles on *Police Woman*. He was the principal, Jim Willis, in *The White Shadow* from 1978 to 1981. He had key roles in the television films *Reflections of Murder* in 1974 and *Act of Violence* in 1979.

BERNARD, JASON. Jason Bernard played Wilma Rudolph's coach in *Wilma* and Daddy Ben Ross in *A Woman Called Moses* in 1978, both made-for-television films. Then, in the first episode of *The White Shadow* in 1978, he was the principal, Jim Willis. He played Deputy Inspector Marquette in the series *Cagney and Lacey* from 1982 to 1983. He was the boss, Mr. Bracken, in the sitcom *Herman's Head* from 1991 to 1994. He had key roles in the made-for-television films *The Night the City Screamed* in 1980, *High Performance* in 1983, and *Sophie and the Moonhanger* in 1996. He had a key role in *V—The Final Battle*, a 1984 miniseries. Bernard died in 1996 at the age of 58.

BERNIE MAC SHOW, THE (*FOX, 2001–*). Comedian **Bernie Mac** starred in this sitcom as a man with a wife (Kelita Smith) but no children—by choice. Then circumstances forced him to take in his sister's children: teenage Vanessa (**Camille Winbush**) and elementary schoolers Jordan (Jeremy Suarez) and Bryanna (Dee Dee Davis). Bernie finds that his ideas of raising children did not coincide with society's rules. His philosophy was that he is always right, but the kids taught him otherwise. *See also* FAMILY SERIES.

BERRY, CHUCK. The rock 'n' roll star made many appearances on variety series—*American Bandstand*, *The Ed Sullivan Show*, and *The Midnight Special*. He also appeared in *20 Years of Rock & Roll* in 1975; *The Apollo Theater Hall of Fame* in 1994; *The Rock and Roll Hall of Fame* in 1995; *Hollywood Rocks the Movies: The Early Year (1955–1970)* in 2000; *The History of Rock 'n' Roll*, a 2000 miniseries; and *Christmas in Washington* in 2000. He was an honoree on *The Kennedy Center Honors* in 2000.

BERRY, FRED. A former break-dancer with The Lockers, Berry played the character Freddie "Rerun" Stubbs on the sitcom *What's*

Happening!! from 1976 to 1979 and *What's Happening Now!!* from 1985 to 1986. He appeared in the shows *Star Dates* and MTV's *Doggy Fizzle Televizzle* and had a couple of cameo roles as himself and as the character Rerun. He said he lost more than a million dollars to drugs and luxuries and, with no acting jobs, charged for appearances at shopping malls. Berry died in 2003 at 52 years of age.

BERRY, HALLE. Berry played Debbie Porter on *Knots Landing* in 1991. She played the title role in the miniseries *Alex Haley's Queen* in 1993. In 1999, she starred in the made-for-television movie *Introducing Dorothy Dandridge* and received great acclaim. In 2005, after receiving the Oscar for leading actress, she starred in *Oprah Winfrey Presents: Their Eyes Were Watching God.*

BEST ON RECORD, THE (*NBC, May 18, 1965*). Winners of the 1964 Grammy Awards entertained in this one-hour variety special. Among them were **Louis Armstrong**, **Godfrey Cambridge**, **Sammy Davis Jr.**, Woody Allen, Eddy Arnold, Tony Bennett, Carol Channing, and Arthur Fiedler. *See also* VARIETY SPECIALS.

BEST, WILLIE. Statuesque and upright in stature in real life, Best was the slumped-over, bugged-eyes, slow servant in most of his film and television roles. He was Charlie the elevator boy in *My Little Margie* and Willie the dumb handyman in *The Stu Erwin Show*. It was the work he could get. Best was born in 1915 and died in 1962. *See also* STEREOTYPES.

BET NIGHTLY NEWS (*BET, 2003–*). When it premiered in 2003, this was the only nightly newscast to report the day's national and international headlines with a black perspective. **Jacque Reid** was anchor of **Black Entertainment Television**'s 11:00 P.M. newscast. *See also* NEWS ON TELEVISION.

BET TONIGHT WITH TAVIS SMILEY (*BET, 1996–2001*). This was a nightly news and talk show hosted by popular radio personality **Tavis Smiley**. His popularity was not as apparent while the show was on the air as it was when he was fired. **Black Entertainment Television** (BET) chairman Robert Johnson fired him after he sold an interview to ABC News, a rival of Viacom that owned BET and CBS.

Johnson said BET should have had the opportunity to refuse the interview before it was offered to ABC's *Primetime Live*. Smiley said his appearance on ABC plugged BET because he was identified as a talk show host from BET in the segment and in the promotion for it. At any rate, after the firing, Smiley's loyal viewers and radio listeners flooded BET with angry e-mails, letters, and telephone calls protesting his termination. The press covered it widely; people who had never heard of the show heard about Smiley being fired.

BETWEEN BROTHERS (*FOX, 1997–1999*). Dondre T. Whitfield, Kadeem Hardison, and **Tommy Davidson** starred in this ensemble buddy sitcom about two brothers who share an apartment with two other men. Charles (Hardison) and James (Whitfield) were the brothers; Charles was a very responsible and meticulous sportswriter, and James was a woman-chasing, scheming real estate agent. Sharing their apartment was Mitchell Ford (Davidson), a high school teacher whose second wife had just thrown him out.

BEULAH (*ABC, 1950–1953*). The Beulah character began in radio as a domestic who was the voice of reason in a white household of zany misadventures. **Hattie McDaniel**, who won an Oscar for her role in *Gone with the Wind*, played the role on radio and the show was a big hit. It was expected that, like so many other radio shows, *Beulah* would also become a television series, and it was also expected that McDaniel would play the role. However, when ABC-TV announced the show, **Ethel Waters** was to play the title role. There were rumors that Waters and McDaniel feuded over the role, but there were also numerous denials of the rift between the two actresses. The *New York Times* (October 4, 1950) said the TV show "suffered from a trite story and was regrettably stereotyped in concept." Yet the ratings remained high for both the radio and the television show. Then Ethel Waters decided to leave the show, claiming at least partly that she disliked living on the West Coast, where the show was produced. A Californian, McDaniel was then cast in the role, and she planned to continue to play the radio character too. Carlton Jackson, her biographer, said that McDaniel had fought to keep stereotypes off the radio show, and that fight carried into the television show. However, although McDaniel taped six episodes of the television series, she became ill (some reports said she had a heart attack) and was replaced by her friend **Louise Beavers**. McDaniel's shows were never seen, according to some historians, although at least one is available on videotape today. Beavers kept the role until she quit in 1953. Some sources say **Lillian Randolph** played the television roles, while others disagree. Nevertheless, Randolph definitely did play radio's **Beulah**. Whether on television or radio, Jackson said that McDaniel's influence was apparent even when Beavers and Randolph played the role; they also fought to avoid stereotypes. When Randolph quit, ABC gave up on the series. Jackson said that when television began to "move away from depicting black Americans in false and unfair roles of dialect, shuffles, and other demeaning characterizations," credit went to black pressure groups but that these groups would not have been so successful were it not for "the pioneering efforts of Hattie McDaniel and radio '*Beulah*'."

Beulah critics say the show did include negative stereotyping—all black women are fat maids. Another black character in the series was Beulah's friend, Oriole, also a maid in the neighborhood played by **Butterfly McQueen** (1950–1952) and by **Ruby Dandridge** (1952–1953). McQueen was also in *Gone with the Wind*, and like McDaniel, she played a maid in the film too. In fact, these actresses made their careers playing maids—when they could get work as actresses at all. All had problems with their roles but reportedly felt it was a matter of playing a maid or being a maid.

BEXLEY, DON. Bexley played Bubba in *Sanford and Son* from 1972 to 1977 and in *The Sanford Arms* in 1977. He was born in 1910 and died in 1997 of heart and kidney failure.

BIAS AND THE MEDIA (*ABC, 1968*). Six hour-long specials which exposed racism in the journalistic ranks aired under this title. *See also* DOCUMENTARIES.

BIG BAND AND ALL THAT JAZZ, THE (*NBC, November 29, 1972*). This was an hour of jazz with **Count Basie**, **Duke Ellington**, **Ella Fitzgerald**, **Dizzy Gillespie**, **Lionel Hampton**, **Teddy Wilson**, The Dave Brubeck Quartet, Benny Goodman, Bobby Hackett, Gene Krupa, and Benny Goodman.

BIG HOUSE, THE (*ABC, 2004*). This sitcom was called the reverse of *The Fresh Prince of BelAir*. Comic Kevin Hart played a college student who had to leave his plush home in Malibu and live with his uncle's family in working-class Philadelphia. **Keith David** and **Arnetia Walker** played Uncle Clarence and Aunt Tina. **Faizon Love** was rotund cousin Warren. Aaron Grady was C.J.; Yvette Brown was Eartha. The series was loosely based on Hart's personal life.

BILL COSBY SHOW, THE (*NBC, 1969–1971*). This sitcom starred Bill Cosby as Chet Kincaid, a coach and physical education teacher at a school in a lower-middle-class area of Los Angeles. Story lines involved Chet's students and associates at the school as well as his family. Key characters were his mother, Rose, played by **Lillian Randolph** (1969–1970) and **Beah Richards** (1970–1971), his brother and sister-in-law (Lee Weaver and **Olga James**), the principal (**Sid McCoy**), and the guidance counselor (Joseph Perry). *See also* COSBY; COSBY MYSTERIES; COSBY SHOW.

BILL COSBY'S SPECIALS. Actor/comedian **Bill Cosby** hosted several specials in the 1960s and 1970s; all featured sketches and monologues tailored to Cosby's comedic style. They were the following: *The Bill Cosby Special* (March 20, 1968) had Sheldon Leonard and Janice Robinson as guests. The special won the **Emmy Award** for Outstanding Variety or Music Program. *Bill Cosby Does His Thing* (February 9, 1969) had the Art Reynolds Singers and the Donald McKayle Dancers as guests. *The Second Bill Cosby Special* (March 11, 1969) was also titled *A Special Bill Cosby Special*, probably because it was the third special. Again, the Art Reynolds Singers were guests. *The Third Bill Cosby Special* (April 1, 1970), even though it was the fourth, had **Roberta Flack** as a guest star and a black director, Vantile Whitfield. *The Bill Cosby Special, Or?* (March 2, 1971) had **Johnny Brown**, John Denver, **Billy Eckstine**, Herb Edelman, **Dizzy Gillespie**, **Bill Henderson**, Burgess Meredith, and **Nancy Wilson** as guest stars. Cosby was producer; **Ivan Dixon** was director. *Cos: The Bill Cosby Special* (CBS, November 10, 1975) had Loretta Lynn, Tony Randall, and Karen Valentine as guests. *See also* VARIETY SPECIALS.

BILLINGS, EARL. Billings played Leon in the sitcom *New Attitude* (1990) and had key roles in the following TV films: *Minstrel Man* (1977), *Kids Don't Tell* (1985), *The George McKenna Story* (1986), *Perry Mason: The Case of the Ruthless Reporter* (1991), and *Nails* (1992).

BILLY: PORTRAIT OF A STREET KID (*CBS, September 19, 1977*). LeVar Burton played Billy Peoples, a ghetto youth whose efforts to escape from dismal life leads him to look toward a future as a veterinarian's assistant in this two-hour television film. Key roles were played by **Ossie Davis**, **Tina Andrews**, **Roxie Roker**, and **T. K. Carter**.

BINGHAM, TRACI. Bingham was Jordan Tate, a *Baywatch* beauty (1996–1998). She was a regular on the spy series *The Deam Team* (1999) and a feature reporter on the sports show *Battlebots* (2001). She was one of the housemates on *The Surreal Life* (2003).

BIOPICS. Numerous motion pictures made for television and miniseries were produced to depict the lives of famous and great people—entertainers, politicians, and notable persons in African-American history. Biopics are popular fare during February, **African American History Month**. Among the television film biographies are the following: *Solomon Northrup's Odyssey* (1985); *The Court-Martial of Jackie Robinson* (1990); *The Jacksons: An American Dream* (1992), about the singing Jackson family including Michael and Janet; *The Ernest Green Story* (1993), the story of one of the students who integrated Little Rock schools in 1957; *The Vernon Johns Story* (1994), the story of the minister who became a civil rights leader; *Introducing Dorothy Dandridge* (1999), the life of the African-American actress; *Hendrix* (2000), the story of musician Jimi Hendrix; *The Little Richard Story* (2001); *Bojangles*, the life of entertainer Bill "Bojangles" Robinson (2001); *Lumumba* (2002), the life of the first prime minister of the Congo, Patrice Lumumba; and *Keep the Faith, Baby* (2002), the life of legendary New York Congressman Adam Clayton Powell. The film *Lackawanna Blues* (2005) was a "self-biopic" written by Ruben Santiago-Hudson about the people in his early life. *See also* ATHLETES' BIOPICS.

BIRACIAL CHARACTERS. Characters of mixed race have appeared in most television genres. For example, Winifred "Freddie" Brooks of the situation comedy *A Different World*, numerous characters of mixed species in the multiple *Star Trek* series in syndication, and *Queen* portrayed by **Halle Berry** in the miniseries sequel to Alex Haley's *Roots* offer a sample of mixed-race characters seen on television since the 1980s. Several TV films had biracial characters; among them were *A House Divided* (2000).

In her study of television situation comedy, soap opera, and science fiction, scholar Michele Foss found that being of mixed race was tragic or unfortunate and could lead to death, especially if the character chose not to consider mixed heritage as an affliction. Foss uncovered evidence of this view in her review of the story arc of Ziyal in the syndicated program *Star Trek: Deep Space Nine*. Ziyal, daughter of a military commander and a member of a population conquered by that military force, is killed by one of her father's soldiers. The soldier sees her as a traitor.

Foss argued that at first glance, biracial characters appear to offer alternative or progressive inroads for viewers. But the characters often faced a tormented life. For instance, Chad Harris of the daytime drama *Passions* fell in love with his half sister, a tragedy brought about by the indiscretion of his parents, a white man and a black woman. *See also* PUDD'N HEAD WILSON; OPRAH WINFREY PRESENTS: THE WEDDING.

BLACK AND BLUE *(PBS, February 17, 1993)*. Singers **Ruth Brown** and **Linda Hopkins** were the stars of this Tony Award–winning Broadway musical directed for television by Robert Altman. Bunny Briggs, Bernard Manners, Jimmy Slyde, Carrie Smith, and Dianne Walker were also in the company. *See also* BROADWAY PLAYS AND MUSICALS.

BLACK ENTERTAINMENT TELEVISION. Robert L. Johnson launched Black Entertainment Television (BET) on cable across the United States on January 25, 1980. It started small, airing only two hours per week. Johnson said the new cable network would offer black viewers as well as nonblack viewers the kinds of programming commercial television "can't, don't or won't." He was quoted in the *Washington Post* as saying, "The black consumer market is a $75-

billion consumer market. It generates more revenues than 114 nations in the world, and television sells products to that black audience—and yet blacks still have trouble getting jobs in television. . . . What the black audiences want is, I think, pretty much the same things as white audiences. more choices. They want to see J.J. of *Good Times*, but they want a sensitive drama about blacks too . . . blacks watch more television on the average than whites. And we know that blacks like to watch programs with black actors and actresses in them."

In the same year, BET reached 3.8 million households; in 1982, it transmitted six hours per day. In 1984, it gained 7.6 million subscribers and began transmitting 24 hours per day. In 11 years, BET became the first black-owned company traded on the New York Stock Exchange. In 1996, revenues reached $132 million. Then, in 2000, Johnson sold BET to Viacom for close to $3 billion. Included in the sale were BET on Jazz: The Cable Jazz, BET International, BET Books, BET Holding's interest in BET.com, BET's programming interest in two Radio Satellite program channels (Urban AC and Jazz), and BET Pictures, Inc. A condition of the sale was that, for five years, Johnson would remain chairman and chief executive officer and that Debra Lee would remain president and chief operating officer. According to *Black Enterprise*, African Americans had mixed feelings about the sale. "[They] lamented the loss of so significant a black-owned company. But at the same time, there was a collective, 'Bravo' in salute to a man who had shown the world that a black company can garner such a price."

BLACK HISTORY: LOST, STOLEN, OR STRAYED (*CBS, 1968*).
Bill Cosby narrated this one-hour documentary that examines how historians have ignored or improperly documented achievements by black Americans. Evidence is offered through negative media images in films and newsreels. This documentary won the **Emmy Award** for Outstanding News Documentary—Individual Achievement for the 1968–1969 season. *See also* DOCUMENTARIES.

BLACKMON, EDAFE. Blackmon played Reggie in the sitcom *For Your Love* (1998–2002).

BLACK OR WHITE (*BET, FOX, MTV, VH1, November 16, 1991*).
The premiere of **Michael Jackson**'s "Black or White" video (or "short film," as Jackson describes the video).

BLACK VIEW OF SOUTH AFRICA, A (*CBS, 1970–1971*). Nana Mahomo narrated this documentary and won the **Emmy Award** for Outstanding Achievement in Cultural Programming—Individuals.

BLACKS IN AMERICA: WITH ALL DELIBERATE SPEED (*CBS, July 24–25, 1979*). A news special on *CBS Reports* examining 25 years of desegregation since the *Brown v. Board of Education* decision. **Ed Bradley** hosted.

BLACQUE, TAUREAN. Blacque played toothpick-chewing Detective Neal Washington in *Hill Street Blues* from 1981 to 1987 and Henry Marshall in the daytime drama *Generations* in 1989. Prior to his *Hill Street Blues* role, he played key roles in *The Night the City Screamed* and *The $5.20 an Hour Dream*, both in 1980. He had a key role in the TV films *She Stood Alone* in 1991, *Murder without Motive: The Edmund Perry Story* in 1992, and *Soul Survivors* in 1995.

BLEDSOE, TEMPESTT. Bledsoe was Vanessa Huxtable, next to the youngest of the daughters on *The Cosby Show*, from 1984 to 1992. She starred in the drama special *The Gift of Amazing Grace* in 1986. After the sitcom ended, she completed a degree in finance at New York University and, in 1995, at 22, became host of a syndicated talk show *Tempestt*. The show was canceled in 1996. Later, she had a recurring role on *The Practice* as a tough-talking single mother. In 2000, she costarred in the USA Network film *The Expendables* as a gun-toting prisoner on a secret mission. The director of the latter project spoke about how meticulous Bledsoe was in researching the character she portrayed, that she spoke with prison inmates who had been in gangs. Said Bledsoe, "It's hard for a television actor to reinvent himself and even harder for a [former] child actor to do it."

BLIGE, MARY J. Blige sang "I Guess That's Why They Call It the Blues" with Elton John on his special on December 1, 2000. She performed in the halftime show for Super Bowl XXXV in 2001. She performed on *MTV 20: Live & Almost Légal* in 2001, the *Source Awards* in 2001, *VH1 Divas Live 2001: The One and Only Aretha Franklin* in 2001, and the *Tony Awards* in 2004.

BLUES, THE (*PBS, September–October 2003*). This series, in seven parts, was aired in consecutive days and consisted of interpretive and impressionistic films by seven directors. The films traced the roots of blues from Africa to its heyday in the 1920s and 1930s, its demise in the 1940s, and its resurrection in the 1960s, when British rock bands like the Rolling Stones and Led Zeppelin were inspired by American blues artists. Highlights included performances by and vintage footage of **B. B. King, Muddy Waters, Bessie Smith, Leadbelly, Ray Charles,** Sister Rosetta Tharpe, **Duke Ellington,** Oscar Peterson, **Fats Domino,** and numerous others. Contemporary young blues singer Shemika Copeland performed. Charles Burnett was the sole black director who was responsible for "Warming by the Devil's Fire," a drama about a young boy taken by his uncle to 1956 New Orleans, where he was introduced to "dirty blues." Martin Scorsese was executive producer.

BLUES FOR A JUNK MAN (*NBC, 1962*). This episode of *Cain's Hundred* starred **Dorothy Dandridge** in her final dramatic role. She played a jazz singer with a drug problem fighting to build her career and keep her jazz musician husband (**Ivan Dixon**). The dialogue between the two was tense and emotional, a rare opportunity for black actors on television at that time.

BLUES: IN PERFORMANCE AT THE WHITE HOUSE, THE (*PBS, November 3, 1999*). **Della Reese** hosted and **B. B. King** was featured in this performance show for President Bill and Mrs. Hilary Clinton. Performers were selected to span races, gender, and ages to represent the widespread appreciation of the musical art form.

BOBATOON, STAR-SHEMAH. Using merely Star-Shemah as her stage name, she played a key role in *The Seven Wishes of Joanna Peabody* in 1978. Then, with a last name added, she played Diana Freeman in *Palmerstown, U.S.A.* in 1980–1981.

BOBBY MCFERRIN: LOOSELY MOZART, THE NEW INNOVATORS OF CLASSICAL MUSIC (*PBS, December 10, 1996*). Host **Bobby McFerrin** showed how classical music can be fun as he improvised Mozart with players like Yo-Yo Ma. Marcus Roberts reinvented "Rhapsody in Blue."

BOJANGLES (*SHO, February 4, 2001*). **Gregory Hines** starred as Bill "Bojangles" Robinson, the performer who was once an orphan and became one of the greatest tap dancers of his time. The biopic explored his earliest performance as a street dancer and his rise in vaudeville and Hollywood overcoming some racial barriers and fighting others. The film showed his problems as a womanizer and gambler and his financial difficulties. The end credits showed Hines's choreography on a dance routine situated on the screen opposite Bojangles's original routines. **Kimberly Elise** played Robinson's wife, Fannie. Broadway star **Savion Glover** danced in the film based on the book *Mr. Bojangles—Biography of Bill Robinson* by Jim Haskins and N. R. Mitgang. Hines said that he realized he did not resemble Robinson and that there was some experimentation with trying to make him look more like him. "We were never able to get the right look with the budget that we had. So I had to try to do it from the inside out," he said.

BOND, JAMES III. In series television, Bond played Josh, a recurring role on The Waltons from 1978–1980 and Doc in The Red Hand Gang (1977). In TV films, he had roles in The Sky is Gray (1980), *The Color of Friendship* (1981), Booker (1984), and *Go Tell It On the Mountain* (1985).

BONET, LISA. Bonet starred in the sitcom *A Different World* (1987–1988) playing Denise Huxtable, the role she created in *The Cosby Show* in 1984. Her TV films included *New Eden* (1994) and *Lathe of Heaven* (2002). She appeared on *Motown Returns to the Apollo* (1985), *Battle of the Network Stars XVIII* (1985), and *Walt Disney World Celebrity Circus* (1987).

BONNELL, VIVIAN. Bonnell played key roles in the telefilms *Christmas in Connecticut* (1992), *In the Arms of a Killer* (1992), *Switched at Birth* (1991), *The Josephine Baker Story* (1991), *Daughter of the Streets* (1990), *The Women of Brewster Place* (1989), *Addicted to His Love* (1988); *Elvis and Me* (1988), and *Convicted: A Mother's Story* (1987).

BOOK OF DAVID; THE CULT FIGURE'S MANIFESTO STARRING DAVID ALAN GRIER, THE (*COM, April 25, 2003*). This one-hour special was a showcase for Grier's comedy. His subjects were drugs and youth, marriage, and world domination.

BOSTON PUBLIC (*FOX, 2001–2004*). Chi McBride starred as Principal Steven Harper in this dramatic series, often with comedic subplots, about the faculty, staff, and students at a fictional public high school in Boston. The cast was racially integrated with key African-American characters. Music teacher Marilyn Sudor (**Sharon Leal**) became Harper's love interest in the fourth season. Special education teacher Marla Hendricks (**Loretta Devine**) was often comic foil but could also be a very serious character. In the first and second seasons, Louisa Fenn (**Rashida Jones**) was the school secretary. The series often dealt with racial issues and won a Peabody Award in 2003 for an episode about using the word "nigger" in the classroom. *See also* SERIES ABOUT SCHOOL LIFE.

BOWE, RIDDICK. *See* RIDDICK BOWE FIGHTS.

BOWERS, WILLIAM. Bowers was the bailiff to Judge Larry Joe Doherty on the syndicated courtroom series *Texas Justice* (2001–).

BOWIE, PHYLLIS C. G. Interior designer Bowie was host of *Living with Soul* on TV One (2004–).

BOXING MATCHES ON TELEVISION. Boxing was television's first major sport. Long before pay-for-view was even a dream, in the 1940s, boxing was popular television fare, even though basketball and wrestling were televised too. Before people had television "sets" in their homes, the invention was seen in almost every bar. It was common to have five or six network boxing shows on during any given week. NBC had the first televised boxing matches on its *Gillette Cavalcade of Sports* airing on Monday and Friday nights as early as 1947 (it lasted for 14 years). Then, in 1948, NBC had *Boxing from St. Nicholas Arena* on Monday nights at 9:30 and Tuesday nights at 10:00. The Dumont Network had *Boxing from Jamaica Arena* on Wednesdays at 9:00 P.M. opposite CBS's *Boxing from Westchester*. At first, all originated from arenas in the New York area.

Whereas boxing fans today are concerned primarily with the heavyweight class, boxers in other classes had appeal to viewers in early television. In 1949, ABC's first boxing show was *Tomorrow's Boxing Champions* with unranked boxers. The broadcast originated from Chicago. In 1952, there was *Meet the Champ*, a series of bouts involving members of the military. There was *Boxing from Ridgewood Grove*, *Motor City Boxing from Detroit*, *Boxing from Eastern Parkway*, the *CBS Blue Ribbon Bouts*, and *The Fight of the Week*. The *Fight of the Week*, on ABC, was the final regularly televised boxing show, and it ended in September 1964. Thereafter, ABC's *Wide World of Sports* aired boxing as well as other sports. Top matches have been pay-for-view in recent years. The black boxers of the 1940s and 1950s were the outstanding sportsmen of the era, the Great Black Hopes to follow Joe Louis's accomplishments on radio. The great boxers of the early years of television included Sugar Ray Robinson and Archie Moore. *See also* EVANDER HOLYFIELD FIGHTS; GEORGE FOREMAN FIGHTS; JOE FRAZIER FIGHTS; KEN NORTON FIGHTS; MARVIN HAGLER FIGHTS; MIKE TYSON FIGHTS; MUHAMMAD ALI FIGHTS; RIDDICK BOWE FIGHTS; SUGAR RAY LEONARD FIGHTS; and STEREOTYPES.

BOYCOTT (*HBO, February 24, 2001*). This made-for-television film told the story of the Montgomery Bus Boycott in 1955 and how the black Americans in the city were united in their act of defiance and a new national leader, Martin Luther King Jr., emerged. **Jeffrey Wright** (as King), **Terrence Howard** (as Ralph Abernathy), **C. C. H. Pounder** (as JoAnn Robinson), and **Carmen Ejogo** (as Coretta Scott King) starred. Erik Dellums played Bayard Rustin, and **Whitman Mayo** played the Rev. Banyon. *See also* HISTORICAL EVENTS DRAMATIZED.

BRADLEY, ED. Bradley joined CBS's *60 Minutes* as coeditor in the 1981–1982 season. He also anchored and reported special broadcasts on *60 Minutes II*. Bradley's first full-time work in television was as a war correspondent for CBS News during the Vietnam War. He was injured during this period and returned to the United States after the fall of Saigon. Prior to joining *60 Minutes*, he was a principal correspondent (1978–1981) for *CBS Reports*, a White House correspondent for CBS News (1976–1981), and anchor of the *CBS Sunday Night News* (1976–1981). He also anchored the CBS newsmagazine *Street Stories* from 1992 to 1993 and was host of *Blacks in America:*

With All Deliberate Speed in 1979. He has received numerous **Emmy Awards** for his work, one for a 1981 interview with Lena Horne. *See also* NEWS ON TELEVISION.

BRADLEY, KATHLEEN. Bradley was one of Barker's Beauties on the game show *The Price Is Right* (1990–2000).

BRADY, WAYNE. Brady starred as one of two "music cops" in *Vinyl Justice* (1998–1999), a takeoff of the show *Cops* on which the criminals they cited were unmusical people. He was a regular on the improvisational comedy series *Whose Line Is It Anyway* (1998–2001). Also, he starred in *The Wayne Brady Show*, an improvisational comedy series, from 2001 to 2002, and in *The Wayne Brady Show*, a syndicated talk/variety series, from 2002 to 2004. In 2003, he won the **Emmy Award** for Outstanding Talk Show Host, and his series won the award for Outstanding Talk Show.

BRANDY. Recording artist Brandy (aka Brandy Norwood) played Danisha on the sitcom *Thea* (1993–1994) and the title role in the sitcom *Moesha* from 1996 to 2001. She used her singing talents in at least two special productions: *Cinderella*, the Rodgers & Hammerstein musical in 1997, and *Double Platinum* in 1999. She had executive producer credits in the latter.

BRAUGHER, ANDRE. Braugher played Detective Winston Blake in *Kojak* from 1989 to 1990. For playing another detective, Frank Pembleton, in *Homicide: Life on the Street*, he won the **Emmy Award** for Outstanding Lead Actor in a Drama Series. He again played the detective in *Homicide: The Movie* in 2000. He starred in a segment of the trilogy TV film *Love Songs* and directed another in 1999. Braugher played Marcellus Washington, friend and former partner to the series' central character (played by David Morse), in *Hack* (2003–2004).

BRAVE NEW WORLD (*NBC, March 7, 1980*). Based on the novel by Aldous Huxley, this three-hour miniseries was about life in a place called Savageland 600 years in the future when no one ages past 35, babies are mass-produced, and sexual activity is compulsory. The large cast consisted of **Ron O'Neal** as Mustapha Mond, **Dick Anthony Williams** as Helmhotz Watson, **Jonelle Allen** as Fanny

Crowe, **Lee Chamberlin** as Head Nurse, **Bill Overton** as Chief Manager, and **Carol Tillery Banks** as Compu-to-Structress.

BRAZLETON, CONNI MARIE. Brazleton played Nurse Connie Oligario on *ER* (1994–).

BREAK THE BANK (*ABC, 1948–1949; NBC, 1949–1952, 1953; CBS, 1952–1953***).** In this quiz show, contestants answered questions in a specific category and could potentially win $250,000 (although no one ever did). In the beginning, contestants were selected from the studio audience. Then, later, the show featured experts on various categories answering questions. It was during this period (1956) when singer/actress **Ethel Waters** was a contestant. In dire financial circumstances, she sorely needed money to pay an IRS debt. Answering questions in the category of music, she won $10,000.

BREWSTER PLACE (*ABC, 1990***).** This drama series spun off of the 1989 hit TV movie *The Women of Brewster Place*, which was based on the novel of the same title by Gloria Naylor. **Oprah Winfrey** starred as Mattie Michael, who lived on Brewster Place and ran a restaurant with her friend, Etta Mae (played by Brenda Pressley). **Olivia Cole** played the neighborhood's gossipmonger. **Oscar Brown Jr.** was Miss Sophie's husband, Jessie. The series aired for two months in the summer of 1990.

BRIAN'S SONG (*ABC, November 30, 1971***).** Based on Gale Sayers's book *I Am Third*, this biographical dramatization of the friendship between Chicago Bears football players Brian Piccolo and Sayers starred James Caan and **Billy Dee Williams.** The emotional story dealt with Piccolo's fight with cancer. **Bernie Casey** was also featured. The two-hour TV film won the **Emmy Award** for Outstanding Single Program, Drama or Comedy. It also won Emmy Awards for writing and film editing.

BRIAN'S SONG (*ABC, December 2, 2001***).** The story of the friendship between football players Gale Sayers and Brian Piccolo during Piccolo's fight with cancer was produced again with actors **Mekhi Phifer**, Sean Maher, Paula Cale, **Elise Neal**, and Ben Gazzara.

BRIDGES, JAMES. As a youngster, Bridges played Young Shadrack Davis in *A Woman Called Moses* in 1978. He is the older brother of **Todd Bridges**.

BRIDGES, TODD. Known primarily for his role of Willis, the older brother in the sitcom *Diff'rent Strokes* (1978–1986), Bridges first played the character Loomis in the sitcom *Fish* (1977–1978) and had a recurring role in *The Waltons*. He had roles in *Roots* (1977) and *High School, USA* in 1983 and *A Killing Affair* in 1977.

BROADWAY PLAYS AND MUSICALS. Broadway musicals and plays have often been mounted for television, especially after the leads became stars of television series. The musical *Ain't Misbehavin'* was broadcast in 1982 with the original Broadway cast after **Nell Carter** starred in the hit sitcom *Gimme a Break*. The musical *Purlie* was aired in 1979 after its lead, **Robert Guillaume**, starred in *Soap* and was scheduled to star in *Benson* and featured performer **Sherman Hemsley**, who was starring in *The Jeffersons*. Carter, Guillaume, and Hemsley were cast in their television series as a result of their Broadway performances. *See also* FOR COLORED GIRLS WHO HAVE CONSIDERED SUICIDE WHEN THE RAINBOW IS ENUF; GREEN PASTURES; RAISIN IN THE SUN; SMOKEY JOE'S CAFÉ; WHEN HELL FREEZES OVER, I'LL SKATE.

BROOKS, AVERY. Brooks was a regular on the detective drama series *Spenser: For Hire* (1985–1988) playing the character Hawk. In 1989, his character was spun off into his own series, *A Man Called Hawk* (1989). In 1991, he narrated the documentary *Marian Anderson*. From 1992 to 1999, he was Commander Sisko, the lead character in *Star Trek: Deep Space Nine*. Brooks played a key role in the 1993 TV film *The Ernest Green Story*.

BROOKS, CLAUDE. Comic Brooks played Anthony Harper in the sitcom **Homeroom** in 1989, played one of the teenage sons in the sitcom *True Colors* (1990–1992), and starred in the sitcom *Claude's Crib* (1996–1997).

BROOKS, GOLDEN. Brooks was a regular playing Maya Wilkes in the sitcom *Girlfriends* (2000–). She played CeCe Jennings on the series *Lincs* (1998) and had a role in the TV film *Drive By: A Love Story* (1997).

BROOKS, RANDY. Brooks had key roles in the made-for-television movies *Rage* and *Scared Straight! Another Story*, both in 1980.

BROWN, CANDY ANNE. Brown played Candy Beaumont in the made-for television film *Dallas Cowboys Cheerleaders II* in 1980 and had a key role in *Don't Look Back: The Story of Satchel Paige* in 1981.

BROWN, CHARNELE. Brown played Kim in the sitcom *A Different World* (1988–1993).

BROWN, CHELSEA. Dancer/singer Brown was a member of the cast of the first season of *Rowan and Martin's Laugh-In* in 1968–1969.

BROWN, GEORG STANFORD. Brown played Terry Webster, an idealistic rookie cop, when he starred in *The Rookies* from 1972 to 1976. He had key roles in several miniseries and motion pictures made for television including *Roots* in 1977, *Roots: The Next Generations* in 1979, *The Night the City Screamed* in 1980, *The Kid with The Broken Halo* in 1982, and *The Jesse Owens Story* in 1984. He played Johnnie B. Goode in the series *Lincs* (1998–2000). He was director of an episode of *Roots: The Next Generations*. He won the **Emmy Award** for Outstanding Directing in a Drama Series for an episode of *Cagney and Lacey* in 1986. He had a key role in the TV film *Murder without Motive: The Edmund Perry Story* in 1992.

BROWN, GOLDEN. Brown played waitress Cece Jennings in the series *Lincs* (1998–2000).

BROWN, JAMES (the entertainer). Nicknamed The Godfather of Soul, James Brown made numerous appearances on *The Ed Sullivan Show*. He said the show gave him a plaque reading "The Hardest Working Man in Show Business," a claim with which he agrees. In 2003, **Black Entertainment Television** gave him its Lifetime

Achievement Award. That same year, he was an honoree of *The Kennedy Center Honors*.

BROWN, JAMES (the sportscaster). Brown joined Fox Sports in 1994 after 10 years with CBS Sports. As cohost of *Fox NFL Sunday*, his assignments included three Super Bowls. He also was host of *World's Funniest!* (a weekly show of home videos from all over the world) and *America's Black Forum*. He won two **Emmy Awards** as Best Studio Host for his work and was named the National Sportscaster of the Year in 1999 by the American Sportscasters' Association. He also hosted a National Hockey League pregame show. At CBS, he hosted two Winter Olympics, the National Basketball Association Finals, and NCAA Tournament coverage. He was reporter/correspondent on *Real Sports with Bryant Gumbel* on HBO and host of *Basketball: The Dream Teams* on the History Channel (2000) and *Amazing Science of Sports* on the Learning Channel (2000).

BROWN, JOHNNY. A man of numerous talents who had been on the Broadway stage, Brown was a regular playing Leslie Uggams's brother in the "Sugar Hill" sketch on *The Leslie Uggams Show* in 1969 before joining the cast of *Rowan and Martin's Laugh-In* from 1970 to 1972. He went on to play Bookman, the building superintendent in *Good Times*, in 1977–1979. An impressionist, he was popular as a guest on variety series and specials. In TV films, he had roles in *The TV Show* (1979) and *Jackie's Back!* (1999).

BROWN, LES. Brown, an internationally recognized motivational speaker known for his high-energy presentations, hosted a syndicated talk show, *The Les Brown Show*, from 1993 to 1994.

BROWN, OLIVIA. Brown was Trudy Joplin, a female lead in the drama series *Miami Vice* (1984–1989), Denise in the sitcom *Dear John* (1990–1991), Patricia Hamilton in the drama *7th Heaven* (1996–2000), and Barbara Lee, Q's mother, in *Moesha* (2001). In TV films, she had roles in *I Can Jump Puddles* (1981), *Memories of Murder* (1990), and *Kids Killing Kids* (1994).

BROWN, ORLANDO. Brown played EJ in the sitcom *Family Matters* from 1996 to 1998.

BROWN, OSCAR, JR. Brown was one of the performers in the drama *Zora Is My Name* (1990). He played Miles Taylor on the sitcom *Roc* (1992–1993) and Jessie on the sitcom *Brewster Place* (1990).

BROWN, RENEE. Brown played Liz, one of the Harris children, in the 1978 TV film *Love Is Not Enough* and reprised the same role in the 1979 series *Harris & Company*.

BROWN, ROGER AARON. Brown had a key role in 1981's *Thornwell*, a made-for-television film. He played Gordon Ormsby in the sitcom *On Our Own* (1994–1995) and Deputy Chief Joe Noland in *The District* beginning in 2000.

BROWN, RUTH. In sitcoms, the singer was Leona in *Hello Larry* (1979–1980) and Betty in *Checking In* (1981). She headlined *Black and Blue* (1993), the televised Broadway musical.

BROWN, SHARON. Brown, the daughter of actor/entertainer **Johnny Brown**, played Daisy Allen in the daytime drama *Love of Life* (1971) and Chantel Marshall in the daytime drama *Generations* (1989–1990). In TV films, she had key roles in *Mr. Music* (1998), *Introducing Dorothy Dandridge* (1999), and *The Defectors* (2001).

BROWN SUGAR (*PBS, February 8, 1980*). This 60-minute documentary hosted by **Billy Dee Williams** centered on the personal and professional lives of black female entertainers. Film clips, still photos, and interviews made up the production. Donald Bogle was writer/director and producer. *See also* DOCUMENTARIES.

BROWN, TONY. Brown was the first black person to host a long-running network minority affairs program, *Black Journal*. The program was funded in 1968 by the Corporation for Public Broadcasting and aired on PBS. Brown was hired as executive producer and host in 1970. Among his many awards was an NAACP Image Award in 1991.

BROWNE, ROSCOE LEE. Browne played the Ghost of Christmas Past in "John Grin's Christmas" in 1986. He played the arrogant, sarcastic Harold Neistadter on the sitcom *Miss Winslow and Son* in 1979 and Saunders on *Soap* (1980–1981). He had key roles in the TV films

The Big Ripoff in 1975, the miniseries *King* in 1978, *Lady in the Corner* (1989), *You Must Remember This* (1992), *Crosstown* (1996), *The Notorious 7* (1997), and *Hard Time: The Premonition* (1999). He was Rosemont in the drama series *Falcon Crest* from 1988 to 1990. He was the spokesman of the American Cheese Industry, saying, "Ah, the power of cheese!" in commercials.

BRUCE, BRUCE. He was host of *Comicview* from 2001 to 2002. He appeared on *Def Comedy Jam: All Stars* (1999).

B. SMITH WITH STYLE (*SYN, 1997–*). B. (Barbara) Smith, the owner of caterics of the same name in New York City, Washington, D.C., and the Hamptons, led conversations of various subjects as well as cooking. Living well was the general theme. The host took her viewers around the United States to take a look at various lifestyles. Celebrities were interviewed along the way; among them were **Little Richard, Holly Robinson Peete, Chaka Kahn, Steve Harvey, Raven-Symone**, Al Jarreau, **Kevin Eubanks**, Henry Winkler, and many others.

BUFFALO SOLDIERS (*TNT, December 7, 1997*). Danny Glover portrayed Sgt. Wyatt of the Black Cavalry known as the Buffalo Soldiers, a fierce fighting unit of the post–Civil War, a cavalry troop who fought for a country that did not recognize their rights as citizens. **Glynn Turman, Mike Warren**, and **Mykelti Williamson** also had key roles.

BURTON, LEVAR. Burton was a student at the University of Southern California when he was launched as the young Kunta Kinte in the miniseries *Roots*. Later, he starred in the made-for-television movie *One in a Million: The Ron LeFlore Story* in 1978. He was the voice of Kwame (Earth) in *Captain Planet and the Planeteers*. He had starring or key roles in numerous made-for-television motion pictures including *Billy: Portrait of a Street Kid* in 1977, *Battered* in 1978, *Dummy* in 1979, *Grambling's White Tiger* in 1981, and *The Jesse Owens Story* in 1984. His recent credits include being host and co–executive producer of *Reading Rainbow*, an award-winning daily show urging literacy in children. In 1995, he hosted a special designed to encourage children to find ways to avoid violence, *LeVar Burton Presents—A Reading Rainbow Special: Act Against Violence*.

BUSIA, AKOSUA. Busia had key roles in the TV films *Badge of the Assassin* in 1985 and *The George McKenna Story* in 1986.

BUSTIN' LOOSE *(SYN, 1987–1988)*. Like *Stir Crazy* in 1985–1986, this was an effort to make a TV sitcom based on a **Richard Pryor** film but without Pryor. **Jimmie Walker** starred as Sonny Barnes, a con man known for telling lies. One of his lies got him into trouble, and the judge sentenced him to community service. He had to work with a social worker (**Vonetta McGee**) who cared for orphans (Larry Williams, Tyren Perry, Aaron Lohr, and Marie Lynn Wise). While he did the physical work around the house, he told outrageous lies to the kids, and they loved them.

BYRD, EUGENE. Byrd was Jelani on *Sesame Street* (1987–1990) and L.T. in *Promised Land* (1998–1999). He began playing Uncle Omar in *For Your Love* (2002). He had roles in TV films *Murder in Mississippi* (1990), *Bad Attitudes* (1991), *Perfect Harmony* (1991), *Color of Justice* (1997), and *Enslavement: The True Story of Fanny Kemble* (2000).

BYRON ALLEN SHOW, THE *(SYN, 1989–1992)*. Byron Allen hosted this one-hour weekly late night talk show. It later became a half-hour comedy show with sketches and guest comics. Allen traveled out of the studio looking for funny bits. *See also* ENTERTAINERS.

– C –

CAESAR, ADOLPH. With credits in film and theater, Caesar guest-starred in many television series. His voice was deep and mellow, so he was a natural to be narrator of the documentaries *Men of Bronze* (1977) and *I Remember Harlem* (1981). He had a key role in the *ABC Afterschool Special* "Getting Even." He was born in 1934 and died in 1986.

CALHOUN, MONICA. Calhoun played teenager Debbie in the sitcom *Bagdad Café* (1990) and played Linda in the TV film *The Ditchdigger's Daughters* in 1997.

CALL ME CLAUS (*TNT, December 2, 2001*). In this TV film, **Whoopi Goldberg** starred as a successful TV producer who was a Scrooge about Christmas until she met a Santa Claus from her own childhood.

CALLOWAY, CAB. Singer Calloway played Gabriel in "The Littlest Angel," a *Hallmark Hall of Fame* musical drama in 1969. In 1980, he and other entertainers paid tribute to the Apollo Theater in *Uptown*. In 1986, he participated in a salute to the composer in *Irving Berlin's America*. In 1987, he was in a command performance for President and Mrs. Ronald Reagan to preserve Ford's Theatre in *All Star Gala at Ford's Theatre*. In 1991, he performed on *A Capitol Fourth*, an annual Independence Day celebration in Washington, D.C., with the National Symphony Orchestra. Calloway was born in 1907 and died in 1994.

CALLOWAY, SWAY. Calloway joined MTV News in 2000 as the channel's resident hip-hop correspondent. His credits include hosting the live interactive hip-hop show *Direct Effect (DFX)*, cohosting the pre- and postshows of the *MTV Video Music Awards*, and hosting MTV's *News Now* specials. He interviewed such acts as Master P, Scarface, Mystikal, and P. Diddy.

CALLOWAY, VANESSA BELL. Calloway had a role in the daytime drama *All My Children* (1970). In 1992, she played Dorothy in the TV film *Stompin' at the Savoy*. In 1995, she played the teacher in "The Boy Who Painted Jesus Black," one of the *America's Dream* trilogy. In 1996, she had a key role in the TV film *The Cherokee Kid*. In 1998, she played Johnnie Mae Matthews in the TV film *The Temptations*. Calloway played the mother of the character played by singer **Monica** in *Love Song* in 2000. Also, in 2000, she started cohosting the BET talk show *Oh Drama!*

CAMBRIDGE, GODFREY. Comedian/actor Godfrey Cambridge was one of the winners of the 1964 Grammy Awards who performed in *The Best on Record* (1965). He was part of an hour of music and comedy in *A Last Laugh at the 60's* in 1970. He helped relate the history of humor through humor in *The Many Faces of Comedy* in 1973. Cambridge was born in 1933 and died in 1976.

CAMPBELL-MARTIN, TISHA. Singer/actress Campbell (aka Tisha Campbell), as a teen, played the smart-mouthed adopted daughter of Joseph Bologna's character, the lead in *Rags to Riches*, a 1987–1988 sitcom. Then she played Gina, girlfriend and then wife to Martin Lawrence, in the sitcom *Martin*. During the final years of the series, she was married in real life and shortly thereafter left the series because of a conflict with Lawrence. She returned for the series' final episode (in the script, she was said to be out of town) but never appeared in a scene with Lawrence. She played Rosalee in the series *Lincs* and Nicole in *Cousin Skeeter*, both in 1998–2000. She returned to series television in 2001 as the wife (to Damon Wayans) in *My Wife and Kids*. Her TV film credits include the role of Ruby Wilson in *The Sweetest Gift* (1998).

CANADA, RON. Canada played a doctor in *City of Angels* (2000), a coach in *Hangin' with Mr. Cooper* (1994–1995), Donald Preston in *The Preston Episodes* (1995), and Richard Barnes in *One on One* (2000–).

CANNING, LISA. Canning was announcer of *Into the Night* (1990–1991), cohost of *Knights and Warriors* (1992–1993), and host of *Destination Stardom* (1999–2000). She played Dori in *P.S. I Luv U*, a detective drama, in 1991–1992.

CAPERS, VIRGINIA. Capers had key roles in the made-for-television motion pictures *White Mama* in 1980, *Inmates: A Love Story* in 1981, and *The George McKenna Story* in 1986. Capers died of pneumonia in 2004.

CAPITOL FOURTH, A (*July 4, various years*). These musical specials originated from Washington, D.C., to celebrate Independence Day. The National Symphony Orchestra provided music for the 90-minute shows. Each show had one or two hosts and guests. **Pearl Bailey** hosted in 1981 (it was repeated in 1982) and 1989. Opera singer **Leontyne Price** and Willie Stargell hosted in 1983. **Sarah Vaughn** and others were guests in 1986. **Roberta Flack** and others were guests in 1987. **Cab Calloway, Diahann Carroll,** and **Bill Cosby** were guests in 1991. **Patti LaBelle** was a guest in 1992. **Duke**

Ellington was saluted in 1999. **Ossie Davis** hosted in 2003 and again in 2004. *See also* VARIETY SPECIALS.

CAPTAIN PLANET AND THE PLANETEERS (*TBS, 1990–*). This was an animated series about superheroes—environmental superheroes who wanted to rid the world of all the pollutants and polluters and anyone and anything that abused natural resources. **Whoopi Goldberg** was the voice of Gaia; **LeVar Burton**'s voice was used for Kwame (Earth). Beginning in the fourth season, the series was retitled *The New Adventures of Captain Planet*.

CAPTIVE HEART: THE JAMES MINK STORY (*CBS, April 14, 1996*). **Louis Gossett Jr.** was the black Toronto businessman who posed as his Irish wife's slave in order to rescue their daughter who had been kidnapped and sold into slavery in 1854 Virginia. Kate Nelligan (as Elizabeth, Mink's wife), **Ruby Dee** (as the slave Indigo), **Michael Jai White** (as Indigo's son Elroi), and Rachel Crawford (as Mink's daughter, Mary) also starred. *See also* BIOPICS.

CARA, IRENE. Cara played Bertha Palmer in *Roots: The Next Generations* in 1977 and starred in the TV film *Sister, Sister* in 1982. She made several appearances as a singer on *The Midnight Special* (1980).

CARNEGIE HALL SALUTES THE JAZZ MASTERS (*PBS, May 18, 1994*). **Vanessa L. Williams** and **Herbie Hancock** hosted this special all-star jazz concert featuring Betty Carter, Jimmy Smith, Abbey Lincoln, Jackie McLean, and Joe Henderson. *See also* VARIETY SPECIALS.

CARNEY, KAT. Carney joined CNN in 2001 as a health news anchor for *CNN Headline News*. After the September 11, 2001, terrorist attacks, she reported extensively on the anthrax threats and provided reports on precautions against the virus. Before joining CNN, she hosted the documentary series *The Body Invaders* for the Discovery Health Channel, hosted *Vacation Living* for Home & Garden Television, and was cohost with Richard Simmons of the nationally syndicated series *DreamMaker*.

CAROL, CARL, WHOOPI, AND ROBIN (*ABC, February 10, 1987*). This comedy special consisted of skits highlighting the talents of Carol Burnett, Carl Reiner, **Whoopi Goldberg**, and Robin Williams.

CAROL CHANNING AND PEARL BAILEY ON BROADWAY (*ABC, March 16, 1969*). This was a musical variety hour spotlighting the talents of Carol Channing and **Pearl Bailey**.

CARPENTER, THELMA. Carpenter played Mabel in the sitcom *Barefoot in the Park* (1970–1971) and appeared in *The Apollo Hall of Fame* in 1993.

CARROLL, DIAHANN. Carroll played the title role in *Julia* (1968–1971) and was the first black woman to actually star in a sitcom throughout its run; three actresses played the title role in *Beulah*. Also, the story line always had *Julia* as its center, whereas in *Beulah* the story centered on the white family for which Beulah worked as a maid, and Beulah was the voice of reason.

Her first national television appearance was in "Crescendo" on *The DuPont Show of the Month* in 1957. Carroll also starred in *The Diahann Carroll Show*, a four-week variety series (1976), and played Dominique Deveraux in the prime time soap opera *Dynasty* (1984–1987) and on *The Colbys* (1985–1986). She was Ida Grayson in the western drama *Lonesome Dove: The Series* in the 1994–1995 season. Carroll played a recurring role in the sitcom *A Different World* (1989 and 1991–1993) and *Soul Food* (2003, 2004). In variety programs, she was a guest on the special *Francis Albert Sinatra Does His Thing* in 1969, on *The Flip Wilson Special* in 1974, and in two George Burns specials in 1984 and 1986. She hosted her own variety special, also titled *The Diahann Carroll Show* in 1971. In TV films and miniseries, she played key roles in *I Know Why the Caged Bird Sings* in 1979, *Sister, Sister* in 1979, *From the Dead of Night* (1989), *Murder in Black and White* (1990), *Having Our Say* in 1999, *The Courage to Love* (2000), *Sally Hemings: An American Scandal* (2000), *Livin' for Love: The Natalie Cole Story* (2000), and *The Court* (2002).

CARROLL, LARRY. Carroll, a local Los Angeles newscaster, played news commentators in several television productions, including the 1981 miniseries about the Watergate crisis, *Blind Ambition*.

CARROLL, ROCKY. Carroll played Joey Emerson on the sitcom *Roc* (1991–1994) and Dr. Keith Wilkes in the sitcom *Chicago Hope* in 1996. He was Carl Reese in the drama series *The Agency* (2001–2003). In TV films, he had key roles in *Money, Power, Murder* (1989) and *Five Desperate Hours* (1997).

CARSON, LISA NICOLE. Carson played Carla Reese/Simmons on *ER* beginning in 1996 and Renee on *Ally McBeal* (1997–2001) but left both series before they ended. She had a key role in the miniseries *After Shock: Earthquake in New York* (1999) and the TV film *No Visible Bruises: The Katie Koestner Story* (1992). As Lisa Carson, she was a regular on *The Apollo Comedy Hour* (1992–1993).

CARSON, T. C. Carson played Kyle Barker on the sitcom *Living Single* (1993–1998) and Abednigo ("JoJo") on the sitcom *Key West* (1993).

CARTER, CHRIS. After a 15-year National Football League (NFL) career, Carter joined HBO's *Inside the NFL* in 2003.

CARTER COUNTRY (*ABC, 1977–1979*). This sitcom had racial story lines and centered on a police chief (Victor French) publicized as a "lovable redneck." Jimmy Carter was the U.S. president when the show aired, so it was significant that the show was set in a small town in Georgia near Carter's hometown of Plains. **Kene Holliday** was the second banana playing Sgt. Curtis Baker, the smart deputy who had training in New York City police methods. There was conflict over how to get the job done, but the two had mutual respect. Curtis had a crush on Lucille (**Vernee Watson**), the mayor's secretary. In the last season of the series, the characters were married.

CARTER, NELL. A Broadway Tony Award winner, Nell Carter's (aka Nell-Ruth Carter) first major network television appearance was in the black musical version of Cinderella, *Cindy*, in 1979. Her first series was *Lobo*, a police comedy starring Claude Akins on which she played Sgt. Hildy Jones in the 1980–1981 season. The following year, she got her own series, *Gimme a Break*, a sitcom in which she played Nell, a housekeeper/surrogate mother to a widowed police chief and his teenage daughters. Carter also sang the theme song. The series ended in 1987. In 1993, she joined the cast of the sitcom *Hangin' with Mr. Cooper* as Ms. P. J. Moore, the principal, a role she played for a year. She also played a psychiatrist in the 2001 sitcom *Reba*. In TV films, she had a key role in *Final Shot: The Hank Gathers Story* (1992).

In variety programming, while *Gimme a Break* was on the air in 1982, NBC mounted the musical that made Carter famous, *Ain't Misbehavin'*, with the original Broadway cast. For her work, she won the **Emmy Award** for Outstanding Individual Achievement—Special Class. In 1986, she starred in the special salute to music *Nell Carter—Never Too Old to Dream*. She also sang on the special *My Favorite Broadway: The Leading Ladies: Great Performances* in 1999. Four-time Tony winner **Audra McDonald**, who also performed in the latter production, said of Carter, "She had the ability to be such an incredible comedic musical-theater actress, blow a song all the way to the back of the wall, and then come down and be so intimate and beautiful in a ballad."

Carter was a guest on numerous variety and musical celebration specials including the following: *Baryshnikov on Broadway*, a 1980 tribute to American musical theater; *Night of 100 Stars I and II* (1982 and 1985) for the Actor's Fund; a *Dean Martin Celebrity Roast* of Mr. T (1984); *Christmas in Washington* (1984); *Las Vegas: An All Star 75th Anniversary* (1987); *Irving Berlin's 100th Birthday Celebration* (1988); *Freedom Festival '89*, an Independence Day celebration; *The Presidential Inaugural Gala for President George H. W. Bush*; *Sammy Davis Jr.'s 60th Anniversary Celebration* (1990); and *Welcome Home, America*, honoring the USO and the military (1991). She also performed in *Circus of the Stars* (1985). Carter was a regular on one of the later versions of *The Match Game*.

Carter was born in 1948 and died in 2003 of natural causes; she had suffered from aneurysms and diabetes. The latter was diagnosed during the *Gimme a Break* years. At the time, she was told that her body was producing insulin but not enough for so large a body and that if she lost weight, she might rid herself of the disease. Her weight was up and down for the rest of her life. *See also* DOMESTIC WORKERS IN THE 1980s.

CARTER, RALPH. Carter played Michael Evans on *Good Times* (1974–1979).

CARTER, TERRY. Carter, as a child, was Gabriel in 1957's **"The Green Pastures."** In 1970, as a young man, he played Sgt. Joe Broadhurst in *McCloud: Who Killed Miss U.S.A?* and in the series *McCloud* (1970–1977), which followed the successful film. He played Col. Tigh in *Battlestar Galactica* from 1978 to 1979. He became a producer.

CARTER, THOMAS. Carter played Ray Gun in *Szysznyk* (1977–1978) and James Hayward in *The White Shadow* (1978–1980). He won the **Emmy Award** for Outstanding Directing in a Drama Series for the "Promises to Keep" episode of *Equal Justice* in 1990. He won in the same category in 1991 for the "In Confidence" episode of *Equal Justice*. As executive producer of **Don King: Only in America**, he won the Emmy in 1998 for Outstanding Made-for-Television Movie.

CARTER, T. K. Carter, primarily a comedic actor, played some serious dramatic roles. He played a key role in **Billy: Portrait of a Street Kid** (1977) and Carter in *Yesterday's Target* (1996). In 2000, he starred in the miniseries **The Corner** as Gary McCullough. In sitcoms, he starred as the genie Shabu in the 1983 sitcom *Just Our Luck*. He was the teacher, Mike Fulton, in *Punky Brewster* (1985–1986) and Clarence Hall in **The Sinbad Show** (1993–1994). He recurred as T-Bone in **The Steve Harvey Show** (1996–1998).

CARTER'S ARMY (*ABC, January 27, 1970*). This 90-minute motion picture for television was about an all-black rear-echelon service company under the command of a redneck commanding officer. The unit was ordered to hold an important dam against the enemy. Starring were **Robert Hooks** as Lt. Edward Wallace, **Rosey Grier** as Big Jim, **Moses Gunn** as Doc, **Richard Pryor** as Jonathan Crunk, **Glynn Turman** as George Brightman, and **Billy Dee Williams** as Lewis. Stephen Boyd played Capt. Carter.

CASABLANCA (*ABC, 1955–1956; NBC, 1983*). "Casablanca" was one of two rotating shows under the umbrella title *Warner Brothers Presents*. It was based on the classic film of the same title and, in the 1950s, starred Charles McGraw as Rich, the character created by Humphrey Bogart in the feature film. When Rich said, "Play it again,

Sam," he said it to a Sam played by actor **Clarence Muse**. There was another version on NBC in 1983, and **Scatman Crothers** played Sam; David Soul played Rich.

CASEY, BERNIE. He starred as Joe Louis in the TV film *Ring of Passion* in 1978 and in the same year in the two-hour film *Love Is Not Enough*. The latter was the pilot for the 1979 half-hour dramatic series *Harris and Company*. He had a starring role as Ozzie Peoples in the 1983 drama series *The Bay City Blues*. He had key roles in *Mary Jane Harper Cried Last Night*, a 1977 TV film about child abuse; the Emmy-winning TV movie *Brian's Song* in 1971; and *Panic on the 5:22* in 1974. Other key roles included *Roots: The Next Generations* in 1979; *The Martian Chronicles* in 1980; *The Sophisticated Gents* in 1981; and *The Fantastic World of D.C. Collins* in 1984.

CASH, ROSALIND. Cash had key roles in *Ceremonies in Dark Old Men* in 1975, *A Killing Affair* in 1977, *Guyana Tragedy: The Story of Jim Jones* in 1980, *The Sophisticated Gents* in 1981, *Special Bulletin* in 1983, a starring role in *Sister, Sister* in 1982, and *Go Tell It on the Mountain* in 1985. All were made-for-television films. She was playing the continuing role of Mary Mae Ward in the daytime drama *General Hospital* when she died of cancer in 1995. She had a role in the TV film *Circle of Pain*, which aired after her death in 1996.

CBS SUNDAY MORNING (*CBS, 1979–*). In this newsmagazine, jazz musician **Billy Taylor** began reporting segments on jazz in 1981. Beginning in 2004, **Wynton Marsalis** opened the newsmagazine with his trumpet sounding "The Abblasen Fanfare" by Gottfried Reiche.

CEDRIC THE ENTERTAINER. Cedric was host of the variety series *Cedric the Entertainer Presents* (2002–2003). He won the NAACP Image Award for doing the voice of Uncle Bobby in **The Proud Family** (2001–), an animated cartoon about a black family. He was cohost of *Motown 45* in 2004. He was host of *Comicview* (1993–1994), and he played Cedric Robinson on *The Steve Harvey Show* (1996–2002).

CEDRIC THE ENTERTAINER PRESENTS (*FOX, 2002–2003*). Comedian **Cedric the Entertainer** hosted a variety series reminiscent of big comedy variety series like *The Flip Wilson Show* of the 1970s. This variety show was the highest-rated show among African Americans in the 2002–2003 season, but it was canceled by the network because of **ratings**. In the overall rankings of series, the show was near the bottom at number 94. A series must have high overall ratings and sell the products advertised to stay on the air. A network executive said that Fox was willing to find another series for him that would better showcase his talents. However, Cedric's representatives had other plans. Cedric said the cancellation "disregards what's popular among a culture of people. The decision [to cancel] borders on some very blatant racism. We were the No. 1 show." *See also* VARIETY SERIES.

CELEBRATE THE DREAM: 50 YEARS OF EBONY MAGAZINE (*ABC, November 28, 1996*). The 50th anniversary of *Ebony* magazine was celebrated in comedy and music as well as tributes. Among the celebrities participating were the following: **Muhammad Ali, Brandy, Bill Cosby, Whitney Houston, Quincy Jones, Patti La Belle, Sinbad, Will Smith, Cicely Tyson, Luther Vandross, Oprah Winfrey**, and **Stevie Wonder**.

CELEBRITY AND THE ARCADE KID, THE (*ABC, November 9, 1983*). **Darnell Williams** starred in a dual role in this one-hour comedy, which was an *ABC Afterschool Special*. He was Kyle Rhoades, a celebrity, and also Johnny Grant, a video game whiz who looked exactly like Kyle. To escape from fans, Kyle got Johnny to switch places with him, and they lived each other's lives. **Roxie Roker** portrayed Aunt Helen, **Hal Williams** was Tony Grant, and **Debbi Morgan** was Jennifer Sanders.

CEREMONIES IN DARK OLD MEN (*ABC, 1975*). Based on the classic award-winning play by Lonne Elder III, this TV movie was about the Parker family, particularly the patriarch who felt trapped and defeated with his plight in life. His business had failed, and he agreed to a scheme that threatened to negatively affect his entire family. **Robert Hooks**, who was playwright Elder's roommate in the early 1960s, played the role of Blue Haven. **Rosalind Cash** played Adela. **Michele Shay** was the Young Girl. **Glynn Turman** was Theo. **Douglas Turner Ward** was Russell B. Parker.

CHAMBERLIN, LEE. In daytime drama series, Chamberlin played Pat Baxter on *All My Children* from 1982 to 1991 and the same role on *Loving* (1983). In prime-time series, she played Lucy Daniels in *All's Fair* (1976). In children's programs, she was Brenda and Gladys Glowworm in *The Electric Company* (1971–1973). In classic drama, she was Cordelia in *King Lear* (1974). In made-for-television films and miniseries, she had key roles in *Long Journey Back* (1978), ***Roots: The Next Generations*** in 1979, ***Brave New World*** in 1980, *Once upon a Family* (1980), and *Willing to Kill: The Texas Cheerleader Story* (1992).

CHAPMAN, TRACY. Chapman performed on the musical special *One Love: The Bob Marley All-Star Tribute* in 1999.

CHAPPELLE, DAVE. Chappelle starred in the short-lived sitcom *Buddies*, a spin-off of *Home Improvement*, in 1996 and then made a hit of *Chappelle's Show* in 2003. He headlined the specials *Dave Chappelle: Killin' Them Softly* (2000) and *Dave Chapelle: For What It's Worth* (2004).

CHAPPELLE'S SHOW (*COM, 2003–*). Comedian **Dave Chappelle** starred in this half-hour comedy/variety series featuring comedy sketches videotaped in New York City's tristate area and some popular musical guests. The show's staff called the show "the comedy equivalent of crack; one try and you're hooked." A sketch in one show was a satire of a McDonald's commercial, MacArnold's; another was a junkie giving an antidrug speech to kids in grade school. Still another featured the streetwise "President Black Bush." Charlie Murphy talked about the feud between his brother, **Eddie Murphy**, and singer Rick James with Chappelle playing James; James himself also appeared in the segment (which aired before his 2004 death). Comedian **Paul Mooney**, who made multiple appearances, forecast the future as "Negrodamus." Another sketch centered on a 1950s white family with the last name "Niggar." In another sketch about the "racial draft," delegates from various races chose celebrities forcing them to be 100 percent of one race. The black delegation chose Tiger Woods. The Jewish delegation chose Lenny Kravitz. The white delegation chose Colin Powell, but the black delegation forced it to also accept Condoleezza Rice in the process.

The show, known for profanity, used the "N" word profusely and also the word "bitch," and Chappelle made no apologies. He said the TV networks' theory of adding white characters to broaden appeal has "f— — blown out of the water." A warning before one episode reads that the show was "deemed more offensive than usual." Yet Chappelle was praised by *TV Guide* for being "the funniest man on TV . . . he's rude, he's crude . . . and he's absolutely brilliant." *TV Guide* and *USA Today* compared him with **Richard Pryor**. Each show usually ended in the performance of a musical artist, making the series variety as well as comedy. As of January 2005, the first season, uncensored, was the best-selling TV series on DVD ever, selling more than two million copies. The series was nominated for three **Emmy Awards** in 2004. In 2005, Chappelle voluntarily disappeared from the series, and its future was questionable.

CHARLES, KEITH. Charles was a regular in the sitcom *Six Feet Under* (2003–).

CHARLES, RAY. Charles (née Ray Charles Robinson) was a guest entertainer on numerous variety series and specials. Among them were the following: *It's What's Happening, Baby!* in 1965; *Andy Williams Kaleidoscope Company* in 1968; *The Bob Hope Special* in 1969; *Sammy and Company, Duke Ellington . . . We Love You Madly* in 1973; *Cotton Club '75* in 1974; *Celebration: The American Spirit* in 1976; *The Beatles Forever* and *The All-Star Gong Special* in 1977; *Barbra Streisand and Other Musical Instruments* in 1973; *50 Years of Country Music*, *The Second Barry Manilow Special*, and *Johnny Cash: Spring Fever* in 1978; *The Kenny Rogers Special* in 1979; *Linda Carter's Celebration*, *A Special Kenny Rogers*, and *Country Comes Home* in 1981; *A Salute to Lady Liberty* in 1984; *Walt Disney World's 15th Birthday Celebration* in 1986; *The Beach Boys—25 Years Together* and *Las Vegas: An All-Star 75th Anniversary* in 1987; *Sesame Street . . . 20 Years and Still Counting* in 1989; *A Tribute to John Lennon* in 1991; and *Willie Nelson: The Big Six-O* in 1993. In 1983, Charles received the Hall of Fame Award by the *NAACP Image Awards*. He was an honoree at *The Kennedy Center Honors* in 1986 and one of six entertainers honored on the 1987 special *The Grammy Lifetime Achievement Awards*. He performed in *Irving*

Berlin's 100th Birthday Celebration in 1988 and *The Apollo Hall of Fame* in 1993. He also headlined his own specials, such as *Gladys Knight and the Pips with Ray Charles* in 1987 and *Ray Charles: 50 Years of Music, Uh-Huh!* in 1991.

In 1994, Charles received the Lifetime Achievement Award as part of the *Black Achievement Awards* televised by Johnson Publishing Company. In 2001, he received the Trumpet Award on behalf of Turner Broadcasting Systems. That same year, he sang "America, the Beautiful" at the Super Bowl. In 2003, he sang "America, the Beautiful" on *A Capitol Fourth* in Washington, D.C. In 2004, he received the Hall of Fame Award, the second time, at the NAACP Image Awards. In 2004, he was posthumously celebrated in the concert *Genius: A Night for Ray Charles* hosted by Jamie Foxx, who starred in the film *Ray* that same year. Charles died in 2004 of liver disease at 73.

CHARLIE & COMPANY (*CBS, 1985–1986*). Flip Wilson and **Gladys Knight** played Charlie and Diana Richmond, a married couple with three children: Lauren (Fran Robinson), Charlie Jr. (**Kristoff St. John**), and Robert (**Jaleel White**). The Richmonds lived on the South Side of Chicago; Charlie worked as an administrative assistant for a city government office, while Diana was an elementary school teacher. **Della Reese** played Diana's aunt, Rachel. Some scenes depicted Charlie at work, while most were of the family. Critics charged that the series was an attempt to duplicate the success of *The Cosby Show*. Wilson walked away from the series after a white writer said to him, "Don't change my words." A producer later said, "Didn't he know we could get rid of the writer?"

CHARLOTTE FORTEN'S MISSION: EXPERIMENT IN FREEDOM (*PBS, February 25, 1985*). The two-hour film is the story of a pioneer African-American educator Charlotte Forten (**Melba Moore**), who traveled from north of the Mason-Dixon line to Port Royal, South Carolina, to teach newly freed slaves during the Civil War. Her mission was made more difficult because the slaves somehow mistrusted her lighter complexion and "fancy airs." **Mary Alice, Moses Gunn, Anna Maria Horsford**, and **Glynn Turman** also starred.

CHASE, ANNAZETTE. Chase played Anne in the TV films *Goldie and the Boxer* in 1979, Cathy in *The 11th Victim* in 1979, and Loretta in *Marriage: Year One* in 1971.

CHASING A RAINBOW: THE LIFE OF JOSEPHINE BAKER (*PBS, February 25, 1989*). The life of the international singer/dancer was highlighted in this documentary.

CHEADLE, DON. Cheadle was the district attorney, Jonathan Littleton, on *Picket Fences* from 1993 to 1995. He played a starring role in the made-for-television movies *Rebound: The Legend of Earl "The Goat" Manigault* in 1996 and *A Lesson before Dying* in 1999. He starred in *Things behind the Sun* in 2001.

CHECKER, CHUBBY. Checker, born Ernest Evans, got his start on television after Dick Clark signed him to a recording contract in 1959. Already nicknamed Chubby, Clark's wife added the "Checker" to his name. After other artists failed to make a hit of "The Twist," Checker's version became a hit, and he worked hard at promoting it in interviews, TV, and live appearances from June 1959 to August 1960. A number one hit, it became a dance sensation, and many other twist tunes followed; these were followed by numerous other dance crazes, many introduced by Checker. Among them was "The Pony" from the song "Pony Time," which had been recorded by another group, and Checker covered it. His version went to number one and stayed there for 16 weeks in 1961. In 1961, "The Twist" reentered the charts, and by 1962 it became number one again. No other record had accomplished this feat. Checker was also a headliner in the halftime show for Super Bowl XXII in 1982.

CHECKING IN (*CBS, 1981*). **Marla Gibbs** starred in this sitcom as Florence, the character she played in *The Jeffersons* (1975–1985). In this series, Florence left her job as George and Weezy's maid to become head of the housekeeping department at the St. Frederick Hotel in Manhattan. **Ruth Brown** played Betty. Gibb's son, Jordan, played Dennis, the bellboy.

CHEETAH GIRLS, THE (*DIS, August 13, 2003*). This made-for-television film centered on a multiethnic group of girls who formed a band and were determined to succeed. The movie followed their challenges as they learned the music industry and were determined to remain friends throughout the stressful journey. **Raven-Symone, Lynn Whitfield,** Adrienne Bailon, Kiely Williams, and Sabrina Bryan were primary cast members. Whitfield played Raven's mom. Oz Scott was director. The TV film was based on the book of the same title by Deborah Gregory. **Whitney Houston** was one of the executive producers.

CHEROKEE KID, THE (*HBO, December 14, 1996*). Sinbad starred in the title role of this comedy western TV film. As a child, Isaiah saw his family killed by Bloomington (James Coburn), a land baron. He vowed to get revenge. The grown-up Isaiah trained to get Bloomington and called himself the Cherokee Kid as he encountered fictional and historical characters along the way. **Gregory Hines, Ernie Hudson, Vanessa Bell Calloway,** Burt Reynolds, **Hal Williams, Obba Babatunde, Dawnn Lewis,** and **Lorraine Toussaint** played key roles.

CHESTNUT, MORRIS. Chestnut played the title role in the TV film *The Ernest Green Story* in 1993.

CHICO AND THE MAN (*NBC, 1974–1978*). This sitcom set in a blue-collar Hispanic neighborhood of Los Angeles followed, on Friday nights, **Redd Foxx's** *Sanford and Son*, set in a black blue-collar Los Angeles neighborhood. The pair were a kind of minority block and finished the year with *Sanford* in second place of all series and *Chico* in third place. *Chico and the Man* starred Jack Albertson and Freddie Prinze (Sr.). The man, Ed Brown (Albertson), was a crotchety old garage owner who hired Chico (Prinze), a problem kid with more charm than problems, to clean the garage and help communicate with customers. Black regulars were **Scatman Crothers** as Louie Wilson, the garbage man, and **Della Reese** (1976–1978) as the owner of a neighborhood diner. The show struggled to keep its audience after Prinze committed suicide during the 1977 season but could not.

CHILD ACTORS WHO MAINTAINED SUCCESS AS ADULTS IN SHOW BUSINESS. Few child actors are able to make the transition to success as adult actors. Desire has a lot to do with it. Some child actors are anxious to have real lives. Others would love to continue their acting careers, they like being recognized, and/or they realize that the salaries are perhaps greater than most occupations. And some say that acting is all they know, all they can do, and all they want to do. But the transition is not easy. The biggest hurdle is the teen years. These children must have teachers and social workers on the film or TV set, a cost that production companies can avoid by hiring young-looking actors over 18. Also, the number of hours a child can work is limited, making production schedules difficult.

Still, persistent former child actors have overcome the problems and have made some success as adults. Some are **Kim Fields** (Tootie in *The Facts of Life*) and **Regina King** (Brenda in *227*). Some child actors chose to go into behind-the-scenes work, like **Kevin Hooks** (*Just an Old Sweet Song*) and also **Mario Van Peebles** (the feature film *Sweet Sweeetback's Badasssss Song*); both are actors, directors, and producers. **Leslie Uggams** (*Sing Along with Mitch*) and **Janet Jackson** (*The Jacksons*) were singers first and became actors while continuing to sing. **Michael Jackson** (*The Jacksons*) was a child singer and remained a singer with a few experiences as an actor. **Kristoff St. John**, who plays Neil Winters in *The Young and the Restless*, was the boy Christopher St. John in the 1982 TV film *Sister, Sister* and the teenager in the sitcom *Charlie & Company* (1985–1986). **Malcolm-Jamal Warner**, Theo, one of the kids in *The Cosby Show* (1984–1992), grew up to star in *Malcolm and Eddie* (1996–2000) and to be a director. **Terry Carter** and **Demond Wilson** were child actors in **"The Green Pastures"**; Carter starred later in *McCloud* and Wilson in *Sanford and Son*.

CHILDRESS, ALVIN. Childress played Amos, the taxi driver and peacemaker in *Amos 'n' Andy* (1951–1953). He guest-starred in series episodes and had roles in made-for-television films including *Sister, Sister* in 1982. He had a recurring role in both *Sanford and Son* (1972–1977) and *Good Times* (1976–1979) as the minister. Childress was born in 1908 and died in 1986.

CHONG, RAE DAWN. Chong played Peggy Fowler in the supernatural series *Mysterious Ways* beginning in 2000. She had a key role in the TV film *Badge of the Assassin* (1985) and the TV projects *Valentine's Day* (1998), *The Alibi* (1997), and *Prison Stories: Women on the Inside* (1991).

CHRIS ROCK: BIGGER AND BLACKER (*HBO, July 10, 1999*). From the legendary Apollo Theater, Chris Rock entertained before a live audience.

CHRIS ROCK: NEVER SCARED (*HBO, April 17, 2004*). Rock delivered his comedic takes on social and political issues, religion, gay marriage, and more. The show was taped before an audience in DAR Constitution Hall in Washington, D.C.

CHRISTMAS DREAM, A (*NBC, December 16, 1984*). Mr. T starred in this musical special as a sidewalk Santa Claus who tries to make a young boy believe in Christmas. **Emmanuel Lewis** played the young boy. Also in the cast were ventriloquist **Willie Tyler** and his dummy Lester, **Tai Babilonia**, and Randy Gardner.

CHRISTMAS IN WASHINGTON (*annually, various networks, December 1982– *). These one-hour variety specials were shown during the Christmas season each year and were broadcast from Washington, D.C., usually with the current president and his wife present. At least one black entertainer was on the bill plus the Eastern High School choir, a primarily black choir from a local high school. The dates of each year's broadcast and the black entertainers were the following: December 13, 1982, **Diahann Carroll**; December 15, 1983, **Leslie Uggams**; December 16, 1984, **Nell Carter**; December 15, 1985, **Natalie Cole**; December 21, 1987, **Marilyn McCoo**; December 21, 1988, soprano opera singer **Kathleen Battle**; December 18, 1989, Diahann Carroll for the second time; December 19, 1990, **Aretha Franklin**; December 18, 1991, **Anita Baker** and **Johnny Mathis**; December 19, 1992, Peabo Bryson; December 15, 1993, **Patti LaBelle**, **Wynton Marsalis**, and **Aaron Nelville**; December 13, 1994, Anita Baker and the Sounds of Blackness; December 10, 1995, Al Green; December 19, 1996, **Luther Vandross** and Cece Winans; December 14, 1997, Aaliyah and Shirley Caesar; December 16, 1998, **Aretha Franklin**; December 12, 1999, **B. B. King**; December 17, 2000, **Chuck Berry**; December 16, 2001, **Usher**; December 19, 2002, Yolanda Adams; December 14, 2003, Ashanti; and December 15, 2004, Ruben Studdard and Vanessa L. Williams.

CHRISTMAS LILIES OF THE FIELD (*NBC, December 16, 1979*). This made-for-television movie was a sequel to the 1963 film *Lilies of the Field* starring **Sidney Poitier**. In the TV film, **Billy Dee Williams** played Homer Smith, a jack-of-all-trades who visited the chapel he helped build in the Arizona desert for German nuns. **Fay Hauser** played Janet Owens. Maria Schell played Mother Maria.

CHRISTMAS STARFEST (*SYN, annually*). Beginning in 1998, this special featured performances by recording artists and cameo appearances and message vignettes by actors in popular series. This was a special from the producers of *Soul Train* and was also called *The Annual Sears Soul Train Christmas Starfest*.

CINDERELLA (*ABC, November 2, 1997*). Airing as an episode of *The Wonderful World of Disney*, this Rodgers & Hammerstein musical starred **Whitney Houston** as the fairy godmother and **Brandy** as Cinderella. It was the first time a black actress played the role in the Rodgers & Hammerstein version, although there was a black musical version of the story, *Cindy*, starring **Charlaine Woodard**. Houston was originally slated to play the title role, but when it was finally developed, she felt too old for the part. So executive producer Craig Zadan suggested Brandy; Houston telephoned her immediately and said, "Hi, this is your fairy godmother." **Whoopi Goldberg** played the queen. The cast was intentionally multiethnic. Houston was also credited with being executive producer.

CINDY (*ABC, March 24, 1978*). This two-hour musical production was a black version of the classic story of Cinderella and the handsome prince, only this version takes place in World War II Harlem with an all-black cast. **Charlaine Woodard** played Cindy, and **Clifton Davis** played Capt. Joe Prince. **Scoey Mitchll** was the father, Mae Mercer was the stepmother, and the stepsisters were

Nell Carter and **Alaina Reed**. **Cleavant Derricks** played Michael Simpson.

CITY OF ANGELS (*CBS, 2000*). An inner-city medical drama, many viewers held great hope that *City of Angels* would emerge as the first successful primarily black-cast drama. It did air for nearly a year, which was longer than most. **Blair Underwood, Vivica A. Fox,** and **Michael Warren** headed the cast. Dr. Ben Turner (Underwood) was acting chief of surgery at Angels of Mercy Hospital in Los Angeles. Dr. Lillian Price (Fox) was his superior; she was also his former lover, which did not help their professional relationship. Harris (Warren) was the chief executive officer of the hospital. Dr. Wesley Williams (Hill Harper) was a resident, as was Jackson (T. E. Russell). **Maya Rudolph**, Octavia L. Spencer, and **Viola Davis** were nurses. **Harold Sylvester, Ron Canada,** and **Gabrielle Union** were doctors. White actor Robert Morse played the chairman of the board. In the second season, Dr. Price left the hospital, and a rapist (**Bokeem Woodbine**) terrorized the hospital. Numerous black writers, directors, producers, and crew members were employed by the series.

CLAIBORNE, RON. Claiborne's credits at ABC News include being a general assignment correspondent based in Boston and reporting for *World News Tonight with Peter Jennings*, *World News This Weekend*, and *Good Morning America*.

CLARENCE THOMAS'S SUPREME COURT CONFIRMATION HEARINGS. The controversial U.S. Senate hearings in October 1991 led to the confirmation of Clarence Thomas to the U.S. Supreme Court, though many Americans preferred a different outcome. Anita Hill, a law professor and a former employee of Thomas, was the star witness of the controversy about sexual harassment. The hearings dominated television for that weekend, interrupting regularly scheduled programs. The controversy pitted men against women, conservative against liberal, old against young, the educated against the uneducated, and people with business experiences against those uninitiated.

CLARK, MYSTRO. Clark hosted *Soul Train* (1997–1998).

CLASH, KEVIN. A Jim Henson puppeteer for many years, Clash provided the voice for Elmo on *Sesame Street*. He also did the voice for Hoots, the Owl. He was part of the *Sesame Street* production team that won the **Emmy Award** for Outstanding Pre-School Children's Series in 2002, 2003, and 2004. He was nominated each year from 1999 to 2004 for the Emmy for Outstanding Performer in a Children's Series. He also provided voices for characters in *The Muppet Family Christmas* (1987), *The Jim Henson Hour* (1989), *Dinosaurs* (1991), *The Torkelsons* (1991), *Mr. Willowby's Christmas Tree* (1995), *Elmo's Musical Adventure* (2000), *It's a Very Merry Muppet Christmas Movie* (2002), and others.

CLEROW WILSON AND THE MIRACLE OF P.S. 14 (*November 12, 1972*). This was a 30-minute animated children's special featuring characters created by **Flip Wilson** on his popular variety series. There was Clerow Wilson (Flip's real name), Geraldine Jones (a girl on which Little Clerow had a crush), Rev. Leroy, Herbie, and Freddy. The story was loosely based on Wilson's childhood in Jersey City, New Jersey, when a teacher told the class at P.S. 14 that the Statue of Liberty, which has its back turned to Jersey City, would turn around and face the city if any of them ever accomplished anything great.

CLUB COMICVIEW PRESENTS. *See* COMICVIEW.

COBB, KEITH HAMILTON. Cobb played Noah Keefer in *All My Children* (1994–1996). Then, in 2003, he joined the cast of another daytime drama, *The Young and the Restless*, as businessman Damon Porter. In prime time, he played Tyr Anasazi in the sci-fi drama *Gene Roddenberry's Andromeda* (2000–2003). In 1996, *People* named him one of the 50 most beautiful people in the world.

COBBS, BILL. Cobbs played father to the lead character in the sitcom *The Gregory Hines Show* (1997–1998). He was Right Burke in the two-hour made-for-television film *Always Outnumbered* in 1988 and played a key role in the 1996 TV film *Nightjohn*.

COCAINE AND BLUE EYES (*NBC, January 2, 1983*). A two-hour pilot for a dramatic series, this **O. J. Simpson** vehicle centered on a private investigator in San Francisco. Michael Brennen (Simpson) gets involved with a drug-smuggling ring and a politically prominent family. Simpson was executive producer for his own company, Orenthal Productions. **Tracy Reed** played Chris Brennen.

COLEMAN, GARY. Coleman played Arnold in the sitcom *Diff'rent Strokes* (1978–1986). During the hiatus periods from the series, he starred in five TV films catering to children and families. They were the following: *The Kid from Left Field* (1979), *Scout's Honor* (1980), *The Kid with the Broken Halo* and *The Kid with the 200 I.Q.* (1983), *The Fantastic World of D.C. Collins* (1984), and *Playing with Fire* (1985).

COLEMAN, MARILYN. Coleman had roles in TV films: *A Woman Called Moses* (1978), *Nowhere to Run* (1978), *No Other Love* (1979), *Something So Right* (1982), *Don't Go to Sleep* (1982), *The Atlanta Child Murders* (1985), *Heat Wave* (1990), and *Better Off Dead* (1993). She recurred as Bookman's wife on *Good Times* (1977–1978) and as Mrs. Hayward on *The White Shadow* (1978 and 1981).

COLE, NATALIE. The daughter of **Nat "King" Cole** starred in her first variety special, *The Natalie Cole Special*, in 1978. She also performed in numerous specials as a guest of other headliners. She was one of several entertainers who showed the music, fashions, and fads of *Yearbook: The Class of 1967* in 1985. In 1976, she was a guest in *Hi, I'm Glen Campbell*, and in 1977, she was a guest of Frank Sinatra in his special *Sinatra and Friends*. That same year, Cole joined other guests at the Hollywood Palladium for the special *Paul Anka . . . Music My Way* and helped salute Super Bowl XI in *Super Night at the Super Bowl*. In 1980, she and other celebrities who were alumni of the Apollo Theater paid tribute to the Harlem landmark in *Uptown*. She was in the cast of *Christmas in Washington*, an annual holiday musical celebration, in 1985. She was in *Motown Merry Christmas* and *Grammy Lifetime Achievement Awards* as a performer, both in 1987. Then she sang for *Irving Berlin's 100th Birthday Celebration* in 1988. In 1990, in *A Tribute to John Lennon*, Cole performed his songs. In 1994, she was one of the headliners in the special *Rhythm*

Country and Blues, and she sang the National Anthem at *Super Bowl XXVII*. In 1997, she sang for President Bill Clinton in the *Gala for the President at Ford's Theatre*. In 1999, she read bedtime classics in *Goodnight Moon*, a children's program. In 1988, she had a rare dramatic role when she played the romantic interest in the two-hour made-for-television film *Always Outnumbered*.

COLE, NAT "KING." Cole was the first major black star to head-line a network variety series when *The Nat "King" Cole Show* premiered in 1956 and lasted for a little more than a year. In series starring other entertainers, he was a guest star on *The Pat Boone-Chevy Showroom*, which aired from1957 to 1960. Even before his series, he sang on *The Perry Como Show* (which ran from 1948 to 1963), and on *Ford Star Jubilee*, which aired from 1955 to 1956. In variety specials, he was one of the stars who saluted America in *I Hear America Singing* in 1955, then he was one of the singing stars who saluted spring in song in *Five Stars in Springtime* in 1957. He sang songs that won Oscar Awards on *Academy Award Songs* in 1960. He was a guest on *The Dinah Shore Special* in 1961. During the 1991–1992 season, his daughter, Natalie Cole, starred in a special tribute to him, *Unforgettable, with Love: Natalie Cole Sings the Songs of Nat "King" Cole*, on PBS's *Great Performances*. Cole was born in 1919 and died in 1965 of lung cancer.

COLE, OLIVIA. Cole played Mathilda in the miniseries *Roots* (1977) and won the **Emmy Award** for Outstanding Single Performance by a Supporting Actress in a Drama or Comedy Series. Also in miniseries, she starred in *Backstairs at the White House* as Maggie Rogers, a domestic in the White House (1979), and Maum Sally in *North and South* (1985). In 1989, she was Miss Sophie in the miniseries *The Women of Brewster Place* and the same role in the short-lived drama series that followed, *Brewster Place* (1989). In other made-for-television films, she had key roles in *Children of Divorce* (1980), *Mistress of Paradise* in 1981, *Something about Amelia* (1984), and *Go Tell It on the Mountain* (1985). Cole's credits also include sitcoms; she played Blanche in *Report to Murphy* in 1982 and Ms. Harrison in *Szysznyk* in 1977–1978.

COLES, CHARLES "HONI." Coles had a key role as Old Shady in the TV film *Charleston* in 1979.

COLES, KIM. Coles, a stand-up comedienne, got her start as a contestant on *Star Search*. Then she performed sketches as part of the regular cast of the comedy show *In Living Color* in 1990, its premiere year. She did a hip comedy segment called "Girl Talk" on *Friday Night Videos*. From 1993 to 1998, she played Synclaire James in the sitcom *Living Single*. She was also host of *New Attitudes,* a magazine format show on Lifetime.

COLLEGE HILL (*BET, 2004*). Promoted as the first African-American reality series, this was basically a series of documentaries, continued visits with eight students at the historically black Southern University in Louisiana. Unlike other reality series like *Big Brother* and *Survivor* or *Real Life*, this series did not place its participants in the university; these were real students matriculating at Southern; however, for the series, they were all housed in one suite with cameras observing them constantly. The unscripted half hour was spent observing the students' academic and social lives and the drama associated with problems like flunking out of school, romantic entanglements, pregnancy, and attempted suicide. Veronica and Gabe were a romantic couple, both from Texas and both achievers. Veronica (from Houston) was considered the spoiled rich girl, beautiful and aware of it. Gabriel (from Dallas) was active with his fraternity and the band and proud that he could do all of it and keep his grades up. Kinda (from Baton Rouge, Louisiana) was hot for the opposite sex and not hot on attending classes. Pregnant Shalondrea (from Shreveport, Louisiana) was an outspoken honor student and a troublemaker. Kevin (from Los Angeles) liked the girls, more than one at a time. Nina (from Shreveport) said she went to Southern to be a cheerleader. She enjoyed her social life and was called the group diva. Delano (from Los Angeles) was a rapper and aspiring actor. A big teddy bear of a guy, he was a charmer who liked to clown. His mother had died shortly before the show began taping. Dreadlocked Jabari (from Chicago) was academically a genius who took some teasing by the others and had no problems seeking counseling if he felt it necessary. Avery was the resident adviser who resigned during the 13 episodes, ostensibly because he was rarely in the dorm. Tracey Edmonds and her husband, singer Kenneth "Babyface" Edmonds, created the series. She was executive producer. The series made its debut on January 28 with 1.5 million viewers, a record for **Black Entertainment Television** (BET). BET selected one college-bound or college-enrolled viewer to receive a $2,004 scholarship after each episode. Students seeking the scholarships watched the episode for an on-screen password, then logged on to BET's *College Hill* Web page. The 2005 series took place on the campus of Langston University in Oklahoma.

COLORED MUSEUM, THE (*PBS, February 1, 1991*). This 10-scene production was based on a stage revue making fun of black stereotypes and also dealing seriously with the pain of being black. **Danitra Vance, Linda Hopkins, Victor Love**, Kevin Jackson, Reggie Montgomery, Vickilynn Reynolds, **Loretta Devine, Tommy Hollis**, and **Phyllis Yvonne Stickney** starred. *See also* BROADWAY PLAYS AND MUSICALS.

COLOR OF COURAGE, THE (*USA, February 10, 1999*). **Lynn Whitfield** played Minnie McGhee, a black woman whose family moved into a previously all-white neighborhood. She bonded with a white woman (Linda Hamilton), and together they became a landmark civil rights case in 1944.

COLOR OF FRIENDSHIP, THE (*ABC, November 11, 1981*). **James Bond III** starred in this one-hour *ABC Afterschool Special* as Joel Garth, the sole black student in his junior high school class. Garth develops a friendship with a classmate, David Bellinger (Chris Barnes). Despite the racial prejudice that exists in the school, the friendship between the two boys is colorless.

COLOR OF FRIENDSHIP, THE (*DIS, February 5, 2000*). This TV film was based on the true story of an African girl learning to cope with racism and her own prejudices during a visit to the United States. Set in 1977, the film was based on a true story about African-American Congressman Ron Dellums, who volunteered to take in a South African exchange student. He and his family expected a black student, but Mahree Bok (Lindsey Haun) arrived. She had lived with apartheid and believed that blacks were inferior. **Carl Lumbly** played Dellums. The Dellums family was played by Shadia Simmons (as Dellums's daughter Piper), **Penny Johnson**, Anthony Burnett, and Travis Kyle Davis. The production won the **Emmy Award** for Outstanding Children's Program and the prestigious Humanitas Prize for the script. **Kevin Hooks** was producer and director. This film aired as an offering of **African-American History Month**. It was rerun in 2005, also as part of African-American History Month.

COLOR OF LOVE: JACEY'S STORY, THE (*CBS, March 19, 2000*). **Louis Gossett Jr.** and Gena Rowlands starred in this TV film as a paternal grandfather and maternal grandmother, respectively, who overcame their long-standing negative attitudes about each other to care for their orphaned young granddaughter.

COMEDY CENTRAL PRESENTS: THE FIRST KENNEDY CENTER MARK TWAIN PRIZE CELEBRATING THE HUMOR OF RICHARD PRYOR (*COM, January 20, 1999*). Comedian Richard Pryor was presented this first annual award for humor.

COMEDY STORE'S 20TH BIRTHDAY (*NBC, September 24, 1992*). **Arsenio Hall**, **Jimmie Walker**, and **Damon Wayans** were among the comedians who got their start onstage at the famed Comedy Store in Hollywood. These three and numerous others paid tribute to the club and its 20th anniversary.

COMICVIEW (*BET, 1992– *). In a flashy nightclublike setting, primarily black comedians who did not have a sitcom were offered a chance to get national exposure while entertaining a primarily black studio audience, one that could respond with raves or boos. In that respect, the series approximated the black theaters of the 1940s and 1950s—the Howard Theatre in Washington, D.C., and the Apollo in New York—where the interplay with the all-black crowd could make or break the entertainer. If the audience accepted a comedian, he or she knew he or she was funny. There were no polite laughs. The comedian had the freedom to make jokes about anything—race, politics, sex, even persons in the audience. Each year, the series had a different comedian host who had successfully defeated others for the job. J. Anthony Brown was the host for 2003–2004 season; other hosts were Bruce Bruce (2001–2002), Rickey Smiley (2000–2001), Montana Taylor (1997–1998), Don "D.C." Curry (1995–1996), Sommore (1994–1995), **Cedric the Entertainer** (1993–1994), and **D. L. Hughley** (1992–1993). Reynaldo Rey was cohost. Laura Hayes appeared as Miss Laura. Angelique Perrin was the narrator. Online critics of the series (www.imdb.com, December 31, 2001) say it began as a "wonderful showcase of up and coming black comedians strutting their stuff . . . [and became] a display of buffoonery and sex talk in poor taste." The series title became *Club Comicview* in 2003.

COMMON GROUND (*CBS, March 25 and 27, 1990*). **C. C. H. Pounder** (as Rachel Twymon) starred in this miniseries about three families caught up in the conflict surrounding the desegregation of public schools in Boston. Jane Curtin and James Farentino also starred.

CONCERT FOR THE ROCK AND ROLL HALL OF FAME (*HBO, September 2, 1995*). The live six-hour concert emanating from Cleveland starred **Chuck Berry** and **Little Richard** as well as others.

CONVERSATION WITH MAGIC, A (*NIK, March 25, 1992*). Basketball great **Magic Johnson** was interviewed by Linda Ellerbee and a group of youth. This was shortly after he announced he was HIV positive.

COOK, NATHAN. Cook played Billy Griffin in *Hotel* (1983–1988) and Milton Reese in *The White Shadow* (1978–1980).

COPAGE, MARC. Young Copage played Corey Baker on the sitcom *Julia* (1968–1971) and recurred on the musical police drama *Cop Rock* (1990).

COP AND THE KID, THE (*NBC, 1975–1976*). This sitcom centered on an aging white policeman who became the guardian to a black boy, an orphan with a penchant for street crimes. The unlikely duo was Charles Durning as Officer Murphy, the cop, and **Tierre Turner** as Lucas, the kid. **Eric Laneuville** played Mouse.

CORA UNASHAMED (*PBS, October 25, 2000*). In this character study, a TV film from *Masterpiece Theatre*'s American Collection, **Regina Taylor** starred as a domestic worker who forms a motherly bond with her employer's daughter in 1920s Iowa. A conflict with the natural mother ensued. **C. C. H. Pounder**, Cherry Jones, Ellen Muth, and Michael Gaston also starred. The script was based on a Langston Hughes story. **Deborah Pratt** was director.

CORNELIUS, DON. Cornelius was the host of *Soul Train* (1971–1994), a show of soul music and dancing. He remained executive producer after he stepped away from the host position. The series was his idea when it debuted in Chicago in 1970 and got into syndication the following year. With Tribune Entertainment Company, Don Cornelius Productions coproduced *The Soul Train Music Awards*, *The Soul Train Lady of Soul Annual Awards*, and *The Christmas Starfest*.

CORNER, THE (*HBO, April 16 and May 21, 2000*). Based on a popular nonfiction book, this six-hour miniseries centered on residents of Fayette Street in West Baltimore, Maryland. The focus was on a couple (**T. K. Carter** and **Khandi Alexander**) as they battled to save their family from the drug culture in the neighborhood. **Charles S. Dutton**, who grew up in Baltimore, was director.

COS (*ABC, 1976*). This was a comedy/variety series designed for children. Each show began with a **Bill Cosby** monologue. There were skits by a cast of repertory child actors and celebrity guest stars.

COSBY (*CBS, 1996–2000*). This **Bill Cosby** sitcom centered on the character Hilton Lucas, a 60-year-old blue-collar worker who, as the series opened, was laid off from his longtime job with an airline. **Phylicia Rashad**, who played Cosby's devoted wife on *The Cosby Show* (1984–1992), played his devoted wife, Ruthie, in this series. **T'Keyah Crystal Keymah** played Hilton's daughter, Erica, a lawyer who later became a chef and even later a teacher. **Doug E. Doug** played Erica's platonic friend, Griffin, who would be her romantic interest if he could. Hilton, in the 1998–1999 season, took care of 11-year-old Jurnee (played by **Jurnee Smollet**) after school. Others in the series were Madeline Kahn, Angelo Massagli, and Darien Sills-Evans.

COSBY, BILL. Cosby was the first black actor to star in a drama series when he played Alexander Scott in *I Spy* from 1965 to 1968, co-billed with Robert Culp. (Cicely Tyson had a regular role in *East Side/West Side* in 1963, but she was not the star of the series; George C. Scott was.) From 1969 to 1971, he starred in *The Bill Cosby Show* as high school teacher Chet Kincaid. In 1971, he played characters in the children's program *The Electric Company*. From 1972 to 1973, he was the star of *The New Bill Cosby Show*, a **variety** series. From 1984 to 1992, he was Cliff Huxtable, father, husband, grandfather, and obstetrician, on *The Cosby Show*. In 1992, he hosted the game show *You Bet Your Life*. In 1994–1995, he was Guy Hanks, criminologist, in *The Cosby Mysteries*. From 1996 to 2000, he played Hilton Lucas, 60 years old and unemployed, in *Cosby*. He hosted and talked to children in *Kids Say the Darndest Things* from 1996 to 2002. Cosby headlined many of his own specials, and he made numerous guest appearances on specials, talk shows, and sitcoms headed by others. Among them were *The Andy Williams Show* in 1962; *Diana!* in 1970; *The Flip Wilson Show* in 1970 and 1971; *Harry Belafonte in Concert* in 1985; the special simply titled *Comedy* and a George Burns special, both in 1986; and *The Roseanne Show* in 1998. He starred in *Aesop's Fables* in 1971 and hosted *The Apollo Hall of Fame* in 1993. He starred in the made-for-television movie *Top Secret* in 1978.The Fat Albert animated programs were based on characters in Cosby's childhood. His voice was used for several characters. He was executive producer of the *Fat Albert Christmas Special* in 1977 and writer/creator of *Fat Albert and the Cosby Kids* in 1972. The animated series *Fatherhood*, which premiered in 2004, was based on his book of the same title. His credits are sometimes listed under various names: Dr. William H. Cosby Jr., William H. Cosby Jr., Dr. William H. Cosby, and William H. Cosby.

In 1966, he cohosted the **Emmy Awards** telecast, the first black actor/performer to do so. In those days, the show was bicoastal; Danny Kaye was the Los Angeles host, and Cosby hosted from New York. He also won the Emmy that year for Outstanding Continued Performance by an Actor in a Dramatic Series, the first of his three straight wins (1965–1966, 1966–1967, and 1967–1968) for *I Spy*. In his speech, he praised the network for having the courage to hire him. His *The Bill Cosby Special* won an Emmy for Outstanding Variety or Musical Program in 1968–1969. Cosby received the Kennedy Center Honor in 1998 and was inducted into the Television Academy's Hall of Fame in 1991. In 2003, he won the Bob Hope Humanitarian Award, one of the highest honors presented by the Academy of Television Arts and Sciences. Cosby asked not to be considered for the Emmy Award during *The Cosby Show*.

COSBY MYSTERIES, THE (*NBC, 1994–1995*). Bill Cosby starred in this detective drama series as Guy Hanks, a retired forensics expert who loved his work so much that he could not fully retire. He didn't need the salary (he was a lottery winner), but he continued to handle interesting cases. **Lynn Whitfield** played Barbara Lorenz, the widow of Hanks's former partner. Others in the series were James Naughton, Dante Beze, Rita Moreno, and Robert Stanton. The pilot film aired on January 31, 1994. *See also* DRAMA SERIES.

COSBY SALUTES AILEY (*NBC, December 24, 1989*). Bill Cosby, **Roberta Flack**, and Judith Jamison celebrated Alvin Ailey's 25th anniversary with music and dance.

COSBY SHOW, THE (*NBC, 1984–1992*). This sitcom was **Bill Cosby**'s fifth series and third sitcom, following the drama series *I Spy* (1965–1968), *The Bill Cosby Show* (1969–1971), *The New Bill Cosby Show* (1972–1973), and the children's prime-time variety series *Cos* (1976). *The Cosby Show* proved that a series about a black middle-class, buffoonless family could be successful with viewers and critics. It also disproved the networks' belief, at the time, that the black sitcom was dead. It pulled NBC from the ratings cellar. This did not happen without battles. The pilot episode was shown to the nation's TV editors gathered in Los Angeles; they were high on it immediately. When Cosby spoke to the editors at a press conference, he was asked, "Why do you plan to tape the show in New York?" Cosby, whose last two series had not been ratings winners, responded, "So I can get canceled closer to home." NBC executives at the press conference groaned, but Cosby was confident he had a winner.

He played Dr. Heathcliff (called Cliff) Huxtable, an obstetrician-gynecologist in New York. His wife, Clair, a lawyer, was played by relative newcomer to television **Phylicia Ayers-Allen** (she married later and changed her name to Phylicia Rashad), who had had featured roles in Broadway musicals. In the pilot episode, there were four children, and Clair, in a moment of exasperation, asked Cliff, "Why do we have four children?" Soon, however, there were five children, reflecting the makeup of Cosby's own family of one boy and four girls. The older of the original four were high schoolers Denise, played by **Lisa Bonet** (who kept the pronunciation of her name but changed the spelling from Boney to avoid jokes about being skinny), and Theo (**Malcolm-Jamal Warner**), the sole son, who liked bacon burger dogs and girls. Denise was sometimes eccentric and always individualistic; she frequently left her parents stupefied. Theo was growing up like most teenage boys—forming his ideas about school, girls, and life. The elementary school–aged child was Vanessa (played by **Tempestt Bledsoe**), who was smart and cute and had given up her position as the baby of the family to adorable pre-schooler Rudy (played by **Keshia Knight-Pulliam**). Later, another daughter, Sandra (played by Sabrina LaBeauf), was added to the cast as the eldest daughter who was away at Princeton University.

The comedy came from Cosby's interactions with the children as well as the children's interactions with each other. The lovable banter between Cliff and Clair was an integral part of the series with Clair's signature loving laughter at Cliff's antics. Some episodes found Cliff interacting with his patients, mothers-to-be. Because Cosby is a jazz aficionado, the series often featured singers, dancers, and musicians playing either roles or themselves. **Dizzy Gillespie, Sammy Davis Jr., B. B. King, Nancy Wilson**, Mavis Staples, Miriam Makeba, **Lena Horne**, Howard "Sandman" Sims, **Stevie Wonder**, and **Melba Moore** were some of the musical performers who appeared on the series. Joe Williams played the recurring role of Clair's father. In addition, the Huxtable family serenaded Cliff's parents by lip-syncing to **Ray Charles**'s and the Raelets' "Night and Day" in the "Happy Anniversary" episode on October 10, 1985. This episode was named one of *TV Guide*'s best ever and was number 1 among Nick at Nite viewers. The following year, the family did James Brown's "I Got the Feeling" in the "Golden Anniversary" episode on October 9.

As the show began, network officials, fearful that a black family sit-com was doomed, suggested to Cosby and other producers that the family adopt a white child. Racially integrated families series like *Dif-f'rent Strokes* and *Webster* had been successful. Cosby, who had significant control, refused. It was suggested that the family have a non-black live-in housekeeper. Again, Cosby refused. There was a move to change the family name Huxtable to Brown. It was feared that America would not remember the name. At first Cosby agreed, but minds were changed. (In Cosby's animated series *Fatherhood*, which began in 2004, the family name is even more difficult: Bindlebeep.)

Cosby and the other producers were determined that the show be a successful sitcom about a middle-class family, but race was not an issue in the story lines. Numerous nonblack guest stars were featured in the series. They were primarily friends of the children, Cliff's patients, and others. Sonia Braga played Theo's teacher. Criticism arose, often in black circles, that it was not realistic to have a family with a physician/father and a lawyer/mother. Then numerous black families spoke up, saying they were headed by parents who were a physician and a lawyer. On the other side, many middle-class black families complained that the Huxtables did not live as well as they should. The house was rather ordinary; the Huxtables should have had a live-in housekeeper or nanny, and the house should have more bedrooms. There were subtle signs of the family's affluence. For example, the walls of the brownstone were adorned with the works of contemporary African-American artists, especially Varnette Honey-wood.

Clarice Taylor and **Earle Hyman** played Cliff's parents. **Carl Anthony Payne II** played Theo's friend, Cockroach (1986–1987). **Troy Winbush** was Theo's friend, Denny (1987–1991). **Deon Richmond** played Rudy's friend, Bud (1986–1992).

As time passed, Sandra married Elvin (**Geoffrey Owens**, 1986–1992). Denise graduated from high school and went to fictitious Hillman College, where her parents had met as students. This move was the core of the spin-off sitcom *A Different World* (1987–1993). She dropped out of college and married Martin, a military man (**Joseph C. Phillips**, 1989–1992) who had a precocious daughter, Olivia (**Raven-Symone**, 1989–1992), providing a young child for conversations with Cliff. Theo went to New York University. Vanessa went to Lincoln University and became engaged to a campus maintenance man, Dabnis (William Thomas Jr., 1991–1992). Pam Tucker (**Erika Alexander**, 1990–1992) joined the cast as Clair's teenage cousin who was used to a less privileged life before she moved in with the Huxtables.

The Cosby Show is one of the 20 top-rated series of all time. It ran for eight seasons. It was the number one series each season from 1985 to 1989. It won the **Emmy Award** in 1985 for Outstanding Comedy Series. *See also* FAMILY SERIES; LONG-RUNNING SERIES; SERIES RANKINGS AND RATINGS (Appendix A).

COTTON CLUB '75 (*NBC, November 23, 1974*). This one-hour variety special paid tribute to the famed Cotton Club in Harlem. Performers were **Franklyn Ajaye, Jonelle Allen, Ray Charles**, Johnny Dankworth, **Clifton Davis, Redd Foxx, Rosey Grier**, Cleo Laine, Buddy Rich, and **Jimmie Walker**.

COUNTRY COMES HOME (*CBS, May 3, 1984*). **Charley Pride** hosted with Glen Campbell a show of performances by country-western entertainers. Included were the following: Chet Atkins, Roy Clark, The Charlie Daniels Band, Tennessee Ernie Ford, Willie Nelson, Minnie Pearl, Lee Greenwood, Barbara Mandrell, and Asleep at the Wheel.

COURAGE TO LOVE, THE (*CBS, January 24, 2000*). **Vanessa L. Williams** starred in this made-for-television movie about Henriette Delille, the founder of the Sisters of the Holy Family, an international order of nuns in the 1800s. She was a mulatto daughter of a wealthy white entrepreneur and his black mistress. In those days in New Orleans, interracial relationships were not rare; a black woman could garner some wifelike respect if she were a mistress to a wealthy white man. Henriette's position was dissolved, however, during the Civil War, when her father acquired a more socially acceptable partner and dumped Henriette's mother. Henriette fought to right all of society's wrongs, including racism and tradition, that had thrown her into poverty. She became a nurse in a charity hospital. In the midst of her fight, she also fell in love with a white man whose morals she approved, but that was not the end of the battle. **Diahann Carroll**

played Pouponne. Williams was also credited as executive producer. *See also* BIOPICS; INTERRACIAL ROMANCES/RELATION-SHIPS.

COURT-MARTIAL OF JACKIE ROBINSON, THE (*TNT, October 15, 1990*). This story was based on facts centered on an intellectually and athletically gifted young man who challenged institutionalized bigotry in the U.S. military. **Andre Braugher** was Jackie Robinson; **Stan Shaw** played Joe Louis, and **Ruby Dee** played Robinson's mother. Others in the cast were **J. A. Preston** and Steven Williams. *See also* BIOPICS.

COURTROOM REALITY SERIES. Courtroom series, usually syndicated, became popular reality-type shows in the 1990s. Most starred real-life judges hearing small-claims-court cases in which the dispute was limited to a few thousand dollars (cities vary). Usually, the litigants, when filing for cases in their own cities, were offered the chance to have the case tried by a television judge. The litigants agree to bide by the judge's decision. Actually, no one lost because the participants in the case (plaintiff, defendant, and witnesses) shared a lump-sum payoff from the show. *People's Court* and *Judge Judy* were so successful that numerous others followed. *Judge Joe Brown*, *Judge Mathis*, *Judge Hatchett*, *Curtis Court*, and *Texas Justice* were the most popular. If the judges were African American, their bailiffs were white. If the judges were white, the bailiffs were black. Most, if not all, of the bailiffs were also real-life bailiffs. Other than small-claims cases, *Moral Court* made determinations of whether a defendant was morally wrong. Court TV aired real-life high-profile courtroom trials.

COUSIN SKEETER (*NIK, 1998–2000*). This was a live-action sitcom with a puppet named Skeeter (voice of **Bill Bellamy**). Skeeter was a loud, hip kind of New York teenage guy who loved women. He led Bobby (**Robert Ri'chard**), his shy, withdrawn unhip cousin from Los Angeles, into all kind of adventures. Bobby's parents, Andre and Vanessa Walker, were played by **Rondell Sheridan** and Angela Means. The talkative Nina was played by Megan Good. Nicole was played by **Tisha Campbell**, and Sweetie was Christine Flores.

COWBOYS OF COLOR (*TV1, 2004–*). This weekly series introduced viewers to the competitive world of cowboys of color. Rodeo competitions of African-American, Hispanic, and Native American cowboys were featured along with profiles of these cowboys and behind-the-scenes looks at their world. The show traveled to various cities participating in the Cowboys of Color Invitational Rodeo.

CRESCENDO (*CBS, September 27, 1957*). This variety special told a story of an English gentleman, Mr. Sir (Rex Harrison), who visited the United States and learned a lesson in culture when introduced to various kinds of music. Among the singers were **Louis Armstrong**, **Diahann Carroll**, **Mahalia Jackson**, Dinah Washington, Ethel Merman, Benny Goodman, and Peggy Lee.

CRISIS AT CENTRAL HIGH (*CBS, February 4, 1981*). This made-for-television film told the story of the historic 1957 federal government/state government controversy over the integration of Central High School in Little Rock, Arkansas. The story was told from the point of view of a teacher/vice principal. Joanne Woodward played that role, but black cast members played the Little Rock Nine. They included **Calvin Levels**, who played Ernest Green; **Tamu**, who played Caroline Fuller; **Irma Hall** as Lulu Richards; Riona Martin as Carlotta Walls; and **Regina Taylor** as Minniejean Brown. *See also* HISTORICAL EVENTS DRAMATIZED.

CRISIS—BEHIND A PRESIDENTIAL COMMITMENT (*ABC, October 21, 1963*). This **documentary** centered on the June 1963 integration crisis at the University of Alabama.

CROSS CURRENT (*CBS, November 19, 1971*). **Robert Hooks** starred as Inspector Lou Van Alsdale (with Jeremy Slate) in this two-hour made-for-television film centering on two police detectives searching for the contract killer of a shipping tycoon's son on a San Francisco cable car. The film was an unsold pilot for a series that would have starred Hooks. The film was also called *The Cable Car Murder*. Actors **James McEachin**, **Ta-Tanisha**, and **Mario Van Peebles** also had roles.

CROSS, IRV. Cross was a CBS sportscaster for 15 years. He was co-host and commentator on *NFL Today* and a game analyst. He also covered track and field, gymnastics, and the National Basketball Association.

CROSSE, RUPERT. Crosse starred in the series *The Partners* (1971–1972) and made appearances on other series. After a long film career, he was nominated for an Oscar in 1970 for his supporting role in *The Reivers*. In 1967, he played the funeral director in the TV film *The Final War of Oily Winter*. He died of cancer in 1973 at 46.

CROTHERS, SCATMAN. Comedian/dancer/actor Crothers played the piano player, Sam, in TV's *Casablanca* in 1983. In the same year, he was one of the older performers in the variety special, *Grandpa, Will You Run with Me*, which examined how the old and the young enjoy each other's company. He played Louie Wilson, the garbage man in *Chico and the Man* (1974–1978). In variety specials, he performed on *Jonathan Winters Presents 200 Years of American Humor*, a comedy special in 1976. He helped roast Ted Knight and Angie Dickinson in productions of the *Dean Martin Celebrity Roast* in 1977. He had a key role in *Roots* in 1977, *The Harlem Globetrotters on Gilligan's Island* in 1981, and *Missing Children: A Mother's Story* in 1982; all were made-for-television film projects. Crothers was born in 1910 and died of lung cancer in 1986.

CULLY, ZARA. Cully was Mother Jefferson on *The Jeffersons* from 1975 until her death in 1978. She played Beth Rogers in *A Dream for Christmas*, a 1973 TV film.

CUMBUKA, JI-TU. Cumbuka played The Wrestler in the miniseries *Roots* in 1977. He was Brother Lateef in the TV film *The Jericho Mile* (1979) and Moody Shaw in the miniseries *Flesh and Blood* (1979).

CURRY, MARK. Comedian Mark Curry starred as Mark Cooper in the sitcom *Hangin' with Mr. Cooper* (1992–1997). He also hosted the quiz show *Don't Forget Your Toothbrush* (2000) and *It's Showtime at the Apollo* (1992–1993). He headlined the special *Mark Curry: The*

Other Side (1996) and appeared on *Comic Relief VI* (1994) and *The Apollo Theater Hall of Fame* (1993).

CURTIS COURT (*SYN, 2000–2001*). This half-hour syndicated courtroom reality show originating from New York City was headed by **James Curtis**, a former California prosecutor with a tough stance on crime. He had specialized in juvenile crime working toward community involvement as a deterrent to crime. He brought police officers, educators, and parents together in a community-based program to fight crime; the program became a model for other areas, and Curtis toured the United States as a motivational speaker on the subject. *Curtis Court*, with small-claims types of cases, had as its goal to explain how and why things in law happen and to enable people to understand the legal system. He urged litigants, usually with family problems, to take responsibility for their actions.

CURTIS, JAMES. An anchor for Court TV's daytime trial coverage, Curtis joined the network in 1995. He was a former prosecutor who had appeared on numerous television networks—NBC, CNBC, MSNBC, and ABC—as a legal commentator. He provided comment on high-profile cases: the Jon-Benet Ramsey murder, the impeachment of President Clinton, and the Columbine school shootings. His first television appearance was on Court TV during the **O. J. Simpson** trial in 1995. He was the judge on *Curtis Court*.

CURTIS-HALL, VONDIE. A Broadway musical veteran, Curtis-Hall played Dr. Dennis Hancock on the medical drama *Chicago Hope* from 1995 to 1999 and Cmdr. Warren Osborne on the police musical drama *Cop Rock* in 1990. In made-for-television movies, he played Cliff Turpin in *Heat Wave* in 1990, Father Willis in *One Good Cop* in 1991, Vinnie in *What She Didn't Know* in 1992, Danforth in *There Was a Little Boy* in 1993, Jessup Bush in *Dead Man's Revenge* in 1994, Davis in *Zooman* in 1995, Lloyd Price in *Don King: Only in America* in 1997, Edward Morgan in *Sirens* in 1999, Daniel Wall in *Freedom Song* in 2000, and Drew "Bundini" Brown in *Ali: An American Hero* in 2000. He had a key role in the TV film *Deceit* in 2004, and he directed the TV film *Redemption*, starring **Jamie Foxx**, in 2004.

– D –

DAGGS, PERCY, III. Daggs, who was sidekick to Shaquille O'Neal in the Nestle Crunch TV commercials, had a role on the drama series *Veronica Mars* (2004–).

DAKTARI (*CBS, 1966–1969*). This adventure drama centered on an American veterinarian (Marshall Thompson) who operated an African center to study and treat animals. **Hari Rhodes** was Mike, the capable native African intern, a key part of the team, though viewers never learned much about Mike's life outside the center. *See also* SERIES WITH ONE BLACK SUPPORTING ACTOR/ PERFORMER BEFORE 1980.

DAMON (*FOX, 1998*). **Damon Wayans** starred in this sitcom as Detective Damon Thomas, undercover cop with the Chicago Police Department. Witty, dedicated Damon dressed up in outrageous disguises to smash inner-city criminals, such as´ drug smugglers. His brother, Bernard (**David Alan Grier**), was a security guard and an undercover cop "wannabe," but he was destined not to succeed. The series also did not succeed as far as longevity was concerned; it lasted four months.

DAMON WAYANS: THE LAST STAND (*HBO, May 25, 1991*). The comedian performed his stand-up act and said it would be his last on television. He said that unless somebody came to him with "an incredible amount of money," he was finished with stand-up. In the final shot of this special taped at the Apollo Theater in Harlem, he dropped the microphone to the floor, and it shattered. "I'm hoping it's over," he said. It wasn't. He headlined another HBO special, *Damon Wayans—Still Standing*, in 1997.

DANCE BLACK AMERICA (*PBS, January 25, 1985*). African-American dance companies—Alvin Ailey Dance Theater, Bucket Dance Theater, and Charles Moore Dance Theatre—performed 300 years of black American dance history. **Geoffrey Holder** was narrator.

DANCING IN SEPTEMBER (*HBO, February 3, 2001*). This made-for-television film was the story of an idealistic writer who wanted to sell a sitcom to TV about a realistic African-American family and an ambitious executive looking for a hit show. **Nicole Parker, Isaiah Washington, Vicellous Reon Shannon**, and **Malinda Williams** starred.

DANDRIDGE, DOROTHY. She starred with **Ivan Dixon** in *Blues for a Junk Man* (1962) under the umbrella title of *Cain's Hundred*, her last dramatic role. She also appeared in *Light's Diamond Jubilee*, a 1954 special on four networks to celebrate the 75th anniversary of Thomas Edison's invention of the lightbulb. In 1956, she was a guest when **Louis Armstrong** hosted *You're the Top*, a special celebrating the music of Cole Porter. Dandridge was born in 1923 and died in 1965.

DANDRIDGE, RUBY. Dandridge, Dorothy's mother, played Oriole in *Beulah* from 1952 to 1953. She was born in 1899 and died in 1987.

DANELLE, JOHN. Danelle played Dr. Frank Grant in the daytime drama *All My Children* from 1972 to 1982.

DANGEROUS EVIDENCE: THE LORI JACKSON STORY (*LIF*, *April 12, 1999*). **Lynn Whitfield** starred in this fact-based story of Lori Jackson, a 1980s activist who defended a U.S. Marine Corp battalion's only African-American corporal who was wrongly charged with raping a white officer's wife. *See also* BIOPICS.

DANNY THOMAS SHOW, THE (*ABC, 1953–1957, 1970–1971; CBS, 1957–1965*). This family sitcom, originally called *Make Room for Daddy*, centered on the family of nightclub entertainer Danny Williams (Thomas). There were the necessary adorable kids and a maid named Louise, played by **Louise Beavers** from 1953 to 1954 and **Amanda Randolph** from 1955 to 1964. Former football star **Roosevelt Grier** recurred as Rosey Robbins, Danny's accompanist, from 1970 to 1971. *See also* SERIES WITH ONE SUPPORTING ACTOR/PERFORMER BEFORE 1980.

DASH, STACEY. Dash played Monique in the drama series *TV 101* in 1988–1989; then, after appearing in the film *Clueless* in 1995, she and other cast members stayed in the cast when it went to television in the sitcom of the same name (1996–1999). She was Vanessa Weir in the drama series *The Strip* (1999–2000).

DAVE CHAPPELLE: FOR WHAT IT'S WORTH *(SHO, September 4, 2004)*. Comedian **Chappelle** taped this comedy show for an audience at the Fillmore Hotel in San Francisco.

DAVE CHAPPELLE: KILLIN' THEM SOFTLY *(HBO, August 5, 2000)*. Comic **Chappelle** entertained in an all-comedy show from Lincoln Theater in Washington, D.C.

DAVID, KEITH. David starred in the sitcom *The Big House* (2004).

DAVIDSON, TOMMY. Davidson was a regular on *In Living Color* (1990–1994), played Mitchell Ford in the sitcom *Between Brothers* (1997–1999), and provided the voice of Oscar, the father, in *The Proud Family*, the animated cartoon series (2001–).

DAVIS, ALISHA. Davis joined CNN-TV as prime-time culture and entertainment anchor for *CNN Headline News*. She also was previously guest commentator on *CNN Headline News*, CNN International, MSNBC, Fox News Channel, and Oxygen.

DAVIS, BILLY, JR. First a member of the singing group **The Fifth Dimension**, Davis and his real-life wife and singing partner later formed a duo. They hosted the summer variety series *The Marilyn McCoo and Billy Davis Jr. Show* (1977).

DAVIS, CHARLES. Serving as analyst for American Football League (AFL) telecasts, in 2002, Davis also contributed analysis to NBC Sports coverage of the Bayou Classic, a longtime rivalry between Grambling and Southern Universities. He was also an analyst on TBS Superstation's *Big Play Saturday*, sportscasts of Big 12 and Pac 10 college football games. In 2001 and 2002, he was a sideline reporter for CBS's coverage of the NCAA Basketball Tournament.

DAVIS, CLIFTON. Davis was a member of the repertory company of *Love, American Style* in 1971. In 1972, he starred in *The Melba*

Moore-Clifton Davis Show, a musical variety summer series. He had the lead in the sitcom *That's My Mama* from 1974 to 1975. Davis retired from show business for a few years, earned a master's degree, and became a Seventh-Day Adventist minister. Then he was cast as the Rev. Reuben Gregory in *Amen* from 1986 to 1991. In television films, Davis had important roles in *Little Ladies of the Night* in 1977, *Cindy* in 1979, *The Night the City Screamed* in 1980, and *Don't Look Back: The Story of Satchel Paige* in 1981.

DAVIS, OSSIE. Davis had a key role in the 1969 *Night Gallery* TV movie, which spawned the series and later a feature film. He played Ponder Blue in the sitcom *Evening Shade* (1990–1994). He had starring or key roles in the following TV films: *Billy: Portrait of a Street Kid* (1977), *King* (as Martin Luther King Sr.) (1978), *Roots: The Next Generations* (1979), *Freedom Road* (1979), *Don't Look Back: The Story of Satchel Paige* (1981), *Alex Haley's Queen* (1993), *Miss Evers' Boys* (1997), *The Ernest Green Story* (1999), *Anne Rice's "The Feast of All Saints"* (2001), and *Deacons for Defense* (2003). The TV (1981) and Broadway musical *Purlie* were based on the play he wrote, *Purlie Victorious*. Davis hosted the Fourth of July celebrations, *A Capitol Fourth*, in Washington, D.C., in 2003 and 2004. He and his wife, **Ruby Dee**, were honorees at *The Kennedy Center Honors* in 2004. Davis was born in 1917 and died in 2005 of natural causes.

DAVIS, SAMMY, JR. The super-talented Davis was popular as a guest star in musical variety series and talk shows; some of these shows were *The Big Party* (1959), *The Jerry Lewis Show* (1963 and 1967–1969), *Dionne* (Warwick) *and Friends* (1990), and several appearances on *The Flip Wilson Show* (1970–1974) and *The Ed Sullivan Show* (1948–1971). He was frequently guest host and star of *The Hollywood Palace* (1964–1970) and appeared in nearly all episodes of *NBC Follies* (1973). He made guest appearances on sitcoms including *The Cosby Show* and *All in the Family*; his kissing bigot Archie Bunker (Carroll O'Connor) became one of the highlights of that series just as his catchphrase "Here come de' judge!" was to *Rowan and Martin's Laugh-In*. The "Sammy's Visit" episode of *All in the Family* won the **Emmy Award** for Directing.

In the early 1950s, Davis was preparing to star in a sitcom that would have been part drama and part musical and centered on a family of entertainers. ABC, reportedly, had trouble finding a sponsor, then after NBC had so much difficulty getting advertisers for *The Nat "King" Cole Show*, the plans were abandoned. He had two series, *The Sammy Davis Jr. Show*, a musical variety series that aired on NBC for four months in 1966, and *Sammy and Company*, a syndicated talk show with variety acts that aired, mostly in late night hours, from 1975 to 1977.

Davis sang the theme songs for at least two series, *Baretta* (1975–1978) and *Hell Town* (1985), both starring Robert Blake. His voice was used in the animated special *The Funtastic World of Hanna-Barbera Arena Show* in 1981. In 1969, he starred as a detective in the 90-minute made-for-television movie *The Pigeon*, which was a pilot for a series that never developed, as was *The Trackers* in 1971, when Davis played a frontier scout helping to find the killer of a rancher's daughter. He headlined numerous specials, including the 1982 special *Texaco Star Theater*, a salute to musicals, guested on *The Henry Fonda Special* in 1973 and *The Flip Wilson Special* in 1975. With Frank Sinatra and Liza Minnelli, he starred in the special *Frank, Liza, and Sammy* in 1989. He appeared in specials starring co–Rat Packer Sinatra in 1969 and 1980. His final starring appearance was on *Sammy Davis Jr.'s 60th Anniversary Celebration* (February 4, 1990), a tribute to his lifetime achievements. He died of throat cancer shortly afterward in 1990. (He was born in 1925.) The special won the **Emmy Award** for Outstanding Variety, Music, or Comedy Special for the 1989–1990 season.

DAVIS, VIOLA. Davis played Nurse Lynette Peeler in the drama series *City of Angels*.

DEACONS FOR DEFENSE (*SHO, February 16, 2003*). This two-hour made-for-television film told the story of African-American men in 1960s Louisiana who armed themselves against the Ku Klux Klan. This true story is significant in that most civil rights movements in the 1960s were about passive resistance and nonviolence. **Forrest Whitaker** and **Ossie Davis** were stars.

DEADLOCK (*NBC, February 22, 1969*). This two-hour film was a pilot for a segment of the series *The Protectors* (1969–1970), one of three rotating segments of the series *The Bold Ones* (1969–1973). The film was about the conflict between a black district attorney (Hari Rhodes as Leslie Washburn) and a white policeman (Leslie Neilsen as Sam Danforth). Both were committed to uphold the law, but their approaches were different. **Ruby Dee**, **Beverly Todd**, Max Julien, **Mel Stewart**, and **James McEachin** also had roles. Rhodes and Neilsen were central characters again in the series, but Rhodes's character's name was changed to William Washburn.

DEADLY VOYAGE (*HBO, 1996*). **Omar Epps** starred in this drama of nine African men who were stowaways on a ship bound for America. They dreamed of a new life, but the dream became a nightmare when they were discovered and hunted down and murdered by the ship's vicious crew. Only one man (Epps) escaped the crew's wrath, and a thrilling cat-and-mouse chase on the high seas results. The story comes from real-life testimony.

DEAN MARTIN CELEBRITY ROASTS (*NBC, various dates*). These roasts, patterned after the roasts held at the Friars Club, were at first segments of *The Dean Martin Show* (1965–1974). Then, when that show ended, the roasts continued as specials. Celebrity participants, gathered at a head table, fired insult jokes at the guest of honor. **Redd Foxx** was a guest of honor on November 26, 1976. **Mr. T** was a guest on March 14, 1984. Celebrity roasters often included **Jimmie Walker**, **Lawanda Page**, **Nipsey Russell**, and Foxx.

DEAN MARTIN PRESENTS (*NBC, 1968–1973*). During summers, these musical variety series were replacements for *The Dean Martin Show* time slot. **Stu Gilliam** (1968) and **Lou Rawls** (1969) were regulars.

DEAN MARTIN SHOW, THE (*NBC, 1965–1974*). In this variety series, Dean Martin crooned and starred in comedy sketches with guest stars and a cast of regular performers. Comedian **Nipsey Russell** was a regular from 1972 to 1973. At first, Martin had a group of lovelies who sang and danced and were called the Golddiggers, then most of them were dropped except four who became the Ding-a-Ling Sisters. **Jayne Kennedy** was one of four Ding-a-Ling Sisters (1967–1973) who sang with him, danced, and adorned the stage. *See also* VARIETY SERIES.

DEBBIE ALLEN SPECIAL, THE (*ABC, March 5, 1989*). Actress/dancer **Debbie Allen** headlined an hour of music and comedy with **Whoopi Goldberg, Robert Guillaume, Little Richard, Barbara Montgomery, Phylicia Rashad, Philip Michael Thomas,** and others. Norman Nixon was producer. Allen earned two **Emmy Award** nominations for the production—for direction and choreography. *See also* VARIETY SPECIALS.

DEE, RUBY. Dee was one of a very few black performers to appear on the now classic game show *What's My Line?* (1950–1967) as a panelist. She and her husband, actor **Ossie Davis**, also appeared together on the series as mystery guests, a highlight of each show. In 1968–1969, she played Alma Miles, the doctor's wife, in the drama *Peyton Place* (1964–1969). She played Queen Haley in *Roots: The Next Generations* in 1978–1979 and was nominated for an **Emmy Award**. She had a key role, as did Davis, in the TV movies *All God's Children* in 1980 and *Anne Rice's "The Feast of All Saints"* in 2001. She produced and led the performance of the drama special *Zora Is My Name* in 1990. Other key roles Dee performed in TV movies are *Deadlock* (1969), *It's Good to Be Alive* (1974), *I Know Why the Caged Bird Sings* (1979), *The Ernest Green Story* (1993), *Captive Heart: The James Mink Story* and *Mr. and Mrs. Loving* (1996), *Having Our Say* (1999), and *Oprah Winfrey Presents: Their Eyes Were Watching God* (2005). Dee and Davis were honorees at *The Kennedy Center Honors* in 2004.

DEF COMEDY JAM. *See* RUSSELL SIMMONS' DEF COMEDY JAM.

DEF, MOS. The rapper starred in the TV film *Something the Lord Made* (2004) and was nominated for an **Emmy Award** for Lead Actor in a Miniseries or Movie. He had a singing role in the 2005 TV film *Lackawanna Blues*.

DEF POETRY JAM. *See* RUSSELL SIMMONS' DEF POETRY JAM.

DELAIN, MARGUERITE. DeLain had a key role in *Man from Atlantis* in 1977. She was one of the singing/dancing Flipettes on *The Flip Wilson Show*.

DERRICKS, CLEAVANT. Derricks was Rembrandt "Crying Man" Brown in the drama series *Sliders* (1995–1997) and the TV film that preceded the series. Other series credits include the following sitcoms: *Something Wilder* (1994–1995), *Thea* (1993–1994), *Drexell's Class* (1991), and *Good Sports* (1991). A Broadway singer, he was a member of the cast for the TV version of the musical *When Hell Freezes Over I'll Skate* (1979).

DERRICKS-CARROLL, CLINTON. Derricks-Carroll (aka Clinton Derricks), the twin brother of Cleavant Derricks, played Cliff Anderson in the sitcom *Sanford* in 1980–1981. Also a singer, he had a key role in the black musical version of Cinderella, *Cindy*, in 1979, and was a member of the cast for the TV version of the musical *When Hell Freezes Over I'll Skate* (1979).

DESERT, ALEX. Desert played Jake Malinak on the sitcom *Becker* (1998–). Earlier roles include playing Holden Hines in the drama series *TV 101* (1988–1989), Julio in the fantasy adventure series *The Flash* (1990–1991), Stan Lee on the dramatic series *The Heights* in 1992, and Eli on the sitcom *Boy Meets World* (1996).

DESHIELDS, ANDRE. DeShields was a member of the four-person musical ensemble of *Ain't Misbehavin'* in 1982; for his work, he won the **Emmy Award** for Outstanding Individual Achievement— Special Class.

DE SOUSA, MELISSA. De Sousa played Coco in the sitcom *Second Time Around* beginning in 2004.

DESSELLE-REID, NATALIE. Desselle-Reid (aka Natalie Desselle) was a regular in the sitcom *Eve* beginning in 2003. She had a role in the short-lived sitcom *Built to Last* in 1997. She had a role in TV's 1997 *Cinderella* with **Whitney Houston** and **Brandy**.

DESTINY'S CHILD. The popular group made appearances on various variety specials and award shows. Among them were the following: *Nobel Peace Prize Concert* (2001), *Christmas in Rockefeller Center* (2001), *The Teen Choice Awards* (2001), *Michael Jackson: 30th Anniversary Celebration* (2001), *The 43rd Annual Grammy Awards* (2001), and *The 28th Annual American Music Awards* (2001). *See also* KNOWLES, BEYONCE.

DETOUR TO TERROR (*NBC, February 22, 1980*). **O. J.** Simpson starred and was executive producer of this TV film about the driver of a Las Vegas–bound tour bus who tried to save the passengers after would-be kidnappers terrorized the passengers.

DEVINE, LORETTA. After a career in Broadway musicals, Devine played guest roles and regular roles in television series, key roles in television motion pictures, and voice-overs in animated productions. Among her credits are Stevie, the dorm house adviser, in *A Different World* from 1987 to 1988 and Janine in the 1991 television production of the stage play *The Colored Museum*. She had a key role in the TV film *Freedom Song* (2000). She was Marla Hendricks in the drama series *Boston Public* (2000–2004). She was the star of the short-lived sitcom *Sugar and Spice* in 1990. In TV films, she was Missy in *Rebound: The Legend of Earl "The Goat" Manigault* (1996), Connie Harper in *Don King: Only in America* (1997), Snookie Tate in *Jackie's Back* (1999), and Ruby Dandridge in *Introducing Dorothy Dandridge* (1999). She also had roles in the TV films *Funny Valentines* (1999) and *Best Actress* (2000). Hers was the voice of Muriel in *The PJs* beginning in 1999. She joined the series *Wild Card* in 2004.

DE WINDT, SHEILA. De Windt was Angie in *B.J. and the Bear* (1979) and Sue in the miniseries *Wheels* (1978) and had a recurring role as Joan Hopkins in *Days of Our Lives* (1983–1984). She had a recurring role as Lt. Dietra in *Battlestar Galactica* (1978).

DIAHANN CARROLL SHOW, THE (special) (*NBC, April 5, 1971*). The star of *Julia* headlined her own special with special guests **Harry Belafonte**, Tom Jones, and Donald Sutherland. *See also* VARIETY SPECIALS.

DIAHANN CARROLL SHOW, THE (series) (*CBS, 1976*). This four-week summer series starred singer/actress Carroll with guest stars, dancers, and an orchestra. *See also* VARIETY SERIES.

DIANA! (*ABC, April 18, 1971*). Shortly after **Diana Ross** left **The Supremes**, she hosted this special with **Bill Cosby**, the Jackson Five, and Danny Thomas.

DIANA! (*CBS, March 2, 1981*). Nearly 10 years after the first special titled *Diana*, **Diana Ross** starred in another special with the same title. This one had guests **Michael Jackson**, **Quincy Jones**, The Joffrey Ballet, and Larry Hagman.

DIANA ROSS, AN EVENING WITH (*NBC, March 6, 1977*). Diana was host of this special, which traced her life and career through song.

DIANA ROSS IN CENTRAL PARK (*SYN, February 1985*). A two-hour special featuring highlights of a concert originating from Central Park in July 1983 was aired later. This concert was memorable because despite a rainstorm, Ross continued to sing and then urged the crowd to disperse peaceably. (There had been riots after concerts.)

DIANA ROSS IN CONCERT (*HBO, July 27, 1982*). This 75-minute special featured the Eddie Kendrix Singers (Kendrix was former lead singer of **The Temptations**).

DIANA ROSS . . . RED HOT RHYTHM AND BLUES (*ABC, May 20, 1987*). In this music special, Ross's guests were **Etta James**, **Little Richard**, **Billy Dee Williams**, Bernadette Peters, Dick Shawn, and others.

DIANA ROSS WORLD TOUR '89 "WORKIN' OVERTIME"
(*HBO, September 8, 1989*). Ross starred in a concert featuring old tunes as well as her new hit "Workin' Overtime." She performed before a live audience at Wembly Stadium in England.

DICK VAN DYKE SHOW, THE (*CBS, September 25, 1963*). Episode number 64, "That's My Baby," is the episode producers of the series named as the most memorable. It is probably best remembered by African-American viewers in that it had black actors in it. In this episode, **Greg Morris** made one of his two appearances on the show. As creator-producer Carl Reiner said in recent years, "Television was a lily white neighborhood in those days." However, Reiner was proud of this episode in which Rob Petrie (Van Dyke) thinks he and his wife brought home the wrong baby from the hospital. He believes he has the baby belonging to the Peters couple (played by Morris and Mimi Dillard) and that they have his baby. The story involved primarily Rob's discussion and antics over his belief, but the culmination of the story comes when the Peters couple arrives at the house and they are black. Sponsor Procter & Gamble and CBS were afraid the scene would look as if the show were making fun of the black couple, but producer Sheldon Leonard convinced them that fun was being made of Rob; the black couple was smart and dignified. Some African Americans argue that a baby born to Morris and Dillard would look white too, that black babies often do not get their complexions until later, and that the babies could have been switched. However, the viewing public laughed, and that made CBS and the producers happy. And black viewers were happy to see black actors on-screen even though for only 30 seconds. Morris appeared on another episode as Rob's Army buddy who had written the music to a song. **Bernie Hamilton** and **Godfrey Cambridge** also had roles in episodes of this series. Hamilton was Patrolman Nelson on the December 11, 1963, episode. Cambridge was a cop who set up a stakeout in Ritchie's bedroom on April 20, 1966.

DIFFERENT WORLD, A (*NBC, 1987–1993*). This spin-off of *The Cosby Show* was about life at fictional predominantly black Hillman College. The original lead was **Lisa Bonet** (1987–1988) as Denise Huxtable, who followed her proud parents, who were alumni of Hillman. Denise's roommates were Jaleesa (**Dawnn Lewis**, 1987–1992), a divorcée who provided the sound judgment in the room's chatter, and Maggie (Marisa Tomei, 1987–1988), a talkative white coed. In the same dorm was their nemesis, the spoiled snobbish Whitley (**Jasmine Guy**, 1987–1993). Dwayne Wayne (**Kadeem Hardison**, 1987–1993) was a bright math major who had an early crush on Denise. Ron Johnson (**Darryl Bell**, 1987–1993) was Dwayne's buddy. Stevie (**Loretta Devine**, 1987–1988) was the housemother at Gilbert Hall, where most of the action took place in the early seasons.

Perhaps more than any other sitcom in history, this series had cast changes, and no matter who left or who was added, the series remained successful in the ratings. At first, the series, which aired following *The Cosby Show*, was believed to be a hit because *The Cosby Show*'s audience merely stayed tuned. Then, in the 1991–1992 season, *A Different World* finished the season as number 17 (with a 15.2 rating), while *The Cosby Show* was number 18 (with a 15.0 rating). Bonet, Tomei, and Devine were dropped from the cast before the second season. Lettie Bostic (**Mary Alice**, 1988–1989) became the new housemother. Col. Taylor (**Glynn Turman**, 1988–1993), a professor called "Dr. War," was added, as was Walter Oakes (**Sinbad**, 1987–1991), Freddie (**Cree Summer**, 1988–1993), and Kim (**Charnele Brown**, 1988–1993). A new set, The Pit, a student eatery, was added with its owner Mr. Gaines (**Lou Myers**, 1988–1993). In later years, Lena (**Jada Pinkett**, 1991–1993), Charmaine (**Karen Malina White**, 1992–1993), and Shazza Zulu (**Gary Dourdan**, 1992) were added as students. Byron Douglas III (**Joe Morton**, 1991) became a professor. Jalessa married Dr. War. Others in the cast from time to time were Marie-Alise Recasner, Amir Williams, Beebe Smith, Kim Wayans, Cory Tyler, Reuben Grandy, Dominic Hoffman, Ajai Sanders, and Michael Ralph. The series also lasted after the central cast graduated. Near the end of the series, Whitley and Dwayne, once two people who couldn't bear each other, were married. *See also* LONG-RUNNING SERIES.

DIFF'RENT STROKES (*NBC, 1978–1985; ABC, 1985–1986*). This sitcom was born during a period before *The Cosby Show* in which networks believed that shows with all-black casts would not be successful in the ratings. Precocious, diminutive, chubby-cheeked,

10-year-old **Gary Coleman**, with excellent comedy timing, had guest-starred on *The Jeffersons*, and Norman Lear's company snatched him up to be cast into the sitcom. Conrad Bain, who had played Arthur on *Maude* (1972–1978), another Lear show, was considered a classy actor with whom to work. He was suddenly available as that show went off the air.

The back story to *Diff'rent Strokes* was that Philip Drummond's (Bain) former housekeeper had died and left two young sons— Arnold (Coleman) and Willis (**Todd Bridges**)—whom he had promised to care for should the need arise. So, wealthy Drummond, who had a perky daughter, Kimberly (Dana Plato), took the boys in and adopted them. The stories centered on how two poor black boys from Harlem adjusted to life in a Manhattan penthouse with a rich white father. In the beginning, one of the benefits of the boys' new life was the housekeeper, Mrs. Garrett (Charlotte Rae), who was also part friend and part mother.

Bridges and Plato were more experienced than Coleman, but Coleman quickly emerged as the attraction of the series. As soon as that was apparent, Coleman's newly acquired business managers and lawyers negotiated a contract that brought his salary from $15,000 per episode to over $40,000 in the final season.

His parents—Sue, a nurse, and Willie, an assembly-line worker in a pharmaceutical plant in Illinois—had never contemplated such earnings and took the advice to turn over money management to professionals. Coleman had the kidney ailment when the series began, and it was known that a defective kidney caused him to be short, but most if not all network and production executives were unaware that he had only one kidney. Sue said she introduced her son Gary to modeling so that he would have something to do while other kids played sports; the modeling quickly turned into the acting career.

For four years, Sue stayed in Los Angeles with Gary while the series was in production, and Willie remained on his job in Illinois. During holidays and vacations, they flew home to Zion, Illinois. Occasionally, Willie Coleman would fly out to Los Angeles. Then, in 1981, Gary's only kidney failed, and he needed both parents with him in Los Angeles. When the kidney failed, Coleman decided that rather than go to a dialysis treatment center regularly, he would undergo a portable dialysis treatment, which meant draining fluid into his body through a stint surgically inserted into his abdomen. His nurse-mother helped him with the treatments at first, and then he learned to do them himself. An arrangement, with young Coleman's participation, was made to provide reasonable salaries for the parents, who had given up their careers and pensions back in Zion to provide their son this opportunity. NBC and producers offered Coleman and his parents the option of curtailing the series, but Coleman, never a person who hesitated to express himself, wanted to continue. He enjoyed the series and the privileges fame brought, and he had an ambition to be a writer or director. He wrote the story for a *Diff'rent Strokes* script and watched every move of series director Gerren Keith in preparation for his future career.

Coleman's stardom brought him not only more earnings than Bridges and Plato but also more attention. This did not cause conflict between the kids, but some of the parents felt their kids were being sidelined. Bain, who understood the dynamics of such a series, had a contract from the beginning that provided him with one dollar more than any other actor in the series. So, when Coleman's salary went up, so did his. He knew he was the straight man, primarily, so if there was any concern about Coleman's taking the show, Bain just went to the bank. Still, he was the strength of the series' relationships. When Bain spoke, everyone listened; no one wanted to upset "Connie." During the series, Bain said he would not have permitted his own children to be child actors. "What if they wake up one morning and say they don't want to go to work?" he asked. "They have contracts."

Growing through the teenage years in a television series proved to be problematic to Bridges and Plato. Both experimented with drugs. Bridges, whose parents divorced during the series, had some adjustment problems going from toys to cars and childhood to adulthood and got into trouble with the law. Plato, being raised by a sickly single mother, became pregnant and was dropped from the series in 1984.

The series was in the top 30 for the first three years it was on the air, a bona fide hit. In 1982–1983, NBC ran the series' reruns in daytime. It had reasonable ratings thereafter, but NBC canceled it in 1985. ABC felt the series still had possibilities and picked it up for another year but ended it in 1986. Arnold's friend Dudley (**Shavar Ross**) joined the cast in 1981 with Le Tari playing his father, Ted.

Janet Jackson (1981–1982) played a recurring role as Willis's girlfriend, Charlene. Nikki Swasey played Lisa (1982–1986). Dixie Carter joined the cast (1984–1985) to play Drummond's new wife, Maggie, a role later played by Mary Ann Mobley (1985–1986). Maggie had a son, Sam (Danny Cooksey). *The Facts of Life* was a spinoff of *Diff'rent Strokes*, taking Mrs. Garrett (Rae) into the new series. *See also* FAMILY SERIES; LONG-RUNNING SERIES.

DIGGS, TAYE. Diggs played the title role in the drama series *Kevin Hill* (2004–2005). He was Jackson Duper on *Ally McBeal* in 2001. He played Adrian "Sugar" Hill in the daytime drama *The Guiding Light* in 1997.

DIONNE WARWICK IN LONDON (*SYN, February 27, 1988*). This one-hour **Dionne Warwick** concert originated from London's Royal Albert Hall. Guests were **Gregory Hines**, Peter Allen, and Rita Coolidge.

DIONNE WARWICK SPECIAL, THE (*CBS, September 17, 1969*). **Dionne Warwick**'s first television special was an hour of music and comedy with guests **George Kirby**, Burt Bacharach, and Glen Campbell. *See also* VARIETY SPECIALS.

DISAPPEARING ACTS (*HBO, December 9, 2000*). Based on the novel by Terry McMillan, this made-for-television film starred **Wesley Snipes** and **Sanaa Lathan** as a struggling romantic couple. He was a construction worker and she an independent woman with a career. They met challenges that tested their love and their relationship. **John Amos**, **C. C. H. Pounder**, Regina Hall, and Michael Imperioli also starred.

DISNEY'S GREAT AMERICAN CELEBRATION (*CBS, July 4, 1991*). **Robert Guillaume** hosted this Independence Day celebration with Connie Selleca. The two-hour **variety special** originated from Disneyland and Disney World and featured several musical artists.

DISTRICT, THE (*CBS, 2000–2004*). This drama series starred Craig T. Nelson as Police Chief Jack Mannion of Washington, D.C., a city with a predominantly black citizenry. Even though that city had not had a white police chief in many years, many key members of the regular cast were black, as were recurring players, guest stars, and behind-the-scenes professionals. **Lynne Thigpen**, from 2000 to 2003, was Ella Farmer, Mannion's right hand who could locate any information he needed on her computer. During the course of the series, Ella battled to get custody of her nephew (Segun Ajaga, 2000–2001, and William Turner, 2001–2003), whose father had killed his mother. Ella also had a romance with Clive (Gregalan Williams). In another story line, Ella had a recurrence of breast cancer. The character Ella died suddenly of a stroke in 2003, when actress Thigpen died of a heart attack. **Roger Aaron Brown**, as Deputy Chief Joe Noland, was the man who had hoped to get the job as chief and showed his displeasure when Mannion prevailed. He later came to like Mannion and was his staunch supporter, even when Mannion was fired and he became acting chief of police. **Sean Patrick Thomas** played Detective Temple Page, a young, ambitious, determined man who admired Mannion and Noland. **John Amos** played the mayor from 2000 to 2001, and **Joseph C. Phillips** was the mayor from 2002 to 2004. **Ving Rhames** was Attorney General Troy Hatcher (2002–2004). Christopher B. Duncan was Sgt. Roy Cutter (2001–2004). Oz Scott directed several episodes and was supervising producer the last two seasons.

DITCHDIGGER'S DAUGHTERS, THE (*FAM, February 23, 1997*). **Carl Lumbly** starred in this TV film based on a true story about a ditchdigger, Donald Thornton, who wanted the best for his six daughters. Thornton was extremely demanding; he not only insisted on high grades but also forbade dating and demanded that the girls aim for careers as doctors. It was all based on his perceptions of what it meant to be poor and black and his own failure to get an education. The daughters as children were played by Adrienne Monique Coleman, Rae'ven Kelly, Jameelah Nuriddin, Malaika Jabali, Kiara Tucker, and Niaja Cotton. As adults, the daughters were played by Shelley Robertson, Kimberly Elise, Rosalyn Coleman, **Monica Calhoun**, Erika L. Heard, and Denice J. Sealy. **Dule Hill** played Young Donald. Elise as Jeanette won a CableACE Award for Supporting Actress in a Movie or Miniseries. **Lynne Moody** played Kathryn.

DIVA'S CHRISTMAS CAROL, A (*VH1, December 13, 2000*). Singer/actress **Vanessa L. Williams** starred in this TV movie as Ebony Scrooge, a self-centered singing star who learns the true meaning of Christmas in this adaptation of Dickens's *A Christmas Carol*. Rozonda "Chili" Thomas played Marli Jacob.

DIVAS LIVE '99 (*VH1, April 1999*). Divas from pop, soul, rock, and country took turns onstage. **Whitney Houston, Tina Turner, Brandy, Chaka Khan, Mary J. Blige**, Cher, and Faith Hill were all headliners. David Nathan, author of *The Soulful Divas*, described a diva as "someone who has accomplished something and has really been around for a while and might have some temperament." These divas managed to get together for some duets. Tina and Cher sang "Proud Mary." Brandy and Faith sang "Everything I Do I Do for You." Whitney and Mary sang Aretha's hit "Ain't No Way." Whitney and Chaka sang "I'm Every Woman," which Chaka originally recorded. The special show was annual; the 2004 show was titled *VH1 Divas*.

DIVORCE COURT (*FOX, 1999– *). Trial attorney/mediator **Mablean Ephraim** presided over this half-hour reality program designed to determine settlements between bickering couples. The settlements were legally binding because the litigants agreed to abide by the decision. The settlements could be child support, spousal support, or unpaid bills. Before Judge Mablean made her ruling, each litigant explained his or her side of the argument, and the judge expressed her opinion of the usually sleazy partner. The show, taped in Los Angeles, was a kind of remake or update of a 1950s courtroom series that sought to persuade couples not to divorce. Ephraim was once a correctional officer at the Women's Division of the Federal Bureau of Prisons in Terminal Island, a deputy city attorney in Los Angeles, and domestic violence coordinator for spousal, parent, and child abuse, also in Los Angeles.

DIXON, IVAN. Dixon played Sgt. James Kinchloe in the sitcom *Hogan's Heroes* from 1965 to 1970 and was disappointed that most television viewers recognized him from "that bit part" and not from his work in dramas in which he had major roles. Even before *Hogan's Heroes*, he played opposite **Dorothy Dandridge** in the

"Blues for a Junk Man" episode of *Cain's Hundred* (1962) and with Diane Baker and Oscar Homolka in the "Arrowsmith" episode of *The DuPont Show of the Week*. He left *Hogan's Heroes* in 1970 and guest-starred in TV shows and features films. He also turned to directing films and television. His 30 years of credits include 15 episodes of *The Waltons*, 12 episodes of *Magnum P.I.*, *The Bill Cosby Show*, *Get Christie Love*, *Brewster Place*, *The Rockford Files*, *The Mod Squad*, *Starsky and Hutch*, *In the Heat of the Night*, and many others.

DIXON, N'GAI. The son of **Ivan Dixon**, N'Gai played 10-year-old Herman Washington in *A Storm in Summer*, a TV film that won the **Emmy Award** in 1970.

D. L. HUGHLEY: GOING HOME (*HBO, August 7, 1999*). From his hometown of Charlotte, North Carolina, comedian **D. L. Hughley** performed a monologue about his childhood, his upbringing, his mother, relationships, race, school violence, marriage, the National Rifle Association, the U.S. Constitution, and religion.

DOC AND GLADYS CELEBRATE (*NBC, January 1, 1977*). Doc Severinsen and **Gladys Knight** celebrated the New Year in a three-hour special consisting of music and comedy. The show aired from 1:00 A.M. to 4:00 A.M., intending to entertain viewers still celebrating after midnight. Guests included Gladys Knight's Pips.

DOCUMENTARIES. Most documentaries with African-American themes have been about the struggles for civil rights, battles of racism, or accounts of the lives of famous or successful black people. Some were produced by news departments of television networks, while others were done by production companies. Documentaries about racism and civil rights included *American Revolution of '63* (1963); *Crisis—Behind a Presidential Commitment* (1963), about the University of Alabama integration crisis; *Africans in America: America's Journey through Slavery* (1998); and *America Beyond the Color Line* (2004).

Documentaries about the lives or careers of various people included *A Man Named Mays* (1963), about baseball great Willie Mays; *Black History: Lost, Stolen, or Strayed* (1968), about achievements of blacks; *POWs: The Black Homecoming* (1973), about black prisoners of war; *Shadowboxing: The Journey of the African-American Fighter* (1991), about boxers; *Aretha Franklin: The Queen of Soul* (1988); and *Beah: A Black Woman Speaks* (2004). Exceptions were informational shows that targeted black people as well as nonblacks like *Scared Straight! 20 Years Later* (1999). *See also* BIOPICS; HISTORICAL EVENTS DRAMATIZED.

DOMESTIC WORKERS IN THE 1950s. From the early days of television, African-American actors entered American living rooms as domestic workers. Several, such as **Eddie Anderson**'s Rochester, valet to Jack Benny, and **Lillian Randolph**'s Birdie Lee Coggins from *The Great Gildersleeve* arrived straight from radio. *Beulah*, named for a character created for radio's *Fibber McGee and Molly*, holds the distinction as the first television series about an African-American character. Actors **Ethel Waters**, **Hattie McDaniel**, and **Louise Beavers** each played Beulah in the show's three-year run (1950–1953).

April Peterson, in her dissertation, pointed out that the early television stereotypical "mammy" role, as Beulah was, was so fixed within the American imagination that it did not matter who played the role. It was not until the 1980s that actors like Robert Guillaume in *Benson* and Joseph Marcell in *Fresh Prince of Bel Air* in the 1990s were able to develop their roles to include their own perceptions of what the characters should be. This did not mean that the actresses playing Beulah did not have that ability, but they did not have the freedom to add dignity and depth to characterizations.

According to scholar Lahn Sung Kim, the presence of the African-American maid on television allowed mainstream America to maintain a fantasy of race, gender, and class privilege of the antebellum South. The television show *Beulah* historicized and romanticized domestic service, glossing over larger social issues going on outside the television screen, such as the disparities of post–World War II, where freedom remained guaranteed for some but not all, Jim Crow laws maintained a segregated society, women and people of color expected layoffs to accommodate returning soldiers, and mainstream America fled cities for the suburbs.

DOMESTIC WORKERS IN THE 1960s. The face of domestic work changed color for a short time. In *Hazel, Family Affair,* and *The Brady Bunch,* white, vaguely ethnic servants came to work in mainstream households. However, the black domestic worker did not disappear. For example, the character Louise played by **Amanda Randolph** kept house for the nuclear family on *The Danny Thomas Show/Make Room for Daddy* into the middle of the decade. And other people of color, such as Mrs. Livingston in *The Courtship of Eddie's Father* and Hop Sing of *Bonanza,* portrayed by Miyoshi Umeki and Victor Sen Young, respectively, took on domestic work.

DOMESTIC WORKERS IN THE 1970s. Television viewers of the 1970s witnessed the return of the African-American domestic worker in Florida Evans of *Maude,* Florence Johnson in *The Jeffersons,* and Benson of *Soap.* Confident, wisecracking, and outspoken, these images of servants were updated but not necessarily new. Scholar Michele Johnson writes of the character Florida Evans, "She had to seem to be complex, her character had to appear to be layered and certainly her role as a servant had to look as if it rose above caricatures from a tradition of racial prejudice." Florida held her own in verbal jousts with Maude; Benson displayed obvious contempt for the Tates, for whom he worked; and Florence was a maid for an African-American nuclear family on the exclusive Upper East Side of Manhattan. Race was not ignored or taken for granted but instead was prominently featured as key to these characters.

DOMESTIC WORKERS IN THE 1980s. Domestic work as an occupation for African Americans on television continued into the 1980s through characters such as *Gimme a Break*'s Nell and the unseen mother of Arnold and Willis Jackson/Drummond who asked her employer, Mr. Drummond, to take in her sons on her death in the comedy *Diff'rent Strokes.* **Roscoe Lee Browne**'s Saunders replaced **Robert Guillaume**'s Benson on *Soap* when the latter's character was spun off into the situation comedy *Benson.* Saunders's opinion of the Tates was comparable to that of his predecessor in the job.

DOMESTIC WORKERS IN THE 1990s. In the 1990s, Geoffrey took care of the Banks' home in *Fresh Prince of Bel-Air*, and Lilly Harper worked for the Bedfords in the South during the civil rights era in *I'll Fly Away*. Interestingly, the story of the life of domestic worker Lilly Harper played by Regina Taylor was a critical success and an example of quality network television, though it was short-lived. *Homefront* lasted two years and starred **Hattie Winston** and **Dick Anthony Williams** as domestic employees to a white family who was determined to improve their status in life. This drama was set in the midwest right after World War II. The program later moved to public television. Lilly Harper's life outside the home of the Bedfords where she worked was central to the plot. A mother and budding civil rights activist, Lilly's actions propelled the story lines. Her voice framed most episodes as she shared excerpts from her diary and other writings in voice-overs that opened and closed each show.

DOMESTIC WORKERS' NAMES. In domestic worker roles, African-American workers suffered indignities dictated by the traditions of a life in the service of others. Employers referred to Beulah (*Beulah*), Louise (*The Danny Thomas Show/Make Room for Daddy*), Florence (*The Jeffersons*), Florida (*Maude*), and Lilly (*I'll Fly Away*) by their first names. The Baxters and the Bradys called Hazel (*Hazel*) and Alice (*The Brady Bunch*) by their first names too. As maids and, even worse, as general maids, the lowest position on the hierarchy of domestic service, these women did not rate the dignity of their full names, according to Michele Johnson. Moreover, these maids meddled in their employers' affairs, symbolic of their emotional attachment to the families they served. Meanwhile, television butlers, standing at the zenith of the domestic service hierarchy, remained aloof, professional, and somewhat superior, especially if they were British and white, such as Mr. French (*Family Affair*), Mr. Higgins (*Our Man Higgins*), or Mr. Belvedere (*Mr. Belvedere*).

Names were tricky for African-American butlers on television. For example, Geoffrey worked for the Banks family on *Fresh Prince of Bel-Air*. He was British, a hallmark of the best type of servant. He also was black, relegating him to be called by his first name even by Will, the outsider from the inner city. Saunders of *Soap* also was British. And it was not until Benson left the Tate household on *Soap* for his own show that he obtained his last name, DuBois.

DOMINO, FATS. Domino was one of six entertainers presented with awards on the 1987 special *The Grammy Lifetime Achievement Awards*. Vintage footage of Domino performing was a highlight of *The Blues*, a 2003 seven-part series about the music genre.

DONALDSON, NORMA. Donaldson had a key role in *Inmates: A Love Story*, a 1981 TV film.

DONELAN, JENNIFER. Donelan was named the Chicago-based correspondent for CBS *Newspath* in 2003.

DON KING: ONLY IN AMERICA (*HBO, 1997*). **Ving Rhames** played the infamous boxing promoter Don King, whose sports savvy made him one of the most successful and most controversial in his field. This was the story of his life and his rise to fame from being a small-time numbers runner to a big-time promoter in the corners of champions. It is also the story of the men he turned into champs. The TV film also starred **Vondie Curtis Hall** as Lloyd Price, **Darius McCrary** as Muhammad Ali, **Loretta Devine** as Connie Harper, **Bernie Mac** as Bundini Brown, **Lou Rawls** as Harold Logan, and **Donzaleigh Abernathy** as Henrietta King. **Thomas Carter** was executive producer, and the production won the **Emmy Award** for Outstanding Made-for-Television Movie in the 1997–1998 season. Writer Kario Salem also won the Emmy for Outstanding Writing in a Miniseries or a Special. Rhames won the Golden Globe Award for his role, and during the award ceremony, he accepted the statuette, then gave it to Jack Lemmon, a fellow nominee. This was the first time anyone ever gave away the Golden Globe Award on camera. The Hollywood Foreign Press Association reportedly gave Rhames another. *See also* ATHLETES' BIOPICS; BIOPICS.

DONNA RICHARDSON: MIND, BODY, & SPIRIT (*TV1, 2004– *). Fitness expert Donna Richardson, who made several appearances on *Oprah* and had best-selling workout tapes and books, developed these broadcasts of workouts that included crunches, sit-ups, and so on but also nutritional tips and advice leading to healthy minds and spirits.

DONNA SUMMER SHOW, THE (*ABC, January 27, 1980*). The Queen of Disco, **Donna Summer**, hosted this one-hour special, which also featured **Robert Guillaume**, Twiggy, and Debralee Scott. *See also* VARIETY SERIES.

DON'T LOOK BACK: THE STORY OF SATCHEL PAIGE (*ABC, May 31, 1981*). This story is a biopic of Leroy "Satchel" Paige, the legendary baseball player, a pitcher who played first with the black leagues and then, at the age of 43, after Jackie Robinson had broken baseball's color barrier, became a member of the Cleveland Indians team. **Louis Gossett Jr.** played Paige. Paige himself did the introduction to the film and was also seen in the epilogue. He died a year after the film aired. Others in the cast included **Beverly Todd**, **Cleavon Little**, **Ernie Barnes**, **Clifton Davis**, and **Hal Williams**. *See also* ATHLETES' BIOPICS; BIOPICS.

DOQUI, ROBERT. DoQui played key roles in the TV films *Green Eyes* (1977), *How the West Was Won* (1978), *Centennial* (1978), *The Child Stealer* (1979), *Andrea's Story: A Hitchhiking Tragedy* (1983), *Dark Mirror* (1984), *Between the Darkness and the Dawn* (1985), *The Court-Martial of Jackie Robinson* (1990), *Original Intent* (1992), and *A Case for Murder* (1993). He was Detective Cliff Sims in the police drama *Felony Squad* (1968–1969) and George Briggs in *A Dream for Christmas* (1973).

DORN, MICHAEL. Dorn is probably best known for his portrayal of Lt. Commander Worf in the sci-fi series *Star Trek: The Next Generation* (1987–1994) and *Star Trek: Deep Space Nine* (1995–1999). He played Jimmy in *The Days of Our Lives* (1986–1987) and Officer Turner in the police drama *Chips* (1980–1982). He has done numerous voice-overs, including the voice of Weasel in the cartoon *I Am Weasel*, which premiered in 1997, and the voice of Rufus in *Kim Possible: A Stitch in Time* (2003). In TV films, he had roles in *The Girl Next Door* (1998) and *Through the Fire* (2002).

DOUBLE PLATINUM (*ABC, May 16, 1999*). **Diana Ross** and **Brandy** starred in this made-for-television story of Olivia King (Ross), a talented singer who left her husband and infant daughter to pursue her dream of becoming a famous singer. She succeeded and became a legendary recording star. Nineteen years later, her daughter, Kayla (Brandy), had the same dream of becoming a great singer.

The two met, but Kayla did not realize that Olivia, the great singer who helped her with her career, was the mother she despised for leaving her as a child. The scenes in Olivia's apartment were actually shot in Ross's New York City apartment. Both artists sang songs from their then most recent albums. Ross sang four songs from "Every Day Is a New Day," and Brandy sang three songs from "Never S-A-Y Never." Broadway superstar **Brian Stokes Mitchell** played Adam Harris. Ross, Brandy, and Brandy's mother, Sonja Norwood, had credits as executive producers.

DOUG, DOUG E. Doug (aka Douglas Bourne) starred in the **sitcom** *Where I Live* (1993) and played Griffin Vesey in the sitcom *Cosby* (1996–2000).

DOUGLAS, SUZZANNE. Douglas played Yvette, the researcher in the legal drama series *Against the Law* (1990–1991), and Jerri, the wife, in *Parent'hood* (1995–1999).

DOURDAN, GARY. Dourdan had a starring role as Warrick Brown in *CSI: Crime Scene Investigation* (2000–). He was Detective Randall Paterson in the drama *Swift Justice* in 1996, Bobby Harold in the sitcom *The Office* in 1995, and Shazza Zulu in *A Different World* in 1992. In TV films, he played Malcolm X in *King of the World* in 2000.

DOW, HAROLD. Dow joined CBS as a correspondent for the newsmagazine *48 Hours* in 1990 after serving as a contributor to the program since its premiere in 1988. He was a contributing correspondent for *48 Hours on Crack Street*, the 1986 documentary that launched *48 Hours* newsmagazine. He was also a correspondent for the CBS magazine *Street Stories* from 1992 to 1993 and reported for the *CBS Evening News* with Dan Rather, *CBS Sunday Morning*, and the CBS legal news series *Verdict*.

DRAKE-HOOKS, BEBE. Drake-Hooks (aka Bebe Drake-Massey) was a regular on *The Sanford Arms*. She played a key role in *Scared Straight! Another Story* in 1980.

A DREAM FOR CHRISTMAS (*CBS, December 24, 1973*). This TV film was a pilot for a proposed drama series about a black family.

Created by Earl Hamner, who also created *The Waltons* (1972–1981), it was the 1950 story of the Rev. Will Douglas (**Hari Rhodes**), a Baptist preacher in Sweet Clover, Arkansas, who, with his wife, Sarah (**Lynn Hamilton**); mother; Grandma Bessie (**Beah Richards**); and four children, drove to Los Angeles, where he was promised an inner-city church. When they arrived in Los Angeles, they found that business developers were planning to raze the church to build a shopping center. The family had to convince the developers not to destroy the church and convince the parishioners to remain. George Spell played the oldest son, Joey. **Robert DoQui** as George Briggs, **Juanita Moore** as Fannie Mitchell, **Joel Fluellen** as Arthur Rogers, and **Zara Cully** as Beth Rogers were among the cast. Reviewers praised the actors; *Variety* (December 14, 1973) said, "This is a series just waiting to get out." The series did not get out.

DUBOIS, JA'NET. DuBois is known to television viewers primarily as Willona Woods, the feisty neighbor to the Evans family in the sitcom *Good Times* from 1974 to 1979. She later received an **Emmy Award** for her voice-overs of Avery in *The PJs* in 1999. She played a key role in the children's drama *J.T.* in 1969. She also had key roles in several made-for-television movies, including *The Blue Knight* in 1973; *The Sophisticated Gents* in 1981; *Hellinger's Law*, the 1981 pilot film for the series *Kojak*; and *Sophie and the Moonhanger* in 1996.

DUBOIS, MAURICE. DuBois' credits include substituting as news anchor and cohost on *NBC's Weekend Today* and on MSNBC. He also substituted as news anchor on *NBC News at Sunrise* and has hosted special programming for Court TV called *Mind over Media* to help students understand media images.

DUKE, BILL. Duke played Luther Freeman in *Palmerstown, U.S.A.* He is also a director and producer.

DUKE ELLINGTON . . . WE LOVE YOU MADLY (*CBS, February 11, 1973***).** This 90-minute music special was a tribute to **Duke Ellington** with top black stars performing his music: **Sammy Davis Jr., Roberta Flack, Ray Charles, Sarah Vaughn, Count Basie, James Cleveland, Paula Kelly, Quincy Jones, Billy Eckstine,**

Aretha Franklin, and Peggy Lee. **Quincy Jones** was producer. It was Jones's first experience as a television producer. Ellington was 75 and not well. Jones had for years tried to get networks to do a special on Ellington "while he's still with us." There were no takers until 1972, when CBS gave him the green light but told him he must choose between five top production companies. He wound up with Norman Lear and Bud Yorkin, who later would produce *All in the Family* and *Sanford and Son*. The special went well, but according to Jones, there was a near glitch in that Roberta Flack, Sarah Vaughn, and Peggy Lee had a problem with Aretha. "They ragged on Aretha and complained that she couldn't read music and wouldn't wear a black dress like they did. . . . [Then] the four of them did an Ellington medley and she [Aretha] smoked it. . . . Lord knows, they knew how to do it, and they all did. They got a standing ovation." Ellington was so ill with pneumonia that he was taken to the hospital after the show was taped. He died a few months later. *See also* VARIETY SPECIALS.

DUMMY (*CBS, May 27, 1979*). LeVar Burton starred in this two-hour made-for-television film as an illiterate "deaf-and-dumb" youth who was charged with murdering a prostitute. The story was concerned with the relationship between the youth, Donald Lang, and Lowell Myers (Paul Sorvino), his court-appointed lawyer who was also deaf.

DUNBAR, ROCKMOND. Dunbar played Kenny in *Soul Food* (2000–2004).

DUNCAN, ART. Duncan was the tap dancer on *The Lawrence Welk Show* from 1971 to 1982, the only regular black performer on the series.

DUNGEY, MERRIN. Dungey played Francie Calfo on *Alias* from 2001 to 2003. Prior to that, she played Sara Spooner in *The King of Queens* from 1999 to 2001. She was in the cast of *Summerland* (2004–). She recurred as Joan from the Network in *Grosse Pointe* from 2000 to 2001 and played Wanda in the brief sitcom *Party Girl* (1998).

DUTTON, CHARLES S. Dutton starred as Roc Emerson on the sitcom *Roc* (1991–1994). He starred in *Zooman*, a 1995 TV film, and *The Piano Lesson*, in the same year. He also starred as Mayor Lincoln of New York City in *Aftershock: Earthquake in New York*, a 1999 miniseries. He also became a director and won the **Emmy Award** in 2000 for Outstanding Directing for a Miniseries for *The Corner*. He won the Emmy again in 2002 for Outstanding Guest Actor in a Drama Series for a role in *The Practice*.

– E –

EARTHA KITT SHOW, THE (*SYN, September 1969*). This was a half-hour concert by Eartha Kitt.

EARTH, WIND AND FIRE IN CONCERT (*HBO, September 7, 1982*). Earth, Wind, and Fire (Johnny Graham, Anthony Wollfolk, Philip Bailey, Roland Bautista, Fred White, Larry Dunn, Ralph Johnson, Verdone White, and Maurice White) performed in a one-hour concert. Michael Schultz, Maurice White, and Gloria Schultz were producers. Schultz was director.

EAST SIDE/WEST SIDE (*CBS, 1963–1964*). Cicely Tyson was the first black woman in a regular role on a drama series in *East Side/West Side*, filmed in New York. The main characters were the staff of a welfare agency tackling the problems of the inner city— race relations, drug abuse, crime, and child abuse. The star, George C. Scott, was the social worker. Elizabeth Wilson was his boss; Tyson was their secretary, Jane Porter. The series only lasted one season because CBS could not totally sell the show to sponsors; it was said to be too controversial, particularly with its treatment of race relations. And the serious social issues with which the series dealt were not tied up into tidy little solutions by the end of each episode. This was unheard of at the time. *See also* SERIES WITH ONE BLACK SUPPORTING ACTOR/PERFORMER BEFORE 1980.

ECKSTINE, BILLY. Eckstine, in 1971, appeared on the special *Bill Cosby, Or?* and in 1972 on *Portrait of Nancy Wilson*. The following year, he was part of the musical jazz tribute in *Duke Ellington . . . We Love You Madly* and a Tony Bennett special. In 1988, he was in the cast of *Irving Berlin's 100th Birthday Celebration*. Eckstine was born in 1914 and died in 1993.

EDMUNSON, WILLIAM. Edmunson was a member of the gospel singers **Southernaires Quartet**, also the title of the quartet's show in 1948.

ED SULLIVAN SHOW, THE (CBS, 1948–1971). *The Ed Sullivan Show* was *the* variety show of its time. It lasted for 23 years, and except for the orchestra and dancers, only the host, newspaper columnist Ed Sullivan, was there every week, every stiff but classy inch of him. Every entertainer wanted to do the Sullivan show. You hadn't made it to the top unless you had been on Sullivan's "really big shew," as he pronounced it. Acts were from all kinds of entertainment—recording artists, Broadway stars, opera singers, dancers of all kinds, comedy acts of all kinds including ventriloquists, acts of miniature dogs, and acts of greyhounds. Singers **Cab Calloway, Billy Eckstine, Pearl Bailey,** and **Sarah Vaughan** made appearances on the show as early as 1949. **William Warfield** and **Muriel Rahn** appeared on the show in 1951, as did **Sammy Davis Jr.** as part of the Will Maston Trio. **Marian Anderson** appeared in 1952. Just a few of the other black entertainers were **Lena Horne, Flip Wilson, Harry Belafonte, Richard Pryor, Little Richard, James Brown,** and **The Temptations. The Supremes** made their first appearance on December 27, 1964, and made numerous appearances until December 21, 1969, when they made their last TV appearance with Diana Ross.

Ebony magazine wrote about Sullivan's liberal attitude toward booking artists. Sullivan said, "Recognizing the place of the black in television is not generosity. It is just common sense and good business." However, there was at least one crisis. Sam Cooke was scheduled to make his first appearance on the show on November 3, 1957. When Sullivan introduced him, Cooke came onstage to sing "You Send Me" and was cut off. Actually, time had run out, and someone should have known that there was not enough time for Cooke to complete the song. African Americans were incensed and called it racial discrimination; Cooke was miffed too, and apparently no one explained what had happened. Sullivan received many phone calls and letters charging him with prejudice. He booked Cooke again and this time he sang "You Send Me" as he planned before. Then, later in the show, he came back, and Sullivan said to the audience, "I did wrong one night here on our stage by young Sam Cooke and I never received so much mail in my life." Then he introduced his new hit record *For Sentimental Reasons*, and Cooke sang it to great applause. Black Americans felt this was a classy apology and a triumph for Cooke and black entertainers.

Mary Wilson of The Supremes said that of all the shows on which the group performed, Sullivan was her favorite host. "We were booked for his show so often that I began to think of it as The Supremes Show. Mr. Sullivan made no secret of the fact that he was crazy about us. The Supremes were the only act he let keep the special gowns from the production numbers."

In his quest for success, Richard Pryor's ambition, dating back to his childhood in Peoria, Illinois, was to be on *The Ed Sullivan Show*. He realized that dream in 1965. Pryor said Sullivan saw him perform in Greenwich Village and sent for him the next day. He did a monologue about how military officers speak and a routine on submarines.

Smokey Robinson had a funny memory of being on the show. He said that Sullivan went to the mike as he and The Miracles waited in the wings and he said, "Ladies and gentlemen. Let's have a warm welcome for a great group of guys from Detroit, Michigan—Smokey and the Little Smokeys!"

EDWARDS, GLORIA. Edwards had a key role as Nurse Mary in the made-for-television film *Sister, Sister* in 1982. She was born in 1944 and died of cancer in 1988.

EDWARDS, JAMES. James Edwards, according to historian Donald Bogle, was a major dramatic actor in the early days of television, though his name never became particularly well known. In 1954, he starred in the half-hour drama "The Reign of Amelika Jo" on the dramatic anthology series *Fireside Theatre*. In 1955, he played Ralph Bunche in "Toward Tomorrow" on the *DuPont Cavalcade Theater*. He was in "D.P." on *General Electric Theater* and "Breakdown" on *Alfred Hitchcock Presents*. The latter is still seen in reruns. In it, Edwards was one of three convicts who encountered a paralyzed man (Joseph Cotton) in an auto accident. They thought he was dead and took his clothes. Edwards, the only black convict, had problems stealing from a dead man. Edwards was born in 1918 and died in 1970.

EDWARDS, TAMALA. Edwards joined ABC News as a White House correspondent in August 2001.

EJOGO, CARMEN. Ejogo played the title role in *Sally Hemings: An American Tragedy* (2000) and had key roles in *Boycott* in 2001 and *Lackawanna Blues* in 2005.

ELDER, JUDYANN. Elder played Bernette Wilson in the miniseries *A Woman Called Moses* in 1978 and Helen in the made-for-television movie, *The Oklahoma City Dolls*, in 1981.

ELDER, LARRY. Lawyer/radio talk show host Elder hosted television's *Moral Court* (2000–2001) and began hosting *The Larry Elder Show*, a talk show, in 2004.

THE ELECTRIC COMPANY (*PBS, 1971–1978*). This production of the Children's Television Workshop (CTW) was developed following the success of *Sesame Street*, also a CTW production. The program was designed to help teach reading skills to slow readers in the second, third, and fourth grades. It was intended to supplement school-reading curricula. In addition to support materials such as teaching guides, books, magazines, and puzzles, the show's primary teaching methods were entertainment techniques—comic vignettes, animation, electronic effects, and music. Star teachers on the show were **Bill Cosby**, who was already a television star who had gone back to academia to earn a doctorate in education, and **Morgan Freeman**, who would be a dramatic film star later. **Hattie Winston**, who has had key roles in numerous television shows and films, also broke into television and film from her work on *The Electric Company*. The educational experiment was a success according to PBS reports that the show reached 6.5 million youngsters regularly and was seen both in homes and in schools.

ELLINGTON, DUKE. Ellington was one of the stars of *All Star Jazz* in 1957 and headlined *The Barbara McNair and Duke Ellington Special* (1968). He was one of the highlights of . . . *And Beautiful* (1970), *The Big Band and All That Jazz* (1972), and *All Star Swing Festival* (1972). He was saluted in *Duke Ellington . . . We Love You Madly* (1973) and posthumously in *Ellington at 100* and *A Capitol Fourth* (1999) and at the halftime show of Super Bowl IX (1975). Vintage footage of Ellington was an important part of the series *The Blues* in 2003. Ellington was born in 1899 and died in 1974.

ELLINGTON AT 100 (*PBS, April 7, 1999*). **Wynton Marsalis** and the Lincoln Center Jazz Orchestra joined with the New York Philharmonic to perform Ellington masterpieces including the swinging Ellington–Strayhorn arrangement of the "Peer Gynt Suite."

ELISE, KIMBERLY. Elise played Jeanette and won a CableACE Award for Supporting Actress in a Movie or Miniseries for *The Ditchdigger's Daughter* (1997). In other television films, she played the title role in *The Loretta Claiborne Story* (2000) and the female lead, the wife, in the TV film *Bojangles* (2001).

EMMANUEL LEWIS: MY VERY OWN SHOW (*ABC, 1987*). **Emmanuel Lewis** had been the star of the ABC sitcom *Webster* for more than four years. In the final year of the sitcom, he hosted a variety special. The special was about how a network variety special is produced and had as guest stars **Debbie Allen**, **Sammy Davis Jr.**, Bob Hope, Siegfried and Roy, Rene Auberjonois, Shelly Berman, Frank Gorshin, and others.

EMMY AWARDS. The Emmys are television's equivalent of film's Oscars; the prime-time entertainment awards are presented in a television special each September by the Academy of Television Arts and Sciences in southern California. The first Emmys were offered in 1949; Harry Belafonte was the first black Emmy winner in 1960.

Categories of awards include but are not limited to performers, writers, directors, hairstylists, costumers, and makeup artists. Producers enter nominations for shows; individuals enter themselves. In June of each year, nominations ballots go out to members of the Academy, and at least two but usually five nominees are selected by popular vote. A blue-ribbon panel of judges is made up of members who volunteer to watch videos or DVDs of programs/episodes of nominated individuals or shows in their categories. Only peers in each category are on the blue-ribbon panels. Directors judge directors, performers judge performers, and costumers judge costumers. All members are qualified to judge programs. Votes from the peer judging go to an accounting firm for final and secret tabulations. Some awards are presented on the September telecast, while others are presented a week prior at a banquet.

African-American performers who have won multiple Emmy Awards are **Bill Cosby, Cicely Tyson, Flip Wilson, Robert Guillaume, Alfre Woodard, James Earl Jones, Laurence Fishburne, Chris Rock, Charles S. Dutton, Beah Richards**, and **Ja'net DuBois**. The National Academy of Television Arts and Sciences presents Emmy Awards in other categories including news, sports, and daytime and local programming. *See also* EMMY AWARDS (appendix B).

ENGLISH, ALEX. English's credits in the sports field range from basketball player to being a color commentator for the Denver Nuggets on the Fox Sports Network in 1997–1998. He was also cohost of *This Week in the NBA* on CNNSI. He also worked as a basketball analyst for NBC.com TV.

ENNIS' GIFT: A FILM ABOUT LEARNING DISABILITIES (*HBO, November 23, 2001*). Inspired by **Bill Cosby**'s son Ennis, who was devoted to working with children with special needs, this film introduced children to great people who succeeded despite their physical, mental, and emotional challenges. Ennis Cosby, at 27, was mysteriously shot and killed while changing a tire at a Los Angeles freeway exit on January 16, 1997. *See also* DOCUMENTARIES.

ENTERTAINERS (*SYN, 1994– *). **Byron Allen** hosted this weekly celebrity interview show. This show was different from other celebrity interview shows in that instead of the celebrities coming to him, he went to them—sometimes in their homes, in restaurants, on sets, anywhere seemingly that the celebrity might be at ease.

EPHRAIM, MABLEAN. Ephraim presided over *Divorce Court* (1999–).

EPPERSON, SHARON. Epperson went to CNBC Business News in 1996 covering personal and corporate finance. Her credits include reports on *NBC Weekend Nightly News*, *NBC Weekend Today*, *Early Today*, and MSNBC.

EPPS, OMAR. Epps played Dr. Dennis Gant on *ER* from 1996 to 1997. He joined the medical drama *House* in 2004. In TV films, he was in the following: *Daybreak* (1993), *Deadly Voyage* (1996), and *First Time Felon* (1997).

ER (*NBC, 1994–*). This medical drama series is notable in African-American history for numerous black actors in central roles in its large racially integrated cast. Prime among them would be **Eriq LaSalle**, who played Dr. Peter Benton from 1994 to 2001. Benton was a master surgeon who made interns shiver in their shoes. One of them committed suicide. Benton had an ailing mother, Mae (played by **Beah Richards**, 1994–1995), who was cared for by physical therapist Jeanie Boulet (played by **Gloria Reuben**, 1995–1999), who had contracted the HIV virus from her wayward husband (played by **Michael Beach**, 1995–1997). Benton had a brief affair with Jeanie, but he remained virus free. Then he learned that he was the father of Carla's (**Lisa Nicole Carson**) baby, Reese (Matthew Watkins), who was born deaf. He was devoted to the baby, but after Carla died in an accident, he discovered that he was not Reese's father. Still, he fought for and got custody of the child and chose to quit the hospital when he could not work reduced hours. Actually, LaSalle left the series to pursue other interests. Reuben left the series to sing with Tina Turner.

Other African Americans in the cast and their roles were the following: **Conni Marie Brazleton** as Nurse Connie Oligaro, **Yvette Freeman** as Nurse Haleh Adams, **C. C. H. Pounder** (1994–1995) as Dr. Angela Hicks, **Omar Epps** (1996–1997) as Dr. Dennis Gant, **Cress Williams** (1998–2000) as Officer Reggie Moore, **Michael Michele** (2000–2001) as Dr. Cleo Finch; and **Mekhi Phifer** as Dr. Gregory Pratt (2002–).

ERNEST GREEN STORY, THE (*DIS, January 17, 1993*). This TV film was based on the true story of Ernest Green, who at 15 was one of the Little Rock Nine, the black students who integrated an Arkansas high school in 1957. Green was the only senior in the group of nine, and the TV film tells the story of his harrowing year and how he survived. **Morris Chestnut** played Green. **Ossie Davis** played Green's grandfather. Eric Laneuville was director. Others in the cast included **Avery Brooks** as Rev. Lawson, **Ruby Dee** as Mrs. Lydia Wilson, **Omar Gooding** as Marcus, and **C. C. H. Pounder** as Daisy Bates. *See also* HISTORICAL EVENTS DRAMATIZED.

ESCAPE ROUTE (*CBS, 1957*). "Escape Route" was one of the *Studio One* anthology dramas. It is significant in that it featured **Juano Hernandez.** The story was about a white college professor who was mysteriously shot and, just before he died, whispered something to a colleague named Tucker. Hernandez portrayed the detective, Calador, whose job was to interrogate Tucker. According to historian Donald Bogle, Hernandez played the role with "great self assurance . . . oblivious to the fact that he was a black man challenging a white suspect," a rare role for a black man in the 1950s. Bogle said, "'Escape Route' was neither great nor compelling drama. But it afforded Juano Hernandez, one of America's unacknowledged great dramatic actors, a rare opportunity to play a shrewd, ironic character on television."

ESSENCE AWARDS, THE (*various networks, 1987–*). *Essence* magazine annually honors outstanding women in the African-American community as selected by the editors of the magazine.

ETHEL WATERS SHOW, THE (*NBC, 1939*). This one-time show was most likely the first televised show with an African-American star. It was a test broadcast for the television industry and, in a sense, a pilot for television itself. Waters had appeared in the play *Mamba's Daughters*, so part of the show was scenes from the play with cast members Fredi Washington and Georgette Harvey. There were also skits, slapstick comedy, and even serious lectures.

EUBANKS, KEVIN. The bandleader on *The Tonight Show with Jay Leno* (1995–) was composer for the TV film *Rebound: The Legend of Earl "The Goat" Manigault* (1996).

EVANDER HOLYFIELD FIGHTS. Holyfield's second professional fight, against Eric Winbush, was televised on January 20, 1985. He won his first title with a 15-round decision against Dwight Qawi for the WBA Junior Heavyweight crown; the bout aired live from Atlanta on July 12, 1988. He lost to Riddick Bowe by an 11th-round knockout on March 6, 1993, in Las Vegas. *See also* BOXING MATCHES.

EVANS, ART. Evans played A. D. King in the miniseries *King* (1978). He had a key role in the TV film *Minstrel Man* (1977), *I Know Why* *the Caged Bird Sings* (1979), *World War II* (1982), *Long Time Gone* (1986), *Adventures in Babysitting* (1989), and *Always Outnumbered* (1998).

EVANS, DAMON. Evans was the second actor to play Lionel on *The Jeffersons* (1975–1978). A singer as well as an actor, he played Sportin' Life in *Porgy & Bess*, the Gershwin opera in 1993, and performed in *Evening at Pops: A Tribute to the Music of George Gershwin* in 1995.

EVANS, MICHAEL. Evans played the original Lionel Jefferson in *All in the Family* (1971–1975) and in *The Jeffersons* (1975 and 1979–1981).

EVE (actress). This Grammy Award–winning singer, who had roles in motion pictures and guest-star roles in television productions, starred in her own sitcom *Eve* beginning in 2003. She was one of the divas in *VH1 Divas* (2004).

EVE (sitcom) (*UPN, September 2003– *). Grammy Award–winning Hip Hop artist **Eve** starred as Shelly Williams, a single woman who, with beauty and intelligence, tried to juggle love, sex, romance, and career. Her best friends were Rita (Ali Landry) and Janie (**Natalie Desselle-Reid**). The men in this sitcom about relationships were J. T. Hunter (**Jason George**) and Nick (**Brian Hooks**).

EVENING WITH DIANA ROSS, AN. *See* DIANA ROSS, AN EVENING WITH.

EVENING WITH JULIE ANDREWS AND HARRY BELA-FONTE. *See* JULIE ANDREWS AND HARRY BELAFONTE, AN EVENING WITH.

EVERYBODY HATES CHRIS *(UPN, 2005–)*. This series starred Chris Rock.

EYES ON THE PRIZE *(PBS, 1987 and 1990)*. This 14-part documentary series centered on the American civil rights movement and included historic film footage and interviews with persons involved in the movement. The first six installments, *America's Civil Rights*

Years (1954–1965), were broadcast in January and February 1987. Included were such events as Rosa Parks's arrest for refusing to give up a seat, which was the spark for the Montgomery Bus Boycott; the passage of the Voting Rights Act; James Meredith's tumultuous enrollment at the University of Mississippi; the 1963 March on Washington; and other civil rights efforts. The 1990 sequel aired in eight parts and was called *Eyes on the Prize II: America at the Crossroads* (1965–1985) and included later topics such as the Nation of Islam, busing, and affirmative action. The series was seen by more than 50 million viewers and won numerous awards.

– F –

FACTS OF LIFE, THE (*NBC, 1979–1988*). Actress **Kim Fields** was Tootie, a child so short she had to wear skates to be the same height as the other children in camera shots, in this sitcom, which was a spin-off of *Diff'rent Strokes*. Yet she was the black hook to the show about the girls boarding at Eastland School, their housemother (Charlotte Rae, who had been the housekeeper on *Diff'rent Strokes*), their friends, and their families. Lori L. Tharps, editor of the San Francisco women's magazine *Bitch*, said that she felt a keen connection to 1970s and 1980s female characters like Tootie because black women were so rare in television fare.

FAISON, DONALD ADEOSUN. Faison played Tracey on *Felicity* for two seasons and Murray on *Clueless* for three seasons. Murray was the hip boyfriend of the central character's best friend, Dee (**Stacey Dash**). The role in *Clueless* was reprised from the film of the same title. He later played Chris Turk on *Scrubs* (2001–).

FAISON, FRANKIE. Faison starred in the sitcom *True Colors* (1990–1992) as Ron Freeman, a dentist. He played Detective Ray Peterson in the sci-fi series *Prey* (1998).

FALANA, LOLA. Singer/dancer/actress Falana made numerous appearances on musical variety series and specials. She headlined her own special, *Lola*, in 1976. She was a regular on the limited summer series *Ben Vereen . . . Comin' at Ya* (1975) and also on *The New Bill*

Cosby Show, a 1972–1973 comedy variety series. She was also the announcer on the latter series. She was a guest star on *The Lou Rawls Special* in 1976. Falana made numerous appearances on *The Tonight Show with Johnny Carson* and *Hullabaloo*. She was victimized by multiple sclerosis in 1987. She said she turned to God and retired from show business except for a few appearances. One of the exceptions was for her longtime friend **Sammy Davis Jr.** She was present at the *Sammy Davis Jr. 60th Anniversary Celebration* (1990).

FALLEN CHAMP: THE UNTOLD STORY OF MIKE TYSON (*NBC, February 12, 1993*). This documentary centered on the life and times of former heavyweight champion Mike Tyson.

FAME (drama series) (*NBC, 1982–1983; SYN, 1983–1987*). This drama series, based on the feature film of the same title, was about the students and faculty of the High School of the Performing Arts in New York City. **Debbie Allen** and **Gene Anthony Ray** were among the cast members who reprised their roles in the film. Allen was dance teacher Lydia Grant; Ray was student Leroy Johnson. **Erica Gimpel** played Coco in the 1982–1983 season, and she sang the theme song. **Janet Jackson** joined the cast in the 1984–1985 season as student Cleo Hewitt. The episodes dealt with the students' dreams and efforts to succeed as singers, dancers, actors, and musicians. According to the *New York Times* (December 18, 1982), the series was much more popular in Great Britain than in the United States. During its first and only season on network TV, in December 1982, the show ranked 60th out of 77 regular programs in the United States, while it was in the top 10 on BBC. Two record albums of the show's music sold more than two million copies each in Britain. Ten concerts featuring Allen and Ray and other cast members played in London and other cities, and all seats were sold within three days of the announcement.

FAME (reality series) (*NBC, 2003*). In other times, this limited series would have been called a variety series or a talent show, but in 2003, "reality" was the buzzword, so that is what it was called. Dancer/choreographer/actress **Debbie Allen** (who was an actor on both the original movie and the 1980s television series) was a producer who gathered 24 young people who performed before judges (among them was celebrity manager Johnny Wright and singer Carnie Wilson). Dancing was the essential talent, although Allen explained the necessity of being multitalented, a triple threat: dancing, singing, and personality. Someone on each show was eliminated by the judges until there were eight left standing, then viewers' votes left one winner, Harlemm Lee, whose final appearance included a recap of how hard it is in his Asian culture to be a creative artistic person and not a businessman. Finalists were Serena Henry, Brandon O'Neal, and Shannon Bex. *See also* REALITY SERIES.

FAMILY MATTERS (*ABC, 1989–1997; CBS, 1997–1998*). This sitcom, a spin-off of *Perfect Strangers*, centered on the Winslow family, headed by Chicago Police Officer Carl Winslow (**Reginald VelJohnson**) and his wife, Harriette (**JoMarie Payton**). The show was built around Payton's character who was first the elevator operator on *Perfect Strangers*. The Winslow children were Eddie (**Darius McCrary**), Laura (**Kellie Shanygne Williams**), and Judy Winslow (**Jaimee Foxworth**). For the 10th episode, the script called for a gangly boy who was infatuated with Laura. Enter Steve Urkel (**Jaleel White**), a nerd who wore glasses, hitched up his pants and recited his lines in a whiny nasal-sounding voice.

So-so ratings zoomed; the formerly number 40 show joined the top 20 and became the highest-rated show among kids ages 2 to 11. There was no question that the nerdy neighbor was there to stay. For years, the family was tortured by Urkel. As torturous as Steve was, the Winslow family cared about him, even Laura, who turned down his childhood crushes until the final season of the series. Grandma Winslow was played by **Rosetta LeNoire**; Rachel Crawford by **Telma Hopkins**; Richie Crawford, first by twins Joseph and Julius Wright, then by Bryton McClure; Maxine by **Cherie Johnson**; Weasel by **Shavar Ross**; Myra by Michelle Thomas; and 3J by **Orlando Brown**. In later episodes, when Urkel, Laura, and Eddie were in college, episodes dealt with their college lives. Some shows centered on White's portrayal of his alter ego, debonair Stefan Urquelle and other characters, and Urkel's fantastic time-travel inventions.

Family Matters was one of the longest-running sitcoms in television history. *Jet* (June 2, 1997) said, "The show has lasted so long because it is not only funny but it also delivers valuable messages on such issues as family, education, black pride, respect, and the importance of being responsible." VelJohnson noted that the show was successful because of its emphasis on family ties. "It's a message that family is important, that morality is important and doing the right thing is important." Though pleased with their good fortune, Payton and VelJohnson were not happy with the direction of the show. It started out as their show, their opportunity for a big break, and for seven years they worked in the shadow of a cartoonish character. VelJohnson complained primarily about how difficult it was to "come in the door feeling refreshed every day." But he announced that he would "stick it out until the studio breaks down the Winslow living room set for good." Payton, on the other hand, announced she would leave. She wanted to show her talents elsewhere. "She felt there should be more stories about the mom and dad and their relationship with the children," according to the director, John Tracy. "*Family Matters* had been stagnating my creativity," she said. "The Monday after I left, I felt happier and lighter than I'd felt in years." She was replaced by **Judyann Elder**, who played the same role. *See also* FAMILY SERIES; LONG-RUNNING SERIES.

FAMILY SERIES. The term "family series" has two meanings. It could be a show for family viewing, or it could be a show about a family. Generally, shows about families are shows based on a parent or parents with young or teenage children. (Therefore, *Amos 'n' Andy* in the 1950s was not a family show; there were no children. Later series like *Sanford and Son*, *That's My Mama*, and *The Jeffersons* were primarily about parents with adult children.) It was 1968 when a black family show emerged and enjoyed any longevity. *Julia* (1968–1971) was a single widowed mother with a young son; the character Julia (**Diahann Carroll**) was written as a single mom so that dating would create script possibilities. And the first series with any longevity based on an intact family with a mother and father was in 1974, when *Good Times* made its debut. **Esther Rolle**, the star, insisted on having a two-parent family (**John Amos** played the father). She felt that it was important to portray positive images of two parents and loving families. *Good Times* had good ratings and lasted until 1979, although the parents were written out of the series before it ended. In 1976, *What's Happening* premiered with a single mother, but the father visited and truly cared for his children. In the late 1970s and 1980s, there were three successful sitcoms with interracial families: *Diff'rent Strokes* (1978–1986), *Gimme a Break* (1981–1987), and *Webster* (1983–1987). Networks feared that black family shows in which the cast was all black would not garner high ratings. Then *The Cosby Show*, about a middle-class black family, was born in 1984. Though NBC took a chance on it, there was fear in the executive ranks. During a press conference prior to the launching of *The Cosby Show*, **Bill Cosby** told reporters that he wanted to do the series in New York "so I can get canceled closer to home." NBC executives in the room groaned, thinking that was exactly what would happen. The show was an immediate hit, but Cosby fought numerous battles. It was suggested to him that the Huxtable family adopt a white child or that there could be a white housekeeper. He refused. He was the first black series star who was financially able to walk away from a possibly lucrative series, so he got his way on most matters. When the network objected to a sign on the son's bedroom saying "End Apartheid," Cosby was appalled, saying, "There is no question about how this family feels about apartheid." Yet the sign did not appear on the show; NBC felt it was too political. Yet without regular white cast members, the show was the third most popular series for 1984–1985 and the top show for the next three years. Consequently, black family shows *227* (1985–1990), *Family Matters* (1989–1998), and *Fresh Prince of Bel-Air* (1990–1996) were launched. John O'Connor of the *New York Times* (May 20, 1996) observed progress when he said, "With the milestone of 'Cosby' [*The Cosby Show*] paving the way, '*Fresh Prince*' reached the point where a black family could have a picture of Malcolm X on the wall and both James Brown and Mozart on the stereo."

When UPN and the WB were launched, in 1995 and 1994, respectively, they soon became the networks of black sitcoms. The black family sitcoms on UPN were *Moesha* (1996–2001) and *All of Us* (2003–). *Minor Adjustments* went from NBC to UPN in 1996. *The Hughleys* went from ABC to UPN in 2000. The WB had *The Parent'hood* (1995–1999), *The Steve Harvey Show* (1996–2002), and *All about the Andersons* (2003–2004). *Sister, Sister* went from ABC to the WB in 1995. Fox had *The Sinbad Show* (1993–1994), *The Tracy Morgan Show* (2003–2004), and *The Bernie Mac Show*

(2001–). ABC aired *My Wife and Kids* (2001–). CBS aired *The Gregory Hines Show* (1997–1998).

Animated series about black families emerged in the late 1990s and later. *Waynehead* (1996–1997) was on the WB. *The P.J.s* began on Fox in 1999. *The Proud Family*, a Disney offering, began in 2001. Bill Cosby's *Fatherhood* began on Nickelodeon in 2004.

In the area of family drama series, a 1979 effort was *Harris and Company* starring **Bernie Casey**. Critics and the viewing public were not prepared for a black drama series, and many believed it was an unfunny sitcom because of its half-hour format. It stayed on the air for less than a month. *Palmerstown*, starring **Jonelle Allen** and **Bill Duke**, a Norman Lear drama, lasted a little more than a year. **James Earl Jones** attempted a family drama, *Under One Roof*, in 1995; it lasted for a month. Several pilot films for proposed black family series, like *A Dream for Christmas* (1973), were not bought by networks. *Soul Food* lasted from 2000 to 2004 on Showtime, where ratings demands are not as great as on the networks. *See comments of Casey and Jones in listing for* HARRIS AND COMPANY *and* UNDER ONE ROOF.

FANN, AL. Fann played Raymond in the two-hour biopic *Thornwell* in 1981 and had a key role in *Scout's Honor*, a 1980 television film. He played Alvin in *He's the Mayor*, a 1986 sitcom, and Detective Stratton in *Bodies of Evidence*, a 1992–1993 police drama.

FANTASTIC WORLD OF D. C. COLLINS, THE (*NBC, February 10, 1984*). **Gary Coleman**, in his fifth television film produced during the hiatus period of *Diff'rent Strokes*, played D. C. Collins, the son of a United Nations diplomat (**Bernie Casey**). D. C. daydreamed that he was his favorite movie heroes. Then he got the opportunity to be a hero on his own. **Marilyn McCoo** played his mother, Vanessa.

FARGAS, ANTONIO. Fargas played Les Baxter in the daytime drama *All My Children* (1982–1983 and 1987). He was Huggy Bear, the informer, in *Starsky and Hutch* (1975–1979) and played a memorable cameo as a jailhouse transsexual in *The Ambush Murders* in 1982. He played Leroy in *Soul Survivors* (1995), Eddie in *Maid for Each Other* (1992), Spider in *Percy and Thunder* (1993), and Elijah Muhammad in *Ali: An American Hero* (2000), all TV films.

FAT ALBERT AND THE COSBY KIDS (*CBS, 1972–1984; NBC, 1984–1989*). This animated series was one of the longest-running cartoon series in television history. It was based on people **Bill Cosby** knew in his childhood in Philadelphia and characters in his monologues. Cosby said, "It was anti-stereotype. Fat Albert and his friends were fully-functioning bright kids." Fat Albert was heavyset but basically a role-model kid. Mush Mouth, another character, got his name because he had a speech impediment, but he was intelligent. Clarence Waldron of *Jet* said, "The cartoon's appeal was based on its sense of humor and fun and its pro-social messages and characters." The series was retitled *The New Fat Albert Show* in 1979.

FAT ALBERT CHRISTMAS SPECIAL (*CBS, December 18, 1977*). This 30-minute cartoon special featured the characters created by **Bill Cosby** and based on his childhood friends in the series *Fat Albert and the Cosby Kids* (1972–1979). In a modernized version of the Nativity, Fat Albert and his buddies—Bill, Mush Mouth, Dumb Donald, Weird Harold, Russell, and Rudy—were afraid that mean Tyrone, the owner, would destroy their clubhouse. The kids met a family stranded by a car with mechanical failure; the kids took the pregnant mother and the family to the clubhouse, where the baby was born. The birth revealed a nicer side to Tyrone. Cosby did most of the voices and was producer. Jan Crawford was the voice of Russell; Eric Suter was the voice of Rudy.

FAT ALBERT HALLOWEEN SPECIAL, THE (*CBS, October 24, 1977*). In this half-hour cartoon special based on characters created by **Bill Cosby**, Fat Albert and his friends tried to protect the elderly people in the neighborhood from a troublemaking prankster. Cosby provided most of the voices and was producer.

FATHER FOR CHARLIE, A (*CBS, January 1, 1995*). Louis Gossett Jr. played Walter Osgood, a Depression-era father whose concern for an abandoned boy broke racial barriers in an Ozarks town.

FATHERHOOD (*NIK, 2004– *). This animated series based on **Bill Cosby**'s book of the same title centered on family life and raising children. Specifically, the series was about the Bindlebeep family with three children and two parents. The parents were Norman and

Arthur with voices provided by **Sabrina LeBeauf** and **Blair Underwood**. The children were Roy (Marc John Jefferies), Katherine (Jamai Fisher), and Angie (Giovonnie Samuels). Arthur, a high school professor, learned from his children and from his own parents, Louise and Lester. **Ruby Dee** did the voice of Louise; **Lou Rawls** did the voice of Lester. Cosby was creator.

FESTIVAL OF MUSIC (*NBC, January 30, 1956*). Contralto **Marian Anderson** was one of an impressive list of opera and concert artists who were featured in this 90-minute special of performances. Roberta Peters, Isaac Stern, Arthur Rubinstein, and Rise Stevens performed.

FIELDS, ALEXIS. Fields played Sheila Hendricks on the sitcom *Roc* (1993–1994), Nicole Wilson on *The Secret World of Alex Mac* (1994), and Diavian Johnson on the sitcom *Sister, Sister* (1997–1999). She is the sister of **Kim Fields**.

FIELDS, CHIP. Chip had key roles in the television movies *Battered* in 1978 and *The Night the City Screamed* in 1980. She played the roles of Penny's (**Janet Jackson**) cruel mother on *Good Times* and Regine's (**Kim Fields**) eccentric mother on *Living Single*. Alexis Fields and Kim Fields are her daughters.

FIELDS, KIM. After appearing on a popular commercial for Mrs. Butterworth's syrup, Fields (aka Kim Fields Freeman) played Angie Ellis in the sitcom *Baby I'm Back* in 1978. She was Tootie on *The Facts of Life* from 1979 to 1988 and played early episodes on skates so that she could be as tall as the other characters for the cameras. She played a key role in the television film *The Kid with the Broken Halo* in 1982. After earning a college degree, she returned to television grown up and played sexy Regine on *Living Single* from 1993 to 1998.

FIFTH DIMENSION, THE. The popular singing group appeared on *Francis Albert Sinatra Does His Thing* in 1969, headlined *The Fifth Dimension Special: An Odyssey in the Cosmic Universe of Peter Max* in 1970, and did *The Fifth Dimension Traveling Show* in 1971.

FIFTH DIMENSION SPECIAL: AN ODYSSEY IN THE COSMIC UNIVERSE OF PETER MAX, THE (*CBS, May 21, 1970*). The popular singing group **The Fifth Dimension**—Marilyn McCoo, **Billy Davis Jr.**, Florence Larue, Lamont McLemore, and Ron Townsend—provided an hour of music with guests **Flip Wilson**, Glen Campbell, and Arte Johnson.

FIFTH DIMENSION TRAVELING SHOW, THE (*ABC, August 18, 1971*). **The Fifth Dimension** hosted an hour of song with guests **Dionne Warwick** and Karen and Richard Carpenter.

FIGHT FOR JENNY, A (*NBC, 1986*). This two-hour made-for-television movie starred **Philip Michael Thomas** and Lesley Ann Warren as a married couple enduring the woes of being interracial. David (Thomas) was a model stepfather to Kelsey's (Warren) seven-year-old daughter, Jennifer, but Jennifer's father sued for custody, charging that the child's environment was improper. Kelsey's lawyer argued that the case was about race and took the issue to the Supreme Court. *New York Times* critic John O'Connor wrote, "Some of the carefully-posed love scenes might still strike a good many viewers as being surprisingly daring. Television has a long way to go to catch up with certain realities. . . . Mr. Thomas, the costar of 'Miami Vice,' [delivers] a performance nicely restrained and even charming. [He] is clearly capable of more than the action-adventure capers of Crockett and Tubbs [in *Miami Vice*, his popular series]." *See also* INTERRACIAL ROMANCE/RELATIONSHIPS.

FINAL SHOT: THE HANK GATHERS STORY (*SYN, April 1992*). This biopic follows the brief career of basketball star Hank Gathers from the ghettos of Philadelphia to Loyola Marymount University, where he collapsed during a game and died of a heart ailment. Ahmad Stoner played the child Gathers, while **Victor Love** played Gathers as an adult. **Nell Carter** played his supportive mother. Others in the cast included **Kimberly Russell**, **Reynaldo Rey**, and **Whitman Mayo**. *See also* ATHLETES' BIOPICS.

FINNEY, SHIRLEY JO. Finney played a key role on the *CBS Schoolbreak Special* "15 and Getting Straight" in 1989. She played Olympic champion sprinter Wilma Rudolph in *Wilma*, a 1977 TV film. She had a key role in the 1981 TV film *Thornwell*. She became a director.

FIREHOUSE (*ABC, January 2, 1973*). **Richard Roundtree** starred in this made-for-television motion picture as Shelly Forsythe, a recruit for a big-city fire department who clashes with a bigoted white veteran fireman. **Sheila Frazier** played his wife, Michelle. The film was a pilot for a short-lived series.

FIRES IN THE MIRROR (*PBS, April 28, 1993*). **Anna Deavere Smith** played 19 characters in this piece about racial conflict in Brooklyn. The characters were based on her interviews with witnesses and victims of conflict.

FIRST TIME FELON (*HBO, 1997*). **Omar Epps** starred as Greg Yance, a 23-year-old first-time offender who was arrested and given a choice of five years in prison or four months in a rigorous Marine-style prison boot camp program. The obvious choice ends up changing his life. **Delroy Lindo** played Ransom, the tough guard who was instrumental in helping Yance make his life transition. This marked the directorial debut of **Charles S. Dutton**, who, before launching his acting career, served more than seven years in prison for manslaughter committed in a street fight when he was 17. Dutton also played a cameo as a jailed gang elder with blood in his eye.

FISHBURNE, LAURENCE. Fishburne played Lieutenant Stone in the two-hour TV motion picture *Thornwell* in 1981. He won the **Emmy Award** for "The Box" episode of *Tribeca* in the 1992–1993 season. Fishburne hosted the documentary *Who Killed Martin Luther King?* in 1993. He starred and was executive producer of the two-hour drama *Miss Evers' Boys* in 1997. The production won the Emmy Award for Outstanding Made-for-Television Movie. His credits for made-for-television films also include his starring role in *Always Outnumbered* in 1998. He starred in the children's program *What's Going On* in 2004.

FISHER, GAIL. Fisher was one of the first African-American women to play a key role in a dramatic series and was regarded as a role model to aspiring African-American actresses when she played Peggy Fair, secretary to Joe Mannix, the private detective and lead in *Mannix* (1968–1975). In addition, she won an **Emmy Award** for Outstanding Performance by an Actress in a Supporting Role for her portrayal of Peggy Fair in 1970. Despite the accomplishment, her roles were few after *Mannix*. In the late 1970s, she and a once-popular African-American female recording artist together sought work as secretary and housekeeper from comedian **Redd Foxx**. Fisher, with emphysema and diabetes, died of cardiac arrest in 2001 at the age of 65.

FITTS, RICK. Fitts played Councilman Blake in the daytime drama *General Hospital* (1994) and had a regular or recurring role in *Generations* (1989) and *Santa Barbara* (1984). Other TV credits include the following: *The Kid with the Broken Halo* (1982), *Hunter* (1984), *Streets of Justice* (1985), *The Case of the Hillside Strangler* (1989), *Liz: The Elizabeth Taylor Story* (1995), *A Nightmare Come True* (1997), *You Lucky Dog* (1998), and *Miracle in Lane 2* (2000).

FITZGERALD, ELLA. Honored as The First Lady of Song, jazz singer Fitzgerald was Frank Sinatra's guest on specials airing in 1959, 1967, and 1990 as well as many specials and variety shows. She helped pay tribute to **Louis Armstrong** in the halftime extravaganza of Super Bowl VI (1972). She was saluted in the tribute special *It's Black Entertainment* (1997). She was honored in *The Apollo Hall of Fame* (1993). Ella Fitzgerald was born in 1918 and died in 1996. *See also* TELEVISION PIONEERS.

FLACK, ROBERTA. Flack sang on *Duke Ellington . . . We Love You Madly* in 1973. She played the young girl in *Free to Be . . . You and Me* (1974). She sang on the *19th Annual American Music Awards* (1992), *Juke Box Saturday Night* (1979), and the *20th Annual Grammy Awards* (1973). She made an appearance on the daytime drama *Another World* as herself, sang the theme song for the sitcom *The Hogan Family* (1986–1991), and made numerous guest appearances on *The Rosie O'Donnell Show* in 1996–1997.

FLIP WILSON SHOW, THE (*NBC, 1970–1974*). This was the first hit variety series with a black star. The show was done "in the round" with the studio audience surrounding two-thirds of the stage. Wilson opened the show with a monologue and then participated in comedy sketches with three guest stars or groups. He avoided political humor since the series embraced entertainers and viewers regardless of their politics. Wilson felt that a show like that would bring people together, and it did on Thursday nights. The series was an immediate hit and completed its first year as the number two show, topped only by *All in the Family*. Musical groups sang their latest hits or performed whatever they did best. Wilson played various characters; the most memorable of them was sassy Geraldine, who wore Pucci prints and a well-coiffed wig and demanded respect from everyone. There was also the Reverend Leroy of the Church of What's Happening Now; Freddy, the Playboy; Jiva Koolit, the white-haired guru; regular Marvin Lattimer; Sonny, the White House janitor; and Herbie, the ice cream man. In 1973, the series added the Flipettes, a chorus line of black dancers who also acted in comedy sketches. They were Ka-ron Brown, Marguerite DeLain, Bhetty Waldron, Mary Vivian, Edwetta Little, and Jaki Morrison. The series won two **Emmy Awards** its premiere year: Outstanding Variety Series and Outstanding Writing Achievement in Variety or Music. The latter award was for a show airing December 10, 1970, with guest stars **Lena Horne** and Tony Randall.

The biggest names in show business appeared in the series. "It was so hot, celebrities asked to be on the show," said producer Bob Henry. Some of the stars who guested on the series were Bing Crosby, **Louis Armstrong, Lena Horne, Bill Cosby**, The Jackson Five, Lucille Ball, Ed Sullivan, **Ray Charles, The Temptations, The Supremes**, and **B. B. King**. It was not widely known that Wilson, his manager Monte Kay, and producer Henry owned the series. Consequently, his was the first TV series owned by the star. In the fourth season, Wilson announced he would not do a fifth season.

FLIP WILSON SPECIALS. Comedian **Flip Wilson** hosted the following specials: *Flip Wilson . . . Of Course* (NBC, October 17, 1974) with guest stars **Richard Pryor, Martha Reeves**, Peter Sellers, and Lily Tomlin; *The Flip Wilson Special* (NBC, December 11, 1974) with guest stars **Diahann Carroll**, Freddie Prinze, and Paul Williams; *The Flip Wilson Special* (NBC, February 27, 1975) with guest stars **Sammy Davis Jr.**, William Conrad, and Helen Reddy;

and *The Flip Wilson Special* (NBC, May 7, 1975) with guest stars **Richard Pryor**, McLean Stevenson, and Cher. *Travels with Flip* (CBS, October 1975) was a special about the comedian's travels to Atlanta, Los Angeles, San Francisco, Hawaii, Nashville, and Boley, Oklahoma, a black town he adopted. Guest stars were **Muhammad Ali** and Loretta Lynn. *The Flip Wilson Comedy Special* (NBC, November 11, 1975) featured guests **The Pointer Sisters**, George Carlin, and Ruth Buzzi.

FLUELLEN, JOEL. Fluellen played "Unc" Isom in *The Autobiography of Miss Jane Pittman* in 1974, Arthur Rogers in *A Dream for Christmas* in 1973, and James Allenby in the miniseries *Freedom Road* in 1979. An actor in films and TV whose first television role was in an episode of *Ramar of the Jungle* in 1952, Fluellen died of a self-inflicted gunshot wound in 1990.

FOR COLORED GIRLS WHO HAVE CONSIDERED SUICIDE/WHEN THE RAINBOW IS ENUF *(PBS, February 23, 1982).* The hit Broadway show was directed by director Oz Scott and featured then relatively inexperienced actresses **Alfre Woodard** and **Lynn Whitfield** among the cast of seven black women. The performances—monologues with song and dance about the challenges of black women—were to an explosive, vivid choreopoem written by Ntozake Shange (who was also one of the performers). Unlike the stage production, the televised version had men in it. Shange, who had been criticized for putting down men in the choreopoem, said that the show is a "strongly feminist, woman-centered play." *See also* BROADWAY PLAYS AND MUSICALS.

FORD, THOMAS MIKAL. Ford was Tommy in the sitcom *Martin* (1992–1997) and Lt. Malcolm Barker in New York Undercover (1994–1998). He played the recurring role of Mel Parker on *The Parkers* (1999–2001).

FOREMAN, GEORGE. Foreman played George Foster, a husband and father and an ex–heavyweight boxer who trained high school boys in *George*, a 1993–1994 sitcom. *See also* GEORGE FOREMAN FIGHTS.

FORGIVE OR FORGET (*SYN, 1998–2000*). Mother Love, a former syndicated radio personality and actress, hosted this one-hour syndicated talk/relationship show in which guests confessed their wrongdoings in relationships. These could be romantic partners, siblings, friends, parent and child, or any personal relationship on the skids because of someone's transgressions. After the guest poured his or her heart out to Mother Love and the studio audience, he or she would go to the "forgiveness" door on the stage, and if the wronged person was in the doorway when the door opened, it meant that the guest was forgiven. If there was no one in the doorway, the rejected guest (and TV viewers) would view a videotaped message from the unforgiving person. The result was often emotional, and Mother Love would offer solace. In 2000, actress **Robin Givens** briefly assumed the hosting position on this series.

FOR LOVE OF OLIVIA (*CBS, March 18, 2001*). Louis Gossett Jr. and **Lonette McKee** starred in this two-hour film about a small southern town lawyer running for Congress who finds that, to protect his wife, he must defend a young man charged with murder.

FOR THE PEOPLE (*LIF, 2002–2003*). Debbi Morgan starred as strong-willed Los Angeles District Attorney Lora Gibson who battled her more ideologically liberal chief deputy, Camille Paris (Lea Thompson), as they worked together to convict criminals. This one-hour drama series was obviously female centered, but Professor Thomas Gibson (**Derek Morgan**) was in Lora's corner, while Public Defender Michael Olivas (A. Martinez) was Camille's ex-husband and ally.

FOR YOUR LOVE (*NBC, 1998; WB, 1998–2002*). This sitcom centered on three couples who lived in an upscale Chicago suburb; one couple was black, **James Lesure** and **Holly Robinson Peete**, who played happy newlyweds Mel and Malena Ellis. **Edafe Blackmon** was Mel's brother, Reggie. Mel was a lawyer, Malena was a psychiatrist, and Reggie was a restaurant owner. Reggie started out in the series as a confirmed bachelor, but he married Bobbi (**Tamala Jones**) eventually. Mel and Malena lived next door to the white couple, Dean and Sheri (D. W. Moffett and Sheri Winston), who were an integral part of the series. Uncle Omar Ellis (**Eugene Byrd**) joined the series in 2002. **Chaka Khan** and Michael McDonald sang the theme song written by Ed Townsend. *Variety* (September 21, 1998) called the show "a cute show with a good heart . . . not weighed down by stereotypes and stereotypical situations."

FOSTER AND LAURIE (CBS, November 13, 1975). Dorian Harewood, Jonelle Allen, Eric Laneuville, and Robert Aaron Brown had key roles in the two-hour made-for-television movie chronicling the story of two policemen who, in 1972, were killed in a brutal ambush by militant extremists terrorizing the New York City Police Department.

FOSTER, FRANCES. Foster played Mrs. Alberta King in the miniseries *King* in 1978.

FOSTER, GLORIA. Among Foster's numerous featured roles was *Top Secret* in 1978 and the role of an outspoken mother of a slain child in the made-for-television film *The Atlanta Child Murders* in 1985. She was born in 1933 and died of complications of diabetes in 2001.

FOSTER, JEAN RENEE. Foster had key roles in the TV films *Beulah Land* in 1980 and *Freedom Road* in 1979. She played Young Harriet Tubman in *A Woman Called Moses* in 1978.

413 HOPE STREET (*FOX, 1997–1998*). This drama series, created by **Damon Wayans** (who was also executive producer), was centered in a teen crisis center with the address 413 Hope Street in a low-income section of Manhattan. The unsalaried administrator was a lawyer, Phil Thomas (**Richard Roundtree**), and his wife, Juanita (**Shari Headley**). Others in the cast were **Jesse L. Martin**, Kelly Coffield, and Michael Easton.

FOUR TOPS, THE. The Motown group appeared in the Motown specials including *Motown 25 Yesterday, Today, and Tomorrow* (1984) and *Motown 45* (2004). It also entertained in the special *It's What's Happening* (1965) and numerous other specials and variety shows.

FOX, VIVICA A. Fox joined the cast of the FBI drama *Missing* in 2004, its second season. She had a key role in the miniseries *Solomom* and the TV film *Hendrix*, both in 2000. She had roles in several short-lived series including the daytime drama *Generations* (1989), the sitcom *Arsenio* in 1997, the sitcom *Getting Personal* in 1998, and the medical drama *City of Angels* (2000). She played **Patti LaBelle**'s daughter in the sitcom *Out All Night* (1992–1993).

FOXWORTH, JAIMEE. Foxworth played Judy Winslow in *Family Matters* (1989–1993).

FOXX, JAMIE. Foxx was a regular in the comedy-variety series *In Living Color* from 1991 to 1994. He played the recurring role of Crazy George on the sitcom *Roc* in 1992–1993. The stand-up comic had his own sitcom, *The Jamie Foxx Show* (1996–2001). He was interviewed in the tribute special *It's Black Entertainment* in 1997. He starred in a serious role in the TV film *Redemption* in 2004 and at the same time was making important moves toward feature film stardom. A week before his feature film *Ray* opened, he hosted the star-studded TV tribute concert *Genius: A Night for Ray Charles* (2004).

FOXX, REDD. Redd Foxx's first series was the sitcom *Sanford and Son* (1972–1977), followed by *Redd Foxx* (1977–1978), *Sanford* (1980–1981), *The Redd Foxx Show* (1986), and *The Royal Family* (1991–1992). He was a popular guest on variety series and specials, and even though he was known for his off-color, "blue" jokes, he was proud of the fact that he had never been "bleeped" on television during the era when censors would bleep profanities out of videotaped or time-delayed shows. He made several appearances on the Dean Martin roasts and was roasted himself on March 1, 1974. He entertained the troops abroad with Bob Hope in 1980; had his own special, *Redd Foxx*, in 1977; and was a guest on **Lola Falana**'s special in 1976. He appeared in the special *Motown Merry Christmas* in 1987 and was a part of the documentary *Amos 'n' Andy: Anatomy of a Controversy* (1986). He was a presenter at the *Prime Time Emmy Awards* in 1976 and was nominated for the **Emmy Award** but never won. He did win a Golden Globe for Best TV Actor in a Musical or Comedy in 1973 for his *Sanford and Son* role. Foxx was born in 1922 and died of a heart attack on the set of *The Royal Family* in 1991. *See also* REDD FOXX SPECIAL.

FRANCIS, CHERYL. Francis played a key role in the TV film *Sooner or Later* in 1979.

FRANKLIN, ARETHA. Aretha Franklin and Gloria Loring shared a special in 1968 titled *The Singers*. She sang in *Duke Ellington . . . We Love You Madly* in 1973. In 1990, she was celebrated along with other recording artists who had won Grammy Awards in the special *Grammy Legends*. She was the subject of a documentary *Aretha Franklin: The Queen of Soul* in 1988. Franklin was headliner and guest of honor as she sang duets with other famous singers in *Aretha Franklin: Duets* in 1993.

FRANKLIN, CARL. Franklin played the Bible-quoting runaway slave, Joshua Brown, in the western pilot *The Legend of the Golden Gun* in 1979.

FRANK, LIZA, AND SAMMY: THE ULTIMATE EVENT (*SHO, May 20, 1989*). **Sammy Davis Jr.**, Frank Sinatra, and Liza Minnelli sang solos and also sang together in this special originating from the Fox Theatre in Detroit.

FRANK'S PLACE (*CBS, 1987–1988*). **Tim Reid** starred as Boston professor Frank Parrish, who inherited a New Orleans Creole café, Chez Lousiane, from the father he never knew. Frank (Reid) ran the café surrounded with interesting characters played by **Daphne Maxwell Reid** (a mortician and love interest), **Frances Williams** (Miss Marie, former waitress), **Virginia Capers** (funeral parlor owner), Charles Lampkin, **Lincoln Kilpatrick** (Rev. Deal), Tony Burton (Big Arthur, the head chef), Don Yesso (Shorty, the assistant chef), Francesca P. Roberts (the waitress), and others. The show lasted only one season, but it was the subject of much talk in African-American settings during its run. It also was significant in that it did not have a laugh track. The Dixieland music in the background and **Louis Armstrong** singing "Do You Know What It Means to Miss New Orleans" were an important part of the series; in fact, the song was a resurrected hit. Critics were primarily positive about the show, though some admitted they didn't know what to think. *People Weekly* (September 14, 1987) said, "The cast is delightful. The food looks scrumptious. The jazz sounds delicious."

FRAZIER, JOE. *See* JOE FRAZIER FIGHTS.

FRAZIER, SHEILA. Frazier played a key role in the 1973 TV film *Firehouse*. She was Gloria St. Clair in the medical drama series *The Lazarus Syndrome* in 1979.

FREDERICK, HAL. Fredrick played Dr. Cal Barrin, one of five interns featured in the medical drama series *The Interns* (1970–1971). He was Makedde in the adventure series *Born Free* (1974).

FREEDOM EXPLOSION, THE (*CBS, February 15, 1960*). This news program on *CBS Reports* centered on Nigeria, which was scheduled to became independent from Great Britain the following October.

FREEDOM ROAD (*NBC, October 29 and 31, 1979*). **Muhammad Ali** starred in a four-hour historical drama, a miniseries about Gideon Jackson, a man who rose from slavery to the U.S. Senate. Consummate actor **James Earl Jones** said of Ali, "When given his own words, [he] was a great performer, but given somebody else's words, there was a self-consciousness he was unable to overcome." This, perhaps, explained Ali's performance in this miniseries, in which the well-known powerful personality and voice were reduced to nearly an inaudible whisper. Kris Kristofferson, who also starred in the production, said, "In my view he could have had a career as an actor, but nobody took the time to train him properly." The film's director, Jan Kadar, died shortly after production wrapped, and speculation arose that perhaps he was too ill to take the time or take on the task of helping Ali become an actor. The miniseries also costarred **Barbara O.** and **William Allen Young**. Kristofferson also recalled an incident that occurred during filming. "There was a scene in the film that Muhammad asked me to rehearse all the time with him. I don't know how many times we did it. I played a Georgia cracker, and it was where I called him a 'nigger.' Something about that tickled him to death; maybe because I was a skinny little white guy, and he could have torn me apart if he'd wanted." *See also* BIOPICS.

FREEDOM SONG (*TNT, February 27, 2000*). **Danny Glover** starred in this drama, the story of a civil rights movement in a small town as seen through the eyes of an African-American teenager Owen Walker **(Vicellous Reon Shannon)** growing up in racist Mississippi in the 1960s. Owen was impatient with his father's **(Vondie Curtis Hall)** passivity, so he joined the Student Nonviolent Coordinating Committee (SNCC) as it struggled to lead blacks to fight for their rights. **Loretta Devine** played Owen's mother. Laura Fries's review in *Variety* read, "The film mainly showcases Shannon—who proves his emotional turn in 'The Hurricane' was no fluke—and Curtis-Hall, whose understated turn is one of his best to date. Glover gets top billing, and his performance is powerful despite limited screen time. Picture is further enhanced by a cappella performances of spirituals and protest songs by Grammy Award winners Sweet Honey in the Rock."

FREEMAN, AL, JR. Freeman starred in *My Sweet Charlie*, a 1970 made-for-television film. He played Charles Bingham in the sitcom *Hot L Baltimore* in 1975 and Damon Lockwood in the miniseries *King* in 1978. He was Malcolm X in the miniseries *Roots: The Next Generations* in 1979. For many years, he played Ed Hall in the daytime drama *One Life to Live*. He won the **Emmy Award** for Best Actor for that role in 1979 and while accepting the statuette said, "Wouldn't you know it? After 24 years of being an actor, they tell me we're jammed for time."

FREEMAN, MORGAN. Children recognized Morgan Freeman long before adults because he was a regular feature, Easy Reader, on *The Electric Company*. He was a founding member of the Frank Silvera Writers' Workshop, named after noted black actor **Frank Silvera**. He appeared in the special *Alan King's Energy Crisis* in 1974, and he played Dr. Roy Bingham in the daytime drama *Another World* (1982–1984). In 1992, Freeman helped honor **Sidney Poitier** in an American Film Institute (AFI) Life Achievement Award in "AFI Salute to Sidney Poitier." He was the narrator of *The Atlanta Child Murders* (1985). In TV films, Freeman starred in *Hollow Image* (1979), *Attica* (1980), and *The Marva Collins Story* (1981).

FREEMAN, YVETTE. Freeman played Nurse Haleh Adams on *ER* (1994–) and Evelyn Smalley in the sitcom *Working* (1997–1998).

FRESH PRINCE OF BEL-AIR (*NBC, 1990–1996*). **Will Smith,** a rap artist who had never been an actor prior to this sitcom, starred as the character Will Smith, a kid from tough West Philadelphia. His mother sent him to live with his well-to-do Uncle Philip (**James Avery**) and Aunt Vivian (**Janet Hubert-Whitten**, 1990–1993) in the tony Bel-Air suburb of Los Angeles. **Quincy Jones**, whose company produced the sitcom, recalls having a meeting with Will Smith and NBC executives at his home. In selecting the lead for the series, there was concern that a rapper would be risky. Jones disagreed. Though Smith had no previous acting experience, Jones said, he "was asked to read a few pages of dialogue . . . after 15 minutes, he was hired." Jones added, "The first day of shooting, Will didn't know where the camera was—but he learned fast, and grew like a weed."

Uncle Phil and Aunt Viv had three children: stuffy, preppy teen Carlton (**Alfonso Ribeiro**); typical spoiled California brat Hilary (**Karyn Parsons**); and the youngest, a sweet impressionable grade schooler, Ashley (**Tatyana M. Ali**). The Banks family must have had income beyond Philip's salary as a judge and Vivian's as a college professor, but it was never revealed how the family could afford the lifestyle they enjoyed and the kids often abused. There was even a properly haughty British butler, Geoffrey (**Joseph Marcell**).

Smith's rapping partner in the Grammy Award–winning team Jazzy Jeff (**Jeff Townes**) and the Fresh Prince played Jazz from 1990 to 1994. He was Will's best buddy from the wrong side of the tracks, and Philip literally threw him out of the house on a regular basis.

Though they provided the children, including Will, with the comforts as well as the luxuries of life, Philip and Viv tried to instill in them a sense of earning one's own. Neither Philip nor Viv was born into wealth. Phil tried to be the strong, wise, male figure Will needed in his life. Will, on the other hand, taught the Banks family, especially the kids, about life in the ghetto, a world the parents had forgotten and a culture the kids had never known.

There was growth of the characters over the years of the series. Shallow Hilary got a job as a TV weather girl and became engaged to Trevor, a newscaster (**Brian Stokes Mitchell**) who later died in a bungee jump. Will and Carlton grew to understand each other better, graduated from high school, enrolled in college, and moved into a bachelor pad in the pool house. Vivian was pregnant and gave birth to little Nicky, who was played by Ross Bagley (1994–1996).

In the 1993–1994 season, several changes were made. The most noticeable to viewers was the change of actresses playing Vivian. Hubert-Whitten was fired. At first, she felt she was fired because of a vendetta waged by the network and the officials of the series; she had first been reduced to 13 episodes per season from 25, and her salary was also cut, according to *Jet* (August 9, 1993). After she fought back, she said she was fired. She admitted to being moody on the set because she was enduring a difficult pregnancy and had gained 65 pounds. A few weeks later, Will Smith was quoted as saying that Hubert-Whitten brought a lot of problems to work and that the problems lasted well beyond her pregnancy. He said, "I can say straight up that [she] wanted the show to be the 'The Aunt Viv of Bel Air Show'" (*Jet*, August 30, 1993). At the time of the cast change, Smith's production team took control of the series. At this point, Hubert-Whitten said she realized Smith played a role in her termination. She sued Smith and NBC, but the suit was not successful. Avery said later that Hubert-Whitten's departure was painful, that he missed the friendship. But he also said the series was "the best job in the world." The show continued with **Daphne Maxwell Reid** in the role of Vivian. She said the cast members "welcomed me with hugs."

Also in the 1993–1994 season, **Tyra Banks** played Jackie Aimes, Will's girlfriend from Philadelphia. In the 1994–1995 season, Ashley became a singer (paralleling Ali's actual debut as a recording artist with Smith coproducing her CD *Kiss the Sky*). Will had a new girlfriend, Lisa (**Nia Long**) in the final season, and the pair canceled their marriage and wedding as the series ended. At this point, Smith had completed filming of the feature film *Independence Day* and was ready for a big screen career. When he and wife **Jada Pinkett Smith** were executive producers of the sitcom *All of Us* (2003–), Smith saw to it that Ribeiro was hired as one of the directors. *See also* LONG-RUNNING SERIES.

FUNNY VALENTINES (*BET/Starz, February 14, 1999*). Alfre Woodard starred in this TV film as a well-to-do woman who walked away from her troubled marriage and moved to the South, where she grew up. Once there, she made efforts to mend a relationship with a cousin who was once her best friend. Others in the cast were **Loretta Devine, C. C. H. Pounder**, and **Yolanda King**. This was the first original production of BET Movies and Starz Pictures. The magazine *New York* (February 15, 1999) praised Devine and the production saying, "The resonant performance is Devine's, as Dearie, who is supposed to be slow but who is glorious. Devine's eye lights up everything in the natural world. . . . And it's precisely this rich texture that director [Julie] Dash, an African-American Matisse, has always sought with her sensuous camera."

– G –

GABRIEL'S FIRE (*ABC, 1990–1992*). **James Earl Jones** starred in this drama series as Gabriel Bird, a former policeman who was sent to prison for an act of heroism that was mistaken as an act of murder. After serving 20 years, he was released and became a private investigator for the attorney (Laila Robins) who was instrumental in getting him released. Empress Josephine (**Madge Sinclair**) was his longtime friend and the owner of a café where the angry Bird spent a lot of time. David Hiltbrand, in *People Weekly* (September 17, 1990), raved about the first episode but said, "As the series moves further from prison and more into your standard TV plots, Jones won't be afforded the substance to exercise his talents." The series did return for second season retitled *Pros and Cons* with a no-longer-angry Bird. He teamed up with another private eye (Richard Crenna) and eventually married Josephine, but the series ended.

GAINES, SONNY JIM. Gaines (aka James Gaines) played Trunk in the drama *Just an Old Sweet Song* in 1976. In 1979, he had roles in *I Know Why the Caged Bird Sings* and *Freedom Road*. In 1981, he was a key player in *The Sophisticated Gents*.

GALA FOR THE PRESIDENT AT FORD'S THEATRE (*ABC, March 27, 1997*). **Natalie Cole** hosted this evening of entertainment for President Bill Clinton at historic Ford's Theatre in Washington, D.C. **Gregory Hines** was among the performers.

GARRETT, SUSIE. Garrett, the sister of actress **Marla Gibbs**, played Betty Johnson on the **sitcom** *Punky Brewster* (1984–1986).

GARVIN, G. (*TV1, 2004–*). Gerry Garvin is the former executive chef of the Ritz Carlton and Morton's and more recently owner of the Los Angeles restaurant G. Garvin. He hosted this series of cooking techniques for the "culinary challenged." Offered were recipes and hints for both traditional and nontraditional dishes in African-American households.

GATHERING OF OLD MEN, A (*CBS, May 10, 1987*). Based on the Ernest Gaines novel of the same title, the plot centered on the murder of a white Louisiana farmer in the late 1970s. The farmer was hit with a single bullet from a shotgun. At the scene were a white woman and a group of elderly black men each holding a shotgun and each telling a conflicting and confusing story. Each man claimed to be the shooter, but the sheriff believed that not one of them could hit the side of the barn if they were in it. The situation taught the old men a lesson in what power they could have when they courageously stick together. **Louis Gossett Jr.** played Mathu. **Julius Harris** played Coot. **Joe Seneca** played Clatoo. Woody Strode played Yank. Papa John Creach, the jazz-rock violinist, played Jacob. Richard Widmark was the sheriff. The script was adapted by Charles Fuller.

GAYLE KING SHOW, THE (*SYN, 1997–1998*). Oprah's best friend, **Gayle King**, a popular news anchor in Hartford, Connecticut, hosted this half-hour talk/interview show with information about health, travel, parenting, and family life. The syndicated show reportedly had been approved by many stations for a second season, but all the contracts included performance clauses requiring higher ratings than the series earned.

GENDER AND TELEVISION. The display of gender in entertainment television often attracts media scholars as a topic of study, particularly scholars engaged in feminist or women's studies research. More recently, researchers and the entertainment industry have begun to delve into the presentation of masculinity, producing television programs such as *Queer Eye for the Straight Guy*.

In their respective works, Beretta E. Smith-Shomade and Sandra Dickerson examined African-American women on television. Dickerson examined sexual and racial stereotypes of African-American women. Dickerson argued that mainstream filmmakers created stereotypes of African-American women later picked up by television, including but not exclusive to the mammy, Aunt Jemima, and Sapphire, a character from the *Amos 'n' Andy* radio program described by Dickerson as wielding "a tongue as fast and furious as a jackhammer [who] dominated, emasculated and denigrated her husband." In her study of six popular network television programs, including *Amen*, *The Cosby Show*, and *A Different World*, Dickerson found Sapphire alive but better educated and communicating with "just one menacing glance, tilt of the head, or finger snap" rather than by emasculating insults.

Landmark representations of African-American women on television have occurred in all television genres including situation comedies, the news, music video, and the talk show, according to Smith-Shomade. For example, Anita Hill's testimony brought live coverage to **Clarence Thomas's Supreme Court Confirmation Hearings** and opened up the national discussion of sexual harassment in the workplace. Smith-Shomade also examined the rise and fall of the first African-American "Miss America," **Vanessa L. Williams**, a news story without peer in coverage of men no matter their race. And Oprah Winfrey's presence as talk show host "Queen of All Media," as crowned by *Newsweek*, must be noted. And lastly, it must be recalled that *Beulah*, a television show about an African-American maid, ranks among the first television shows ever.

Meanwhile, black masculinity as portrayed on television also prompted study, including portrayals of African-American males in the news. For example, in her discussion of major news stories of the 1990s, Diane McDaniel noted that African-American men often were in the center of what she calls media spectacles, news events often marked as "reveal[ing] the country in a light that it does not want the rest of the world to see." Moreover, most of the stories spoke to the long-held stereotypes of African-American men as threatening and brutish (Rodney King and **O. J. Simpson**) and highly sexual (**Magic Johnson** and Clarence Thomas). However, at the same time, such spectacular stories put African Americans at the center of national issues such as police brutality, the viability of the justice system, sexual harassment in the workplace, and the HIV/AIDS crisis.

Scholars also review African-American masculinity in entertainment programming. In her study of *A Different World*, Venita Ann Kelley found African-American male characters, including Dwayne Wayne, Ron Johnson, and Colonel Taylor, portrayed as intelligent, respectful of women, and showing a healthy sense of self-value and self-worth, a contrast to the characters such as Kingfish of *Amos 'n' Andy*, who plotted to keep his elaborate schemes from his wife, and the strutting and often obnoxious George Jefferson. Scholar Herman Gray found a particular bright spot in the presentation of black masculinity in an episode of the television show *Roc* in which Roc's Uncle Russell tells Roc and the rest of the family that he is gay and plans to marry his partner, a white man. **Richard Roundtree**, star of the *Shaft* movie franchise, played Russell. "By casting Roundtree as a gay black man in an interracial relationship, the producers both represented and then deconstructed black film constructions of black masculinity and heterosexuality," wrote Gray.

Sometimes, however, old ways of portraying gender persist. Kristal B. Zook noted that the female characters in *Fresh Prince of Bel-Air* often functioned in secondary story lines revolving around "shopping, dating, marriage, pregnancy and childrearing." Vivian, Ashley, and Hilary, asserted Zook, often remained objects of desire for men, not complex individuals with their own ideas. The Banks women often helped or needed help from the male characters, and such events generally received comic treatment. More dramatic events remained in the hands of the male characters Will, Geoffrey, Carlton, and Judge Philip Banks. And in his study of MTV's *The Real World*, Mark P. Orbe found that portrayals of black masculinity as "inherently angry, potentially violent, and sexually aggressive," traits emanating from long-standing stereotypes about black men as violent highly sexual brutes, persisted thanks to a variety of factors including nonsequential editing to create high drama, casting certain types to optimize conflict, and creative use of techniques such as montage and black-and-white film. In the six seasons Orbe studied, he found that *The Real World* lacked images presenting black masculinity in nonstereotypical ways and instead, arguably, strengthened "the justification of a general societal fear of black men."

GENE, GENE, THE DANCE MACHINE. This NBC stagehand danced on *The Gong Show* whenever host/producer Chuck Barris felt it appropriate. Gene Patton (his real name) was spotted by Barris dancing backstage, so Barris put him in front of the cameras. Patton said he earned enough to finance his children's college education.

GENERATIONS (*NBC, 1989*). *Generations* was the first daytime drama centering on an entire black family and not isolated black characters with few if any family connections. It also dealt with a white family, so TV critics called it a "desegregated soap." At the time, viewership statistics showed that blacks watched 14 hours a week during daytime hours compared to nine and a half hours watched by nonblacks. As John O'Connor of the *New York Times* said, "The time has come for a very profitable segment of commercial television to go beyond tokenism." The Marshalls (black) and the Whitmores (white) were linked once because the matriarch of the Marshalls, Vivian, had been a live-in housekeeper to the wealthy Rebecca Whitmore. However, that was in the past. Vivian retired, was going to college, and had a son-in-law with a successful business. The Marshalls had three generations of characters for story lines: Vivian, played by **Lynn Hamilton**; Vivian's daughter, Ruth, played by **Joan Pringle**; Ruth's husband, Henry, played by **Taurean Blacque**; and Ruth and Henry's children, Adam, played by **Kristoff St. John**, and Chantel, played by **Sharon Brown**. Pat Crowley played Rebecca Whitmore. The drama was canceled in 1991 because of low ratings. Various black groups campaigned to save the series, but to no avail. *Generations* was sold into foreign syndication and was licensed to **Black Entertainment Television** in 1991.

GENIUS: A NIGHT FOR RAY CHARLES (*CBS, October 22, 2004*). This one-hour tribute to 12-time Grammy Award winner **Ray Charles** aired four months after his death and one week before the nationwide opening of *Ray*, the feature film about his life starring **Jamie Foxx**. Foxx also hosted the TV concert. Considering Charles's music extended into rhythm and blues, country, patriotic, and pop, that diversity was reflected in the artists performing, who included **Stevie Wonder** ("I Got a Woman"), **Usher** ("Georgia on My Mind"), Al Green ("What'd I Say"), Elton John and **Mary J. Blige** ("Night

Time Is the Right Time"), Reba McIntire ("I Can't Stop Loving You"), and Kenny Chesney ("You Don't Know Me").

GENTRY, MINNIE. Gentry played Aunt Velvet in the drama *Just an Old Sweet Song* in 1976 and had a key role in *Hollow Image* in 1979.

GEORGE (*ABC, 1993–1994*). Champion boxer **George Foreman** starred in this **sitcom** as George Foster, a former heavyweight champion who decided to form an after-school boxing club at an inner-city high school. **Sheryl Lee Ralph** played his feisty wife, a guidance counselor at the same school. Tony T. Johnson and Lauren Robinson played their children.

GEORGE FOREMAN FIGHTS. George Foreman's first professional fight, against Don Waldheim, was televised on June 28, 1969. He fought Ken Norton and won by a second-round technical knockout on a telecast on March 31, 1974. He lost to **Muhammad Ali** in "The Rumble in the Jungle" fight from Zaire, Africa, on January 5, 1975. *See* BOXING MATCHES ON TELEVISION.

GEORGE, JASON. George (aka Jason Winston George) played J. T. Hunter in the sitcom *Eve*, which began in the fall of 2003. He had roles in the daytime drama *Sunset Beach* for three years and played a regular role in the short-lived prime-time drama *Titans* in 2000. In the spring of 2003, he had a lead role in the serial drama *Platinum*. He played the rap-singing neighbor in the sitcom *Off Centre* (2001–2002).

GEORGE KIRBY SPECIAL, THE (*ABC, December 18, 1970*). The comedian hosted the special with comedy sketches and music with guests the Mills Brothers, Lainie Kazan, Joe Higgins, The Lighthouse, and the Poppy Family.

GEORGE MCKENNA STORY, THE (*CBS, 1986*). **Denzel Washington** starred in the title role as the new principal of an infamously violent high school in Los Angeles. McKenna, with the help of his girlfriend, played by **Lynn Whitfield**, was determined to turn the school around and get rid of the gangs, the drugs, and the weapons.

Akosua Busia and **Virginia Capers** had key roles. **Eric Laneuville** was director.

GET CHRISTIE LOVE (TV film) (*ABC, January 22, 1974*). **Teresa Graves** starred as a super-undercover lady cop in the Special Investigations Division of the Los Angeles Police Department in this TV movie, which also became a series (1974–1975). In the film, Graves was a policewoman who went undercover to break up a drug empire. **Davis Roberts** had a key role in the film.

GET CHRISTIE LOVE (TV series) (*ABC, 1974–1975*). **Teresa Graves** starred in television's first police drama series to headline an African-American actress. It was based loosely on the real-life adventures of a New York City detective and was reportedly written for **Cicely Tyson**. Sexy Christie Love was skilled at karate and was charming, witty, and hip. She called everyone, including criminals, "Sugah." Many of today's female police officers say their ambitions to join law enforcement stemmed from watching this series when they were children. After one season, Graves quit acting to be a devout Jehovah's Witness.

GET THE HOOK-UP (*TV1, 2004– *). In this updated, soulful dating game, the African-American player always got the date because all the contestants were black. To be selected, the contestant had to show evidence of a skill (like baking a perfect cake) or display a talent (like seductive dancing). Hosts were Russ Parr and Aldredas, personalities from Radio One (parent company of TV One). The vocal studio audience added to the partylike atmosphere.

GIBBS, MARLA. Gibbs earned television fame as Florence on *The Jeffersons* (1975–1985). She went on to star in *Checking In* (1981), her own spin-off series, and *227* (1985–1990). In TV films, she had key roles in *Menu For Murder* (1990) and Lily In Winter (1994). She provided voices for the animated series *Happily Ever After: Fairy Tales For Every Child* (1995) and 1*01 Dalmatians: The Series* (1997).

GIBSON, KENDIS. Gibson joined CNN in January 2002 as entertainment and culture anchor and correspondent for *CNN Headline News*. He started his career in local television and with NBC's *Today Show*.

GIFT OF AMAZING GRACE, THE (*ABC, November 19, 1986*). A drama special, this one-hour program was about a family of gospel singers, the Williams family. For generations, the family members had been known for their voices. However, Grace, the youngest daughter, would lip-sync with the family because she felt her voice was inadequate. A crisis occurred when the family was scheduled to appear on a television show and was offered a recording contract. Should Grace admit her problem or quit? **Tempestt Bledsoe** played Grace, **Della Reese** played Aunt Faith, and Sam Wright played Morris.

GILLESPIE, DIZZY. Gillespie performed in the *Timex All-Star Jazz Show IV* (1959), in *Bill Cosby Special, Or?* (1971), and in the *All-Star Swing Festival* and the *Big Band and All That Jazz* specials (1972). He performed in the *Original Rompin' Stompin' Hot and Heavy, Cool and Groovy All-Star Show* (1976). In 1990, he was among the honored musicians and singers in *Grammy Legends*, and in the same year he was honored in *The Kennedy Center Honors*. Born in 1917, Gillespie died of pancreatic cancer in 1993. *See also* TELEVISION PIONEERS.

GILLIAM, STU. A veteran stand-up comedian and ventriloquist, Gilliam was a regular on the summer variety series *Dean Martin Presents* in 1968. He starred as Corporal Sweet Williams on *Roll Out* in 1973 and played Charlie in the TV movie *Love Is Not Enough* in 1978 and the subsequent drama series *Harris and Company* in 1979. In afternoon children's dramas, Gilliam had roles in *The Haunted Trailer* in 1977 and *Henry Hamilton, Graduate Ghost* in 1984. In TV movies, he had a key role in *Three's a Crowd* in 1969.

GILYARD, CLARENCE, JR. Gilyard was Officer Webster in the police drama *Chips* (1982–1983), Conrad McMaster in the drama *Matlock* (1989–1993), and Jimmy Trivette in the western drama *Walker, Texas Ranger* (1993–2001). In TV films, he had roles in *The Kid with the 200 I.Q.* (1983), *L.A. Takedown* (1989), and *The Big One: The Great Los Angeles Earthquake* (1990).

GIMME A BREAK (*NBC, 1981–1987*). Tony Award–winning musical star **Nell Carter** starred as housekeeper Nell Harper, who worked for a widowed police chief (Dolph Sweet) who had three daughters (Lara Jill Miller, Lauri Hendler, and Kari Michelson) ranging in age from preteen to nearly adult. She was a friend to the chief and a nanny to the girls. When the series began, an NBC executive was asked why a show developed for Nell had to have her play a housekeeper. The executive responded, "What else could she play?" There were various additions to the cast as the show attempted to attract viewers. In 1984, **Telma Hopkins** joined the regular cast as Addy, Nell's best friend. In 1986, **Rosetta LeNoire** was added as Maybell "Mama" Harper. In February 1985, the series was the first situation comedy in 30 years to go on the air live. Television sitcoms generally retape or refilm scenes in which actors flub lines or make the wrong moves. Most of the cast had theater experience and was professional enough to perform without making errors. Several taped episodes had already been done without error. So producers agreed to try the live broadcast before an audience of friends, relatives, and network executives. It worked right down to the curtain call, and Carter yelled, "We did it!" Sweet died later that same year; the series lasted one more year with more cast additions. *See also* DOMESTICS IN THE 1980s; LONG-RUNNING SERIES.

GIMPEL, ERICA. Gimpel played Coco Hernandez in the series *Fame* (1982–1983) and played Adele Newman in the series *ER* beginning in 1997. She had a recurring role as Suzanne Duff in *Roswell* (1999). In TV films, she had roles in the following: *Intimate Betrayal* (1999), *The Price of Love* (1995), *Women & Wallace* (1990), *Case Closed* (1988), and the miniseries *North and South* (1985) and *North and South II* (1986).

GIRLFRIENDS (*UPN, 2000–*). This sitcom centered on four friends facing problems with relationships, careers, and family. Joan (**Tracee Ellis Ross**), Maya (**Golden Brooks**), Toni (**Jill Marie Jones**), and Lynn (**Persia White**) were the girls, and William (Reggie Hayes) was their honorary boyfriend.

GIST, CAROL ANNE-MARIE. Gist was the first black woman to be crowned Miss U.S.A. on March 2, 1990. Later, she was first runner-up in the Miss Universe pageant.

GIVENS, ROBIN. After playing a guest-star role on *The Cosby Show*, Givens's stock went up in Hollywood. Hers became a recognizable face when she portrayed Darlene, the rich girl, on the popular teeny-bopper sitcom *Head of the Class* from 1986 to 1991. While playing Darlene, she played Kiswana Browne in the miniseries *The Women of Brewster Place* in 1989. She had a starring role in the police drama *Angel Street* in 1992, but the series lasted less than a month after reports that Givens and costar Pamela Gidley were as hostile with each other offscreen as on. The ratings were also very low. In 1995, she was investigator Suzanne Graham in *Courthouse*, a legal drama that lasted two months. Her next series lasted two years, 1996 to 1998; it was the sitcom *Sparks*, on which she played Wilma Cuthbert, the sexy law school grad working in an inner-city law firm. She was the host of the syndicated relationship show *Forgive or Forget* in 2000.

GLADYS KNIGHT AND THE PIPS: MIDNIGHT TRAIN TO GEORGIA (*NBC, June 21, 1974*). The popular recording group starred in a one-hour variety special with Tom T. Hall as a guest.

GLADYS KNIGHT AND THE PIPS SHOW, THE (*NBC, 1975*). This musical-variety series highlighting the popular musical group (**Gladys Knight**), her brother Merald "Bubba" Knight, and her cousins William Guest and Edward Patten ran for a planned four weeks in the summer. They sang their hits and performed comedy sketches with guest stars who also performed their specialties.

GLADYS KNIGHT AND THE PIPS WITH RAY CHARLES (*SYN, August 1987*). This one-hour musical concert was videotaped at the Greek Theatre in Los Angeles and featured Gladys Knight and the Pips and the great Ray Charles.

GLASS, RON. Glass earned television fame playing Detective Ron Harris on the sitcom *Barney Miller* (1975–1982). Following that, he starred in the black version of the sitcom *The Odd Couple* as Felix Unger (1982–1983). He was Don Phillips in the brief sitcom *Rhythm and Blues* (1992), Ronald Felcher in *Mr. Rhodes* (1996–1997), and The Head who called himself God's cousin in the sitcom *Teen Angel* (1997–1998). He was Book in the sci-fi series *Firefly* (2002) and the voice of Randy Carmichael in *Rugrats* beginning in 1991. In television films, he had key roles in *Crash* (1978), *Gus Brown and Midnight Brewster* (1985), and *Incognito* (1999).

GLENN, ROY. Glenn played various sophisticated roles, like businessmen, on *Amos 'n' Andy*. He may be best known for his portrayal of **Sidney Poitier**'s father in the feature film *Guess Who's Coming to Dinner*. Glenn played Lieutenant Frank Miller in the TV movie *The Pigeon* starring **Sammy Davis Jr.** in 1969. *See also* TELEVISION PIONEERS.

GLOVER, DANNY. Glover had guest-star roles in television dramas and sitcoms, then starred in the 1987 biopic *Mandela*. In 1989, he played Walter Lee, the son in *A Raisin in the Sun*. He had key or starring roles in the TV films *The Face of Rage* in 1983, *Alex Haley's Queen* in 1993, *Buffalo Soldiers* in 1997, *Freedom Song* in 2000, and *Good Fences* in 2003. Glover was also a producer of *Good Fences*. He was a guest on the special *All-Star Tribute to Kareem Abdul-Jabbar* in 1989. He hosted the documentary series *Civil War Journal* in 1993–1995. In 1995, he was executive producer of HBO's *America's Dream* and played the role of Silas.

GLOVER, SAVION. Tap dancer Glover performed in *It Just Takes One*, a special addressing tolerance, discrimination, and hate through dance, poetry, and song, in 1997. Also in 1997, he performed at *The 53rd Presidential Inaugural Gala: An American Journey*. The following year, he headlined *In Performance at the White House: Savion Glover—Stomp, Slide, and Swing*. In 2001, he danced in the TV film *Bojangles*, starring his mentor, **Gregory Hines**, and in 1998, he played Bracey Mitchell in *The Wall*. He made appearances on *Sesame Street* from 1990 to 1995. In 1989, he was one of the stars of *Tap Dance in America*.

GOING PLATINUM WITH CHARLEY PRIDE (*SHO, October 11, 1980*). The *Going Platinum* series of six specials aired in 1980. Each was a one-hour solo performance by a recording artist with record sales that had gone platinum. **Charley Pride** was the center of the final special of the series. Others were the Beach Boys, Journey, Stephen Stills, Charlie Daniels, and **Smokey Robinson** (see next entry).

GOING PLATINUM WITH SMOKEY ROBINSON (*SHO, May 15, 1980*). The *Going Platinum* series of six specials aired in 1980. Each was a one-hour solo performance by a recording artist with record sales that had gone platinum. This one starred **Smokey Robinson**, who had hits as a solo artist as well as when he was leader of the group **Smokey Robinson and the Miracles**.

GOLDBERG, WHOOPI. Goldberg starred in the three-hour benefit for the homeless, *Comic Relief* in 1986, and subsequently cohosted several more with Billy Crystal and Robin Williams. She starred in "My Past Is My Own," a *CBS Schoolbreak Special* in 1989, the same year she guest-starred on the special *All-Star Tribute to Kareem Abdul-Jabbar*. She starred in the sitcom *Bagdad Café* (1990). She played Gaia in *Captain Planet and the Planeteers* in 1990. She played a recurring role for five seasons on *Star Trek: The Next Generation* as Guinan (1988–1993). Goldberg played the queen in the musical *Cinderella* in 1997. She sat in the center square of the revived *The Hollywood Squares* game show (1998–2002) and was coexecutive producer. She hosted *Here's to You Charlie Brown: 50 Great Years!* in 2000. She starred in the TV film *Call Me Claus* in 2001. She starred in and produced the TV film *Good Fences* in 2003. She hosted the *Academy Awards Ceremonies* in 1994, 1996, 1999, and 2002.

Goldberg hosted her own syndicated talk show, *The Whoopi Goldberg Show* (1992–1993). She had HBO specials of her stand-up comedy act, like 1985's *Whoopi Goldberg—Direct from Broadway*. In 1997, Goldberg played Nurse Myrna in the TV dramatic film *In the Gloaming*. She starred in *A Knight in Camelot* in 1998 as Dr. Vivien Morgan, a computer research scientist who gets zapped back to A.D. 589 and Camelot. In 1999, Goldberg played the Cheshire Cat in the three-hour Disney production of *Alice in Wonderland*. She was creator and executive producer of the drama *Strong Medicine*, which premiered in 2000. Hers was the voice of Deborah Samson in the animated series *Liberty's Kids* (2002–2003). In the 2003–2004 season, she starred in the sitcom *Whoopi*.

GOLDEN AGE OF JAZZ, THE (*CBS, January 7, 1959*). This hour of music was hosted by Jackie Gleason with guests **Louis Armstrong**, **Duke Ellington**, **Dizzy Gillespie**, Gene Krupa, and George Shearing.

GOLDEN MOMENT—AN OLYMPIC LOVE STORY, THE (*NBC, May 25–26, 1980*). This four-hour miniseries was supposed to build up the anticipation of the 1980 Olympic Games and was centered on a romance between an American decathlon aspirant (David Keith) and a Russian gymnast (Stephanie Zimbalist). **Richard Lawson** and **James Earl Jones** played key roles. **Bryant Gumbel, O. J. Simpson**, Charlie Jones, Dick Enberg, and Bruce Jenner played themselves. The film did not achieve its goal because the United States withdrew from the games.

GOLDIE AND THE BOXER (*NBC, December 20, 1979*). **O. J. Simpson** starred with Melissa Michaelsen in this TV film in which unknown boxer Joe Gallagher (Simpson) is encouraged by Goldie (Michaelsen), the 10-year-old daughter of his best friend, a deceased boxing champion. Joe goes on to win the title. Vincent Gardenia and Phil Silvers played key roles. Ratings were high enough to warrant a sequel, *Goldie and the Boxer Go to Hollywood*, in 1981.

GOLDIE AND THE BOXER GO TO HOLLYWOOD (*NBC, February 19, 1981*). **O. J. Simpson** starred in this two-hour film and was executive producer. It was the sequel to 1979's *Goldie and the Boxer*. The story centered on heavyweight champ Joe Gallagher (Simpson) and his 10-year-old manager (Melissa Michaelsen) who fled to Hollywood to evade a crooked promoter who lost money on a fight and wanted revenge. **Lynne Moody** had a key role.

GOLER, WENDELL. Goler joined Fox News Channel at its inception in 1996. As White House correspondent, he has covered stories ranging from President Bill Clinton's impeachment to President George W. Bush's post–September 11, 2001, policy initiatives and all presidential news conferences.

GOODE, MALVIN "MAL." Goode was the first black news correspondent for a television network when he was hired by ABC News in 1962. Jackie Robinson had recommended him for the position based on his years of experience in newspapers and local television news in Pennsylvania. He was known for his coverage of the Cuban missile crisis and United Nations activities. He retired after 20 years but remained an ABC news consultant. He was a mentor to **Bernard Shaw** and George Strait. He also became the first black member of the National Association of Radio and Television News Directors in 1971.

GOOD EVENING, CAPTAIN (*CBS, August 21, 1981*). This special airing in prime time celebrated a longtime star of morning television: Captain Kangaroo. Bob Keeshan, who had played Captain Kangaroo for 25 years, was the host. His guests included **Todd Bridges, Ja'net DuBois, Kim Fields, Ted Lange**, and **LaWanda Page**.

GOOD FENCES (*SHO, February 2, 2003*). This two-hour made-for-television film centered on an ambitious 1970s African-American attorney who, with his family, moved into an upscale all-white neighborhood. The family adapted to its new community until a new neighbor moved next door and a shocking legacy of racism arose. **Danny Glover, Whoopi Goldberg**, and **Mo'Nique** were the stars. **Spike Lee**, Sam Kitt, Goldberg, and Glover were producers.

GOODING, CUBA, JR. Gooding played Tyree in the TV film *Murder without Motive: The Edmund Perry Story* (1992). He was listed as one of "12 Promising New Actors of 1991." The promise was good because he won the Academy Award for his supporting role in the 1996 feature film *Jerry Maguire*. Earlier, he was a noncelebrity contestant on *The New Dating Game* (1986); he did not get the date. A dancer who once backed up Paula Abdul, he performed a break dance in the 1984 closing ceremonies of the Olympic Games in Los Angeles. Cuba and **Omar** are brothers and sons of Cuba Gooding Sr., lead singer of the Main Ingredient.

GOODING, OMAR. Gooding played Mo in the sitcom *Smart Guy* (1997–1999) and Earvin in the sitcom *Hangin' with Mr. Cooper* (1992–1997). He played Marcus in the TV film *The Ernest Green Story* (1993). He also starred in the sitcom *Barbershop* beginning in 2005. Omar and **Cuba** are brothers and sons of Cuba Gooding Sr., lead singer of the Main Ingredient.

GOOD NEWS (*UPN, 1997–1998*). Nicknamed "Amen 2," this sitcom was set in a Christian church, specifically The Church of Life, in

Compton, California. Unlike *Amen* (1986–1991), this series concentrated on the music of the church more than the business of the church. The central character, the new pastor, David Randolph (David Ramsey), tried to rebuild the church and started with the choir. **Roz Ryan**, a singer-actress who was a member of the *Amen* cast, played Mrs. Dixon, the church cook in this series. She said, "Our show takes place mostly in the sanctuary and we deal much more with the music. . . . The issues are also a lot deeper." The issues were condoms, homosexuality, racism, and teen pregnancy—all presented in a comedy story line. Alexa Robinson, Tracey Cherelle Jones, Guy Torrey, Jazsmin Lewis, and **Billy Preston** were also cast members.

GOOD TIMES (*CBS, 1974–1979*). When this sitcom made its debut on February 1, 1974, it was the great black hope for television. There had never been a show about a black family on television with a mother and father and children under the same roof. *Julia* had aired from 1968 to 1971, but there was no father in the family, and most of the cast was white. *Sanford and Son* aired from 1972 to 1977, but there was no mother, and the son was an adult. In addition, there had been complaints by black people that Julia and her son Corey (**Diahann Carroll** and **Marc Copage**) lived too well, that the situation was unrealistic (though that was not the case). So *Good Times* was to be the answer to all of these problems. The series was created by Eric Monte and **Michael Evans** and was a spin-off of **Maude**, which was a spin-off of **All in the Family**. All of them were Norman Lear productions. Florida Evans, played by **Esther Rolle**, had been Maude's housekeeper.

The series was basically about Florida's home life—her loving husband, James (**John Amos**), and their three children: 17-year-old J.J. (**Jimmie Walker**), 16-year-old Thelma (**BernNadette Stanis**), and grade schooler Michael (**Ralph Carter**). They lived in a Chicago housing project and struggled to get ahead. Willona Woods (**Ja'net DuBois**) was their neighbor who always got applause from the studio audience on both her entrance and her exit. Most Norman Lear comedies dealt with serious issues, and *Good Times* was no exception. Viewers would listen to the catchy opening song about how lucky we are to have good times. Then they would watch an episode dealing with the most depressing aspects of ghetto life. There was gang violence, crime, illness, no heat in a cold tenement, much unemployment, substance abuse, welfare, and child abuse. J.J., the senior and best deliveryman for a chicken franchise, lost his job. James, expecting a promotion, was fired. On another occasion, James spent Thelma's college fund for Florida's surgery. The Evans family was never lucky. It was always one step forward and two steps backward. But love abounded among family members despite bickering among the children.

Then problems happened within the show. John Amos and Esther Rolle became disenchanted with the direction of the show. They expected episodes about serious issues with lessons and positive role models for viewers, all within the realm of comedy. Instead, the J.J. character grew popular with the studio and home audiences, especially his catchphrase "Dy-no-mite!" This is a frequent occurrence in television; one character "breaks out" as the most popular character. It was Fonzie in *Happy Days*. It was Steve Urkel in **Family Matters**. Although it was not the series the producers planned, producers generally run with the breakout character hoping for sustained popularity and high ratings. High ratings trump quality. That is what happened with J.J. He was the comic relief in the dismal life of the Evans family, and viewers liked him. This was not a personal attack on Jimmie Walker, who stayed out of the debate, saying, "I'm no actor. I'm a comic who lucked into a good thing."

Critical viewers sided with Amos and Rolle, saying that the J.J. character was a buffoon not unlike the clownish dumb coon types of the old minstrel shows. Both actors expressed their discontent, but to no avail. After they told their story to *Ebony* magazine, Lear was reportedly so upset that he released Amos from his contract in 1976. Amos worried about the stereotypical nature of the characters and later told interviewer Margretta Browne, "It was an ongoing struggle to say no, I don't want to be a part of the perpetuation of this stereotype. . . . It ultimately reached a point where it was inflammable. . . . They killed my character off and, as God would have it, just when they told me I would never work again, I got cast in a little program called **Roots**, and as they would say, the rest is history. I could have begged and they made it obvious to me that if I wanted to come back and be a good boy . . . but I'd rather say 'Toby be good nigger in *Roots*' than 'Toby be good nigger on *Good Times*.'"

When Amos left, the character James Evans died in a car accident, making the Evans family another fatherless television family, something Rolle fought against from the beginning. Rolle left in 1977, and the character Florida, always a loving mother, married again, leaving her children with neighbor Willona, who had already adopted a girl (**Janet Jackson**) who had been abused by her natural mother. The building super (**Johnny Brown**) was also added to the cast for comedic value. Then Rolle returned in 1978 after producers promised to tone down the J.J. character. J.J. was already established as a talented artist; African-American artist **Ernie Barnes** was the real creator of the paintings displayed frequently in the series. The Evans daughter Thelma married a pro football player, and life looked up; then her husband suffered a leg injury that ended his career. The series ended original episodes in 1979. *See also* LONG-RUNNING SERIES.

GOODWIN, KIA JOY. Goodwin (aka Kia Goodwin) was Tiffany Holloway, Rose's daughter, in the sitcom *227* (1985–1986). In TV films, she played Latisha Jordan in *Strapped* (1993) and Lady Bryce in *Platinum* (2003).

GORDON, CARL. Gordon played Andrew Emerson on the sitcom *Roc* (1991–1994). He was a key player in the TV drama *The Piano Lesson* in 1995. He had a key role in the three-part TV film *Love Songs* in 1999.

GORE, GEORGE O., II. Gore's first regular role in a television series was as "G" (alias Gregory), the young son of J.C. (Malik Yoba), in *New York Undercover* (1994–1998). He was later cast as the teenage Junior in the comedy series *My Wife and Kids* in 2001.

GOSPEL CHALLENGE (*TV1, 2004– *). This one-hour, weekly gospel music competition featured leading black church choirs in performance battles. Host Jonathan Slocumb traveled across the United States searching for outstanding choirs. Gospel experts judged videotaped performances until one winner was selected. The culmination of the contests presented four finalist choirs in a live championship concert in Richmond, Virginia, when the winning choir received a recording contract.

GOSPEL OF MUSIC WITH JEFF MAJOR, THE (*TV1, 2004–*). This weekly hour of gospel music featured contemporary artists as Mary Mary, Kirk Franklin, and Yolanda Adams as well as such traditional gospel artists as Odetta, Shirley Caesar, the Blind Boys of Alabama, and Albertina Walker. Also included was gospel hip-hop, gospel folk music, quartets, and large urban megachoirs. Gospel harpist and radio personality Jeff Majors was host/performer.

GOSSETT, LOUIS, JR. The actor (aka Lou Gossett) played Fiddler in the 1977 miniseries *Roots* and won an **Emmy Award** for the second episode for Outstanding Lead Actor for a Single Appearance in a Drama or Comedy Series. In the 1979 miniseries *Backstairs at the White House*, Gossett was Levi, the butler and footman. He was nominated for the Emmy Award for this role. In 1983, he played the title role in the miniseries *Sadat*.

In 1979, Gossett starred in the short-lived drama series *The Lazarus Syndrome*. Gossett had starring or key roles in numerous TV films including 1974's *Sidekicks* based on the 1971 feature film *Skin Game*, in which he also starred. The film was a pilot for a series that was not sold. He had a major role in the made for television films *Little Ladies of the Night* in 1977, *To Kill a Cop* in 1978, *This Man Stands Alone* in 1979, *Benny's Place* in 1982, *It's Good to Be Alive* in 1984, and *A Gathering of Old Men* in 1987. He was an actor in the drama special *Zora Is My Name* in 1990. He starred in the 1995 TV films *Zooman* and *A Father for Charlie*, the 1996 TV film *Captive Heart: The James Mink Story*, the 2000 TV film *The Color of Love: Jacey's Story*, the 2001 TV film *For Love of Olivia*, and the 2003 film *Jasper, Texas*. Gossett starred in a segment of the trilogy TV film *Love Songs* and directed another in 1999. In 2004, he joined the cast of *Half & Half* as Spencer's long-lost father. Gossett had a key role in the 2005 TV film *Lackawanna Blues*.

GOSSETT, ROBERT. The actor, who is also Lou Gossett's cousin, had roles in *Heartbeat* (1989), *Silk Stalkings* (1992–1993), and *The Closer* (2005–).

GO TELL IT ON THE MOUNTAIN (*PBS, January 14, 1985*). Paul Winfield, James Bond III, Olivia Cole, and Rosalind Cash starred in this television film based on the novel of the same title by James Baldwin. Largely autobiographical, it told the story of a poor black boy growing up in Harlem under the tyranny of his father, a rigidly autocratic preacher who hated his son. This was an *American Playhouse* presentation. The film spanned the lives of three generations, using flashbacks to tell the searing stories of love and loss and the damage wrought by hypocrisy and racism. Baldwin said the book "is the book I had to write. I had to deal with what hurt me most. I had to deal, above all, with my father. He was my model; I learned a lot from him. Nobody's ever frightened me since."

GOTTA MAKE THIS JOURNEY: SWEET HONEY IN THE ROCK (*PBS, February 15, 1984*). This one-hour film about the a cappella singing group Sweet Honey in the Rock showed quick looks at the lives of the members and showed how their music and their backgrounds, personal lives, and politics were related. Black notables were interviewed, including Alice Walker, the Rev. Ben Chavis, Angela Davis, and others. The original members in their 1973 debut performance were Evelyn Harris, Patricia Johnson, Carol Lynne Maillard, Bernice Johnson Reagon (founder), and Louise Robinson.

GRACE BUMBRY AND SHIRLEY VERRET IN CONCERT AT COVENT GARDEN (*PBS, April 25, 1984*). Sopranos Bumbry and Verret hosted a 90-minute special celebrating the 250th anniversary of Covent Garden in London. The concert was taped at London's Royal Opera House. The program included duets and arias by Verdi, Bellini, and Ponchielli.

GRADY (*NBC, 1975–1976*). This sitcom was a spin-off of the popular **Sanford and Son** and starred **Whitman Mayo** as Grady, Fred Sanford's buddy. The plotline was that Grady's son-in-law (Joe Morton) accepted a position as a professor at UCLA and moved his family—wife (Carol Cole) and children (Rosanne Katon and **Haywood Nelson**)—to Westwood. Grady moved with them and found living out of the ghetto odd. This series was an attempt to sell the public on a sitcom with a middle-class black family, but viewers didn't buy it. It lasted three months.

GRAMBLING'S WHITE TIGER (*NBC, October 4, 1981*). This two-hour made-for-television film was about a white quarterback on the previously all-black legendary football team at Grambling College in Louisiana. Grambling, with a record of turning out professional football players, was appealing to Jim Gregory (Bruce Jenner) even though he had to learn lessons in being a minority. **Harry Belafonte** played Coach Eddie Robinson. **Dennis Haysbert** was James "Shack" Harris. **LeVar Burton** was Charles "Tank" Smith. **Bill Overton, Deborah Pratt**, and **Ray Vitte** played key roles. Several notable blacks were in behind-the-scenes positions; among them were **Georg Stanford Brown** as director, **Scoey Mitchlll** as associate producer, and Joseph M. Wilcotts as director of photography. *See also* BIOPICS.

GRAMMY AWARDS, THE. This annual extravaganza, which began in 1958, celebrates the music industry and is sponsored by the National Academy of Recording Arts and Sciences.

GRAMMY LEGENDS (*CBS, December 11, 1990***).** A two-hour special paying tribute to recording artists who won Grammy Awards, this special was hosted by **Oprah Winfrey, Stevie Wonder**, Larry Gatlin, and James Woods. The honored guests included **Aretha Franklin, Quincy Jones**, Andrae Crouch, **Dizzy Gillespie, Lionel Hampton, Ice T** and Quincy D, James Ingram, Eddie Kendricks, Chaka Khan, Ben E. King, and **Smokey Robinson.**

GRAMMY LIFETIME ACHIEVEMENT AWARDS (*CBS, December 9, 1987***).** This two-hour tribute special honored six recording artists with the Grammy Lifetime Achievement Award. They were the following: **Ray Charles, Fats Domino, B. B. King**, Roy Acuff, Benny Carter, and Isaac Stern. **Dionne Warwick** and Beverly Sills were hosts. Guests praising the six in words or song included the following: **Ed Bradley, Natalie Cole, Carmen McRae**, and James Moody.

GRANT, SARINA. Grant had a key role in the 1978 television film *Ring of Passion*. Other TV films in her list of credits include *A Dream for Christmas* (1973), *A Guide for the Married Woman* (1978), *A Matter of Life and Death* (1981), *Money on the Side* (1982), *Life of the Party: The Story of Beatrice* (1982), and *My Mother's Secret Life* (1984).

GRAVES, TERESA. Graves was a regular on *Rowan and Martin's Laugh-In* (1969–1970), one of the bikini-clad girls whose bodies were painted with catch phrases like "Sock it to me." After *Laugh-In*, she starred in 1971's comedy-variety series *The Funny Side* about married couples. Then she got the starring role in the drama series *Get Christie Love* (1974–1975) as a lady cop. She appeared on a Bob Hope special in 1982, but she had already decided to drop her acting career to be a faithful Jehovah's Witness. She died in a fire at her home in the Hyde Park area of Los Angeles in 2002. She was 54.

GREAT GILDERSLEEVE, THE (*SYN, 1955*). This sitcom starred Willard Waterman as Thockmorton Gildersleeve, a utilities commissioner in a fictitious town. Gildersleeve was a bachelor who had been charged with caring for his niece and nephew. **Lillian Randolph** played the housekeeper, Birdie, who took on the responsibilities of the woman of the house. *See also* SERIES WITH ONE BLACK SUPPORTING ACTOR/PERFORMER BEFORE 1980.

GREEN EYES (*ABC, January 3, 1977*). **Paul Winfield** starred in this two-hour made-for-television film as Lloyd Dubeck, a Vietnam War veteran who returns to Southeast Asia to search, among thousands of war orphans, for the son he left behind. **Royce Wallace** played Mrs. Dubeck, and **Robert DoQui** played Hal.

GREEN PASTURES, THE (*NBC, October 17, 1957*). Under the umbrella title of the *Hallmark Hall of Fame*, this comedy-drama, which had already been a hit on Broadway and had an all-black cast, was about life in heaven. The stories came to life as a Sunday school teacher preached to students. **William Warfield** was "de Lawd" (the Lord), **Earle Hyman** (later to be Cliff Huxtable's father on *The Cosby Show*) was Adam, **Eddie "Rochester" Anderson** was Noah, **Frederick O'Neal** was Moses, **Richard Ward** was Pharaoh, **Terry Carter** was Gabriel, **Rosetta LeNoire** was Noah's wife, and **Estelle Hemsley** was Mrs. Deshee. It aired twice to positive reviews but was not a ratings hit either time. Critical black people disliked the dialect and other **stereotypes**. *See also* BROADWAY PLAYS AND MUSICALS.

GREGORY, DICK. Comedian and activist Gregory made appearances on *Comic Relief* (1986), *A Party for Richard Pryor* (1991), *The Real*

Malcolm X (1992), and the 1998 miniseries *Cold War* as himself. He made several appearances on *ESPN Sports Century* (2000) and *The Tonight Show Starring Johnny Carson* (1970–1972). He was on *Rowan and Martin's Laugh-In* in 1968.

GREGORY HINES SHOW, THE (*CBS, 1997–1998*). Supreme tap dancer Hines starred in this sitcom as Ben Stevenson, a widowed father of a 12-year-old son (Brandon Hammond). Wendell Pierce played his brother. **Bill Cobbs** played his father.

GRIER, DAVID ALAN. Grier became recognizable as a cast member of the comedy series *In Living Color* from 1990 to 1994. However, prior to that, in 1986, he had a regular role in the short-lived sitcom *All Is Forgiven.* After *In Living Color*, in 1995, he starred as Professor David Preston in the sitcom *The Preston Episodes.* He took Dennis Rodman shopping in the comedic *The Rodman World Tour.* Grier was the host of *Comedy Central's Premium Blend* in 1997. Then, in 1998, he played the sidekick/brother in the sitcom *Damon.* He starred in his own special, a solo performance titled *The Book of David: The Cult Figure's Manifesto Starring David Alan Grier*, in 2003. He had a regular role as David Bellows, the producer on *Life with Bonnie*, beginning in 2003.

GRIER, PAM. Grier had a key role in *Roots: The Next Generations* in 1979, in *Badge of the Assassin* in 1985, and in *Anne Rice's "The Feast of All Saints"* in 2001. She played Eleanor in the series *Lincs* (1998–2000).

GRIER, ROOSEVELT. A former pro football player, Grier played Rosie Robbins, the accompanist to entertainer Danny Williams (Danny Thomas), on *The Danny Thomas Show* in 1970–1971 and then again in *Make Room for Granddaddy* (1970–1971). He was a guest on *Super Comedy Bowl I* in 1971. He had recurring roles in *The White Shadow* (as Ezra Davis, 1980–1981) and *Movin' On* (as Benjy, 1975–1976). He had key roles in the made-for-television movies *Second Chance* in 1972, *Carter's Army* in 1970, *The Desperate Mission* in 1971, *To Kill a Cop* in 1978, and *The Seekers* in 1979. He also had roles in the miniseries *Roots: The Next Generations* in 1979 and *The Sophisticated Gents* in 1981. He was one of the celebrities speaking out in the public service special *Get High on Yourself* in 1981.

GRIFFIN, EDDIE. Griffin starred in the sitcom *Malcolm and Eddie* (1996–2000).

GUARDIAN, THE (*HBO, 1984*). Louis Gossett Jr. and Martin Sheen starred in a two-hour drama in which John Mack (Gossett), a no-nonsense former military man, was hired to be a security guard for a Manhattan building plagued with violent crime. Mack is meticulous and totally dedicated to his task. Soon the tenants believe that Mack has taken his authority too far. So one tenant, Hyatt (Sheen), sets out to get rid of Mack.

GUILLAUME, ROBERT. Known primarily for his role of Benson on the popular sitcom *Soap* and its spin-off *Benson*, Guillaume won the **Emmy Award** for Outstanding Supporting Actor in a Comedy-Variety or Music Series for his *Soap* role in 1979 and the Emmy for Outstanding Lead Actor in a Comedy Series for the role in *Benson* in 1985. He played Isaac Jaffee in *Sports Night* from 1998 to 2000. He suffered a stroke in 1999 but returned to the series to play Isaac. His credits also include singing, dramatic roles, and narration. In 1981, he starred in the title role of the televised version of the Broadway musical *Purlie*, a role he played on Broadway. Guillaume guest-starred in *'S Wonderful, 'S Marvelous, 'S Gershwin* in 1972 and in *The Donna Summer Special* in 1980. In 1982, he sang in the *Texaco Star Theater*, a salute to musicals. He and Gary Coleman starred in three made-for-television family films: *The Kid from Left Field* in 1979, *The Kid with the Broken Halo* in 1982, and *The Kid with the 200 I.Q.* in 1983. In 1986, he was the star, director, and producer of *John Grin's Christmas*. The same year, he narrated *Passion and Memory*, a PBS **documentary** about the careers of black film pioneers. In 1991, he co-hosted *Disney's Great American Celebration*, an evening of July 4 festivities. In 1995, Guillaume and his wife, Donna Brown Guillaume, produced a series of ethnically diverse fairy tales, *Happily Ever After: Fairy Tales for Every Child*; he also was narrator. In 1996, he had a key role in the TV film *Run for the Dream: The Gail Devers Story*. He said, "If I had to identify what led me to success, I would have to say that I was never afraid of the English language. Many young people cannot speak English and seem to think there is some kind of nobility in not being able to speak well." *See also* DOMESTIC WORKERS.

GUILTY OF INNOCENCE: THE LENELL GETER STORY (*CBS*, *February 3, 1987*). A two-hour made-for-television movie, this script was based on a *60 Minutes* segment about a black man who was "positively identified" by a victim of a crime and then, years after serving time in prison, was found to be innocent. *60 Minutes* was instrumental in vindicating Lenell Jeter. **Dorian Harewood** played the title role. *See also* BIOPICS.

GUMBEL, BRYANT. He was with NBC for nearly 25 years, 15 as host of *The Today Show* (1981–1996)—making him the first black person to host a network morning show. Prior to *Today*, his work was primarily in sports broadcasting, which he continued to do. He was chief anchor of NBC's televised football games. In 1977, Gumbel was cohost of Super Bowl XI. In 1988, he was host of the Olympic Games in Seoul, South Korea. He was also cohost of NBC's Rose Bowl Parade for several years. In 1980, he played himself in the television movie *The Golden Moment—An Olympic Love Story*. Gumbel signed with CBS in 1997 to anchor the CBS newsmagazine *Public Eye with Bryant Gumbel*. The show won two Peabody Awards, two **Emmy Awards**, and an Overseas Press Club Award. In 1999, he agreed to host *The Early Show*, a position he kept for two and a half years before announcing his resignation in 2002. While at CBS, he hosted *The 49th Annual Emmy Awards*. signed with CBS in 1997 to anchor the CBS newsmagazine *Public Eye with Bryant Gumbel*. The show won two Peabody Awards, two **Emmy Awards**, and an Overseas Press Club Award. In 1999, he agreed to host *The Early Show*, a position he kept for two and a half years before announcing his resignation in 2002. While at CBS, he hosted *The 49th Annual Emmy Awards*. His credits also include hosting HBO's *Real Sports*. He won numerous awards including three Emmys and two NAACP Image Awards. He was named Journalist of the Year in 1993 by the National Association of Black Journalists. He is **Greg Gumbel**'s brother.

GUMBEL, GREG. Gumbel's sports broadcast career began in local television in 1973 and quickly broadened. He joined CBS Sports for the second time in 1999 to serve as host of NCAA Men's Basketball Championships. As play-by-play announcer for the 2001 Super Bowl, Gumbel was the first black commentator to serve as play-by-play announcer for a major sports championship in the United States. When asked to comment about the milestone, he said, "I'd like to think it's an acceptance of me not as an African-American but as a broadcaster. The first African-American? I'm not going to downplay that. It's significant." He had called play-by-play for NBC since 1994. Prior to NBC, Gumbel was with CBS from 1989 to 1994 as host of *The NFL Today*. He was also prime-time anchor of CBS Sports' coverage of the 1994 Olympic Winter Games and was coanchor for the morning broadcasts of the 1992 Olympic Winter Games. He also hosted major league baseball and college football for CBS Sports. He is **Bryant Gumbel**'s brother.

GUNN, MOSES. Gunn had a role in *Carter's Army*, a 1970 made-for-television movie. He played the ranch foreman who supervised seven teenage boys who fought rustlers in the 1974 western drama *The Cowboys*. Adept at comedy as well as drama, Gunn, in 1977, played Carl Dixon, Florida's romantic interest after her husband James (**John Amos**) died in *Good Times*. That same year, he played Kintango in the African scenes of the miniseries *Roots*. He was a regular on the drama series *The Contender* in 1980 and a miner named Moses Gage who was sidekick to the title character in the drama series *Father Murphy* from 1981 to 1984. Gunn had a key role in *Charlotte Forten's Mission: Experiment in Freedom* in 1985. He was the Old Man in *A Man Called Hawk* and Ben in the miniseries *The Women of Brewster Place*, both in 1989. Gunn was born in 1929 and died of asthma in 1993.

GUY, JASMINE. Guy's first major television role was as the "stuck-up" Whitley with the extreme southern accent on the sitcom *A Different World*. She began the series as a supporting regular player in 1987, but before the series ended in 1993, hers was the lead character. She appeared in the tribute special *The Funny Women of Television* in 1991 and *It's Black Entertainment* in 1997. She played Elna Du Vaul in "Long Black Song" on *America's Dream* in 1995. She had key roles in the made-for-television films *Stompin' at the Savoy* in 1992, *Alex Haley's Queen* in 1993, and *Anne Rice's "The Feast of All Saints"* in 2001. In 2003, she was in the cast of *Dead Like Me* as the sassy, outspoken Roxy.

GUYANA TRAGEDY: THE STORY OF JIM JONES (*CBS, April 15–16, 1980*). This miniseries chronicled the charismatic minister who led many people, mostly blacks, to a "promised land" in South America and then forced them to drink poisoned punch. Powers Boothe played the Rev. Jim Jones; **James Earl Jones** and **Ron Cash** also starred.

– H –

HAGINS, MONTROSE. Hagins played Grandmother Davis in *Homefront* (1991–1993) and Miz Coretta Jackson in the series *The Famous Jett Jackson* (1998–) and the TV film *Jett Jackson: The Movie* (2001). She had roles in the following TV films: *On Fire* (1987), *The Women of Brewster Place* (1989), and *Hijacked: Flight 285* (1986).

HAIRSTON, JESTER. Hairston played various roles on *Amos 'n' Andy*, particularly Sapphire's cousin, Leroy, and Henry Van Porter, a well-dressed self-styled socialite. The cast of *Amos 'n' Andy* was criticized for portraying demeaning depictions of blacks. Later, Hairston explained, "We had a hard time fighting for dignity. We had no power. We had to take it, and because we took it, the young people today have greater opportunities." In the 1974–1975 sitcom *That's My Mama*, he played Wildcat, one of the barbershop regulars. From 1986 to 1991, he played Rolly Forbes, the wisecracking deacon on the sitcom *Amen*. In 1935, he was assistant conductor of the Hall Johnson Choir, which sang in the film *The Green Pastures* and later in the television production. In an alliance with Dmitri Tiomkin, Hairston composed and arranged the song "Amen" and dubbed the singing for Sidney Poitier in the film *Lilies of the Field*. He was successful worldwide primarily as a choir director and a writer of religious songs and hymns; he composed or arranged more than 300 choral spirituals. As an official goodwill ambassador for the United States, Hairston conducted an international choir of 1,500 voices in Estonia in 1991. He was born in 1901 and died in 2000 of natural causes.

HALF & HALF (*UPN, 2002–). In this sitcom, Dee Dee (**Essence Atkins**) and Mona (Rachel True) were half sisters who had the same father. Their mothers were the comedic problem. Mona's mother, Phyllis (**Telma Hopkins**), was outspoken and wanted the best for her daughter. Dee Dee's mother, Big Dee Dee (**Valerie Pettiford**), was status conscious and wanted the best for her daughter. The mothers hated each other. Both sisters ended up living in the same apartment building with the feuding mothers always on hand. Mona worked for a record company and was practical and not very sociable. Dee was in law school and lively. Chico Benyman played Spencer, Mona's best friend. In 2004, **Louis Gossett Jr.** joined the cast; his character dated Phyllis and was Spencer's long-lost father.

HALL, ALBERT. Hall had a key role in the 1981 miniseries *The Sophisticated Gents*. He played Dr. Terry Wilson in the series *Ryan's Four* in 1983 and Judge Seymore Walsh on *Ally McBeal* from 1998 to 2002.

HALL, ARSENIO. The comedian hosted his own late night series, *The Arsenio Hall Show*, from 1989 to 1994 and was the first black to do so successfully. Prior to having his own series, he was a regular on the summer series *The Motown Revue* in 1985 and *Thicke of the Night* from 1983 to 1984, a late night talk show. He was one of the stars of *Uptown Comedy Express* in 1987. He starred in a short-lived sitcom *Arsenio* in 1997. He hosted the amateur talent show *Star Search* in 2003 and 2004.

HALL, ED. Hall played Col. Dickey on the sitcom *Baby I'm Back* in 1978.

HALL, IRMA P. Hall played Big Mama in flashbacks on *Soul Food*, the series, and had key roles in the made-for-television movies *An Unexpected Love* (2003), *Miss Lettie and Me* (2002), *Something to Sing About* (2000), *A Lesson before Dying* (1999), *The Love Letter* (1998), *To Sir with Love II* (1996), *In the Shadow of a Killer* (1992), and *Crisis at Central High* (1981).

HALL, KEVIN PETER. Hall was Dr. El Lincoln on the adventure series *Misfits of Science* (1985–1986). He played Warren on the sitcom *227* (1989–1990). He was Harry, the pet Sasquatch, a tall apelike, smart creature, on the first season (1990–1991) of the series *Harry and The Hendersons*. Hall first played the character in the 1987 feature film of the same title. Hall died in 1991, and the series continued for two more years with other actors.

HAMILTON, BERNIE. Hamilton's first television role was in 1953 in *Ramar of the Jungle*. From 1969 to 1970, he played various roles in *The Name of the Game*. He may be best known for his role as Captain Harold Dobey in *Starsky and Hutch* (1975–1979). In TV films, he had key roles in *A Clear and Present Danger* (1970) and *Me and Benjie* (1970).

HAMILTON, KIM. Hamilton played key roles in made-for-television films *Doctors' Private Lives* and *A Family Upside Down*, both in 1978. She also had a role in the TV film *Stone*, the 1979 pilot of a short-lived series of the same title.

HAMILTON, LISA GAY. Gay was a regular cast member playing Rebecca Washington, the paralegal turned lawyer, on *The Practice* (1997–2003). She had key roles in *Hamlet* and *A House Divided* in 2000. She produced and narrated *Beah: A Black Woman Speaks* (2004), a documentary of the late actress/activist **Beah Richards**.

HAMILTON, LYNN. Hamilton played recurring roles on *Sanford and Son* as Donna, Fred Sanford's girlfriend (1972–1977), and *The Waltons* (as neighbor Verdie Foster, 1972–1981). In 1972, she had a leading role in *A Dream for Christmas*. Hamilton played Cousin Georgia in *Roots: The Next Generations* in 1979. She played Mrs. Ellis in *The Hero Who Couldn't Read* in 1984. She was Vivian in the daytime drama *Generations* in 1989. In made-for-television motion pictures, Hamilton played the mother of a teenager charged with murder in *The Marcus-Nelson Murders*, the 1973 pilot for the *Kojak* series, which starred Telly Savalas. She had a key role in *The Jesse Owens Story* in 1984. She also had roles in the TV films *Elvis and Me* (1988), *A Walton Thanksgiving Reunion* (1993), and *A Walton Easter* (1997). She had regular or recurring roles in the following series: *Rituals* (1984), *227* (1988–1989), *Dangerous Women* (1991), *Sunset Beach* (1997), *Port Charles* (2002–2003), and *The Practice* (1997).

HAMPTON, LIONEL. In 1990, Hampton was celebrated, along with other recording artists who had won Grammy Awards, in the special

Grammy Legends. He was born in 1908 and died of heart failure in 2002.

HANCOCK, HERBIE. Hancock was a guest star in the special *All-Star Tribute to Kareem Abdul-Jabbar* in 1989. He cohosted *Carnegie Hall Salutes the Jazz Masters* in 1994.

HANGIN' WITH MR. COOPER (*ABC, 1992–1997*). Billed as an updated version of *Three's Company* (1977–1984), this sitcom began as two girls and a guy sharing a house. **Mark Curry** played Mark Cooper, a high school teacher and basketball coach. His platonic housemates were Vanessa (**Holly Robinson**), who worked for a brokerage firm, and Robin (**Dawnn Lewis**), a music teacher. In the second season, **Nell Carter** was added to the cast as the principal. Lewis was dropped from the series in 1993. She said she was told her exit would allow the show to bring in a child with a mother, who was too similar to her character. In the series, Mark Cooper's cousin Geneva (Sandra Quarterman) and her seven-year-old daughter Nicole (**Raven-Symone**) moved in. Others in the cast were **Omar Gooding** as Earvin and **Roger E. Mosley** as a rival coach (1992–1993).

HAPPILY EVER AFTER: FAIRY TALES FOR EVERY CHILD (*HBO, 1995*). This was an animated family series featuring retold classic fables with characters of various ethnicities. **Robert Guillaume** was narrator of the 13 episodes with voices of leading performers, also of various ethnic backgrounds reading scripts. "Rumplestiltskin," for example, was a West Indian conjurer with the voices of **Roscoe Lee Browne** and **Jasmine Guy**. "Little Red Riding Hood" was a Chinese girl named "Little Red Happy Coat" with the voices of Brian Tochi and B. D. Wong. Guillaume and his wife, Donna Brown Guillaume, were producers.

HAPPY ENDINGS (*ABC, April 10, 1975*). This special consisted of four comedy skits that made fun of modern American life. In one story, **James Earl Jones** was the star in a segment titled "Big Joe and Kansas." Jones was Big Joe; Alan King was Kansas.

HARDEN, ERNEST, JR. Harden (aka Ernest Hardin Jr.) was Marcus in the sitcom *The Jeffersons* (1977–1979) and had a key role in the made-for-television movie *White Mama* in 1980.

HARDISON, KADEEM. Hardison earned television fame playing Dwayne Wayne on *A Different World* (1987–1993). He starred as Charles Winston in the sitcom *Between Brothers* (1997–1999). He played Will Jefferies in *Abby* in 2003 and was host of *Livin' Large* (2002). In TV films, he had roles in *The Color of Friendship* (1981), *Go Tell It on the Mountain* (1985), *Fire and Ice* (2001), and *Red Skies* (2002).

HAREWOOD, DORIAN. Harewood had key roles in numerous motion pictures made for television including *Foster and Laurie* in 1975, *Roots: The Next Generations* in 1979, *American Christmas Carol* in 1979, and *Beulah Land* in 1980. Harewood starred in *The Ambush Murders* in 1981. The actor played Lenell Jeter in *Guilty of Innocence: The Lenell Geter Story* in 1987. He played Jesse Owens in *The Jesse Owens Story*, a 1984 TV film, and the Rev. Morgan Hamilton in the drama series *7th Heaven* (1996–2001).

HARLEM GLOBETROTTERS ON GILLIGAN'S ISLAND (*NBC, May 15, 1981*). The Harlem Globetrotters' plane crashed on Gilligan's Island, and they were marooned with the castaways from the old series. They played a basketball game with a specially programmed team of robots controlled by a mad scientist.

HARPER, HILL. Harper, playing a forensics expert, was in the regular cast of *CSI: NY* when it premiered in 2004. His previous series roles were Tommy in the drama series *Live Shot* (1995–1996), Dr. Wesley Williams in *City of Angels* (2000), and Christopher Bell in the legal drama *The Court* (2002). He had a key role in the 2005 TV film *Lackawanna Blues*.

HARRIS AND COMPANY (*NBC, 1979*). Bernie Casey starred in the one-hour drama series as Mike Harris, a widower and father of five children. After his wife died, blue-collar worker Harris moved from Detroit to Los Angeles to start a new life. His cousins Charlie (**Stu**

Gilliam) and Angie (**Carol Tillery Banks**) helped him with the children: David (David Hubbard), Liz (Renee Brown), J.P. (Lia Jackson), Tommy (Eddie Singleton), and Richard Allen (Dain Turner). Mike Harris handled family decisions with a family board meeting. The board members were the children who discussed issues before taking a vote. This was an effort to launch a black family drama. Series star Casey said, "The series was important because it was a handsome family with no coons. The casting was done by [director] Ivan Dixon and [producer] Stanley Robinson, both black professionals. The characters were articulate; there was not that sarcastic in-your-face-humor, no 'Your hair's so nappy' jokes. The interplay with the family was easily likeable. The father was a master mechanic and he was compassionate, loving, with his children. The children came to him saying, 'Dad, I want to talk to you about something.' This man was controlling his own destiny and the family was mutually supportive. This was not an image white television decision-makers were used to with black families. Remember, this was five years before *The Cosby Show*."

Many TV critics and editors had difficulty understanding that this was a drama show and not an unfunny sitcom. So their readers never got the idea either, and viewers waited for the jokes that were never intended to come. The series lasted only a few episodes. Looking back, Casey said, "It was never intended to succeed because they only gave it four episodes. You can't get an audience in such a short run." **James Earl Jones** made a similar comment when his family drama *Under One Roof* failed in 1995. Both Casey and Jones agreed that a successful black family drama requires time to develop characters and scripts and time to build an audience.

HARRIS, JULIUS. Harris played key roles in the TV films *To Kill a Cop* in 1978, *Ring of Passion* in 1978, *Thornwell* in 1981, *Missing Pieces* in 1983, and *A Gathering of Old Men* in 1987. He played Idi Amin in the 1976 film *Victory at Entebbe*. Harris was born in 1923 and died in 2004 of heart failure.

HARRIS, LEON. Harris joined CNN in 1983 as a video journalist and after several promotions became reporter and anchor on numerous CNN programs including *CNN Live Today*, *Early Edition*, *CNN Presents*, and *Prime News and the World Today*. He was on the air just minutes after the September 11, 2001, attacks and reported throughout the day. He also covered the search for John F. Kennedy Jr.'s plane, Election 2000, and the 1991 Los Angeles riots. He was voted Best Newscaster twice by the CableACE Awards. He became news anchor of the Washington, D.C., ABC-TV-station in 2004.

HARRIS, STEVE. Harris played Eugene Young, senior lawyer in the firm depicted on *The Practice* (1997–2004). He starred as Sonny Liston in the TV film *King of The World* in 2000. He was the voice of Detective Bennett in *The Batman* animated series in 2004.

HARRIS, WOOD. Harris starred as Jimi Hendrix in the biopic *Hendrix* in 2000. He played Ellis in *Spenser: Small Vices* (1999) and Billy Dixon in *Rhapsody* (2000), both TV films. He played Avon Barksdale in the series *The Wire* (2002–).

HARRY AND LENA (*ABC, March 22, 1970*). **Harry Belafonte** and **Lena Horne** headlined this semiautobiographical special of singing. The songs took the audience into the lives of the performers, a kind of musical history. Belafonte's songs included "My Old Man," "If You Ever Lived in a Ghetto," and "Abraham, Martin and John." Horne sang "I Want to Be Happy," "It's Always Somewhere Else," and "Brown Baby." Together, they sang "Don't It Make You Want to Go Home" and "The First Time."

HARRY BELAFONTE IN CONCERT (*HBO, October 10, 1985*). **Harry Belafonte** was the host and star with guests **Bill Cosby**, Dick Cavett, Marge Champion, Lee Grant, and Alan King.

HARRY, JACKEE. Harry (aka Jackee) played Sandra on the sitcom *227* from 1985 to 1990 and won the **Emmy Award** for Outstanding Supporting Actress in a Comedy Series for the 1986–1987 season. In 1989, she played Etta Mae Johnson in the miniseries *The Women of Brewster Place*. She was Ruth in the sitcom *The Royal Family* from 1991 to 1992 and Lisa in the sitcom *Sister, Sister* from 1994 to 1999. In variety specials, Harry was a guest on the *All-Star Tribute to Kareem Abdul-Jabbar* in 1989. In 2005, she was one of those losing weight on *Celebrity Fit Club.*

HARVEST OF SHAME (*CBS, November 25, 1960*). This news program on *CBS Reports* was about the many migrant farmworkers in the United States. Many of them were African Americans who worked farms in Florida and along the East Coast and lived in squalor. The special also described the plight of the migrant children who also worked in the fields and were not being educated.

HAUSER, FAYE. Hauser had a key role in the made-for-television film projects *Inmates: A Love Story* in 1981, ***Roots: The Next Generations*** in 1979, and ***Christmas Lilies of the Field*** in 1979. She had a recurring role in the daytime drama *The Young and the Restless*. She is also a director and producer.

HAVING OUR SAY (*CBS, April 18, 1999*). Based on the lives of the two Delaney sisters, Sadie and Bessie, and the popular stage production of the same title, this TV film starred **Diahann Carroll** and **Ruby Dee**. The centenarian sisters experienced struggles and triumphs in their long lives and successful careers. The sisters' story arose from an interview with a writer (Amy Madigan). Others in the cast were **Mykelti Williamson**, **Lonette McKee**, **Audra McDonald**, **Richard Roundtree**, Lisa Arrindell Anderson, and **Della Reese**. McDonald and Arrindell played the sisters when they were younger. *See also* BIOPICS; BROADWAY PLAYS AND MUSICALS.

HAWKINS-BYRD, PETRI. Called "Byrd" by Judge Judy Sheindlin on the syndicated courtroom show *Judge Judy*, he is the bailiff. He had the same job in real life in her courtroom.

HAYES, ISAAC. Composer/actor Hayes's unmistakable voice was used as the voice of Jerome "Chef" McElroy on the cartoon series and special productions *South Park* (1997), *South Park Rally* (1999), and *South Park: Bigger Longer & Uncut* (1999). In TV films, he played Jonah Parks in *Book of Days* (2003), Vernon Holland in *Soul Survivors* (1995), Detective Stubbs in *Acting on Impulse* (1993), Prophet in *Hallelujah* (1993), Hammer in *Hammer, Slammer, and Slade* (1990), and Frank Moreno in *Betrayed by Innocence* (1986). He composed the theme music for the TV series *Shaft* (1973) and *As-*

signment Vienna (1972). He was a highlight of *Wattstax 1973*, a filmed special that aired on television in 2004.

HAYMAN, LILLIAN. Hayman was Leslie Uggams's mother in the "Sugar Hill" sketch on *The Leslie Uggams Show* in 1969.

HAYNES, LLOYD. Haynes starred as history teacher Pete Dixon in the series *Room 222* (1969–1974) and John Stevens in the miniseries *Harold Robbins' '79 Park Avenue* in 1977. He played Ken Morgan on the daytime drama *General Hospital* (1984–1986) and had roles in numerous TV films from 1966 through 1981. He was born in 1934 and died from cancer in 1986.

HAYSBERT, DENNIS. Haysbert was the first African American to play the role of the president of the United States in a successful drama series in his role as President David Palmer in the series *24* (2001–). Simultaneously, he was the spokesperson for Allstate Insurance in television commercials. Previously, he played Dr. Theodore Morris in the sci-fi series *Now and Again*, Stuff Wade in the adventure series *Code Red* from 1981 to 1982, Cletus Maxwell in the sitcom *Off the Rack* in 1985, and Coach Duane Johnson in the sitcom *Just the Ten of Us* from 1988 to 1989. In made-for-television movies and miniseries, he had a key role in *Grambling's White Tiger* in 1981, *The Return of Marcus Welby, MD* in 1984, and *Alex Haley's Queen* in 1993.

HAZEL SCOTT SHOW, THE (*DUM, 1950*). This 15-minute music summer show, starring popular nightclub singer **Hazel Scott**, aired at first on Friday evenings, then on Mondays, Wednesdays, and Fridays. Scott was the second wife of New York Congressman Adam Clayton Powell. Most reviewers termed the show "dignified," which was positive news to African Americans concerned with what fare might make it to television, especially considering the predominance of domestic workers portrayed on radio and in film. The show had not been on the air long when, during the McCarthyism era, Scott's name was listed in the publication *Red Channels* as being either a Communist or a Communist sympathizer. She fought the charge and the publication before the House Un-American Activities Committee and urged other entertainers to fight. People admired her courage, but *The Hazel Scott Show* was cancelled.

HEAT WAVE (*TNT*, August 13, 1990). This drama was based on the observations of a *Los Angeles Times* reporter-trainee, Bob Richardson, who watched the 1965 Watts uprising in Los Angeles. It also looked at the incident from the eyes of Richardson's grandmother and the white family that employed her as a domestic worker. The cast included **James Earl Jones** (who won an **Emmy Award** for his portrayal), **Blair Underwood, Cicely Tyson, Margaret Avery, Vondie Curtis Hall**, and **Paris Vaughn**. *See also* HISTORICAL EVENTS DRAMATIZED.

HEAVY D. The rapper (aka Dwight Myers) made 11 appearances on *Boston Public* as Mr. Luck/Big Boy. He had annual roles on *Living Single* as Darryl (1994–1996) and four episodes on *Roc* as Calvin. He composed the themes for *The Tracy Morgan Show* (2003) and *In Living Color* (1990).

HEMPHILL, SHIRLEY. Hemphill played Shirley Wilson in the sitcoms *What's Happening!!* (1976–1979) and *What's Happening Now!!* (1985–1988). In between, she starred as Shirley Simmons on the sitcom *One in a Million* (1980). In comedy variety, she appeared in *The Richard Pryor Special* (1977), the comedy show *The Comedy Spot* in 1978, and the weekly stand-up comedy show *Comic Strip Live* (1989–1994). Born in 1947, she died of kidney failure in 1999.

HEMSLEY, ESTELLE. Ms. Hemsley played Mrs. Deshee in "The Green Pastures" on *The Hallmark Hall of Fame* in 1957.

HEMSLEY, SHERMAN. After a career in Broadway musicals, Hemsley hit television as a guest star playing George Jefferson on *All in the Family*. Then his character was spun off into the sitcom *The Jeffersons*, which ran for 11 seasons (1975–1985), becoming the longest-running show with an African-American cast. He was Deacon Frye in *Amen* from 1986 to 1991 and played the lead in the short-lived sitcom *Goode Behavior* (1996–1997). He reprised his Broadway role of Gitlow in the television version of the musical *Purlie* (1981).

HENDRIX (*SHO,* September 17, 2000). **Wood Harris** starred in this TV film about the life and career of Jimi Hendrix beginning with his performing in Greenwich Village and ending with his performing at Woodstock. **Vivica A. Fox** also starred. *See also* BIOPICS.

HENSON, DARRIN DEWITT. A choreographer who won the MTV Video Music Award for Best Choreographer of the Year in 2000, Henson played Lem in the drama series *Soul Food.* He taught dance steps to N'Sync and Christina Aguilera for their videos.

HENTON, JOHN. Henton played Overton Jones on the sitcom *Living Single* (1993–1998) and Seth Milsap on the sitcom *The Hughleys* (1998–1999).

HERNANDEZ, JUANO. Black and Puerto Rican, Hernandez was able to get roles not necessarily written for black Americans in the late 1950s and 1960s, especially roles as Native Americans or other nonblack but "ethnic" roles. He had a key role in "The Decision at Arrowsmith" on *Medallion Theatre* in 1953; in "Escape Route" in the *Studio One* anthology series in 1957; in "Goodwill Ambassador" for *Studio 57,* also in 1957; and in "An Occurrence at Owl Creek Bridge" on *Alfred Hitchcock Presents* in 1959. He played several episodes of the series *Adventure in Paradise* (1959). He played Standing Bear in *Westinghouse Presents: The Dispossessed* in 1961. He also had roles in *Naked City, Route 66, The Dick Powell Show, The Defenders,* and many other series as well as films and radio. Hernandez was born in 1901 and died in 1970 of a cerebral hemorrhage.

HERO WHO COULDN'T READ, THE (*ABC,* January 9, 1984). This *ABC Afterschool Special* centered on Freddie Ellis, a high school superathlete who could not read and managed to slide through most of high school because he had easy classes and his girlfriend wrote his papers. Then Mr. Simpson, a new teacher, came to the school and was not satisfied with the situation. Eric Wallace played Freddie, and **Clarence Williams III** played Mr. Simpson. **Kareem Abdul-Jabbar** played himself. **Lynn Hamilton** played Mrs. Ellis. **Renee Jones** was Cynthia.

HESHIMU. He was Jason Allen, one of the key students in *Room 222* (1969–1974).

HE'S THE MAYOR (*ABC, 1986*). This sitcom, which lasted only two months, is significant in that a black actor (**Kevin Hooks**) played the lead and the main character was a mayor. Mayor Carl Burke was only 25. His father, Alvin (**Al Fann**), was the City Hall janitor, and his best buddy, Wardell (Wesley Thompson), was his chauffeur. Both of them were his advisers. *See also* OCCUPATIONS OF TV CHARACTERS.

HEY HEY HEY—IT'S FAT ALBERT (*NBC, November 12, 1969*). **Bill Cosby**'s childhood stories were the basis of this animated special.

HEY MONIE (*BET and OXY, 2003–*). An adult animated series produced jointly by **Black Entertainment Television** (BET) and Oxygen, *Hey Monie* was aired first on BET and later on Oxygen. The central character in the half hour was Simone, or Monie (voice of Angela V. Shelton), as she was called, a young African-American professional woman living in the big city. Monie's best friend was Yvette (voice of Frances Callier). There were numerous other characters in the stories. It aired first as a series of comedy shorts on Oxygen in 2000. Oxygen's target audience is women, while BET's is African Americans. Initially, both networks planned to debut the show at the same time, but Oxygen decided the show should be offered to the African-American market first, so the series opened on BET a few months earlier.

HICKMAN, FRED. Hickman cohosted the first *Sports Tonight* on CNN in 1980. He did the first play-by-play of a National Basketball Association (NBA) game on TBS. He left to work at a local station in 1984 but returned in 1986 and again hosted *Sports Tonight*. He signed a five-year contract and also hosted *This Week in the NBA* and TBS's *NBA Preview*. In 1994, he won the CableAce Award for best sports anchor in cable television.

HICKS, HILLY. Hicks played Pfc. Jed Brooks in the 1972 sitcom *Roll Out*. He also played Lewis in the miniseries *Roots* in 1977.

HIGH CHAPARRAL, THE (*NBC, 1967–1971*). This western series is listed because **Frank Silvera**, a black actor who often played other ethnic roles, portrayed Don Sebastian Montoya, a wealthy landowner and cattle baron in Arizona Territory. Montoya's daughter, Victoria (Linda Cristal), married the central character, rancher Big John Cannon (Leif Erickson). Silvera died before the series ended. *See also* SERIES WITH ONE BLACK SUPPORTING ACTOR BEFORE 1980.

HILL, DULE. Known to television audiences primarily as Charles Young, the president's personal aide on *The West Wing*, Hill started his show business career as a child when he understudied **Savion Glover** in Broadway's *The Tap Dance Kid*. He went on to star in the national tour of the musical, had other roles in musicals and commercials, and then was cast as one of the *City Kids*, a Saturday morning series. He had roles in the TV films *The Ditchdigger's Daughters* (1997), *Color of Justice* (1997), and *Love Songs* (1999).

HILL STREET BLUES (*NBC, 1981–1987*). This was the first police drama played in a serialized format where the several intertwined stories did not tie up in a neat little package at the end of the episode. *Hill Street Blues* was popular with African-American viewers. The setting was the chaotic Hill Street station of a fictional city where crime in the vicinity was rampant. The primary characters were realistic, imperfect cops trying to do their jobs and live their lives. It was considered drama, but there was comedy also in the fast-paced and intentionally choppy series. Each episode began with roll call and the warning from the sergeant, "Be careful out there!" There were two black regulars: **Michael Warren** as Officer Bobby Hill and **Taurean Blacque** as Lt. Neal Washington. **J. A. Preston** played the mayor from 1982 to 1985. There were also numerous black guest stars ranging from criminals to family members. The series was a product of MTM Enterprises headed by Grant Tinker, who believed strongly that if you make quality shows, high ratings will result. Ratings on this series began very low, then the series won six **Emmy Awards**, including Outstanding Drama Series, an award won again for four consecutive seasons. Ratings climbed, and the show peaked at number 21 of all shows in its third season.

HILTON-JACOBS, LAWRENCE. Jacobs was Freddie "Boom Boom" Washington in the sitcom *Welcome Back Kotter* from 1975 to 1979. He had key roles in the TV film projects *Roots* in 1977 and *For the Love of It* in 1980. In 1992, he played Joe Jackson, the patriarch of the singing Jackson family, in *The Jacksons: An American Dream*.

HINES, GREGORY. As a young adult, Hines was a third of the tap-dancing trio Hines, Hines, and Dad with his older brother, Maurice Jr., and his father, Maurice. The trio danced on the special *Soul* in 1968 and on *The Dionne Warwick Special* in 1969 and other variety series and specials. Hines starred in the 1992 informational special *Jammin': Jelly Roll Morton on Broadway*. He had a key role in the television film *The Cherokee Kid* in 1996 and starred in *The Gregory Hines Show*, a 1997 series. That same year, he danced for President Bill Clinton in the *Gala for the President at Ford's Theatre* and was interviewed in *It's Black Entertainment*. He was one of Grace's boyfriends on the sitcom *Will & Grace* in 1998. He starred in the biopic *Bojangles* in 2001. He won the **Emmy Awards** for the 1989 PBS special *Dance in America*. Hines was born in 1946 and died of cancer in 2003.

HISTORICAL EVENTS DRAMATIZED. African-American history proved to be fertile ground for dramatization in the television movie and miniseries formats. Particularly popular with moviemakers were those events taking place during the modern civil rights movement of the latter 20th century. These dramatized efforts met with varying degrees of success with viewers and critics. However, it could be argued that the dramatizations of real events brought into American homes aspects of African-American history and life otherwise overlooked and unacknowledged. Both cable and network television presented such works. HBO tackled the bus boycotts in Montgomery, Alabama, in *Boycott* (2001). In 1990, NBC aired *Murder in Mississippi* about the murder by the Ku Klux Klan of civil rights workers James Chaney, Andrew

Goodman, and Mickey Schwerner. The dramatic story of the Little Rock Nine, the nine African-American students called on to desegregate Central High School in Little Rock, Arkansas, was presented by the Disney Channel in 1993 in *The Ernest Green Story* and in 1981 by CBS in *Crisis at Central High*, the latter told from the point of view of teacher and vice principal Elizabeth Huckaby. *Heat Wave*, in 1990, was TNT's presentation about the 1965 Watts uprising. In 1995, HBO presented *The Tuskegee Airmen*, a dramatic rendering of the story of the all-black U.S. fighter group in World War II.

Stories of crimes and innocent people convicted included 2003's *D.C. Sniper: 23 Days of Fear* about the military-style sniper attacks in several suburbs of Washington, D.C., when 10 people died in the attacks. Montgomery County Police Chief Charles Moose, an African American, became a nationally recognized law enforcement official. *Guilty of Innocence: The Lenell Geter Story*, in 1987, was about a black man who served time in prison for a crime of which he was innocent but positively identified.

Smaller and quieter stories also received movie treatment. In 1996, Showtime aired the movie *Mr. and Mrs. Loving*. The movie told the story of the Supreme Court decision outlawing antimiscegenation laws nationwide. Mildred Jeter, a black woman, and Richard Loving, a white man, appealed their case through the Virginia state courts after they were arrested and thrown in jail on their wedding night in 1958. The case was argued before the Supreme Court in 1967.

Of particular note is the ABC production *Separate but Equal* (1991) about the historic Supreme Court case *Brown v. Board of Education*, which ended legal segregation and thrust Thurgood Marshall into the national spotlight and on the road to his own Supreme Court tenure. Other events in dramas were *Race to Freedom: The Underground Railroad* (1994) about the escapes of slaves in 1850. *See also* DOCUMENTARIES.

HOGAN'S HEROES (*CBS, 1965–1971*). *Hogan's Heroes* was a hit half-hour sitcom about prisoners in Stalag 13, a Nazi prisoner-of-war camp supposedly commanded by Col. Wilhelm Klink (Werner Klemperer) but actually under the control of the POWs headed by Col.

Hogan (Bob Crane). The show's longtime black character was Sgt. James Kinchloe played by **Ivan Dixon**. Dixon said he was happy to do the series but disturbed that everyone recognized him from "such a bit part" when he also played meatier roles, "roles I was more proud of," in anthology dramas like *CBS Playhouse*'s "The Final War of Ally Winter." He left the series after the fifth year and was replaced by **Kenneth Washington**, who played Sgt. Richard Baker. *See also* SERIES WITH ONE BLACK SUPPORTING ACTOR/ PERFORMER BEFORE 1980.

HOLDER, GEOFFREY. Holder played the Ghost of Christmas Future in *John Grin's Christmas* in 1986. He also narrated *Dance Black America* in 1985.

HOLIDAY HEART (*SHO, December 10, 2000*). The made-for-television film based on a play of the same title was about a drag queen who cares for a young girl whose mother battles a drug addiction. **Ving Rhames**, **Alfre Woodard**, and **Mykelti Williamson** starred.

HOLLIDAY, BILLIE. Holliday was honored posthumously in *The Apollo Hall of Fame* in 1993. She was born in 1915 and died of heart and liver disease on July 17, 1959.

HOLLIDAY, KENE. Holliday had an important role in *Roots: The Next Generations* in 1979 and *The Badge of the Assassin* in 1985. He played Sgt. Curtis Baker in the sitcom *Carter Country* (1977–1979) and Tyler Hudson in *Matlock* (1986–1995).

HOLLIS, TOMMY. Hollis played a key role in *Alex Haley's Queen* (1993), *The Piano Lesson* (1995), and *Zooman* (1995).

HOLLOWELL, TODD. Hollowell played Jeff Williams in *The Facts of Life* (1987–1988).

HOLLOW IMAGE (*ABC, June 24, 1979*). Saundra Sharpe starred in this televised play as Harriet Gittens, a black woman who worked her way up from humble beginnings in Harlem to a key position in the world of fashion. She had all the signs of the good life—a chic apartment in a prestigious neighborhood, beautiful clothes, and a successful lawyer-boyfriend (**Robert Hooks**), who also worked his way out of Harlem. However, she returned to Harlem on a visit and encountered old boyfriend (**Dick Anthony Williams**), an idealistic man who still loved her but wanted to remain in the neighborhood to improve life for those living there. **Morgan Freeman** played a ghetto poet. **Hattie Winston** played a singer.

HOLLY, ELLEN. Holly was the first black actress to play a running role on a daytime drama when she made her debut on *One Life to Live* as Carla Benari, a black woman passing for a white woman in 1968. She played the role from 1968–1980 and from 1983–1985. She also played Regan in *King Lear* in 1974 and had key roles in *Sergeant Matlovich vs. the U.S. Air Force* in 1978 and *10,000 Black Men Named George* in 2002.

HOLT, LESTER. Holt's credits include being lead anchor for the daytime news and breaking news coverage on MSNBC (NBC News on cable).

HOLYFIELD, EVANDER. The champion prizefighter was also a contestant on *Dancing with Stars* (2005). *See also* EVANDER HOLYFIELD FIGHTS.

HOMEBOYS IN OUTER SPACE (*UPN, 1996–1997*). **Flex Alexander** and **Darryl Bell** starred in this sitcom as Ty and Mo, respectively, spacemen of the 23rd century who hopped from planet to planet in a raggedy spaceship that resembled a raggedy car. They had been expelled from Starship Commander Community College and were trying to make successes of their lives with the limited knowledge of space travel they had acquired. They took odd jobs on each planet they reached. Also in the series were Rhona L. Bennett, Kevin Michael Richardson, Paulette Braxton, and Peter Mackenzie. Rick Ellis, in an online review on AllYourTV.com, said, "It's not as if these people aren't talented. . . . But apparently some giant show-biz leech has grabbed the cast and crew and sucked all of the good sense out of them."

HOMEFRONT (*ABC, 1991–1993*). This drama series took viewers back to 1945 as soldiers in River Run, Ohio, returned home after World War II. The continuing stories dealt with the town's families touched by sons and brothers killed in the war, soldiers returning to girlfriends who had married others, and the operation of the local factory where women who had worked during the war were let go so that returning soldiers could go to work. Returning soldiers were guaranteed jobs, but the only job offer Cpl. Robert Davis (Sterling Macer Jr.), a young black soldier, could get was as a janitor. His father, Abe Davis (**Dick Anthony Williams**), was chauffeur to the town's most wealthy family, and his mother, Gloria Davis (**Hattie Winston**), was the same family's maid. Drama was intense as the Davis family fought for a better life.

HOMICIDE: LIFE ON THE STREETS (*NBC, 1993–1999*). This police drama premiered after the 1993 Super Bowl and opened with the line "Life is a mystery." It ended with the same line in 1999. The series centered on teams of homicide detectives in Baltimore. The cast was large, and there were many comings and goings of cast members. **Andre Braugher** stayed with the series all but the last season, when his character, Detective Frank Pembleton, resigned from the police force. Earlier, his stressful character had suffered a stroke, but throughout the series he was masterful at interrogating suspects. The Academy of Television Arts and Sciences considered him masterful at acting too; in 1998, he won the **Emmy Award** for Outstanding Lead Actor in a Drama Series. **Yaphet Kotto** stayed with the series the entire run as Lt. Al Giardello. In the final year, his estranged son, Mike (played by Giancarlo Esposito), joined the story line as an FBI agent. In the series' final episode in 1999, Giardello was promoted to captain. There were numerous African-American guest stars; among them were **James Earl Jones** and **Charles Dutton**. Reviewer Erik Arneson, on MysteryNet.com, said the show's cast "could not be better" and that Kotto and Braugher "led what was perhaps the finest ensemble in television history." The series won two Peabody Awards, two Writers Guild of America Awards, three Emmy Awards, and was proclaimed by *TV Guide* to be "the best show you're not watching." Ratings were generally low, and one critic claimed the show was "probably too good for American television." There were few car chases and shoot-outs.

HOMICIDE₁ THE MOVIE (*NBC, February 13, 2000*). Andre Braugher and Yaphet Kotto headed the reunited cast of *Homicide: Life in the Streets* in this TV film about the mysterious public shooting of Giardello (Kotto), who had become a candidate for mayor. As he battled for life, former cases from the series were recalled in flashbacks.

HOOKS, BRIAN. Hooks played a regular role in the sitcom *Eve* beginning in 2003. He had a key role in the TV film *Runaway Car*.

HOOKS, CHRISTOPHER CARTER. Hooks (aka Christopher Carter) played Andre Bailis in *Hangin' with Mr. Cooper* (1992–1994). He is also a writer. He is the son of **Robert Hooks**.

HOOKS, DAVID. Hooks played key roles in the TV films *The Autobiography of Miss Jane Pittman* in 1974 and *The Miracle of Kathy Miller* in 1981.

HOOKS, ERIC. Hooks played Highpockets in the drama *Just an Old Sweet Song* in 1976. He is the son of **Robert Hooks**.

HOOKS, KEVIN. Hooks played Junior in the drama *Just an Old Sweet Song* in 1976. He was Mayor Carl Burke in *He's the Mayor* (1986) and Morris Thorpe in *The White Shadow* (1978–1981). He learned to direct while doing *The White Shadow* and started his directing career doing episodic television in 1982. He directed *Murder without Motive: The Edmund Perry Story* (1992) and was director and producer of the television film *The Color of Friendship* (2000). He won the **Emmy Award** in 2000 for Outstanding Children's Program for *The Color of Friendship*. He has numerous credits as director and executive producer of series episodes as well as TV films. Asked what excites him, Hooks responded, "For me, it's about having spent the time to tell a story that is significant and compelling in some way. But I also am a socially-conscious person, and I'm also, being an African-American, very aware of the fact that there are tremendously compelling stories about African-American culture that have never been explored." He is the son of **Robert Hooks**, of whom he says, "He's been my mentor since day one in this business, and he continues to be a great source of inspiration and influence."

HOOKS, ROBERT. Hooks, an alumnus of New York's Negro Ensemble Company, was one of the first black dramatic actors to make a mark in Hollywood. His first television role was in an episode of *East Side, West Side* (1963–1964); then he played a starring role (as young Frederick Douglass) in an episode of the anthology series *Profiles in Courage* (1964–1965). Hooks played key roles in numerous made-for-television films including the following: *Carter's Army* in 1970, *Trapped* in 1973, *Ceremonies in Dark Old Men* in 1975; *To Kill a Cop* in 1978, *Can You Hear the Laughter? The Story of Freddie Prinze* in 1979, *Hollow Image* in 1979, *The Oklahoma City Dolls* in 1981, *The Sophisticated Gents* in 1981, and *Sister, Sister* in 1982. He was the male lead, Nate Simmons, in the 90-minute drama *Just an Old Sweet Song* in 1976. He was William Still in the miniseries *A Woman Called Moses* in 1978. He is the father of **Kevin, Eric**, and **Christopher Carter Hooks**.

HOPKINS, LINDA. Primarily a singer, Hopkins was an actress in *Roots: The Next Generations* in 1979. She headlined the televised production of the Broadway musical *Black and Blue* (1993). In TV films, miniseries, and specials, she also had roles in *King* (1978), *Purlie* (1981), *Go Tell It on the Mountain* (1985), and *The Colored Museum* (1991).

HOPKINS, TELMA. Hopkins was a member of the popular singing group *Tony Orlando and Dawn*, which was also the title of the 1974–1976 variety show. She played a recurring role as Felix's wife, Frances, in *The New Odd Couple* (1980–1993). She played Jess Ashton in the short-lived series *A New Kind of Family* (1979–1980). Hopkins played Isabelle in *Bosom Buddies*

(1980–1984), Addy in *Gimme a Break* (1984–1987), Rachel Crawford in the sitcom *Family Matters* (1989–1995), and Dolores in *Getting By* (1993–1994). She played divorcée Phyllis Thorne in the sitcom *Half & Half* (2002–). In television movies, Hopkins had roles in *Roots*, *The Next Generations* in 1979 and *The Kid with the Broken Halo* in 1982.

HORNE, LENA. Lena Horne sang on *Your Show of Shows* (1951), was a mystery guest on *What's My Line* (1953), and sang on *The Ed Sullivan Show* (1957). She made multiple appearances on all of the series shows. In 1960, Horne was Frank Sinatra's guest on a special. In 1962, she made a guest appearance on *The Milton Berle Show*, and in 1970, she and **Harry Belafonte** had a special, *Harry and Lena*. She made guest appearances on *The Flip Wilson Show* and *Sanford and Son* in the 1970s. Then she was one of the headliners in the musical special *Carnegie Hall: The Grand Reopening* in 1987. She was saluted in 1997's *It's Black Entertainment*.

HORSFORD, ANNA MARIA. Horsford had key roles in the TV films *Charlotte Forten's Mission: Experiment in Freedom* (1985), *Nobody's Child* (1986), *If It's Tuesday, It Still Must Be Belgium* (1987), *Who Gets the Friends?* (1988), *Taken Away* (1989), *A Killer Among Us* (1990), *Murder without Motive: The Edmund Perry Story* (1992), *Mr. Jones* (1993), *Baby Brokers* (1994), *Widow's Kiss* (1996), and *Circle of Pain* (1996). She played Thelma Frye in the sitcom *Amen* (1986–1991) and had key roles in two short-lived sitcoms: Veronica in *Rhythm & Blues* in 1992 and Lainie in *Tall Hopes* in 1993. She also played Dee Baxter in *The Wayans Bros.* (1995–1999) and Dorothea in *Method & Red* beginning in 2004.

HOUSE DIVIDED, A (*SHO, July 30, 2000*). **Jennifer Beals** starred in this post–Civil War drama as a young woman struggling with her racial identity who eventually becomes a staunch leader against racism. **Lisa Gay Hamilton** also stars. *See also* BIRACIAL CHARACTERS.

HOUSTON, CISSY. Cissy Houston, **Whitney Houston**'s mother, was Rose in *The Vernon Johns Story* (1994).

HOUSTON, WHITNEY. Houston sang the National Anthem at 1991's Super Bowl XXV. She played the fairy godmother in Rodgers and Hammerstein's musical "Cinderella," a segment of *The Wonderful World of Disney* in 1997. She was interviewed in *It's Black Entertainment* in 1997. Some of her specials were *Welcome Home Heroes with Whitney Houston* (1990), *Whitney Houston: The Concert for a New South Africa* (1994), *Whitney Houston: Classic Whitney* (1997), *Whitney T.V.* (2000), and *Whitney Houston: The True Story* (2002).

HOWARD, TERRENCE DASHON. Howard played Lucius in *Street Time* beginning in 2003 and played Cassius Clay in *King of the World* in 2000. He played Bill, the wandering husband, in the 2005 TV film *Lackawanna Blues*.

HUBERT-WHITTEN, JANET. Hubert-Whitten (aka Janet Hubert) played Vivian Banks in the sitcom *Fresh Prince of Bel-Air* (1990–1993). She played Esther Hayes in the drama *Lawless*, which was canceled after only one episode aired in 1997. She played Alice Dawson in the daytime drama *All My Children* (1999). In TV films, her credits are the following: *New Eden* (1994) and *What about Your Friends* (1995).

HUDSON, ERNIE. Hudson played the warden on the late night drama *Oz* (1997–2003). In television films, Hudson had roles in *White Mama* in 1980 and *The Cherokee Kid* in 1996. In 2003, he starred in the drama series *10-8* as a senior deputy who oversaw the training of a former punk turned police officer.

HUGHLEY, D. L. The star (pronounced Hu-glee) of *The Hughleys* (1998–2002) also starred in a one-man comedy special *D. L. Hughley: Going Home* in 1999. He considers his appearance on HBO's *Def Comedy Jam* as a big break. He was chosen as the first host of *Comic View* (1992–1993). He played Marlon on the TV series *Double Rush* (1995) and was also host of *VH1 Big in 03* (2003) and the series *Premium Blend* (1997).

HUGHLEYS, THE (*ABC, 1998–2000; UPN, 2000–2002*). Comedian **D. L. Hughley** (pronounced Hu-glee) starred in this sitcom as Darryl

Hughley, a husband and father who wanted the good life for his family, so he moved them into a formerly white suburb of Los Angeles. Wife Yvonne (**Elise Neal**) tried to keep him calm when he felt the children—Sydney (Ashley Monique Clark) and Michael (Dee Jay Daniels)—adjusted so well that they seemed to be losing their blackness. Also, the neighbors, Dave and Sally (Eric Allen Kramer and Marietta Deprima), though friendly, were very "WASPy." *See also* FAMILY SERIES.

HULLABALOO (*NBC, 1965–1966*). On this rock 'n' roll show, recording artists sang their hit songs. The Hullabaloo Dancers also performed. There was a different host each week. Several black acts, like the Marvelettes (the first successful Motown girls' group), **The Supremes,** and the Ronettes, performed on this show; some made their national television debuts on this show.

HUNTER-GAULT, CHARLAYNE. Hunter-Gault was the first black woman anchor on a nationally televised newscast, *The MacNeil/Lehrer Report* on PBS in 1978. After 20 years, she joined National Public Radio as a correspondent in South Africa. In 1999, she joined CNN in Johannesburg, South Africa, as bureau chief. Viewers of newscasts saw her heckled and harassed when she became one of the first two black students enrolled at the University of Georgia in 1962.

HUNTER-GAULT, CHUMA. Hunter-Gault, the son of **Charlayne Hunter-Gault**, played Greg Sparks in a recurring role on *Girlfriends* beginning in 2001. He also frequented on *The Parkers.*

HYMAN, EARLE. Hyman's first network television role was Jim in the *U.S. Steel Hour*'s production of "The Adventures of Huckleberry Finn" in 1957. He played Adam in **"The Green Pastures"** on *Hallmark Hall of Fame.* He is known to younger viewers as Russell, Cliff Huxtable's father in *The Cosby Show* (1984–1992). In 1959, he played Hopkins in "Simply Heavenly" on *Play of the Week.* In TV films, he had roles in *Hijacked: Flight 285* (1996) and *The Moving of Sophia Myles* (2000). *See also* TELEVISION PIONEERS.

– I –

ICE T. Rapper-turned-actor Ice T played Detective Odafin "Fin" Tutuola in *Law and Order: Special Victims Unit* beginning in 1999. In TV films, he had roles in *Players* (1997), *Exiled* (1998), and *The Disciples* (2000). His was the voice of Dr. Scratch in *The Magic 7*.

IFILL, GWEN. Ifill became moderator of PBS's *Washington Week* in 1999 after being a panelist on the program. Her title also was managing editor of *Washington Week* and senior correspondent for *The NewsHour with Jim Lehrer*. In 2004, she was moderator of the debate between vice-presidential candidates John Edwards and Dick Cheney. Prior to joining PBS, she was chief congressional and political correspondent for NBC News.

IGUS, DARROW. Igus played Jersey in 1973's sitcom *Roll Out*. He was a regular on the comedy/variety series *Fridays* from 1980 to 1982.

I HATE MY JOB *(Spike, 2004–)*. Right after running as Democratic Party candidate for U.S. president, the Rev. Al Sharpton hosted this reality series in which eight men quit their jobs to pursue their dream jobs. Each got a chance at doing things like being a comedian or a hockey coach. Sharpton and a therapist advised the candidates, and some were eliminated along the way. Sharpton told Jay Bobbin on Zap2it, "Other than being president, it is exactly where I think I can do some good and inspire people to do what I did: pursue their goals and their dreams. I think it's a good thing."

I HEAR AMERICA SINGING *(CBS, December 17, 1955)*. A 90-minute variety special, this was a salute to America with performers **Nat King Cole**, **Ella Fitzgerald**, Eddie Fisher, and Debbie Reynolds.

I KNOW WHY THE CAGED BIRD SINGS *(CBS, April 28, 1979)*. This was a two-hour biopic based on the early life of **Maya Angelou** and Angelou's book of the same title. In the telepic, Marguerite Johnson (played by Constance Good), a southern girl during the Depression, lived with her grandmother and older brother, Bailey, in a very segregated town where everybody knew their places. While visiting her mother, Marguerite was raped by her mother's boyfriend. The rest of the film is concerned with how the rape impacted her life. **Paul Benjamin** played Freeman, and **Diahann Carroll** played Vivian. **Ruby Dee** was Grandmother Baxter, while **Esther Rolle** was Momma. **Madge Sinclair** played Miss Flowers, **Sonny Jim Gaines** was Uncle Willie, John M. Driver II was Bailey Jr., and **Roger Mosley** was Bailey Sr. **Art Evans** was the principal.

I'LL FLY AWAY (*NBC, 1991–1993*). Although **Regina Taylor** did not have top billing (Sam Waterston did), her character, Lily Harper, was pivotal in this dramatic story about life in a small southern town on the cusp of the civil rights movement. Lily, the black housekeeper to a family headed by a liberal-minded prosecutor (Waterston), was also nanny to his three children, whose mother was in a mental institution. She quietly educates the family members about the issues of the struggle. The show lasted two seasons, and the year following its cancellation (1993), the cast did a PBS movie finale wrapping up loose ends. *See also* DOMESTIC WORKERS IN THE 1990s; DOMESTIC WORKERS' NAMES.

INGRAM, REX. A Broadway and movie actor, Ingram played De Lawd in *Hallmark Hall of Fame*'s **"The Green Pastures,"** a fantasy about an all-black heaven. Other Ingram credits include *The Emperor Jones* in 1955 and various episodic roles. His last television appearance was ***The Bill Cosby Show***, but he also had roles in ***Daktari***, *Gunsmoke*, *I Spy*, and *Playhouse 90*. He was more successful in film than in TV; he spoke about being denied roles because of racism. Still, after enjoying some success, Ingram made a promise to himself that he would not accept any roles that were demeaning to blacks. He was born in 1895 and died of a heart attack in 1969. *See also* TELEVISION PIONEERS.

IN LIVING COLOR (*FOX, 1990–1993*). This primarily black, controversial, totally irreverent show of fast-paced sketch comedy featured an ensemble cast headed by creator **Keenen Ivory Wayans**, also the show's executive producer and head writer. The cast introduced and also starred as regulars Wayans's siblings: **Damon,**

Dwayne, Shawn, Marlon, and **Kim Wayans**. Others in the repertory cast during the run of the series included Jim Carrey, **Kim Coles, Tommy Davidson, David Alan Grier, T'Keyah "Crystal" Keymah, Jamie Foxx, Anne-Marie Johnson**, and **Chris Rock**. A frenetic troupe of dancers called The Fly Girls (one was Jennifer Lopez) were included in transition between sketches. A popular skit was Damon and Grier as gay critics who trashed any and all art forms but especially "Men on Film." Another was "The Homeboy Shopping Network," in which two hoods (Keenen and Damon) sold stolen goods. "Hey, Mon" was a West Indian family in which all the members had numerous jobs. Keenen left his own hit series in 1992. Newspapers said Wayans had a growing rift with Fox officials. Soon, all his siblings left also. Carrey and Kelly Coffield were the resident white characters, and Carrey became star of the series in the fall of 1993; the series ended after that year. The series earned 17 **Emmy Award** nominations and won two Image Awards for Outstanding Variety Series.

IN PERFORMANCE AT THE WHITE HOUSE: AN EVENING OF SPIRITUALS AND GOSPEL MUSIC (*PBS, December 14, 1983*). Though this title indicates the special was performed at the White House, it was not. It was taped two weeks prior to air at Shiloh Baptist Church in Washington, D.C. **Leontyne Price** was the host of the show, which consisted entirely of spiritual and gospel music. With the Howard University Choir, Price sang "His Name Is Sweet." Unaccompanied, she sang "Go Tell It on the Mountain." Other performers were Lillias White, Kevette Cartledge, David Weatherspoon, and the Richard Smallwood Singers. President Ronald and Mrs. Reagan sat in the front pew. *New York Times* critic John J. O'Connor (December 14, 1983) wrote about the music as "extremely moving" and "bursting with handclapping." He said even the president joined in the spirit, "although his clapping appears to be decidedly off the beat."

IN PERFORMANCE AT THE WHITE HOUSE: CECE WINANS, GLORIOUS GOSPEL (*PBS, February 3, 1999*). Singer **Cece Winans** was host of this special concert of American gospel music, ranging from traditional to contemporary. President Bill and Mrs. Clinton were special guests.

IN PERFORMANCE AT THE WHITE HOUSE: SAVION GLOVER—STOMP, SLIDE, AND SWING (*PBS, September 16, 1998*). Tap dancer **Savion Glover** was host of a White House concert for President Bill and Mrs. Clinton showcasing four forms of American dance: tap, Irish step, Lindy Hop, and jazz. Performers spanned three generations.

INSIDE TV LAND: AFRICAN AMERICANS IN TELEVISION (*TVL, 2002*). The network of classic television series produced a documentary-type show framing the history of African Americans in the network television industry in programs, each centering on one of three genres—drama, variety, or comedy.

INTERNS, THE (*CBS, 1970–1971*). **Hal Frederick** played Dr. Cal Barrin, the black character among five young interns in New North Hospital who reported to Dr. Goldstone (Broderick Crawford). The series' scripts centered on the professional and personal lives of the interns.

INTERRACIAL ROMANCES/RELATIONSHIPS. Television genres, including news, talk shows, soap operas, and television movies, look at interracial romance from a variety of angles and with varying degrees of success, accuracy, and urgency.

In news coverage, for example, the interracial romance of **O. J. Simpson** and the late Nicole Brown Simpson factored into the media blitz surrounding her murder as well as the 2004 rape charges against basketball star Kobe Bryant.

Perhaps the best-known dramatized interracial couple is that of Franklin Cover's Tom Willis and **Roxie Roker**'s Helen Willis on the long-running sitcom *The Jeffersons*. Tom and Helen lived in the same apartment building as the Jeffersons and were their best friends. The Willis' daughter, Jenny (**Berlinda Tolbert**), looked and lived black, but later in the series, there emerged a son who looked white and was played by white actor Jay Hammer. Audiences, black and white, seemed to accept Tom and Helen, possibly because there was no physical passion and very little touching. Entertainer **Lenny Kravitz**, Roker's son, after her 1995 death, spoke of his mother seeking the role of Helen; he said when she was asked if she could play a woman in an interracial marriage, she pulled out a photo of herself and her Jewish husband as proof.

Prime-time series also tackle interracial romance. Actress **Denise Nicholas** said the interracial romance between her character, Harriet DeLong, and Carroll O'Connor's character, Police Chief Bill Gillespie, in *In the Heat of the Night* was planned early in the series. When she auditioned for the role, O'Connor told her of his plan for the romance, which started with loving but fleeting glances and tender touches before culminating in a marriage during the final season of the series. "Carroll purposely brought the relationship along slowly to bring viewers—black and white—along with us," said Nicholas, who wrote six of the series' episodes.

Nicholas, contemplating the issue years later, felt that Carroll probably wanted to expand his own image after playing Archie Bunker, the most famous TV racist. She said there was some hate mail, but that mail did not deter O'Connor. "He [O'Connor] read me one letter which was pretty dreadful but I never saw the others. He was completely surprised that some black people weren't that happy about my character being in love with Gillespie. I had told him about responses I had gotten from people—men and women—across the country."

Daytime drama series have similar experiences. Peter Bergman and **Debbi Morgan** received racist hate mail when they played lovers on *All My Children* in the 1980s. **Kristoff St. John**, who plays Neal Winters on *The Young and the Restless*, recalls that in the 1990s his character had a very brief affair with Victoria, the boss's daughter (who is white). "I received horrible letters," said St. John, "some even to my home address."

Jack Smith, executive vice president and head writer on *The Young and the Restless*, said, "Romance is a keystone of daytime drama, but we don't write inter-racial romance to be titillating or provocative; it's always story-driven—something that naturally would develop between characters. When I first started with the series, 25 years ago, it would have been very risky to show an inter-racial romance, but now the racist mail has decreased. However, it has not gone away. Even if we get one letter, it is disturbing. Racism is not dead. We know that."

Smith said the series, in 2004, received a very racist letter from a woman in a northern city, that the racist reactions are not confined to geographical regions. He suspects that young people are more tolerant than older viewers. Sharon Bramlett-Solomom's research agrees with Smith; she found that 75 percent of university students had seen interracial couples on television and that 50 percent of those felt there was no reason for concern.

Smith also cited objections from African-American women to the 2004 romance between black hunk Damon (**Keith Hamilton Cobb**) and white beauty Phyllis (Michelle Stafford). "I think that's more pride than racism," said Smith, who is white, "more territorial than racially driven." Nicholas agreed and said, "Black people find each other precious too. The erroneous take is that only white people get upset with inter-racial relationships."

In 1977, O. J. Simpson and Elizabeth Montgomery played a pair of detectives having an affair in *A Killing Affair*. In 1996, the cable movie channel Showtime brought to television the true story of *Mr. and Mrs. Loving* starring Timothy Hutton and **Lela Rochon**. The movie followed the story of Richard Loving and Mildred Jeter, both of Virginia. The couple was jailed on their wedding night for violating state law prohibiting mixed marriage. The Lovings took their case to the U.S. Supreme Court. The ruling in their case outlawed antimiscegenation laws in the United States.

Other series with interracial romance and relationships include the following: **Eriq LaSalle**'s Dr. Peter Benton and Alex Kingston's Dr. Elizabeth Corday, Ming-Na's Dr. Ming-Mei Chen and **Mekhi Phifer**'s Dr. Gregory Platt, and Thandie Newton's Makemba and Noah Wylie's Dr. John Carter on *ER*; **Richard Roundtree**'s Russell Emerson and Stephen Poletti's Chris Daily on *Roc* (also a gay romance); Wren T. Brown's Courtney Rae and Elizabeth Regen's Rita on *Whoopi*; Amy Acker's Fred Burkle and J. August Richards's Charles Gunn on *Angel*; **Blair Underwood**'s Dr. Robert Leeds and Cynthia Nixon's Miranda Hobbes on *Sex and the City*; Rachel True's Mona Thorne and Nick Stabile's Nick Tyrell on *Half & Half*; Jill Marie Jones's Toni Childs and Jason Pace's Dr. Todd Garrett on *Girlfriends*; **Robert Guillaume**'s Edward Sawyer and Wendy Philips's Ann Sheer on *The Robert Guillaume Show*; and the various romantic twists involving **Diahann Carroll**'s Dominique Deveraux in the shows *Dynasty* and *The Colbys*. There were also interracial romances or relationships on *The West Wing* (with **Dule Hill**), *Whoopi*, *Scrubs* (with **Donald Faison**), *Will & Grace* (with **Gregory Hines**), and *24* (with **Dennis Haysbert**). *See also* OPRAH WINFREY PRESENTS: THE WEDDING; STAR TREK.

IN THE HEAT OF THE NIGHT (*NBC and CBS, 1988–1994*). Carroll O'Connor (as Police Chief Bill Gillespie) starred in this police drama series based on the 1967 Sidney Poitier film *They Call Me Mister Tibbs*. Playing the Poitier character, secondary only to O'Connor, was **Howard Rollins** as Chief of Detectives Virgil Tibbs. Gillespie and Tibbs were very different in their crime-fighting methods in their small southern town, Sparta, Mississippi. Gillespie was more traditional; Tibbs had learned "big-city ways" as a cop in Philadelphia. Yet they learned to work together and became friends. **Anne-Marie Johnson** played Tibbs's devoted wife, Althea. In a rare continuing interracial romance, **Denise Nicholas** played Gillespie's classy girlfriend, Harriet; they were married in the final season of the series. The episodes dealt with crime and racism. The crimes ranged from murder to robbery to drug busts.

Drugs were a problem not only in fictional Sparta but also among some of the cast and crew members of the series. Rollins fought a drug addiction for years, and O'Connor (who was also executive producer) supported him in his battle for a long time. In 1988, when the show filmed in Louisiana, Rollins pleaded guilty to driving under the influence and cocaine possession. In 1992, he pleaded guilty to driving under the influence of a tranquilizer; he served two days in jail and lost his driver's license. Rollins even served half of a 70-day jail sentence in 1993 for driving under the influence and reckless driving. He admitted he had a problem he couldn't beat and said he almost committed suicide in 1989. He was dropped from the series in 1993, a year before the series ended, and was replaced by **Carl Weathers** as Chief Hampton Forbes (Gillespie had become sheriff). Rollins died in 1996 of complications from lymphoma, a cancer he discovered only six weeks before his death. The series' hairdresser died of a drug overdose while the series was on location in Georgia. O'Connor's son, Hugh (who played Jamison, the deputy), died of a drug overdose in 1995 shortly after the series had ended. O'Connor, said friends, never recovered from the loss of his son, and he died in 2001 of a heart attack. *See also* INTERRACIAL ROMANCE/RELATIONSHIPS; LONG-RUNNING SERIES.

IN THE HOUSE (*NBC, 1995–1996; UPN, 1997–1998*). This black-cast sitcom starred rap star **LL Cool J** (née James Todd Smith) as Marion Hill, an Oakland Raiders star who suffered an injury. To **Quincy Jones**, whose company produced the series, "LL Cool J was another multitalented rapper [Will Smith preceded him] we inducted into television. . . . He has a very centered mind and is a consummate pro. His grandma raised him right." In the scripts, central character Marion rented his house to a divorced mother, Jackie (**Debbie Allen**), with two small children, Tiffany (Maia Campbell) and Austin (**Jeffrey Wood**). When Jackie could not find day care for the children, Marion agreed to take on the duties. When the series moved to UPN, Jackie had moved to Nashville with son Austin, leaving Tiffany in Marion's care. Then Marion went into partnership in a sports clinic with Tonia (**Kim Wayans**) and Dr. Stanton (**Alfonso Ribeiro**). Other actors in the cast were Dee Jay Daniels as Rodney, **John Amos** as Coach Sam, Ken Lawson as Carl, Gabrielle Carmouche as Raynelle, Derek McGrath as Bernie, Paulette Braxton as Natalie Davis, and Lark Voorhees as Mercedes Langford. *See also* RAP ARTISTS WHO BECAME TV ACTORS.

INTRODUCING DOROTHY DANDRIDGE (*HBO, August 21, 1999*). **Halle Berry** starred in and was executive producer of this biopic about the beautiful African-American movie star whose life ended so early, so tragically. The made-for-television film spans the life of Dandridge, whose successes included an Oscar nomination for the movie *Carmen Jones*. It included the sadness and low points of Dandridge's life as well as the passions and pleasures. **Obba Babatunde** (as Harold Nicholas), **Loretta Devine** (as Ruby Dandridge), Tamara Taylor, LaTanya Richardson, Brent Spiner, Alexia Carrington, Cynda Williams, and Klaus Maria Brandauer were the central cast. Berry won a Golden Globe Award for Best Actress in a Miniseries or Movie Made for Television. Martha Coolidge, director of the film, when asked about Berry's participation as executive producer, replied, "She was involved with the development of the script. She was involved with hiring me. She had a lot of strong feelings about the material, and a very strong interpretation of what she was interested in and why, and who Dorothy was. But once we started in rehearsals, preproduction and production, she understood what a huge challenge the role was and really took on the role of actor." Coolidge, who is white, said that working on the film gave her a greater understanding of exclusion. "Never has my awareness been higher of discrimination in our country, in our world, and certainly in this business."

IRONSIDE (*NBC, 1967–1975*). Robert Ironside (Raymond Burr) was a former San Francisco police chief of detectives who took a would-be assassin's bullet in the spine and was left paraplegic. He became a special crime-solving consultant to the Police Department, and Mark Sanger was the former delinquent who pushed his wheelchair and was his bodyguard. **Don Mitchell** played Sanger. Later in the series, Sanger went to law school; he graduated and got married during the series' final season. *See also* SERIES WITH ONE BLACK SUPPORTING ACTOR/PERFORMER BEFORE 1980.

IRVIN, MICHAEL. A retired Dallas Cowboy, Irvin joined ABC to provide analysis and commentary on NBC's Arena Football League studio show during pregame and halftime coverage. His credits include appearing on the panel on Fox Sports Net's *Best Damn Sports Show, Period* and as a member of the Fox Sports Network's pregame show, *The NFL Show*.

I SPY (*NBC, 1965–1968*). This one-hour drama starred **Bill Cosby** and Robert Culp as undercover agents working in foreign countries where there was some threat to U.S. security. The series made history because it was the first time a black star and a white star shared equal billing and the first time a black actor had a lead role in a drama series. Cosby's acting career was given a head start by a teenage Rob Reiner (who would later play Mike "Meathead" Stivic on *All in the Family*), who saw him doing a comedy routine on *The Tonight Show*. Reiner told his father, producer Carl Reiner, how funny Cosby was. The elder Reiner asked Cosby to come in and do a routine for him and other associates. Cosby did his "Noah and the Ark" monologue, and Reiner offered him the costarring role on *I Spy*. When someone asked if the comedian could act, Reiner said Cosby had done all the acting he needed to see in the comedy routine. Even though in many episodes Robinson (Culp) was portrayed as the leader of the twosome, Scott (Cosby) was clearly not a servant. The two characters had fun doing their espionage work, and that fun added humor to the series. *See also* SERIES RANKINGS (Appendix A).

IT'S BLACK ENTERTAINMENT (*SHO, 1997*). A cast of dozens appeared in this program of interviews and entertainment focusing on black entertainers in music, film, and television throughout the 20th century. **Vanessa Williams** was host. Interviewed were Whitney Houston, **Debbie Allen, Smokey Robinson, Gregory Hines, Jasmine Guy**, Snoop Dogg, **Jamie Fox, Little Richard, Spike Lee**, and **Billy Dee Williams**. Footage of performances included the following talent: **Louis Armstrong**, Josephine Baker, **Sammy Davis Jr.**, Ella Fitzgerald, Lena Horne, Michael Jackson, Billie Holiday, Otis Redding, **Diana Ross**, The Notorious B.I.G., **Dorothy Dandridge, Billy Eckstine, Duke Ellington, Tina Turner**, and numerous others. Kage Alan, reviewing the DVD of the production, said, "The people who are interviewed seem genuinely interested in the subject matter and reflect very fondly on those who have influenced their lives and careers, even when the stories have tragic endings." Stan Lathan was director.

IT'S GOOD TO BE ALIVE (*CBS, February 22, 1974*). This two-hour made-for-television film was the story of Roy Campanella, the Brooklyn Dodgers' catcher, and his struggle to adapt to life in a wheelchair after he was paralyzed in a 1959 auto accident. **Paul Winfield** played Campanella. **Lou Gossett, Ruby Dee, Ty Henderson, Ketty Lester**, and **Stymie Beard** had key roles. Campanella appeared in the film as well as members of his real-life family. *See also* AFRICAN-AMERICAN HISTORY MONTH; ATHLETES' BIOPICS.

IT'S SHOWTIME AT THE APOLLO (*SYN, 1987–*). Taped before a live audience from the Apollo Theater, this series was seen in more than 100 markets, usually in late night. The show originally opened with the Apollo Dancers. It featured Apollo regular dancer Sandman Sims, who, dressed in an outrageous costume, would shoo off unworthy contestants in the Amateur Night competition. This contest in which the audience booed and Sandman shooed was an Apollo tradition. The understanding among black performers at the Apollo was that the audience was so tough that "if you can make it at the Apollo, you can make it anywhere." Most shows also had an Amateur Kids segment; the audience was supportive of the kids, talented or not. At first there were celebrity hosts for each telecast and celebrity entertainers, then comedian **Sinbad** was host for 1989–1991. **Mark Curry** was host from 1992 to 1993. At other times, the show used celebrity hosts until 1994, when comedian **Steve Harvey** took over hosting duties. During a labor dispute, Harvey and the series regular hostess Kiki Shepard hosted a series of shows showing highlights of the series. Harvey left in 2003, and comedy actress **Mo'Nique** got the job. Percy Sutton's Inner City Broadcasting was the original production company for the series, but it lost the rights. Sutton continued with a similar show for a while, then he backed away, and Suzanne Depasse, who had won an **Emmy Award** in 1985 as producer of *Motown Returns to the Apollo*, produced the series.

IT'S WHAT'S HAPPENING (*CBS, June 28, 1965*). This was a 90-minute variety special with big-name entertainers. Among them were the following: **Ray Charles**, **Bill Cosby**, The Drifters, The Four Tops, Marvin Gaye, Little Anthony and the Imperials, Martha and the Vandellas, **Johnny Mathis**, **The Supremes**, **The Temptations**, and **Dionne Warwick**. Also featured were Herman's Hermits, Gary Lewis and the Playboys, Johnny Rivers, The Righteous Brothers, and others.

IYANLA (*SYN, 2001–2002*). Iyanla **Vanzant**, a best-selling author and self-help expert, hosted this show centering on helping viewers cope with the challenges of life. Each one-hour show covered a single topic and involved the studio audience. Some of these challenges were difficult relationships, financial problems, and parenting. The canceling of the show was announced in January 2002, and Vanzant, though not making excuses, said, "Our show was launched three weeks before September 11, after which most of the country understandably spent the next three weeks watching the news." *See also* TALK SHOWS.

– J –

JACK BENNY SHOW, THE (*CBS, 1950–1964, 1977; NBC, 1964–1965*). This comedy show evolved from a hit radio show starring comedian Jack Benny. **Eddie Anderson** was hired for a one-time appearance as a railway porter on the radio show in 1937 and was so popular that he was hired to play Benny's valet, Rochester, on a regular basis. Unlike most black characters in early television, there was never much objection from black Americans to this character, probably because the character was not played by a white actor imitating a black servant. Many people thought Anderson was actually Benny's servant. His gravelly voice was his distinctive trademark, but he never spoke in dialect. He stood erect, never moving like a wimpish frightened houseman as his predecessors had to play. Surely, he was playing a servant, as did black actors in most programs, but Rochester was different. His trademark line was "What's that, Boss?" Yet as the series continued, Anderson became a valued member of the cast, and the show's writers eliminated some stereotypes. He had a level of dignity and sophistication. In fact, he usually got the best of Benny, who could only utter afterward, "Well!"

Los Angelenos during that time called him "Rochester," and he answered gladly. He and his family lived in a large house that occupied much of a cul-de-sac in a neighborhood of smaller houses occupied primarily by blacks who were proud to be his neighbors. The famous Hollywood maps of the stars homes never included Anderson's house, but African Americans visiting Los Angeles were frequently brought by friends to see "where Rochester lives."

JACKSON, JANET. The singer-actress-dancer played herself on *The Jacksons* (1976–1977), Jojo Ashton in *A New Kind of Family* (1979–1980), Penny Gordon Woods in *Good Times* (1977–1979), Charlene DuPrey on *Diff'rent Strokes* (1981–1982), and Cleo Hewitt in *Fame* (1984–1985). Jackson appeared in the variety special the *Sounds of Summer* in 1993. In 2001, she was one of the divas in the tribute show *VH1 Divas Live 2001: The One and Only Aretha Franklin*. She was a headliner in the halftime show of Super Bowl XXXVIII in 2004 and dominated the news with a controversial exposure. *See also* SUPER BOWL HALFTIME SHOWS.

JACKSON, REVEREND JESSE. The Reverend Jesse Jackson recited his poem *I Am Somebody* in *Wattstax 1973*, a film documentary with limited distribution that aired in 2004. He appeared in the comedy *All-Star Celebration: The '88 Vote* in 1988 and the tribute special **Sammy Davis Jr.'s 60th Anniversary Celebration** in 1990. On *Saturday Night Live*, he hosted and recited the lyrics to "Bonnie Jean" in 1984. He was host of *The Jesse Jackson Show*, a weekly program on which he and a panel of experts discussed a preselected topic (1990–1991). He hosted another weekly discussion show *Both Sides with Jesse Jackson* in 1992; that show centered on a variety of social and political issues.

JACKSON, LATOYA. LaToya Jackson appeared in variety specials *Command Performance* in 1989, *Bob Hope's USO Road Tour to the Berlin Wall and Moscow* in 1990, and *Mary Hart Presents Love in the Public Eye* in 1990.

JACKSON, LIA. Jackson played one of the Harris kids in the 1978 TV movie **Love Is Not Enough** and the short-lived black family drama series it spawned, **Harris and Company**, in 1979.

JACKSON, MAHALIA. The gospel singer appeared in variety specials "Crescendo" (*A DuPont Show of the Month* production) in 1957, . . . *And Beautiful II* in 1970, and *Captain EO—Backstage* in 1988. She appeared in the *Bing Crosby Special* in 1958, three airings of *The Bell Telephone Hour* (one in 1960 and two in 1962), two airings of *The Dean Martin Show* in 1966, and *Westinghouse Presents: The Sound of the Sixties* (1961). She was the mystery guest on the game show *What's My Line?* in 1961. She also appeared through film in the tribute special *MTV: Music Television's 10th Anniversary* in 1991 and the documentary *Michael Jackson . . . The Legend Continues* in 1992. She was born in 1911 and died in 1972 of heart disease.

JACKSON, MEL. Jackson played Ira Lee Williams III ("Tripp") in the sitcom **Living Single** (1997–1998) and had a key role in **The Little Richard Story** in 2000.

JACKSON, MICHAEL. In addition to numerous appearances with the Jackson Five in variety series and specials, Michael Jackson, as a solo performer, headlined numerous specials. In 1987, he headlined the special *Michael Jackson—Mega Star*; in 1992, the special *Michael Jackson: In Concert in Bucharest*; in 1995, *Michael Jackson: One Night Only*; in 1999, *A Concert for Kosovo's Children*; in 2001, *Michael Jackson: 30th Anniversary Celebration*; and in 2004, *Michael Jackson: Number Ones*. He also appeared in specials headlined by other performers including *Marlo Thomas and Friends in Free to Be . . . You and Me* in 1974, *Disneyland's 25th Anniversary* in 1980, *Diana* in 1981, *Captain EO—Backstage* in 1988, and *A Night at the Apollo* in 2002. Jackson also appeared in tribute specials *It's Black Entertainment* in 2002, *Sammy Davis Jr.'s 60th Anniversary Celebration* in 1990, and *A Tribute to John Lennon* in 1990. The Gloved One's video *Black or White* premiered in 1991. He starred in *MTV 10*, the 10th anniversary tribute to MTV, the music cable channel, in 1991.

He was the subject of an interview by **Oprah Winfrey** in 1993, when he was the subject of sensational news stories about charges that his behavior with children was improper. *Michael Jackson Talks . . . to Oprah: 90 Primetime Minutes with the King of Pop* was the top-rated special of the 1992–1993 season. His early videos (he calls them short films) were history making, especially *Thriller* (1983) and *Bad* (1987). He appeared in the documentary *Michael Jackson . . . The Legend Continues* in 1992.

JACKSON, SAMUEL L. Jackson starred or had key roles in the TV films *Against the Wall* (1994), *Assault at West Point: The Court-Martial of Johnson Whittaker* (1994), *Dead and Alive: The Race for Gus Farace* (1991), *Dead Man Out* (1989), *Uncle Tom's Cabin* (1987), and *The Displaced Person* (1976). Jackson was interviewed on black Hollywood for the documentary *America Beyond the Color Line* (2004). He made appearances as presenters in various awards shows and was host of the 2002 ESPY Awards. His was the voice of Johnson in *Unforgivable Blackness: The Rise and Fall of Jack Johnson* in 2005.

JACKSON, STONEY. Jackson played Black Jack Savage on *Disney Presents the 100 Lives of Black Jack Savage* (1991), James Mackey in *The Insiders* (1985–1986), Travis Filmore in *227* (1989–1990), and Jesse B. Mitchell on *The White Shadow* (1980–1981).

JACKSONS: AN AMERICAN DREAM, THE (*ABC, November 15–18, 1992*). This made-for-television film dramatized the lives of the famous singing family including superstar **Michael Jackson**. Wylie Draper and Jason Weaver played Michael. **Angela Bassett** portrayed Katherine Jackson, and **Lawrence Hilton-Jacobs** was Joe Jackson, who was determined his kids would be successful. **Holly Robinson Peete** played Diana Ross; **Billy Dee Williams** played Berry Gordy. Academy Award nominee **Margaret Avery** was also in the cast. Suzanne de Passe was executive producer of the film. This was the highest-rated television movie of the 1992–1993 season. *See also* BIOPICS.

JACKSONS, THE (*CBS, 1976, 1977*). The Jackson siblings— **Michael**, Jackie, Tito, Marlon, Randy, **LaToya**, Rebie, and **Janet**— starred in this musical variety series, which also included comedy. The series was launched before Michael's album *Off the Wall* catapulted his career into stardom. Each week, young Janet, long before she launched her successful acting or singing career, often did an impression of Mae West, "Why don't you come up and see me sometime." The brothers sang as the Jackson Five doing their hits. There were also solos and comedy sketches featuring guest stars like Betty White and Lynda Carter. The series aired for four weeks for two consecutive summers.

JACKSONVILLE AND ALL THAT JAZZ (*PBS, October 15, 1983*). This one-hour special featured highlights of the jazz festival in Jacksonville, Florida, with **Dizzy Gillespie**, **Wynton Marsalis**, Art Blakey and the Jazz Messengers, the **Billy Taylor** Trio, Freddie Hubbard, and Buddy Rich. At the festival, Gillespie was designated the King of Jazz.

JACQUET, JEFFREY. A child actor, Jacquet played Eugene in *Mork and Mindy* in 1978–1979 and Jeremy Saldino in *Whiz Kids* in 1983–1984. He was one of the kids in the 1982 special *Goldie and the Kids: Listen to Me* starring Goldie Hawn. He became a lawyer.

JAMES BALDWIN: THE PRICE OF THE TICKET (*PBS, August 14, 1989*). Authors **Maya Angelou** and William Styron, musician

Bobby Short, and Baldwin's brother, David, appeared in this comprehensive biography of author/civil rights activist James Baldwin.

JAMES BROWN: SOUL SURVIVOR (*PBS, October 29, 2003*). One of the *American Masters* series, the show tracked James Brown's climb to superstardom with performances, rare archival footage, and interviews with musicians, friends, and the "Godfather of Soul" himself.

JAMES, OLGA. James was the sister-in-law in the sitcom *The Bill Cosby Show* (1969–1971).

JAMES, PETER FRANCIS. James played Alfred Livingston, the father of the character played by singer **Monica**, in *Love Song* in 2000 and Raymond Parks, Rosa Parks's husband, in *The Rosa Parks Story* in 2002.

JAMES-REESE, CYNDI. After winning the acting competition on *Star Search*, James-Reese had key roles in *The Face of Rage* and *The Return of Marcus Welby, M.D.*, both in 1983.

JAMIE FOXX SHOW, THE (*WB, 1996–2001*). Comedian **Jamie Foxx** starred in this sitcom as Jamie King, an aspiring actor from Texas who moved to Hollywood to find fame and fortune in the entertainment industry. While waiting for his big break, he decided to work at the King's Towers, a small hotel owned by his Aunt Helen (Ellia English) and Uncle Junior (**Garrett Morris**). The hotel staff, particularly accountant Braxton P. Hartnabrig (Christopher B. Duncan), was not happy about the new employee. Jamie was attracted to Fancy (Garcelle Beauvais), the sexy desk clerk who at first couldn't care less. Then later, she was more interested. Foxx was creator, director, and producer and sang the theme song. He won an NAACP Image Award in 1998 for Outstanding Lead Actor in a Comedy Series for this show. He was nominated again in 1999, 2000, and 2001.

JAMIE FOXX: STRAIGHT FROM THE FOXXHOLE (*HBO, November 6, 1993*). Comedian Foxx starred in this one-man show of his stand-up act. It was taped in San Diego at the Spreckels Theatre.

JAMMIN' (*SYN, 1992–1993*). **Byron Allen** hosted this one-hour show featuring interviews of music celebrities. Most, but not all, of the entertainers interviewed were black.

JAMMIN': JELLY ROLL MORTON ON BROADWAY (*PBS, November 2, 1992*). This documentary starring **Gregory Hines** included a profile of Morton but also a look at the process of putting together the Broadway musical *Jelly's Last Jam*, based on Morton's work.

JANET JACKSON: IN CONCERT FROM HAWAII (*HBO, February 17, 2002*). **Janet Jackson** sang and danced at Aloha Stadium in Honolulu. The performance included a multimedia production, numerous sets and costumes, support dancers and singers, and musicians.

JANET: THE VELVET ROPE (*HBO, October 11, 1998*). **Janet Jackson** headlined a show of music and dance, her final concert of her sold-out world tour. Featured were songs from her double platinum album "The Velvet Rope."

JANET'S WORLD TOUR SPECIAL (*HBO, November 26, 1993*). This was a behind the scenes look, with performances, at **Janet Jackson**'s world tour on opening night in Cincinnati.

JASPER, TEXAS (*SHO, June 8, 2003*). This TV motion picture told the story of the 1998 murder of James Byrd Jr., a black man who was chained to the back of a truck and dragged by three young white supremacists. **Louis Gossett Jr.** (as the town's first black mayor, R. C. Horn), **Joe Morton** (as Walter Diggles), Emily Yancy (as Stella Byrd), Bokeem Woodbine (as Khalid X), and Jon Voight (as Billy Rowles, the town's white sheriff) starred.

JAZZ AT LINCOLN CENTER: ARMSTRONG—WHEN THE SAINTS GO MARCHING IN (*PBS, December 13, 2000*). **Wynton Marsalis** and the Lincoln Center Jazz Orchestra celebrated **Louis Armstrong**.

JAZZ AT LINCOLN CENTER WITH WYNTON MARSALIS (*PBS, July 1, 1998*). Marsalis's recent Opus "Big Train" was performed, as was the music of **Duke Ellington** and **Louis Armstrong**. The Lincoln Center Jazz Orchestra performed with singer/pianist Shirley Horn and Broadway tap dancer Baakiri Wilder.

JAZZ COMES HOME TO NEWPORT (*PBS, February 13, 1984*). This special was an hour-long compilation of two days of jazz performances at the Newport, Rhode Island, festival the previous August. **Dizzy Gillespie**'s quintet was a highlight. Ron Carter's bass solo was praised by critics for the combination of camera work and performance.

JEAN-BAPTISTE, MARIANNE. Actor-musician-songwriter-composer Jean-Baptiste played Vivian Johnson, an investigator in the drama series *Without a Trace* beginning in 2003. Her TV film credits include the following: *The Wedding* (1998), *The Murder of Stephen Lawrence* (1999), *The Man* (1999), *Men Only* (2001), and *Loving You* (2003).

JEFF, JAZZY. *See* TOWNES, JEFF.

JEFFERSON, HERBERT, JR. Jefferson played Boomer in *Battlestar Galactica*, a series similar to *Star Wars* that lasted only one season (1978–1979) but later became a cult hit. His first regular series role was as Ray Dwyer in *Rich Man, Poor Man—Book 1* (1976–1977), and he was Otis Branes in *The Devlin Connection* (1982).

JEFFERSONS, THE (*CBS, 1975–1985*). This was the longest-running black-cast series with original episodes and still continues in reruns. **Sherman Hemsley** and **Isabel Sanford** played George and Louise "Weezy" Jefferson, characters originated in the popular sitcom *All in the Family*. George's dry-cleaning business expanded to such a successful chain that the couple had to "move on up to the East Side," according to the theme song (written by **Ja'net DuBois** and sung by DuBois and Jeff Barry). Neighbors in the upscale high-rise building were Helen (**Roxie Roker**) and Tom Willis (Franklin Cover). Willis was white and the object of racial jokes from the bigoted George; this was a character trait established on *All in the Family*. George was doubly incensed when his young adult son, Lionel (first played by **Mike Evans**, then by **Damon Evans**, then again by Mike Evans), fell in love with Jenny (**Berlinda Tolbert**), the daughter of the Willises. George referred to her as "zebra," half black and half white.

Through all of George's racial slurs, Willis and George were not enemies; Willis seemed to ignore George's remarks, but occasionally he would fight words with words. Mostly, Willis judged George by his actions rather than his big mouth; there were acts of kindness between the two. Yet their relationship was still grounded in the close friendship of their wives. George was arrogant and a social climber, but Louise was down-to-earth and concerned about the effects of new money and privilege on the family, particularly George. Louise had an often-hidden strength to take control, and George had an often-hidden weakness to turn to mush if Louise chose to attack.

Central to the life of the Jeffersons was Florida, their cynical maid (**Marla Gibbs**), who was as outspoken as George; she was the only character who could always put him in his place. The others tolerated George's mouth; Florida did not. In fact, it was debatable who was head of the household. Bentley (Paul Benedict) was the neighbor with the proper English accent. Ralph (Ned Wertimer) was the doorman who was never seen opening a door; he visited the Jeffersons' apartment delivering packages and mail and tried effortlessly to get gratuities from the penny-pinching George. For the first three seasons, George's cantankerous mother (Zara Cully) added conflict and humor; Louise was never good enough for her son.

As the series progressed, Lionel and Jenny became engaged, then married, and eventually had a daughter, Jessica (Ebonie Smith). Jessica was the pride and joy of both sets of grandparents and a reason for George and Willis to argue and try to be most important in her life. Jenny and Lionel separated; only Jenny and the daughter remained in the series. In the 1977–1979 season, young Marcus (**Ernest Harden Jr.**), who worked in one of George's dry cleaners, frequently visited the apartment. In 1978, Allan, also a son of Tom and Helen, returned home to his parents after being in a commune. Unlike his sister Jenny, who looked black, Allan looked white (Jay Hammer, a white actor, played the role). In 1984, George and Willis became partners in Charlie's Bar, a neighborhood hangout. Charlie was played by Danny Wells.

Lear comedy series dealt with serious social issues and controversy, and so did *The Jeffersons*; there were situations and lessons in
race, gender, class, and urban strife. The controversies generally were
about race or racism. In one episode, George charges that Louise's
uncle, who was a butler, was an Uncle Tom because black people
were obligated to rise above subservient jobs. However, the show's
goal was obviously to be funny first and serious, perhaps, later. *See
also* INTERRACIAL RELATIONSHIPS, LONG-RUNNING SE-
RIES.

JEFFRIES, ADAM. Jeffries played one of the Freeman sons in the sitcom *True Colors* (1990–1992) and Jarvis, another teenage son, on
the sitcom *Thea* (1993–1994).

JENKINS, LARRY FLASH. Jenkins played Lynwood Scott on *The
Bay City Clues* (1983), Lyman Whittaker in *Finder of Love Lost*
(1985), and Wardell Stone on *The White Shadow* (1980–1981).

JERICHO MILE, THE (*ABC, March 18, 1979*). **Richard Lawson,
Roger E. Mosley, Beverly Todd**, and **Ji-Tu Cumbuka** played supporting roles in this much-praised two-hour film about an inmate (Peter Strauss) at Folsom prison who earns an opportunity to compete in
the Olympics as a runner.

JERK TOO, THE (*NBC, January 6, 1984*). This two-hour telefilm
was a sequel to the theatrical film *The Jerk* starring Steve Martin. The
story was that white Navin Johnson (Mark Blankfield) leaves the
black sharecropping family that reared him and goes on one misad-
venture after another in his quest to make life successful. The large
cast had several black actors. Among them were **Thalmus Rasulala,
Mabel King, Jimmie Walker, Al Fann, Todd Hollowell**, and **Helen
Martin**. George Crosby was associate producer.

JESSE OWENS STORY, THE (*SYN, July 9 and 16, 1984*). A miniseries about the Olympic track star, the story traces 40 years of his
life from his childhood in Alabama through his tax battles with the
federal government. Filmed to air during the excitement of the 1984
Olympics, **Dorian Harewood** played Owens, who won gold medals

in the 1936 Olympics and infuriated Adolf Hitler. **Georg Stanford Brown**, who played a parole officer investigating Owens's background for the government, narrates the story. **Debbi Morgan** played Ruth Solomon Owens. **Lynn Hamilton** played Mamma Solomon, and **LeVar Burton** played Prof. Slade Preston. **Greg Morris** was Mel Walker. **Ben Vereen** was Herb Douglas. *See also* ATHLETES' BIOPICS.

JESSYE NORMAN SINGS CARMEN (*PBS, November 13, 1989*). Opera singer **Jessye Norman** sang the role of Carmen for the first time. Accompanied by the Orchestre National de France, she performed in Paris in a closed recording studio.

JESSYE NORMAN: WOMEN OF LEGEND, FANTASY AND LORE (*PBS, April 27, 1994*). Soprano **Jessye Norman** starred in this program, which highlighted the great women of opera and literature. The broadcast was live from Lincoln Center in New York.

JIMMY B. & ANDRE (*CBS, March 19, 1980*). **Madge Sinclair**, **Barbara Meek**, **Hank Rolike**, and young Curtis Yates played key roles in this two-hour dramatic film about the actual relationship between Detroit restaurateur Jimmy Butsicaris (Alex Karras) and a black boy (Yates) he tried to adopt.

JOBS IN THE TELEVISION INDUSTRY. African Americans work in all aspects of the television industry, from appearing in front of the camera to writing scripts, developing and producing shows, and running television stations. Scholars have looked into various aspects of the work life of African Americans in television. Marginalization to specific shows or networks, lack of power in board and staff meeting rooms, and an overriding myth of a lack of African-American creative talent rank high among challenges faced by African-American production assistants, writers, directors, producers, and executives working in television. In interviews with figures such as actor/producer/director **Tim Reid**, writer/producer Vida Spears, and former CBS executive Frank Dawson, Gregory Adamo's study found that "for African-American creators economic, creative and racial issues are tightly connected."

African-American writers in Adamo's study told of their agents being unwilling to seek jobs for them on mainstream or established and award-winning network shows. Instead, writers interviewed said, agents pursued work for their black writers on black-themed programs. On the rare occasion when hired for mainstream shows, black writers in Adamo's study described themselves as translators or cultural informants about black life for white writers and not as members of the creative team to help produce a good show. Some writers spoke of being viewed by others on staff as the affirmative action writer hired to fill minority quotas rather than as a qualified member of the staff.

According to the 1998 Hollywood Writers' Report titled *Telling All Our Stories* and commissioned by the professional organization Writers Guild of America, minority writers made up 7 percent of all writers working on television overall in 1997. In the same study, researchers reported that the bulk of minority writers worked for Fox, UPN, and the WB networks. In the 1997–1998 season, 13 percent of minority writers credited on-screen worked for Fox. Meanwhile, 19 percent of minority writers with on-screen credit worked for the WB network, and 29 percent worked for UPN. The online executive summary of the report also notes that of the 168 shows analyzed for the report, 80 percent had no minority writer or only one minority writer credited on-screen. The report continues, "Despite gains made in employment and earnings since the 1980s, in the entertainment industry today [the late 1990s], 94 percent of the writing is done by nonminorities. Among those working in the industry, non-minorities outnumber minorities by more than 16 to 1."

African-American broadcast station managers confront challenges as well. Researcher Gwendolyn Taylor learned that African-American women often encounter obstacles such as racism and the glass ceiling obstructing promotion to upper-level management jobs. In in-depth interviews with a dozen station managers, Taylor found that African-American women called on strategies such as seeking out mentors, modeling behavior of others, and joining professional organizations to gain footing in their careers, especially in work environments where they were "the first and/or only" African-American woman to have that job in a field traditionally dominated by older white men. Several spoke of success in their careers coming at a price, impacting their health and relationships with their children and other family members.

Meanwhile, creators of shows carried burdens, such as expectations of any one show serving to represent the full African-American experience. Critics of the highly successful *The Cosby Show*, for example, scolded the show for not addressing issues of working-class black America and overt racism, according to researchers Sut Jhally and Justin Lewis. The same was not expected of an equally successful mainstream show.

JOE AND MAX (*Starz, March 9, 2002*). This two-hour docudrama was about the championship boxing bouts and lives of American champ Joe Louis (Leonard Roberts) and challenger German Max Schmeling from 1938 to 1952. The two, who expressed respect for each other, were victims of their environment—Jim Crow America and Nazi Germany. *See also* ATHLETES' BIOPICS.

JOE FRAZIER FIGHTS. Frazier lost to Buster Mathis in the U.S. Olympic Boxing Trials televised on May 30, 1964. Mathis broke a knuckle prior to the Olympic Games, and Frazier substituted for him and went on to win a gold medal. Frazier was victorious in his fight with Jerry Quarry for the New York World Heavyweight Championship televised on June 28, 1969. Frazier beat Bob Foster in a second-round knockout for the World Heavyweight Championship on November 21, 1970. He fought George Foreman for the World Heavyweight Championship and lost in a televised bout on January 27, 1973. **Muhammad Ali** defeated him on March 2, 1974. He lost the "Thrilla in Manila" to Ali on January 11, 1976. *See also* BOXING MATCHES ON TELEVISION.

JOHN GRIN'S CHRISTMAS (*ABC, December 6, 1986*). **Robert Guillaume** starred in this drama, an African-American version of Dickens's *A Christmas Carol*. This Scrooge, John Grin (Guillaume), was a wealthy toy maker who earned his fortune the hard way. He was stingy, grumpy, did not get along well with the people in the neighborhood, and was against celebrating Christmas. Then he was visited by three ghosts. These ghosts turned his life around and thereby improved the plight of the community. **Roscoe Lee Browne**

was the Ghost of Christmas Past; **Ted Lange** the Ghost of Christmas Present; and **Geoffrey Holder** the Ghost of Christmas Future. **Alfonso Ribeiro** played Rocky. Guillaume was producer and director.

JOHNNIE MAE GIBSON: FBI (*USA, 1986*). **Lynn Whitfield** starred in this TV film based on fact about a woman who worked undercover for the FBI, Johnnie Gibson. Her husband (**William Allen Young**) would prefer that she concentrate on being a wife and mother, but she was determined. She and her partner (**Howard Rollins**) headed up a dangerous operation in which she, working undercover, encounters an overly charming suspect (**Richard Lawson**).

JOHNNY MATHIS: CHANCES ARE (*PBS, March 2, 1991*). Singer Mathis's career was highlighted in this 90-minute musical retrospective with Larry Gatlin and the Gatlin Brothers, Patti Austin, and the First Baptist Church Choir of Capitol Hill, Nashville.

JOHNNY MATHIS IN THE CANADIAN ROCKIES (*SYN, 1975*). Mathis headlined this variety special, which was taped in Canada.

JOHNSON, ANNE-MARIE. Johnson played Aileen Lewis in the sitcom *Double Trouble* (1984–1985), portrayed Nadine Hudson Thomas in the sitcom *What's Happening Now!!* (1985–1988), played Althea Tibbs in the drama series *In the Heat of the Night* (1988–1993), was a regular on the comedy/variety show *In Living Color* (1993–1994), and was Alicia Barnett in *Melrose Place* (1995–1996). She had a recurring role as Rep. Bobbie Latham on the drama series *JAG* (1995–) and a recurring role as Sharon on *Girlfriends* (2000–). In TV films, she had key roles in *His Mistress* (1984), *Dream Date* (1987), *Lucky/Chances* (1990), *Asteroid* (1997), and *Through the Fire* (2002).

JOHNSON, CHERIE. Johnson played Cherie in *Punky Brewster* from 1984 to 1986 and Maxine on *Family Matters* (1992–1998). She had a key role in the 1985 TV film *Playing with Fire*.

JOHNSON, GUS. Johnson joined CBS Sports in 1995 as a play-by-play announcer for coverage of college basketball, including the

NCAA Men's Basketball Championship. His credits also include play-by-play for college football, bobsled, and luge at the 1998 Olympic Winter Games. He also hosted *Black College Sports Today* and was the radio voice of the National Basketball Association's New York Knicks.

JOHNSON, LEWIS. Johnson joined NBC Sports in 1999 to cover the Track and Field World Championships in Seville, Spain. He also worked as a reporter at the 2000 Sydney Olympic Games. He was a sideline reporter for NBC during Notre Dame football games and also covered the basketball and the bobsled venue at the Winter Olympics in Salt Lake City. A college track star, he got into broadcasting for ABC and ESPN while competing on the pro track circuit in Europe.

JOHNSON, MAGIC. In addition to basketball games and talk shows, Magic Johnson appeared in *The Jimmy McNichol Special* in 1980 and was one of the celebrities speaking out in the public service special *Get High on Yourself* in 1981. He appeared in *Muhammad Ali's 50th Birthday Celebration* in 1992.

JOHNSON, PENNY. Johnson (aka Penny Johnson Jerald) played Sherry Palmer, the wife of the president of the United States, in *24* (2000–). She played Virgina "Vicki" Harper in *Homeroom* in 1989 and Beverly in *The Larry Sanders Show* in 1992. In TV films, she had roles in *Road to Galveston*, *Death Benefit*, and *The Writing on the Wall* in 1996; *The Color of Friendship*, *A Secret Life*, and *Deliberate Intent* in 2000; and *DC 9/11: Time of Crisis* (2003).

JONES & JURY (*SYN, 1994–1995*). In this one-hour courtroom series, **Star Jones** presided as litigants presented small-claims-court cases. At the end of the presentation of evidence, Jones instructed the studio audience to cast votes that were legal and binding.

JONES, CLARENCE. Jones was pianist and arranger to *The Southernaires* (1948).

JONES, JAMES EARL. Successful on the Broadway stage first, Jones played Alex Haley in *Roots: The Next Generations* (1979). He was the star of the one-man drama *Paul Robeson* (1979). He starred in the police drama *Paris* (1979–1980). He played Gabriel in the detective drama series *Gabriel's Fire* (1990–1992) and starred in the family drama *Under One Roof* (1995). He had a key role in the brief series *Me and Mom* (1985). He had starring roles in numerous television films, including *Judge Horton and the Scottsboro Boys* (1976), *The Golden Moment—An Olympic Love Story* (1980), *Guyana Tragedy: The Story of Jim Jones* (1980), *The Atlanta Child Murders* (1985), *The Vernon Johns Story* (1994), *Rebound: The Legend of Earl "The Goat" Manigault* (1996), and *Anne Rice's "The Feast of All Saints"* (2001).

He starred in dramas *Amy and the Angel* in 1982, *Soldier Boys* in 1987, and *The Parsley Garden* in 1993. In television specials, he appeared on *Happy Endings* in 1975, *Night of 100 Stars* in 1982, *America's All-Time Favorite Movies* in 1988, *The Presidential Inaugural Gala* in 1989, *The National Memorial Day Concert* in 1990, and *Save the Planet: A CBS/Hard Rock Special* in 1990. Jones made an appearance on *AFI Salute to Sidney Poitier* (1992). He made an appearance on *The Magic of David Copperfield XIV: Flying . . . Live the Dream* in 1992.

He was spokesman for Cable News Network, saying, "This is CNN," and Verizon Wireless. Jones won two **Emmy Awards** in 1991—one for Lead Actor in a Drama Series for *Gabriel's Fire* and the other for Outstanding Actor in a Miniseries or Special for his role in *Heat Wave* in 1990. In 2004, he was nominated for the Emmy for Outstanding Guest Actor in a Drama for his role in an episode of *Everwood*.

JONES, JILL. Jones was part of the regular cast of *Girlfriends* (2000–).

JONES, QUINCY. In addition to his enormous list of credits in the music world as arranger, producer, conductor, composer, and music supervisor, Jones scored the music for more than 30 feature films, music videos, and animated films. His credits also include the television scores and themes for seven television series: *Sanford and Son*, *Oprah*, *The Bill Cosby Show*, *The New Bill Cosby Show*, *Ironside*, *NBC Mystery Movie*, and *Hey, Landlord*. He also scored the music for made-for-television movies *Split Second to an Epitaph* (the pilot for *Ironside*) in 1967, *Jigsaw*, *The Counterfeit Killer*, and *Killer by Night*.

Jones was producer of the 1973 tribute special **Duke Ellington . . . We Love You Madly**, his first producing position. He won an **Emmy Award** for music composition of **Roots** in 1976–1977. He was Frank Sinatra's guest on his birthday special, **Sinatra 75: The Best Is Yet to Come** in 1990. In the same year, he was celebrated along with other recording artists who had won Grammy Awards in the special **Grammy Legends**.

He made appearances in numerous specials and series; they are the following: *The Rat Pack*, a 1965 concert with Frank Sinatra, **Sammy Davis Jr.**, and Dean Martin on which Jones conducted the Count Basie Orchestra; the "Eat Drink and Be Buried" episode of *Ironside* in 1967; **Saturday Night Live**, which he hosted in 1990; the "Someday Your Prince Will Be in Effect" episode of *Fresh Prince of Bel-Air*; *Mad TV* in 1995; and the "Kill the Noise" episode of *New York Undercover* in 1996.

His production company was responsible for **The Fresh Prince of Bel-Air** (1990–1996) and **In the House** (1995–1998). In 1996, he was executive producer and coproducer with David Salzman of the **68th Annual Academy Awards** telecast.

His credits also include the **AFI Salute to Sidney Poitier** in 1992, **Rodgers and Hart Today** in 1967, **Diana** in 1981, **Sammy Davis Jr.'s 60th Anniversary Celebration** in 1990, **Ray Charles: 50 Years of Music, Uh-Huh!** in 1991, **The Kennedy Center Honors** in 1986, and the documentary **Michael Jackson . . . The Legend Continues** in 1992.

JONES, RASHIDA. The daughter of **Quincy Jones**, Rashida played the school secretary, Louisa Fenn, on **Boston Public** (2000–2002). She had roles in the TV film projects *If These Walls Could Talk 2* (2000) and *The Last Don* (1997). She sang in *Rocky Horror 25: Anniversary Special* (2000).

JONES, RENEE. Jones began playing Lexie Carver on the daytime drama *Days of Our Lives* in 1993. She played the recurring role of Diana Moses on *L.A. Law* from 1989 to 1990.

JONES, RICHARD T. Jones played Bruce Van Exel, the court services officer, in *Judging Amy* beginning in 1999.

JONES, STAR. Star Jones, first a lawyer and then an assistant district attorney in Brooklyn, made her network television debut in 1991 as a studio commentator on the William Kennedy Smith rape trial on Court TV. Soon after, she became legal correspondent for *The Today Show* and *NBC Nightly News*, where she covered both the Rodney King police brutality trial and the Mike Tyson rape case. Success from these led to her own syndicated show *Jones & Jury*. In 1995, she was named chief legal analyst and senior correspondent for *Inside Edition* and covered the **O. J. Simpson** criminal and civil trials. In 1997, she and other female hosts launched the ABC talk show *The View*.

JONES, TAMALA. Jones played Lucile in *The Little Richard Story* in 2000 and was a regular on *For Your Love* (1998–2002).

JOSEPHINE BAKER STORY, THE (*HBO, March 16, 1991*). Lynn Whitfield starred in the title role of this made-for-television movie about Josephine Baker, who was a major entertainer in the cabarets of Paris in the 1920s and 1930s. The film followed her struggle to become a performer in St. Louis, her triumphs as an internationally celebrated African-American entertainer, and her death in 1975. **Louis Gossett Jr.** played Sidney Williams, **Kene Holliday** played Sidney Bechet, and **Vivian Bonnell** played Josephine's mother. George Faison was the emcee in the Harlem club. *See also* BIOPICS.

JOYCE, ELLA. Joyce played Eleanor Emerson on *Roc* from 1991 to 1994. She was Betty Webb in the TV film *Selma, Lord, Selma* (1999).

J.T. (*CBS, December 13, 1969*). This drama, aired under the title *CBS Children's Hour*, was set in Harlem and starred **Kevin Hooks** and **Ja'net DuBois**. It later aired in prime time.

JUDGE HATCHETT (*SYN, 2000– *). This courtroom reality show was presided over by Judge Glenda Hatchett. Hatchett was the first

African-American chief presiding judge in Georgia and headed the Fulton County Juvenile Court for eight years. She became known for showing youthful offenders what their lives would be like should they continue to live as criminals. She brought this type of justice to her television courtroom. Known for her hugs and for admonishing litigants that they need "a reality check," Judge Hatchett's style was that of a loving and strong mother practicing tough love as she sent youth to spend a day in prison or to visit drug rehab clinics or to talk with AIDS patients.

JUDGE JOE BROWN (*SYN, 1998–*). Judge Joe Brown, a product of a tough South Central Los Angeles neighborhood, worked his way through both a bachelor's degree and a law degree at UCLA before becoming the first African-American prosecutor. Later, he was a state criminal courts judge. He became known for his unconventional sentences of making the punishment fit the crime. For example, he sentenced a thief to have his victim steal something from him. He also presided over the reopening of the case of convicted Martin Luther King Jr. assassin James Earl Ray. The producers of *Judge Judy* learned of Brown, and the daily half-hour TV courtroom reality series *Judge Joe Brown* was born. It dealt with small-claims cases and originated from Los Angeles in a studio across the hall from Judge Judy Sheindlin's studio. His efforts in court seemed to be urging litigants to make a change in their lives.

JUDGE MATHIS (*SYN, 1999–*). Judge Greg Mathis presided over this daily courtroom reality show originating from Chicago. There were usually four small-claims-type cases in this one-hour show in which the judge left the courtroom to deliberate and returned with his verdict, unlike other similar court shows in which the verdicts were delivered immediately following testimony. Mathis, who was a former gang member/drug dealer/high school dropout, decided to alter his lifestyle while awaiting trial on a drug offense when his mother announced she was dying. He went to college and law school and became an attorney and then a popular elected judge in Detroit. He took pride in being able to speak the lingo of the troubled youth who found themselves in his courtroom, for he had "been there, done that."

JULIA (*NBC, 1968–1971*). *Julia* was a landmark sitcom in that it was the first sitcom with a black female who was not a domestic worker in the title role. It also proved that white viewers would watch black actors in television series. **Diahann Carroll** starred as Julia Baker, a registered nurse and widowed mother rearing her young son, Corey (**Marc Copage**), in Los Angeles. Julia spoke well, dressed well, and lived well but not extravagantly.

Singer/actress Carroll had already enjoyed success on Broadway and was a headliner in the then-flourishing nightclub circuit. She sang in top clubs. She saw her future in New York theater, and even though she had guest-starred on TV variety series and specials, she was not anxious to do a sitcom.

Julia's producer, Hal Kanter, had, in his early career, written scripts for *Amos 'n' Andy*. He wrote, then, for laughter and laughter alone. Then, in 1967, he saw NAACP Executive Director Roy Wilkins make an impassioned plea to support the NAACP's battle for equality. Kanter was so moved by the speech that he decided he wanted to do his part for the American Dream through his greatest ability, laughter. He said, "I reasoned that if I could create a television show that featured black characters as people first and black only incidentally—in time a white audience would see blacks as people, not as black people . . . and if they could laugh *with* and not *at* my characters, as we once laughed at Stephen Fetchit, *Amos 'n' Andy*, and *Beulah*, sooner or later, some of the verities of African-American life would become apparent, some of the myths exploded." He said that such "a bold dream would take a bold network to implement it," and he found that in NBC.

His first draft was called *Mamma's Man*, and NBC's head of talent, David Tebet, suggested Carroll for the role. Tebet telephoned to urge her to come to Los Angeles to talk with producer Hal Kanter about *Julia*; he prefaced his request with, "I know you're not fond of Los Angeles and you're unimpressed with television, but . . ." Carroll knew she would have battles. Television sitcoms up to this time had not portrayed black people in a way she saw as upstanding or even accurate. If she were to do a series, some changes would have to be made.

The first step was the initial meeting with Kanter, arranged for the Polo Lounge at the Beverly Hills Hotel. "I wore a Givenchy dress because that's how I pictured the character Julia . . . not necessarily in a Givenchy but with a similar look in a dress purchased at a department store." Kanter and Carroll's agent were already seated at a table when she arrived. Kanter had never met her or seen her, nor was he familiar with her work. When she appeared in the door, he said to the agent, "There's a young lady there at the door. If Julia could have that kind of look, it's what I'm looking for." Of course, it was Diahann Carroll. So they were in instant agreement on the look of the character. At that meeting, they discussed the characters and the direction of the series. "I gave him my thoughts. He gave me his and at the end of the meeting, we were both very excited. I began to trust him and I was ready to jump over the moon to get *Julia* on the air," said Carroll.

After Carroll was announced as the star of the upcoming series *Mamma's Man*, James Baldwin and **Harry Belafonte** complained about the title, saying it suggested that black women dominate the men in their families. So *Julia* became the title because the series was about the character.

The battles did not end there. Hollywood was inexperienced in coping with a black female star who knew what she wanted and was outspoken enough to express it. No one had figured that hairdressers, makeup artists, wardrobe masters, lighting technicians, and numerous other professionals would require techniques and skills they had never known. "I wanted to get it right! I didn't want to be difficult but it was very important to get it right," she said.

She and Kanter decided that the two of them alone would discuss problems and issues and that he would take them back to studio and network heads. The character Julia was single so that her dating would provide script possibilities. One issue Carroll recalls was how Julia's boyfriends would be introduced to her son. (**Paul Winfield** and **Fred Williamson** played boyfriends.) "My parents were Southerners and Baptists and I saw Julia as having the same upbringing. There are certain things that a devoted mother does not do. She won't allow a man in her home until she knows how to introduce him to her child. There can't be numerous men in and out of the house. Corey's dialogue was extremely important. There could be nothing inappropriate for a black child in the late 1960s. America saw him as my child and we could not insult black parenthood." The scripts were written according to her wishes.

The clothes Julia wore were from the designer Travilla; it was part of the story line that she made her own elegant clothes. An arrangement was made with a pattern company so that women who admired Julia's attire could purchase patterns for the fashions she wore on the show and duplicate them. Julia and Corey lived in a one bedroom apartment, and Corey had the bedroom, not luxurious living even in the 1960s. Still, the series had complaints—the usual and expected racist complaints from whites but also complaints from blacks that Julia lived too well and dressed too well, "that she was not black."

Carroll and Kanter were disturbed by the complaints, particularly from blacks. She said, "You will always find others who will disagree with you and those who will understand what we were trying to do. People have a right to their opinion, but I am very proud of what we did."

Still, viewers watched. Julia ranked number 7 out of all shows in its first year and remained in the top 30 in the second year.

JULIE ANDREWS AND HARRY BELAFONTE, AN EVENING WITH (*NBC, November 9, 1969*). This was an hour of song with Julie Andrews and **Harry Belafonte** as hosts and stars.

JUST AN OLD SWEET SONG (*CBS, September 14, 1976*). This 90-minute drama starred **Cicely Tyson** and centered on a contemporary Detroit black family on a two-week family vacation in the South and how the experience impacted the family members. Tyson played Priscilla Simmons, and **Robert Hooks** played Nate Simmons. Hooks's real-life sons **Kevin Hooks** and **Eric Hooks** played the roles of Junior and Highpockets, respectively. **Beah Richards** played Grandma, **Lincoln Kilpatrick** played Joe Mayfield, **Minnie Gentry** played Aunt Velvet, **Mary Alice** played Helen Mayfield, and **Sonny Jim Gaines** played Trunk. **Melvin Van Peebles** wrote the teleplay and theme song and performed the theme song with Ira Hawkins. A second one-hour film was produced in 1978 with the same basic cast, except **Madge Sinclair** played Tyson's role.

– K –

KAHN, CHAKA. Singer Chaka Kahn appeared in the musical-variety series *Motown Revue* in 1985 and the tribute special *Grammy*

Legends in 1990. She sang the theme song with Michael McDonald for *For Your Love*, a 1998–2002 sitcom.

KATHLEEN BATTLE & JESSYE NORMAN SING SPIRITUALS *(PBS, December 7, 1990).* **Kathleen Battle** and **Jessye Norman** sang the spiritual songs passed down from generation to generation, songs that they had sung since their childhoods. **Marian Anderson** introduced them.

KEENEN IVORY WAYANS SHOW, THE *(SYN, 1997–1998).* Wayans, a comedian, was host and executive producer of this talk show. The guest stars were mostly African-American celebrities in film, TV, music, and sports. They chatted with Wayans in a set resembling a living room that was obviously designed to create a feeling of familiarity and intimacy between the on-camera subjects and viewers. Wayans did a monologue to open each show, and there was a hip, cute, all-female band called Ladies of the Night in a party setting before moving to the living room set. Recording artists performed their latest music numbers.

KEEP THE FAITH, BABY *(SHO, February 17, 2002).* This made-for-television motion picture was based on the life and legend of Adam Clayton Powell Jr., the charismatic black U.S. congressman who was popular among his constituents in Harlem but controversial in Washington. Harry Lennix and **Vanessa L. Williams** starred. *See also* BIOPICS.

KELLEY, JON. A weekend anchor and correspondent for the daily show on WB's *Extra*, Kelley was the main anchor of *The National Sports Report* and the lead anchor for the weekly series *Baseball Today* on the Fox Sports Network. He is the author of *Breaking into Broadcasting*, a guide to getting an on-air job in television news.

KELLOGG, CLARK. Kellogg joined CBS in 1997 as a full-time studio game analyst for college basketball coverage. He had been an analyst for NCAA Men's Basketball Championships for 11 years. He cohosted the Final Four beginning in 1997.

KELLY, MALCOLM DAVID. Kelly had a key role in the drama series *Lost* (2004–).

KELLY, PAULA. Dancer/singer/actress Paula Kelly was a performer on *Duke Ellington . . . We Love You Madly* in 1973. She was Tiger Lily in "Peter Pan" on a 1976 *Hallmark Hall of Fame* production and sang on *Peter Marshall Salutes the Big Bands* in 1981. She played Liz Williams in the sitcom *Night Court* in 1984 and earned an **Emmy Award** nomination but was dropped from the cast the following season. She had a key role in *The Women of Brewster Place* in 1989. Kelly was one of the performers in the drama special *Zora Is My Name* in 1990. In 1996, she played a key role in *Run for the Dream: The Gail Devers Story*.

KENNEDY CENTER HONORS (*CBS, 1978– *). Each year within days of Christmas, *The Kennedy Center Honors* recognized performers who have made significant contributions to the culture of the United States. The two-hour specials originated from the Kennedy Center for the Performing Arts in Washington, D.C. News icon Walter Cronkite began hosting the specials in 1979 and did through 2001, except for 1999, when he had laryngitis. Caroline Kennedy took his place that year and hosted in 2003 and 2004. Each honoree's life and work was highlighted by performances of notable entertainers, film and video clips, and photos. The honorees sat in the balcony surrounded by family and friends and stood to an ovation after the tribute. African-American honorees have been the following: **Marian Anderson** (1978), **Ella Fitzgerald** (1979), **Leontyne Price** (1980), **Count Basie** (1981), Katherine Dunham (1983), **Lena Horne** (1984), **Ray Charles** (1986), **Sammy Davis Jr.** (1987), Alvin Ailey (1988), **Harry Belafonte** (1989), **Dizzy Gillespie** (1990), Harold and Fayard Nicholas (1991), **Lionel Hampton** (1992), Marion Williams and Arthur Mitchell (1993), **Aretha Franklin** (1994), **B. B. King** and **Sidney Poitier** (1995), Benny Carter (1996), **Jessye Norman** (1997), **Bill Cosby** (1998), **Stevie Wonder** and Judith Jamison (1999), **Chuck Berry** (2000), **Quincy Jones** (2001), **James Earl Jones** (2002), **James Brown** (2003), and **Ossie Davis** and **Ruby Dee** (2004).

KENNEDY CENTER PRESENTS: A TRIBUTE TO MUDDY WATERS: KING OF THE BLUES *(PBS, January 27, 1999).* Billy Dee Williams hosted this show consisting of musical performances and documentary vignettes chronicling the works of blues king Muddy Waters, who is credited with the invention of modern urban blues. Performers were Bo Diddley, Buddy Guy, Koko Taylor, Phoebe Snow, Gregg Allman, Nick Gravenites, and John Hiatt. Bob Dylan and Keith Richards were interviewed. Waters died in 1983.

KENNEDY CENTER PRESENTS: THE CONCERT OF THE AMERICAS *(ABC, December 14, 1994).* Quincy Jones hosted a musical celebration of the many rich cultures of the Western Hemisphere. This was part of President Bill Clinton's Summit of the Americas.

KENNEDY-OVERTON, JAYNE. After participating in the 1970 Miss U.S.A./Universe Pageant as Miss Ohio, Kennedy-Overton (aka Jayne Kennedy) was cast as one of the party girls on *Rowan and Martin's Laugh-In* (1972–1973). She was one of the Golddiggers and then one of the Ding-a-Ling Sisters on *Dean Martin Presents* and *The Dean Martin Show* from 1967 to 1973. She appeared in variety specials *Bob Hope for President* in 1980, *Men Who Rate a "10"* in 1980, *The All-Star Salute to Mother's Day* in 1981, and *Happy Birthday, Hollywood* in 1987. She became a sportcaster for CBS's *NFL Today* (1978–1980), one of the first women to do so. She appeared in game specials *The Celebrity Football Classic* in 1979, *Circus of the Stars* in 1980, and the *Battle of the Video Games* in 1983. In TV films, she had roles in *Cover Girls* (1977), *Mysterious Island of Beautiful Women* (1979), and *Big Time* (1989).

KEN NORTON FIGHTS. Norton fought **Muhammad Ali** in a bout televised from San Diego on March 31, 1973. Norton won in a 12th-round decision. Then he lost the rematch to Ali in 12 rounds on September 15, 1973. He lost to George Foreman by a second round technical knockout in a World Championship bout on March 31, 1974. *See also* BOXING MATCHES ON TELEVISION.

KEVIN HILL *(UPN, 2004–2005).* Taye Diggs starred in the title role of this drama series as a super lawyer, a 28-year-old bachelor who enjoyed his lifestyle. Then a cousin died and left an infant daughter for Kevin to rear. He accepted the responsibility, and in order to have time to be a parent, he resigned from a time-demanding law firm to work at a flex-time, boutique law office owned and staffed by women. His life changed completely to coping with the women at the office and the little woman at home. Others in the cast were the following: Jon Seda as Kevin's buddy, Dame; Patrick Breen as the gay nanny, George; **Michael Michele** as the boss Jessie, a single mom; Christina Hendricks as Nicolette; and Kate Levering as Veronica.

KEYMAH, T'KEYAH "CRYSTAL." Keymah was a regular on *In Living Color* (1990–1994) and played Scotti on *On Our Own* (1995), Erica on *Cosby* (1996–2000), and Raven's mother on *That's So Raven* (2003–).

KID FROM LEFT FIELD, THE (*NBC, September 30, 1979*). This television remake of a feature film starred **Gary Coleman** as J. R. Cooper, a batboy for the San Diego Padres. Aided by his father (**Robert Guillaume**), a baseball has-been who sells refreshments in the stands, J.R. guides the team to the World Series. Coleman and Guillaume (who had the same lawyer/managers) starred in two later TV movies: *The Kid with the Broken Halo* in 1982 and *The Kid with the 200 I.Q.* in 1983.

KID 'N' PLAY. Kid 'n' Play appeared in variety specials *NBC All-Star Stay in School Jam* in 1991 and *The Olsen Twins Mother's Day Special* in 1993.

KIDS KILLING KIDS/KIDS SAVING KIDS (*SYN, April 26, 1994*). **Malcolm Jamal-Warner** hosted this children's program, which followed four fictional teens who carried guns and allowed them to retrace their steps and avoid making the worst mistakes of their lives.

KIDS SAY THE DARNDEST THINGS (*CBS, 1998–2002*). **Bill Cosby** hosted this half-hour show featuring interviews with children. The show was based on a segment with the same title on Art Linkletter's *House Party* series beginning in the 1950s. Like Linkletter, Cosby urged honest and often hilarious comments from the children.

The show's staff preinterviewed the kids and wrote questions, but Cosby insisted on not meeting the children before the show so that the interchange would be natural.

KID WITH THE BROKEN HALO, THE (*NBC, April 5, 1982*). This two-hour made-for-television film starred **Gary Coleman** as Andy LeBeau, a 12-year-old angel who must prove himself worthy of admittance to Heaven by saving three souls. **Robert Guillaume** played his guardian angel, Blake. **Telma Hopkins, Kim Fields**, and **Georg Stanford Brown** played key roles. This was the pilot for a Saturday morning animated series of the same title (1982–1983).

KID WITH THE 200 I.Q. (*NBC, February 6, 1983*). **Gary Coleman** starred as Nick Newell, a 13-year-old genius who learned to adjust to being a college student, not so much the academics as the social life, and one difficult faculty member, Professor Mills (**Robert Guillaume**). **Mel Stewart, Harrison Page**, Starletta DuPois, and Harriet Nelson played roles. Guillaume was an executive producer.

KILLING AFFAIR, A (*CBS, September 21, 1977*). This TV film starred **O. J. Simpson** and Elizabeth Montgomery and was about a white female detective, Viki Eaton, and her black partner, Woodrow York, who found themselves in a love affair while working on a series of cases. Making the interracial relationship more complicated was the fact that he was married. **Rosalind Cash** played Beverly York, and **Todd Bridges** played Todd York. **Charlie Robinson** played Buck Fryman. *See also* INTERRACIAL ROMANCES/ RELATIONSHIPS.

KILPATRICK, ERIK. Kilpatrick played Ricky Duran in *Jessica Novak* (1981) and Curtis Jackson in *The White Shadow* (1978–1980). In TV films, he had roles in *The Color of Friendship* (2000), *Mama Flora's Family* (1998), *False Arrest* (1991), *Heat Wave* (1990), and *83 Hours 'til Dawn* (1990). He is the son of **Lincoln Kilpatrick**.

KILPATRICK, LINCOLN. Lincoln Kilpatrick was **Leslie Uggams**'s husband, BJ, in the "Sugar Hill" sketch on *The Leslie Uggams Show* in 1969. He played Joe Mayfield in the drama *Just an Old Sweet*

Song in 1976 and Jerry Waring in the miniseries *King* in 1978. He was Det. Lt. Michael Hoyt in *Matt Houston* from 1983 to 1985. Kilpatrick died in 2004 of lung cancer; he was 73.

KILPATRICK, LINCOLN, JR. Kilpatrick appeared in the TV films *Alexander: The Other Side of Dawn* (1977) and *Dead Men Tell No Tales* (1971). **Lincoln Kilpatrick** was his father; Erik, his brother.

KING (*NBC, February 12–14, 1978*). This miniseries was a biopic about the life of Martin Luther King Jr. from his days as a Baptist minister in the 1950s until his assassination in 1968. **Paul Winfield** played the title role with **Cicely Tyson** as Coretta Scott King. **Roscoe Lee Brown** played Philip Harrison, **Ossie Davis** was Martin Luther King Sr., **Al Freeman Jr.** was Damon Lockwood, **Lincoln Kilpatrick** was Jerry Waring, **Howard Rollins** was Andrew Young, **Dick Anthony Williams** was Malcolm X, **Frances Foster** was Mrs. Alberta King, **Ernie Banks** played Ralph Abernathy, and **Art Evans** was A. D. King. Dr. King's daughter, **Yolanda King**, played Rosa Parks. Martin Luther King III, Dexter King, and Bernice King were also seen in the film, as were other members of the King family and the daughter of the Rev. Abernathy, Donzaleigh. Tony Bennett, Julian Bond, and Ramsay Clark played themselves. Cliff DeYoung played Robert F. Kennedy, Dolph Sweet played J. Edgar Hoover, and David Speilberg played David Beamer. The production had numerous **Emmy Award** nominations including Tyson, Whitfield, and Davis for acting and the production for Outstanding Limited Series. There were no Emmy wins; the production competed against the blockbuster nine-and-a-half-hour miniseries *The Holocaust*, which had also earned high ratings and high praise among reviewers and viewers.

KING, B. B. The blues singer was one of six honorees on the 1987 special *The Grammy Lifetime Achievement Awards*. B. B. King appeared in variety specials *... And Beautiful II* in 1970, *The Captain and Tennille Songbook* in 1979, *The Crystal Gayle Special* in 1979, *The Apollo Hall of Fame* in 1993, and *Willie Nelson: The Big Six-O* in 1993. King appeared in the tribute special *The Grammy Lifetime Achievement Awards* in 1987. He was in the documentary *Elvis: The*

Echo Will Never Die in 1986. King had voice-overs in the special *Garfield Gets a Life* (1991). He was one of the headliners of the special *Rhythm Country and Blues* (1994). In 1999, he was the highlight of the special *The Blues: In Performance at the White House*, and in the same year he performed in the special *Christmas in Washington*, playing Black Bluesman in *Shake, Rattle and Roll*.

KING, BEN E. King appeared in variety specials *Whatta Year . . . 1986* in 1986 and *The Gordon MacRae Show* in 1971.

KING, DEXTER SCOTT. King, the son of Martin Luther King Jr., played his father in the made-for-television film *The Rosa Parks Story* in 2002.

KING, FREEMAN. King was a regular on *The Sonny and Cher Comedy Hour* (1971–1974) and played roles in the brief series *Semi-Tough* (1980) and *Driving Me Crazy* (2000). He was born in 1943 and died of a heart attack in 2002. He played Jack in *King's Pawn* (1999).

KING, GAYLE. King hosted *The Gayle King Show* in syndication in 1997. Known as **Oprah Winfrey**'s best friend, she made numerous appearances on *Oprah* and cohosted *Cover to Cover,* a daytime magazine series, with Robin Wagner (1991).

KING, MABEL. King played Mrs. Thomas (Mama) on the sitcom *What's Happening!!* from 1976 to 1979. She had roles in the TV films *The Jerk, Too* (1984) and *All the Money in the World* (1983). She was born in 1932. She lost both legs to diabetes and died in 1999 of complications of diabetes.

KING OF THE WORLD (*ABC, January 10, 2000*). This made-for-television film, based on the Pulitzer Prize–winning book of the same title, depicted young boxer Cassius Clay from the 1960s to becoming **Muhammad Ali**, Heavyweight Champion of the World. The film dealt with his religious growth and the impact of a changing America. **Terrence Howard** (as Cassius Clay) and **Steve Harris** (as Sonny Liston) starred. **Gary Dourdan** played Malcolm X. *See also* ATHLETES' BIOPICS.

Amos 'n' Andy was not television's first black cast series; however, it was the first national broadcast after families in big cities began purchasing television sets. Alvin Childress (left) played Amos Jones, a taxi driver and an upstanding family man who was the series narrator. Spencer Williams, Jr. (right) played Andy Brown, a nice guy who loved the women, usually had money but never had a job, and was an easy dupe for the swindles of the con artistry of the Kingfish (played by Tim Moore). The characters had been played by white actors on the popular radio series, so when television brought real black actors into homes of black viewers, the hilarious show was very popular. However, discerning viewers and the NAACP were instrumental in getting the series cancelled because of its negative stereotypes.

Temple Hatton, pictured here as the prosecutor in the 1959 film *Epistle from the Koreans*, was an aspiring actor with small roles in the 1950s and early 1960s. He had acted on radio in nonracial roles and had done numerous plays in the legitimate theatre. "I had learned my craft both in college and later, but preparation was not enough," he said. He said that in Hollywood film and television, darker-skinned actors like Sidney Poitier, Bernie Hamilton, Roy Glenn, and Greg Morris began to get most of the roles and casting people told him, "We never have calls for your type." He says, even today, "I didn't get turned down on the basis of auditions; it was only my look. At one time, I was the most interviewed black actor in Hollywood." Hatton became a producer for a local Los Angeles television station and was a network censor for nearly 20 years.

Ed Sullivan poses with actresses who were stand-ins on the 1965 feature film *The Singing Nun*. Some stand-ins and extras, who usually do not speak lines, have made a more consistent income than many actors. Toni Vaz (far right), who was head of the NAACP committee that conceived the Image Award, was stand-in for actress Juanita Moore. Other actresses (left to right) were stand-ins for Debbie Reynolds, Agnes Moorhead, and Greer Garson.

Natalie Cole was a child when she attended the funeral for her father, legendary singer Nat "King" Cole, in 1965. *The Nat King Cole Show*, a musical variety series, ran for a little more than a year, from 1956 to 1957. News coverage was frequent as he was dying from lung cancer in a Southern California hospital and continued through the well-attended funeral. Jerry Lewis and other notables are seen in the background.

Redd Foxx, as star of *Sanford and Son* (1972–1977), insisted upon hiring his friends as guest stars. Some were not actors or performers. Foxx knew many of the men in this photo from his younger days in the streets of the Watts area of Los Angeles, even before he recorded his famous party albums, when he worked days painting signs and worked nights in clubs. They are listed here by their street names and their real names. Front row (left to right): Little Beaver (Gayle H. Dooms); Nature Boy (Lee Andrews); Redd Foxx (John Elroy Sanford); Little Caesar (Harry Caesar); Jonesy (Ocie Jones). Back row (left to right): actor Louis Guss; actor Ray Herndon; Hucklebuck (Marlin Jackson); actor Tony O'Dare; Black Dot (Elihu McGee); Shelley (Sheldon Slusman); Bogart (Jose Busby).

Lynn Hamilton played neighbor Verdie Foster on the long-running series *The Waltons*. The series creator Earl Hamner developed a pilot for a black family drama series to star Hamilton, but the network did not buy it. The pilot aired as a made-for-television movie, *A Dream for Christmas*, in 1973. Pictured here at a 1996 reunion of *The Waltons* are the following: (left to right) Lisa Harrison Walmsley (Toni Hazleton Walton); Richard Thomas (John Boy Walton); Lynn Hamilton; Hamner's wife, Jane; and Earl Hamner.

Flip Wilson bows in appreciation to Redd Foxx, who told Johnny Carson about how funny he was—a move that subsequently landed Wilson a spot on *The Tonight Show*, a job guest-hosting for a week, and his own hit variety show, *The Flip Wilson Show* (1970–1974). Author Kathleen Fearn-Banks, then an NBC publicist on both *The Flip Wilson Show* and *Sanford and Son* (1972–1977), is seen in the foreground.

Jan'et DuBois of *Good Times* (left) poses with Adella Farmar and Gloria Vinson at the costume party attended by the series' cast and crew. Farmar began her career as a costumer and designer on *Good Times* (1974–1979) and went on to numerous series including *Sanford*, *Gimme a Break*, *227*, *Jones & Jury*, and *The Carol Duvall Show*. Vinson was a script supervisor on *Good Times*, *Diff'rent Strokes*, *The Facts of Life* and others. She was probably the first black woman to be producer of a network primetime series when she held that title with the Redd Foxx sitcom, *Sanford* (1980–1981).

Esther Rolle (right), when not doing *Good Times*, often traveled doing a one-women show. When she did, she usually was accompanied costume designer Adella Farmar (left) and makeup artist Billie Jordan (center); both of them also worked on *Good Times*. This photo was taken when she made an appearance in Atlanta.

Sylvia O'Gilvie (standing, second from right) was production associate on *The Jeffersons* for eight years and associate producer for one year. She also was production associate for *Sanford and Son*, *Checking In*, *Benson*, and 15 pilots for series. She was script supervisor on many other series and specials. Pictured with her are the cast and production staff of *The Jeffersons*, who posed on a day Billy Dee Williams guest-starred. Front row (left to right): Roxie Roker (Helen), Billy Dee Williams, Isabel Sanford (Louise), Marla Gibbs (Florence). Back row (left to right): Jay Moriarty (producer), Paul Benedict (Bentley), Sherman Hemsley (George), Mike Milligan (producer), Jack Shea (director), Silvia O'Gilvie, and Ned Wertimer (Ralph, the Doorman).

Roxie Roker, who played Helen Willis on *The Jeffersons* **for 10 seasons, is pictured here as one of four generations of her family. Left to right are Zoe Kravitz, her granddaughter; singer/musician Lenny Kravitz, her son; Albert Roker, her father; and Roxie Roker.**

The Sophisticated Gents was a mini-series starring many of the leading black actors in 1981. It centered on a reunion of members of a high school social club and a long-unsolved mystery. Next to *Roots*, the *Gents* had one of the largest black casts of any television film up to that date. Melvin Van Peebles (seated, front row, right) wrote the script and the theme song. Also seated on the front row, left to right, are Rosey Grier and Paul Winfield. On the back row, left to right, are Ron O'Neal, Thalmus Rasulala, Bernie Casey, Dick Anthony Williams, Raymond St. Jacques, and Robert Hooks.

The Gents' ladies, wives and girlfriends, also attended the reunion. The actresses are also the top actresses of the time. Left to right are Janet McLachlan, Rosalind Cash, Bibi Besch, Denise Nicholas, Alfre Woodard, Joanna Miles, Ja'net DuBois, and Marlene Warfield.

Toni Vaz, who as a committee chairperson for the Beverly Hills/Hollywood branch of the NAACP, wanted a way to praise positive images of black people in film and television and conceived of the Image Awards, which originated in 1967, and began being televised annually in 1982. She is pictured here with Image Award winner Louis Gossett Jr.

Kim Fields, as a young teen in *The Facts of Life* (1979–1988), heads to the podium as a presenter in a broadcast of the *NAACP Image Awards*. Partly hidden behind her is Gary Coleman, star of *Diff'rent Strokes* (1978–1986), and approaching right is Danielle Spencer, of *What's Happening* (1976–1979) and *What's Happening Now* (1985–1988).

Charles Floyd Johnson (at the podium) accepts an award at the 7th Annual Awards Banquet of the Minorities in Broadcasting Training program in 2000. Looking on are presenters/actors James Garner and Robert Guillaume. Even though he had a law degree, Johnson began his career in television in the mailroom at Universal Studios "because it was the only job available." Three days later, he was out of the mailroom and on his way to a career, first in public affairs, then as an associate producer on *The Rockford Files* (starring Garner), and then as producer and supervising producer.

Charles Floyd Johnson (right) talks to Tom Selleck, star of *Magnum P.I.*, on location with the series in Hawaii. *Magnum PI* was one of several series, including *Evening Shade*, *JAG*, and *NCIS*, on which Johnson was coexecutive producer, supervising producer, or executive producer.

Marla Gibbs is surrounded by the writers of her 1985–1990 sitcom *227*. Going clockwise beginning at the top is Reynaldo Rey, Booker Bradshaw, Bobby Crawford, Fred Johnson, and Christine Houston. Not pictured were Sarah Finney and Vida Spears. The series was based on a stage play written by Houston.

Howard Bingham was one of the first black still photographers in the motion picture/television industry. In 1969, Bill Cosby, then star of *The Bill Cosby Show*, was instrumental in getting him into the union. Since then, he has shot numerous television and film projects for publicity and promotion purposes. He is primarily known for his photos of Muhammad Ali, his friend since 1962, though he was never on Ali's payroll. His photos of Ali were seen in Bingham's book *Muhammad Ali: A Thirty-Year Journey* (1993).

The Parkers creators, producers, and cast members celebrate the 100th episode of the popular sitcom (1999–2004). Pictures left to right are: Vida Spears (creator); Jenna Von Oy (Stevie); Sara Finney-Johnson (creator and executive producer); Countess Vaughn James (Kim); Ralph Farquhar (creator); Mo'Nique (Nikki); Dorien Wilson (Professor Oglevee); Yvette Wilson (Andel); Ken Lawson ("T"). Spears, Finney-Johnson, and Farquhar also created and executive produced *Moesha*.

Living with Soul, a design lifestyle series on television, gives viewers a look at homes designed with Afro-centric style while offering practical advice for creating an authentic personal space. Pictured here are the following: Shirley Neal, executive producer of the series; Phyllis C. G. Bowie, interior designer; George Faison, host/producer of the series, director/choreographer, and Tony Award winner, whose home was featured on one segment; and Fay Hauser-Price, producer of the series and also an actress and writer.

Dr. Jannette Dates, dean of the John H. Johnson School of Communications, Howard University, poses with actor/director Bill Dukes, who taught at Howard University from August 1998 through June 2002. He held the Time Warner Endowed Chair in Media.

Nell Carter (foreground) played housekeeper to a police chief played by Dolph Sweet (left) in *Gimme a Break*. Carter's character was also surrogate mother to the chief's teenaged daughters. Carter felt the role was not demeaning because her character was part of the family, that there was no subservient behavior, and she was rarely seen cleaning house. Carter said she imagined, as she played the character, that she was not a housekeeper at all but was having an affair with the police chief. Author Kathleen Fearn-Banks, then a network publicist, is seen at right.

KING, REGINA. King was teenager Brenda Jenkins in the sitcom *227* (1985–1990) and Cynthia in the 2002 sitcom *Leap of Faith*. In TV films, she had key roles in *Damaged Care* (2002), *If These Walls Could Talk 2* (2000), and *Where the Truth Lies* (1999). See also CHILD TV ACTORS/PERFROMERS WHO MAINTAINED SUCCESS AS ADULTS IN SHOW BUSINESS.

KING, REINA. Reina King played Carolyn on the sitcom second *What's Happening!!* from 1985 to 1986. She is **Regina King**'s sister.

KING, YOLANDA. King, the daughter of Martin Luther King Jr., played Rosa Parks in the miniseries *King* in 1978. Hers was the voice of Elizabeth Freeman in the animated series *Liberty's Kids* (2002–2003). She played Mrs. Crawford in one of the trilogy of dramas on *America's Dream* in 1995. She played Miss Bright in the TV film *Selma, Lord, Selma* in 1999 and in that same year had a role in the TV films *Funny Valentines* and *The Silent Path*.

KIRBY, GEORGE. George Kirby was a regular on the program "The Copycats," part of the *ABC Comedy Hour* (1972), and did impressions. He starred in his variety series, *Half the George Kirby Comedy Hour*, which originated from Canada and lasted less than a year. In 1975, he tried a sitcom *Rosenthal and Jones*, which lasted only a few episodes. He starred in **The George Kirby Special** in 1970. He was a guest star on **Dionne Warwick**'s first special in 1969. He appeared in the satirical special *Alan King in Las Vegas, Part II* in 1973. He appeared in *Bob Hope's USO Christmas Show* in 1983, the **Dean Martin Celebrity Roast** of Gabe Kaplan in 1977, *A Special London Bridge Special* in 1972, and *Saga of Sonora* in 1973. He had a key role in the television movie *Sunset Limousine* in 1983. He hosted *Amos 'n' Andy: Anatomy of a Controversy* in 1984. Kirby was born in 1924 and died in 1995 of Parkinson's disease.

KITT, EARTHA. Kitt played the title role in "Salome" on *Omnibus* (1955). She had a key role in the TV films *Lieutenant Schuster's Wife* (1972), *To Kill a Cop* (1978), *A Night on the Town* (1983), and *Desperately Seeking Roger* (1991). She appeared in *Anne Rice's "The*

Feast of All Saints" in 2001. She was once a mystery guest on the original *What's My Line?* in the 1950s. She was one of three actresses who played Catwoman on the fantasy series *Batman* in the late 1960s. In the mid-1960s, according to Steve Hosey (*Michigan Chronicle*, May 11, 1999), Kitt was essentially "whiteballed" by President Lyndon Johnson. Apparently, at a White House ceremony, she expressed concern that Lady Bird Johnson's program of beautifying America with flowers and shrubs was trivial when there were so many other more important issues, like the nation's poor. The president was so infuriated that his wife had been insulted that he reportedly sent the word out that "he didn't want to see that woman's face on television."

KNIGHT, GLADYS. As a seven-year-old, Knight was discovered as a singer on Ted Mack's *Original Amateur Hour*, a competition she won easily. In 1985–1986, she starred with Flip Wilson in the sitcom *Charlie & Co.* She appeared with her brother and cousins as Gladys Knight and the Pips or as a solo artist in numerous television specials. Among them were the following: *Doc and Gladys Celebrate*, a New Year's special with Doc Severinsen, in 1977, *Gladys Knight and the Pips: Midnight Train to Georgia* in 1974; *Doc and Gladys Celebrate* in 1977; *The George Burns One-Man Show* in 1977; *Rolling Stone Magazine: The 10th Anniversary* in 1977; *Uptown* in 1980; *Marvin Hamlisch: They're Playing My Song* in 1981; *100 Years of Golden Hits* in 1981; *The Suzanne Somers Special* in 1982; *The Mac Davis Special: The Music of Christmas* in 1983; *Sisters in the Name of Love* in 1986; *Walt Disney World's 15th Birthday Celebration* in 1986; *Gladys Knight and the Pips with Ray Charles* in 1987; *Super Night at the Super Bowl* in 1987; *All-Star Tribute to Kareem Abdul-Jabbar* in 1989; and *Motown 30: What's Going On?* in 1990. She sang on the special *Motown 45* in 2004. She also starred in the drama *An Enemy among Us* in 1987.

KNIGHT, GLADYS, AND THE PIPS. The quartet with lead singer Gladys Knight performed on the special *The George Burns One-Man Show* in 1977. The group headlined its own specials *Gladys Knight and the Pips: Midnight Train to Georgia* in 1974 and *Gladys Knight and the Pips with Ray Charles* in 1987. In 1975, the group had a four-week summer replacement on NBC titled *The Gladys Knight and the Pips Show*.

KNOWLES, BEYONCE. Knowles sang the National Anthem at Super Bowl XXXVIII in 2004. She made appearances on numerous musical award shows including the *46th Annual Grammy Awards* (2004), *The Essence Awards* (2003), the *American Music Awards* (2003), the *MTV Video Music Awards* (2003), and the *Spike TV VGA Video Game Awards* (2003). She performed on *Christmas in Rockefeller Center* (2003) and was one of the divas on *VH1 Divas Duets* (2003). As a member of Destiny's Child, she made appearances in earlier specials and award shows.

KOBE BRYANT SEXUAL ASSAULT CASE. The 24-year-old Los Angeles Lakers all-star guard was charged with sexual assault of a 19-year-old Colorado woman; he claimed that the June 30, 2003, encounter was consensual. If found guilty, he could have received a sentence ranging anywhere from probation to life in prison. The story was prominent in national newscasts that sensationalized each step he and his lawyers made and each step the unnamed accuser and her lawyers made. Public sentiment was affected when the defense revealed that DNA showed the woman had sex with another man soon after the encounter with Bryant. Then, days before the trial was to begin, prosecutors dropped the charges according to the accuser's wishes. Bryant issued an apology while still maintaining innocence. This story would be in the top 10 of news stories ranked according to the numbers of hours of TV airtime allotted to them in 2003–2004.

KODJOE, BORIS. Kodjoe played Damon on the drama series *Soul Food* (2000–2004). In 2004, he began a starring role of Jackson Muse in the sitcom *Second Time Around*.

KOJAK (CBS, 1973–1990). This long-running drama starring Telly Savalas as a New York City police inspector also introduced to television **Andre Braugher**, as Detective Winston Blake, from 1989 to 1990.

KOTTO, YAPHET. Kotto starred as Idi Amin in *Raid on Entebbe* in 1977. He played Sgt. China Bell in the drama series *For Love and*

Honor in 1983. Kotto had key roles in the TV films *Rage* in 1980 and *Women of San Quentin* in 1983. He starred with James Woods in the TV film *Badge of the Assassin* in 1985 and in the same year played a key role in the TV film *Playing with Fire*. He played Lt. Al Giardello in *Homicide: Life on the Street* from 1993 to 1999 and the same role in *Homicide: The Movie* in 2000.

KRAVITZ, LENNY. Kravitz appeared in the tribute special *A Tribute to John Lennon* in 1990, *The Beatles Revolution* (2000), *Being Mick* (2001), and various talks shows, specials, and music awards shows. He is the son of **Roxie Roker** (*The Jeffersons*).

– L –

LABELLE, PATTI. Grammy Award winner LaBelle starred in the 1992–1993 sitcom *Out All Night* as a former singer who owned a nightclub. She had a recurring role on *A Different World* as Dwayne Wayne's mother. She also appeared in variety specials: *Rolling Stone Magazine: The 10th Anniversary* in 1977, *The Kraft All-Star Salute to Ford's Theatre* in 1985, *Musical Comedy Tonight* in 1985, *Placido Domingo . . . Stepping Out with the Ladies* in 1985, *Liberty Weekend: Closing Ceremonies* in 1986, *Sisters in the Name of Love* in 1986, *Happy Birthday, Hollywood* in 1987, *We the People 200: The Constitutional Gala* in 1987, *The Songwriter's Hall of Fame* in 1989, *Tommy—The Who* in 1989, *Motown 30: What's Going On?* in 1990, *The Bob Hope's Yellow Ribbon Celebration* in 1991, *Disney World's 20th Anniversary Celebration* in 1991, and *A Country Music Celebration: The 35th Anniversary of the Country Music Association* in 1993. She also appeared in the musical special *A Capitol Fourth: 1992.* She hosted her own variety special, **The Patti La-Belle Show**, in 1985. LaBelle was a headliner at the halftime show for Super Bowl XXIX in 1995. She sang in *Goodnight Moon*, a 1999 children's program.

LACKAWANNA BLUES (*HBO, February 12, 2005*). S. Epatha Merkerson starred in this dramatic cable film based on Ruben Santiago-Hudson's play about characters in his early life in upstate

New York in the 1950s. Merkerson played Nanny, a boardinghouse owner with an open house as well as an open heart to various colorful and eccentric people who told their stories to young Ruben, Nanny's "son," after she convinced his problematic parents (**Carmen Ejogo** and **Jimmy Smits**) that the boy would be better off in her loving, supporting home.

Ruben, as a child, was played by Marcus Carl Franklin. As a young adult, he was played by **Hill Harper**. Others in the cast included **Mos Def** as a nightclub singer who had the joint jumping when he sang "Caldonia"; **Louis Gossett Jr.** as Mr. Taylor, who left a mental institution to live at Nanny's place; **Terrance Dashon Howard** as Nanny's womanizing husband, Bill; **DelRoy Lindo**; **Jeffrey Wright**; Rose Perez; **Charlayne Woodard**; and others.

Halle Berry, who was instrumental in getting HBO to make the film, was executive producer. Broadway's George C. Wolfe was director. *See also* BIOPICS.

LADY FROM PHILADELPHIA: THROUGH ASIA WITH MARIAN ANDERSON, THE (*December 30, 1957*). This episode of *See It Now* was a documentary on singer Marian Anderson's goodwill tour of Asia sponsored by the U.S. State Department.

LAND OF THE GIANTS (*ABC, 1968–1970*). **Don Marshall** was the sole black actor in this science fiction drama about seven Earthlings who traveled into space and landed on a planet where the inhabitants were 12 times their size. Marshall was Dan Erickson, the copilot. *See also* SERIES WITH ONE BLACK SUPPORTING ACTOR/ PERFORMER BEFORE 1980.

LANEUVILLE, ERIC. Laneuville started his TV career as an actor playing the student Larry on *Room 222* (1969–1974). He was Mouse in *The Cop and the Kid* (1975–1976) and had key roles in the TV dramatic films *Foster and Laurie* in 1975 and *Scared Straight! Another Story* in 1980. Then, he was Luther Hawkins, the orderly on *St. Elsewhere* (1982–1988). He directed an episode of *St. Elsewhere* in 1982 and thereafter piled up numerous credits as a director. He won an **Emmy Award** in 1992 for Outstanding Directing in a Drama Series for his work on an episode of *I'll Fly Away*.

LANGE, TED. Lange played Junior in the 1974–1975 sitcom *That's My Mama* and Harvard in the 1976 sitcom *Mr. T and Tina*, and is recognized primarily for his role as bartender Isaac Washington in the nine years of the one-hour sitcom *The Love Boat*. Ted Lange appeared in game *The Celebrity Football Classic* in 1979 and the TV special *Circus of the Stars* in 1980. He appeared in variety specials *Good Morning, Captain* in 1981, *The Love Boat Fall Preview Special* in 1983, and *The ABC All-Star Spectacular* in 1985. He played the Ghost of Christmas Present in *John Grin's Christmas* in 1986. Even before *That's My Mama*, Lange appeared in the film project *Wattstax 1973*, which had limited film release and was aired on television as a classic in 2004.

LANGHART, JANET. Langhart was a newscaster who played a newscaster in the miniseries *Blind Ambition* in 1979. Her credits include being correspondent for *Entertainment Tonight* and **Black Entertainment Television**.

LARRY ELDER SHOW, THE (*SYN, 2004–*). Elder's talk format was based on themes. He tackled a subject and brought in experts or persons who had personal experiences to talk about that subject. Among the subjects discussed were teachers having affairs with pupils, obesity as a disease, and various other life choices and lifestyles. *See also* TALK SHOWS.

LASALLE, ERIQ. LaSalle played Dr. Peter Benton on *ER* (1994–2001) and Michael Stoven in the medical drama *The Human Factor* (1992). He played Diego in the 1996 TV film *Rebound: The Legend of Earl "The Goat" Manigault*. Other TV films in his list of credits include the following: *Mind Prey* (1999), *Empty Cradle* (1993), *Eyes of a Witness* (1991), *Hammer, Slammer & Slade* (1990), and *When We Were Young* (1989). In 1987, he played Charles Thompson in the daytime drama *Another World*. He became a director, producer, and writer.

LATHAN, SANAA. Lathan was the female lead in the TV film *Disappearing Acts* (2000).

LATIFAH, QUEEN. A rapper, turned TV actress, turned movie star, Latifah (nee Dana Owens) was the star of the sitcom *Living Single* (1993–1998) and played the granddaughter in the miniseries *Mama Flora's Family* (1998). She appeared in the Motown salute in the halftime show of 1998's Super Bowl XXXII. She performed on the musical special *One Love: The Bob Marley All-Star Tribute* in 1999. She also hosted a talk show, *The Queen Latifah Show*, in 1999–2000. Latifah was featured in MTV's documentary show *Biorhythm* in 1998. In 2005, she was host of the *Grammy Awards*.

LAUREL AVENUE (*HBO, July 10 and 11, 1993*). This miniseries starring **Mary Alice** and **Malinda Williams** depicted three days in the lives of a middle-class African-American family and its struggles.

LAWRENCE, MARTIN. Lawrence was a contestant on the 1980s version of *Star Search*. He played Maurice Warfield on the sitcom *What's Happening!!* (1987–1988). He played Martin Payne and various other characters in his starring role on the sitcom *Martin* (1992–1997). In TV films, he had a key role in *Hammer, Slammer, & Slade* (1990). He was host of *Def Comedy Jam: All Stars* in 1999 and appeared on *Def Comedy Jam: Primetime* in 1994.

LAWRENCE, SCOTT. Lawrence played Commander Sturgis Turner in the military drama series *Jag* beginning in 2001. He had a recurring role on the daytime drama *One Life to Live*. Speaking of his role on *Jag*, Lawrence said, "Sometimes the fact that I am black comes in to the script. It's good to be 'the' black character on a show because you can make the decisions that are fundamental for what they eventually can do with the black character. It's a big responsibility and I welcome it."

LAWRENCE WELK SHOW, THE (*ABC, 1955–1971; SYN, 1971–1982*). This musical variety series became relevant to African-American history when tap dancer **Art Duncan** was added to the regular cast of entertainers. He hoofed onto the Welk show in 1964 and remained there through the syndicated shows of 1971–1982. *See also* SERIES WITH ONE BLACK SUPPORTING ACTOR/ PERFORMER BEFORE 1980.

LAWS, ELOISE. Singer Laws appeared in a Tom Jones special in 1971. Briefly, she was a member of the singing group **The Fifth Dimension** and made an appearance on *The Tonight Show with Johnny Carson*. She also made two 1971 appearances on the show as a solo singer.

LAWSON, BIANCA. Lawson had a role in the TV movie *Anne Rice's "The Feast of All Saints"* in 2001.

LAWSON, KEN. Lawson played Thaddeus "T" Radcliffe in the sitcom *The Parkers* (1999–2004). He was Carl in *In the House* (1996–1999).

LAWSON, RICHARD. Lawson played Nick Kimball in the prime-time soap *Dynasty* in the 1986–1987 season and Det. Nathaniel Hawthorne in the dramedy series *The Days and Nights of Molly Dodd* in the 1987–1988 season. He was Lucas Barnes on the daytime soap *All My Children* from 1992 to 1994. He had key roles in the 1979 motion pictures for television *Charleston* and *The Jericho Mile*, the 1980 TV film *The Golden Moment—An Olympic Love Story*, and *Johnnie Mae Gibson, FBI* in 1986.

LAYTONS, THE (*DUM, 1948*). This sitcom, which lasted only about two months, starred **Amanda Randolph**, who would later have a key role in the more successful but also controversial *Amos 'n' Andy*.

LAZARUS SYNDROME, THE (*ABC, 1979*). Although it lasted only a month, African-American critics of then-current television fare were pleased to see this series air. It was a medical drama starring **Louis Gossett Jr.**, an actor with an impressive background. There was hope that it would survive because the cast was racially integrated and therefore not truly a black drama. Perhaps it would be a way to get the public used to a black man playing a professional character in a drama series. The character (MacArthur St. Clair) portrayed by Gossett was a man trying to be the best as chief of cardiology at Webster Memorial Hospital. At the same time, he wanted to please his wife, Gloria (**Sheila Frazier**), who wanted him to spend more time with the family. Ronald Hunter played the hospital administrator. The series lasted one month.

LEADBELLY. Vintage footage of Leadbelly performing was a highlight of *The Blues*, a seven-part series about the music genre in 2003.

LEAL, SHARON. Leal played Marilyn Sudor, the music teacher on *Boston Public* (2001–2004). She was Marita in the drama *Legacy* (1998–1999) and Dahlia in the daytime drama *The Guiding Light* (1996–1999).

LE BEAUF, SABRINA. After playing Sandra, the eldest daughter in *The Cosby Show* (1984–1992), Le Beauf later provided the voice of the mother, Norma Bindlebeep, in another Cosby production, *Fatherhood*, the animated series that began in 2004. In TV films, she played Maresha Fisher on *Howard Beach: Making a Case for Murder* in 1989.

LEE, JOHNNY. Lee played Algonquin J. Calhoun, the Kingfish's lawyer, on *Amos 'n' Andy*. He also played a key role in the half-hour drama "The Reign of Amelika Jo" in 1954.

LEE, SPIKE. The film director was interviewed in *It's Black Entertainment* in 1977. He was conarrator with **Debbie Allen** of 1990's *Spike & Co.*, a search for New York a cappella groups. He also directed the 2003 made-for-television film *Good Fences* starring **Whoopi Goldberg** and **Danny Glover**.

LEHMAN, LILLIAN. Lehman played Letty Gilmore on the sitcom *Fay* (1975–1976). She also played Ruth Tenafly in the drama series *Tenafly* (1973–1974) and had a recurring role as a judge on *L.A. Law* (1990–1994). She played Lena Hart on *Sunset Beach* (1997–1998). In TV films, she had roles in the following: *The President's Plane Is Missing* (1973), *Anatomy of an Illness* (1984), *Miracle of the Heart: A Boys Town Story* (1986), *The Last Fling* (1987), *In My Daughter's Name* (1992), and *Sawbones* (1995).

LEMON, DON. Lemon joined MSNBC in 2002 as a news correspondent based in the network's New York bureau. He contributed to both NBC and MSNBC programs.

LENA HORNE: IN HER OWN VOICE (*PBS, November 25, 1996*). A documentary, part of the *American Masters* series, this production traced **Lena Horne**'s life from the Cotton Club in Harlem to MGM Studios in Hollywood. The entertainer revealed the prejudices she faced in her career. Horne said she wasn't anxious to see the production because "I can't bear to see myself perform, have never wanted to hear myself sing. I always wanted to be like **Aretha Franklin** or **Ella Fitzgerald**."

LENA HORNE: THE LADY AND HER MUSIC (*SHO, December 2, 1984*). **Lena Horne** headlined this variety special in which she was a solo performer. The special was based on her Tony Award–winning Broadway show, and she sang songs for which she was most famous. *See also* BROADWAY PLAYS AND MUSICALS.

LENOIRE, ROSETTA. Longtime stage actress/producer LeNoire played Noah's wife in **"The Green Pastures"** in 1957 and had a key role in *Mandy's Grandmother* in 1980. She joined the cast of the daytime drama *A World Apart* in the late 1960s and recurred in *Another World* from 1971 to 1973. She was Leola in the sitcom *Amen* from 1987 to 1989 and Grandma Winslow in *Family Matters* from 1989 to 1997. She founded New York's AMAS Repertory Theatre Company in 1968 and established the Eubie Blake Children's Theatre in 1976. In 1988, Actors' Equity created the Rosetta LeNoire Award to recognize theaters and producers who hire ethnic minorities. She was born in 1911 and died in 2002.

LEON. Leon played the title role in the TV movie *The Little Richard Story* in 2000.

LEONARD, SUGAR RAY. The champion boxer joined the search for the next great boxer in the reality show *The Contender* (2005).

LES BROWN SHOW, THE (*SYN, 1993–1994*). Motivational speaker Les Brown hosted this short-lived talk show. King World Productions, which brought **Oprah Winfrey** to national television in 1986, had been looking for another big hit for six years when it launched *The Les Brown Show*, saying it "will do away with the four J's—Joan Rivers, Jenny Jones, Jane Whitney, and Jerry Springer."

LESLIE (*ABC, May 1, 1968*). Leslie Uggams starred in this special of music and songs with guest performers Noel Harrison, Robert Morse, and the Young Rascals.

LESLIE UGGAMS SHOW, THE (*CBS, 1969*). Singer Leslie Uggams was the star of this musical variety series with guest stars as well as regular performers. She was the first black female performer since **Hazel Scott** (1950) to host her own music/variety series. A feature of the show was the sketch "Sugar Hill" about the lives of a middle-class black family. Uggams was Henrietta. **Lincoln Kilpatrick** was her husband, BJ; **Lillian Hayman** was her mother; **Johnny Brown** was her brother, Lamar; and **Allison Mills** was her sister, Oletha. Dennis Allen was the token white regular in the series. Werner Klemperer, a white actor who had played Col. Klink in *Hogan's Heroes*, said he guest-starred on this show and felt so good about it that he wanted to kiss Uggams. The network brass, he said, told him this was a no-no, that no white man had ever kissed a black woman on television before. The network denied that anyone had said that and cited other interracial kisses—Flip Wilson kissed Carol Burnett, and Danny Kaye kissed **Diahann Carroll**, both on CBS shows. However, Klemperer, who in real life was married to African-American actress Kim Hamilton, said that the warning did take place and that he did not insist because he didn't want a recurrence of the furor that erupted when Petula Clark touched **Harry Belafonte**'s arm on the Petula Clark special the year before. *See also* PETULA.

LESSON BEFORE DYING, A (*HBO, May 22,1999*). **Don Cheadle**, **Cicely Tyson**, **Mekhi Phifer**, and **Irma Hall** starred in this TV film based on Ernest Gaines's best-selling novel about race relations, capital punishment, and human dignity in a bayou town in 1940s Louisiana. College graduate Grant Wiggins (Cheadle) returned to his hometown to teach in the colored school. While there, a former student, Jefferson (Phifer), was falsely accused and convicted of murder, and Wiggins was asked to help teach Jefferson to die with dignity. It was not a task he relished, but Tante Lou (Tyson) and his mother (Hall) urged him to rise to the occasion. Reviewer David Loftus said of this film, "An excellent drama that is nearly worthy of the superb book on which it is based. . . . The acting, particularly by Cheadle, Phifer . . . is excellent."

LESTER, KETTY. Lester played Helen Grant on the daytime drama *Days of Our Lives* (1965), Nora Blake on the drama series *Morningstar/Eveningstar* (1986), and Hester Sue Terhune on *Little House on the Prairie* (1978–1983). She had key roles in the made-for-television motion pictures *It's Good to Be Alive* (1974), *Louis Armstrong—Chicago Style* in 1976, *Battered* in 1978, *The Night the City Screamed* (1980), *Percy and Thunder* (1993), and *Jack Reed: A Search for Justice* (1994).

LESURE, JAMES. Lesure played Mel on the sitcom *For Your Love* in 1998–2002. He starred in the drama series *Las Vegas* as Mike Cannon beginning in 2003.

LET'S MAKE A DEAL (*various networks and SYN, 1967–1971, 1971–1976, 1980, 1984, 1990–1991, 2003*). From the beginning, black people were seen in great numbers on this audience participation game show. Would-be contestants arrived at the show's studio dressed in outrageous gimmicky costumes hoping to be selected to sit on "the trading floor." If selected, host Monty Hall might choose them to trade some item they brought with them for a "deal." The deal might be money, furs, trips, or cars, or it might be what the show called "zonks"—worthless junk, such as burned-out trucks or bunches of bananas. The idea was that the contestant usually did not know whether he or she would win something valuable or a zonk. Greed played its part in the excitement of the show. The two contestants who had won the most valuable prizes at the end of the show would compete for the "Big Deal" by choosing door number 1, number 2, or number 3.

As different variations of the show were developed, the prizes increased in value. The show moved from time to time—Las Vegas, Vancouver, and Orlando were production sites. Hall, not only an emcee of the original version but also a creator and producer, either hosted or produced most versions, including the 2003 version, which aired occasionally but in no particular time slot.

LET THE GOOD TIMES ROLL WITH B. B. KING (*PBS, June 14, 1984*). Blues king **B. B. King** and his guitar, Lucille, starred in this 60-minute concert peppered with King's minilessons in the mastery of the guitar. He talked about how he "trills" or gets vibrato effects on his treble strings. Each of his principal musicians was spotlighted in brief solo performances.

LE VAR BURTON PRESENTS A READING RAINBOW SPECIAL: ACT AGAINST VIOLENCE (*PBS, October 19, 1995*). Burton hosted a special program designed to help children make decisions to avoid violence. It showed how the Watts community of Los Angeles empowered its children to do this.

LEVELS, CALVIN. Levels played a key role in the television film *Crisis at Central High* in 1981. He played Wayne Williams in *The Atlanta Child Murders* in 1985, and he was Mark "Burn" Johnson in the 1988–1989 drama series *Knight Watch*.

LEWIS, ANANDA. Lewis became recognizable to television viewers as a veejay on **Black Entertainment Television** and then on MTV shows like *Hot Zone*. She cohosted major events like MTV's *New Year's Eve Bash* and also MTV *Cribs*.

LEWIS, DAWNN. Lewis starred as Jalessa in the sitcom *A Different World* (1987–1992). She played Robin in the sitcom *Hangin' with Mr. Cooper* (1992–1993). She had a key role in the made-for-television film *The Cherokee Kid* in 1996. She provided the voices of two characters on the animated series *Sistas 'n the City* (2004).

LEWIS, EMMANUEL. Lewis became a TV star in the sitcom *Webster*, which aired from 1982 to 1987. He was one of the celebrities at *The 50th Presidential Inaugural Gala* held two days prior to the inauguration of President Ronald Reagan in 1985. He headlined his own special, aptly titled *Emmanuel Lewis: My Very Own Show*, in 1987. Lewis appeared in variety specials *The Love Boat Fall Preview Special* in 1983, *A Salute to Lady Liberty* in 1984, *The ABC All-Star Spectacular* in 1985, *Christmas in Washington* in 1985, and *Walt Disney World's 15th Birthday Celebration* in 1986 and in the musical *A Christmas Dream* in 1984. He also appeared in TV specials *Circus of the Stars* in 1984 and *The Secret World of the Very Young* in 1984; the comedy special *The World's Funniest Commercial Goofs* in 1983,

1984, 1985; and *Life's Most Embarrassing Moments* in 1986. He was one of the regulars on the first season (2003) of the reality series *The Surreal* Life.

LEWIS, JENIFER. Lewis played Charlaine on the sitcom *Roc* (1993), Judge Rosetta Reide on the legal drama sitcom *Courthouse* (1995), and Bebe Ho on the animated sitcom *The PJs* (1999). She played a key role in the TV film *The Little Richard Story* in 2000 and played Lana Hawkins in the medical drama series *Strong Medicine* beginning in 2000.

LEWIS, PHILL. Lewis was T.C. in *The Wayans Bros.* (1995–1998) and starred in *Teech* (1991).

LEWIS-HALL, JENNIFER. Lewis-Hall joined CNBC in 1999. Her credits include covering stories ranging from the markets to music for various CNBC programs. Her credits also include substitute anchor on many *CNBC Business Day* programs, *NBC's Early Today*, and *The Wall Street Journal Report*.

LIFE WITH THE ERWINS. *See* THE STU ERWIN SHOW.

LIGHT'S DIAMOND JUBILEE (*ABC, NBC, CBS, DUM, October 24, 1954*). This special was significant in that it appeared on all four networks. It was two hours of music and comedy in celebration of the 75th anniversary of Thomas Alva Edison's invention of the electric lightbulb. The top names in show business appeared. Especially significant in African-American history was the appearance of **Dorothy Dandridge**, who made few television appearances. Among others were the following: Lauren Bacall, Walter Brennan, Joseph Cotton, Helen Hayes, and David Niven.

LIKE FAMILY (*WB, 2003– *). As the WB attempted racial integration in its series, this sitcom was developed starring **Holly Robinson Peete** and Kevin Michael Robinson as Tanya and Ed, a loving married couple with a 16-year-old daughter (Megalyn Echikunwoke) and a 12-year-old son (B. J. Mitchell). Diversity occurs because Tanya's best friend, Maddie (Diana Farr, who is white), moved in with her 16-year-old son (J. Mack Slaughter).

LINCS (*SHO, 1998–2000*). **Tim Reid** cocreated, executive-produced, directed, and played a role in this dramedy series set in a Washington, D.C., bar and grill called Lincs. Russell "Linc" Lincoln (played by **Steven Williams**) was the proprietor of Lincs. The primarily black patrons were played by the ensemble cast. **Pam Grier** was a children's rights advocate, Eleanor. **George Stanford Brown** was lobbyist Johnnie B. Goode. **Daphne Maxwell Reid** was Eartha, a prostitute with clients in high places. **Tisha Campbell** was Linc's beloved daughter, Rosalee, who was in the Army. **Golden Brown** was Cece Jennings, a waitress who did not mince words. Tim Reid played the priest. Adewale Akinnuoye-Agbaje was Winston Iwelu, a Nigerian taxi driver. Joe Inscoe was the token white character, Harlan Hubbard III, who worked for a pedophile senator. The conversation at Lincs was about problems and issues the characters had faced as minorities in America.

LINDO, DELROY. Lindo starred in the 1999 TV film *Strange Justice* as Clarence Thomas. He starred in the TV film *Profoundly Normal* in 2003 and played a key role in the TV films *First Time Felon* in 1997 and *Lackawanna Blues* in 2005.

LISARAYE. Lisaraye played Neesee in the sitcom *All of Us* beginning in 2003.

LITTLE ANTHONY AND THE IMPERIALS. Little Anthony and the Imperials appeared in the variety specials *It's What's Happening, Baby!* in 1965 and *Fabian's Good Time Rock and Roll* in 1985. They also appeared in the music special *American Bandstand's 40th Anniversary Special* in 1992.

LITTLE BILL (*NIK, November 1999–). This was an animated series about the adventures of a five-year-old boy learning about life. The series stressed the importance of friendship and how to solve problems fairly. Educational consultants designed the series to teach kids to make choices that will enhance their lives. The series was based on a book series by **Bill Cosby**. **Phylicia Rashad** provided the voice of Little Bill's mother.

LITTLE, CLEAVON. After being a Broadway star, Little was a regular on the program of satirical skits, *The David Frost Revue*, in 1971. He starred in the sitcom *Temperatures Rising* in 1972–1974, appeared in the TV special *Once upon a Brothers Grimm* in 1977, and appeared in the drama *The Color of Friendship* in 1981. He had key roles in ***Don't Look Back: The Story of Satchel Paige***, a 1981 television movie, and *In the Nick of Time*, a 1991 Christmas film. He had a key role in the miniseries ***Separate but Equal*** in 1991. He made recurring appearances on the sitcom ***Bagdad Café*** in 1990. In 1989, he won an **Emmy Award** for Outstanding Guest Actor in a Comedy Series for his role on *Dear John*. Little died of colon cancer in 1992 at 53.

LITTLE JOHN (*CBS, May 5, 2002*). **Gloria Reuben** and **Ving Rhames** starred in this *Hallmark Hall of Fame* production about a family court judge whose life is changed when a son she gave up for adoption at birth returns as a 12-year-old.

LITTLE LADIES OF THE NIGHT (*ABC, January 16, 1977*). **Lou Gossett** and **Clifton Davis** had key roles in this made-for-television film about a former pimp-turned-cop (David Soul) who tried to help a teenage runaway drawn into prostitution.

LITTLE RICHARD. Little Richard (aka Richard Pennyman) appeared in *A Tribute to Woody Guthrie and Leadbelly* in 1988, *Happy Anniversary, Bugs: 50 Looney Years* in 1990, and *The Chipmunks—Rockin' through the Decades* in 1990. He also appeared in *33 1/3 Revolutions Per Monkee* in 1969, *Night Dreams* in 1975, *Diana Ross . . . Red Hot Rhythm and Blues* in 1987, *A Rock 'n' Roll Christmas* in 1988, *The Debbie Allen Special* in 1989, and *Muhammad Ali's 50th Birthday Celebration* in 1992. In TV films, he was in *Goddess of Love* (1988). He played the choir director in the pilot of the sitcom *Amen* (1986), but it never aired. His life was dramatized in ***The Little Richard Story*** (2000).

LITTLE RICHARD STORY, THE (*NBC, February 20, 2000*). This two-hour biopic of the flamboyant rock 'n' roll pioneer starred **Leon** (as Little Richard), **Jenifer Lewis** (as Muh Penniman), **Carl Lumbly** (as Father Bud Penniman), **Tamala Jones** (as Lucille), **Mel Jackson** (as Bump Blackwell), and **Garrett Morris** (as Preacher Rainey). The story included his battles against racial barriers, his family life, and his decision to become a Christian minister while at the height of his musical career. Robert Townsend was director. Little Richard was credited as executive producer, but in interviews he complained about the accuracy of certain aspects of the picture, aspects that Larry Katz of the *Boston Herald* (February 17, 2000) said were included in Richard's own autobiography. Katz also said, "It's a well-acted, musically thrilling and rare look at the rock 'n' roll era from a black perspective . . . it highlights Richard's role as 'the architect of rock 'n' roll—without his blueprint, Elvis wouldn't have had a kingdom.'"

LIVE FROM LINCOLN CENTER (*PBS, May 1989*). Promoted as "Ballet Meets R&B," this live one-hour variety show starred **Ray Charles** and his orchestra with the Raelettes on stage with the New York City Ballet performing "A Fool for You," a ballet. Danish choreographer Peter Martins said he wanted to showcase his "American hero." The ballet company danced to several Charles numbers including "Hit the Road Jack," "Drown in My Own Tears," I Got a Woman," and "What'd I Say?"

LIVE FROM LINCOLN CENTER: ANDRE WATTS IN RECITAL (*PBS, February 20, 1985*). Pianist Watts played solo: Scarlatti, Beethoven, Chopin, Gershwin, Debussy, and Ravel.

LIVE FROM LINCOLN CENTER: A CLASSICAL JAZZ CHRISTMAS WITH WYNTON MARSALIS (*PBS, December 22, 1989*). Jazz trumpeter **Wynton Marsalis** performed holiday songs; Duke Ellington's band performed Tchaikovsky's "Nutcracker Suite."

LIVING IT UP WITH PATTI LA BELLE (*TV1, 2004– *). Singer **Patti LaBelle** also talks. In this series, she entertained famous friends in her kitchen. She shared tips on cooking soul food and tips on shopping (especially for shoes which are her passion), shared her personal joys and disappointments, and simply engaged in down-home conversation. Both **Phylicia Rashad** and **Sheryl Lee Ralph** appeared in one segment.

LIVING SINGLE (*FOX, 1993–1998*). Former rap star-turned-actor **Queen Latifah** starred in this sitcom with **Kim Coles, Kim Fields (Freeman)**, and **Erika Alexander** as four professional black women living in Brooklyn. Khadijah James (Latifah) was editor of a magazine, and Synclaire (Coles) was her somewhat dim cousin and secretary. Sexy, shallow Regine (Fields), reminiscent of Sandra in *227*, worked in a boutique. Max (Alexander) was a lawyer with a quick tongue. Kyle (**T. C. Carter**) and Overton (**John Henton**) were their neighbors and sometime boyfriends. Other characters—Terrence (Cress Williams); Khadijah's old boyfriend, Ivan (Bumper Robinson), a college student working at the magazine; Russell (Shaun Baker), a Jamaican with a crush on Regine; and Tripp (Mel Jackson), a jingle writer—were added to the cast. Latifah wrote and performed the theme song.

The series was the most popular sitcom among black viewers but failed to attract the mainstream audience after several seasons. When it was canceled in 1997, there was an outcry from black viewers, and the series was kept on the air for another half season, ending in January 1998. After the show ended, star Latifah did not look back. She told *Jet* magazine (July 20, 1998), "There's always going to be life after 'Living Single.' That was just one part, one thing, one venture that I undertook for my life and it was successful. But it was not the first thing that I've done and it won't be the last." She was certainly right.

LIVING WITH SOUL (*TV1, 2004– *). This design lifestyle series hosted by interior designer Phyllis C. G. Bowie gave viewers a look at homes designed with Afrocentric style while offering practical advice for creating an authentic personal space. Some were the homes of celebrities, and others were not. Each episode took viewers on a "cultural journey to discover then capture the essence of who they are and the spirit of how far they've come," according to Bowie. Pairing instruction with inspiration, viewers learned the art of soulful living through cultural design. **Fay Hauser**-Price was producer.

L, KEN. Ken L played the girl-chasing friend of Kim on *The Parkers* (2000 2001). He also played a recurring role on the sitcom *In the House*.

LL COOL J. The former rapper (née James Todd Smith) played Marion Hill in the sitcom *In the House* (1995–1998). In TV films, he was Charles Red Taylor in *The Right to Remain Silent* (1996). He appeared in numerous music awards shows and cohosted *The 28th Annual American Music Awards* (2001). He also hosted *Mad TV* (1997).

LOCKE, KIMBERLY. Locke, who placed third in 2003 in *American Idol*, was in the performing cast of the special *Motown 45* (2004).

LOLA (*ABC, 1975–1976*). Lola Falana starred in a series of one-hour variety specials with various guests. On December 18, 1975, she was joined by **Muhammad Ali** and Hal Linden. On January 29, 1976, her guests were **Bill Cosby** and Dinah Shore. On March 9, 1976, **Redd Foxx** and Dick Van Dyke guested. And on March 23, 1976, she was joined by Art Carney and Dennis Weaver. Ventriloquist **Willie Tyler** was among the regulars on the specials.

LONG, AVON. Long had a key role in the miniseries *Roots: The Next Generations* in 1979.

LONG, LORETTA. Long played Susan on *Sesame Street* beginning in 1970.

LONG, NIA. In series television, Long played Sasha in the drama *Third Watch* (2003–), Andrea in the drama *Judging Amy* (2001–2002), Ramona in the drama *Live Shot* (1995–1996), Lisa in the sitcom *Fresh Prince of Bel-Air* (1994–1995), and Kat Speakes in *The Guiding Light* (1991–1993). In TV films, she played Karen in *If These Walls Could Talk 2* (2000) and Lou in *Sightings: Heartland Ghost* (2002) and had a role in *Black Jaq* (1998). She was interviewed on the state of black Hollywood in the 2004 documentary *America beyond the Color Line*.

LONG-RUNNING SERIES. Considering the genres situation comedy, drama, and variety, the sitcom *The Jeffersons* was the longest-running series with a black cast or a black actor in a leading role; it aired for 11 seasons with original programming. *Family Matters* ran for nine seasons. *The Cosby Show*, *Diff'rent Strokes*, and *Mannix* ran for eight seasons each. *Benson* was on the air for seven seasons, as was *In the Heat of the Night. A Different World, Fresh Prince of Bel-Air*, *Good Times*, *Gimme a Break*, *Moesha*, *Real People*, *Sanford and Son*, *Sister, Sister*, and *The Steve Harvey Show* aired for six seasons.

LOST CLASS OF '59, THE (*CBS, January 21, 1959*). This news documentary hosted by Edward R. Murrow was about the closing of six Norfolk high schools to forestall federally ordered desegregation.

LOUIS ARMSTRONG—CHICAGO STYLE (*ABC, January 25, 1976*). **Ben Vereen** played jazz trumpeter/singer **Louis Armstrong** in a depiction of a 1931 incident in which Armstrong was the victim of gangsters and a manager bribed to frame him on a marijuana charge. This was Broadway singer/dancer Vereen's dramatic acting debut. **Margaret Avery** played Alma Rae, **Janet MacLachlan** played Lil Armstrong, **Bill Henderson** played Charles Rudolph, **Ketty Lester** played Mrs. Thomas, and **Stack Pierce** played Cummins. *See also* BIOPICS.

LOU RAWLS PARADE OF STARS. *See* UNITED NEGRO COLLEGE FUND TELETHON: AN EVENING OF STARS.

LOU RAWLS SPECIAL, THE (*ABC, April 21, 1977*). Singer **Lou Rawls** starred in this variety special with guests **Lola Falana** and Crystal Gayle.

LOVE, AMERICAN STYLE (*ABC, 1969–1974*). This comedy anthology series consisted, each week, of several short plays with a love theme. The playlets usually starred recognizable Hollywood actors in comedic situations. The premier show (September 29, 1969) featured

Flip Wilson as a pool shark who gives lessons to a "novice" girl in "Love and the Hustler." Between playlets, repertory players performed even shorter "comedic blackouts." **Tracy Reed** (1969–1970 and 1972–1974), **Clifton Davis** (1971), and **James Watson Jr.** (1972–1974) were members of the repertory company.

LOVE BOAT, THE (*ABC*, 1977–1986). Each voyage of the luxury cruise ship had three or four stories, stories usually about romance that goes astray, and by the end of the show, the lovers are united and living happily ever after. The one-hour sitcom was one of those series that black people watched primarily because of the appeal of one black character; in this case, it was bartender Isaac Washington played by **Ted Lange**. Isaac served drinks and was also involved in several story lines. Occasional stories had black actors in addition to Lange. *See also* SERIES WITH ONE BLACK SUPPORTING ACTOR/ PERFORMER BEFORE THE 1980s.

LOVE, FAIZON. Before Love played Warren on the sitcom *The Big House* in 2004, he played Wendell, the handyman on the first three (1995–1998) of four seasons on *Parent'hood*.

LOVE IS NOT ENOUGH (*NBC*, August 12, 1978). Bernie Casey starred in this made-for-television motion picture as Mike Harris, a working-class father and widower trying to raise five children. This was the pilot for the drama series *Harris and Company*. **Stu Gilliam** was Charley, and **Carol Tillery Banks** was his wife, Angie. The Harris children were played by Stuart K. Robinson, **Renee Brown**, **Dain Turner**, Lia Jackson, and Eddie Singleton. Stanley G. Robinson was producer, and **Ivan Dixon** was director.

LOVE, MOTHER. Mother Love hosted her own syndicated advice show *Forgive or Forget* from 1998 to 2000. She was a regular panelist on the 2000 version of *To Tell the Truth*. She was a guest star in numerous episodic roles in series.

LOVE SONG (*MTV*, December 1, 2000). Pop singer **Monica** made her acting debut in this made-for-television motion picture about interracial romance. She played Camille, the overly protected daughter of prosperous New Orleans African-American parents. Camille had a steady African-American boyfriend who passed her parents' (played by **Vanessa Bell Calloway** and Peter James Francis) approval, but her eyes and her heart fell on a white gas station attendant who was a struggling blues musician. Monica (Arnold) sings "What My Heart Says," her single released at the time. The actress/singer said promotion of the film was difficult because just before it was released, her first love and two close relatives passed away. Julie Dash directed. *See also* INTERRACIAL RO-MANCE/RELATIONSHIPS.

LOVE SONGS (*SHO, April 25, 1999*). This was a made-for-television film with three intertwining segments starring **Robert Townsend**, **Louis Gossett Jr.**, and **Andre Braugher**. Each one directed one of the segments, but not the one in which he was acting. The stories were all about life in the city, and some characters showed up in more than one segment. Townsend was the star of "A Love Song for Champ," Braugher starred in "A Love Song for Jean and Ellis," and Gossett was the lead in "A Love Song for Dad." **Carl Gordon**, **Lynn Whitfield**, and **Dule Hill** were members of the supporting cast.

LOVE THY NEIGHBOR (*ABC, 1973*). This sitcom starred **Harrison Page** and **Janet MacLachlan** as Ferguson and Jackie Bruce, a young middle-class couple moving into a previously all-white housing development. The early 1970s hook was that Ferguson had a white-collar job at a local company, while his white next-door neighbor was a blue-collar slob. The jokes were about racial differences. The series, like several others in the 1970s, was based on a British hit of the same title. It was a summer trial series that never made it to fall.

LOVE, VICTOR. Love played the title role in *Final Shot: The Hank Gathers Story* in 1992 and was one of the stars of *The Colored Museum* in 1991.

LUMBLY, CARL. Lumbly played Petrie, a key role in the TV movie *Cagney and Lacey*, and the same role in the 1982–1988 series the movie spawned. He played Dr. Michael Norris in *Going to Extremes* from 1992 to 1993. Lumbly was the star of the science fiction series *M.A.N.T.I.S.* from 1994 to 1995. He played Cal in one of the trilogy of dramas on *America's Dream* in 1995. He was the lead in *The Ditchdigger's Daughters* and Mayor Christian Davidson in *EZ Streets*, both in 1997. He starred in the TV film *The Color of Friendship* and had a major role in *The Little Richard Story*, both in 2000. He played Agent Dixon, a key role in the drama series *Alias* beginning in 2001. Lumbly was the voice of Martian Manhunter in the cartoon *Justice League*.

LUMUMBA (*HBO, February 2002*). A political thriller, this was the story of the rise and fall of Patrice Lumumba (played by Eriq Ebouaney), the first prime minister of the Congo. Having achieved the position as a young man, Lumumba helped lead his country to independence from Belgium in the late 1950s. His foes were Belgian authorities, who wanted to keep a connection, and the Central Intelligence Agency (CIA), which wanted to protect U.S. business interests in the Congo's resources. Lumumba was eventually betrayed by his former friend, Joseph Mobutu (played by Alex Descas), whom he had appointed head of the army. Lumumba suffered a brutal death only nine months after becoming prime minister. A review in the *Atlanta Journal and Constitution* (February 15, 2002) praised the film, saying it "tears through the bloody conflicts and devious politics with a ferocity matched by Ebouaney's fierce charismatic performance . . . because the film is in French (with English subtitles), it's a particular challenge. But it's a challenge worth accepting." Lumumba was a Black History Month offering. *See also* AFRICAN-AMERICAN HISTORY MONTH FILMS; BIOPICS.

LUTHER VANDROSS: IN THE SPOTLIGHT "AN EVENING OF SONG." (*BET, November 28, 1994*). This musical was singer Vandross's first televised U.S. special, and it was filmed at the Royal Albert Hall in London. The songs included "Endless Love," "Evergreen," and "Killing Me Softly."

LYN, NICOLE. Lyn played a key role in *Anne Rice's "The Feast of All Saints"* in 2001.

– M –

MAC, BERNIE. Comedian Bernie Mac played Drew "Bundini" Brown in *Don King: Only in America* in 1997. He starred in the sitcom, *The Bernie Mac Show* (2001–).

MACLACHLAN, JANET. MacLachlan played Naomi Speare in the TV film *Trouble Comes to Town* (1973). She was Mrs. Jane Summerfield in 1979's *Friends* series, Jackie Bruce in the sitcom *Love Thy Neighbor*, and Polly Swanson in *All in the Family* (1980–1981). She had key roles in the made-for-television films *Louis Armstrong —Chicago Style* in 1976, *She's in the Army Now* in 1981, and *The Sophisticated Gents* in 1981.

MACNEIL, CLAUDIA. Theater actress MacNeil played a leading role in the televised play *The Member of the Wedding* in 1958 and was also a member of the cast of *A Salute to the American Theater* in 1959.

MCBRIDE, CHI. McBride starred as Principal Steven Harper in the high school drama *Boston Public* (2000–2004). He was Heavy Gene in the sitcom *The John Larroquette Show* (1993–1996). In 1998, he played the lead, a butler in Abraham Lincoln's White House, in a controversial sitcom titled *The Secret Diary of Desmond Pfeiffer*.

MCCLARIN, CURTIS. McClarin starred in *Murder without Motive: The Edmund Perry Story* in 1992.

MCCLOUD (*NBC, 1971–1977*). *McCloud* was one of those shows with one black actor playing a sidekick. This appealed to black audiences who were still excited about seeing other black people on television. The show was a police drama starring Dennis Weaver in the title role. Weaver had been the popular television character Chester in *Gunsmoke*, so he brought his own widespread appeal to the series. However, his associate, Sgt. Joe Broadhurst, was played by African-American actor **Terry Carter**, and the two solved crimes in New York City. *See also* SERIES WITH ONE BLACK SUPPORTING ACTOR BEFORE 1980.

MCCOO, MARILYN. McCoo sang, at first, with the **Fifth Dimension**, then she went solo. She and her husband starred in *The Marilyn McCoo and Billy Davis Show* in 1977. McCoo appeared in numerous variety specials: *The Fifth Dimension Special: An Odyssey in the Cosmic Universe of Peter Max* in 1970, *The Fifth Dimension Traveling Show* in 1971, *Christmas around the World* in 1976, *State Fair America* in 1977, *I Love You* in 1978, *Anne Murray's Ladies' Night* in 1979, *Men Who Rate a "10"* in 1980, *Placido Domingo . . . Stepping Out with the Ladies* in 1985, *Christmas in Washington* in 1987, We the People 200: The Constitutional Gala in 1987, Happy Birthday, Hollywood in 1987, and *The Songwriter's Hall of Fame* in 1989. She also hosted *Celebrate the Miracles* in 1988. She played Gary Coleman's mother in the made-for-television film *The Fantastic World of D.C. Collins* in 1984.

MCCORMICK, LARRY. Local Los Angeles newscaster McCormick played a newscaster in numerous TV productions including the 1979 miniseries *Blind Ambition*.

MCCOY (*NBC, 1975–1976*). Tony Curtis and **Roscoe Lee Browne** starred in this detective drama series. Curtis played McCoy, a con man who robbed rich criminals and returned the stolen items to victims. His sidekick was a nightclub comedian named Gideon Gibbs, played by Browne. McCoy was one of four series that rotated under the banner title of *NBC Mystery Movie*; only four episodes ever aired. *See also* SERIES WITH ONE BLACK SUPPORTING ACTOR BEFORE 1980.

MCCOY, SID. McCoy played the principal, Mr. Langford, in *The Bill Cosby Show* (1969–1971) and Prof. Olanga in the TV series *Lazer Tag Academy* (1986). He was the announcer on *Soul Train* and other shows. He had a role in the TV film *A Question of Guilt* (1978). He became a director and producer as well.

MCCRARY, DARIUS. McCrary played Eddie Winslow in *Family Matters* from 1989 to 1998. He also played Muhammad Ali in *Don King: Only in America* in 1997.

MCDANIEL, HATTIE. McDaniel, the first African American to win an Academy Award (for her role in *Gone with the Wind*) was Beulah in *Beulah* on radio and was the second actress to play Beulah on television. Like **Ethel Waters**, who played the television role before her, she fought for dignity in the portrayal. McDaniel was born in 1895. She became ill after three episodes and died from breast cancer on October 26, 1952.

MCDANIEL, JAMES. McDaniel was Lt. Arthur Fancy in *NYPD Blue* (1993–2001) and Officer Franklin Rose in *Cop Rock* (1990). He was **Nat "King" Cole** in the TV film *Livin' for Love: The Natalie Cole Story* (2000). Other TV film credits include the following: *Adventures of Huckleberry Finn* (1985), *Murder in Black and White* (1990), *Silencing Mary* (1998), *Deliberate Intent* (2000), *Taken* (2002), and *Edge of America* (2003).

MCDONALD, AUDRA. Multiple Tony Award winner/singer McDonald had a key role in the television musical *Annie* in 1999. She was one of the leading ladies performing in *My Favorite Broadway: The Leading Ladies* in 1999. She had key roles in the drama *Having Our Say* (1999) and the made-for-television film *Wit* (2001). She played a key role, as Jackie Brock, a U.S. senator's chief of staff, in the drama series *Mister Sterling* in 2003.

MCEACHIN, JAMES. A guest star in many series, McEachin starred in *Tenafly* (1973–1974) as a private detective who chased crooks and not skirts. He also had key roles in many made-for-television motion pictures including *Cross Current* in 1971, *This Man Stands Alone* in 1979, *Samurai* in 1979, and *Gridlock* in 1980. He was a Supreme Court justice in the drama series *First Monday* (2002).

MCFERRIN, BOBBY. McFerrin hosted *Bobby McFerrin: Loosely Mozart, the New Innovators of Classical Music* in 1996.

MCGEE, VONETTA. McGee played the female lead in the sitcom *Bustin' Loose* (1987–1988) and had a regular role in the series *Hell Town* (1985). She had key roles in the made-for-television motion pictures *The Norliss Tapes* (1973), *Superdome* (1981), *Scruples* (1981), *Brother Future* (1991), *Stormy Weathers* (1992), *You Must*

Remember This (1992), *Cagney & Lacey: The Return* (1994), and *The Man Next Door* (1996).

MCGINTY, DEREK. McGinty was named coanchor of the ABC News overnight broadcast *World News Now* in March 2001. Prior to that, he was a correspondent for CBS's *Public Eye with Bryant Gumbel*. His credits also include being a correspondent for HBO Sports.

MCINTOSH, DOUGLAS. McIntosh was Judge Milian's court officer on *The People's Court* (2002–).

MC K, MISHA. Misha Mc K starred in the sitcom *Me and Mrs. C* from 1986 to 1987.

MCKEE, LONETTE. McKee played Lorraine in the miniseries *The Women of Brewster Place* (1989) and *Alex Haley's Queen* (1993). She had a key role in the drama *Having Our Say* (1999).

MCNAIR, BARBARA. McNair headlined *On Stage with Barbara McNair* in 1970. In 1968, she was part of the starring team in *The Barbara McNair and Duke Ellington Special*. She was a frequent guest star on the Bob Hope specials; she appeared in five between 1968 and 1972, more than any other black entertainer during that period. She was a guest on many other specials including the following: *On Stage with Phil Silvers* in 1968, *Where the Girls Are* in 1968, *The Gordon MacRae Show* in 1971, and *The Boots Randolph Show* in 1972.

MCNEIL, CLAUDIA. McNeil appeared in the variety special *A Salute to the American Theater* in 1959. She portrayed Mamie in the television play *Simply Heavenly* (1959), Josepha in *Do Not Go Gentle into That Good Night* (1967), Odessa in *Incident in San Francisco* (1971), Sara in *Moon of the Wolf* (1972), Big Ma in *Roll of Thunder, Hear My Cry* (1978), and Sister Will Ada in *Roots: The Next Generations* (1979). She was born in 1917 and died of complications of diabetes in 1993.

MCQUEEN, ARMELIA. McQueen was a member of the four-person musical ensemble of *Ain't Misbehavin'* in 1982.

MCQUEEN, BUTTERFLY. McQueen, who in *Gone with the Wind* said, "I don't know nothin' 'bout birthin' babies," played Oriole, a domestic and friend to Beulah in *Beulah* from 1950 to 1952. Butterfly McQueen was born in 1911 and died in 1995. *See also* TELEVISION PIONEERS.

MCRAE, CARMEN. The singer had the role of Lila in *Roots: The Next Generations* in 1979. She starred in *Carmen McRae: Live* in 1986. She sang the theme song for *A Circle of Children* in 1977. McRae was born in 1922 and died of respiratory illness and complications from a stroke in 1994.

MAD TV (*FOX, 1995– *). This regularly scheduled late Saturday night series featured humor relating to any current subject or person, especially in politics. The show tended to feature parodies and emphasize political incorrectness. The show was reminiscent of *Saturday Night Live* but made its own place and its own audience. It has been the number 1 scheduled late night show among teens and the number 2 among adults 18 to 34. **Quincy Jones** served the show as an executive producer. Some of the regular African-American performers were Orlando Jones (1995–1997), Phil LaMarr (1995–2000), Debra Wilson (1995–2003), Aries Spears (1997–2005), and Danielle Gaither (2003–).

MAKE ROOM FOR DADDY. *See* THE DANNY THOMAS SHOW.

MAKING THE BAND (*ABC, 2000–2002; MTV, 2002*). This documentary series, reality television, was about 1,700 young men who came from all over the country to audition to be members of a rock band. Five were to be chosen. Then the band toured and recorded music. Shows dealt with their personal and family problems. Trevor Penick was the likable, energetic black musician. *See also* REALITY TELEVISION.

MAKING THE BAND 2 (*MTV, 2003– *). The series was picked up for second season with Sean "P. Diddy" Combs as the leader. The crew was made up of the following: Chopper, the youngest and a rapper; Dylan, the reggae performer; Ness; the group leader; Fred, the member with the growl in the voice; Babs, the female emcee; and Sara, the singer.

MALCOLM AND EDDIE (*UPN, 1996–2000*). **Malcolm Jamal-Warner** and **Eddie Griffin** starred in this sitcom as two young men, Malcom McGee and Eddie Sherman, who managed to be friends even though they had very little in common. They shared a Kansas City apartment above a sports bar that they eventually bought. Malcolm was the upstanding serious one who wanted to be a sports commentator. He always tried to contain Eddie, a car mechanic, and his impulsive behavior and get-rich schemes. Nicolette (**Karen Malina White**) was, in the beginning, a meter maid who frequented the bar and had a crush on Eddie. Later, she was a cop, then she worked for the partners. Malcolm was attracted to Holly (Angelle Brooks, 1996–1997), who was not interested in him. Later, Malcolm hired Simone (Michelle Hurd, 1997—1998) as the chef for the bar. During the 1998–1999 season, the partners had sold the building and opened a jazz club where Doug (Ron Pearson, 1998–2000) worked as a bartender and Leonard (Christopher Daniel Barnes, 1998–2000) was the waiter. Adding conflict was T. R. Hawkins (Tucker Smallwood), a problematic businessman who died in the final season leaving everything to his daughter Ashley (Alexa Robinson, 1999–2000) if she married Eddie within 30 days.

MAMA FLORA'S FAMILY (*CBS, November 8 and 10, 1998*). A four-hour miniseries based on Alex Haley's family after the *Roots* sagas, this story centered on Mama Flora, the matriarch of a large black family during three generations. Mama Flora (**Cicely Tyson**) was determined to keep her family together during challenging times. **Blair Underwood** played her youngest son, Willie, while **Mario Van Peebles** was the oldest son, Luke. **Queen Latifah** was the granddaughter, Diana. **Novella Nelson**, **Shemar Moore**, **Lou Myers**, and **Erika Alexander** played key roles. Tyson said that just before Haley died, in 1992, he told her manager to tell her he was working on something for her. "It wasn't until years later," said Tyson, "when I got the script from Jon Avnet and he told me the project's history, that I realized what Alex meant."

MAN CALLED HAWK, A (*ABC, 1989*). **Avery Brooks** starred in this spin-off of the drama series *Spenser for Hire*. Brooks played Hawk, a man who could track down the evildoers, in both series. There was plenty of action and violence, and Hawk was a person to be feared. He had a cool exterior, but his alter ego was a person who loved music—he was a jazz pianist—quality cuisine, and reading. He had a friend who also had a strange name—Old Man (**Moses Gunn**). Old Man was a philosopher of sorts. The series was set in Washington, D.C.

MAN IN THE MIRROR (*VH1, August 6, 2004*). Flex Alexander starred in this television motion picture about the life of entertainer **Michael Jackson** from his Motown years until then-current times. Alexander said that he would not have done the film if it bashed Jackson, that the film showed a Michael whom the public has no opportunity to see, and that it showed his sensitivity and how fans affect him.

MAN IS TEN FEET TALL, A (*NBC, 1955*). This drama aired under the title *Philco Television Playhouse*, an anthology series. Not many of the anthologies had black stars, but occasionally one surfaced. About a friendship between a white army deserter and a black longshoreman (**Sidney Poitier**), this garnered praise and was an asset to Poitier's budding career. The production was problematic to Philco when disturbed viewers mistakenly believed that the light-skinned actress (**Hilda Simms**) playing Poitier's wife was white.

MAN NAMED MAYS, A (*NBC, October 6, 1963*). This was a documentary profile of baseball great **Willie Mays** featuring Mays interviews. The show began with the ticker tape parade for the 1954 World Champion Giants. Then, when the team moved to San Francisco, Mays felt he had to prove himself all over again for fans there. The show covered his childhood in Birmingham, Alabama, batting in the minor leagues, his first days in the majors in 1951. Highlights covered on video were when Mays hit four home runs in one game; Willie Mays Night at the Polo Grounds; his signing of the newsmaking $105,000 contract; the All-Star Game in 1963; his 400th home run on August 27, 1963; and his 2,000th hit five days later. His home in Forest Hills, New York, was seen, as were scenes in the Giants clubhouse and training room. This project was made in 1963 in the heat of the Giants's pennant race.

MANDELA (*HBO, September 20, 1987*). This biopic of the first black president of South Africa starred **Danny Glover** and **Alfre Woodard**. Glover played Mandela, the heroic South African whose fight for civil rights landed him in prison for 27 years. His popularity among his people and people all over the world continued to grow even when he was in prison. His stand against injustice of apartheid awakened the conscience of the world. The film spans more than 30 years and dramatized Mandela's struggle against apartheid and his arrest and imprisonment on charges of high treason. It also chronicled Winnie Mandela's (Woodward) continued efforts to speak out after he was imprisoned. The TV film was the first of several projects sympathetic to Mandela and the African National Congress airing before his release. Conservative leaders like the Rev. Jerry Falwell urged followers to boycott it. *See also* BIOPICS.

MANDELA AND DE KLERK (*SHO, February 16, 1997*). Sidney Poitier starred in this TV movie as Nelson Mandela, while Michael Caine played Frederik W. de Klerk. It was a character study of the two men and the postapartheid period that ushered in the historic administration. De Klerk, in 1990, released Mandela after 27 years in prison. Howard Rosenberg of the *Los Angeles Times* wrote that the film "is never more vivid or entertaining than when showing their private haggling over a release date. Surprisingly, Mandela is the one who wants it delayed to give his wife Winnie (played by Tina Lifford) and other supporters more time to prepare for his liberation." The production was filmed in South Africa and meshed footage of real-life events with the dramatized scenes. *See also* BIOPICS; HISTORICAL EVENTS DRAMATIZED.

MANNIX (*CBS, 1967–1975*). Black Americans tuned in to this drama to see **Gail Fisher**, who joined the cast in the second season to play Peggy Fair, girl Friday to Joe Mannix (Mike Connors), a private detective with powerful fists. Fair was more than just a pretty face, and Fisher won an **Emmy Award** for her portrayal. *See also* LONG-RUNNING SERIES; SERIES WITH ONE BLACK SUPPORTING ACTOR.

M.A.N.T.I.S. (*FOX, 1994–1995*). **Carl Lumbly** starred in this sci-fi series as Dr. Miles Hawkins, a genius scientist, paralyzed when he was shot by a corrupt policeman. Hawkins invented a suit, the M.A.N.T.I.S. (Mechanically Automated Neuro Transmitter System), which enabled him not only to walk but also to possess super speed and strength. In the suit, he was a crime-fighting hero. The series was a spin-off of a 1994 TV film with a black cast; all but Lumbly were replaced in the series.

MARCELL, JOSEPH. Marcell played Geoffrey, the butler, in the sitcom *Fresh Prince of Bel-Air* (1990–1996). He also played Hudson in the daytime drama series *The Bold and the Beautiful* (2003–). Marcell, who is British, also played roles in British series and specials.

MARCH ON WASHINGTON (*NBC, August 28, 1963*). NBC-TV News covered live the now-famous civil rights march at the U.S. Capitol grounds attended by thousands of black Americans and supporters who watched Martin Luther King Jr. deliver the famous "I Have a Dream" speech.

MARCUS-NELSON MURDERS, THE (*CBS, March 8, 1973*). This was a three-hour TV film about a detective who fought to keep Lewis Humes, a black teenager (**Gene Woodbury**), from being wrongly convicted of murder. This film was the pilot for the long-running series *Kojak*; both starred Telly Savalas. **Lynn Hamilton** played Humes's mother.

MARIAN ANDERSON (*PBS, May 8, 1991*). Avery Brooks narrated this one-hour documentary celebrating the life, career, and musical legacy of contralto Marian Anderson.

MARILYN MCCOO AND BILLY DAVIS JR. SHOW, THE (*CBS, 1977*). This was a summer variety series airing after the husband/wife duo's hit "You Don't Have to Be a Star to Be in My Show." Regular performers in the series included Jay Leno and **Tim Reid**.

MARSALIS, BRANFORD. Branford Marsalis appeared in the variety special *The Best of Disney Music* in 1993. From 1992 to 1995, he was bandleader/music director of *The Tonight Show with Jay Leno*. He was composer for the TV films *Mr. and Mrs. Loving* (1996) and *To*

My Daughter with Love (1994). Marsalis participated in the following TV productions: *The Best of Disney Music: A Legacy in Song—Part 1* (1993), *Motown 40: The Music Is Forever* (1998), the miniseries *Jazz*, and *Apollo at 70: A Hot Night in Harlem* (2004).

MARSALIS, WYNTON. Wynton Marsalis performed the National Anthem at Super Bowl XX in 1986. He appeared in the variety special *The Presidential Inaugural Gala* in 1993. He directed the orchestra in *Swingin' with Duke: Lincoln Center Jazz Orchestra* and *Ellington at 100*, both in 1999. He and his jazz orchestra joined with the New York Philharmonic in *Nutcracker Swing!* in 2001. Beginning in 2004, it was Marsalis's piccolo trumpet solo of Gottfried Reiche's "Abblasen" that opened *CBS Sunday Morning*.

MARSHALL, DON. Marshall was the copilot Dan Erickson in the series *Land of the Giants* (1968–1970). He had key roles in the made-for-television motion pictures *The Reluctant Heroes* in 1971, *Benny & Barney: Las Vegas Undercover* in 1977, and *The Suicide's Wife* in 1979.

MARSHALL, WILLIAM. Marshall starred in "Othello" on *Omnibus* and in various other dramatic roles. He also appeared in comedy *Pee Wee's Playhouse Christmas Special* in 1988. He died in 2003 at the age of 78.

MARTHA AND THE VANDELLAS. Martha and the Vandellas appeared in the variety special *It's What's Happening, Baby!* in 1965 and numerous other musical variety series.

MARTIN (*FOX, 1992–1997*). Comedian **Martin Lawrence** starred in this sitcom as Martin Payne, a talk show host on a Detroit radio station. In addition to the character Martin, Lawrence played other characters who satirized black ghetto life. Among them were the following: Otis, the insecure security guard; Jerome, the self-proclaimed player; Sheneneh, the feisty female character, and Elroy, the performing auto mechanic. Primarily, the scripts dealt with his relationships with his girlfriend, Gina (**Tisha Campbell**), a marketing executive; his buddies Cole (**Carl Anthony Payne II**) and Tommy (**Thomas Mikal Ford**); and Gina's best friend, Pam (**Tichina**

Arnold). When Martin was at the radio station, he encountered Stan (**Garrett Morris**, 1992–1994), the station owner, and Shawn (Jonathan Gries, the token white actor, 1992–1994), the handyman. Each show was chock full of lines based on insult humor: Martin was short and had big ears. In one episode, Gina said to Martin, ". . . those satellite dishes on the side of your head." The rest of the cast was not exempt: Gina had a big head, Tommy didn't have a job, and Martin called Pam ugly with doglike qualities. During the second season, Gina moved into Martin's apartment, and they became engaged. Martin lost his job and was hired as an associate producer of a local TV talk show. During the 1994 to 1995 season, Gina and Martin were married, but the trouble was just beginning. In real life, Campbell accused Lawrence of sexual harassment, of sexual battery, of making violent threats toward her, and of being so volatile and unpredictable that she feared for her life. She sued Lawrence and the show's producers. She refused to do the series, and in the scripts, her character was working in Los Angeles. Lawrence issued a statement saying that he regretted that he was "being used as a pawn in a contract dispute between Tisha Campbell and producers of the show, that he had "long been Tisha's champion and protector," and was "thus deeply hurt by these allegations." He said there was no merit to the lawsuit. Campbell did appear in the series' final episode but never in a scene with Lawrence.

MARTIN, DUANE. Martin played Vidal Thomas in the 1992–1993 sitcom *Out All Night*, B. J. Teach in the two-hour TV film *Mutiny* in 1999, and Robert, star of the sitcom *All of Us*, beginning in the 2003–2004 season.

MARTIN, HELEN. Martin was a regular on the sitcoms *Baby, I'm Back* (1978) and *227* (1985–1990). She had key roles in the made-for-television movies *J.T.* in 1969; *Dummy* and *This Man Stands Alone*, both in 1979; *A Raisin in the Sun* in 1989; and *Something to Sing About* in 2000. She was born in 1909 and died in 2000.

MARTIN, JESSE L. Martin played Dr. Greg Butters (1998–1999) in the comedy-drama *Ally McBeal*, Antonio Collins in *413 Hope Street* (1997–1998), and Detective Edward Green in *Law and Order*

(1999–). He played the singing, dancing role of the Ghost of Christmas Present in *A Christmas Carol: The Musical* in 2004.

MARTIN LUTHER KING JR. ASSASSINATION (*CBS, April 4–9, 1968*). At the news and documentary **Emmy Awards** in 1969, Coretta Scott King, King's widow, was the presenter when CBS News won the Emmy statuette for "its intensive and sobering coverage" of the aftermath and funeral of the assassination of the civil rights leader. She said, "No matter how you measure it, 1968 was a most extraordinary year . . . the shock and tragedy of two assassinations [presidential candidate Sen. Robert Kennedy also], the violence of riots and demonstrations, the first rays of hope for peace, and the first orbit of the moon."

MARTIN, MICHEL. Martin joined ABC News in 1992 after being a reporter for the ABC newsmagazine program *Day One*. Later, she was named correspondent and guest anchor for *Nightline*. She received an **Emmy Award** for her reporting.

MARVA COLLINS STORY, THE (*CBS, December 1, 1981*). This two-hour made-for-television film depicted the achievements of teacher Marva Collins, who made remarkable progress in teaching "unteachable" students in poor areas of Chicago. A 1979 *60 Minutes* segment had spotlighted her scholars. **Cicely Tyson** played Collins and was nominated for an **Emmy Award** for her portrayal. Others in the cast were **Morgan Freeman** as Clarence Collins, **Marsha Warfield** as Lela Boland, Roderick Wimberly as Martin Luther Jones, and others. *See also* BIOPICS.

MARVIN HAGLER FIGHTS. "Marvelous" Marvin Hagler fought Alan Minter in a live telecast of the WBA/WBC Middleweight Championship on September 27, 1980. Hagler won with a third-round technical knockout. The bout between Hagler and John "The Beast" Mugabi was a delayed broadcast on March 29, 1986. Hagler won with an 11th-round knockout.

MARY TYLER MOORE SHOW, THE (*CBS, 1970–1977*). John Amos portrayed Gordy, the weatherman, a recurring role in this half-hour sitcom about a 30-something liberated lady (Mary Tyler Moore) trying to make a success of working in a previously all-male television newsroom. The Gordy character as a weatherman was interesting because at that time, in real television news, black men were primarily sportscasters. Gordy was also the most respected of the two on-air personalities on WJM-TV News (the other was the inept Ted Baxter played by Ted Knight). So, in this respect, the show took the high road. There were few black guest stars. (**Janet MacLachlan** as a political candidate's campaign manager and **Tamu** as a troubled teenager in a big-sister program are memorable.) In 1973, Amos left the series to star in *Good Times*. See also SERIES WITH ONE BLACK SUPPORTING ACTOR BEFORE 1980.

MASTER P. Hip-hop artist Master P played Percy Miller on the children's program *Romeo* (2003–).

MATHIS, JOHNNY. Mathis headlined his own specials, *Johnny Mathis in the Canadian Rockies* (1975) and *Johnny Mathis Live by Request* (1998). He was one of a few black performers to be a mystery guest on the early version of the game show *What's My Line?* (1959). He was a guest on numerous specials, including *The Frances Langford Show* in 1960, *It's What's Happening, Baby* in 1965, *Monsanto Presents Mancini* in 1971, *The Natalie Cole Special* in 1978, *Marvin Hamlisch: They're Playing My Song* in 1981, *American Bandstand's 33 1/3 Celebration* in 1985, *American Bandstand's 40th Anniversary Special* in 1992, and *Christmas in Washington* in 1991. He also appeared in the specials *I Love You* in 1978, *The Music of Your Life* in 1985, *Mary Hart Presents Love in the Public Eye* in 1990, and *Holiday Greetings from The Ed Sullivan Show* in 1992. He played himself in the TV films *Ray Alexander: A Menu for Murder* (1995) and *Get Happy* (1973). He made 38 guest appearances on *The Tonight Show with Johnny Carson* from 1971 to 1990 and 10 appearances on *The Ed Sullivan Show* from 1957 to 1970. He sang the theme song for the 1980s sitcom *Family Ties*.

MATNEY, BILL. After a career in newspapers, Matney joined NBC News in 1963. He covered Capitol Hill and the White House and at some point in the 1970s also worked for ABC News. Matney died in 2001 of respiratory failure.

MATT WATERS (*CBS, 1996*). **Montel Williams** starred in this high school drama series as a career Naval officer who retired and became a science teacher in New Jersey. The school was tough with armed guards and security equipment, but Waters was tougher with his disciplinary policies. Kriston Wilson played the African studies teacher. The show aired six episodes, and fans said it was not enough time to grow an audience.

MAUDE (*CBS, 1972–1978*). This sitcom was a spin-off of *All in the Family* starring Beatrice Arthur as a liberated, independent-thinking woman. Maude had a maid who was as witty as she was, and that maid, Florida (**Esther Rolle**) was spun off in 1974 into her own series, *Good Times*. In 1977, **Marlene Warfield** joined the cast as the maid, Victoria Butterfield. *See also* SERIES WITH ONE BLACK SUPPORTING ACTOR/PERFORMER BEFORE 1980.

MAYA ANGELOU; RAINBOW IN THE CLOUDS (*PBS, May 22, 1992*). Poet/actress/activist **Maya Angelou** talked about the importance and the impact of faith.

MAYO, WHITMAN. Mayo played Grady in *Sanford and Son* from 1973 to 1977 and in *The Sanford Arms* (1977). He was the star of the *Sanford and Son* spin-off *Grady*, which ran for a few weeks (1995–1996). Mayo played a role in the TV film *Final Shot: The Hank Gathers Story* (1992). He had a key role in the TV film *Boycott* in 2001. Mayo was born in 1930 and died in 2001 of a heart attack.

MAYS, WILLIE. The baseball great helped pay tribute to the "Peanuts" comic strip in the live-action and animated children's program *Here's to You Charlie Brown: 50 Great Years!* in 2000.

MEADOWS, TIM. Meadows was a regular on *Saturday Night Live* (1991–2000).

MEEK, AARON. Meek played Ahmad in *Soul Food*.

MEEK, BARBARA. Meek had a key role in the TV film *Jimmy B. & Andre* in 1980, and she played Archie Bunker's housekeeper

(1980–1982), hired after his wife, Edith, died, in *All in the Family*. She played mother to **Melba Moore**'s character in *Melba* in 1986.

MEETING, THE (*PBS, May 3, 1989*). This *American Playhouse* 90-minute production reveals what may have happened when Martin Luther King Jr. and Malcolm X met. This was "nonviolence" versus "by any means necessary." Considering their very contrasting philosophies of the racial struggle, what were the points of agreement and the points of conflict? Both were later assassinated, but how did they view their futures? Based on the Jeff Stetson play, the film starred **Jason Bernard** as King and **Dick Anthony Williams** as Malcolm X. *USA Today* wrote, "The drama soars, greatly aided by expert acting from Dick Anthony Williams . . . and Jason Bernard." *See also* BIOPICS.

MELBA (*CBS, 1986*). Melba Moore starred in this sitcom as the director of the Manhattan Visitors' Center. Her character, Melba Patterson, was a divorcée with a nine-year-old daughter, Tracy (Jamilla Perry), and a live-in mother, Rose (**Barbara Meek**). One episode of the show aired, and it was yanked from the CBS lineup until summer, when the rest of the episodes were aired. Many felt the show was unrealistic because of the white character, Susan (Gracie Harrison), who was considered a sister because she, too, was raised by Rose. It was a time when the networks had long felt that only racially integrated shows could be successful, but *The Cosby Show* had premiered in 1984 and proved that theory wrong.

MELBA MOORE-CLIFTON DAVIS SHOW, THE (*CBS, 1972*). This summer variety series starred Broadway musical stars and then-sweethearts **Melba Moore** and **Clifton Davis**. With regulars **Timmie Rogers**, Ron Carey, Liz Torres, and Dick Libertini, they performed comedy skits and sang musical numbers.

MEMBER OF THE WEDDING, THE (*CBS, June 12, 1958*). This 90-minute drama was based on the Carson McCullers stage play. Set in 1945 Georgia, a 12-year-old girl was anxious to grow up and become a woman. Berenice was instrumental in helping her grow up. **Claudia McNeil** played Berenice. *See also* BROADWAY PLAYS AND MUSICALS. *See the next two listings.*

MEMBER OF THE WEDDING, THE (*NBC, December 20, 1982*). **Pearl Bailey**, **Howard Rollins Jr.**, and **Bill Cobbs** starred in this live television version of the Carson McCullers stage play. Dana Hill played Frankie.

MEMBER OF THE WEDDING, THE (*USA, January 29, 1997*). This production was not a mounting of the stage play but an adaptation of the Carson McCullers novel. **Alfre Woodard** played Berenice, the maid who raised the troubled 12-year-old Frankie (Anna Paquin). Frankie believes that all the problems in her life will be solved if she goes to live with her unsuspecting brother and his bride after they marry and that it is up to Berenice to prevent a disaster from occurring. Lloyd Rose of the *Washington Post* (January 29, 1997), wrote, "Woodard is an excellent Berenice, but it's the kind of role she could do in her sleep."

MERCER, MAE. Mercer played Aunt Juba in *A Woman Called Moses* in 1978 and had a key role in the black musical version of Cinderella, *Cindy*, in 1978.

MERKERSON, S. EPATHA. A veteran of the legitimate theater, Merkerson is best known to television audiences as Lt. Anita Van Buren on *Law and Order* (1993–). She was a regular on *Pee Wee's Playhouse*, where she played Reba, the Mail Lady. She was a regular in the short-lived sci-fi series *Mann & Machine* in 1992, then went right onto the comedy series *Here and Now* as the director of the youth center where star **Malcolm-Jamal Warner's** character worked. In TV films and miniseries, Merkerson had roles in the following: *A Place for Annie* (1994), *A Mother's Prayer* (1995), *Breaking Through* (1996), *An Unexpected Life* (1998), *Exiled* (1998), *A Girl Thing* (2001), and *Lackawanna Blues* (2004).

MERRITT, THERESA. Merritt played the mama, Eloise Curtis, in the sitcom *That's My Mama* from 1974 to 1975. In TV films, she had roles in *J.T.* (1969), *Concealed Enemies* (1984), and *Miracle at Beekman's Place* (1988). Merritt was born in 1924 and died of cancer in 1998.

METHOD & RED (*FOX, 2004–*). This sitcom starred rappers **Method Man** and Redman as streetwise rap artists who try to fit into a previously predominantly white and affluent neighborhood in New Jersey and cause funny confusion. But Method Man, who was also credited as executive producer, said that despite his title, he had been unable to have enough creative control to make the show what he wanted, that the network had "taken the ghetto out" of the series. The hip-hopster/actor said, "There's a way for it to be both ghetto and intelligent." A reported eight million viewers saw the premiere episode on June 16, 2004, a reasonable statistic for a summer series. Critics generally charged that the series was nothing more than a collection of racial stereotypes. An online reviewer on IMDb (July 4, 2004) criticized the black and the white characters and said, "The show has never met a stereotype it didn't like." This critic also warned that judging a show after a few episodes is probably unfair. **Anna Maria Horsford** also starred.

METHOD MAN. The rap artist starred with Redman in the sitcom *Method & Red* beginning in 2004.

MIAMI VICE (*NBC, 1984–1989*). This action/police drama series was hot with black and mainstream viewers. The two leads were reminiscent of Robert Culp and **Bill Cosby** in *I Spy* (1965–1968) in that they were a black guy and a white guy partnered to solve crimes. The white guy, in both series, had top billing, but the black guy was very much a draw for black viewers. *Miami Vice's* black star was **Philip Michael Thomas** (as Det. Ricardo Stubbs), and the white lead was Don Johnson (as Det. Sonny Crockett). They worked undercover to solve crimes in the drug world. And they looked cool. Their wardrobes became as much of a draw as they were. They wore Italian tropical-type fashions in pastel colors. Linen jackets by designers like Versace and Vittorio Ricci were worn over T-shirts and white linen pants. They shunned socks, ties, and belts, and soon male viewers were dressing similarly. Crockett had snazzy sports cars—once a black Ferrari Spider and at another time a Ferrari Testaroosa. Women and men liked their lifestyles. Equally appealing was sexy Det. Trudy Joplin (**Olivia Brown**), who, with Det. Gina Navarro Calabrese

(Saundra Santiago), formed a female undercover partnership. The series was also hip in the music department with rock music prominently heard, actually too prominent to be called background music. Others in the regular cast were Edward James Olmos as Lt. Martin Castillo and Michael Talbott as Det. Stan Switek. Uncommon celebrity guests doing cameos included **James Brown**, **Little Richard**, and **Don King**.

MICHAEL JACKSON: IN CONCERT IN BUCHAREST (*HBO, October 10, 1992***).** This musical special starring Jackson was taped in Romania.

MICHAEL JACKSON TALKS . . . TO OPRAH—90 PRIMETIME MINUTES WITH THE KING OF POP (*ABC, February 10, 1993***).** This was an informational special consisting of **Oprah Winfrey**'s exclusive live interview with Jackson. It included a tour of his Neverland Ranch.

MICHAEL JACKSON: THE MAGIC RETURNS (*CBS, August 31, 1987***).** This musical special starring the King of Pop announced the release of the *Bad* album and the premiere of the *Bad* video. This was the first music video to be premiered in a network prime-time special. The show also featured one of Jackson's early performances with the Jackson Five, concert footage of the Jackson's Victory Tour, his moonwalk to "Billie Jean," and excerpts of the *Beat It* and *Thriller* videos. The special was the highest rating CBS had achieved in that time period (Monday, 8:00–8:30 P.M.) since November 1986.

MICHAEL JACKSON: 30TH ANNIVERSARY CELEBRATION (*CBS, November 12, 2001***).** This two-hour musical special celebrated the 30th anniversary of **Michael Jackson**'s career as a solo performer. It also served as the first reunion in more than 16 years of the Jackson Five.

MICHELE, MICHAEL. Michele played Dr. Cleo Finch in the drama series *ER* (2000–2001) and had a regular role as Jessie in the drama series *Kevin Hill* (2004–2005). She had a role in *Homicide: The Movie* (2000) as well as *Homicide: Life on the Street.* She was a regular on the series *Central Park West* and had a recurring role on *New York Undercover*. In TV films, she had roles in *Trade Winds* (1993) and *Creature* (1998).

MICKEY MOUSE CLUB'S 200TH EPISODE SPECIAL (*DIS, December 3, 1992*). The theme of this children's program was racial harmony. The **Rev. Jesse Jackson** was a guest, and children were honored for improving race relations. The Mousketeers discussed their experiences with racism.

MIDDLE SCHOOL CONFESSIONS (*HBO, January 4, 2002*). **Samuel L. Jackson** hosted this documentary about adolescents and how adults can be instrumental in making young lives turn in the right direction.

MIDNIGHT SPECIAL (*NBC, 1973–1981*). This series was 90 minutes of primarily rock music recording artists in concert; Wolfman Jack was announcer. Late in the series, there was a segment with a panel of comics. At first, there were different guest hosts each week, then Helen Reddy became host from 1975 to 1976. Then the series went to guest hosts again. Some of the black performers who appeared as entertainers or hosts were Edwin Hawkins (1973), **Johnny Mathis** (1973 and 1976), **Chuck Berry** (1973), **Franklyn Ajaye** (1974 and 1976), **Tina Turner** (1974, 1975, and 1979), **Jimmie Walker** (1975 and 1976), **Donna Summer** (1976–1980), the Jackson Five (1979), and **Irene Cara** (1980).

THE MIGHTY CLOUDS OF JOY. The Mighty Clouds of Joy gospel singers appeared in *Johnny Cash—A Merry Memphis Christmas* in 1982 and *Texas 150—A Celebration* in 1986.

MIKE TYSON FIGHTS. On July 26, 1986, "Iron" Mike Tyson defeated Marvis Frazier in a first-round knockout in a heavyweight fight live from Glenn Falls, New York. He then defeated Donovan "Razor" Ruddock by a technical knockout on a show airing on June 1, 1991, but taped on March 18, 1991. The referee stopped the fight in a controversial decision in the seventh round, and after the two hugged, a fight broke out in their corners. A special report on Tyson's trial and conviction of rape aired on *Wide World of Sports* on February 1, 1992.

MILLER, CHERYL. A member of the Basketball Hall of Fame and former head coach, Miller, at TNT, became the first female analyst to call a nationally televised National Basketball Association (NBA) game. She had joined Turner Sports in 1995 as an analyst and reporter covering the NBA on TNT and TBS. She served as women's basketball analyst for NBC's coverage of the 1996 Olympic Games in Atlanta and in 1997 was named head coach and general manager of the WNBA's Phoenix Mercury. In 2002, she returned to TNT and TBS as a sideline reporter and studio analyst.

MILLER, TANGI. Miller played Elena Tyler in the drama series *Felicity*. She had roles in the HBO sports comedy *Arli$$* and the **Black Entertainment Television** movie *Playing with Fire*.

MILLS, ALLISON. Allison Mills was Leslie Uggams's sister, Oletha, in the "Sugar Hill" sketch on *The Leslie Uggams Show* in 1969.

MILLS BROTHERS, THE. The quartet was popular in variety series and specials. It appeared frequently on *The Ed Sullivan Show* and was seen in *The George Kirby Special* in 1970, *One More Time* in 1974, *The Bing Crosby Special, Bing! . . . A 50th Anniversary Gala* in 1977, and *100 Years of Golden Hits* in 1981.

MINSTREL MAN (*CBS, March 2, 1977*). A primarily black cast depicted the era of black minstrel entertainment in this one-hour made-for-television movie. The story centered on brothers, one an extroverted song-and-dance man who wanted to own his own minstrel troupe in a field dominated by white performers in blackface. The other brother was introverted and wanted to break away from the stereotypes. **Glynn Turman**, **Ted Ross**, Stanley Clay, **Saundra Sharp**, **Art Evans**, Gene Bell, and **Earl Billings** had key roles.

MINOR ADJUSTMENTS (*NBC, 1995; UPN, 1996*). Comic **Rondell Sheridan** played Dr. Ron Aimes, a child psychologist with a skill at interacting with children, in this sitcom reminiscent of Bill Cosby's conversations with children both on *The Cosby Show* and on *Kids Say the Darndest Things*. Aime's wife, Rachel, was played by **Wendy Raquel Robinson**. The son, Trevor, was played by Bobby E. McAdams II. Emma, the daughter, was played by **Camille Winbush**. The physicians who shared an office with Dr. Aimes—Dr. Bruce Hampton and Dr. Francine Bailey—were played by Mitchell Whitfield and Linda Kash. Sara, Aimes's niece and receptionist, was played by Sara Roe. *See also* FAMILY SERIES.

MISS AMERICA PAGEANT. The first black state winner in the Miss America pageant was Miss Iowa, Cheryl Brown Hollingsworth, in 1970. **Vanessa Williams**, as Miss New York, was the first black beauty crowned Miss America in 1984. When suggestive photos of her were published in *Penthouse* magazine, she was replaced, 10 months into her term, by Suzette Charles, Miss New Jersey. Despite the furor, Williams became the most successful former Miss America, black or white, as she soared in her singing and acting career. Though pageant officials had asked for her resignation in 1984, the broadcasts, in later years, proudly showed her photo when displaying former winners. Debbye Turner was crowned in 1990, Marjorie Vincent in 1991, Kimberly Aiken in 1994, Erika Harold in 2003, and Ericka Dunlap in 2004.

MISS EVERS' BOYS (*HBO, February 22, 1997*). This TV film was based on the actual Tuskegee Experiment, a controversial 40-year U.S. government study (which began in 1932) in which African-American men infected with syphilis went untreated so that the fatal course of the disease could be tracked. The men had no knowledge that the government was basically watching them die when they could have been cured with penicillin. **Alfre Woodard** played Miss Eunice Evers, a dedicated nurse caught in the web of official lies. **Laurence Fishburne** played Caleb Humphries, one of the victims, and was also executive producer. **Joe Morton** played Dr. Brodus, who treated the dying patients. The production won the **Emmy Award** for Outstanding Made-for-Television Movie. Woodard won the Emmy for Outstanding Lead Actress in a Miniseries or Special. Fishburne was nominated for outstanding lead actor. **Obba Babatunde** and **Ossie Davis** also had roles and were nominated for the

Emmy in the Supporting Actor category. There were numerous other nominations including one for the Presidents Award, which recognizes programming that explores social or educational issues and encourages changes that help society cope with the situation. *See also* HISTORICAL EVENTS DRAMATIZED.

MISSION IMPOSSIBLE (*CBS, 1966–1973; ABC, 1988–1990*). The primary attraction to African-American audiences in this original drama series was Barney Collier, the electronics expert, played by **Greg Morris**. Morris had played roles on television, but this was the series that made him famous. Collier was one of the agents of the U.S. government's Impossible Missions Force, or IMF, which each week at the top of the hour received a recorded message detailing the secret and dangerous assignment. The tape recorder self-destructed after it played. The IMF would track down foreign powers that threatened the United States. In 1988, the series was revived with Greg's son, **Phil Morris**, playing the role his father created. The revival ended in 1990.

MITCHELL, BRIAN. Mitchell (aka Brian Stokes Mitchell) played second-banana roles like Dr. Justin "Jackpot" Jackson on the medical drama series *Trapper John M.D.* from 1979 to 1986 and Nat Holliday on the police drama *Houston Knights* from 1987 to 1988. He had a role in the miniseries *Roots: The Next Generations* in 1979. In 1992, he played Hilary's boyfriend, the recurring role of Trevor, on *The Fresh Prince of Bel-Air*. Mitchell went to New York, changed his name to Brian Stokes Mitchell, and became one of the most sought-after black Broadway stars, winning numerous awards including the Tony and playing leads in numerous musicals. In 1999 TV film projects, he played Adam Harris in *Double Platinum* and Duke Kahanamoku in *Too Rich: The Secret Life of Doris Duke*. He had a role in 1993's *The Ernest Green Story*, and he played Earl Delacroix in the TV film *Ruby's Bucket of Blood* in 2001. He provided voice-overs for numerous animated projects.

MITCHELL, DARYL. Mitchell played Eli, the bowling alley manager in the series *Ed*. Previously, he was a regular in the series *Veronica's Closet* and *The John Larroquette Show*. In 2001, he was in a motorcycle accident that left his spinal cord damaged. Producers of *Ed* wrote the character of Eli into the series because they admired his intensity, passion, and determination for acting despite his injury.

MITCHELL, DON. Mitchell played Mark Sanger, bodyguard to Chief Ironside (Raymond Burr), in *Ironside* (1967–1975).

MITCHELL, FINESSE. Mitchell joined the cast of *Saturday Night Live* in 2003.

MITCHELL, RUSS. Mitchell was a correspondent for the CBS newsmagazine *Eye to Eye* (1993–1995) and was the network's overnight news broadcast coanchor on *Up to the Minute* (1992). In 1996, he covered the presidential election. In 1997, he became coanchor of the *Saturday Early Show* and one of the primary anchors of *CBS Evening News Saturday Edition*. He also served as news correspondent contributing to various broadcasts. He won the **Emmy Award** in 1997 for his coverage of the crash of TWA Flight 800.

MITCHLLL, SCOEY. Mitchlll played Paul Bratter, a lawyer and newlywed in the sitcom *Barefoot in the Park* in 1970. He was Cindy's father in the 1978 version of Cinderella, *Cindy*. He was instrumental in getting the Christine Houston play *227* to television in 1985. He was executive producer of the sitcom *Me & Mrs. C* (1986–1987). He produced and had roles in the TV projects *Miracle at Beekman's Place* and *Gus Brown and Midnight Brewster*. He was a frequent celebrity player on *The Match Game*.

MOD SQUAD, THE (*ABC, 1968–1973*). In this one-hour drama, three young hippie types, after having conflicts with the law, get work as undercover cops. The stories dealt not only with their solving crimes and cornering the bad guys who prey on youth but also with their relationships with each other. An unlikely trio, Linc (**Clarence Williams III**) was the black guy from Watts. Pete (Michael Cole) was white and from a wealthy Beverly Hills family. Julie (Peggy Lipton) had run away from her San Francisco home, where her mother was a prostitute. *See also* SERIES WITH ONE BLACK SUPPORTING ACTOR/PERFORMER BEFORE 1980.

MOESHA (*UPN, 1996–2001*). Popular pop singer **Brandy** (aka Brandy Norwood) starred in this sitcom as Moesha Mitchell, a Los Angeles teenager transitioning into adulthood. Each episode began with the theme performed by Brandy and a monologue of Brandy introducing this chapter of her life. Her monologues also closed each episode. The adults in her life were her father, Frank Mitchell (**William Allen Young**), a car salesman, and her new stepmother, Dee Mitchell (**Sheryl Lee Ralph**), a teacher at Crenshaw High School, where Moesha matriculated. She also had a younger brother, Myles (Marcus Mitchell). Moesha's friends were Hakeem (**Lamont Bentley**), Kim (**Countess Vaughn**), and Niecy (Shar Jackson). The friends hung out at The Den, a restaurant run by Andell (**Yvette Wilson**). Mo, as Moesha was often called, dated Quenton "Q" (Fredro Starr) during the first years of the series. The scripts centered on aspects of her aspirations to become a journalist, confrontations with her parents, graduating from high school, and going on to college. At home, she once moved out because of a clash with her father, Frank. Frank moved a nephew, Dorian (Ray J. Norwood, Brandy's brother), into the home; eventually, Dorian, much to his surprise, was revealed to be his son. Moesha didn't like this and moved out again but later made up with her father. In 2000, she had a roommate, Alicia (**Alexis Fields**). She eventually became engaged to Q, but they broke up, and Starr left the series. She helped Dorian find his birth mother, who was Barbara Lee (**Olivia Brown**), and the reunited mother and son tried to form a relationship. Dorian was seeking a career in the music business and met some shady guys, and Myles was kidnapped. The series was canceled without resolution. The show spawned the sitcom *The Parkers* spinning off the regular character Kim and her mother, Nikki (**Mo'Nique**), who had guest-starred. The show was not without its problems. In 1999, Brandy was away from the show for three weeks. Some reports said she suffered from dehydration. She told **Oprah Winfrey** that she had had an emotional, physical, and spiritual breakdown, that she had begun to hate the character she played. In 2004, long after the series ended, *People* (July 26) said that she admitted that "an eating disorder had been at the heart of the crisis," that she had dropped to a dangerous 105 pounds. Executive producer Vida Spears said *Moesha* was UPN's first hit. Sara V. Finney was also an executive producer. *See also* LONG-RUNNING SERIES.

MO' FUNNY: BLACK COMEDY IN AMERICA (*HBO, February 9, 1993*). This special program chronicled the history of black comedians from blackfaced comics in Vaudeville to the Def Jam generation of the 1990s. Seen were **Charles Dutton, Della Reese**, Norma Miller, **Paul Mooney**, and Donald Bogle. Archival footage of the following was featured: **Eddie "Rochester" Anderson, Pearl Bailey, Louise Beavers, Willie Best, Godfrey Cambridge, Bill Cosby, Redd Foxx, Whoopi Goldberg**, Dick Gregory, Robin Harris, **Hattie McDaniel**, Mantan Moreland, **Eddie Murphy, Richard Pryor**, Moms Mabley, Dewey "Pigmeat" Markham, **Timmie Rogers, Sinbad, Damon Wayans, Keenen Ivory Wayans, Marsha Warfield, Flip Wilson**, and many others. **Richard Pryor** was one of the co–executive producers.

MONICA. Monica (Arnold) made her acting debut in the 2000 television film *Love Song*. She also debuted a single, "What My Heart Says," in the film.

MO'NIQUE. After doing stand-up comedy on various comedy revue shows, Mo'Nique was known to television viewers primarily as Nikki in *The Parkers* (2000–2004). Mo'Nique also starred in the TV film *Good Fences*. She won the NAACP Image Award twice for Outstanding Lead Actress in a Comedy Series for her portrayal of Nikki. She hosted *It's Showtime at the Apollo* beginning in 2003. In 2005, she was the host and executive producer of *Mo'Nique's Fat Chance*.

MONTEL (*SYN, 1991– *). **Montel Williams** hosted this talk show (once titled *The Montel Williams Show*), the longest-running national daytime talk show hosted by an African-American man. The series was test-marketed in numerous American cities and received high marks. Williams was also executive producer of the daily show. All the guests were people who shared their problems and issues—health, relationship, crime, and so on—with Montel, who offered advice. Critics said he was too preachy; fans said he had a great heart and seemed to care about the guests and their problems. The show won the 1999 Genesis Award for outstanding television talk show. It was nominated numerous times for the **Emmy Award**.

MONTGOMERY, BARBARA. Montgomery played Casietta Hetebrink in the sitcom *Amen* from 1986 to 1990 and Olivia in the sitcom *Married People* (1990–1991). She was Eva Turner in the miniseries *The Women of Brewster Place* in 1990. Her roles in TV films include Mrs. Martin in *A Fight for Jenny* (1986), Mrs. Conloy in *Polly* (1989) and *Polly: Comin' Home* (1990), Juvy Judge in *Bloodlines: Murder in the Family* (1993), and Geneva in *Daddy's Girl* (1996).

MOODY, LYNNE. Moody played Tracy in the first episodes of the 1974–1975 sitcom *That's My Mama*. She was Polly Dawson in the sitcom *Soap* from 1979 to 1981, nurse Julie Williams in the sitcom *ER* from 1984 to 1985, and Patricia Williams in the prime-time soap opera *Knots Landing* from 1988 to 1990. Moody had key roles in the made-for-television movies *Charleston* in 1979, *The Oklahoma City Dolls* in 1981, *Wait 'Til Your Mother Gets Home* in 1983, *Agatha Christie's "A Caribbean Mystery"* also in 1983, and *The Toughest Man in the World* in 1984. Her roles in motion pictures for television include 1997's *The Ditch Diggers Daughters* starring **Carl Lumbly** and *A Taste for Justice* starring **Louis Gossett Jr.** She had an important role, Irene Harvey, in the legendary miniseries *Roots* in 1977 and in *Roots: The Next Generations* in 1979. Other miniseries roles include *The Atlanta Child Murders* (1985).

MOONEY, PAUL. Comedian Paul Mooney was a performer and/or writer on *The Richard Pryor Special?* in 1977, *The Richard Pryor Special* in 1982, variety specials *The Patti LaBelle Show* in 1985, and *Sisters in the Name of Love* in 1986.

MOORE, JUANITA. Moore made her first national television appearance in an episode of *Ramar of the Jungle* in 1953. She acted in several anthology series: *Alfred Hitchcock Presents* (1961) and *The DuPont Show with June Allyson* (1960). Many longtime television viewers recall the excitement of seeing a black woman on *Dragnet* when she played Mrs. Esther Jenkins in the episode "The Missing Realtor" in 1967. She was a nominee for an Academy Award (for *Imitation of Life*) and appeared on that broadcast in 1959. In TV films, she had roles in *The Whole World Is Watching* (1969), *A Dream for*

Christmas (1973), and *The Notorious Jumping Frog of Calaveras County* (1981).

MOORE, MELBA. Moore starred in *The Melba Moore-Clifton Davis Show*, a summer variety series in 1971. In 1981, she starred in the televised version of the Broadway musical *Purlie* as Lutiebelle, the role that made her famous. She also starred in the sitcom *Melba* in 1986. Moore appeared in *Bing Crosby's Christmas Show* in 1970, *Doug Henning's World of Magic* in 1980, *The Adventures of a Two Minute Werewolf* in 1985, *Opryland Celebrates America's U.S.A.* in 1973, *The Beatrice Arthur Special* in 1980, *How to Be a Man* in 1985, and *Night of 100 Stars II* in 1985. Moore also starred in the drama special *Seasonal Differences* in 1987.

MOORE, SHEMAR. Moore was first known to television viewers for his role on the daytime drama *The Young and the Restless*, then he became host of *Soul Train* (1999–2003). He played a key role in *Mama Flora's Family*, a 1998 TV film, and *Scott Turow's Reversible Errors*, a 2004 film. In 2005, he was one of the stars of the new series *Criminal Minds.*

MOORE, TIM. Moore played the Kingfish, the central character in the controversial sitcom *Amos 'n' Andy*. Moore was born in 1888 and died in 1958. *See also* TELEVISION PIONEERS.

MORAL COURT (*SYN, 2000–2001*). Los Angeles radio talk show host **Larry Elder** hosted this one-hour courtroom reality show with a twist. The litigants explained each side of the conflict. The verdicts centered on whether the litigants were morally right or wrong rather than legally right or wrong. If Judge Elder found one party to be morally wrong, the victimized party was awarded $500. If the misdeed was more serious, it was deemed offensive, and the award was $1,000. If the victim had behaved horribly, the deed was termed outrageous and the award was $2,000. All judgments were paid by the producers.

MORGAN, DEBBI. Debbi Morgan (aka Deborah Morgan-Weldon) appeared in the comedy special *The Celebrity and the Arcade Kid* in

1983 and the drama *The Less Than Perfect Daughter* in 1991. She had an important role (Elizabeth Harvey) in *Roots: The Next Generations* in 1979. She had key roles in the television movies *Love's Savage Fury* in 1979, **Thornwell** in 1981, *The Jesse Owens Story* in 1984, and **"The Runaway"** on *Hallmark Hall of Fame* in 2000. She played Dr. Angie Baxter Hubbard in the daytime drama *All My Children* from 1982 to 1990. She was the school superintendent in the drama series *Boston Public*.

MORGAN, TRACY. Morgan was a member of the cast of *Saturday Night Live* (1996–2003). He had his own sitcom, *The Tracy Morgan Show*, in 2003. He did the voice of Spoonie Luv on *Crank Yankers* (2002) and hosted *Comic Groove* (2002) and *Uptown Comedy Club* (1992).

MORRIS, GARRETT. Morris was the first African-American regular in the Not Ready for Prime Time Players during the first seasons of *Saturday Night Live* (1975–1980). His most memorable character was an ex–baseball player whose catchphrase was "Baseball has been very very good to me." After his *Saturday Night Live* departure, Morris was in a series every season, except one, for more than 20 years, an admirable accomplishment for any actor, especially an African American. Prior to *Saturday Night Live*, he played the character "Wheels" on the sitcom *Roll Out* (1973–1974). Most of his series roles were in sitcoms but not exclusively so. He was Principal Dwight Ellis in *It's Your Move* from 1984 to 1985, Arnold "Sporty" James in the police drama *Hunter* from 1986 to 1989, Wiz in *Roc* from 1991 to 1992, Stan Winters in *Martin* from 1992 to 1994, Sidney Carlson in *Cleghorne* from 1995 to 1996, and Uncle Junior in *The Jamie Foxx Show* from 1996 to 2001.

MORRIS, GREG. Morris had the distinction of being the only black actor to play two roles on the *The Dick Van Dyke Show*. He played a songwriter who was in the Army with Rob Petrie (Van Dyke) and also a new father who Rob thought had accidentally taken the Petrie baby home from the hospital. The producers of *The Dick Van Dyke Show* have spoken proudly of the latter casting. Carl Reiner said, "Television was a lily-white neighborhood then." From 1966 to 1973,

Morris became well known as Barney Collier, the electronics guru on *Mission Impossible*, a rare dramatic role for a black actor. From 1978 to 1981, he was Lt. David Nelson in *Vegas*. He guest-starred in the special *Swing Out, Sweet Land* in 1971. He had key roles in the miniseries *Roots: The Next Generations* in 1979 and *The Jesse Owens Story* in 1984. He was born in 1934 and died in 1996.

MORRIS, PHIL. The son of **Greg Morris**, he played, in 1988–1990, the same role (Barney Collier) that his father played on the original *Mission Impossible* series. Prior to that, he had played Jerry Stockton in the syndicated sitcom *Marblehead Manor*. In 1990, he played Eddie Bock, a TV newsman lacking in ethics in *WIOU*. In 2003, he played Bradley in the sitcom *Wanda at Large*.

MORRIS, VALERIE. Morris was hired by CNN in 1996 after more than 25 years in broadcast journalism. She anchored CNN's *The Flip Side* and was the anchor of CNN's personal finance segment *Smart Assets*.

MORTON, JOE. Morton played Ron Langston in the black family drama series *Under One Roof* in 1995, Officer Thomas in the dramatic anthology series *Tribeca* in 1993, and Michael James on *Equal Justice* in 1990–1991. He starred in *Mercy Point*, a sci-fi medical series, in 1998 and in the sitcom *Grady* in 1975–1976. He had a role in the sitcom *A Different World* in 1991. He was Dr. Brodus in *Miss Evers' Boys* in 1997. He was Thurgood Marshall in the TV film *Mutiny* in 1999. He was Walter Diggles in the TV film *Jasper, Texas* in 2003.

MOSLEY, ROGER E. Mosley had a starring role, Cotton Crown, in *The Jericho Mile* in 1979. In the miniseries *Roots: The Next Generations*, in 1979, he was Lee Garnett. He had key roles in the TV films *I Know Why the Caged Bird Sings* in 1979 and *Attica* in 1980. He played T.C. in the drama series *Magnum P.I.* from 1980 to 1988, was Michael Kirkland in the short-lived sitcom *You Take the Kids* in 1990, was one of the performers in the drama special *Zora Is My Name* in 1990, and starred as Coach Ricketts in the sitcom *Hangin' with Mr. Cooper* from 1992 to 1993.

MOTOWN 40: THE MUSIC IS FOREVER (*ABC, February 15, 1998*). This four-hour special anniversary celebration aired in two parts and featured entertainment as well as commentary and archival footage of Motown's beginnings. The first half covered the birth of the record label in Detroit and the company's efforts to teach dance and etiquette to the performers to prepare them for stardom and the skilled songwriters. The second half centered on Motown's move to Los Angeles in the 1970s and its expansion into television and film. Among the large cast of participants were the following: **Diana Ross** (host), Sean "P. Diddy" Combs, **Don Cornelius, Aretha Franklin,** Berry Gordy, **Smokey Robinson, Little Richard, Russell Simmons, Luther Vandross,** Mary Wilson, and many others.

MOTOWN 45 (*ABC, May 17, 2004*). The Motown record label celebrated 45 years of Motown songs. **Lionel Richie** and **Cedric the Entertainer** were hosts, but both also performed. Richie sang "All Night Long" and sang a duet of "Endless Love" with Kelly Rowland. Cedric helped Bubba Knight as a Pip in the background as **Gladys Knight** sang "Neither One of Us" and "I Heard It through the Grapevine." Cedric and **Kimberly Locke** sang "It Takes Two." **The Four Tops** sang a medley of their songs. The Commodores sang "On The Night Shift." Thelma Houston sang "Don't Leave Me This Way." Several popular non-Motown singers sang Motown songs: Macy Gray sang Marvin Gaye's "Let's Get It On." **Raven-Symone** sang Stevie Wonder's "Superstitious." The Funk Brothers, **Smokey Robinson,** Brian McKnight, **Wayne Brady,** Mary Wilson, Cindy Birdsong, and others made up the show.

MOTOWN LIVE (*SYN, 1998–2000*). **Robert Townsend** was host of the first season of this live variety series in which Motown performers of the past and current recording artists entertained. Townsend's humor was an integral part of the series. Montell Jordan took over the second season. The Motown Live Dancers and Rickey Minor and The Band were also featured. **Patti LaBelle,** the Temptations, and Earth, Wind and Fire were among the entertainers.

MOTOWN MERRY CHRISTMAS (*NBC, December 14, 1987*). **Philip Michael Thomas** was host of the variety special of Motown music and some Motown stars. Former Motown executive Suzanne de Passe was producer. Guests included **Natalie Cole, Lola Falana, Redd Foxx,** Darlene Love, Stephanie Mills, **The Pointer Sisters, Smokey Robinson, The Temptations,** and **Marsha Warfield.** This aired again in syndication in 1989.

MOTOWN ON SHOWTIME: SMOKEY ROBINSON (*SHO, February 17, 1990*). This look at the life of the singer/producer/songwriter featured interviews with Berry Gordy, **Luther Vandross,** and Linda Ronstadt.

MOTOWN REVUE (*NBC, 1985*). Smokey Robinson starred in this brief musical variety series that came on the heels of the highly rated *Motown 25*. The show had famed Motown artists plus others including Natalie Cole and **Chaka Khan. Arsenio Hall,** and other comics were regulars, too.

MOTOWN 30: WHAT'S GOING ON? (*CBS, November 25, 1990*). Following the success of *Motown 25* in 1983, this special also celebrated the Motown sound and Motown artists. The stars of this event were **Debbie Allen, Tracy Chapman, The Four Tops, Marla Gibbs, Gladys Knight, Patti LaBelle, Dawnn Lewis, Smokey Robinson, Sinbad, Meshach Taylor, Denzel Washington, Damon Wayans,** and **Stevie Wonder.** Suzanne de Passe produced with Don Mischer and was a member of the team of writers.

MOTOWN 25: YESTERDAY, TODAY, AND FOREVER (*NBC, May 16, 1983*). Top Motown acts of the past and the present starred in this celebration of the 25th anniversary of Motown Records. **Michael Jackson** did his now-famous moonwalk for the first time on television. **Diana Ross** and **The Supremes** were briefly united though persons in the studio audience saw a near fight between Ross and fellow Supreme Mary Wilson. **The Temptations, The Four Tops, Smokey Robinson** and The Miracles, the Jackson Five, **Stevie Wonder,** and Linda Ronstadt were the headliners.

MOVIE STARS WHO STARTED ON TV SERIES. The following film stars once starred or were regulars on popular television series:

Denzel Washington, *St. Elsewhere*; Will Smith, *Fresh Prince of Bel-Air*; Martin Lawrence, *Martin*; Queen Latifah, *Living Single*; Morgan Freeman, *The Electric Company*; Eddie Murphy, *Saturday Night Live*; Regina King, *227*; and Jamie Foxx, who started his TV career on *In Living Color*.

MOVING OF SOPHIA MYLES, THE (*CBS, November 26, 2000*). Della Reese starred in this TV film about forgiveness and faith as a widow who not only has trouble coping with her minister-husband's death but also must come to forgive him for dying.

MOWRY, TAHJ. Mowry starred as T. J. Henderson in *Smart Guy* (1997–1999), played Teddy in *Full House* (1991–1995), and was the voice of Wade in *Kim Possible* (2002–).

MOWRY, TAMERA. Tamera Mowry and her twin sister, Tia, played the leads in the sitcom *Sister, Sister* (1994–1999). Tahj Mowry is their brother. Tamera played Dr. Kayla Thornton in the drama series *Strong Medicine* beginning in 2004.

MOWRY, TIA. Tia Mowry and her twin sister, Tamera, played the leads in the sitcom *Sister, Sister* (1994–1999). Tahj Mowry is their brother.

MR. AND MRS. LOVING (*SHO, March 31, 1996*). Lela Rochon and Timothy Hutton starred in this made-for-television film about an interracial couple whose love for each other encourages them to fight miscegenation laws. This fight for justice culminates in a 1967 U.S. Supreme Court decision that ended the laws in 17 states. Richard Loving (Hutton) and Mildred Jeter (Rochon) grew up as neighbors in a small Virginia town. The two date, and when Mildred, nicknamed Bean, got pregnant, Richard wanted to marry her. Bean's brother Leonard (**Bill Nunn**) warned him that it was against the law for blacks and whites to marry. Believing that the law would never be enforced, they married, but they were arrested on their wedding night. The judge asked them to choose jail or banishment from the town; they chose banishment and moved to Washington, D.C. Bean met Blue (**Isaiah Washington**), an organizer with the Southern Christian

Leadership Conference, and Sophia (**Ruby Dee**) and two hairdressers named Leanne (Suzanne Coy) and Marcelle (Sharon Lewis). Through them, she learned about the civil rights movement and wrote Attorney General Robert Kennedy explaining her marital situation. Young lawyer Bernie Cohen (Corey Parker), who did pro bono work for the American Civil Liberties Union, made the problem his own. *See also* HISTORICAL EVENTS DRAMATIZED; INTERRACIAL ROMANCES/RELATIONSHIPS.

MR. T. Born Laurence Tureaud, he changed his name to Lawrence Tero in 1970. He said he renamed himself Mr. T so that people would call him Mister. Mr. T earned fame as an actor in the film *Rocky III*. He starred in *The A-Team* (1983–1987) as Sgt. Bosco B. A. (officially Bad Attitude but commonly known as Bad Ass) Baracus. He also appeared frequently in the *WWF Superstars of Wrestling* (1985–1986 and 1988). From 1987 to 1990, he starred in *Mr. T. and T.*, a detective drama. He was one of the celebrities at *The 50th Presidential Inaugural Gala* held two days prior to the inauguration of President Ronald Reagan in 1985. Mr. T appeared in TV specials *The Battle of the Network Stars* in 1983 and *The Secret World of the Very Young* in 1984. He starred in the musical special *Mr. T and Emmanuel Lewis in a Christmas Dream* in 1984. Mr. T also appeared in variety specials *Hollywood's Private Home Movies II* in 1983, and he headlined *Mr. T . . . Going Back Home* in 1984. He was the star of the TV film *The Toughest Man in the World* in 1984.

M SQUAD (*NBC, 1957–1960*). This police drama was about plain-clothes detectives (played by Lee Marvin and Paul Newlan) fighting organized crime. The series is significant in African-American history in that from 1958 until the end of the series, the jazzy theme song used was composed by **Count Basie**. Titled "Theme from M Squad," it was also a recording hit.

MTV. *See* MUSIC TELEVISION.

MTV AWARDS (*MTV, annually*). Musical recording artists gather to celebrate outstanding achievement in music and music video. **Samuel L. Jackson** was host in 1998. **Will Smith** was host in 1994.

MTV MOVIE AWARDS *(MTV, annually).* This ceremony is MTV's version of the Academy Awards with musical stars.

MTV 10 *(ABC, November 27, 1991).* This special marked the 10th anniversary of MTV, the music cable channel. **Michael Jackson** starred, as did Madonna.

MTV VIDEO MUSIC AWARDS, THE *(MTV, annually).* This awards ceremony, usually held in September each year, honored the best in rock videos with a statuette called Moon Men. The show claims to cater to a hipper audience than the Grammys or the American Music Awards. The show started in 1984 and has taken place at various locations in Los Angeles and New York over the years of its existence. Pop singers **Brandy** and Monica introduced their song "This Boy Is Mine" on the 1998 show.

MUHAMMAD ALI'S 50TH BIRTHDAY CELEBRATION *(ABC, March 1, 1992).* A variety special, this two-hour production benefited the United Negro College Fund and also celebrated the boxing champ's 50th birthday. It was taped at the historic Wiltern Theatre in Los Angeles. Ali was host, and his guests were **Ella Fitzgerald**, **The Four Tops**, **Whitney Houston**, **Magic Johnson**, **Little Richard**, **The Pointer Sisters**, **Raven-Symone**, **Diana Ross**, **Sinbad**, **Blair Underwood**, Sylvester Stallone, Dan Aykroyd, Howard Cosell, Billy Crystal, Dustin Hoffman, and Arnold Schwarzenegger.

MUHAMMAD ALI FIGHTS. Highlights of Ali fights on home television include the following: As Cassius Clay, on a fight airing on April 11, 1964, he defeated Sonny Liston in a bout taped from Miami Beach. This was the first World Heavyweight Championship fight to be televised on ABC's *Wide World of Sports*. He had a rematch with Liston on a bout airing on May 29, 1965, and originating from Lewiston, Maine. Ali won with a punch in the first round. On May 21, 1966, ABC aired the championship fight between Ali and Henry Cooper. Ali won with a technical knockout in the sixth round. It was the first fight beamed from Europe and the first live heavyweight title fight on home television; the preceding fights were pretaped. Ali defeated Jerry Quarry on October 31, 1970, from Atlanta. He ended

Floyd Patterson's boxing career with a seventh-round knockout on September 23, 1972. Ali was beaten by Ken Norton on March 31, 1973, from San Diego. Then he won the rematch with Norton on September 15, 1973. "The Rumble in the Jungle," the title fight between Ali and George Foreman, originated from Zaire, Africa, and aired on January 5, 1975, with Ali knocking out Foreman in the eighth round. "The Thrilla from Manila" was telecast on January 11, 1976; Ali won when Frazier failed to answer the bell for the 14th round. *See also* BOXING ON TELEVISION.

MUHAMMAD ALI: THE WHOLE STORY (*TBS, September 3, 1996*). The special six-hour documentary included never-before-seen clips and insightful comments about the life of the boxing champion in and out of the ring. The first hour told the story of Ali's childhood, his Golden Gloves bouts, and his winning of the gold medal in the Olympics in Rome. Many of his fights were highlighted, including "The Rumble in the Jungle." Interviews of Ali on TV talk shows were included; one was hosted by **Sammy Davis Jr.** Also, Ali appeared as a mystery guest on *What's My Line?* His trainer, Angelo Dundee, as well as his family, friends, and professional associates, including some opponents, were also interviewed.

MUHAMMAD ALI VARIETY SPECIAL, THE (*ABC, September 13, 1975*). World heavyweight boxing champion Muhammad Ali was the headliner in this variety special in which entertainment celebrities performed and sports celebrities made appearances. **Aretha Franklin** and **Flip Wilson** were among the entertainers. The sports guests included Jim Brown (football) and Satchel Paige (baseball). Clarence Avant was a producer.

MURDER IN MISSISSIPPI (*NBC, February 5, 1990*). A made-for-television movie, this story was based on the 1964 murders of three civil rights workers—James Chaney, Mickey Schwerner, and Andrew Goodman. The film centers on the deaths of James Chaney and Mickey Schwerner. **Blair Underwood** and Tom Hulce played the subjects, Chaney and Schwerner, who travel to Mississippi for a civil rights training camp. According to the film, Goodman (Josh Charles) was simply a young man who begged to go along; the bigots who killed the three were targeting Chaney and Schwerner. Tom Shales of the *Washington Post* (February 5, 1990) said the film "succeeds in fleshing out the characters of James Chaney and Mickey Schwerner." He praised Underwood, saying that he "does enough acting for everybody. He graduates from pretty to handsome, from stylish to powerful." **C. C. H. Pounder** played Fannie Lee Chaney. *See also* HISTORICAL EVENTS DRAMATIZED.

MURDER IN MISSISSIPPI: THE PRICE OF FREEDOM (*ABC, 1994*). This was a one-hour documentary about the disappearance and murders of the three civil rights workers—James Chaney, Mickey Schwerner, and Andrew Goodman in the summer of 1964. The final third of the program was devoted to the investigation of the crime by the FBI (Federal Bureau of Investigation) and the eventual convictions of seven of the defendants on charges of violating the civil rights of the three young men. An interview with Chaney's younger brother, Ben, was included, as were interviews with other relatives of the three.

MURDER WITHOUT MOTIVE: THE EDMUND PERRY STORY (*NBC, January 6, 1992*). **Curtis McClarin** starred in this TV film as Edmund Perry, a Harlem teenager who, shortly after graduating with honors from a principally white exclusive prep school, is killed by a policeman who claimed he was attacked by the youth and his brother, Jonah (Guy Killum). The film, directed by **Kevin Hooks**, shows what pressures and forces led the killer and the victim to the fateful and tragic point. **Taurean Blacque** played the boys' father, Jonah Sr. **Georg Stanford Brown** played Darwin Tolliver. **Anna Maria Horsford** played Anna Perry. Cuba Gooding Jr. played Tyree.

MURPHY, EDDIE. Murphy's television stardom began when he joined the cast of *Saturday Night Live* in 1981. After he left the late night series in 1984, he went on to star in feature films. Yet he remained in television as a producer and guest star. Murphy appeared in variety specials *The Joe Piscopo Special* in 1984, *The Joe Piscopo*

New Jersey Special in 1986, and *Disney World's 20th Anniversary Celebration* in 1991. He also hosted the comedy special *Uptown Comedy Express* in 1987 and the tribute special *Sammy Davis Jr.'s 60th Anniversary Celebration* in 1990. He produced the comedy special *What's Alan Watching?* in 1989. He was the voice of the lead character, Thurgood Stubbs, in the claymation series he created, *The PJs* (1999–2001).

MUSE, CLARENCE. Muse played the piano player, Sam, in TV's "Casablanca," a rotating series of *Warner Brothers Presents* dramas in 1955–1956. He played Donald Freeland in the TV film *A Dream for Christmas* in 1973. Muse died of a cerebral hemorrhage in 1979, one day short of his 90th birthday.

MUSIC TELEVISION. When the cable channel Music Television (MTV) made its debut on August 1, 1981, the music video channel strictly adhered to an album-oriented rock format. Few music acts featuring African Americans received airplay, prompting charges of discrimination from record labels and artists, among them Rick James, who appeared on ABC's late night news show *Nightline* and in the pages of the *Los Angeles Times* blasting the cable channel as racist (Banks 1996; Denisoff 1988). MTV maintained that few black artists fit the definition of rock music the cable channel used. It was not until March 1983, about 18 months after the channel's debut, that the music video by **Michael Jackson** for his song "Billie Jean" went into heavy rotation on the channel, a moment often marked as a breakthrough for African-American artists on MTV. "Billie Jean" was a single from Jackson's release *Thriller*, a crossover success story that sold multiple millions of copies and spawned the hit videos *Beat It*, featuring a guitar solo by rock guitarist Eddie Van Halen and an extended dance number to rival the Jets and the Sharks in *West Side Story*, and *Thriller*, a big-budget elaborate miniature movie directed by Hollywood filmmaker John Landis. Interestingly, it was Jackson's younger sister, Janet, who the channel named the first MTV Icon in 2001. In between those MTV moments, video clips by artists such as Run DMC, Macy Gray, Living Color, **Whitney Houston**, Prince, En Vogue, **Tina Turner**, Dr. Dre and Snoop

Dogg, Missy Elliott, Lauryn Hill, Tupac Shakur, TLC, Puff Daddy/ P. Diddy, Public Enemy, **Queen Latifah**, M. C. Lyte, and **Lenny Kravitz** garnered fans and expanded the station's play list to include rap, hip-hop, and pop. J. J. Jackson, an African American, was one of the five original video jockeys or veejays. He was older and more robust and, according to veejay Mark Goodman, "the wise veejay." He left the network in 1986, lost weight, quit smoking, had triple-bypass surgery, and seemed in good shape until he died of a heart attack in 2004. Programming on MTV went on to include reality shows such as *The Real World, Road Rules, Fraternity Life*, and *Sorority Life*; celebrity-driven programs including *The Osbournes, Punk'd, Newlyweds: Nick and Jessica*, and *Making the Band*; cartoons and animated programs; dating shows; and game shows. All the shows targeted MTV's young audience. In his study of MTV's long-running reality program *The Real World*, Orbe (2004) wrote, "They (MTV) have also served as a media source . . . for alternative images that are typically not available on network television" (314). *See also* REALITY TELEVISION.

MUSIC VEEJAYS. African-American disc jockey J. J. Jackson was the only black veejay in the first class of video jockeys, or veejays, on **Music Television (MTV)**. Jackson stayed with the channel until 1986. Other African-American veejays and show hosts on the channel include comic and actor **Bill Bellamy**, who hosted a variety of programs including *MTV Jams*; **Ananda Lewis**, who hosted the channel's *Total Request Live* from 1999 to 2001, among other programs; and **Sway Calloway**, a correspondent for MTV News and host of the programs *Direct Effect* and *Chart Attack* on the channel. Fab Five Freddy, Ed Lover, and Doctor Dre hosted various editions of *Yo! MTV Raps*, the rap and hip-hop program and one of the first stand-alone shows on the channel.

MUSIC VIDEO. The modern music video circa 1980 was designed primarily as an advertising tool. Record labels featured artists in videos to boost record sales. Record companies promoted African-American artists through videos, and music fans soon became watchers and fans of the videos. In their essay on the cable channel **Black**

Entertainment Television (BET), scholars Tait and Barber (1996) note that BET founder Robert Johnson banked on music video as his channel's debut programming because of the popularity of music videos with African-American music listeners and television audiences. Premier venues for music videos on television include BET, specializing in African-American artists; MTV, focused on mainstream pop, hip-hop, and rock music; MTV2, featuring alternative rock, rap, and dance music styles; and Video Hits One (VH1), the adult contemporary companion to MTV's youth-oriented programming. The music video genre may include clips featuring concert footage of musicians in live or simulated live performance, elaborate miniature movies showcasing flashy special effects, promotional clips for music featured in Hollywood movies, and surreal concept videos.

MUTINY (*NBC, March 28, 1999*). This two-hour made-for-television film told the fact-based story of 323 predominantly black sailors who were killed during World War II while loading munitions onto a ship at a San Francisco naval base. The ship exploded, causing the deaths and the injuries of 390 more. Two hundred of the dead were African Americans, as were 200 of the injured. Three weeks later, 50 sailors were court-martialed and given dishonorable discharges because they, fearing their safety, refused to load another shipment. The stars of the film were **Michael Jai White** as Ben Cooper and **Duane Martin** as B. J. Teach. **Joe Morton** played Thurgood Marshall, who was the young defense attorney in the case. **Morgan Freeman** was an executive producer and played a role. **Kevin Hooks** was director. *See also* HISTORICAL EVENTS DRAMATIZED.

MY BROTHER AND ME (*NIK, 1994*). This short-lived sitcom was significant in that it was the first on the Nickelodeon cable channel about a black family. Dee Dee Parker (Ralph Woolfolk IV) was the central character in that the story unfolded from his point of view. He was an eight-year-old North Carolina kid who had a cool older brother (Arthur Reggie III) and a snotty sister (Aisling Sistrunk). His buddies were played by Keith Naylor and Stefan Wilbur. Karen E. Fraction and Jim R. Coleman played his parents. Jimmy Lee Newman, Amanda Seales, and Kym Whitley were also in the cast. Ilunga Adell and Calvin Brown Jr. were creators.

MYERS, DWIGHT "HEAVY D." Myers played Bernard on *The Tracy Morgan Show* beginning in 2003.

MYERS, LOU. Recognized by television viewers primarily as Vernon Gaines, who ran the campus restaurant on *A Different World* (1988–1993), Myers played a key role in *Mama Flora's Family*, a 1998 TV film, and *The Piano Lesson* in 1995.

MYERS, PAULINE. Myers had a key role in the TV film *Benny's Place* in 1982.

MY FAVORITE BROADWAY: THE LEADING LADIES: GREAT PERFORMANCES (*PBS, December 1, 1999*). Among the leading ladies performing were **Jennifer Holliday** doing "And I'm Telling You I'm Not Going" from *Dreamgirls*, **Nell Carter** doing "Mean to Me" and "Ain't Misbehavin'" from *Ain't Misbehavin'*, and **Audra McDonald** doing "Down with Love" from *Hooray for What?*

MY LITTLE MARGIE (*CBS, then NBC, in 1952; CBS, 1953, then NBC, later in 1953–1955*). In this half-hour sitcom, **Willie Best** played Charlie, the elevator operator whose assistance Margie (Gale Storm) sought in her efforts to keep designing women away from her handsome eligible father (Charles Farrell). *See also* SERIES WITH ONE BLACK SUPPORTING ACTOR.

MY PAST IS MY OWN (*CBS, January 24, 1989*). This dramatic special aired under the umbrella title of *CBS Schoolbreak Special*. The story was about two black teenagers who traveled in time to the 1960s, where they were exposed to racial prejudice in a small southern town. **Whoopi Goldberg** played mystical Mariah Johnson, who through hypnotic regression she learned in India, took them on the journey. Allison Dean played Kerry; Phil Lewis, Justin; **C. C. H. Pounder**, Renee; **Thalmus Rasulala**, Marshall; and **William Allen Young**, the Rev. Jordan.

MY SWEET CHARLIE (*NBC, January 20, 1970*). **Al Freeman Jr.** and Patty Duke were stars of this made-for-television movie, a drama about a special relationship between a black man and a white woman. Al Freeman Jr. played a New York City attorney who befriended a pregnant southern girl (Duke). The two-hour made-for-television film won the **Emmy Award** for Outstanding Writing Achievement in Drama. Duke won the Emmy for Outstanding Single Performance by an Actress in a Leading Role.

MY WIFE AND KIDS (*ABC, 2001– *). **Damon Wayans** was star, cocreator, and executive producer of this sitcom also starring **Tisha Campbell-Martin**. The story centered on Michael Kyle (Wayans) and his interactions with his wife, Janet (Campbell-Martin), and three kids, Claire, Michael Jr., and Kady. Michael Jr. (George O. Gore II) liked gangsta rap artists more than his father. His teenage daughter, Claire (played by Jazz Raycole the first season and then by Jennifer Freeman), would rather go shopping than spend time with her dad. And young Kady (Parker McKenna Posey) was bringing up dad. Michael was owner of a successful delivery truck company, while Janet was a part-time stockbroker. Wayans, as executive producer and cocreator, said the show was "about simple family values with a strong father figure and love as the glue that keeps everyone together." In 2001, the *Los Angeles Times* reported that this sitcom was the first starring a black comedian to achieve wide popularity with white audiences since *The Cosby Show*. Wayans admitted that one of the objectives of the show was to utilize some of the best elements of *The Cosby Show* and update them for the new millennium.

– N –

NAACP IMAGE AWARDS (*annually*). The NAACP (formerly titled National Association for the Advancement of Colored People) honors positive images of African Americans in film, television, and music. The annual ceremony is based in Hollywood. The Image Award was conceived in the mid-1960s by a coordinating committee of the Beverly Hills/Hollywood branch of the NAACP. Toni Vaz, an actress and member of the Screen Extras Guild, headed the committee consisting of Eddie Smith (founder of the Black Stuntmen's Association), Lil Cumber (Hollywood's first black talent agent), Dorothy Farley, Elmer Alexander, Ernie Robinson, and Alex Brown. Vaz said initially that "the award was to honor individuals and production companies for hiring black actors in positive roles."

The first Image Award ceremony was held at the Beverly Hilton Hotel in 1967, and the following series were among those honored: *I Spy*, *Hogan's Heroes*, *Star Trek*, and *Mission Impossible*. In later years, awards were granted to performers in all areas of the entertainment industry.

Willis Edwards became president of the branch in 1978 (he remained in the position for 10 years) and made it his mission to get the ceremony televised nationally. After some setbacks, the outlook was optimistic in the early 1980s, when NBC President Brandon Tartikoff told Edwards he would air the ceremony if the show could get a bonded production company acceptable by the network and if the show could raise $150,000 collateral. Johnny Carson, already connected to NBC with *The Tonight Show*, offered his production company, Carson Productions. Jeffrey Katzenberg, then president of the Walt Disney Company, raised the $150,000. Edwards said, "Both Carson and Katzenberg helped without wanting fanfare, praise or publicity. If it were not for them, we wouldn't be on television." The first telecast of the *NAACP Image Awards* was in 1982; Edwards was executive producer.

Others active in the NAACP branch worked to make the *Image Awards* successful. Among them was Maggie Hathaway, an actress/singer, also popular in golf circles, who used her association with Hollywood personalities and other movers and shakers to advance the production.

Billie J. Green, president of the Beverly Hills/Hollywood Branch from 1995 to 2000, said that after the ceremony aired successfully for nine years, the NAACP national organization took over the production.

Edwards and Green agree that Toni Vaz was never given the credit she deserved for creating the award, which became a way of praising not only companies and networks for racially sensitive hiring and programs but also, more important, for performers and actors who say with great pride, "I won an Image Award."

NATALIE COLE SPECIAL, THE (*CBS, April 27, 1978*). Singer **Natalie Cole** led this hour of music, her first television special. Guest stars were **Earth, Wind and Fire, Johnny Mathis**, and Stephen Bishop.

NATALIE COLE'S UNTRADITIONAL TRADITIONAL CHRISTMAS (*PBS, December 5, 1994*). **Natalie Cole** performed holiday songs including jazz tunes and pop favorites. Elmo of *Sesame Street* was the guest star.

NAT "KING" COLE SHOW, THE (*NBC, 1956–1957*). Cole was the first African-American performer to headline a variety series that lasted more than a few weeks, though the show was never a secure hit. Two musical variety series preceded Cole's: *Sugar Hill Times* in 1949 and *The Hazel Scott Show* in 1950. Neither lasted more than three months. *The Nat King Cole Show* was on the air for 13 months. No variety series with a black star would do better until 1970, when *The Flip Wilson Show* ended its first season as the number 2 show of the year. Cole's series began on Monday, November 5, 1956, and was a 15-minute showcase of Cole with various backup groups and an orchestra. Later the show expanded to a half hour with guest stars who were so supportive that they volunteered to make appearances for small salaries or for gifts like televisions and cameras. There was high praise from critics. The problem was that many southern affiliate stations would not carry the show. One even said he personally liked Cole but that he was afraid that irate viewers would bomb his house and station. Sponsors were also a problem, so NBC took the high road and kept the show going without a sponsor until December 17, 1957. After the show was canceled, Cole said, "Madison Avenue is afraid of the dark." **Pearl Bailey, Sammy Davis Jr.**, Tony Bennett, Peggy Lee, the **Mills Brothers, Ella Fitzgerald, Billy Eckstine**, and **Count Basie** were some of the guest stars. A chain smoker, Cole died of lung cancer in 1965 at age 45.

NBC FOLLIES (*NBC, 1973*). **Sammy Davis Jr.** and Mickey Rooney, though not actually the hosts of this comedy-variety series, appeared on most if not all episodes. The show consisted of music performers and comedy skits. Each show had guest stars in addition to Davis and Mickey Rooney and singers and dancers.

NEAL, ELISE. Neal played Tia, the wife on *All of Us*, beginning in 2003; Yvonne in *The Hughleys* (1998–2002); and Lt. J. J. Fredericks (1995) in the sci-fi series *Seaquest DSV*. In TV films, she had roles in *Brian's Song* (2001), *Chance of a Lifetime* (1998), *Daddy's Girl* (1996), *There Was a Little Boy* (1993), and the miniseries *Tales of the City* (1993).

NEIGHBORHOOD, THE (*NBC, April 25, 1982*). This 90-minute made-for-television film, an unsold pilot, was about a blue-collar neighborhood in Queens, New York. Residents become concerned when several black families moved in and changed the ethnic makeup of the area. **Howard E. Rollins Jr.** played Allen Campbell, and **Sheryl Lee Ralph** played his wife, Doris.

NELL CARTER—NEVER TOO OLD TO DREAM (*NBC, March 22, 1986*). Singer-actress Nell Carter was the host and star of this one-hour special set in a speakeasy and a disco. She and guest stars sang music from the Jazz Age to the Age of Aquarius. The guests were **The Four Tops**, **Phylicia Rashad**, and Harry Anderson.

NELSON, HAYWOOD. Nelson was a regular on *Grady* (1975–1976). He also played Dwayne on *What's Happening!!* (1976–1979) and *What's Happening Now!!* (1985–1988).

NELSON, NOVELLA. Nelson played a key role in *Mama Flora's Family*, a 1998 TV film.

NEVILLE, AARON. Neville sang the National Anthem at Super Bowl XXIV in 1990.

NEW ADVENTURES OF CAPTAIN PLANET, THE. *See* CAPTAIN PLANET AND THE PLANETEERS.

NEW BILL COSBY SHOW, THE (*CBS, 1972–1973*). After being successful in the drama *I Spy* (1965–1968) and the sitcom *The Bill Cosby Show* (1969–1971), comedian Bill Cosby tried this variety series. Regulars on the show included **Lola Falana** and the **Quincy**

Jones Orchestra as well as Foster Brooks, Pat McCormick, and others. The show also featured guest stars, often singers who sang their hits. Each week, there was a Cosby monologue and several comedy sketches. One running sketch was "The Dude," and the other was "The Wife of the Week."

NEW ODD COUPLE, THE (*ABC, 1982–1983*). **Ron Glass** and **Demond Wilson** played Felix Unger and Oscar Madison, respectively, in this black version of *The Odd Couple*. Felix was the extra-neat photographer, and Oscar was the sloppy sportswriter. The Pigeon Sisters were Sheila Anderson and Ronalda Douglas. **Jo Marie Payton** played Mona.

NEWS ON TELEVISION. Television news has long attracted the attention of media and other scholars interested in race and the media. McDaniel (2001), Rada (1997), and Dixon (1998) are among the most recent scholars to tackle the subject. Dixon (1998) examined television news in Los Angeles and Orange counties in California to find out how broadcast news presented African Americans, Latinos, and white Americans. He found African Americans to be overrepresented as lawbreakers on television news and more likely to be portrayed as lawbreakers on television news than actual arrest records in Los Angeles and Orange counties reflect. Meanwhile, whites were overly represented as police officers on television news. In other words, more whites were seen on television as officers than were actually employed as police according to employment records. These and other findings led Dixon to note, "The message of television news appears to be that blacks are the perpetrators of crime, Whites are the defenders of the law, and Latinos do not exist at all."

NICHOLAS, DENISE. She was counselor Liz McIntyre in *Room 222* (1969–1974) and Harriet DeLong in *In the Heat of the Night* (1989–1994); she wrote several scripts for the series. She played Olivia in the sitcom *Baby I'm Back* in 1978. She had key roles in 1978's *Ring of Passion* and 1981's *The Sophisticated Gents*, both TV films.

NICHOLAS, FAYARD. Dancer Fayard Nicholas, with his brother Harold, was honored in *The Kennedy Center Honors* in 1991.

NICHOLAS, HAROLD. Dancer Harold Nicholas, with his brother Fayard, was honored in *The Kennedy Center Honors* in 1991.

NICOLET, DANIELLE. Nicolet played Paula in the series *Second Time Around*, which premiered in 2004.

NICHOLS, NICHELLE. Nichols earned fame as Lt. Uhura in the original series *Star Trek* (1966–1969). Other TV credits included the following: *Great Gettin' Up Mornin'* (1964), *Say Goodbye, Maggie Cole* (1972), *Antony and Cleopatra* (1983), and *The Adventures of Captain Zoom in Outer Space* (1995).

NICKELODEON SPORTS THEATER WITH SHAQUILLE O'NEAL (*NIK, February 23, 1997*). The basketball player starred in this special about a boy who wants to play basketball but is held back because of his height.

NICK O'DEMUS. *See* STEWART, NICK.

NIGHT COURT (*NBC, 1984–1992*). This popular sitcom set in a courtroom in New York starred Harry Anderson as Judge Harry T. Stone. At various times, there were three black actors playing regular roles. **Paula Kelly** played legal-aid lawyer Liz Williams the first season; she was then dropped from the cast and was subsequently nominated for an **Emmy Award**. **Charlie Robinson** joined the cast in 1984 as Mac Robinson, the court clerk, and stayed until the series ended. **Marsha Warfield** was a member of the cast (1986–1992) as Roz Russell, the court officer.

NIGHTJOHN (*DIS, 1996*). **Carl Lumbly** played the title role in this made-for-television film as a slave who, before the Civil War, when teaching slaves was illegal, risks his life to teach a younger slave (Allison Jones) to read and write. **Lorraine Toussaint**, **Bill Cobbs**, and Beau Bridges also starred. Charles Burnett was director.

NIGHT THE CITY SCREAMED, THE (*ABC, December 14, 1980*). This two-hour made-for-television movie explores what might happen during a power failure in a major city when the looters take over the city. Among the long list of cast members are the following: **Georg Stanford Brown** as Charles Neville, **Clifton Davis** as Arnold Clements, **Dick Anthony Williams** as Jim Downs, **Stuart K. Robinson** as Douglas King, **Taurean Blacque** as Oscar, **Jason Bernard** as Dale Wrightson, **Chip Fields** as Young Clements, and **Ketty Lester** as Mrs. King. Raymond Burr, Don Meredith, and Robert Culp played city officials.

NORMAN, JESSYE. Norman appeared in the variety special *Carnegie Hall: The Grand Reopening* in 1987. She headlined *Jessye Norman Sings Carmen* in 1989, *Kathleen Battle & Jessye Norman Sing Spirituals* in 1990, and *Jessye Norman: Women of Legend, Fantasy and Lore* in 1994. She was honored in *The Kennedy Center Honors* in 1997; at the time, she was the youngest performer to be so lauded.

NORMAN, MAIDIE. Norman was the talk of black America on October 11, 1956, when she made an appearance on the series *Dragnet*, the first black actor to do so. She played Ruth Thornwell in the made-for-television film *Thornwell* (1981) and Neddy in *Secrets of a Mother and Daughter* (1983). She also had a role in *Roots: The Next Generations* in 1979. She was born in 1912 and died of breast cancer in 1998.

NORTON, KEN. Boxing great Ken Norton appeared in the specials *Super Night at the Super Bowl* (1977) and *Circus of the Stars* (1979). *See* KEN NORTON FIGHTS.

NORWOOD, BRANDY. Norwood is more commonly known as **Brandy**. *See also* BRANDY.

NORWOOD, WILLIE. Norwood, Brandy's younger brother, played L.J. on *The Sinbad Show* (1993–1994).

NUNN, BILL. Nunn played a key role in the TV film *Mr. and Mrs. Loving* (1967).

– O –

O, BARBARA. Ms. O played the wife of Gideon Jackson (**Muhammad Ali**) in the TV dramatic film *Freedom Road* in 1979.

OCCUPATIONS OF TV CHARACTERS. In their book on *The Cosby Show*, media scholars Sut Jhally and Justin Lewis quoted the character of Edith Bunker, wife of Archie Bunker on the classic situation comedy *All in the Family*, when she was asked for her opinion on African Americans. "Well, you sure gotta hand it to 'em. I mean two years ago they were nothing but servants and janitors. Now they're teachers and doctors and lawyers. They've sure come a long way on TV."

It could be said that Edith was right. African Americans have held a variety of occupations on television since the 1950s, when maids and handymen were the primary roles available. In her study of soap operas featuring multiethnic casts, James found that African Americans frequently appeared as professionals working as physicians, lawyers, police officers, and small-business owners. However, such characters were less often lead characters and more often workplace or business acquaintances of the lead characters, who were white. In popular legal dramas from *L.A. Law* in 1986 until the present, judges are often African American, but the actors who portray them have bit parts rather than the meaty roles actors desire.

At various times, there has been criticism of blacks playing an abundance of roles as drug dealers, drunks, and prostitutes. Then, in response to that criticism, there follows a time when black actors could expect only upstanding roles—the good cop, the clergyman, the dedicated teacher, the nurturing parent. Producers thought they would be criticized if they hired black actors to be negative characters.

Actor Bernie Casey, a longtime advocate of quality television, said the problem was always balance. If there are good guys to compare to the bad guys, there is a kind of balance. In white shows, according to Casey, "for every Gomer Pyle, there was a Marcus Welby. In black television, there has been a plethora of stereotypical images. Actors of color easily fall into the stereotypical roles and function out of terror because there is so much competition for acting jobs. They take the stereotypical role and say, 'I'm getting paid.'"

Since the roles of maids and other domestic workers in the 1950s and leading into the early 21st century, African Americans of both genders have had roles as lawyers (*The Cosby Show*), judges (*Fresh Prince of Bel-Air*), physicians (*ER*), nurses (*Julia*), detectives (*A Man Called Hawk*), teachers (*Boston Public*), forensic experts (the

CSI series), business executives (*Living Single*), college students (*The Parkers*), international spies (*I Spy*), funeral home directors (*Frank's Place*), more domestic workers (*Benson*, *The Jeffersons*), and numerous secretaries, police officers, criminal masterminds, drug dealers, small-time criminals, and prison inmates.

Though television has made progress in the occupations blacks play, there are still improvements to be made in characterizations. Casey spoke about an African-American plastic surgeon on the series *Extreme Makeover*: "They talk of his competence. He's not just an extraordinary black surgeon, but an extraordinary surgeon. We need more of that. This is a real person, but if they created a character to play him, it is likely that he would not have the same dignity. They would have him saying so-called cool things like, "Hey, Honey!"

Arguably, **Dennis Haysbert** held the top job open to American citizens and television viewers when he played David Palmer, president of the United States, in the action adventure series *24*. Haysbert said, "I am gratified to have been chosen to shoulder this responsibility. We don't see characters like this on stage or TV. I want society to begin to see black people in a different light. I want the industry to see the versatility and complexity of the character."

ODETTA. Folk/blues singer Odetta had a key role in the TV film *The Autobiography of Miss Jane Pittman* in 1974.

OH DRAMA (*BET*, 2000–2004). This night-time talk show featured three high-energy opinionated female hosts—Kym R. Whitley, **Vanessa Bell Calloway**, and Julissa Marquez. Mari Morrow was host from 2000 to 2001 and Sheryl Underwood in 2002. Subjects of discussion and guests were varied. The studio audience and the hosts' personalities created the atmosphere of a party in someone's living room.

O. J. SIMPSON MURDER TRIAL VERDICT (*ABC*, *CBS*, *CNN*, *NBC*, *Court TV*, *October 3, 1995*). When the former football great was charged with murdering his ex-wife, Nicole, the trial dominated the news and airwaves interrupting regular television. The only camera in the courtroom was a robotic camera, though coverage looked as if there were several cameras present. Then, at 10:00 A.M., Judge

Ito's court clerk, Diedre Robinson, read the verdict: "We the jury in the above entitled action find the defendant, Orenthal James Simpson, not guilty of the crime of murder." An estimated 10 million viewers watched, one of television's most-watched live events. The pleasure or displeasure of the outcome was largely divided along racial lines. *See also* O. J. SIMPSON "SLOW CHASE."

O. J. SIMPSON "SLOW CHASE" (*NBC, CBS, ABC, June 17, 1994*). After **O. J. Simpson**'s wife, Nicole, and her friend, Ron Goldman, were killed, Simpson became the obvious suspect. Since there is no bail on a murder charge, Simpson knew he would probably be in jail for months before the trial. He was supposed to surrender at 11:00 A.M. where thousands of reporters and others were gathered. Friends said he was trying to get his business in order; others claimed he was contemplating suicide or that he was visiting Nicole's grave site. Nonetheless, he rode around the Los Angeles freeways in his 1993 white Ford Bronco driven by his buddy Al Cowling, and nationwide confusion resulted as police cars, TV news vehicles, and news helicopters followed. News reports called it a "slow-speed chase," but it was not a chase at all but more like a parade. An estimated 95 million Americans watched it. At about 8:00 P.M., Simpson's car arrived at his Brentwood home, where he was arrested. He was held in jail until he was acquitted on October 3, 1995, more than a year later. *See also* O. J. SIMPSON MURDER TRIAL VERDICT.

OKE, FEMI. Oke joined CNN International in 1999 after having been a weather presenter in London television. Her credits at CNN include being weather anchor for CNN International's World Weather service.

OLYMPIC GAMES, 1968 (*ABC, October 16, 1968*). These Olympic Games originated from Mexico City during a time when black Americans were expressing discontent with discrimination in the United States. Martin Luther King Jr. had been assassinated a few months before, and his nonviolent movement was being replaced with rioting in urban areas. Tension enveloped the nation over losses in the Vietnam War. There was a rumor that black athletes would boycott the games. Track champions Tommie Smith and John Carlos, both black

Americans, did not boycott, but their silent protest was seen around the world via television. Smith won the gold medal in the 200-meter race, and Carlos won the bronze. As the National Anthem played during the medal ceremony, they each held up one black-gloved hand in a clinched fist denoting black power and bowed their heads. Smith later said he decided to protest only minutes before the ceremony, that he told Carlos and he agreed to join him as they walked toward the platform. Smith handed Carlos a glove. Smith said he silently said the Lord's Prayer as the music played. "It was a prayer of solidarity," he said. Officials of the Olympic Games and much of white America were angry, to say the least. Smith and Carlos worked in the fringes of sports (Smith as a community college coach), but their careers as athletes ended that day. *TV Guide*, in calling the incident one of television's more memorable moments (in 2004), said the athletes "made a bold statement of past race relations."

OLYMPIC GAMES, 1996 (*NBC, July 19, 1996*). In the opening ceremony of the Olympic Games, probably nothing is more exciting, especially for the host country, than the anticipation and the final recognition of which athlete will light the Olympic torch. In 1996, the games were held in Atlanta, Georgia, a primarily black city with a black mayor, so black viewers expected a black athlete, though that was indeed not promised. During the weeks before the Games, chatter at cocktail parties and around office water coolers was, "Who can it be?" When **Muhammad Ali**'s name was mentioned (he had been an athlete in the 1960 Olympics), it was quickly dismissed because Ali suffered from Parkinson's disease. Also, the identity of the torch lighter is always a secret, and no one could imagine how Ali could sneak into Atlanta without being seen. So, when swimmer Janet Evans ascended the stairs to the platform, Ali stepped into view to take the torch. America—black and white—was in tears. Fans prayed that his trembling hands wouldn't drop the torch. NBC's host Bob Costas, who was unaware, said, "Look who gets it next," and his co-host, Dick Enberg, announced, "The Greatest!" Ali's friend since 1962, photographer Howard Bingham had helped mastermind the elaborate plot. Bingham said he had lobbied for Ali to light the torch for a whole year without telling Ali of his efforts. Finally, in June, producer Don Mischer called him to say he wanted to do it. Bingham said, "I did not tell Ali until just before, but I did tell his wife. Ali can't keep a secret." Mischer had warned that the element of surprise was crucial and that if word got out that Ali would light the torch, there was another athlete standing by to substitute.

OMNIBUS (*CBS, 1953–1956; ABC, 1956–1957*). *Omnibus* was a 90-minute cultural experience featuring documentary, musical theater, historical drama, ballet, opera, symphony, literature, and informational presentation. Sometimes, the show featured excerpts from productions like theatrical dramas. At other times, scripts were written for the *Omnibus* audience. Occasionally, there were black performers. For example, **William Marshall** played the title role in "Othello," and **Eartha Kitt** played "Salome."

O'NEAL, FREDERICK. O'Neal played the role of Moses in **"The Green Pastures"** on *Hallmark Hall of Fame* (1957).

O'NEAL, RON. O'Neal had key roles in the television movies *Freedom Road* in 1979, *Brave New World* in 1980, and *The Sophisticated Gents* in 1981. He was H.H., the Sultan of Johore, in *Bring 'em Back Alive*, the 1982–1983 adventure series. He played Steve Phillips in the TV film *Playing with Fire* (1985). O'Neal died in 2004.

ONE IN A MILLION (*ABC, 1980*). **Shirley Hemphill** starred in this sitcom as taxi driver Shirley Simmons, who, after one of her customers died, inherited a multi-million-dollar corporation. The gutsy Shirley locked horns with a company executive, Mr. Cushing (Keene Curtis), who had hoped to take over as head of the company. She had her own ideas of how to run a company. **Ralph Wilcox** played Duke. **Ann Weldon** and **Mel Stewart** played Edna and Raymond, Shirley's parents. The series lasted six months.

ONE IN A MILLION: THE RON LEFLORE STORY (*CBS, September 26, 1978*). **LeVar Burton** starred in the title role of this biopic, a TV film about the life of a street kid who goes to prison after a life of petty crime. He then turns his life around and becomes a professional baseball player. It also starred **Paul Benjamin**, Larry Scott, and Billy Martin.

ONE LOVE: THE BOB MARLEY ALL-STAR TRIBUTE (*TNT*, *December 12, 1999*). Bob Marley, who is credited with taking reggae music of Jamaica and introducing it to the world, died of cancer in 1981. His family, consisting of seven children (including Stephen, Ziggy, and Damian), was joined by **Erykah Badu**, **Tracy Chapman**, Lauryn Hill, **Queen Latifah**, **Busta Rhymes**, Jimmy Cliff, Sheryl Crow, and others for a celebration of Marley's music on the beach of Oracabessa Bay in Jamaica. The concert consisted of 19 songs including "Get Up, Stand Up," "Redemption Song," and "One Love."

ONE MORE TIME (*CBS, January 10, 1974*). This one-hour variety special featured performances by comedy and music stars. Among them were **Pearl Bailey**, the Jackson Five, **The Mills Brothers**, and **The Pointer Sisters**. Also in the cast were Carol Channing, George Gobel, and the June Taylor Dancers.

ONE ON ONE (*UPN, 2001–*). **Flex Alexander** played Flex Washington, a television sportscaster and former National Basketball Association star who must give up his bachelor life when his teen-aged daughter, Breanna **(Kyla Pratt)** moves in with him. **Tichina Arnold** recurred as Flex' ex-wife who moved to Nova Scotia. **Joan Pringle** and **Ron Canada** also recurred as Flex's parents who believed Flex should exercise more control over his daughter. Duane (Kelly Perine) was Flex's buddy. Spirit (Sicily) was Breanna's best friend.

ON OUR OWN (*ABC, 1994–1995*). This sitcom was unique in that six members of one family played characters in it. The story line was that seven children in one family had been orphaned when their parents were killed in an auto accident. The oldest of the siblings, Josh (Ralph Louis Harris), took care of the others, and when social workers showed up, he donned a disguise as Aunt Jelcinda. The other brothers and sisters were played by the Smolletts: **Jurnee Smollett** (as Jordee), Jojo (as Jimi), Jazz (as Jai), Jussie (as Jesse), Jake (as Joc), and Jocqui (as Jarreau). **T'Keyah Crystal Keymah** played Scotti, a boarder (1995). **Roger Aaron Brown** played the social worker.

ON PROMISED LAND (*DIS, April 17, 1994*). This children's show was the story of a young African-American boy and an elderly white woman who developed a friendship that impacted the lives of both their families. Norman D. Golden II was the boy; Joan Plowright played the woman.

ON STAGE WITH BARBARA MCNAIR (*SYN, January 1970*). Singer **Barbara McNair** headlined her own special with guests **Duke Ellington** and Carlton Johnson.

OPRAH AFTER THE SHOW (*OXY, 2002–)*. Oprah Winfrey conversed with the studio audience, after her syndicated show was taped, in an unscripted, unrehearsed hour. She was said to be less guarded and more candid than she was on the "big show," though the conversation might or might not be about the same subjects.

OPRAH WINFREY PRESENTS: BEFORE WOMEN HAD WINGS (*ABC, November 3, 1997*). This was the first of six TV films produced by **Oprah Winfrey**'s Harpo Films under the banner Oprah Winfrey Presents. This film depicted a dysfunctional white family in 1960s rural Florida. Ellen Barkin was the boozing mother; John Savage, the boozing father; Julia Stiles, the troubled teenage daughter; and Tina Majorino, the spirited but innocent daughter named Bird. Winfrey played Miss Zora, a nice lady who bonded with Bird. The performances were widely praised by critics. *Variety* (November 3, 1997) said, "Clearly, this is a quality piece of work guided by caring hands."

OPRAH WINFREY PRESENTS: DAVID AND LISA (*ABC, November 1, 1998*). Sidney Poitier starred in this TV film, a remake of a 1962 film, about two emotionally disturbed youth aided by a compassionate psychiatrist who runs a school for such teenagers.

OPRAH WINFREY PRESENTS: THEIR EYES WERE WATCHING GOD (*ABC, March 6, 2005*). Halle Berry starred in this film, based on the novel by Zora Neale Hurston. The film centered on Janie Crawford, a beautiful black woman in the 1920s, and her search for love while experiencing both great success and heartbreak. Michael Ealy, Ruben Santiago-Hudson, and **Ruby Dee** also star.

OPRAH WINFREY PRESENTS: THE WEDDING (*ABC, February 22–23, 1998*). **Halle Berry**, Eric Thai, **Lynn Whitfield**, **Carl Lumbly**, and **Michael Warren** starred in this two-part miniseries, which explored race and class in black society on Martha's Vineyard in the 1950s. Berry was Shelby Coles, a debutante from an elite family who wanted to marry a poor white musician (Thai). Her socially significant parents (Whitfield and Warren) are appalled when they learned the groom's family refused to attend the wedding. Lumbly played the single father of mixed-race daughters. Charles Burnett was director. **Marianne Jean-Baptiste** and **Charlayne Woodard** had key roles. *See also* INTERRACIAL ROMANCES/RELATIONSHIPS.

OPRAH WINFREY PRESENTS: TUESDAYS WITH MORRIE (*ABC, December 5, 1999*). Winfrey's company produced this drama starring Jack Lemmon; it did not have a black theme but is significant in that it was an **Oprah Winfrey** production.

OPRAH WINFREY SHOW, THE (*SYN, 1986– *). The talk show (later titled *Oprah!*) starring **Oprah Winfrey** was launched nationally in 1986 and became the highest-rated daytime talk show in television history. In 1994, after talk shows began to concentrate on sensational subjects, Winfrey pledged to focus her show on uplifting, meaningful subjects. In 1996, she begin Oprah's Book Club, a segment of her show designed to get viewers excited about reading. The segment was successful, and each book selected as reading by the book club became an instant best-seller. In 1997, the show launched Oprah's Angel Network, a campaign to encourage donations that were used for scholarships, Habitat for Humanity homes, and the building of schools in 10 countries. In 1999, Winfrey won the National Book Foundation's 50th Anniversary Gold Medal for her influence on reading and books. In 2003, she took gifts to thousands of South African children orphaned by AIDS. She also began building 12 schools in Africa, two in Afghanistan, and one in Mississippi for disadvantaged girls.

One of the most memorable shows was the first show of the 1988–1989 season, when Winfrey, who had been on the Optifast diet during the hiatus, wheeled out 67 pounds of fat in a wagon showing how much weight she had lost to get down to a size 10. It was after this weight loss that *TV Guide*'s cover girl had Oprah's face and Ann Margaret's body. It was obvious to *TV Guide* readers that this was not Oprah's body, thin as she was, and *TV Guide* admitted so later. Oprah's Pop Star Challenge, a singing competition, in the 2003–2004 season, was designed to propel aspiring talented singers possibly older than the *America Idol* contestants into stardom. The winner was LaShell Griffin, who landed a contract with Epic Records. For the opening show of the 2004–2005 season, Oprah gave away new $28,000 Pontiacs to each of 276 members of the studio audience. The series and Winfrey have won numerous **Emmy Awards**.

ORIGINAL AMATEUR HOUR, THE (*CBS, ABC, NBC, 1948–1960*). This talent show hosted by Ted Mack is recognized in black history primarily because it discovered a seven-year-old Atlanta girl with a big voice who grew up to be recording artist **Gladys Knight**. A foreparent to shows like *American Idol* and *Star Search*, the winner was selected by viewers' votes. In those days, votes were entered by telephone calls and postcards. The show was done in what is now the Ed Sullivan Theater in New York City, where, in later years, *Late Night with David Letterman* would be taped. Gladys had to travel back and forth with her mother from Atlanta to New York by train because it took time for the votes to be counted. Singing "Brahm's Lullaby" and "Because of You," she won three consecutive rounds and $2,000.

ORIGINAL ROMPIN' STOMPIN' HOT AND HEAVY, COOL AND GROOVY ALL-STAR JAZZ SHOW, THE (*CBS, April 13, 1976*). **Dionne Warwick** hosted this variety special. It was an hour-long history of jazz and featured the following musicians and singers: **Count Basie**, **Dizzy Gillespie**, **Lionel Hampton**, **Herbie Hancock**, Max Roach, **Joe Williams**, Stan Getz, and Gerry Mulligan.

ORMAN, ROSCOE. Orman was Gordon, one of the early cast members on *Sesame Street*.

OSUNSAMI, STEVE. Osunsami joined ABC News in 1997. As a correspondent, his credits include reports on *World News Tonight with*

Peter Jennings and contributions to *Nightline* and *Good Morning America*, ABC News radio, and other ABC broadcasts.

OUT ALL NIGHT (*NBC, 1992*). Singer **Patti LaBelle** starred in this sitcom as Chelsea Page, a former singer who owned a hip nightclub, Club Chelsea. Other characters included Jeff Carswell (**Morris Chestnut**) the manager-trainee at the club; Chelsea's daughter Charisse (**Vivica A. Fox**), a fashion stylist; Vidal Thomas (**Duane Martin**), who had a crush on Charisse; and Angus (Simon O'Brien), the eccentric neighbor. LaBelle and other performers entertained in the series, which was canceled before it completed its contracted 22 episodes.

OUTCASTS, THE (*ABC, 1968–1969*). This early western had a regular cast of two: Earl Corey (Don Murray), a wealthy gunman who made it his business to catch bad guys, and Jemal David (**Otis Young**), his trusty sidekick, a freed slave. It was a series with one black supporting actor before 1980.

OUT OF DARKNESS (*ABC, January 16, 1994*). **Diana Ross** starred in this made-for-television movie as Pauline Cooper, a woman who, with the help of a new drug, comes out of a 17-year battle with schizophrenia.

OVERTON, BILL. Overton had key roles in *Cover Girls* (1977), *The Night They Took Miss Beautiful* (1977), *Trials of Life* (1977), *Backstairs at the White House* (1979), **Brave New World** (1980), and **Grambling's White Tiger** in 1981, all television movies or miniseries. He played Cal in the TV series *Firehouse* (1974). He later became an author.

OWENS, GEOFFREY. Owens played Elvin on **The Cosby Show** (1986–1992), Robert on the 1997 series *Built to Last*, and the teacher in the 1990 TV film *Stood Up!*

OZ (*HBO, 1997–2003*). This late night drama was about life in fictional Oswald State Penitentiary (nicknamed "Oz"), where violence, rape, drug trade, gangs, intimidation, racism, homosexuality, and even religion reflected life in real hard-time prisons. Like most

U.S. prisons, a great percentage of the population was black. Prisoner Augustus Hill (**Harold Perrineau**) was convicted of murder in the second degree and sentenced to life; Hill was a member of the gang called "The Others" and the series narrator. The warden was Leo Glynn (**Ernie Hudson**). Simon Adebisi (Adewale Akinnoune-Agbaje), a member of the HomeBoys, was convicted of murder in the first degree and sentenced to life without parole. Kareem Said (Eamonn Walker), head of the Muslims, was convicted of arson in the second degree and sentenced to 15 years. The Poet (Mums), a member of the HomeBoys, was first sentenced for armed robbery. He was paroled and then convicted of first-degree murder and sentenced to life. He earned his nickname because he performed his original poetry about people and events at Oz. Burr Redding (Anthony Chisholm), a leader of the HomeBoys, was convicted of 17 counts of attempted murder and was sentenced to life without parole. Other actors and characters were J. D. Williams as Kenny Wangler, a HomeBoy; Michael Wright as Omar White, one of The Others; and Granville Adams as Zahir Arif, assistant to the head of the Muslims.

OZZIE'S GIRLS (*SYN, 1973*). This sitcom spun off of *The Adventures of Ozzie and Harriett*, a popular sitcom from 1952 to 1966. The spin-off is listed in this volume only because one of the key characters was played by **Brenda Sykes**, a black actress very popular at the time. Sykes played Brenda MacKenzie (at first, her name was Jennifer), one of two college girls who boarded with Ozzie and Harriett Nelson (played by themselves). Ozzie was passing on fatherly advice to the boarders much like he did with his natural sons, Ricky and David, in the original series. *See also* SERIES WITH ONE BLACK SUPPORTING ACTOR/PERFORMER BEFORE 1980.

– P –

PACE, JUDY. Pace played Ann Fielding in the television film *The Young Lawyers* and went on to star in the series of the same title in 1970–1971. She had a key role in the highly praised telefilm *Brian's Song* in 1971.

PAGE, HARRISON. Page (aka Harrison Paige) starred in the 1973 sitcom *Love Thy Neighbor*; played Chief Robinson in the sitcom *C.P.O. Sharkey* (1976–1978); played the porter, George Boone, in the 1979 dramatic anthology series *Supertrain*; and played Capt. Trunk in the sitcom *Sledge Hammer* (1986–1988). In TV films, he had key roles in **Backstairs at the White House** (1979), **The Kid with the Broken Halo** (1983), and *Columbo: Undercover* (1994). He had recurring roles as Admiral M. Morris on *JAG* (1995–), John Fox on **Hill Street Blues** (1981), and Hamilton on **Gimme a Break** (1981).

PAGE, KEN. Page was a member of the four-person musical ensemble of *Ain't Misbehavin'* in 1982. He played *Eden Kendall* in the adventure series *Sable* (1987–1988) and Dr. McHenry in the 1994 comedy drama *South Central*.

PAGE, LAWANDA. Page played Aunt Esther in **Sanford and Son** from 1973 to 1977 and in **The Sanford Arms** in 1977. She appeared in **The Richard Pryor Special?** in 1977, the **Dean Martin Celebrity Roast** of Betty White in 1978, *Ladies and Gentleman . . . Bob Newhart* in 1980, and *Good Evening, Captain* in 1981. She had a key role in *Stonestreet: Who Killed the Centerfold Model?* in 1977. Page was born in 1920 and died in 2002 of complications from diabetes.

PALMERSTOWN, U.S.A. (*CBS, 1980–1981*). Coproduced by award-winning author **Alex Haley** ("Roots") and Norman Lear , this one-hour drama was loosely based on Haley's early life during the Depression. The story centered on two boys, one white, David (played by Brian Godfrey Wilson), and one black, Booker T. (played by Jermain Hodge Johnson), who were best friends in a southern town in the 1930s. Most of the story lines in the series were seen through the eyes of the two boys. **Jonelle Allen** and **Bill Duke** played Booker T.'s parents, Bessie and Luther. **Star-Shemah Bobatoon** played his sister, Diana. *See also* ROOTS; ROOTS: THE NEXT GENERATIONS.

PARENT'HOOD, THE (*WB, 1995–1999*). Robert Townsend starred as Robert Peterson, who was married to Jerri (Suzanne Douglas), a law student. The two had four children: teenagers Michael (Kenny Blank) and Zaria (Reagan Gomez-Preston), grade schooler Nicholas (Curtis

Williams), and preschooler Cece (Ashli Adams). They lived in a Manhattan brownstone. Wendell (**Faizon Love**) was Robert's best friend. Robert had been a professor of communications at New York University, but in the second season, he was hosting a public access cable show. The show often included Robert's daydreams in which the characters played other characters. Townsend was co–executive producer.

PARIS (*CBS, 1979–1980*). This drama series was **James Earl Jones**'s first of two efforts in the 1980s to develop a hit drama series. The second was *Under One Roof* in 1985. Paris was a police drama, not a family drama, but Jones's character, Police Captain Woody Paris, had a family, a life. That was unusual in 1979, when black characters on dramas were only sidekicks with no personal lives of their own. **Lee Chamberlin** played Woody's wife, Barbara. At work, Captain Paris ran a special squad of young officers selected to solve difficult cases. **Mike Warren** played one of those officers, Willie Miller. The series did not garner ratings sufficient to stay on the air.

PARKER, NICOLE ARI. Parker played Teri Joseph in *Soul Food* in the series (2000–2004). She played key roles in *Rebound: The Legend of Earl "The Goat" Manigault* (1996) and *Dancing in September* (2001). In 2004, she began a starring role in the sitcom *Second Time Around*.

PARKER, PAULA JAI. Comedienne Parker played Roberta Young in the 1999 detective drama *Snoops* and Monique in the sitcom *The Wayans Bros* (1995–1996). She was a regular on the comedy/variety series *Townsend Television* (1993) and *The Apollo Comedy Hour* (1992–1993). She was the voice of Trudy Proud on the animated series *The Proud Family* (2001–).

PARKERS, THE (*UPN, 1999–2004*). This sitcom, a spin-off of the series *Moesha*, about an outrageous mother-daughter team, starred **Mo'Nique** as outspoken and outlandish Nikki Parker and **Countess Vaughn** (aka Countess Vaughn James) as the hip but not very bright Kim. Nikki and Kim were roommates who attended Santa Monica College, and despite their age differences, both enjoyed the wild social life of the campus. Nikki had a long-standing crush on Professor

Oglevee (**Dorien Wilson**), who refused her advances for years. Throughout the series run, she chased, nearly stalked, him. Though he spurned her, viewers assumed he would someday stop running. Executive Producer Sara V. Finney said that as the series ended, UPN gave them the opportunity to prepare scripts for the ending of the story line. During the final season, Nikki seemed to be preparing to marry Johnnie (Mel Jackson), a businessman. However, on the final original episode on May 10, 2004, Prof. Oglevee realized he loved her, and they were married. As they proceeded down the aisle to live happily ever after, Kim sang "At Last." And the series ended. Nikki's friend Andell was played by **Yvette Wilson**. Kim's friends Stevie and "T" (Tyrell) were played by Jenna von Oy and **Ken L.** (aka Ken Lawson), respectively.

The Parkers had numerous black notables who appeared as themselves; among them were the following: Yolanda Adams, Laila Ali, Shirley Caesar, Magic Johnson, Shaquille O'Neal, and Tavis Smiley. In its first season, *The Parkers* was the number one series in African-American households. Finney, Vida Spears, and Ralph Farquhar were creators. Bill Boulware was also executive producer.

PARROS, PETER. Parros played Reginald Cornelius III (RC3) on the adventure series *Knight Rider* (1985–1986). He was Dr. Ben Harris (1996–) in the daytime drama *As the World Turns* and Dr. Ben Price in *One Life to Live* (1994–1995). He starred in the syndicated 1989–1990 version of *Adam 12* as Officer Gus Grant.

PARSONS, KARYN. Parsons was Hilary Banks in the sitcom *Fresh Prince of Bel-Air* (1990–1996). She also played Margot Hines in the 1996 series *Lush Life* and Toni in *The Job* (2001–2002). She played Lady-in-Waiting in the 1996 telefilm *Gulliver's Travels*.

PARTNERS, THE (*NBC, 1971–1972*). This was a sitcom starring **Rupert Crosse**, an accomplished black actor who died of cancer in his forties shortly after the end of this one-season series. Also starring was Don Adams, and the two were George Robinson (Crosse) and Lennie Crooke (Adams), a bumbling partnership of police detectives who always solved the crime, but the route to the solution was a comedy of errors. Three episodes of *The Partners* made up a film titled

Confessions of a Top Crime Buster, which aired in syndication in the fall of 1972; after that, the series was canceled.

PARTY FOR RICHARD PRYOR, A (*CBS, November 23, 1991*). The party hosted by **Eddie Murphy** celebrated **Richard Pryor** with song and comedy. Attending and praising Pryor were **James Brown, The Pointer Sisters, Robert Townsend, Arsenio Hall, Keenen Ivory Wayans, Stevie Wonder**, Burt Reynolds, Lily Tomlin, Loni Anderson, and Gene Wilder. The variety special earned positive reviews; it was taped about five years after Pryor was diagnosed with multiple sclerosis.

PASSING GLORY (*TNT, February 21, 1999*). This two-hour TV film starred **Andre Braugher, Ruby Dee**, Bill Nunn, and Sean Squire and was the true story of an idealistic young black priest who used the basketball court to challenge the social conventions of a segregationist town. **Magic Johnson** and **Quincy Jones** were executive producers. *See also* BIOPICS.

PASSION AND MEMORY (*PBS, May 11, 1986*). A documentary, this one-hour production hosted by **Robert Guillaume** explored the careers of five black pioneers in film. The five were the following: Lincoln (Stepin Fetchit) Perry, **Hattie McDaniel**, Bill "Bojangles" Robinson, **Dorothy Dandridge**, and **Sidney Poitier**. The central theme was that circumstances forced them to accept demeaning roles at the beginning of their careers, but each actor transcended racial stereotyping in adding richness to American films. Roy Campanella Jr. was producer, director, and cowriter.

PATTI LA BELLE SHOW, THE (*NBC, November 28, 1985*). Singer **Patti LaBelle** hosted this one-hour variety special celebrating Thanksgiving. Her guests were **Bill Cosby, Luther Vandross**, Amy Grant, and Cyndi Lauper.

PAUL ROBESON (*PBS, October 8, 1979*). **James Earl Jones** performed in a one-man show depicting Paul Robeson.

PAYNE, CARL ANTHONY, II. Payne played Cockroach on *The Cosby Show* (1986–1987). He was Rapper #3 in the 1990 musical drama series *Hull High* in 1990. He played *Cole Brown* on the sitcom *Martin* (1992–1997) and Carl in the sitcom *Rock Me Baby* (2003–). In TV films, he had roles in the following: *Good Night, Sweet Wife: A Murder in Boston* (1990) and *Line of Fire: The Morris Dees Story* (1991).

PAYTON, JO MARIE. Payton (aka Jo Marie Payton-Noble and Jo Marie Payton-France) was Harriette Winslow, the smart-mouthed elevator operator, on the sitcom *Perfect Strangers* (1987–1989) and the pivotal character for the spin-off series *Family Matters* (1989–1997). She played Mona in the sitcom *The New Odd Couple* (1982–1983). She was the voice of Suga Mama on the animated cartoon series *The Proud Family*.

PBS HOLLYWOOD PRESENTS: THE OLD SETTLER *(PBS, April 25, 2001).* Natural sisters **Phylicia Rashad** and **Debbie Allen** starred in this made-for-television film as two middle-aged sisters who take in a handsome young boarder.

PEETE, HOLLY ROBINSON. Robinson (aka Holly Robinson) played Tanya West in *Like Family* (2003–2004), Malena Ellis in *For Your Love* (1998–2000), Vanessa Russell in *Hangin' with Mr. Cooper* (1992–1997), and Officer Judy Hoffs in *21 Jump Street* (1987–1990). She appeared in the variety special *Battle of the Bands* in 1993. She had a key role in the TV film *The Jacksons: An American Dream* in 1992.

PENDERGRASS, TEDDY. The singer appeared in variety specials *Men Who Rate a "10"* (1980), *Teddy Pendergrass in Concert* (1982), and *The Apollo Hall of Fame* (1993).

PERINE, KELLY. Perine was Kelly on *The Parent'Hood* (1999), Dusty Canyon on *Between Brothers* (1997–1998), and Duane on *One on One* (2001–), all sitcoms.

PERKINS, TONY. Perkins joined ABC as the weather forecaster on *Good Morning America* in 1999. His broadcasts were unique in that they originated not from a comfortable studio but from the sites of horrific weather.

PERRINEAU, HAROLD. Perrineau had a regular role as one of 48 passengers stranded on a mysterious desert island when their plane crashed in the drama series *Lost*, which premiered in 2004. He was also one of the convicts and the series narrator on the late night drama *Oz* (1997–2003).

PERRY, FELTON. Perry played Jimmy in the medical drama *Matt Lincoln* (1970–1971) and Inspector McNeil in the drama series *Hooperman* (1987–1989).

PERRY, ROD. Perry played Joe Pittman in *The Autobiography of Miss Jane Pittman* in 1974 and Deacon in the police drama *S.W.A.T.* (1975–1976).

PERSON TO PERSON (*CBS, 1953–1961*). Newsman Edward R. Murrow (1953–1959) and Charles Collingwood (1959–1961) interviewed celebrities in various walks of life—entertainment, politics, and science. Among them were Fidel Castro, Senator John Kennedy, and Marilyn Monroe. Though Collingwood took over near the end of the run, people who recall the series think primarily of Murrow. The camera crew usually went to the celebrity's home and shot the interview live. Murrow sat in the studio, watched the subject on the monitor, and fired questions while smoking constantly. If you were interviewed on *Person to Person*, you were indeed hot. Several black Americans were interviewed including **Ethel Waters**, **Cab Calloway**, **Duke Ellington**, and Roy Campanella.

PETERS, BROCK. Peters's first national television role was the adventure series *Adventures in Paradise* in 1960. In series television, he played Frank Lewis on the daytime drama *The Young and the Restless* (1982–1989) and many guest-star appearances. In TV films and miniseries, he had roles in the following: *Welcome Home, Johnny Bristol* (1972), *Seventh Avenue* (1977), *Black Beauty* (1978), *A Bond of Iron* (1979), *The Incredible Journey of Doctor Meg Laurel* (1979),

Denmark Vessey's Rebellion (1982), *A Caribbean Mystery* (1983), *Broken Angel* (1988), *To Heal a Nation* (1988), *Polly* (1989), *The Big One: The Great Los Angeles Earthquake* (1990), *Highway Heartbreaker* (1992), *The Secret* (1992), *An Element of Truth* (1995), and *The Locket* (2002). He was Ab Decker in **Roots: The Next Generations** in 1979. Peters died on August 23, 2005, of pancreatic cancer. He was 78.

PETERS, LOWELL. Peters was a member of the gospel singers **Southernaires Quartet**; the quartet had a show in 1948.

PETTIFORD, VALARIE. Pettiford played Dee on *Half & Half* and Sheila on *One Life to Live* (1990–1994).

PETULA (*NBC, April 9, 1968*). This musical special starred popular British singer Petula Clark. **Harry Belafonte** was the guest star. During the show, Clark held Belafonte's arm and thereby touched off a nationwide alarm of phone calls and mail at NBC. For a white person to touch a black person on television was horrible to the complainers, even though Clark did not even realize she had touched him; it was, to Clark and Belafonte, an innocent gesture.

PHIFER, MEKHI. Former rap artist Mekhi (pronounced Meck-high) Phifer played Dr. Gregory Pratt on the drama series *ER* beginning in 2002. He played a role in the 1995 TV film **The Tuskegee Airmen**. He had a recurring role on **Homicide: Life on the Street** as Junior Bunk (1996–1998).

PHILLIPS, JOSEPH C. Phillips played Martin on **The Cosby Show** (1989–1992). In daytime drama, he was Justus Ward #1 on *General Hospital* (1994–1998) and Cruiser McCulla in *Search for Tomorrow* (1985). He had a recurring role in *The District* (2002–2004) as Mayor Morgan Douglas. In TV films, he played George Murchison in *A Raisin in the Sun* (1989) and Luke Jordan in *Midnight Blue* (2000).

PHILLIPS, JULIAN. Phillips joined Fox News Channel as an anchor and general assignment reporter in 2002.

PIANO LESSON, THE (*CBS, February 5, 1995*). In this August Wilson play, **Charles Dutton** starred as Boy Willie (a role he played on

Broadway), who wanted to sell the family heirloom piano to buy land for financial security saying "that's the only thing God's not making more of," but his sister wants to keep the piano. **Alfre Woodard, Carl Gordon** (who also starred in the Broadway production), **Courtney B. Vance, Tommy Hollis,** and **Lou Myers** also starred. *See also* BROADWAY PLAYS AND MUSICALS.

PICKENS, JAMES, JR. Pickens played Richard Webber in the drama series *Grey's Anatomy* when it debuted at midseason of the 2004–2005 television season. He had roles in the following TV films: *Trial by Fire* (1995), *Little Girl Fly Away* (1998), *A Slight Case of Murder* (1999), *Semper Fi* (2001), *The X-Files: The Truth* (2002), and *The Lyon's Den* (2003). He reprised his role of Terrence Christianson in the later film in the series *The X Files* (2003–2004).

PIERCE, STACK. Pierce had key roles in the TV films *Louis Armstrong—Chicago Style* in 1976, *Flesh and Blood* in 1979, and the miniseries *V—The Final Battle* in 1984.

PIGEON, THE (*ABC, November 4, 1969*). **Sammy Davis Jr.** starred in this 90-minute unsold pilot for a detective drama series. Davis played an eager investigator. **Roy Glenn** played Lieutenant Frank Miller.

PINKETT, JADA. *See* SMITH, JADA PINKETT.

PJs, THE (*FOX, 1999–2001*). **Eddie Murphy** created this, the first stop-motion animation series to air in prime time. The characters were black people who live in an inner-city housing project, Hilton Jacobs. "PJ" is a term for housing projects. Murphy was the voice of the good-natured but grumpy superintendent of the complex, Thurgood Stubbs, who tries to patch up the building and the relationships of the tenants. Mrs. Avery was the senior citizen of the building who had nothing good to say about Thurgood. **Ja'Net DuBois**, formerly of *Good Times*, lent her voice to this character and won an **Emmy Award** for her work in 1999. Muriel was Thurgood's wife (**Loretta Devine**), the voice of reason. The Stubbses were surrogate parents to young Calvin (Crystal Scales). Calvin's buddy (Michael Morgan) had parents who were so obese they could not leave their apartment. Haiti Lady (Cheryl Francis Harrington) was the project's voodoo expert who had a curse and a solution for every problem. Thurgood played chess with his buddy Sanchez (Pepe Serna).

The animated series was done in stop-motion animation, or foamation, by the Will Vinton Studios, which first used claymation. Foam-bodied characters have a distinctively unique appearance. The voices are recorded before the animation is done. Supervising Director Mark Gustafson said that 20 animators, four directors, and eight executive producers (including Murphy) were part of the company; that only two minutes of footage were shot per week; and that each episode took about 12 weeks to animate. There were some complaints from the black community; the *Los Angeles Sentinel* (February 3, 1999) had a review that read, "Along with the distorted images of the characters, the messages in the program demean many facets of African/American culture." And others gave the show a chance; the *Michigan Chronicle* (March 24, 1999) quoted Murphy, who said, "I wanted to do the type of show where people sit around and talk about it afterward, the way they did with shows like *All in the Family*."

PLAYING WITH FIRE (*NBC, April 14, 1985*). In this TV film, **Gary Coleman** played teenage arsonist David Philips, who did not feel accepted or important either at school or at home. So he began to start fires. David's parents were played by **Cicely Tyson** and **Ron O'Neal**. **Yaphet Kotto** played the fire chief. **Cherie Johnson** played Eileen Phillips.

PLUMMER, GLENN. Plummer had a regular role in the medical drama *ER* as Timmy in 1994–1995; he played Squirrel in the TV film *Scott Turow's Reversible Errors* in 2004.

POINTER SISTERS, THE (the group). The original sister group was made up of Ruth, Bonnie, Anita, and June Pointer; then, because of a contractual problem, Bonnie had to drop out. The group headlined *The Pointer Sisters* in 1982, *The Pointer Sisters in Paris* in 1985, and *The Pointer Sisters—Up All Nite* in 1987. It appeared in numerous variety specials: *One More Time* in 1974, a Flip Wilson special in

1975, *The Mac Davis Christmas Special* in 1981, *The Suzanne Somers Special* in 1983, *Disneyland's 30th Anniversary Celebration* in 1985, *Disneyland's Summer Vacation Party* in 1986, *Liberty Weekend: Closing Ceremonies* in 1986, *Motown Merry Christmas* in 1987, *A Star Spangled Celebration* in 1988, *Bob Hope's Christmas Cheer from Saudi Arabia* in 1991, *Welcome Home, America* in 1991, and *Muhammad Ali's 50th Birthday Celebration* in 1992. They made several appearances on *The Midnight Special* and *Soul Train*.

POINTER SISTERS, THE (a special) (*SYN, July 1982*). The Pointer Sisters—Anita, June, and Ruth—performed in a concert taped before a live audience in March 1982.

POINTER SISTERS IN PARIS, THE (*SHO, September 14, 1985*). The sister group—Anita, June, and Ruth Pointer—entertained from Paris, France, in this one-hour special.

POINTER SISTERS SHOW, THE (a series) (*NBC, 1973*). Also titled *Flip Wilson Presents the Pointer Sisters*, this special series aired in the summer for an intended limited run in *The Flip Wilson Show*'s time slot.

POINTER SISTERS—UP ALL NITE, THE (*NBC, January 23, 1987*). The **Pointer Sisters**—Anita, June, and Ruth—went to various night spots in Los Angeles and sang in this one-hour variety special. Guest stars were **Whoopi Goldberg**, The McGuire Sisters, and Bruce Willis.

POITIER, SIDNEY. Poitier had a rare starring role in **"A Man Is Ten Feet Tall,"** a drama on the *Philco Television Playhouse* in 1955. In 1991, he starred in *Separate but Equal*, the life story of Thurgood Marshall. He starred in the miniseries *Children of the Dust* in 1995. In 1997, he starred as South African President Nelson Mandela in *Mandela and De Klerk*, a TV film. In 1992, he was the guest of honor and winner of the American Film Institute's Life Achievement Award on *AFI Salute to Sidney Poitier*. Poitier also appeared in the documentary *The Spencer Tracy Legacy: A Tribute to Katharine Hepburn* in 1986, and he was an honoree on *The Kennedy Center Honors* in 1989. He appeared in variety specials *Night of 100 Stars II* in 1985 and on the *AFI Tribute to Barbara Streisand* in 2001. He starred in *Oprah Winfrey Presents: David and Lisa* and *The Simple Life of Noah Dearborn*, both in 1998.

POITIER, SYDNEY TAMIIA. Sidney Poitier's daughter Sydney joined the regular cast of the drama series *Veronica Mars* as the journalism teacher in 2004. Before that, she had roles in the following TV projects: *Free of Eden* (1999), *Noah's Ark* (1999), *First Years* (2001), and *Abby* (2003).

POPWELL, ALBERT. Popwell had roles in *Steel Cowboy* in 1978 and *Sister, Sister* in 1982, both made-for-television motion pictures.

PORGY & BESS *(PBS, October 6, 1993).* The Gershwin opera—not the musical—came to television with singers Willard White as Porgy, Cynthia Haymon as Bess, Gregg Baker as Crown, Cynthia Clarey as Serena, Marietta Simpson as Maria, **Damon Evans** as Sportin' Life, and Paula Ingram as Clara. Evans was recognizable as having played the second Lionel on the sitcom *The Jeffersons*.

PORTRAIT OF NANCY WILSON *(SYN, March 1972).* Singer **Nancy Wilson** was the headliner in this one-hour special with guest stars **Billy Eckstine** and **Sarah Vaughn**.

POSEY, PARKER MCKENNA. Posey's first regular role in a television series was as Kady Kyle in the sitcom *My Wife and Kids* (2001–).

POUNDER, C. C. H. Pounder played Renee in *My Past Is My Own* (1989). She had key roles in the made-for-television movies *Psycho IV* and *Murder in Mississippi* (1990), *The Ernest Green Story* (1993), *Zooman* (1995), *Funny Valentines* (1999), *Common Ground* (2000), and *Boycott* (2001). She played Dawn Murphy in the sitcom *Women in Prison* (1987–1988), Dr. Angela Hicks on the medical drama series *ER* (1994–1997), and Det. Claudette Wyms in *The Shield* (2002–2004). She had a key role in the 2004 film *Redemption*.

POWELL, CLIFTON. Powell played Andre, the drug dealer who was nemesis to Roc on the sitcom *Roc* (1993–1994), and Bobby Deavers on the comedy/drama series *South Central* (1993). Powell portrayed Martin Luther King Jr. in the TV film **Selma, Lord, Selma** (1999).

POWERS, BEN. Powers played Keith Anderson in *Good Times* (1978–1979) and was a regular on *Laugh-In* (1979). This was not the original *Rowan and Martin's Laugh-In* (1968–1973) but an effort by the producer, George Schlatter, to make a hit of a similar series. Powers played Moochie in *Mickey Spillane's Mike Hammer* (1984–1987).

POWERS OF MATTHEW STAR, THE (*NBC, 1982–1983*). Louis Gossett Jr. and Peter Barton starred in this sci-fi series. Gossett was Walt Shephard, a high school science teacher and guardian to Matthew Star, a teenage prince from another planet who was sent to earth to develop his magical powers—telepathy, telekinesis, and astral projection (he could transport himself to another location) as well as transmutation. He tried to be a normal earthling and go to school and date girls, but he had to hide from his Quadrian enemies and also help the U.S. government fight spies.

POWs: THE BLACK HOMECOMING (*ABC, July 27, 1973*). This ABC News special was a documentary of how black prisoners of war adjusted to life after they returned to the United States.

PRACTICE, THE (*ABC, 1997–2004*). This legal drama centered on a team of young attorneys battling to keep their firm afloat by winning the toughest cases. Legal maneuvering was what they did best, and in the process, they often found themselves coping with serious moral and ethical challenges. Two African-American actors were members of the original cast: **Steve Harris** as Eugene Young, a senior attorney in the firm, and **Lisa Gay Hamilton** as Rebecca, the firm's secretary who went to law school and then joined the firm. Young could find and argue the weakness in the most formidable opponent. Rebecca learned fast and was determined that right should prevail. This popular legal drama series won acclaim as a Sunday night staple. Then, in

2002–2003, ABC moved it to Monday night supposedly to strengthen that night's lineup with two new dramas. This turned out to be a ratings disaster; the other two shows were canceled, and *The Practice* lost some of its audience. The series was moved back to Sunday nights for the 2003–2004 season but without some of its cast. Hamilton was one of the victims of this cut. Steve Harris remained; his character, Young, first became head of the firm. Then, in the series' final episode, Young became a judge.

PRATT, DEBORAH. Pratt had a key role in *Grambling's White Tiger* in 1981. Other TV film credits include *Love Is Not Enough* (1978), *She's with Me* (1982), *Airwolf* (1984), *Three on a Match* (1987), and the narrator in *Quantum Leap* (1989). Pratt was director of the PBS production *Cora Unashamed* in 2000.

PRATT, KYLA. Pratt's voice is used as the voice of Penny Proud in the animated series about a black family, *The Proud Family*. She played Breanna Barnes on the sitcom *One on One* (2001–).

PREMICE, JOSEPHINE. Premice played Madame Gautier in *The Autobiography of Miss Jane Pittman* in 1974. She made recurring appearances on *A Different World* as Desiree Porter (1992–1993). She was born in 1926 and died in 2001 of emphysema.

PRESIDENTIAL INAUGURAL GALA, THE (*CBS, January 19, 1993*). Show business celebrities celebrated the inauguration of President Bill Clinton. They included **Bill Cosby**, **Aretha Franklin**, **James Earl Jones**, **Wynton Marsalis**, Grover Washington Jr., and Kenny Rogers.

PRESTON, BILLY. Singer/pianist/organist Billy Preston appeared in variety specials *Rolling Stone Magazine: The 10th Anniversary* in 1977 and *Liberty Weekend: Closing Ceremonies* in 1986. He was a popular regular entertainer on *Shindig* (1964–1966), a rock 'n' roll music show featuring recording artists. With a big Afro, he was both a vocalist and a pianist on the series. He was a protégé of **Ray Charles** and later worked with the Beatles in their recordings and films. He also collaborated with **Aretha Franklin**, **Quincy Jones**,

Sammy Davis Jr., Syreeta, and others. He had his own hits as well. He was the first black music director for a national television talk show when he took those duties on the syndicated *NightLife* (1986–1987) starring comedian David Brenner.

PRESTON EPISODES, THE (*Fox, 1995*). David Alan Grier starred in this sitcom as David Preston, a divorced college professor who gave up academia to become a great writer in New York. He wanted to win the Pulitzer Prize, but that was unlikely when the only job he could find was writing photo captions for a tabloid-type publication. Much of the comedy centered on his making the job seem more important than it was. **Ron Canada** and **Lynne Thigpen** played David's parents. Deborah Lacey played his ex-wife.

PRESTON, J. A. Preston played the recurring role of the mayor on *Hill Street Blues* (1982–1985). He had a key role in the made-for-television film *High Noon, Part II: The Return of Will Kane* in 1980 and a regular role in the sitcom *All's Fair* (1976–1977).

PRICE, LEONTYNE. The opera singer was the first black to appear in a television version of an opera when she performed in *Tosca* in 1955. In the same year, she was one of several top entertainers who appeared on *Entertainment 1955*, a 90-minute special that aired live from NBC's then-new $3.7 million studios in Burbank, California. She was an honoree on *The Kennedy Center Honors* in 1981. She sang in the music special *A Capitol Fourth* and was host and star of ***In Performance at the White House: An Evening of Spirituals and Gospel Music***, both in 1983.

PRIDE, CHARLEY. Pride appeared in variety specials: *The Sound and the Scene* in 1969, *The Tom Jones Special* in 1971, *The Bob Hope Special* in 1972, *Love Is . . . Barbara Eden* in 1972, *Perry (Como) and His Nashville Friends* in 1975, *The Stars and Stripes Show* in 1975, *Super Night at the Super Bowl* in 1977, *General Electric's All Star Anniversary* in 1978, *A Country Christmas 1981* in 1981, *America— The Great Mississippi* in 1987, *Hee Haw's 20th Birthday Party* in 1988, and *Opryland Celebrates America's Music* in 1988. Pride sang the National Anthem at Super Bowl VIII in 1974. He cohosted with

Glen Campbell *Country Comes Home* in 1981, and alone he hosted *Going Platinum with Charley Pride* in 1978.

PRINGLE, JOAN. Pringle played Diana, who married **Don Mitchell**'s character in the drama *Ironside* (1974–1975). She was Tracy on the sitcom *That's My Mama* in 1975, Nurse Keynes on the medical drama *Rafferty* in 1977, and Polly Dawson on the sitcom *Soap* from 1979 to 1981. Pringle played Sybil Buchanan, the vice principal who, in the course of the series *The White Shadow* (1978–1981), became principal. She was Ruth Marshall in the daytime drama *Generations* in 1989 and also had roles in the daytime dramas *General Hospital* (1963) and *The Bold and the Beautiful* (1987). She played Eunice on the sitcom *One on One* (2001–). Among her TV film credits are *Up, Up and Away* (2000), *Incognito* (1999), *Gia* (1998), *Eyes of Terror* (1994), and *Corey: For the People* (1977).

PROFILES IN COURAGE (*NBC, 1964–1965*). Each episode of this anthology series centered on an American in history who had displayed extraordinary courage and character. The dramatic series was adapted from President John F. Kennedy's book of the same title. The TV series had been in the planning stage for years before the assassination, and Kennedy had urged strongly that producers include heroes that were not included in the book. **Robert Hooks** starred as young Frederick Douglass, the abolitionist leader, journalist, and statesman. Hooks said that Douglass was the only black profiled in the series and that "the NAACP and black organizations and leaders campaigned to get a black hero included."

PROFOUNDLY NORMAL (*CBS, February 9, 2003*). This fact-based TV film told the story of a mentally challenged couple, Donna and Ricardo Thornton, who were unexpectedly released from a government institution and had to learn, with great difficulty, to live in the real world. **Delroy Lindo** and Kirstie Alley were the stars.

PROUD FAMILY, THE (*DIS, 2001– *). This animated series was about a middle-class African-American family. There was teenager Penny Proud (**Kyla Pratt**); her father, Oscar (**Tommy Davidson**), who was in the junk food business; her mother, Trudy (**Paula Jai**

Parker); her grandmother Suga Mama (**Jo Marie Payton**); and twin siblings Bee Bee and Cee Cee (Tara Strong was the voices of both). **Karen Malina White** was the voice of Dijonay. **Cedric the Entertainer** won an NAACP Image Award for his voice work for the character Uncle Bobby. Ralph P. Farquhar was executive producer. Solange Knowles performed the theme song.

PRYOR, RAIN. Rain Pryor (Richard's daughter) played T. J. Jones in the comedy series *Head of the Class* (1988–1991). She was a student in the one-hour drama on the *CBS Afterschool Special* "Frog Girl: The Jennifer Graham Story" in 1989.

PRYOR, RICHARD. Pryor headlined two series, *The Richard Pryor Show* (1977) and *Pryor's Place* (1984). Before getting his own series, he was a frequent variety show guest who made several appearances on *The Flip Wilson Show* and *The Tonight Show with Johnny Carson*. He also was a key entertainer telling stories in the special *Wattstax 1973*, which was aired in 2004. He won an **Emmy Award** for Outstanding Writing in Variety or Music as part of the writing team of the special *Lily* (Tomlin) in 1974. Pryor hosted *The Richard Pryor Special?* in 1977, *The Richard Pryor Special* in 1982, and the documentary *Hollywood: The Gift of Laughter* in 1982. He appeared in variety specials *The Lily Tomlin Show* in 1973, *Flip Wilson . . . Of Course* in 1974, and *Funny* in 1986. He also guest-starred in the tribute special *Sammy Davis Jr.'s 60th Anniversary Celebration* in 1990. He was honored in *The Apollo Hall of Fame* in 1993. In 1992, he was presented with the American Comedy Awards' Lifetime Achievement Honor. In 2003, he poked fun at his own illness (multiple sclerosis) in hosting the special *Richard Pryor: "I Ain't Dead Yet!!"*

PUBLIC EYE WITH BRYANT GUMBEL (*CBS, 1997–1998*). **Bryant Gumbel**, longtime anchor of *The Today Show*, was host of this newsmagazine. It was a difficult year to launch a newsmagazine because there were 10 on the air that fall; the competition was enormous. Gumbel's introduction and closing and his in-studio interviews were live, while most newsmagazines were not, even *Primetime Live*. However, the bulk of the show was taped segments of hard and soft news with various CBS reporters. Gumbel's interviews of celebrities like **Will Smith** and Hugh Hefner were reminiscent of Edward R. Murrow's *Person to Person* in the 1950s.

PUDD'NHEAD WILSON *(PBS, January 24, 1984)*. This drama on *American Playhouse* was based on Mark Twain's "The Tragedy of Pudd'nhead Wilson," an 1894 novel. The story, set in the 1800s on the banks of the Mississippi, is about a mulatto slave woman who looks white and whose infant son has a light complexion. To prevent his being sold, she switches the youngster with her master's white son. The boy born a slave goes to Yale and returns to behave as if he is superior to all—black and white. The white boy can neither read nor write, and he had the appearance and behavior of a slave. A murder 20 years later results in an unraveling of the switched identities. Ken Howard played Pudd'nhead, and Lise Hilboldt was the mother. Lansgton Hughes, writing about Twain's characters, said, "It was a period when most writers who included Negro characters in their work at all, were given to presenting the slave as ignorant and happy, the freed men of color as ignorant and miserable, and all Negroes as either comic servants on the one hand or dangerous brutes on the other. That Twain's characters in *Pudd'nhead Wilson* fall into none of these categories is a tribute to his discernment. . . . Twain shows how more than anything else, environment shapes the man." *See also* BIRACIAL CHARACTERS; STEREOTYPES.

PULLIAM, KESHIA KNIGHT. Keshia Knight Pulliam played Rudy, the youngest daughter on *The Cosby Show* (1984–1992). She guest-starred in the TV special *Andy Williams and the NBC Kids Search for Santa* in 1985. As an adult, she won a celebrity competition on *Fear Factor.*

PURLIE *(CBS, 1981)*. This Broadway musical, based on the Broadway play *Purlie Victorious*, written by **Ossie Davis**, starred **Robert Guillaume** as Purlie, **Melba Moore** as Lutiebelle, **Sherman Hemsley** as Gitlow, Rhetta Hughes as Aunt Missy, and **Clarice Taylor** as Idella. Set on a Georgia cotton plantation in the early days of the civil rights movement, Ol' Cap'n Cotchipee (Don Scardino) virtually holds his workers in slavery. Rev. Purlie, after fleeing the control of Ol' Cap'n, returns home to free his family and friends by any means necessary and tried to gain control of Big Bethel, the church where he plans to ascend to the pulpit and preach to the freed flock his philosophy of having "glory days before we are dead." In the meantime, the plantation workers were always insulting Ol' Cap'n, but he never understood the put downs. He also never knew that a revolt was brewing. **Linda Hopkins** led the song "Walk Him Up the Stairs." Pauletta Pearson (who later became Mrs. Denzel Washington) and Ted Ross (who later played the Cowardly Lion in *The Wiz*) were in the performing company. *See also* BROADWAY PLAYS AND MUSICALS.

– Q –

QUEEN LATIFAH (*SYN, 1999–2000*). Singer-actress **Queen Latifah** (née Dana Owens) hosted this talk show with numerous celebrities. Shaquille O'Neal, Puff Daddy, and Lauryn Hill were among them. A highlight of the series in November 2000 was a series of shows in which a young black man moved in with a white family for two weeks and a young white woman moved in with a black family for two weeks. One critic said, "It was a powerful lesson in race relations." In another show, Latifah went to school with a teenage girl who was considering dropping out because of her weight. Full-figured Latifah, admired by African-American teens, spoke to the students at the school about the problem. The girl subsequently lost weight and remained in school.

QUEENS OF COMEDY, THE (*SHO, January 27, 2001*). Laura Hayes, Adele Givens, **Sommore**, and **Mo'Nique** headlined this special with their monologues of topics—all from a female perspective—ranging from sex to money to relationships.

– R –

R.A.C.E., THE (*NBC, September 5–6, 1989*). An NBC News special, this two-part production took a look at race relations using the Racial Attitudes and Consciousness Exam. **Bryant Gumbel** was host, executive producer, and one of the writers. Six celebrity panelists from different walks of life were asked survey questions about racial attitudes in an effort to raise consciousness of television viewers. The questions were in the areas of work, neighborhood, school, informal social interaction, crime, and politics. The panelists were the following: writer **Maya Angelou**, National Football League quarterback John Elway, film director **Spike Lee**, home economist/businesswoman Martha Stewart, former White House Communications Director Pat Buchanan, and Boston University President John Silber. Two social scientists known for research on racial attitudes were also on the panel. Gumbel said that 13 million Americans watched the shows and that, to him, meant it was successful. Academics, like Columbia University Senior Research Scientist Eleanor Singer, said it was not possible to know whether the exercise raised consciousness of viewers, that viewers who watched might already be sympathetic.

RACE TO FREEDOM: THE UNDERGROUND RAILROAD (*FAM, February 19, 1994*). Before the Civil War, many slaves were prepared to risk their lives for a chance of freedom. This two-hour made-for-television film told the story of a group of slaves who while walking north endured harsh weather and slave catchers to escape from a brutal North Carolina plantation. They were assisted by the network of caring people, like Harriet Tubman, who make up the Underground Railroad. **Courtney Vance** was Thomas, and Janet Bailey was Sarah. **Alfre Woodard** was Harriet Tubman, **Tim Reid** was Frederick Douglas, and **Glynn Turman** was Solomon. *See also* AFRICAN-AMERICAN HISTORY MONTH; HISTORICAL EVENTS DRAMATIZED.

RAHN, MURIEL. A singer who appeared on Broadway in the 1920s, she appeared on *The Ed Sullivan Show* in 1951. She was born in 1911 and died in 1961.

RAID ON ENTEBBE (*NBC, January 9, 1977*). **Yaphet Kotto** starred as President Idi Amin of Uganda in this dramatization of the Israeli rescue of hostages during a Palestinian hijacking at the airport in Entebbe, Uganda, on July 4, 1976. Kotto was nominated for the **Emmy Award**. *See also* VICTORY AT ENTEBBE.

RAISIN IN THE SUN, A (*PBS, February 1, 1989*). This production of *American Playhouse* was adapted from the 1959 Broadway play by Lorraine Hansberry. It centered on a black family living in a housing project and hoping to raise money for a down payment for a house in a previously all white suburban neighborhood. It was the 1950s when many black families were doing just that. **Esther Rolle** played Lena Younger, family matriarch, who wanted a better life for her family. **Danny Glover** played the son, Walter Lee Younger, who wanted the money to start a business; he also was not eager to move where he might not be appreciated. Kim Yancey played Beneatha Younger, the daughter who was determined to go to medical school. Starletta DuPois played Ruth, Walter's pregnant wife. **Bill Duke** was director. Monica Collins of *USA Today* (January 31, 1989) said the cast was "excellent." Walter Goodman of the *New York Times* (February 1, 1989) said, "'Raisin' has lost some of its urgency." *See also* BROADWAY PLAYS AND MUSICALS.

RALPH, SHERYL LEE. Ralph had a regular role in the short-lived drama series *Foxfire* in 1985. She played Ginger St. James in the sitcom *It's a Living* from 1986 to 1989. She was the lead in the sitcom *New Attitude* in 1990, but it lasted only a few weeks. She was Etienne in the sitcom *Designing Women* in the 1992–1993 season. She was star George Forman's wife Maggie in the brief sitcom *George* in 1993. She was the stepmother, Dee, in the sitcom *Moesha* (1996–2000). Her television film credits include the following: *The Jennie Project* (2001), *Witch Hunt* (1994), *No Child of Mine: The Fight for Baby Jesse* (1993), and *The Neighborhood* (1982).

RANDOLPH, AMANDA. Randolph was the star of *The Laytons*, a 1948 sitcom, but since the program aired in a limited area, she was probably best known for her portrayal of the Kingfish's mother-in-law, Mama, on *Amos 'n' Andy* from 1951 to 1953. She was Louise, the housekeeper, on *Make Room for Daddy*, which was later called *The Danny Thomas Show*. She also appeared in *The Danny Thomas TV Family Reunion* in 1965. She was the sister of **Lillian Randolph** and was born in 1902 and died in 1967. *See also* DOMESTIC WORKERS IN THE 1950s, 1960s.

RANDOLPH, LILLIAN. Randolph played the recurring role of Madam Queen in *Amos 'n' Andy* in 1951–1953 and Birdie Bogle, the housekeeper, in the sitcom *The Great Gildersleeve* in 1955. Some television historians say she was one of the actresses playing **Beulah.** Others disagree. She definitely played the role on radio. In 1969–1970, she played the mother, Rose, in the sitcom *The Bill Cosby Show*, and she was Sister Sara in *Roots* in 1977. She was the sister of **Amanda Randolph.** She was born in 1915 and died in 1980. *See also* DOMESTIC WORKERS IN THE 1950s.

RAP ARTISTS WHO BECAME TV ACTORS. "American kids need leadership and wisdom. Rappers have no choice but to be more responsible, but in order to do that they have to live longer than 25 years. It's the first 30 years that are the hardest!" said **Quincy Jones.** "What I tell young musicians is how important it is to be in control of your musical destiny. Here are some standout examples in the younger generation who understand this: **Russell Simmons,** Dr. Dre, QDIII, Sean 'P. Diddy' Combs, Glen Ballard, Babyface, Wyclef Jean, Chuck D., **LL Cool J, Will Smith,** Timbaland, Shekespere, **Queen Latifah,** Damon and Darien Dash, Meryn Warren, Teddy Riley, and John Clayton." Some of these rappers and others have had success in television, among other venues. **Mos Def** starred in the 2004 TV film *Something the Lord Made* and was nominated for an **Emmy Award.** Will Smith, LL Cool J, and Queen Latifah have starred in sitcoms: *The Fresh Prince of Bel-Air*, *In the House*, and *Living Single*, respectively. Latifah had a talk show; Smith and Latifah have made their marks in feature films. **Ice-T** had a key role on the drama *Law and Order: Special Victims Unit*. Babyface became a producer of *Soul Food* on Showtime. Russell Simmons produced *Def Comedy Jam* and *Def Poetry Jam*. Eve starred in a film, *Barbershop*, and then a television series titled simply *Eve*. **Mekhi Phifer** played a key role in the drama *ER*.

RASHAD, AHMAD. Rashad joined NBC Sports in 1983 as a National Football League commentator and host of NBC's *Sports World*. He was weekend host and late night correspondent of the Olympic Games in Atlanta in 1996. He was one of the hosts of the Olympic Games in Barcelona and, in 1988, was studio anchor for the Seoul Olympics. He was a key contributor to coverage of the National Basketball Association since NBC began broadcasting it. He was host of the reality shows *Real TV* (1997), *Mole* (2001–2003), and *Celebrity Mole*; host of *Insport* (1989–1991), a sports magazine series; and host of *NBA Off the Court* on **BET**. He hosted the syndicated *Real TV* (1997).

RASHAD, PHYLICIA. Rashad (aka Phylicia Ayers-Allen) played Clare, **Bill Cosby**'s wife, on *The Cosby Show* (1984–1992) and Ruth, Bill Cosby's wife, on *Cosby* (1996–2000). Prior to *The Cosby Show*, she played Courtney Wright on the daytime drama *One Life to Live*. She guest-starred in the variety special *Nell Carter—Never Too Old to Dream* in 1986, *Texas 150—A Celebration* in 1986, *Our Kids and the Best of Everything* and *Superstars and Their Moms* in 1987, and *The Debbie Allen Special* in 1989. In TV films, she had roles in the following: as Eliza in *Uncle Tom's Cabin* (1987), as Lynne in *False Witness* (1989), as Aunt Polly in *Polly* (1989) and *Polly: Comin' Home!* (1990), Janice Grant in *Jailbirds* (1991), Mayor Turner in *Hallelujah* (1993), Gladys Johnson in *David's Mother*, Dr. Hale in *The Possession of Michael D.* (1995), Detective Kate Jacobs in *The Babysitter's Seduction*, Desiree in *Free of Eden*, and Elizabeth in *The Old Settler*. She was executive producer of *The Old Settler*.

RASULALA, THALMUS. Rasulala (née Jack Crowder) played Lt. Jack Neal in the daytime drama series *One Life to Live* (1968). In TV films and miniseries, he played Eddie Nugent in *The Bait* (1973); Ned in *The Autobiography of Miss Jane Pittman* (1974); Omoro, Kunta's father, in *Roots* (1977); Lt. Gordon in *The President's Mistress* (1978); and Snake in *The Sophisticated Gents* in 1981. He had a key role in *For Us the Living: The Medgar Evers Story* (1983), *The Jerk Too* (1984), *My Past Is My Own* (1989), *The Preppie Murder* (1989), and *Blind Vengeance* (1990). In series television, he was Raj and Dee's father in the sitcom *What's Happening!!!* (1976–1977), Capt. Boltz in the 1989 version of *Dragnet*, and Tangeneva in the daytime drama *General Hospital*. He was born in 1939 and died of a heart attack in 1991.

RATINGS. The fate of television programming pivots on ratings. Ratings set the rates that a network can charge advertisers and thereby create a complicated intersecting relationship between show content and advertiser desires. The relationship is particularly important with regard to entertainment shows, but television news programming also must deal with and account for fluctuations in ratings for news broadcasts. Part of Nielsen Media Research, the Nielsen TV rating service calculates television viewership on a national scale. Researchers use a sample of viewers to estimate how many people watch a show. According to company literature, information is collected through specially designed meters and diaries (among other research tools and methods) used in households that agree to participate in the Nielsen sample.

Nielsen technology and sampling techniques also allow researchers to calculate viewership by racial and ethnic background. For example, the company specifically examines ratings for African-American and Hispanic audiences (for recent research on these audiences, see www.nielsenmedia.com/ethnicmeasure/). Researchers have found that shows popular with mainstream audiences often are not popular with African-American audiences. In other words, mainstream and African-American audiences often do not watch the same programs. For example, while NBC's *Friends* rated as the top comedy and the second most popular show in mainstream households in the opening months of the 1998–1999 season, the same show placed 91st among African-American television viewers. Meanwhile, *The Steve Harvey Show* ranked first for African-American audiences but placed 118th in mainstream households.

In November 2004, the top 10 among African-American viewers included seven series with black lead stars or black casts: *Girlfriends* (no. 1), *Half & Half* (no. 3), *Eve* (no. 4), *America's Next Top Model* (no. 6), *One on One* (no. 7), *All of Us* (no. 8), and *Second Time Around* (no. 9). Not one of those seven series (all UPN series) was in the top 10 among all viewers. The only shows in the top 10 of both lists were *NFL Monday Night Football* (no. 5 among black viewers and no. 8 among all viewers) and *CSI* (no. 10 among black viewers and no. 1 among all viewers). *The American Music Awards*, with numerous black participants, was number 2 among African-American viewers and not in the top 10 among all viewers. The Nielsen Research Company's estimate was made of more than 13 million black households in the United States and nearly 18 million viewers over the age of two.

Low ratings performance may lead to tactics such as changing a show through casting or story lines to attract viewers, moving the show to a different day or time slot in hopes of establishing an audience, and, in some cases, cancellation of the show. Tyus (1999), following focus group and individual interview sessions with African-American viewers, found that "African Americans feel overlooked and disappointed when their programming choices are eliminated for no apparent reason, particularly when European American oriented programs with the same premises are hyped and renewed." Scholars and media watchers frequently cite the **Tim Reid** comedy *Frank's Place* and the drama *I'll Fly Away* starring **Regina Taylor** as among shows falling victim to frequent schedule changes in pursuit of high ratings and a larger audience. Reid told *Jet* magazine that CBS moved *Frank's Place* seven times in one season, making finding the show difficult for fans or potential new viewers. "If they moved *Cosby* [*The Cosby Show*] that much it would drop out of the ratings," *Jet* quoted Reid.

In some cases, shows canceled by one network for poor ratings performance or lack of audience appeal may find new life on other networks. For example, ABC canceled *The Hughleys* after two seasons (1998–2000). UPN picked up the show for its 2000 season and kept it for two seasons. Other shows that jumped from one of the big three networks to a smaller, niche network to complete their runs include *In the House*, moving from NBC (1995–1996) to UPN (1996–1998); *Sister, Sister*, moving from ABC (1994–1995) to the WB (1995–1998); and *Minor Adjustments*, moving from NBC (September–November 1995) to UPN (January–August 1996). Interestingly, two shows moved from Fox to UPN: *The PJs*, an animated show featuring the voices of **Eddie Murphy** and **Loretta Devine**, and *Between Brothers* (Smith-Shomade 2002). Among the more unique moves was that of *I'll Fly Away* from network to public television. NBC canceled the hour-long drama in 1993, and the show finished its run on PBS in a 90-minute episode that fall. In a news article about the cancellation, Associated Press writer Lynn Elber quoted Sam Weisman, a television producer, about the end of the series. "To think, in our society, out of the hundreds of hours of television, there's not room for an hour or two a week for something that beautiful." (April 26, 1993). *See also* CEDRIC THE ENTERTAINER PRESENTS.

RAVEN-SYMONE. Raven-Symone (aka Raven) began with a starring role in *That's So Raven* in 2003. She starred as Galleria Garibaldi in the TV film *The Cheetah Girls* (2003). She was a singer on the special *Motown 45* in 2004. She was discovered as Olivia, a Huxtable grandchild, on *The Cosby Show* from 1989 to 1992. She played Nicole on *Hangin' with Mr. Cooper* from 1993 to 1997. She guest-starred in the tribute *The Chipmunks—Rockin' through the Decades* in 1990, *The Muppets at Walt Disney World* in 1990, and *Muhammad Ali's 50th Birthday Celebration* in 1992.

RAWLS, LOU. Although he had made a name for himself as a singer, Rawls is best known on television for hosting the *Lou Rawls Parade of Stars*, the annual telethon for the United Negro College Fund. The telethon has raised more than $100 million. In 2004, Rawls celebrated his 25th year as host of the broadcast. Rawls was a regular on the summer variety series *Dean Martin Presents* in 1969. Rawls hosted the variety specials *The Lou Rawls Show* in 1971 and *The Lou Rawls Special* in 1977. In 1980, Rawls and other celebrities who were alumni of the Apollo Theater paid tribute to the Harlem landmark in *Uptown*. Rawls also did voice-overs for *Here Comes Garfield* in 1982 and for subsequent Garfield animated specials. He was one of the celebrities at *The 50th Presidential Inaugural Gala* held two days prior to the inauguration of President Ronald Reagan in 1985. He hosted the *Budweiser Showdown* in 1989. Rawls sang on numerous variety specials including the following: *The Bob Hope Special* in 1968, *The Engelbert Humperdinck Special* in 1971, *Tennessee Ernie Ford's White Christmas* in 1972, *The Stars and Stripes Show* in 1975, *The Secret World of the Very Young* in 1984, *Happy Birthday, Hollywood* in 1987, and *The Songwriter's Hall of Fame* in 1989. He was on the bill of *Aretha Franklin: In Performance at the White House* in 1994. Rawls also played Harold Logan in *Don King: Only in America* in 1997 and was a spokesperson for Colonial Penn Insurance.

RAY CHARLES: 50 YEARS OF MUSIC, UH-HUH (*FOX, October 6, 1991*). This 90-minute special was a musical celebration of the career of singer **Ray Charles**. **Whoopi Goldberg**, **Quincy Jones**, and **Robert Townsend** were hosts of the show taped in September 1991 to benefit the Starlight and Starbright Pavilions, nonprofit organizations that granted wishes to seriously ill children. Among other entertainers were **Bill Cosby**, **Gladys Knight**, **James Ingram**, **Stevie Wonder**, Michael Bolton, Gloria Estefan, Paul McCartney, and Willie Nelson. The "Uh-Huh" in the special's title originated from Charles's commercials for Pepsi Cola. Ray Charles Jr. was producer.

RAY CHARLES: THE GENIUS OF SOUL (*PBS, January 3, 1992*). Charles was profiled in this documentary, which celebrated his genius in gospel, blues, rhythm and blues, and jazz.

RAYCOLE, JAZZ. A dancer since she was 22 months old, Raycole was cast as Claire in the sitcom *My Wife and Kids* in 2001.

RAY, GENE ANTHONY. Ray was a dancer who played Leroy, one of the regular characters on *Fame* (1982–1987). He died on November 14, 2003, of complications from a stroke. He was 41.

RAY, MARGUERITE. Ray played Redd Foxx's love interest, Evelyn, in the *Sanford and Son* spin-off *Sanford* (1980–1981). She was Mamie in *The Young and the Restless* (1980–1989). She had a recurring role in *Dynasty* as Jane Mathews (1989).

READING RAINBOW (*PBS, 1983– *). This half-hour daily program hosted by **LeVar Burton** was developed to encourage children ages four to eight to enjoy books. The show won numerous awards including **Emmy Awards** and a Peabody. A magazine-style format, the show featured animation, music, dancing, and interviews with popular personalities. A popular feature was "Kid-on-the Street," in which real kids expressed their attitudes on various issues. The show traveled to interesting locations and shows kids scenes like Hilo, Hawaii, and its erupting volcano. Also featured were various cultures around the world. The series suffered a financial setback in 2003 when corporate sponsors, tightening their budgets, dropped the series, but it did return for a 20th season after Burton made an impassioned plea during the 2003 Daytime Emmy Awards and PBS made a two-year monetary commitment to the series. Unlike other children's shows, the series did not have merchandising of toys and other paraphernalia to help pay production costs.

REALITY TELEVISION. For most of television's years, viewers watched to escape from reality, then in the late 1990s, so-called reality television began to be the prevailing genre. The definition varies. Most refer to reality TV as primarily unscripted programs without professional actors or performers. Most reality programs are competitions (*American Idol*, *Last Comic Standing*), and many of the competitions also include surveillance (*Big Brother, Survivor, The Apprentice*) where cameras are preset to record on videotape all conversations and actions. One contestant is usually eliminated each week. All these could have been called "game shows," but that genre was linked to shows from earlier decades. Other reality shows (some of them surveillance based) were actually documentary series like *Extreme Makeover*, *College Hill*, *The Osbornes*, and *The Real World*. Another type of surveillance show was the show *Cheaters* (2004–), in which hidden cameras spy on spouses suspected of being unfaithful, then the host helps the wronged spouse stage a confrontation, also on camera. An early surveillance-based reality-type show was *An American Family* in 1973. It was a much-talked-about PBS show about the Louds, a white suburban family that lived with cameras filming its every move, including Mrs. Loud asking her husband for a divorce on the March 8, 1973, show.

The Academy of Television Arts and Sciences included reality programs in its 2004 **Emmy Awards**. There were two Emmys in the genre: Outstanding Reality Program (won by *Queer Eye for the Straight Guy*) and Outstanding Reality Competition Program (won by *The Amazing Race*). The surveillance reality program is less work for actors and writers but more work for editors and, of course, no work for actors. In 2004, the makeover shows were abundant. Makeovers were done on people and on residences. Some of them were *Extreme Makeover, Extreme Makeover: Home Edition, Ambush Makeover, The Swan, Merge,* and *Makeover Manor.*

Participants in the reality programs became semicelebrities for a few minutes. Andrejevic (2004), in researching the reality genre, said the appeal seems to be that "one of the promises of the genre is that you don't have to be a professional actor or entertainer—being on a reality show is work that anyone can do. Indeed, this is precisely what makes it easier for fans to identify with cast members." In other words, people can see themselves in the reality program, whereas they cannot in scripted, dramatized programs.

Most reality programs have one or two African-American contestants depending on the format of the show. Deggans (2004), in the *St. Petersburg Times,* said the reality competitions portray "the saga of the assimilated minority vs. the non-assimilated one." He found that the assimilated minority is adept at fitting in with white competitors and blends in, while the unassimilated player "sticks out like a burr on a silk-covered bed, constantly conflicting with the larger group until they are isolated, demonized and eventually ejected." He cited assimilated easygoing Gervase and unassimilated irritable Ramona as examples on *Survivor* and assimilated Kwame and unassimilated Omarosa as examples on the first edition of *The Apprentice.* Similar comparisons occurred on various editions of *Big Brother* and the second edition of *The Apprentice*, in which Stacy was quickly labeled "crazy" and Kevin was accepted. Deggans made no suggestions as to whether the shows recruit candidates likely to be rejected or accepted.

REAL PEOPLE (*NBC, 1979–1984*). This was an early reality series, which at that time was called "human interest." There were various hosts who went through the studio audience looking for people with interesting and unusual occupations and pastimes. The hosts also went on location to find such people and brought filmed looks at these "real people." One of the hosts was black teenage comedian **Byron Allen**, who had been discovered on mike night at a Los Angeles comedy club and performed successfully on *The Tonight Show with Johnny Carson*. Allen made a success of being a celebrity interviewer and producer of syndicated series. *See also* LONG-RUNNING SERIES; SERIES WITH ONE BLACK SUPPORTING ACTOR/PEFORMER BEFORE 1980.

REAL WORLD, THE (*MTV, 1992–*). This series was one of the early 1990s versions of the so-called reality shows. A kind of documentary, it followed seven youth—all in their twenties—who have agreed to live together for three months. They were all strangers to each other when they became roommates. Their whole names were never revealed to viewers throughout the TV season. Cameras followed them wherever they went, except to the bathroom, both inside and outside the apartment. Unlike Big Brother, which would debut in 2000, these residents could and did leave the house and live their lives. Also, they were not voted out by either viewers or housemates. Most of the residents were seeking success in show business, so the viewer saw them auditioning and job hunting in addition to living together.

Real World I (1992). This took place in a New York City apartment in the Soho district. There were two black roommates. Heather B, a hip-hop and rap artist, spent a lot of her *Real World* time getting her first album recorded. Kevin, a poet, writer, and educator, was the oldest of the roommates, and he struggled with issues facing African Americans. He was sensitive to the others but had trouble becoming connected to them.

Real World II (1993). The site was a beach house in Venice, California. Tami worked as an AIDS care specialist helping her clients cope with the processes of getting insurance companies to pay their medical bills. She moonlighted as part of an all-girl rhythm-and-blues group and became pregnant while in the series. David was a stand-up comedian who had made an appearance on *In Living Color* and also enjoyed some success in Los Angeles clubs.

Real World III (1994). This was set in San Francisco, but for the first time, four of the seven roommates came from other places of the United States and had to find jobs. Also, in this season, one of the roommates, Pedro, had AIDS and died later that year. The African-American roommate was Mohammad, who was lead singer of a local band, Midnight Voices, and also did makeovers at a cosmetics store and worked at his father's Bay Area dance club.

Real World IV (1995). This was set in London, and the participants came from England, Germany, Australia, and the United States. During the season, they took a trip to Africa. Their culturally diverse backgrounds and experiences caused heated conversations. A singer/songwriter, Sharon, was the talkative member of the bunch who during the season had surgery to remove nodules on her vocal cords.

Real World V (1996). This took place in a Miami Beach dockside house. Cynthia was the black roommate who worked as a waitress to put herself through San Jose State. She was excited to go to Miami, for she had never been in the southeastern section of the country.

Real World VI (1997). This was set in Boston in a converted firehouse. Kamelah and Syrus were the black residents. Kamelah was a sophomore at Stanford who was very strong willed and outspoken. Syrus had been a basketball player at the University of Hawaii and coached youth basketball.

Real World VII (1998). This was set in a Seattle waterfront loft. All the roommates worked at a radio station hosting a live radio show. Stephen was the black roommate who had been raised by a Black Muslim mother but turned Jewish when he was 15. He was a business major at the University of California at Berkeley.

Real World VIII (1999). This brought the seven residents to Honolulu, where they ran their own café and performance space on Waikiki. Teck had a lot of energy and humor and was a ladies' man whose goal was to become an entertainer and then go into politics.

Real World IX (1999–2000). The Old World charm of a large Greek revival mansion in New Orleans was the set, and the task of the roommates was to host their own cable access television show. Melissa was witty and admitted that she did not get along well with women. She loved eating, drinking, sleeping, personal hygiene, and giggling, in that order. David had high expectations for himself—physically and mentally—and he wanted to be the first black president of the United States.

Real World X (2000–2001). For the second time, the setting was New York. Intelligent, witty Coral spoke her mind and observed people around her. Malil was biracial and was obsessed with music; he was a popular deejay in the San Francisco Bay Area. Nicole was a senior at Morris Brown College in Atlanta with a 4.0 grade-point average.

Real World XI (2001–2002). Chicago was the setting. Aneesa, an admitted lesbian of mixed heritage, was determined and strong, sensitive, and compassionate. Theo was an outspoken ladies' man, but to him, school and church were priorities. The experience was his first in a diverse environment.

Real World XII (2002–2003). In Las Vegas, handsome Alton played the violin and loved the outdoors. He had grown up a Navy brat and had some unresolved pain from a family tragedy. Arissa had brains and beauty, was black and Italian, and was known to put others before herself. Irulean was also mixed race; she was not afraid of conflict, and she was studying at the Parsons School of Design.

Real World XIII (2003). The roommates lived in Paris. Adam, from Beverly Hills, graduated from Stanford with a degree in communications and aspired to being a lyricist.

Real World XIV (2004). The setting was San Diego, California. Jacquese was the African-American cast member who was teased in his past for looking like Urkel in *Family Matters*. He had a quick wit and a quick tongue.

Real World XV (2004–2005). Living in Philadelphia, Karamo and Shavonda were the black roommates. Shavonda, 21, was from California, where she worked at Hooters and attended Grossmont Community College. Karamo, 23, was originally from Houston and attended Florida A&M as a business administration major. Karamo admitted he was gay in the second episode, and Shavonda flirted with white roommate Landon.

Real World XVI (2005). Set in Austin, Texas, the African-American roommate was Nehemiah, a nineteen-year-old from Rancho Cucamonga, California.

REBOUND: THE LEGEND OF EARL "THE GOAT" MANI-GAULT (*HBO, November 23, 1996*). Manigault was a talented basketball player who never hit the big time because of his drug use. Yet he was successful at teaching youth in Harlem about the how-tos of basketball and of life. Stars were **Don Cheadle** as Manigault, **Forest Whitaker** as Mr. Russell, **James Earl Jones** as Dr. McDuffie, **Glynn Turman** as Coach Powell, **Loretta Devine** as Miss Mary, **Nicole Ari Parker** as Wanda, **Eriq LaSalle** as Diego, **Clarence Williams III** as Coach Pratt, and Colin Cheadle as Young Earl. **Kareem Abdul-Jabbar** appeared as himself. LaSalle made his debut as director. *See also* ATHLETES' BIOPICS.

REDD FOXX SHOW, THE (*ABC, 1977*). The popular comedian played a widower named Al Hughes, who owned a black inner-city coffee shop/newsstand. Al was rearing a 15-year-old street urchin, Toni (Pamela Segall), in the first weeks of the series. Then Segall was gone, and Al's outspoken ex-wife Felicia (**Beverly Todd**) joined the cast. **Nathaniel Taylor**, who played Rollo in *Sanford and Son*, briefly played Jim-Jam, a similar character in this sitcom. Then he was replaced with **Theodore Wilson** in the same role. Others in the cast were **Sinbad** as Byron Lightfoot and Iron Jaw Wilson as Duds. *Variety* (January 29, 1985) said, "Foxx is Foxx, with an appeal that so far transcends the lack of laugh lines. . . . All in all, the series does not look too promising." *Variety* was right; the series lasted two months. *See also* FOXX, REDD.

REDD FOXX SPECIAL, THE (*ABC, April 4, 1978*). The comedian was the headliner in this 90-minute variety special also featuring, in skits, **Slappy White**, Susan Anton, Red Buttons, Lorne Greene, Bill Saluga, and Rip Taylor. *See also* FOXX, REDD.

REDEMPTION: THE STAN "TOOKIE" WILLIAMS STORY (*FX, April 11, 2004*). **Jamie Foxx** starred as Stan "Tookie" Williams, who, as a troubled youth, founded the notorious Crips street gang. As an adult murderer on death row at San Quentin, Williams authored inspirational books as well as a "peace protocol" for warring gangs. He earned nominations for the Nobel Prize seven times. Four times he was nominated for literature for writing books to encourage children to avoid joining gangs. The other three nominations were for peace. **Lynn Whitfield** played Barbara Becnal, a journalist writing a book about gangs, who was instrumental in helping him get his writing career started. **C. C. H. Pounder** and Brenden Jefferson also had roles. **Vondie Curtis-Hall** was director. FX made 5,000 copies of the film for distribution to schools and community groups. Executive producer Rudy Langlais called Foxx's performance "greater than spectacular."

RED HOT RHYTHM AND BLUES (*ABC, May 20, 1987*). A musical special, this production starred **Diana Ross**, **Billy Dee Williams**, Etta James, **Little Richard**, and Bernadette Peters.

REECE, BEASLEY. Former National Football League player Reece joined CBS Sports as lead sports anchor for CBS 3's *Eyewitness News* in 1998.

REED, ALAINA. Reed (aka Alaina Reed-Hall) played Rose Holloway, the landlord on the sitcom *227* (1985–1990). She had a key role in the 1978 black version of the musical *Cinderella*, *Cindy*. She played Olivia on *Sesame Street* (1976–1988) and had a recurring role as Ms. Hall in *Harry and the Hendersons* (1991–1993), a series that starred her husband, **Kevin Peter Hall**, until he died in 1991. She was in the TV films *The Cherokee Kid* (1996) and *Me and the Kid* (1993). She was in the special *Eubie* in 1981.

REED, TRACY. Reed played Corie Bratter in the 1970–1971 sitcom *Barefoot in the Park*. Before and after, she was a member of the repertory company on *Love American Style* (1969–1970 and 1972–1974). She played Charlotte Anderson in *Knots Landing* (1990–1991). She had a key role in the TV film *Top Secret* (1978) and *Cocaine and Blue Eyes* (1983).

REESE, DELLA. Reese was the first woman of any race to guest-host *The Tonight Show*. In musical variety, she starred in . . . *And Beautiful*, a special spotlighting performances of black entertainers. She had her own variety series *The Della Reese Show* (1969–1970) and hosted *The Blues: In Performance at the White House* in 1999. In sitcoms, she had key roles in *Chico and the Man* in 1976–1978 and in *The Royal Family* (1991–1992). In drama, she had a role in *Roots: The Next Generations* in 1979, played Aunt Faith in the special *The Gift of Amazing Grace* (1986), and starred in *The Moving of Sophia Myles* (2001), a TV movie. She had a key role in the drama *Having Our Say* (1999) and a starring role in *Touched by an Angel* from 1994 to 2002. She starred in the made-for-television movie *Anya's Bell* in 1999. She guest-starred in variety specials *Dinah Shore Special—Like Hep* in 1969, *Burt and the Girls* in 1973, and *Holiday Greetings from The Ed Sullivan Show* in 1992. Reese appeared in the TV special *The National Love, Sex and Marriage Test* in 1978. Reese has the sad distinction of being one of the few, if not the only actor, who was a regular on two series when the star died. She was in *Chico and the Man* when Freddie Prinze took his own life in 1977, and she was in *The Royal Family* when star **Redd Foxx** died on the set of an apparent heart attack in 1992. Both deaths were reportedly drug related.

REEVES, MARTHA. Once the lead singer of Martha and the Vandellas, Reeves made a solo guest appearance in the special *Flip Wilson . . . Of Course* in 1974. She sang in Super Bowl XXXIII's tribute to 40 years of Motown.

REID, DAPHNE MAXWELL. Reid (aka Daphne Reid and Daphne Maxwell-Reid) and her husband, **Tim Reid**, hosted the *CBS Summer Playhouse* (1987), a lineup of the network's unsold pilots and promotions of their upcoming series *Frank's Place*, in which she played

Hannah Griffin (1987–1988). She played opposite her husband again in the detective drama *Snoops* (1989–1990). She played Vivian Banks during the last three seasons of *The Fresh Prince of Bel-Air* (1993–1996). Reid had a key role in the dramedy *Lincs* (1998–2000). She starred in the children's program *Alley Cats Strikes!* (2000).

REID, JACQUE. Before becoming anchor of the *BET Nightly News,* Reid anchored the morning news at the CNN Headline News network. Prior to that, she worked in local news in Houston. In her career, she has interviewed President George W. Bush, **Jesse Jackson,** John Glenn, Charles Barkley, Garth Brooks, and **Patti LaBelle.**

REID, TIM. Tim Reid was a regular on the summer series *The Marilyn McCoo and Billy Davis Show* (1977) and *The Richard Pryor Show* (1977). He played Gordon Sims (aka Venus Flytrap) on *WKRP in Cincinnati* (1978–1982), Michael Horne in the sitcom *Teachers Only* (1983), and a detective, Marcel "Downtown" Brown, in *Simon & Simon* (1983–1987). He and his wife, **Daphne Maxwell Reid,** co-hosted the *CBS Summer Playhouse* (1987–1988). As they introduced unsold CBS pilots, they also plugged their then-upcoming fall sitcom *Frank's Place* (1987–1988). The two also headlined the detective drama series *Snoops* (1989–1990). Reid narrated the informational series *Save Our Streets* (1995–1999). He starred in the sitcoms *Lincs* (1998) and *Sister, Sister* (1994–1999). He had a key role in the TV film *Race to Freedom: The Underground Railroad* (1994). He starred in the children's program *Alley Cats Strikes!* (2000). He also appeared in variety specials *Little Lulu* (1978), *You Can't Take It with You* (1979), and *Battle of the Network Stars* (1981) and in the documentary *Memories Then and Now* (1988). He joined the cast of *That '70s Show* in 2004 to play Hyde's (Danny Masterson, white actor) long-lost father; Hyde didn't know his father was black.

REIGN OF AMELIKA JO, THE (*NBC, October 12, 1954*). This 30-minute drama was aired on the dramatic anthology series *Fireside Theatre.* It is noteworthy because it had a cast made up largely of blacks and, even more rare, Asians. The central cast was **James Edwards, Nick Stewart, Johnny Lee,** and Keye Luke. The story was set in the South Pacific during World War II. Some historians say this was the first primarily black drama to air on national television. *See also* TELEVISION PIONEERS.

REUBEN, GLORIA. Reuben played Jeanie Boulet in the drama series *ER* (1994–1999). She portrayed Lisa Fabrizzi in the drama series *The Agency* (2001–2003) and had a key role in "Little John" (2002) on *Hallmark Hall of Fame*. Her TV film credits include the following: *Deep in My Heart* (1999) and *Sara* (1999). Her miniseries credits include *Sole Survivor* (2000), *The Feast of All Saints* (2001), and *Salem Witch Trials* (2002).

REVUE WITH LAURYN HILL (*MTV,* October 14, 1998). Singer **Lauryn Hill** was the focal point of a show featuring half documentary and half performance. She spoke about her career and her inspiration. He was also a sitcom writer.

REY, RENALDO. Comedian Rey played a role in the TV film *Final Shot: The Hank Gathers Story* (1992) and was a regular on *ComicView*.

REYNOLDS, HAROLD. A former professional baseball player, a second baseman, Reynolds joined ESPN in 1996. His credits include anchoring *College World Series* and *Baseball Tonight*.

REYNOLDS, JAMES. Reynolds played Abe Carver on the daytime drama *Days of Our Lives* for 21 years. When his character was killed in 2003, Reynolds was the African-American performer with the longest run on daytime dramas. He noted proudly, "Abe was a minority character of tremendous integrity who was not working for somebody else. He was in charge—and that meant a lot to the African-American audience."

RHAMES, VING. Rhames won a Golden Globe Award in 1997 for his portrayal of the title role in the TV film *Don King: Only in America*. He is one of the more memorable Golden Globe winners because when he ascended the stage to pick up the statuette, he insisted on giving it to Jack Lemmon (who was one of his competitors for the award). Other TV film credits are the following: *Sins of the Father* (2002), *Little John*

(2002), RFK (2002), *American Tragedy* (2000), *Holiday Heart* (2000), *Ed McBain's 87th Precinct: Lightning* (1995), *The Way West* (1995), *Deadly Whispers* (1995), *Rising Son* (1990), *When You Remember Me* (1990), and *Go Tell It on the Mountain* (1985).

RHAPSODY AND SONG—A TRIBUTE TO GEORGE GERSHWIN (*PBS, May 9, 1981*). Sarah Vaughan won the **Emmy Award** in the 1980–1981 season for her performance on this musical variety special.

RHODES, HARI. Rhodes played Mike, the medical intern, on *Daktari* from 1966 to 1969. He starred in the 1969 TV film pilot *Deadlock* and the subsequent series *The Protectors* (1972–1973) as a black district attorney who locked horns with a white cop as they made efforts to solve crimes together. He was Horace Speare in the 1973 film *Trouble Comes to Town*, Seki in the TV film *Matt Helm* (1975), and Dr. Belding in *The Return of Joe Forrester* (1975). In 1978, he played Tazwell Robinson in *A Woman Called Moses*.

RHYMES, BUSTA. Rhymes joined the Bob Marley family for *One Love: The Bob Marley All-Star Family Tribute* in 1999.

RHYTHM COUNTRY AND BLUES (*PBS, February 28, 1994*). This show looked at similarities and mutual influences of country music and rhythm and blues. Among the participants were **Natalie Cole**, **Al Green**, **B. B. King**, Aaron Neville, Lyle Lovett, and Trisha Yearwood.

RIBEIRO, ALFONSO. Ribeiro began his career on Broadway in the title role of *The Tap Dance Kid*. His first television acting job was in a PBS drama *Oye Willie* when he was eight. He became recognizable as the kid who danced with Michael Jackson in the Pepsi commercials in 1994. He was Alfonso Spears, Ricky Schroder's buddy, in the sitcom *Silver Spoons* from 1984 to 1986, and he was **Will Smith**'s cousin, Carlton, in *Fresh Prince of Bel-Air* from 1990 to 1996. In that sitcom, he was famous for being a terrible dancer, which was difficult for him to do with his considerable dance talents. He played Rocky in *John Grin's Christmas* in 1986. He had a recurring role on

Magnum P.I. as Kenny (1986), and he hosted *Your Big Break*, a game show. Ribeiro also guest-starred in numerous television specials: *Andy Williams and the NBC Kids Search for Santa* in 1985, *Circus of the Stars* in 1985, *The Wildest West Show of the Stars* in 1986, and *Happy Birthday, Hollywood* in 1987. He also appeared in the drama special *Home Sweet Homeless* in 1987. He became a director. *See also* CHILD ACTORS/PERFORMERS WHO MAINTAINED SUCCESS AS ADULTS IN SHOW BUSINESS.

RICHARD, LITTLE. *See* LITTLE RICHARD.

RICHARD PRYOR: I AIN'T DEAD YET!! (*CC, November 30, 2003*). **Richard Pryor** was saluted in this special, which took a look at his life and career through clips of his sometimes daring performances and interviews with comedy stars. Pryor, who was 62 at the time and a victim of multiple sclerosis, had made that statement, "I have MS, but I ain't dead yet"—thus the title. Among the entertainers were **Jamie Foxx, Whoopi Goldberg, D. L. Hughley**, and George Lopez.

RICHARD PRYOR SHOW, THE (*NBC, September 13–October 18, 1977*). After **Richard Pryor** had been a hit on his own specials, on other entertainers' specials and series, on *Saturday Night Live*, on comedy albums, in Las Vegas casinos, and in films, it was apparent that a television series would be forthcoming. NBC somehow contracted Pryor to a series. There were several problems. The first was that the series, starring a man known for profanity and blue jokes, was scheduled at 8:00 P.M., television's family hour. The network censors would never let him be who he was. Second, at a press conference to announce the series, Pryor did not seem to know he was doing a series. Just prior to meeting the press, he said to then NBC publicist Kathi Fearn-Banks, "But I'm not doing a series, just a series of specials." "No," he was told, "you're doing a series." Once at a meeting with writers, he said, "I can't do this. I don't want to be on TV." He was convinced that he could do four shows, not the 10 in the contract. However, Pryor and the network could never agree. He had problems with the broadcast standards department (censors) when it refused to air a one-minute sketch that joked about how doing a TV show was emasculating him. In the sketch, he appeared on the stage in a bodysuit that made him look like a naked man with no masculine anatomical organs. He did not like having to do a second show without knowing the public reaction to the first. Mostly, he wanted out of the contract; he had movie offers. Finally, the four shows were completed. Real Pryor fans thought the show was too tame even though some outrageous segments remained. Some of the NBC affiliates would not air the show because of offensive material. NBC announced the show was canceled because of poor ratings. Pryor announced he was canceling the contract because he was not given artistic freedom. It was also announced that Pryor would do specials, what he wanted to do in the beginning, but the specials were never developed. Supporting players **Paul Mooney** (also a writer), **Marsha Warfield**, **Tim Reid**, Robin Williams, Sandra Bernhardt, and others were in the series that was not a series.

RICHARD PRYOR SPECIAL?, THE (*NBC, May 5, 1977*). The comedian hosted this, his first comedy special. Guest stars were **Maya Angelou**, Mike Evans, and John Belushi, **LaWanda Page**, and the Pips without Gladys Knight. Pryor played his alcoholic character, Willie; Idi Amin Dada; and a greedy television evangelist, the Rev. James L. White, whose till overflowed when he sought funds for a Back to Africa campaign. The Pips performed their hits without Gladys Knight. In a Willie skit, the drunkard gets into a hilarious brawl in a bar. Then, when Willie gets home to his wife (Angelou), the skit is suddenly very serious. Billy Ingram, a TVParty.com critic said, "This is something you have to see for yourself, truly one of those moments that remind you of the power that television can have." The reviews and ratings were positive, so positive that NBC started making plans for a Richard Pryor series, which is another story. *See also* RICHARD PRYOR SHOW.

RI'CHARD, ROBERT. Ri'chard played Todd McLemore on *Alley Cats Strike!* (2000–), Arnaz on *One on One* (2001–), and Bobby on *Cousin Skeeter* (1998–2000).

RICHARDS, BEAH. Richards played Rose Kincaid (1970–1971) in *The Bill Cosby Show*, Aunt Ethel in *Sanford and Son* (1972),

Grandma in the dramatic TV film *Just an Old Sweet Song* in 1976, and Cynthia Parker in *Roots: The Next Generations* in 1979. She was one of the performers in the drama special *Zora Is My Name* in 1990 and Mae Benton in the medical drama *ER* (1994–1995). In 1992, she played Miss Lula in the sitcom *Hearts Afire*. In 1988, she won the **Emmy Award** for Outstanding Guest Performer in a Comedy Series for her work in *Frank's Place*. In 2000, she won the Emmy Award for her guest-starring role on the drama series *The Practice*. She was the subject of a 2004 tribute documentary, *Beah: A Black Woman Speaks*, directed by Lisa Gay Hamilton. She was born in 1926 and died in 2000 of emphysema.

RICHARDSON, BURTON. Burton was announcer of game shows *Family Feud* and *The Price Is Right*. He was also the announcer on *The Arsenio Hall Show* (1989–1994).

RICHARDSON, LATANYA. Richardson played a key role in the TV film *Within These Walls* in 2001.

RICHIE, LIONEL. Lionel Richie guest-starred in variety specials *Night of 100 Stars* in 1982 and featured music in the cartoon *Disney's DTV Valentine* in 1986. In 2004, he cohosted and performed on *Motown 45*.

RICHMOND, DEON. Richmond played Bud on *The Cosby Show* (1986–1992). He had regular or recurring roles in the sitcoms *Getting By* (1993) and *Sister, Sister* (1997–1999). In TV films, he had roles in the following: *The Child Saver* (1988), *Desperado: The Outlaw Wars* (1989), and *Hallelujah* (1993).

RIDDICK BOWE FIGHTS. Bowe began his rise to prominence in boxing on a *Wide World of Sports* bout on March 2, 1991. Bowe beat Tyrell Biggs. He also beat Evander Holyfield in an 11th-round knockout in a show telecast on March 6, 1993, from Las Vegas. Boxing historians say that round 10 was the greatest round in boxing history. *See also* BOXING MATCHES.

RILEY, LARRY. Riley played Frank Williams in *Knots Landing* from 1988 to 1992.

RING OF PASSION (*NBC, February 4, 1978*). **Bernie Casey** starred as Joe Louis in this dramatization about the 1930s heavyweight boxing matches between Louis and Max Schmeling (Stephen Macht). The film also dealt with how the two fighters became unwilling symbols of pre World War II political ideologies. Key roles were played by **Percy Rodriguez, Julius Harris, Mel Stewart, Denise Nicholas, Beah Richards**, Shaka Cumuka, and **Sarina Grant**.

RIOT (*SHO, April 27, 1997*). This made-for-television film consisted of four stories, each exploring the Los Angeles riots from the points of view of a different ethnic group—Asian, Hispanic, Anglo, and African American. Stars were **Melvin Van Peebles, Mario Van Peebles, Cicely Tyson**, and Luke Perry.

RIVERS, BOBBY. Rivers was host of *Top 5*, a show about food trends and "pop culture foods" on the Food Network.

ROAD TO GALVESTON, THE (*USA, January 24, 1996*). **Cicely Tyson** starred in this TV film as Jordan Roosevelt, a widow who takes care of women coping with the effects of Alzheimer's disease.

ROBERTA FLACK . . . THE FIRST TIME EVER (*ABC, June 19, 1973*). Singer **Roberta Flack** starred in this one-hour special featuring her songs and the songs of guests, Seals and Crofts.

ROBERT GUILLAUME SHOW, THE (*ABC, 1989*). Robert Guillaume played Edward Sawyer, a divorced marriage counselor who was having an affair with his secretary, Ann (Wendy Phillips), who was white. The relationship was not accepted by his teenage children, Pamela and William (Kelsey Scott and Marc Joseph), or his father, Henry (**Hank Rolike**). Before it aired, Guillaume, who was executive producer and suggested the series, said, "The show is not a forum for social change. I just wanted to try things that hadn't been tried before." Guillaume said he was tired of "this is a black show and this is a white show. There are all kinds of people in the world and no one has a lock on love or compassion or truth or beauty." *See also* INTERRACIAL ROMANCE/RELATIONSHIPS.

ROBERTS, DAVIS. Davis was a popular guest star on series, but some of his roles in television films include *Dallas: The Early Years* in 1986, *The Ambush Murders* in 1982, *The Sophisticated Gents* in 1981, *The First 36 Hours of Dr. Durant* in 1975, *A Case of Rape* in 1974, *The Final War of Olly Winter* in 1967, and *Great Gettin' Up Mornin'* in 1962. Davis played Leonard in *Roots* in 1977. He was in films as far back as 1947. He was born in 1917 and died in 1993 of emphysema.

ROBERTS, DEBORAH. Roberts joined the ABC newsmagazine *20/20* in 1995 after being a correspondent for NBC's *Dateline NBC*. On *20/20*, she was the reporter for a Rosa Parks profile. She also was a reporter on the story of the plight of African Americans who travel to sites in Africa where their ancestors were captured and enslaved. She has also served as substitute anchor for *World News Weekend* and *Good Morning America*. Prior to joining ABC, she worked for NBC news, beginning in 1990, as a general assignment correspondent. She covered the Persian Gulf War (1990–1991) and the 1992 Olympics in Barcelona, Spain. Her credits include hosting the live daily news program *Lifetime Live* on Lifetime Television.

ROBERTS, ROBIN. Roberts was ESPN's first on-air black woman when she hosted the network's overnight *SportsCenter*. Shortly afterward, she joined the *Sunday SportsDay* and *NFL Prime Time* broadcasts. Her credits also include being commentator for ESPN's WNBA coverage. In 1995, she joined ABC's *Wide World of Sports* with a dual contract with ABC and ESPN. Roberts was named the news anchor for ABC-TV's *Good Morning America* in 2002 heading the regular hourly newscasts for the morning news show emanating from Times Square in New York. A former athlete, she hosted ABC's *Wide World of Sports*, the first black woman to hold that position.

ROBERTS, TONY. Roberts was named correspondent for CBS-TV's *48 Hours* in 1998. He also covered stories for the *CBS Evening News with Dan Rather*, *CBS This Morning*, and *CBS Sunday Morning*. Earlier, he served as coanchor of the *CBS Morning News*. He joined CBS in 1993 as coanchor of the overnight broadcast *Up to the Minute*.

ROBESON, PAUL. Robeson played the title role in "The Emperor Jones," a *Kraft Television Theatre* drama in 1955. He was born in 1898 and died in 1976.

ROBINSON, BUMPER. Robinson played Ivan on the sitcom *Living Single* (1995–1997), Clarence on the sitcom *Amen* (1990–1991), Jared Harris on the sitcom *Guys Like Us* (1998–1999), and Louis Duncan Jackson on the sitcom *Molloy* (1990).

ROBINSON, CHARLIE. Robinson played Newdell in the acclaimed sitcom *Buffalo Bill* (1983–1984); Mac, the court clerk, on the popular sitcom *Night Court* (1984–1992); Abe in the sitcom *Love & War* (1992–1995); and Ernie in the sitcom *Ink* (1996–1997). In TV films and miniseries, he had roles in the following: *A Killing Affair* (1977), *King* (1978), *The Last Dance* (2000), *Santa Jr.* (2002), and *Secret Santa* (2003).

ROBINSON, HOLLY. *See* PEETE, HOLLY ROBINSON.

ROBINSON, MAX. After a career as a Portsmouth, Virginia, news-reader and a Washington, D.C., anchor, Robinson was the first black network news anchor when he coanchored *World News Tonight* with Frank Reynolds and Peter Jennings beginning in 1978. In 1981, he apparently angered ABC executives with an attack on racism during a speech he made at Smith College. He was also very vocal with network bosses over the way news stories portrayed black America and how these stories did not reflect the black viewpoint. He was admired by the black community and young black journalists for fighting racism and injustice, but the price for him personally was steep. As time progressed, associates say Robinson grew moody and stubborn and developed a drinking problem. Compounding that, he failed to show up for the funeral of Frank Reynolds, where he was scheduled to sit with First Lady Nancy Reagan. He was demoted to anchoring the weekend news, and Jennings was given the prime anchor spot. Robinson resigned from ABC in 1983 and worked for WMAQ-TV in Chicago, where he remained for two years. His excessive drinking and bouts of depression followed him. He vented his anger with coworkers, and according to sources, at the end of a newscast as the credits rolled, he blurted out profanities at the crew. However, he did not realize the microphone was still on, supposedly accidentally, and all of Chicago heard the outburst. His partnerships with WMAQ ended in 1985.

Robinson sought treatment for his alcoholism, and during those treatments discovered he had AIDS. He died at age 49 of complications from AIDS. He did not discuss the nature of his illness, but he apparently expressed the desire that his death be the occasion for emphasizing the importance, particularly to the black community, of education about AIDS and methods for prevention. He won an **Emmy Award** in 1980 for coverage of the national elections. Among the numerous other awards he won was the Capital Press Club Journalist of the Year Award.

ROBINSON, SMOKEY. As a solo singer, Robinson sang in the Super Bowl XXXIII tribute to 40 years of Motown in 1998. He was one of the entertainers on *Motown 45* in 2004 and was interviewed in the tribute special *It's Black Entertainment* (1997). *See* SMOKEY ROBINSON SHOW.

ROBINSON, WENDY RAQUEL. Robinson played Amelia on the sitcom *Me and the Boys* (1994–1995), Rachel Aimes on the sitcom *Minor Adjustments* (1995–1996), and Principal Regina Grier on *The Steve Harvey Show* (1996).

ROC *(FOX, 1991–1994)*. Charles S. Dutton, already known by friends as Roc Dutton, starred as hardworking garbage man Roc Emerson, who lived in Baltimore with his wife, a nurse named Eleanor (**Ella Joyce**); his brother, Joey (**Rocky Carroll**), a musician who rarely worked; and his racially militant father, Andrew (**Carl Gordon**), who was always upset about the latest actions of "the man." All the regular cast members were alumni of August Wilson plays on Broadway or in regional theater and were capable of doing a show without error. So after doing an episode live in the spring of 1992, the series decided to do the entire 1992–1993 season live. During the introduction to the episode, Dutton would display the day's newspaper to prove the show was live, or he might mention scores from a sporting event the night before. Publicity for the series erred when it was said that no show had gone live since the 1950s; *Gimme* *a Break*, starring **Nell Carter**, did a live episode on February 23, 1985. However, *Roc* was the first sitcom to go live for an entire season. In the final season of the series, Eleanor had a baby, and viewers were given a 900 number to call and select a name for the baby, who ended up being Marcus Garvey Emerson. Proceeds went to the National Safe Kids campaign. The show also became engrossed in serious issues. The Emersons took in a girl, Sheila (**Alexis Fields**), whose father was in prison. Roc ran for a local office and lost. He fought crime in the neighborhood, particularly drugs and drug dealer Andre (**Clifton Powell**). Supporting players included **Garrett Morris** as Roc's buddy, Wiz; **Wally Taylor** as Curtis; **Oscar Brown Jr.** as Miles; **Jamie Foxx** as Crazy George; and both **Ann Weldon** (1992–1993) and **Jenifer Lewis** (1993) as Charlaine.

ROCHON, LELA. Rochon starred in the TV film *Mr. and Mrs. Loving* in 1996. She played Lisa in the sitcom *The Wayans Bros.* (1995).

ROCK, CHRIS. The comedian was one of the stars of *Uptown Comedy Express* in 1987. He was in the cast of *Saturday Night Live* from 1990 to 1993 and in the cast of *In Living Color* from 1993 to 1994. He hosted *Chris Rock: Bring the Pain* in the 1996–1997 season. The special won the **Emmy Award** for Outstanding Variety, Music, or Comedy Special, and Rock won the Emmy for Outstanding Writing in a Variety or Music Program. He hosted *Chris Rock: Bigger and Better* in 1999 and the 1999 and 2003 *MTV Video Music Awards*. He headlined *Chris Rock: Never Scared* in 2004 and was nominated for an Emmy Award. He hosted *The 77th Academy Awards* on February 27, 2005 and began a starring role in the series *Everybody Hates Chris* the same year.

RODGERS AND HART TODAY (*ABC, March 2, 1967*). Popular black singers and musicians—**Count Basie**, **Diana Ross and The Supremes**, and the music of **Quincy Jones**—along with The Mamas and the Papas, the Doodletown Pipers (**Teresa Graves** was a member of the group), and host Petula Clark, performed the songs of composers Rodgers and Hart.

RODMAN WORLD TOUR, THE (*MTV, December 29, 1996*). Comedy ensued when Dennis Rodman and **David Alan Grier** went shopping on Melrose Avenue in Los Angeles in search of a "World Tour" wardrobe. They also decided to "do lunch."

RODRIGUEZ, PERCY. Rodriquez appeared in the drama special *Carol for Another Christmas* in 1964. He was Dr. Harry Miles, the husband/father in the black family introduced in the final year (1968–1969) of the first prime-time soap opera, *Peyton Place*. He was Jason in the police drama *Silent Force* (1970–1971), Malcolm in the drama series *Executive Suite* (1976–1977), and Winston in the sitcom *Sanford* (1980–1981).

ROGERS, TIMMIE. Rogers was a performer on *Sugar Hill Times* (1949), *The Melba-Moore-Clifton Davis Show* (1972), and *Redd Foxx* (1977–1978).

ROKER, AL. Roker joined NBC in 1996 as weather and feature reporter for *The Today Show*. He cohosted Christmas at Rockefeller Center in 1999. In 2003, he added to his credits *Al Roker Investigates* on Court TV.

ROKER, ROXIE. Roker was Helen Willis, the wife in the first racially mixed couple to be featured on a prime-time series, *The Jeffersons* (1975–1985). She appeared in *The Celebrity and the Arcade Kid* in 1983 and *The Day My Kid Went Punk* in 1987. Later, she became known as the real-life mother of rock star **Lenny Kravitz**. She was born in 1929 and died in 1995 of cancer.

ROLANDA (*SYN, 1994–1998*). **Rolanda Watts** hosted this talk show, which sometimes featured celebrity guests and sometimes dealt with serious issues and also some not-so-serious issues. On the serious side, she interviewed, in jail, a woman who had killed her young daughter. She also had several shows on racial issues like interracial dating. On the less serious side, she hosted two clowns who met and fell in love. Among the celebrity guests were **Bill Cosby**, **Flip Wilson**, and **James Brown**.

ROLIKE, HANK. Rolike played Sundance in the 1986 sitcom *The Last Precinct*. He played Henry Sawyer in the sitcom *The Robert*

Guillaume Show in 1989. His miniseries roles included *79 Park Avenue* (1977) and *Roots* (1977). His TV film roles included *Crisis in Mid-Air* (1979), *A Woman Called Moses* (1978), *Jimmy B. & Andre* (1980), and *Something Is Out There* (1988). Rolike was born in 1928 and died in 2002.

ROLLE, ESTHER. After a theater career, Rolle became famous to television viewers when she played Florida Evans, the outspoken family maid in *Maude*, starring Beatrice Arthur. *Maude* was a spin-off of *All in the Family*; Rolle took her Maude role to the spin-off series *Good Times* (1974–1979). She starred in the television movie *I Know Why the Caged Bird Sings* (1979). She won an **Emmy Award** for Outstanding Supporting Actress in a Limited Series for her role in 1978's *Summer of My German Soldier*. Rolle guest-starred in *Retrospective CBS: On the Air* in 1978. She played the matriarch in the television version of the Lorraine Hansberry classic *A Raisin in the Sun* (1978). Rolle was born in 1920 and died in 1998 from complications of diabetes.

ROLLING STONE MAGAZINE: THE 10TH ANNIVERSARY (*CBS, November 25, 1977*). Top recording artists who have been featured in the magazine paid tribute to its 10th anniversary in this two-hour special. Among the artists were **Gladys Knight** and the Pips and **Patti LaBelle**.

ROLLING STONE MAGAZINE: 20 YEARS OF ROCK AND ROLL (*CBS, November 24, 1987*). This two-hour special is a celebration of the magazine's 20th anniversary. It featured clips of performers covered in its pages. Guests were **Aretha Franklin, Smokey Robinson, Tina Turner**, and others.

ROLLINS, HOWARD E., JR. Rollins played Andrew Young in the miniseries *King* in 1978 and had a key role in the TV films *My Old Man* in 1979 and *Thornwell* in 1981. He starred in a live television version of the stage play *A Member of the Wedding* in 1982. He played a regular role in a western series, *Wildside*, in 1985, but it lasted only a month. A few years later, he was cast in a series with longevity. He starred as Chief of Detectives Virgil Tibbs in the drama series *In the Heat of the Night* from 1988 to 1993, and then in the final season (1993–1994), he was seen only occasionally. Rollins was born in 1950 and died in 1996.

ROLL OUT (*CBS, 1973–1974*). The sitcom *M*A*S*H*, which premiered in 1972, was a critical success, eventually a ratings success, and still one of the longest-running series; it was a comedy about the Korean War. So it is easy to see how the network thought that a sitcom about World War II might be a good idea. Thus, *Roll Out* premiered the following year featuring the men of the Red Ball Express, an army trucking unit that took supplies to troops on the front line. There had been a feature film called *The Red Ball Express* starring Sidney Poitier in 1952, and there really was such a unit during the war. The unit was primarily black and, in the series, consisted of Cpl. Sweet William (**Stu Gilliam**), Pfc. Jed Brooks (**Hilly Hicks**), Sgt. B. J. Bryant (**Mel Stewart**), Wheels (**Garrett Morris**), Jersey (**Darrow Igus**), and High Strung (**Theodore Wilson**). The actors were praised for their individual comedic abilities, but the series lasted three months.

ROMEO (entertainer). Known first as Lil' Romeo, the young rap artist starred in the Saturday morning live-action series *Romeo* beginning in 2003.

ROMEO (series) (*NIK, 2003–*). Real-life father and son **Master P** and **Lil' Romeo** starred in a live-action show for children about a family held together by music. Perry Miller (Master P) was a single father whose successful career in music means problems for raising his children—Romeo (Romeo), Jodi (Erica O'Keith), and Gary (Zachary Isaiah Williams). The problem was compounded when Percy began to manage Romeo's music career.

ROOKIES, THE (film) (*ABC, March 7, 1972*). This 90-minute made-for-television film about police recruits was the pilot for the series *The Rookies*. Like the series, it starred **Georg Stanford Brown** with Sam Melville and Michael Ontkean. The role played by Kate Jackson in the series was played by Jennifer Billingsley in the film.

ROOKIES, THE (series) (*ABC, 1972–1976*). Georg Stanford Brown starred in this police drama series as one of three young rookie policemen with more humane ideas about law enforcement than their seasoned supervisor. Michael Ontkean and Sam Melville played the other two cops. Kate Jackson played Melville's wife, Jill. Brown and Ontkean did not have wives.

ROOM 222 (*ABC, 1969–1974*). A racially well-integrated "dramedy," this half-hour series was about the faculty and students of fictional Walt Whitman High School in Los Angeles and the issues they faced: racism, sexism, drugs, teen pregnancy, gangs, and illiteracy. The term "dramedy" was not used until more than a decade later, but this show was serious in nature with some comic relief or comedy scenes. Television historians often label it comedy because the 30-minute format is generally comedy. Others call it drama because of the serious subject matter. The black regular characters were Pete Dixon, the history teacher (**Lloyd Haynes**); his girlfriend/school counselor, Liz McIntyre (**Denise Nicholas**); and students Jason (**Heshimu**), Richie (Howard Rice), Pam (**Ta-Tanisha**), and Larry (**Eric Laneuville**). Mr. Dixon was a strong teacher with a gentle demeanor, and students loved him. There was usually a lesson to be learned, but the show was not preachy. The series won the **Emmy Award** for Outstanding New Series in the 1969–1970 season and numerous other awards by community and educational groups for its positive portrayal of important social issues seldom discussed on television at the time. *See also* SERIES ABOUT SCHOOL LIFE.

ROOTS (*ABC, January 1977*). This miniseries of 12 hours aired for eight consecutive days and was the most-watched dramatic show in television. The statistics say that 100 million viewers saw the final episode, which earned a 51.1 rating with a 71 share, one of the highest ratings ever recorded. Most of the major roles were played by black actors, so that was noteworthy to black viewers who recall rushing home every evening to see *Roots*. It was not just loyalty to black actors or the novelty of seeing black actors; it was also the engrossing story.

The script was based on writer Alex Haley's then 12-year-old book *Roots*, in which he claimed to have traced his ancestors back to Gambia, West Africa, and his forefather, Kunta Kinte. The Haley family legend was that the ancestral line began in America when 17-year-old Kunta was captured and brought over on a slave ship. This information was passed down through the generations, the story of "the old African." In the drama, the angry Kunta (played as a boy by **LeVar Burton** and as an adult by **John Amos**) grew up, adjusted to life as a slave, and married Bell (**Madge Sinclair**), who gave birth to a daughter, Kizzy (**Leslie Uggams**). Then Kizzy was taken away to another plantation and bore a son, Chicken George (**Ben Vereen**), fathered by the slave master. The story continued with every generation until the final episode with Kunta's great grandson, Tom (**Georg Stanford Brown**), after emancipation. As each episode ended, the viewer was left in suspense wanting to know what happened to the current character in crisis.

Cicely Tyson and **Thalmus Rasulala** played Kunta's parents, Binta and Omoro. **Louis Gossett Jr.** played Fiddler, who befriended Kunta on the plantation. **Lawrence Hilton-Jacobs** was Noah, and **Olivia Cole** was Matilda. **Lynne Moody** was Irene. Other actors and their roles were the following: **Maya Angelou** as Nyo Boto, **O. J. Simpson** as Kudi Touray, **Ji-Tu Cumbuka** as the wrestler, **Moses Gunn** as Kintango, **Hari Rhodes** as Brima Cesay, **Ren Woods** as young Fanta, **Beverly Todd** as adult Fanta, Raymond St. Jacques as the drummer, **Scatman Crothers** as Mingo, **Lillian Randolph** as Sister Sara, and **Richard Roundtree** as Sam Bennett.

The production was emotional for black viewers. Most can tell where they were and what they were doing when *Roots* aired. It was also emotional for the actors playing in tense scenes; one black actor who played a slave being beaten reportedly told the director, "You had better get this on one take because I'm not doing it again." White actors in the production also spoke of difficulty in playing scenes in which their character was brutal and offered apologies to the actors they had to abuse.

Some of the nonblack actors with key roles were Sandy Duncan as Missy Anne, Chuck Connors as Tom Moore, Edward Asner as Captain Davies (won an **Emmy Award** for supporting actor), Ralph Waite as Third Mate Slater, Robert Reed as Dr. William Reynolds, George Hamilton as Stephen Bennettt, and Lloyd Bridges as Evan Brent.

The miniseries earned 37 nominations for that year's Emmy Award and won a record nine, including for Outstanding Limited Series. Olivia Cole won for Outstanding Single Performance by a Supporting Actress in a Drama or Comedy Series. Three of her four competitors were other actresses in *Roots*. Louis Gossett Jr. won for Outstanding Actor for a Single Performance in a Drama or Comedy Series, and all his competitors were other actors in *Roots*: Amos, Burton, and Vereen. Before the award ceremony, the four actors purchased an ad in the trade papers announcing that no matter who won, they would consider it a victory. When Gossett won, he said, "*Roots* was the most positive thing that has happened for equal rights since Martin Luther King." Vernon Jordan, former president of the Urban League, called it "the single most spectacular educational experience in race relations in America."

The film also won Emmys for supporting actor, writing, directing, film editing, film sound editing, and music composition (**Quincy Jones** and Gerald Fried).

More than 250 colleges and universities planned courses based on *Roots*, and during the broadcast, more than 30 cities declared "*Roots* Weeks.*"

ABC's showing of Alex Haley's ***Roots*** has long been hailed as a watershed for portrayals of African Americans on television and for television in general. Often credited with establishing the consecutive-night miniseries as a viable television genre and setting off a nationwide interest in family genealogy and personal heritage, the series also represented a rare serious drama about African Americans on network television. Sociology researcher Sherry Lynne Cannon found that audience reaction to *Roots* was primarily emotional. In her study of 37 news articles and 134 interviewee responses within those articles gathered around the time the series was aired, Cannon found pride and anger among the emotions most often expressed by African Americans who watched *Roots*. She found that guilt was both a response to the programs and an impetus to tune in among the most frequent emotions mentioned by mainstream or white viewers. Other emotions included sadness and curiosity about personal family history for both groups.

Part of the attraction to the miniseries, according to Cannon, rested in the television friendly formula of *Roots*. The story had violence, sex, multiple cliffhangers, and appearances by well-known African American actors, such as John Amos, Ben Vereen, Cicely Tyson, Leslie Uggams, Richard Roundtree, and Louis Gossett Jr., as well as television veterans Lorne Green, Robert Reed, and Chuck Connors, to keep viewers interested and ensure high emotional impact. In addition, the show tapped into themes such as family unity, justice, freedom, survival against unimaginable odds, and the triumph of the underdog. Moreover, it was based on real-life events in American, particularly African-American, history. "It offered a black perspective which had rarely, if ever, been presented on television," wrote Cannon.

Even though the black actors of *Roots* were praised for their performances, the project was not necessarily a boost to their careers. Uggams said it did make people realize that she was serious about being an actress as well as a singer, but she added, "I think the men fared better than the women. Even though we all had very high expectations and thought the world was going to be everyone's oyster, it didn't happen that way. We expected more."

ROOTS, THE GIFT (*December 11, 1988*). This Christmas special brought back two characters from *Roots*—Kunta Kinte (**LeVar Burton**) and Fiddler (**Louis Gossett Jr.**)—in a story about freedom, the greatest gift of all. The two slaves met Moyer, a free man of color played by **Avery Brooks**, who is being chased by a bounty hunter. **Kevin Hooks** was director.

ROOTS, THE NEXT GENERATIONS (*ABC, February 1979*). With seven nominations, the 14-hour dramatic miniseries, commonly called *Roots II*, won the **Emmy Award** for Outstanding Limited Series in 1978–1979. It was the continuation of the story of Alex Haley's ancestors from 1882 to 1967. **George Stanford Brown** and **Lynn Moody** continued the roles they played in *Roots*, Tom and Irene Harvey. **Al Freeman Jr.** (who played Malcolm X) and **Paul Winfield** (who played Dr. Horace Huguley) were nominees for Outstanding Supporting Actor in a Limited Series but lost out to fellow cast member Marlon Brando, who played American Nazi leader George Lincoln Rockwell. **Ruby Dee** was nominated in the Supporting Actress category for her role as Queen Haley but lost out to **Esther Rolle** in *Summer of My German Soldier*.

Some others in the cast were the following: **Avon Long** as Chicken George, **Greg Morris** as Beeman Jones, **Fay Hauser** as Carrie Barden, **Brian Mitchell** as John Dolan, **Debbi Morgan** as Elizabeth Harvey, **Ja'net Dubois** as Sally Harvey, **Roger E.** Mosley as Lee Garnet, **Stan Shaw** as Will Palmer, **Irene Cara** as Bertha Palmer, **Ossie Davis** as Dad Jones, **Dorian Harewood** as Simon Haley, **Kene Holliday** as Detroit, **Hal Williams** as Aleck Haley, **Bever-Leigh Banfield** as Cynthia Palmer, **Bernie Casey** as Bubba Haywood, **Pam Grier** as Francey, **Rosey Grier** as Big Slew Johnson, **Percy Rodrigues** as Boyd Moffat, **Maidie Norman** as Sister Scrap Scott, **Brock Peters** as Ab Decker, **Beah Richards** as Cynthia Parker, **Lynn Hamilton** as Cousin Georgia, **Christoff St. John** (who later changed his name to Kristoff) as eight-year-old Alex Haley, **Debbie Allen** as Nan Branch Haley, **Damon Evans** as teenager/young adult Alex Haley, **Diahann Carroll** as Mrs. Simon Haley, Rafer Johnson as Nelson, **Carmen McRae** as Lila, **Della Reese** as Mrs. Lydia Branch, **Telma Hopkins** as Daisy, **Lee Chamberlin** as Odile Richards, **James Earl Jones** as mature Alex Haley, **Claudia McNeil** as Sister Will Ada, **Linda Hopkins** as the singer, Bobby Short as the pianist, **Howard Rollins** as George Haley, and Johnny Sekka as Ebou Manga.

ROSA PARKS STORY, THE (*CBS, February 24, 2002*). Angela Bassett starred as Rosa Parks, the catalyst for the 1955 Montgomery bus boycott and the subsequent civil rights struggle led by the Rev. Martin Luther King Jr. and others. The film illustrated Parks's chance meeting with an old friend, which led her to the offices of the National Association for the Advancement of Colored People (NAACP) and history. The story also highlighted the relationship between Rosa and her husband, Raymond Parks (**Peter Francis James**), a lesser-known aspect of her life. **Dexter King** played the role of Dr. King, his father, in a cameo. **Cicely Tyson** played Leona. Julie Dash directed. *See also* BIOPICS; HISTORICAL EVENTS DRAMATIZED.

ROSS, DIANA. Ross made numerous appearances as a member of **The Supremes** on *The Ed Sullivan Show* and *American Bandstand* as well as other variety series and specials including *Rodgers and Hart Today* in 1967, *Tennessee Ernie Ford Special* in 1967, *The Bing Crosby Special* in 1968, and *The Bob Hope Special* in 1969. Also in 1969, Diana Ross and The Supremes shared a bill with **The Temptations** in the special *Diana Ross and The Supremes and The Temptations on Broadway*. In the 1970s and 1980s, she headlined five specials on all major networks; they were the following: *Diana* in 1971 on NBC; *An Evening with Diana Ross* in 1977 on NBC, *Diana* in 1981 on CBS; *Diana Ross in Concert* in 1982 on HBO; *Diana Ross in Central Park*, which was syndicated in 1985; and *Diana Ross . . . Red Hot Rhythm and Blues* in 1987 on ABC. In 1982, Ross sang the National Anthem at Super Bowl XVI, and in 1996, she sang in Super Bowl XXX's halftime show. In 1994, she starred in the television movie *Out of Darkness*. Ross also guest-starred on *The Smokey Robinson Show* in 1970, *Muhammad Ali's 50th Birthday Celebration* in 1992, and *The Apollo Hall of Fame* in 1993. She starred with Brandy in *Double Platinum*, a made-for-television movie, in 1999. In that project, she sang songs from her album *Every Day Is a New Day*; she was listed as executive producer. She was in *VH1 Divas 2000* and the same year in *An Audience with Diana Ross*. In 1997, she was part of *It's Black Entertainment.*

ROSS, SHAVAR. Ross played Dudley in the sitcom *Diff'rent Strokes* (1981–1986) and played Weasel in *Family Matters* (1992–1994).

ROSS, TED. Ross played Sawyer Dabney in the sitcom *Sirota's Court* in 1976–1977 and Sgt. Debbin in *MacGruder and Loud* in 1985. He was part of the company of the televised version of the Broadway musical *Purlie* in 1981. In TV films, he had roles in *F.D.R.: The Last Year* and *Death Penalty*, both in 1980, and *Parole* in 1982. Ross was born in 1934 and died in 2002 of complications resulting from a stroke.

ROSS, TRACEE ELLIS. Ross, daughter of **Diana Ross**, played Joan Clayton in *Girlfriends* (2000–) and Kaycee King in the TV film *Race against Fear* (1998).

ROSS, TRACEY. Ross was the first $100,000 spokesmodel winner on *Star Search*. Later, she played Diana Douglas on the daytime drama *Ryan's Hope* from 1985 to 1987, and then, in 1999, she joined the cast of *Passions* to play Dr. Eve Johnson Russell.

ROUNDTREE, RICHARD. Roundtree starred in the drama series *Shaft* in 1973–1974 after first making the character a cultural icon in the classic film. He starred in the 1973 TV film *Firehouse*. He guest-starred in the TV special *Circus of the Stars* (1977) and appeared in the dramatic special *Daddy Can't Read* (1988). Roundtree starred in the drama series *413 Hope Street* (1997–1998). He played a key role in the drama *Having Our Say* (1999).

ROWAN AND MARTIN'S LAUGH-IN (*NBC, 1968–1973*). This was a fast-paced comedy show featuring numerous performers, catchphrases, sight gags, sketches, and one-liners. The series featured famous people usually in a few seconds of screen time. President Richard Nixon said, "Sock it to me," and **Sammy Davis Jr.** made his popular catch phrase, "Here come de' judge." Numerous other big names made cameo appearances. Comedy partners Dan Rowan and Dick Martin, Goldie Hawn, and Lilly Tomlin were among the cast members. *Laugh-In* brought numerous minority performers to mainstream audiences including comedian Pigmeat Markham as the all-powerful judge. The black members of the regular cast were exceptional talents who went on to other show business work: dancer **Chelsea Brown** (1968–1969), singer **Teresa Graves** (1969–1970), multitalented impressionist **Johnny Brown** (1970–1972), and ventriloquist **Willie Tyler** and his dummy, Lester (1972–1973). *See also* SERIES WITH ONE BLACK SUPPORTING ACTOR/PERFORMER BEFORE 1980.

ROWELL, VICTORIA. Rowell played Drucilla Barber Winters in *The Young and the Restless* (1990–), in daytime, and Dr. Amanda Bentley in *Diagnosis Murder* (1993–2001), sometimes simultaneously. In TV films and miniseries, she had roles in *Ann Rice's Feast of All Saints* (2001), *A Town without Pity* (2002), and *Without Warning* (2002).

ROYAL FAMILY, THE (*CBS, 1991–1992*). This sitcom is most significant in that star **Redd Foxx** died on the set from an apparent massive heart attack. The series had made its debut on September 18, 1991, and Foxx expired during a rehearsal on October 11. Cast and crew members said they thought Foxx was joking and faking "the big one" as his character did on *Sanford and Son*. His employees rushed his body home to Las Vegas, and there was no autopsy. Foxx played a character named Al Royal, an argumentative mailman with a wife, Victoria (**Della Reese**). Foxx and Reese had played a couple in the Eddie Murphy feature film *Harlem Nights*. Murphy obviously liked the chemistry and produced this series for them. The Royals had a daughter, Elizabeth (Mariann Aaida), who divorced and moved back home with her three precocious children (Sylver Gregory, **Larenz Tate**, and Naya Rivera). After Foxx died, the series writers decided that his character would die too. So Victoria's sister Ruth, played by **Jackee** (aka **Jackee Harry**), moved in to help her deal with the loss. Somehow some episodes later, Jackee was recast as Victoria's older daughter, Coco. Before Foxx died, the series ranked in the top 40 of prime-time series. Matt Roush of *USA Today* (September 18, 1991) had said, "*The Royal Family* starts with the makings of a bona fide winner." However, Brian Lowery of *Variety* (September 18, 1991) said, "Don't look for this royalty to be claiming any ratings crowns."

RUBY'S BUCKET OF BLOOD (*SHO, December 1, 2001*). Angela Bassett starred in a drama as Ruby, the owner of a 1960s juke joint who had to cope with a wayward husband (**Brian Stokes Mitchell**), a teenage daughter (**Jurnee Smollet**) who wanted very much to explore life away from home, and her own attraction to a white singer. Kevin Anderson played Billy Dupre, and Glenn Plummer played Johnny Beaugh. *See also* INTERRACIAL ROMANCE/RELATIONSHIPS.

RUDOLPH, MAYA. Rudolph was a cast member on *Saturday Night Live* (2000–). She played Nurse Grace Patterson in the drama series *City of Angels* (2000).

RUNAWAY, THE (*CBS, December 10, 2000*). This production of the *Hallmark Hall of Fame* was about two boys, one black and one white (Cody Newton and Dwayne McLaughlin), who try to solve the mystery of a murder that most people in the town would rather forget. **Debbie Morgan** and **Maya Angelou** starred.

RUN FOR THE DREAM: THE GAIL DEVERS STORY (*SHO, June 16, 1996*). This was the story of Olympic gold medalist Gail Devers and her fight to overcome Grave's disease and still become the fastest sprinter in the world. **Charlayne Woodard** played Devers; **Louis Gossett Jr.,** coach Bob Kersee; **Robert Guillaume**, the Rev. Devers; and **Paula Kelly** Mrs. Devers. Cameo appearances were made by Florence Griffith Joyner and Willie Gault. Neema Barnette was director. *See also* ATHLETES' BIOPICS; BIOPICS.

RUSSELL, BILL. Bill Russell guest-starred in the variety special *Playboy's 25th Anniversary Celebration* in 1979.

RUSSELL, KIMBERLY. Russell played Sarah Nevins on the comedy series *Head of the Class* from 1986 to 1991. In TV films, she played Carole in the TV film *Final Shot: The Hank Gathers Story* in 1992 and Marguerite in *The O. J. Simpson Story* (1995).

RUSSELL, NIPSEY. Stand-up comedian Russell was one of the stars of *Favorite Songs*, a musical songfest, in 1964; *NBC Follies of 1965*, which actually aired in late 1964; and *The Alan King Show* in 1969. In 1980, he, with other alumni of the Apollo Theater, paid tribute to the Harlem landmark. He played Honey in the sitcom *Barefoot in the Park* in 1970–1971 and Vinnie in "Fame," a *Hallmark Hall of Fame* comedy play by Arthur Miller in 1978. Russell was a regular on *The Dean Martin Show* in 1972–1973, and he appeared on many productions of *The Dean Martin Celebrity Roasts*. He also appeared in the dramatic special *My Past Is My Own* in 1989. He was a frequent guest star on variety series, talk shows, and game shows.

RUSSELL SIMMONS' DEF COMEDY JAM (*HBO, 1992–1998*). This half-hour late night series featured up-and-coming comics doing monologues in front of an energetic audience in Manhattan. Former rap star Simmons was producer. Comedian **Martin Lawrence** was the first host (1992–1997). Other hosts were Sommore, Guy Torry, Joe Torry, Rickey Smiley, Bruce Bruce, and Michael Colyar. Frequent performers included **Steve Harvey, Eddie Griffin, D. L. Hughley, Bernie Mac, Paul Mooney, Tracy Morgan, Chris Rock**, George Wallace, and others. Each show began with a monologue from the host. Critics complained that the jokes were vulgar. Supporters agreed but insisted that the comics were so talented that the blue jokes did not matter. Simmons once said, "I wouldn't want to produce the show if I had to clean up the language, because it wouldn't be as real." John O'Connor of the *New York Times* (July 8, 1993) said, "One certain four-letter word, and its extension suggesting incest, is sounded like a communal mantra. . . . That's part of the fun."

RUSSELL SIMMONS PRESENTS DEF POETRY (*HBO, 2001– *). This showcase of recitations performed by well-known and not-so-well-known contemporary urban poets spawned a Broadway show. The first shows were taped before an audience at The Supper Club in New York with **Mos Def** as host. The series won the prestigious Peabody Award. Some of the artists were Jewel, **Dave Chappelle**, Benjamin Bratt, **Cedric the Entertainer**, Sonia Sanchez, Suheir Hammad, Flow Mental, and Mayda Del Valle.

RYAN, ROZ. Ryan played Amelia Hetebrink in the sitcom *Amen* (1986–1991), Mrs. Dixon in the sitcom *Good News* (1997), and Chickie in the 2001 sitcom *Danny*. She began the role of Flo in *All about the Andersons* in 2003.

– S –

SADAT (*SYN, October 31 and November 7, 1983*). **Louis Gossett Jr.** played Egyptian leader Anwar Sadat in this miniseries, which caused great furor in Egypt. All the films made by Columbia Pictures and the film's producers were banned in Egypt for a while. The film depicted Sadat from his youth to his assassination. Gossett was nominated for an **Emmy Award** for his portrayal. *See also* BIOPICS.

ST. ELSEWHERE (*NBC, 1982–1988*). This medical drama was significant primarily in that Academy Award winner **Denzel Washington** got his start as a regular cast member. Washington played Dr. Phillip Chandler, who was always trying to be the best he could in a Boston hospital (St. Eligius) known for not being well equipped;

thus, it was nicknamed by doctors in other hospitals "St. Elsewhere." The show was one of the first to portray life in an entire hospital and not in one specific ward. It also was pioneering in that sometimes patients actually died. The stories were often controversial; it had one of the earliest episodes to depict an AIDS patient. There was also comedy in each episode of the drama that critics sometimes termed "silly." The series never had high ratings, but it enjoyed critical and demographic success. It appealed to young affluent viewers whom advertisers found desirable. The series had a large ensemble cast to play the mostly dedicated hospital staff. The cast included at various times other black actors. **Eric Laneuville** played Luther Hawkins, an orderly (1983–1986). **Alfre Woodard** played Dr. Roxanne Turner (1985–1987). **Saundra Sharpe** played Nurse Peggy Shotwell (1984–1986). **Byron Stewart** played Warren Coolidge, an orderly (1984–1988). Stewart had played the same role in *The White Shadow*; both series were productions of MTM (Mary Tyler Moore) Enterprises. *St. Elsewhere* aired for six seasons and was nominated for 63 **Emmy Awards**, winning 13.

ST. JACQUES, RAYMOND. St. Jacques played a key role in the TV films *The Monk* in 1969, *Search for the Gods* in 1975, and *The Sophisticated Gents* in 1981. He was a member of the regular cast, playing Dr. Hooks, in *Falcon Crest* in the 1983–1984 season. He was born in 1930 and died in 1990 of lymph cancer.

ST. JOHN, KRISTOFF. As a child, St. John's name in cast billing was Christoff. He played Alex Haley as a boy in the miniseries *Roots: The Next Generations* in 1979 and **Rosalind Cash**'s son in *Sister, Sister*, a 1982 television movie. That same year, he had a role in the 1982 dramatic special *Help Wanted*. He also had roles in the following TV films: *The Atlanta Child Murders* (1984), *An Innocent Love* (1980), *Finish Line* (1990), *The Patty Hearst Ordeal* (1979), and *Beulah Land* (1980). As a teen, he played the son of **Flip Wilson**'s and **Gladys Knight**'s characters in the sitcom *Charlie & Co.* (1985–1986). He played Adam Marshall in the daytime drama *Generations* in 1989. He joined the cast of the daytime drama *The Young and the Restless* as the character Neal Winters in 1991.

SAINTLY SWITCH (*ABC, January 24, 1999*). **David Alan Grier** and **Vivica A. Fox** starred in this made-for-television comedy film about a married couple who exchanged personalities through some stereotypical New Orleans old-fashioned magic and learned what it is like to live the other's life.

SALLEY, JOHN. A retired professional basketball player, Salley, in 2001, became one of the hosts of Fox's *Best Damn Sports Show Period.* He has also been a studio commentator for NBC's National Basketball Association pregame show, *NBA Showtime.*

SALLY HEMINGS: AN AMERICAN SCANDAL (*CBS, February 13 and 26, 2000*). This four-hour miniseries exploring the 38-year relationship between Thomas Jefferson and his black slave mistress, Sally Hemings, starred Sam Neill and **Carmen Ejogo**. Others in the cast were **Diahann Carroll** as Betty Hemings and **Mario Van Peebles** as James Hemings. Tina Andrews wrote the script. *See also* BIOPICS; INTERRACIAL ROMANCE/RELATIONSHIPS.

SALUTE TO THE AMERICAN THEATER (*CBS, December 6, 1959*). This one-hour tribute to Broadway theater centered on how Broadway contributed to the cause of freedom and diversity. **Ossie Davis** and **Claudia McNeil** made appearances along with Phyllis Newman, Robert Preston, Eli Wallach, and narrator Franchot Tone.

SAMANTHA SMITH GOES TO WASHINGTON (*DIS, February 19, 1984*). This one-hour documentary featured 11-year-old Samantha Smith, who visited a school in Washington, D.C., and asked children her age what they thought of candidates for the U.S. presidency: **Rev. Jesse Jackson**, John Glenn, and Reuben Askew.

SAMMY AND COMPANY (*SYN, 1975–1977*). A syndicated talk and variety series, *Sammy and Company* was hosted by multitalented **Sammy Davis Jr.** The show, shown primarily in late night, originated from various entertainment meccas, like Las Vegas and Acapulco, and featured entertainers who were ostensibly appearing at nightclubs and casino rooms in these cities. **Flip Wilson** and **Ray Charles** were among the guest performers.

SAMMY AND HIS FRIENDS (*ABC, November 25, 1965*). Sammy Davis Jr. hosted guests **Count Basie** and his Orchestra and Joey Heatherton in this one-hour special.

SAMMY DAVIS JR. AND THE WONDERFUL WORLD OF CHILDREN (*ABC, February 1, 1966*). Sammy Davis Jr. performed sketches, songs, and dances with a group of children.

SAMMY DAVIS JR. IN EUROPE (*SYN, December 1969*). This one-hour special showed highlights of **Sammy Davis Jr.**'s entertainment tour of Europe. Charles Aznavour and Maurice Chevalier were guests.

SAMMY DAVIS JR. SHOW, THE (*NBC, 1966*). Sammy Davis Jr. was host/star of this short-lived musical variety series. His was the first variety program with a black performer as host since *The Nat King Cole Show* of the 1950s. The series started with two snafus that may have hurt its initial impact. Even though the series had guest stars, its primary draw and star was to be Davis, who was adept at singing, dancing, and comedy. However, Davis had a previous contract with ABC-TV for a special that would air three weeks after his new series began. The contract stipulated that he could not appear on other programs during the weeks preceding the airing of the special. This prevented his appearing on the first three weeks of his own series, so Johnny Carson, Sean Connery, and Jerry Lewis were substitute hosts. They were all big names, but it did not help that Sammy Davis Jr. was not on *The Sammy Davis Jr. Show*. The show debuted in January and ended in April. According to Davis's daughter, Tracey Davis, who wrote his biography, the NAACP protested the cancellation charging racism, but Davis himself acknowledged that it was not racism.

SAMMY DAVIS JR.'S 60TH ANNIVERSARY CELEBRATION (*ABC, February 4, 1990*). This two-and-a-half-hour tribute to **Sammy Davis Jr.** was hosted by **Eddie Murphy** with numerous stars entertaining and praising Davis's lifetime career as a performer. On the bill were **Debbie Allen**, Anita Baker, **Diahann Carroll**, **Nell Carter**, **Bill Cosby**, Tony Danza, Clint Eastwood, **Lola Falana**, Ella

Fitzgerald, Goldie Hawn, **Gregory Hines, Whitney Houston, Rev. Jesse Jackson, Michael Jackson, Quincy Jones,** Shirley MacLaine, Dean Martin, Gregory Peck, **Richard Pryor,** Frank Sinatra, **Mike Tyson, Dionne Warwick, Stevie Wonder,** and many more. Davis died shortly afterward.

SAMMY DAVIS JR. SPECIAL, THE (*NBC, February 18, 1965*). This one-hour variety special featured **Sammy Davis Jr.** and his guests Billy Daniels, **Lola Falana**, Peter Lawford, and Mike Silva in song and comedy skits. Davis was also producer.

SANFORD (*NBC, 1980–1981*). After **Redd Foxx** departed from *Sanford and Son* in 1977 to do other projects, he returned to NBC to do his most successful character, Fred Sanford. He was the same irascible junkman, but there was no son in the new series. Lamont was said to be in Alaska working on the pipeline. In the new series, Fred was courting a classy lady from Beverly Hills, Evelyn "Eve" Lewis (**Marguerite Ray**), and planning to marry her. It was Watts meets Beverly Hills. Much of the scripts were set in her house. Rollo (**Nathaniel Taylor**) remained from the older series. Cliff (**Clinton Derricks-Carroll**), Fred's nephew, moved into his house, as did Cal (Dennis Burkley), a white guy from the South who had become Fred's partner in the junk business. Each of these was to replace Lamont, and it was hoped that Foxx playing off of them would be a similar hit. It was not to be. Others in the regular cast of the short-lived series were Suzanne Stone as Cissy, Cathy Cooper as Clara, and **Percy Rodriguez** as Winston.

SANFORD AND SON (*NBC, 1972–1977*). **Redd Foxx** and **Demond Wilson** starred in this popular sitcom. Sixty-five-year-old Fred Sanford (Foxx) was a widower and a junkman living in the Watts section of Los Angeles. His 30-something son, Lamont (Demond Wilson), lived with him and was partner in the junk business but would rather have another profession. Each time Lamont took a step to leave, Fred would fake a heart attack, look up to Heaven, and say, "I'm coming to join you, Elizabeth [his deceased wife]." And though Lamont knew it was fake, he either stayed or left and returned soon. Based on the British sitcom *Steptoe and Son*, *Sanford and Son* was created and produced by Norman Lear and Bud Yorkin. The title of the series and principal character's name came from Foxx's own life. Foxx's real name was John Elroy Sanford. In fact, he had a brother named Fred Sanford. Lear and Yorkin had already an established hit in *All in the Family*. Archie Bunker was racist, and so was Fred Sanford, though at the time the term "reverse racist" was used to describe a black man who did not like white people. Fred did not like Puerto Ricans or Mexicans either. Redd Foxx didn't care for Norman Lear or Bud Yorkin either. Not far into the series, neither ever showed up on the set, and Foxx said it was his decision. As long as the series was a hit, there was no real reason for the owners to be present.

Recurring characters in the series were the following: Donna, Fred's girlfriend (**Lynn Hamilton**); police officers Smitty (**Hal Williams**, 1972–1976), Swanny (Noam Pitlik, 1972), and Hoppy (Howard Platt, 1972–1976); Grady Wilson, Fred's buddy (**Whitman Mayo**); Rollo, Lamont's buddy (**Nathaniel Taylor**); Bubba, Fred's buddy (**Don Bexley**); Woody, Esther's husband (**Raymond Allen**, 1976–1977); and neighbor Julio (Gregory Sierra, 1972–1975).

The show quickly became NBC's number one show, and Foxx wanted credit for it. He boycotted his own show several times. Sometimes he wanted more money; once he wanted a dressing room with a window. The network argued that the studio building had no dressing rooms with windows, but Foxx knew a hole had been cut into the front of one of the buildings to insert a window to provide a dressing room with a view for Johnny Carson. At the end of the third season, when Foxx was boycotting, Mayo, as the character Grady, Fred's friend, was written in as Fred's replacement in the junk business who would also take care of Lamont. The ratings remained high. At another point, Foxx did the show, but he refused to rehearse five days with a taping on the fifth day, which was the normal schedule. He wanted to spend more time in Las Vegas, where he lived and headlined on weekends. He would come in on Thursdays to block the show; cue cards were used to show him the lines. The show was taped on Friday evening, then a helicopter would fly him to the airport where he would catch a plane for Las Vegas to do his show.

Foxx believed in helping his friends, and all those who were performers were given roles at some time. Comedian **Slappy White**, his longtime buddy, played Melvin beginning the first year of the series. **LaWanda Page**, his friend from his days in Los Angeles nightclubs, played his sister-in law, Esther (1973–1977). Fellow comic Pat

Morita played neighbor Ah Chew. Others made guest appearances including **Scatman Crothers**; former Little Rascal **Stymie Beard**; Leroy Daniels and Ernest Mayhand (comedy duo Leroy and Skillet); Dap Sugar Willie; Cha-Cha Hogan; Allan Drake; Timmie Rogers; Norma Miller; Foxx's stepdaughter, Debraca Foxx; his business managers Bardu Ali and Prince Spencer; and his bodyguard, Barry Wright. Once the series went to South Central Los Angeles and picked up about a dozen of Foxx's old cronies basically off the streets and made them actors for the day.

Hal Williams recalls, "Howard [Platt] and I were talking recently about what a good time we had working on *Sanford and Son*. We didn't know it then but those were the good old days. I look at the reruns now and even though I was there and I know what line is coming up, it is still funny. It's the talent and skill of Redd as well as Ilunga Adell [a black writer] and all the other writers and producers and all of Redd's cronies. The show behind the scenes was as funny as the videotaped show." During the time when Foxx refused to rehearse, Williams continued, "I can't tell now which episodes he did or didn't rehearse; he was just funny." The series and Foxx were nominated several times for the **Emmy Award** but never won. Foxx won the Golden Globe Award for Best TV Actor in a Comedy in 1973. *See also* LONG-RUNNING SERIES.

SANFORD ARMS, THE (*NBC, 1977*). Although its run was brief, this spin-off of the popular *Sanford and Son* was set up in several episodes of the parent series in which Fred Sanford and his son, Lamont (played by **Redd Foxx** and **Demond Wilson**), bought a rooming house near his house/junkyard. Then, when Foxx and Wilson left *Sanford and Son*, the network and producers thought *The Sanford Arms* might be a way of using the other popular characters in the new series. **Theodore Wilson** was cast as Phil Wheeler, the new owner of the rooming house. In the script, Fred and Lamont had moved to Arizona. Phil had a girlfriend (**Bebe Drake-Hooks**) and two children (Tina Andrews and John Earl). Playing the roles they played on *Sanford and Son* were the following: **LaWanda Page** as Esther Anderson, **Whitman Mayo** as Grady Wilson; **Norma Miller** as Grady's wife, Dolly; **Don Bexley** as Bubba; and **Raymond Allen** as Woody.

SANFORD, ISABEL. Sanford, in 1981, won the **Emmy Award** for Outstanding Lead Actress in a Comedy Series for her role of Louise "Weezy" Jefferson on the sitcom *The Jeffersons*. She was the first black woman to win the coveted Emmy in that category. She created the character on *All in the Family* and then played for 11 seasons in her starring role on *The Jeffersons*. Sanford guest-starred in the *Dean Martin Celebrity Roast* of **Redd Foxx** in 1976 and in the retrospective special *CBS: On the Air* in 1978. She also appeared in *The Sensational, Shocking, Wonderful Wacky 70s* in 1980 and *Night of 100 Stars* in 1982. Sanford was born in 1917 and died in 2004 of natural causes.

SANTANA, MERLIN. Santana played Marcus Dixon on the sitcom *Getting By* (1993–1994), Marcus on the drama *Under One Roof* (1995), and Romeo Santana on *The Steve Harvey Show* (1996–2002). In *The Cosby Show*, he played Stanley, who had a crush on Rudy. On November 9, 2002, Santana was shot and killed while sitting in a car in Los Angeles. A teenage girl falsely told two men that Santana had "made some sort of physical advance on her." The two men were angered; one shot Santana with a shotgun and the other with a handgun. Later, the girl recanted her story. The two gunmen and the girl received prison sentences.

SARAH VAUGHAN: THE DIVINE ONE *(PBS, July 29, 1991).* This documentary chronicled Vaughan's career beginning with her childhood and including her rise to fame as a premier interpreter of popular song.

SATCHMO *(PBS, July 31, 1989).* This documentary examined the life and career of singer/trumpeter **Louis Armstrong** from his poor beginnings in New Orleans to his success as a jazz superstar. It offered insights into his struggles in a white world and showed scenes from his films.

SATURDAY NIGHT LIVE *(NBC, 1975–).* A Saturday night mainstay for more than a quarter century, this 90-minute comedy/variety, nicknamed SNL, was intended to bring outrageous comedy to the late night audience. In addition, it aired live on the East Coast, signifying that the performers were very professional and very well rehearsed with fine-tuned scripts. The Not Ready for Prime Time Players were not famous when they joined the series, but most became famous on the show. The men have been much more successful than the women. Some went on to movie careers; others showed they were ready for prime time and went into key or starring roles in television series. The African Americans who were regulars on the series were the following: **Garrett Morris** (1975–1980), **Eddie Murphy** (1981–1984), **Danitra Vance** (1985–1986), **Tim Meadows** (1991–2000), **Chris Rock** (1990–1993), Ellen Cleghorne (1991–1995), **Tracy Morgan** (1996–2003), **Maya Rudolph** (2000–), Jerry Minor (2000), Dean Edwards (2001–), Finesse Mitchell (2003–), and Kenan Thompson (2003–). Eddie Murphy's SNL parody of entertainer James Brown was one of *TV Guide*'s 100 Most Memorable TV Moments in 2004.

Numerous celebrities were guest hosts, some of them not from the entertainment world. Memorable was the Rev. Jesse Jackson, who also recited the lyrics to "Bonnie Jean" in 1984. Some African-American guest hosts were **Halle Berry, Oprah Winfrey, Ray Charles, Lou Gossett**, Walter Payton, **Quincy Jones**, and **Michael Jordan**.

SAUNDERS, JOHN. Saunders has credits for both ABC and ESPN sports. He joined ABC Sports in 1990 and anchored the college football scoreboard show and college basketball's studio show. He joined ESPN in 1986 as *SportsCenter* anchor and later hosted *ESPN Magazine's Sports Reporters*.

SCARED STRAIGHT! ANOTHER STORY (*November 6, 1980*). This two-hour dramatic film for television was based on the successful 1979 television documentary *Scared Straight*. It centered on a fictional prison encounter group helping to scare juveniles into leading crime-free, drug-free lives. **Stan Shaw** starred as a hard-time convict, Carl Jones. Other key roles were played by **Randy Brooks, Eric Laneuville, Nathan Cook**, and **Bebe Drake-Hooks**.

SCARED STRAIGHT! 20 YEARS LATER (*SYN, 1999*). *Scared Straight* was a 1979 documentary about convicts at New Jersey's Rahway State Prison who used intimidation and their experiences to stop juvenile delinquents from continuing lives of crime. After winning an **Academy Award**, it aired on television. The juveniles vowed "I don't want to end up here." Later, grown-up viewers of all races who saw the production as kids wrote on Internet sites how the documentary actually scared them into going straight. They spoke about never having heard profanity on television until that time and their realization that prison was indeed not a pleasant place to be. In 1999, *Scared Straight! 20 Years Later* aired on syndicated television; it was a reunion of the convicts and the kids, a kind of where-are-they-now piece. Most of the former troublemakers (15 out of 17) had gone straight. Whereas the original documentary was the first intentional broadcast of the "f-word," by 1999, graphic language was no longer shocking. Social workers say that such documentaries and programs are not a great deterrent to subsequent juvenile crime.

SCOEY MITCHLLL SHOW, THE (*SYN, April, 1972*). Comedian Mitchlll was the star and host of this one-hour variety special also featuring the Carlton Johnson Dancers, Jim Erving, Damita Jo Freeman, Buddy Hackett, Dave Reeves, Dorothy Van, and **Nancy Wilson**.

SCOTT, HAZEL. The singer and pianist was star of *The Hazel Scott Show* in 1950, one of the first shows to star a black person and a boon for women too. Her style of music was stride/boogie-woogie. She was the wife of Adam Clayton Powell, a minister and U.S. congressman. Scott was born in 1920 and died in 1981.

SCOTT, LARRY B. Scott played James Ramsuer, a youth shot by Bernhard Goetz, in *The Trial of Bernhard Goetz* in 1988. He played F. X. Spinner in the syndicated sci-fi series *Super Force* (1990–1992).

SCOTT, STUART. Scott joined ESPN in 1993, when it launched ESPN2. He anchored *SportsCenter* and interviewed Tiger Woods, Sammy Sosa, and President Clinton. His credits also include hosting ESPN's *Edge NFL Matchup* and ESPN2's *NBA 2Night* and serving as a staff member on the *Sunday NFL Countdown* preview program. Commenting on hate mail he received, Scott said the language was scathing. "You're supposed to say it doesn't bother you. But I keep those letters and read them from time to time. They inspire me."

SCOUT'S HONOR (*NBC, September 30, 1980*). **Gary Coleman** starred in this telefilm as Joey Seymour, an orphan who wants, more than anything, to be a Boy Scout. This was child star Coleman's second television movie, and it also featured former child stars playing the parents of fellow scouts. Among them were Angela Cartwright of *Make Room for Daddy*, Lauren Chapin of *Father Knows Best*, Jay North of *Dennis the Menace*, and Paul Peterson of *The Donna Reed Show*. **Al Fann** and **Hope Clarke** also had roles. Coleman's own production company, Zephyr Productions, produced the film.

SEALES, FRANKLYN. Seales was Dexter Stuffins in the sitcom *Silver Spoons* (1982–1986). He was the choir director, Lorenzo Hollingsworth, in *Amen*, from 1986 to 1987. He performed in the children's special *Henry Winkler Meets William Shakespeare* in 1977. Seales was born in 1952 and died in 1990 of complications from AIDS.

SECOND AGONY OF ATLANTA, THE (*NBC, February 1, 1959*). This news special centered on the federal court order to integrate Atlanta's public schools and the conflict with Georgia law to close all schools if one were to be integrated.

SECOND TIME AROUND (*UPN, 2004*). Nicole Parker and **Boris Kodjoe**, who starred as an on-again/off-again couple on the drama series *Soul Food*, began this sitcom in the fall of 2004. They played two former spouses who decide to give marriage another try.

SECRET DIARY OF DESMOND PFEIFFER, THE (*UPN, 1998*). This sitcom aired only a few episodes before it was taken off the air. **Chi McBride** starred as Desmond Pfeiffer, the English butler to President Abraham Lincoln. African Americans headed by the Brotherhood Crusade picketed Paramount Studios, where the show was produced with signs reading, "Slavery is not funny." The spokesperson for the organization, Danny Bakewell, said, "The show trivializes our suffering, exploits our pain, and distorts history." UPN argued that the series did not feature negative images, nor did it find humor in slavery. The network maintained that the show was political satire and that Pfeiffer was the smartest character on the show and was the president's most trusted adviser. Reviews were also negative, and UPN countered them with promos saying, "The critics hate it! You will love it!" The Los Angeles City Council joined the opposition and unanimously called for a delay of the premiere until there could be a community screening to determine whether the show was appropriate for broadcast. NAACP President Kwesi Mfume agreed that the show trivialized a "very painful part of American history." Once the series aired, it lasted only a month.

SELMA, LORD, SELMA (*ABC, January 17, 1999*). This two-hour made-for-television film was based on two little girls and their memories of Bloody Sunday in Selma, Alabama, during the civil rights riots of the 1960s. **Ella Joyce** played Betty Webb; **Jurnee Smollett** played the central character, Sheyann Webb; and **Yolanda King** played Miss Bright. **Clifton Powell** portrayed Martin Luther King Jr. *See also* HISTORICAL EVENTS DRAMATIZED.

SENECA, JOE. Seneca played Wilma Rudolph's father, Ed, in *Wilma* in 1977. He had roles in *Solomon Northrup's Odyssey* (1984), Pluto in *House of Dies Drear* (1984), the Reverend in *Samaritan: The Mitch Snyder Story* (1986), Clatoo in *A Gathering of Old Men* (1987), and Deacon Wilkes in *The Vernon Johns Story* (1994). Seneca was born in 1919 and died in 1996.

SEPARATE BUT EQUAL (*ABC, April 7–8, 1991*). Sidney Poitier starred in this miniseries, a biopic about Supreme Court Justice Thurgood Marshall and the events leading up to the landmark Supreme Court decision to ban segregation in public schools. **Cleavon Little** played Robert L. "Bob" Carter, and **Lynn Thigpen** played Ruth Alice Stovall. Burt Lancaster was John W. Davis, and Richard Kiley was Earl Warren. *See also* HISTORICAL EVENTS DRAMATIZED.

SERIES ABOUT SCHOOL LIFE. Historically, these series set in schools tended to be the most realistically integrated series ethnically. There was no forced casting of one black actor or one white actor to satisfy pressure groups or to avoid criticism. Whether comedy or drama, they approximated the look of real schools in the United States. Among them were *Room 222* (1969–1974), which had white and black teachers and students. *Fame* (1982–1983) not only had black and white faculty members and students but also added Hispanic and foreign cast members, much like the real High School of Performing Arts in New York City. *Boston Public* (2001–2004), again, had a thoroughly integrated cast of characters. *See also* BILL COSBY SHOW; WELCOME BACK, KOTTER.

SERIES WITH ONE BLACK SUPPORTING ACTOR/ PERFORMER BEFORE 1980. From the beginning of television up through the 1970s, seeing a black actor on a dramatic or comedy series was destined to be conversation among blacks. A guest star was unusual, so when black actors were cast as regulars in series that did not have all-black casts, it was big news. At first, these actors played domestic workers like **Willie Best** in *My Little Margie* (1952) and *The Stu Erwin Show* (1950–1955) and Amanda Randolph, who played the maid on *The Danny Thomas Show* (1953–1971). As the NAACP and other pressure groups complained, the domestic roles began to be dropped. Among the first such series were *East Side/West Side* (1963–1964) with **Cicely Tyson**, *Hogan's Heroes* (1965–1970) with **Ivan Dixon**, and *Daktari* with **Hari Rhodes** (1966–1969). Variety and comedy series also had the one black regular in the cast. Among those were *Sing Along with Mitch* (1961–1966) with **Leslie Uggams** and *The Jack Benny Show* (1950–1977) with **Eddie "Rochester" Anderson**. Of course, the one-black-supporting-actor casting still exists, but in the 1980s, the one-black-actor shows ceased to be conversation over the office water cooler. Black super performers like **Sammy Davis Jr.**, **Harry Belafonte**, and **Lena Horne** broke the color barrier in variety series and specials much earlier than actors in sitcoms and drama series.

SESAME STREET (*PBS, 1969–* **).** This education-through-entertainment program for preschoolers, from its inception on November 10, 1969, consisted of live action coupled with Jim Henson's Muppets, cartoons, stories, and songs to encourage children to solve problems, learn concepts, and develop reading skills, particularly learning the alphabet and numbers from 1 to 20. Most shows were said to be "sponsored" by specific letters of the alphabets or numbers, like a commercial. The show, at first, targeted inner-city children, but it quickly proved popular to children of all backgrounds. The black cast members who played characters who lived on magical Sesame Street included Matt Robinson and **Roscoe Orman** (both played Gordon), **Alaina Reed** as Olivia, **Loretta Long** as Susan, Miles Orman as Miles, **Clarice Taylor** as Harriet, David Langston Smyrl as Mr. Handford, Angel Jemmott as Angel, Syvae and Rachel McDaniel as Kayla, and Jou Jou Papailler as Jamal. **Harry Belafonte** was the first of hundreds of celebrities to visit the Street. **Lena Horne** sang "It's Not Easy Being Green" and compared her life as a black person to Kermit's. **Queen Latifah**, in 1993, used rap to teach the "Letter O." **Denzel Washington** was a grouch poet in 1989. Soon after its premiere, the series was reportedly banned for a month in Mississippi because of its racially mixed cast. The series was developed by the Children's Television Workshop with financial support from the U.S. Office of Education, the Ford Foundation, and the Carnegie Corporation.

SESAME STREET . . . 20 AND STILL COUNTING (*NBC, April 7, 1989*). **Bill Cosby** hosted this peek at the history of *Sesame Street* on the occasion of its celebration of two decades on the air. Guest stars were **Ray Charles**, Placido Domingo, and Jim Henson and the Muppets.

SEVEN WISHES OF JOANNA PEABODY, THE (*ABC, September 9, 1978*). **Butterfly McQueen** and **Bobatoon Star-Shemah** starred in this comedy drama, a one-hour production of an *ABC Afterschool Special*. In the story, 12 year-old Joanna Peabody (Star-Shemah) was offered seven wishes by her fairy godmother (McQueen), and conflicts arose as she made efforts to choose the wishes. **Garrett Morris** played Frank. Starletta DuPois played Mother.

SHADOWBOXING: THE JOURNEY OF THE AFRICAN-AMERICAN FIGHTER (*ESPN2, 1999*). This one-hour documentary narrated by **Andre Braugher** centered on the struggles of African-American boxers through the 1950s. It described the racial hostility that denied opportunities to gifted but now forgotten boxers as well as classic footage of greats like Jack Johnson, Sugar Ray Robinson, and Joe Louis. Louis's son, Joe Louis-Barrow, talked about how his father became a true American hero after he beat German Max Schmeling when Adolf Hitler was "marching through

Europe." "The irony," said Louis-Barrow, "was that Louis was representing freedom and democracy across the world when he couldn't live those freedoms and democracies."

SHAFT (*CBS, 1973–1974*). **Richard Roundtree**, who played the legendary private detective John Shaft in the pop culture classic movie *Shaft*, brought the role to television in this 90-minute drama series, which rotated with two other series. Isaac Hayes's **Academy Award**–winning theme music was also used. Black critics said the series failed to understand the cultural context of the hero Shaft, and the series lasted only one season.

SHANGE, NTOZAKE. Ntozake was the author and was one of seven performers in the televised version of the Broadway choreopoem *For Colored Girls Who Have Considered Suicide/When The Rainbow Is Enuf* in 1982.

SHANNON, VICELLOUS REON. Shannon played Keith Palmer on the drama series *24* (2001–2002) and Cornelius Hawkins in the drama series *Dangerous Minds* (1996–1997). He had a key role in the TV film *Dancing in September* (2001).

SHARPE, SAUNDRA. Sharpe (aka S. Pearl Sharpe), also a poet, writer, and producer, starred in the TV film *Hollow Image* (1979) and played Nurse Peggy Shotwell in *St. Elsewhere* (1984–1986). Her poetry was used in *When Hell Freezes Over I'll Skate* (1979).

SHARPTON, AL. The Rev. Sharpton hosted *I Hate My Job*, a 2004 reality show.

SHAW, BERNARD. Shaw, the first anchor at Cable News Network (CNN), took the position in 1980. He was also CNN's chief Washington correspondent. Before joining CNN, Shaw had worked at local radio and television stations. He worked for CBS for three years and ABC for five (as chief of the Latin American bureau). At CNN, he is remembered for anchoring nearly a full day's coverage of the Persian Gulf War. For his work, he received numerous awards including an **Emmy Award** in 1989 in the News and Documentaries category. He was also awarded the CableACE Award for Best Newscaster of the Year in 1991 by the National Academy of Cable Programming. He retired in 2001.

SHAW, STAN. Shaw played Will Palmer in the 1979 miniseries *Roots: The Next Generations*. In 1980, he starred in *Scared Straight! Another Story* playing hard-time convict Carl Jones. He was Lafe Tate in the legal drama *The Mississippi* (1983–1984).

SHAY, MICHELE. Shay played Henrietta Morgan Bingham in the daytime drama *Another World* (1982–1984). She played a key role in 1975's *Ceremonies in Dark Old Men*, Titania in 1982's *A Midsummer Night's Dream*, and Sheila in 1981's *Skokie*. She had a role in *The Neighborhood* (1982).

SHEPHERD, SHERRI. Shepherd had roles in the following sitcoms: Ramona in *Less Than Perfect* (2002–), Melva in *Emeril* (2001), Miranda in *Suddenly Susan* (1999–2000), Miss Boggs in *Holding the Baby* (1998), and Victoria Carlson in *Cleghorne* (1995–1996).

SHERIDAN, RONDELL. Comic Sheridan starred in the sitcom *Minor Adjustments* as Dr. Ron Aimes (1995–1996). He played Andre Walker in the sitcom *Cousin Skeeter* (1998–2000) and Victor Baxter in the sitcom *That's So Raven* beginning in 2003.

SHIRLEY BASSEY SPECIAL, THE (*SYN, September 1968*). Singer Shirley Bassey's solo concert made up this one-hour special.

SHIRLEY BASSEY SPECIAL, THE (*SYN, May 1969*). A one-hour concert of music and song, Bassey was joined by guest Laurindo Almeida.

SHIRLEY BASSEY SPECIAL, THE (*SYN, July 1981*). Twelve years later, Bassey was still the headliner of a one-hour television concert, and this time her songs were complemented by music and singing by Michel LeGrand and Dusty Springfield.

SHOW BIZ (*NBC, October 9, 1955*). **Eartha Kitt** was one of the entertainers on this show, which took a look at music and comedy dating from Vaudeville. Art Linkletter was the host with numerous white entertainers including Rosemary Clooney, Dennis Day, Buster Keaton, and Groucho Marx.

SHOW BUSINESS SALUTE TO MILTON BERLE (*NBC, December 4, 1973*). **Sammy Davis Jr.** was host of this one-hour tribute to comedian Milton Berle, called Mr. Television. Other guest celebrities were **Redd Foxx**, Jack Benny, Lucille Ball, Kirk Douglas, Bob Hope, and others. **Quincy Jones** did the music.

SHOWTIME AT THE APOLLO. There was a show titled *Showtime at the Apollo* in 1954. It was a showcase for black musicians and singers. *See* IT'S SHOWTIME AT THE APOLLO for the show that began in 1987.

SICILY. Sicily played Spirit, Breanna's best friend, on *One on One* (2001–). She also played Aisha the yellow Power Ranger on *Mighty Morphin Power Rangers*.

SIDEKICKS (*CBS, March 21, 1974*). **Lou Gossett** re-created the role he played in the 1971 feature film *Skin Game* in this TV western comedy film also starring Larry Hagman (in the role played by James Garner in the feature). The two were post–Civil War con men on the sagebrush trail trying to collect a $15,000 bounty on an outlaw's head.

SIDNEY, ORELON. Sidney's national credits include being weather anchor for the CNN News Group, specifically for CNN/U.S., CNN International, CNNfn, and CNN Airport Network.

SIDNEY, P. JAY. Sidney (aka Jay P. Sidney) played minor roles in more than 70 productions in early television and was Private Palmer on the sitcom *You'll Never Get Rich* in 1955. In anthology series, he was Cato in "The Plot to Kidnap General Washington" on *Hallmark Hall of Fame* in 1952 and Peterson on "Man in the Corner" on *The U.S. Steel Hour* in 1955. Historian Bogle, citing Sidney's role as a waiter on "Appointment in Samera" on *Robert Montgomery Presents* (1950–1957), said, "No one would think twice about the role—it's so slight—were it not for the fact that it was one of the few that featured a serious Black actor during that era; and the drama itself was one of the few to incorporate the Negro in some manner into American life." Sidney was born in 1915 and died in 1996. *See also* ANTHOLOGY SERIES; TELEVISION PIONEERS.

SILVERA, FRANK. Silvera's lighter skin gave him the opportunity to play other people of color as well as black portrayals. He made 35 guest-star appearances in series between 1957 and 1970. In TV films, he played Carlos in *The Young Loner* (1968). In 1967, in the western *The High Chaparral*, Silvera was a member of the regular cast and played Don Sebastian Montoya, father-in-law to Leif Erickson's character, Big John Cannon, owner of the Arizona ranch called the High Chaparral. Linda Cristal played Montoya's daughter. He was born in 1914 and died in 1970 while the series *The High Chaparral* was still airing. *See also* SERIES WITH ONE BLACK SUPPORTING ACTOR/PERFORMER BEFORE 1980; TELEVISION PIONEERS.

SIMMS, HILDA. Simms played the wife of **Sidney Poitier**'s character in **"A Man Is Ten Feet Tall"** on *Philco Television Playhouse* in 1955.

SIMPLE LIFE OF NOAH DEARBORN, THE (*CBS, May 9, 1999*). **Sidney Poitier** starred as Dearborn, a skilled craftsman who refused to sell his land for modern development. Mary-Louise Parker also starred.

SIMPSON, CAROLE. Simpson joined ABC News in 1982 after first working for NBC News, where she covered the U.S. Congress. At ABC, her credits include being coanchor of *World News Tonight Sunday*, senior correspondent for ABC News on *World News Tonight with Peter Jennings*, and *Good Morning America*. She has also appeared on *20/20*, *Nightline*, and other news broadcasts. She was one of the reporters on the documentary *Black in White America* and was on the *Nightline* team that covered, live, the release of Nelson Mandela from his 27 years of imprisonment in 1990. While covering that event, she was injured during a conflict between blacks and the South African police. She won an **Emmy Award** for her work and numerous other awards for her reporting on social issues including her efforts to improve opportunities for women and minorities in the broadcasting industry. In 2004, she became head of ABC's news initiative in public schools. The job was to urge youth to be informed citizens by reading newspapers and watching TV news.

SIMPSON, O. J. Former football player Simpson starred in the television films *Goldie and the Boxer* (1979) and *Goldie and the Boxer Go to Hollywood* (1981), both produced by his company, Orenthal Productions. He starred with Elizabeth Montgomery in the 1977 TV film *A Killing Affair*. He was part of the cast of the special *Whatta Year . . . 1986*. He tossed the coin for Super Bowl XXVII in 1993. He played Nordberg in *Naked Gun: From the Files of Police Squad* (1988) and *Naked Gun 33 1/3: The Final Insult* (1994). That same year, he was charged with murdering his ex-wife, Nicole Brown Simpson, and was subsequently acquitted. *See also* O. J. SIMPSON MURDER TRIAL VERDICT; O. J. SIMPSON "SLOW CHASE."

SINBAD. Sinbad won the comedy category on *Star Search* in the mid-1980s and made appearances in 1985–1986 on *Comedy Tonight*, a syndicated variety show. In 1986, he was a regular on the sitcom *The Redd Foxx Show*. In 1987, he was cohost of the variety series *Keep on Cruisin'*, and that same year, he began his role as Walter Oakes, the dorm manager and community center director on *A Different World*. He played that role until the series ended in 1991. From 1989 to 1991, he was regular host on *It's Showtime at the Apollo*. He hosted *Comic Strip: Live* from New Orleans Mardi Gras. He got his own series, the sitcom *The Sinbad Show*, from 1993 to 1994 and played a recurring role in *Cosby* in 1996. He was host of *Vibe*, a syndicated talk/music show in 1998. Sinbad hosted the comedy special *Sinbad and Friends* in 1991 and hosted *Sinbad's Summer Jam: 70's Soul Music Festival* in 1998. He guest-starred in variety specials *Motown 30: What's Going On?* in 1990 and *Muhammad Ali's 50th Birthday Celebration* in 1992. He is known for never using profanity and said, "I want people to bring the whole family to my show."

SINBAD AND FRIENDS (*ABC, December 28, 1991*). Comedian **Sinbad** delivered monologues and was host to other entertainers—**Kim Coles**, **Bill Cosby**, and Heavy D and the Boyz—in sketches. Sinbad and Mark Adkins were producers.

SINBAD'S ONE-MAN SHOW: BRAIN DAMAGED (*HBO, January 12, 1991*). The comedian's one-man show was taped on location at Morehouse College in Atlanta, Georgia. It became the second-highest-rated *Comedy Hour* ever.

SINBAD SHOW, THE (*FOX, 1993–1994*). This sitcom starred **Sinbad** as David Bryan, who designed computer game shows and lived in Silicon Valley near San Francisco. As the series started, he became a bachelor foster father to Zana (Erin Davis), a little girl, and L.J. (**Willie Norwood**), Zana's teenage, big-mouthed brother. When the kids moved in, David's roommate and friend Clarence (**T. K. Carter**), who did not share his love for the kids, had to move out. David's parents, Louise and Rudy (**Nancy Wilson** and **Hal Williams**), did appreciate the kids, and they visited often. Later in the series, David became host of a children's television show.

SINBAD'S SUMMER JAM: 70'S SOUL MUSIC FESTIVAL (*HBO, August 5, 1995*). Sinbad, from St. Maarten, hosted musical artists popular during the 1970s including the O'Jays, Earth, Wind and Fire, and **Gladys Knight**. *Sinbad's Summer Jam 2* was broadcast on HBO, August 24, 1996, from Montego Bay, Jamaica, and featured soul artists Kool and the Gang, the Gap Band, Chaka Khan, and Con Funk Shun. *Sinbad's Summer Jam 3* took place in Aruba, also on HBO, and included the Isley Brothers, the Temptations, the Barkays, and P-Funk in July 1997. *Sinbad's Soul Jam 4* aired on HBO also from Aruba on July 11, 1998. It featured 1970s stars Stephanie Mills, Earth, Wind and Fire, the Emotions, Isaac Hayes, KC & the Sunshine Band, and others. *Sinbad's Soul Jam 5* took place in the Virgin Islands in 1999 and featured Smokey Robinson, Chaka Khan, the Sylistics, Eric Benet, and Deniece Williams. Sinbad decided to host these annual specials because he loved the Kool Jazz Festivals in the 1970s. He said, "I would get *Jet* magazine which had the list of where the festival was traveling. That's how we planned our summers. From my home in Benton Harbor, Michigan, I would hit Milwaukee, I'd hit Chicago and I'd hit Cincinnati. And I said then I would like to do something like the Kool Jazz Festival . . . traveling to various places and attracting people who want to have fun . . . just sitting and people would just jam until the sun went down."

SINCLAIR, MADGE. Madge Sinclair played Bell in the miniseries *Roots* in 1977. She played the female lead in the 1978 production of the drama *Just an Old Sweet Song* and that same year played Madge in the sitcom *Grandpa Goes to Washington* and performed in the drama specials *The Rag Tag Champs.* Her longest-running series role was in the medical drama *Trapper John, M.D.*, a role she played from 1979 to 1986. She had a key role in the TV film *Jimmy B. and Andre* in 1980. Sinclair also guest-starred in the variety special *I Love Liberty* in 1982 and had a key role in *Backwards: The Riddle of Dyslexia* in 1984. In 1987, she was Gussie Lemmons in the drama series *O'Hara.* In the 1994–1995 season, she was Mary in the sitcom *Me and the Boys.* She played "Empress" Josephine Austin, Gabriel Bird's (James Earl Jones) friend, and the café owner in the series *Gabriel's Fire* from 1990 to 1992 and earned an **Emmy Award** for Outstanding Supporting Actress in a Drama Series. She had key roles in the miniseries *Alex Haley's Queen* in 1993 and *A Century of Women* in 1994. Sinclair was diagnosed with leukemia in the early 1980s, but she surpassed physicians' predictions and lived and worked until 1995.

SING ALONG WITH MITCH (*NBC, 1961–1966*). For black people, singer **Leslie Uggams** was a reason to watch this musical variety sing-along series. The singers stood on the stage at various spots on the soundstage, and the camera focused each singer for solos. Like old-time movies, the lyrics to the songs were shown on the screen encouraging viewers to actually sing along. Even though rock 'n' roll was growing in popularity, Miller didn't like it, and the singers on his show sang what was called "old standards." Uggams was the youngest and the only black singer on the show, and Miller told newspaper reporters that she never had to sing a song twice; she was called the "one-take girl." She was also the most successful alumna of the series, as she went on to host her own series and had stellar acting roles. *See also* SERIES WITH ONE BLACK SUPPORTING ACTOR/PERFORMER BEFORE 1980.

SINGERS, THE (*ABC, May 11, 1968*). Aretha Franklin and Gloria Loring performed songs from their stellar careers. *See also* VARIETY SPECIALS.

SINGSATION (*SYN, 1989– *). This gospel music program was the first nationally syndicated black-owned and -produced show of its type on commercial television. The show featured established stars and rising stars in the popular gospel music ministry.

SIRENS (*SHO, September 26, 1999*). In this TV film, an African-American college professor (**Vondie Curtis-Hall**) died at the hands of white policemen (Keith Carradine and Justin Theroux) who thought he was raping a white woman. The white woman was his former wife, Sally (Dana Delaney), who took him to a secluded spot with romantic intentions. Sally learns that her eyewitness account of what happened is meaningless when compared with police testimony. Brian Dennehy played the police detective.

SISKEL & EBERT SPECIAL ABOUT THE NEW BLACK CINEMA (*SYN, June 5, 1992*). Gene Siskel and Roger Ebert spoke with guests—**Whoopi Goldberg**, Spike Lee, John Singleton, and **Wesley Snipes**—about the media images of African Americans and what they expect in the future. The guests expressed their opinions about the pressures of being African American in the film industry and their own triumphs and frustrations. One of the frustrations discussed were white directors directing films about African-American culture and life. Included were clips of numerous films. *See also* DOCUMENTARIES.

SISTAS 'N THE CITY (*SHO, March 25, 2003*). This animated parody of *Sex and the City* followed four African-American women who lived in Chicago and are friends. Tamika (voice of **Dawnn Lewis**), Jordan (voice of Marcy T. House), Mercedes (also the voice of

Dawnn Lewis), and Athena (voice of rapper Medusa) were the center of the stories. They were black yuppies who meet at trendy nightspots, work out at health clubs, and struggle with romance. Tamika was a career-driven publicist. Mercedes was an artist. Jordan was a law clerk. Athena was a lesbian singer. Creator/executive producer **Tina Andrews** admitted being "irked by the cable show featuring four white women who have no interaction with anybody of color, and they live in New York City." She added, "I have this thing about watching television and not necessarily seeing black female representation."

SISTERS IN THE NAME OF LOVE (*HBO, July 12, 1986*). Gladys Knight, Patti LaBelle, and Dionne Warwick joined in concert in this one-hour variety special taped over two nights with an audience at the Aquarius Theatre in Hollywood. Among the songs the three ladies sang were "That's What Friends Are For" and "There's a Place for Us." The show won three CableACE awards, and LaBelle was named Entertainer of the Year. **Gladys Knight** and Bubba Knight were producers with Bob Henry. H. B. Barnum did the music.

SISTER, SISTER (TV film) (*NBC, June 7, 1982*). This TV film of a Maya Angelou story starred **Diahann Carroll**, **Rosalind Cash**, and **Irene Cara** as sisters with very different personalities and choices of lifestyle. The extremely domineering prim and proper eldest sister (Carroll) wanted to keep everything as she felt their deceased father would have wished. This caused friction between the sisters since the other two were free spirits. **Paul Winfield, Dick Anthony Williams,** and **Cristoff St. John** also starred.

SISTER, SISTER (sitcom) (*ABC, 1994–1995; WB, 1995–1999*). Identical teenage twins **Tia** and **Tamera Mowry** starred in this sitcom as twins Tamera Campbell and Tia Landry, who were separated from each other as infants when their feuding parents each decided to take one twin. By chance, they met in a shopping mall and after getting acquainted decided they would not be separated again. The decision forced their father, Ray Campbell (**Tim Reid**), recently widowed, and their mother, Lisa Landry (**Jackee Harry**), now a widow, to move into the same house, "platonically," so that the sisters could be together. *See also* LONG-RUNNING SERIES.

SITCOMS. The situation comedy, or sitcom, is the most common television genre, considering not only black programs but all programs as well. *Amos 'n' Andy* was the first milestone sitcom. Many black Americans thought it was funny, and most people who recall the show still praise the talents of the actors. However, the negative stereotypes perpetuated on the show ceased to be regarded as laughable by many vocal persons, and the show was canceled. *Julia*, which premiered in 1968, was the next milestone—the first black female to star in a sitcom as a professional woman and the first sitcom that proved that a white audience would watch a show starring a black person. The Norman Lear sitcoms—*All in the Family*, which gave birth to *The Jeffersons*; *Maude*, which gave birth to *Good Times*; and *Sanford and Son*—sparked a parade of black hit sitcoms in the 1970s. *The Cosby Show* went further and depicted a black family in which both parents were professional and the children were not overly precocious or smart-mouthed. Then, in the mid-1990s, there was a great exodus of black sitcoms from the big three networks, and the new cable networks, UPN and the WB, were the channels to turn to if you wanted to see a black sitcom. Then, in 2004, these stations began to integrate shows casting white actors in what would have been black sitcoms a few years before.

SIT-IN (*NBC, December 20, 1960*). This segment of *NBC White Paper* was a documentary on desegregation in Nashville. The subject was a sit-in of a restaurant that turned out to be one of the first nonviolent sit-ins. *See also* DOCUMENTARIES.

$64,000 QUESTION (*CBS, 1955–1958*). Conversations, in 1955, often centered on a black Baltimore girl, Gloria Lockerman, who spelled "antidisestablishmentarianism" and won $32,000 on this quiz show. Contestants chose the category in which they felt more expert. Each week, the contestant would have the opportunity to answer a more difficult question and double the money he or she had won the week before. Or contestants could take their winnings and quit at any time. Lockerman quit at $32,000. The quiz show scandal of 1958 ended this and all television quiz shows of the era.

60 MINUTES (*CBS, 1968– *). **Ed Bradley** was one of the weekly correspondents on this, the father of newsmagazines, since 1981.

Bradley covered stories about the African-American experience as well as mainstream stories. He interviewed Lena Horne in 1983. He won the Peabody Award in 2000 for his story on Africans and AIDS. The show helped convince drug companies to donate and discount AIDS drugs. He won numerous awards, including several **Emmy Awards**. One was for his 2000 interview with Oklahoma City bomber Timothy McVeigh, and another was his story of the trials of the Catholic Church in 2002. He won numerous other awards. In 2003, he interviewed entertainer **Michael Jackson** after he had been charged with molesting a child and was the only reporter with whom Jackson, who felt harassed by the news media, agreed to speak.

Andy Rooney, who each week wraps up the show with his humorous observations, was suspended for three months in 1990 for alleged racist remarks. Rooney was quoted in the Los Angeles–based *Advocate* magazine as saying, "I've believed all along that most people are born with equal intelligence, but blacks have watered down their genes because the less intelligent ones are the ones that have the most children. They drop out of school early, do drugs and get pregnant." CBS News President David W. Burke apologized. Rooney denied he said it.

SKIN COLOR OF ACTORS. It has long been argued that the media industry prefers light-skinned, European-featured African Americans to those of darker skin. In her research, Jennifer Wood traces this preference to the traditions of slavery when slave owners relegated dark-skinned slaves to fieldwork while lighter-skinned slaves worked in the master's house. The separation translated to movie and television screens where "dark-skinned blacks got roles as servants or comics, while only light skinned . . . actors and actresses could be considered for serious roles," according to Marjorie Garber. Sandra Dickerson traces Hollywood's first portrayals of poles of skin color to a work often hailed as the first feature film, D. W. Griffith's *Birth of a Nation*. White actors in darker blackface portrayed villainous, prickly, and untrustworthy characters, while the light-skinned or mulatto characters remained good, subservient, and physically attractive.

Conversely, when it became politically correct to hire black actors, lighter-skinned actors claim that casting people wanted to make sure viewers knew the actor was black and that these actors failed to get work because they were not dark enough. Temple Hatton was one of those. He acted in college plays and little theater in Santa Barbara, California. Then, in the early 1950s, he tried Hollywood. He worked in theater groups and managed to get an agent (Lil Cumber who was the most recognized, if not the only, black agent) and become a member of Actors Equity and the Screen Actors Guild. He had small roles in two films. He recalled, "I was told by several people who should know that I was a good actor. However, on every interview I would be told, 'We never have calls for your type.' I was the most interviewed man in the world!" During that time **Sidney Poitier**, **Greg Morris**, **Roy Glenn**, and **Bernie Hamilton** were getting a little work. **Sammy Davis Jr.** and **Godfrey Cambridge** got work as actors because they had names as entertainers. But all these actors were at least a few shades darker than Hatton. Hatton said, "They even hired darker Jewish actors and put turbans on their heads to play East Indians. I admired **Frank Silvera** because he had a look that made him able to play other Mexicans and other ethnicities." Hatton gave up the fight in the mid-1960s and got work as a television executive at CBS and NBC. He was a censor at NBC from 1968 to 1986. *See also* DICK VAN DYKE SHOW.

SKIN OF OUR TEETH, THE (*NBC, September 11, 1955*). This two-hour dramatic play was adapted from the play by Thornton Wilder and starred Helen Hayes as Mrs. Antrobus and Mary Martin as Sabrina Antrobus. This is significant in African-American television history in that **Frank Silvera**, a Negro actor who because of his physical appearance was able to play nonblack roles, played Mr. Tremayne in 1955. *See also* BROADWAY PLAYS AND MUSICALS.

SLAVERY AND THE MAKING OF AMERICA (*PBS, February 9 and 16, 2005*). **Morgan Freeman** narrated this four-part series, which told the story of slavery from the point of view of the enslaved. The series highlighted the humanity and dignity of slaves and showed them as proactive fighters for their freedom. Dante James was producer.

SMART GUY (*WB, 1997–1999*). **Tahj Mowry** played the lead, T. J. Henderson, in this sitcom about a 10-year-old high school genius who tried to fit in with the older students, friends of his brother Marcus (**Jason Weaver**) and sister Yvette (**Essence Atkins**). John Marshall Jones played their widower father. **Omar Gooding** played T.J's friend, Mo.

SMILEY, TAVIS. Smiley, in 2004, began a new talk show on PBS titled *Tavis Smiley*. He gained fame as host of his signature show, *BET Tonight with Tavis Smiley* on **Black Entertainment Television**. His later credits include being a contributor to the CNN News Group and appearing on several CNN/U.S. programs offering commentary and analysis to news and political stories. He also filled in as host on *CNN Talkback Live* and contributed political commentary to *Inside Politics*. On radio, he was the popular political analyst on *The Tom Joyner Morning Show*. Smiley is the recipient of several awards including the NAACP Image Award for Best News, Talk or Information Series; the NAACP President's Award; the National Association of Black Journalists (NABJ) Award for International Reporting; and the Mickey Leland Humanitarian Award from the National Association of Minorities in Television.

SMITH, ANNA DEAVERE. Smith played 19 characters in *Fires in the Mirror* in 1993 and performed her one-woman play *Twilight: Los Angeles* in a made-for-television film in 2001. She had a regular role in the medical drama *Presidio Med* (2002–2003).

SMITH, BESSIE. Vintage footage of Smith performing was a highlight of *The Blues*, a seven-part series about the music genre in 2003.

SMITH, IAN. In addition to credits in the medical profession and in charitable causes, Smith's credits include being medical correspondent for the NBC News Network and filing reports for *Nightly News* and *The Today Show*.

SMITH, JADA PINKETT. As Jada Pinkett, she played Lena James in *A Different World* (1991–1993) and Patty in *If These Walls Could Talk* (1996). As Jada Pinkett Smith, she and her husband, actor Will Smith, produced the sitcom *All of Us* (2003–).

SMITH, JAMIL WALKER. Smith was the voice of Mo Money Jr. in the animated series *Waynehead* (1996) and provided voices (Gerald Martin Johanssen, and Peapod Kid) on the animated series *Hey Arnold!* (1996).

SMITH, KENNY. A former player for the National Basketball Association world champion Rockets as well as the Pistons, Kings, and Hawks, Smith joined Turner Sports in 1997–1998 as a studio analyst. He returned to TNT and TBS telecasts to be a studio analyst for the 2001–2002 season.

SMITH, LARRY. Smith, after being hired by CNN in 2001, has worked as prime-time sports anchor for *CNN Headline News*. Previously, he was a sports anchor for CNN/SI and had appeared on most CNN sports programs.

SMITH, WILL. Will Smith was new to television, except as a rapper, when he assumed his starring role in *The Fresh Prince of Bel-Air* in 1990. His own production team eventually took over the series. After the series ended in 1996, Smith went on to films. He guest-starred in the variety special *NBC All-Star Stay in School Jam* in 1991 and hosted *The Chipmunks—Rockin' through the Decades* in 1990. In 2003, he and his wife **Jada Pinkett Smith** produced the sitcom *All of Us*, loosely based on their own lives.

SMOKEY JOE'S CAFÉ: THE SONGS OF LEIBER AND STOLLER (*HBO, September 10, 2000*). The musical revue *Smokey Joe's Café* showcased the popular songs written by Leiber and Stoller. The primarily black cast of the Broadway musical starred in the production taped live on Broadway. At the time, it was the longest-running musical revue in Broadway history. Among the cast were Ken Ard, Adrian Bailey, Matt Bogart, Deb Lyons, Frederick B. Owens, Brenda Braxton, Victor Trent Cook, B. J. Crosby, and DeLee Lively. *See also* BROADWAY PLAYS AND MUSICALS.

SMOKEY ROBINSON SHOW, THE (*ABC, December 18, 1970*). Motown singer **Smokey Robinson** was the host and star of this hour of music. **The Miracles, The Temptations, Diana Ross and The Supremes, Stevie Wonder**, and other Motown artists were guests.

SMOLLETT, JURNEE. Smollett starred as Sheyann Webb in *Selma, Lord, Selma* in 1999 and played Jordee in the sitcom *On Our Own* (1984–1995), Jurnee in the sitcom *Cosby* (1998–1999), Emerald Delacroix in the TV film *Ruby's Bucket of Blood* (2001), and Holly in the sitcom *Wanda at Large* (2003).

SNIPES, WESLEY. Snipes played George DuVaul in "The Boy Who Painted Christ Black" on *America's Dream* (1995). He participated in the discussion about the plight of blacks in Hollywood on *Siskel & Ebert Special about the New Black Cinema* in 1992.

SNOOPS (*CBS, 1989–1990*). Husband-and-wife acting team **Tim Reid** and **Daphne Maxwell Reid** played a husband-and-wife detective team, Chance and Micki Dennis. In Washington, D.C., Chance was a criminology professor, and Micki worked for the State Department. They were not officially detectives, but mysterious murders were committed, and they were able to solve them. Tim Reid II, Tracy Camilla Johns, and Adam Silbar played Chance's students.

SOAP (*ABC, 1977–1981*). **Robert Guillaume** won his first **Emmy Award** for his portrayal of Benson, the butler to the Tate family, in this sitcom. In 1979, the series spawned the sitcom *Benson* (1979–1986) starring Guillaume. The character Benson was very dignified, and that dignity was present partly due to the conception and script written by Susan Harris but also due to the portrayal by Guillaume. "I was frightened to death that I couldn't escape the pitfalls of comedy I had seen in the 30s and 40s," said Guillaume. He was determined that there would be no slow talking, foot shuffling, or eyes bulging that made domestic workers of film and early TV so despicable. "I tried to reduce the mobility of my facial features and I analyzed the character and determined that if a servant has all this responsibility, he has to be smart. The humor could emanate from his intelligence. He didn't have to be dumb as molasses. So, I came to think of Benson as a peer of mine and after that, there was no way I could fall into a stereotypical portrayal." *See also* DOMESTIC WORKERS IN THE 1970s.

SOJOURNER (*CBS, March 30, 1975*). A one-hour drama, *Sojourner* was the story of Sojourner Truth, a former slave who became an abolitionist. Vinnette Carroll played the title role. Thurman Scott played Frederick Douglass. *See also* BIOPICS.

SOLID ROCK (*SYN, 1980–1988*). This show of music counted down the top 10 of the past week. Sometimes the original artists sang the songs, and at other times someone lip-synced the tunes. As popular as the songs were the Solid Gold dancers, a troupe of superkinetic sexy dancers. The show is significant in this volume in that **Dionne Warwick** was the first host (1980–1981) and then again from 1985 to 1986. **Marilyn McCoo**, of Fifth Dimension fame, cohosted with Andy Gibb from 1981 to 1982 and with Rex Smith from 1982 to 1983. McCoo was solo host from 1983 to 1984 and again from 1986 to 1988.

SOLOMON NORTHRUP'S ODYSSEY (*PBS, December 10, 1984*). This production of *American Playhouse* was directed and written by Gordon Parks, who also composed the score. It was based on the life story of Solomon Northrup, a free black man who supported his wife and children through work as a carpenter and a violinist in Saratoga, New York. In 1841, he was kidnapped and sold into slavery in Louisiana and for 12 years worked the plantations until he was able to get a letter to his family. Northrup wrote a book *Twelve Years a Slave*, which became a best-seller and an important tool for abolitionists. Parks admitted that he had to omit some of the violence in the book and said, "I wanted to make it bearable for people to look at." **Avery Brooks** played Northrup; Rhetta Green, Jenny; Petronia Paley, Anne; Joe Seneca, Noah; and Michael Tolan, Henry Northrup. *See also* BIOPICS.

SOMETHING THE LORD MADE (*HBO, May 30, 2004*). Hip-hop poet **Mos Def** starred with classical-trained white actor Alan Rickman in this TV film. They were a medical team that launched the field of heart surgery at Johns Hopkins University in 1944. Prior to their experiments with "blue babies," the heart was considered too delicate for surgery. Def played Vivien Thomas, a carpenter who lost the money he had saved for medical school in the Depression. Dr. Alfred Blalock (Rickman) notices Thomas's innate skills and knowledge and takes him on first as an apprentice and then as a lab technician, but in practice, he was a surgeon. Joseph Sargent, director of the film, said "Mos (who aged 30 years in the film) uses three separate character voices—one as a young man, one as a middle-aged man, and one when he was elderly. For a rapper, that's pretty dammed sophisticated." Def, speaking of his portrayal, said, "I didn't want to come off as an educated bourgeois caricature. He was an unusual man. He was a blue-collar scientist." The film also dealt with the racial discrimination Thomas endured, like entering the lab only through the back door, being paid a janitor's salary, and being left out of celebrations of successes. **Gabrielle Union** played Thomas's wife, Clare. **Charles S. Dutton** played his father, William, and Clayton LeBouef played his educator-brother, Harold. The production won the 2004 **Emmy Award** for Outstanding Made for Television Movie. Mos Def and Rickman were also nominated for Lead Actor in a Miniseries or Movie. *See also* HISTORICAL EVENTS DRAMATIZED.

SOMMORE. The comedienne was one of *The Queens of Comedy* in the 2001 special.

SONNY AND CHER COMEDY HOUR, THE (*CBS, 1971–1977*). The popular musical variety series was basically a showcase for Sonny Bono and Cher with some regulars as backup in comedy skits. One of the regulars was **Freeman King**, who appeared on the show from 1971 to 1974. *See also* SERIES WITH ONE BLACK SUPPORTING ACTOR/PERFORMER BEFORE 1980.

SOPHIE AND THE MOONHANGER (*LIF, 1996*). In this two-hour made-for-television movie, **Lynn Whitfield** and **Jason Bernard** starred in the title roles as a couple who find they are friends with a woman (Patricia Richardson) whose husband is a member of the Ku Klux Klan. **Ja'Net DuBois** also starred.

SOPHISTICATED GENTS, THE (*NBC, September 29–October 1, 1981*). This four-hour miniseries written by **Melvin Van Peebles** was about members of a black sports club who reunited after many years to celebrate their coach and unravel a mystery. Stars were **Bernie**

Casey, **Robert Hooks, Ron O'Neal, Raymond St. Jacques, Paul Winfield, Dick Anthony Williams, Thalmus Rasulala, Denise Nicholas, Beah Richards, Rosalind Cash, Ja'Net Du Bois**, and Van Peebles.

SOUL (*NBC, 1968*). This was a variety special very much like *Rowan and Martin's Laugh-In* (George Schlatter produced both) with black performers; so it was a groundbreaking show. Reviews were highly favorable, and most (but not all) phone calls to the network were also favorable. The cast included **Redd Foxx, Nipsey Russell, Lou Rawls**, Hines, Hines & Dad (**Gregory Hines**, his father, and brother Maurice), Martha Reeves and the Vandellas, **George Kirby**, the Soul Sisters, **Slappy White**, and the H. B. Barnum Orchestra. **Cal Wilson**, Jeanne Taylor, and Larry L. Reed, alumni of the Watts Writers Workshop, were on the writing team with Digby Wolfe. Both *Laugh-In* and *Soul* had a black director, Mark Warren.

SOUL FOOD (*SHO, 2000–2004*). This series was the first successful drama series about an African-American family. Although the series was *about* a family, it was not a program for family viewing since the show had numerous explicit sex scenes. Considering its 10:00 P.M. Wednesday time slot (and even later when the same episode was repeated on Sundays), the show was obviously not targeted to children.

The series, based on the successful 1997 film of the same title, centered on the Joseph family of Chicago (though the series was filmed in Toronto). The matriarch of the family (seen in flashbacks) had died, and the three daughters and their families were the focus of the stories. **Nicole Ari Parker, Malinda Williams**, and **Vanessa Williams** played the three sisters, Teri, Bird, and Maxine, respectively. The three shared a tight bond even though they often disagreed with each other. The men in their lives added to the conflict. Lem (**Darrin Dewitt Henson**) was Malinda's husband. Kenny (**Rockmond Dunbar**) was Maxine's husband. Damon (**Boris Kodjoe**) was usually Teri's boyfriend. Maxine and Kenny's young son, Ahmad (Aaron Meeks), was approaching manhood and was close to his often-conflicting parents as well as his aunts and uncles. He was the narrator of the series, and he also experienced the greatest changes during the life of the series. The three sisters, over the years, faced infidelity, separation, death, and nearly fatal accidents. Like the movie, food was very important to the series. The family gathered each week for the big Sunday soul food dinner similar to Big Mama's big meals.

Reviews were favorable to the cast and the family relationships. *Ebony* called it "an intelligent series that doesn't sell out the Black family image." Some, like *Variety*, in reviewing the pilot, thought the graphic sex scenes were a negative point. The review read, in part, "While passion is a big part of the Joseph family dynamic, writer Felicia Henderson [also executive producer] introduces far too many booty call jokes and gratuitous sex scenes when the real appeal . . . is the sophisticated emotions and relationships, and, of course, the food." The series was canceled in 2004 after having produced 74 episodes. The ratings were apparently solid, but Showtime said it was not living up to financial standards.

Tracey Edmonds, Kenneth "Babyface" Edmonds, and George Tillman Jr. were also executive producers. Oz Scott directed several episodes.

SOUL OF THE GAME (*HBO, May 20, 1996*). **Delroy Lindo**, **Mykelti Williamson**, and **Blair Underwood** played baseball greats Satchel Paige, Josh Gibson, and Jackie Robinson, respectively, in this made-for-television dramatic movie about the Negro leagues. The players were exceptional, but for many years, they were kept from joining the major leagues because of racism and bigotry. Then things began to change. Everyone expected pitcher Paige and catcher Gibson, the most exceptional players in the Negro leagues, to be tapped for the majors. However, it was rookie Robinson who was first. Edward Herrman also starred as Branch Rickey. *See also* ATHLETES' BIOPICS.

SOUL TRAIN (*SYN, 1971– *). This former Chicago variety/dance series went syndicated in 1971. It featured black teenagers dancing and listening to music of top recording artists. Each week, the latest hits and dances were presented to a viewing audience of kids of all races, actually people of all ages. Musical groups were anxious to appear on the show to introduce their latest singles; it usually made the difference for success on the rhythm-and-blues charts. For its first 20 years, the show was hosted and produced by Don Cornelius, who ended each show with "We wish you love, peace, and Sooouuul!" Then **Mystro Clark** hosted (1997–1999), followed by actor **Shemar Moore** (1999–2003). **Dorian Gregory** took over host duties in 2003. Cornelius remained as executive producer. This was the first black television show sponsored by a black business, Johnson Products. When the show began, videotapes were sent to television stations that aired them and then passed them on to other stations in other cities, so airdates varied greatly across the country. This was a common practice in the 1970s. In the 1980s, Tribune Entertainment, responsible for distribution, began using satellites, and standard airdates came about. Singer Jody Whatley and actor **Mykelti Williamson** are former members of the dancers known as the "Soul Train Gang." **Sid McCoy** was announcer.

SOUL TRAIN LADY OF MUSIC AWARDS. This annual show celebrates the accomplishments of women recording artists in soul music—rhythm and blues, hip-hop, jazz, and gospel.

SOUL TRAIN MUSIC AWARDS, THE (*various networks and stations*). *The Soul Train Awards* honor the best recordings in soul, rhythm and blues, rap/hip-hop, and gospel over the previous year. The first special was hosted by **Dionne Warwick** and **Luther Vandross** and earned high ratings and praise. It became an annual special.

SOUL TRAIN 25TH ANNIVERSARY HALL OF FAME SPECIAL (*CBS, November 22, 1995*). Celebrating *Soul Train*'s 25th season, **Arsenio Hall** hosted various musical artists who helped make the show a success. Among them were **Michael Jackson, Stevie Wonder, Diana Ross**, Prince, **Aretha Franklin**, Al Green, and others.

SOUND OF JAZZ, THE (*CBS, December 8, 1957*). **Billie Holliday, Count Basie**, and Thelonius Monk were among what *Time* (December 23, 1957) described as "two dozen of the best jazz vocalists and sidemen worked through eight of the best jazz numbers with the kind of love, wonder, almost mystical absorption they usually sum up in the most free-wheeling jam sessions." The *New York Times* (December 8, 1957) said, "The spontaneity and artistry of modern music were presented with more authenticity, understanding and appreciation than television has ever managed before." Holliday sang the old jazz-cult favorite "Fine and Mellow." Basie and his group performed "I Left My Baby" and "Dickie's Dream." Monk did a solo. Visually, critics talked about the "stunning composition" of close-ups of feet responding to the beat, Miss Holliday's head nodding to the tones of a tenor sax, and the faces of the instrumentalists reflecting their total absorption in the music. The special was made at a recording session for the album *The Sound of Jazz.* The one-hour show was one of 22 shows planned to air as part of The Seven Lively Arts—performances in drama, music, and dance. After 10 aired, CBS announced that the series, executive-produced by John Houseman, would shut down. Houseman said the cause was a lack of sponsors.

SOUTHERNAIRES QUARTET (*ABC, 1948*). A half hour of gospel music, this series starred the Southernaires, a black quartet popular on radio. Members of the group were **Roy Yeates, Lowell Peters, Jay Stone Toney**, and **William Edmunson. Clarence Jones** was the group's pianist and arranger. Alumni of Knoxville College in Knoxville, Tennessee, say that Peters and perhaps other members of the quartet sang first as members of the Knoxville College Quartet in the mid-1930s.

SPECIALS. *See* VARIETY SPECIALS.

SPENCER, DANIELLE. As a child, Spencer played Dee Thomas on *What's Happening!!* (1976–1979) and irregularly on *What's Happening Now!!* (1985–1988). She quit show business and became a veterinarian.

SPENSER FOR HIRE (*ABC, 1985–1988*). Robert Urich, as a private eye, was the star of this detective series, but **Avery Brooks** was his black, tough sidekick, Hawk. The two solved a murder mystery each week. Brooks once told a writer for the Oberlin College of Communications that he initially had problems with the white producers of the series. "They told me just to say my lines and hit my mark," said Brooks, who said he felt strongly about his responsibility as an artist and did more than say his lines. He insisted on infusing the character with the reality of black culture, making the dialogue more "real and representative." Hawk and Brooks were so tough that the character was spun off into a series titled *A Man Called Hawk* starring Brooks. *See also* SERIES WITH ONE BLACK SUPPORTING ACTOR/ PERFORMER BEFORE 1980.

SPIKE & CO. (*PBS, October 5, 1990*). Director **Spike Lee** and **Debbie Allen** took viewers through locations in Brooklyn searching for a cappella singing groups.

SPIN-OFF SERIES. The following series were developed from other series. Generally, one or more characters from a successful series becomes the central character in a new series. The character is "spun off," so these shows are called "spin-offs." **Esther Rolle**'s character, the maid Florida Evans in *Maude*, became a central character in *Good Times*. In *All in the Family*, the Bunkers' neighbors, the Jeffersons (played by **Isabel Sanford, Sherman Hemsley,** and **Mike Evans**), became the central characters in *The Jeffersons*. A short-lived series titled *Checking In* spun off of the Jeffersons with **Marla Gibbs**'s character Florence as the lead. **Robert Guillaume** as butler *Benson* spun off of *Soap*. *Grady* starring **Whitman Mayo**, *Sanford Arms* (starring numerous characters in *Sanford and Son*), and *Sanford* (starring **Redd Foxx** as Sanford without son) all spun off of *Sanford and Son*. *A Different World*, starring Lisa Bonet, was a spin-off of *The Cosby Show*. *Family Matters* was a spin-off of *Perfect Strangers* with **Jo Marie Payton**'s character Harriette Winslow. *A Man Called Hawk*, with **Avery Brooks**, came from *Spenser: For Hire*. *The Parkers* was a spin-off of *Moesha* with **Countess Vaughn**. *See also* DOMESTIC WORKERS.

SPORTS NIGHT (*ABC, 1998*). **Robert Guillaume** was a key player in this sitcom about personnel of a cable television sports program. Guillaume was Isaac Jaffee, the no-nonsense boss. In 1999, Guillaume suffered a slight stroke, so the writers decided that Jaffee too would suffer a stroke and was written out of the scripts for a while. The actor returned to the series, somewhat affected by the stroke, but he remained until the series ended in 2000.

SST: SCREEN, STAGE, TELEVISION (*ABC, May 7, 1989*). **Robert Guillaume** was host of this one-hour documentary, which took viewers on a visit behind the scenes of television, Broadway theater, and motion pictures. Guillaume was one of the producers.

STANIS, BERNNADETTE. Also in credits simply as Bern Nadette, Stanis was introduced to television viewers as Thelma, the Evans daughter on *Good Times* (1974–1979). She also played a key role in the TV film *Hidden Blessings* (2000).

STAR SEARCH (*CBS, 2003*). Arsenio Hall hosted this one-hour talent series inspired by the original *Star Search* program (1983–1985). The categories were adult singer, junior singer, comic, supermodel, and dancer. There was a panel of celebrity judges. This modernized version boasted that it was broadcast live and that viewers could vote, through the Internet, for their favorite contestants. However, the western half of the country was ignored since those viewers saw the show that aired earlier on the East Coast and voting had ended. A highlight of the 21 episodes of 2003 was 10-year old Tiffany Evans, who won the Junior Singers competition ($100,000) and immediately went on to appear on talk-variety series and did a guest spot on *The District*.

STAR SEARCH (*SYN, 1983–1985*). Ed McMahon hosted the original talent competition that was responsible for boosting the careers of numerous celebrities. Among them are **Kim Coles**, **Martin Lawrence**, and **Sinbad** in the comedy category. **Tracey Ross**, a regular cast member on *Passions*, was the first $100,000 spokesmodel winner. In addition to comedy, dancing, spokesmodel, and singing categories, there were dramatic competitions (one won by actress Cyndi James).

STAR-SPANGLED CELEBRATION (*ABC, July 4, 1987*). Oprah Winfrey hosted this Independence Day celebration of music and comedy with guests **Kareem Abdul-Jabbar**, **Chubby Checker**, Jennifer Holliday, **Malcolm-Jamal Warner**, and numerous others including Carol Burnett, Tony Bennett, Loretta Lynn, and the Rockettes.

STAR TREK (*NBC, 1966–1969*). This science fiction drama series was about the adventures of the crew of a 23rd-century starship *Enterprise*. Though never a ratings hit in its original run, it spawned a cult following that continues today. Trekkies, as they are called, have conventions and paraphernalia. The series spawned an animated cartoon (featuring the voices of the original cast members) and some feature films. Fans say the series taught lessons in race relations and differences in people. For example, Mr. Spock (Leonard Nimoy), a central character, was "a half-breed Vulcan." His and other characters, such as the Klingons and Romulans, forced people to interact with alien races. **Nichelle Nichols** played the sole black character, Lt. Uhura, the communications officer. In one memorable episode on November 22, 1968, aliens forced Kirk (William Shatner) to embrace Uhura, making it perhaps the earliest dramatized interracial love scene on television. In 2004, *TV Guide* called this one of TV's 100 most memorable moments, saying it sent "a powerful racial message in the turbulent 60's." The scene was deleted by some NBC affiliates. *See also* INTERRACIAL ROMANCE/RELATIONSHIPS; SERIES WITH ONE BLACK SUPPORTING ACTOR/PERFORMER BEFORE 1980.

STAR TREK: DEEP SPACE NINE (*SYN, 1992–1999*). *Deep Space Nine* was about a Federation space station at the foot of a wormhole that acted as an intergalactic port. **Avery Brooks** played Benjamin Sisko, Starfleet captain in charge of the *Deep Space Nine* space station. When his wife was killed in an attack, Sisko became a single parent raising his son, Jake (Cirroc Lofton), who at 18 had spent all his life aboard starships. Sisko had an affair with and later married Kasidy Yates (**Penny Johnson**), a freighter captain. Later in the series, **Michael Dorn** from *Star Trek: The Next Generation* joined the cast as Commander Worf.

STAR TREK: ENTERPRISE (*SYN, 2001– *). *Enterprise* showcased intergalactic life before the original series in the 22nd century. True to the original premise of space exploration, *Enterprise* began the tale of the famous starship. Anthony Montgomery played Ensign Travis Mayweather, the helmsman aboard the *Enterprise*, who was friendly and at ease with aliens after spending most of his life aboard interstellar ships.

STAR TREK: THE NEXT GENERATION (*SYN, 1987–1994*). This series took place in the 24th century. The explorers of the *Enterprise* crew traveled through the galaxy to further their understanding of the universe. **LeVar Burton** played Lt. Geordi LaForge, a blind chief engineer who could see with the help of a device that sent video signals to his brain. **Michael Dorn** portrayed the Klingon Lt. Worf, a Starfleet tactical officer. **Whoopi Goldberg** played Guinan (1988–1993), a mysterious humanoid bartender.

STAR TREK: VOYAGER (*SYN, 1995–2001*). Diverting from the *Star Trek* legacy slightly, the premise of this show dealt with the starship *Voyager* lost in space. After being propelled 70,000 light years from Earth, the show chronicled the adventures the crew experiences while returning home. Roxann Bigg-Dawson played Chief Engineer B'Elanna Torres, half human and half Klingon, who was a former student at the Starfleet Academy. Her short temper usually put her at odds with the Starfleet command structure and this led to her dropping out of the Starfleet Academy. In contrast, Tim Russ played Tuvok, a calm, logical Vulcan who served as the Starfleet tactical security officer aboard *Voyager*. He was one of the most skilled pilots of his time and uniquely qualified to sit at the helm of Starfleet's first deep-space exploration vessel.

STARSKY AND HUTCH (*ABC, 1975–1979*). This one-hour action drama with much violence centered on two undercover policemen seeking to arrest low-life criminals in the most dangerous areas of Los Angeles. Bernie Hamilton played Capt. Harold Dobey, the cops' boss. **Antonio Fargas** played Huggy Bear, the regular informant.

STEELER AND THE PITTSBURGH KID, THE (*NBC, November 15, 1981*). This one-hour drama was based on a popular commercial that began in 1981 and featured football star **Mean Joe Greene**, who gave a kid admirer his football jersey in exchange for a Coca-Cola. The drama centered on Greene (playing himself) temporarily adopting a nine-year-old boy and teaching him relationships and values. Greene, the defensive tackle for the Pittsburgh Steelers, and his teammates are touched by the boy's love of football. Henry Thomas played the kid.

STEREOTYPES. Actor **Robert Guillaume**, who won two **Emmy Awards** playing the role of the butler Benson on the sitcoms *Soap* and *Benson*, said, "I tried to avoid the stereotypical sociological traps. I wanted children to understand the characters I portray are real people, that the solutions these characters find to life's problems are true and possible. It has always been important to me to stress that the characters had no less power because they were African-Americans." Researcher Mark Orbe defines stereotypes as "implicitly or explicitly judgmental ways of categorizing particular individuals and groups based on oversimplified and over-generalized features or signs." Good and bad or positive and negative, stereotypes exist. For example, the stereotypical soccer mom is marked by her penchant for high-end minivans or behemoth sports utility vehicles, while the stereotypical superwoman works full time in a rewarding career while still finding time to clean the house, attend to the garden, and be caring and attentive to her husband and children.

Before television, critics of the portrayals of black people concentrated on movies. Beginning with the film *Birth of a Nation*, the complaints are varied and many and were carried over immediately to television. Historians like Donald Bogle and Peter Noble list some of the common stereotypes that were or are offensive to blacks. Bogle lists mammies, bucks, jesters, servants, guardian angels, and others. Noble concentrated on 19 stereotypes that encompass the lists of other historians. Some of them have not been as serious a problem in television as they were in early movies. The list follows: 1) the devoted servant, 2) the natural-born musician, 3) the perfect entertainer, 4) the natural-born cook, 5) the vicious criminal, 6) the razor and knife "toter," 7) the superior athlete, 8) the petty thief, 9) the social delinquent, 10) the sexual superman, 11) the savage African, 12) the happy slave, 13) the corrupt politician, 14) the irresponsible citizen, 15) the unhappy nonwhite, 16) the superstitious churchgoer, 17) the uninhibited expressionist, 18) the mental inferior, and 19) the chicken and watermelon eater.

In the early days of television, according to historians and critics, when a black actor appeared on television, he or she was often the devoted servant (*Beulah*), the perfect entertainer and the natural-born musician (all the entertainers on early variety series), or the superior athlete (heroes of boxing matches that were popular fare).

In his films *Ethnic Notions* and *Color Adjustment*, filmmaker Marlon Riggs points to the logic that justified slavery as starting point for the stereotypes that black Americans combat in real life and in film and television screen images. According to Riggs and other scholars, the stereotypes reserved for women included the mammy, a fiction by which enslaved women, usually presented as dark skinned and heavyset, were presented as enjoying working for white plantation owners; the Jezebel, blatantly promiscuous; and the tragic mulatto, subservient, gentle, and tormented by being of mixed race and therefore neither fully black nor completely white. Stereotypes for African-American men included the coon, often presented as violent and susceptible to criminal thoughts or acts; Sambo, lazy and sometimes sneaky; and the uncle, good natured and happy to be a slave, the male version of the mammy. J. Fred MacDonald and Bogle offer detailed examinations of stereotypes in their respective works on television and film.

After battles by organizations like the NAACP and after research revealed that blacks watch a lot of television and buy many consumer products advertised on television, producers and networks developed a degree of sensitivity to the issue of stereotypical roles. Some blacks, especially black actors, say the sensitivity went too far. When actors were being cast for roles generally considered stereotypical, like maids and vicious criminals, black actors were not considered. **Joseph Marcell**, who played the butler on *Fresh Prince of Bel-Air*, said it is the actor's job to take the role he has and treat it as if it were Shakespeare. "It is the Shakespearean role he has at the moment," he said. In the eyes of some casting executives, a black actor could be a hero but not a villain. Jack Smith, executive vice president and head writer on the daytime drama *The Young and the Restless*, said, "If we have a role of a drug dealer, we are more apt to hire a white actor than a black because we don't want to play into negative stereotypes. However, there are black actors out there who want to work. They say, 'Look at prisons. They are crowded with black drug dealers.' So, what do you do?"

Temple Hatton, a longtime network censor who is African American, said that he battled with producers because there were "an abundance of black pimps and prostitutes." He added, "On some shows, like *The Tonight Show*, sometimes there would be jokes that were off-color racially. The show was tape delay, so the show could be edited before it aired. On *Sanford and Son*, in the beginning, I recall arguing about the relationship between the father and son. I felt the son should not show disrespect for the father. Sometimes I won the fights. Sometimes, the network wanted me to back off. A lot of my job was counting 'hell' and 'damn' in the scripts; there couldn't be a lot of those. Today, however the networks are so competitive with cable that they feel they have to be permissive to get over." *See also* GOOD TIMES; HAIRSTON, JESTER; OCCUPATIONS OF TV CHARACTERS; WADE, ERNESTINE.

STEVE HARVEY'S BIG TIME (*WB, 2003–*). Comedian **Steve Harvey** hosted a half-hour talk/variety series that opened with an announcer saying, "Where everyday people do things you don't see every day." In 2004, the series expanded to an hour. Among the bizarre acts on the series was a guy who sucked milk into his nose and released it through his eyes in a spurt; he was trying to break a distance record. A lady bartender opened beer cans by biting the sides of the cans. A physics professor taught Harvey to pull a tablecloth off a table without disturbing dishes. Twin belly dancers demonstrated their art and gave Harvey a lesson. Harvey injected comedy into the acts ranging from charming to hard-to-believe. Harvey was also one of the executive producers.

STEVE HARVEY SHOW, THE (*WB, 1996–2002*). Steve Harvey starred in this sitcom as Steve Hightower, lead singer in a soul music group that fell on hard times. Steve found himself teaching music, drama, and art at a Chicago high school. Even though he was not onstage, he continued to wear the colorful, often garish suits from his days as an entertainer. Regina (**Wendy Raquel Robinson**) was the principal who dated Steve, but the romance did not work. She went back to an old boyfriend, wealthy Warrington Steele (**Dorien Wilson**). Steve's pal and roommate was Cedric Robinson (**Cedric the Entertainer**), who was the sports coach. Cedric had a romance with Regina's secretary Lovita (Terri J. Vaughn), and the pair spent a lot of time at the apartment Steve and Cedric shared; this did not meet Steve's approval. Romeo Santana (**Merlin Santana**), Sophia (Tracy Vilar), Sara (Nefta Perry), Bullethead (William Lee Scott), and Coretta (Robin Yvette Allen) were students at various times in the series. Regina married Warrington even though Steve tried to stop the wedding. During the final episode of the series, Regina and Steve became engaged, and Cedric and Lovita won the lottery. *See also* LONG-RUNNING SERIES.

STEWART, BYRON. He played Warren Coolidge in *The White Shadow* (1978–1981) and an orderly with the same name in *St. Elsewhere* in 1984.

STEWART, MEL. Stewart played Lionel's uncle in *All in the Family* (1971–1973), Sgt. B. J. Bryant in the sitcom *Roll Out* (1973–1974), Mr. Gibson in *On the Rocks* (1975–1976), Marvin in *Tabitha* (1977–1978), Raymond in *One in a Million* (1980), Rodney Blake in *Freebie and the Bean* (1980–1981), and Billy Melrose in *Scarecrow and Mrs. King* (1983–1987). He played the judge in the TV film *Marriage Is Alive and Well* in 1980.

STEWART, NICK. Stewart (aka Nick O'Demus) played Lightning, the shuffling Stepin Fetchit–type janitor in *Amos 'n' Andy* (1951–1953). He played an African native in the series *Ramar of the Jungle* in 1954. He also had a key role in 1954's "The Reign of Amelika Jo" on the dramatic anthology series *Fireside Theatre*. In later years, he operated the Ebony Showcase Theatre in Los Angeles. *See also* STEREOTYPES; UPTOWN COMEDY EXPRESS.

STICKNEY, PHYLLIS. Stickney had a starring role in the short-lived sitcom *New Attitude* in 1990; she played Yvonne St. James. She also played Cora Lee in the miniseries *The Women of Brewster Place* in 1989.

STINSON, PATRICK. After working in Dallas television news, Stinson covered the **O. J. Simpson** trial for the syndicated *A Current Affair* in 1995. Later, he covered the aftermath of the death of Princess Diana for both NBC and MSNBC. In 1997, he began working for E! News Live as a correspondent. He interviewed **Will Smith**, Arnold Schwarzenegger, Madonna, **Denzel Washington**, and others.

STIR CRAZY (*CBS, 1985–1986*). This sitcom was based on the 1980 **Richard Pryor**/Gene Wilder film of the same title. **Larry Riley**

played the lead character, Harry Fletcher, who was best friends with Skip Harrington (Joseph Guzaldo). The two were unjustly convicted of a crime and sentenced to a chain gang. They escaped and went on a wild adventure to find the guy who really did commit the crime.

STOMPIN' AT THE SAVOY (*CBS, 1992*). This two-hour made-for-television film was about four young African-American female domestic workers during the Depression. They tried to improve their lives and achieve their dreams when, at night, they escaped their lives of servitude and went to the Savoy Ballroom. **Vanessa L. Williams, Lynn Whitfield, Jasmine Guy, Vanessa Bell Calloway, Mario Van Peebles**, and **Michael Warren** made up the central cast. **Debbie Allen** directed.

STORM IN SUMMER, A (*NBC, February 6, 1970*). This drama from the *Hallmark Hall of Fame* was about a white deli owner who battled, befriended, and housed a black ghetto youth. It won the **Emmy Award** in the 1969–1970 season for Outstanding Dramatic Program. Peter Ustinov (who also won an Emmy) played the storekeeper who had shut himself off from all emotions after his son died in World War II. **N'Gai Dixon**, son of actor/director **Ivan Dixon**, played 10-year-old Herman Washington, who was shipped to live with Ustinov's character as part of a civic-minded "fresh air" program. Herman dislikes and distrusts the old man, too. It was the younger Dixon's first professional role.

STRANGE JUSTICE (*SHO, August 29, 1999*). The process by which Clarence Thomas was appointed and confirmed by the U.S. Senate to his post on the U.S. Supreme Court is examined in this two-hour made-for-television film starring **Delroy Lindo** and Regina Taylor. The film centers on Anita Hill's (Taylor) charge that Thomas (Lindo) sexually harassed her. **Paul Winfield** played Thurgood Marshall. *See also* CLARENCE THOMAS'S SUPREME COURT CONFIRMATION HEARINGS; HISTORICAL EVENTS DRAMATIZED.

STRANGER INSIDE (*HBO, June 23, 2001*). This made-for-television film is set in a harsh women's prison and tells the story of a young African-American woman's search for the mother she never knew.

Yolanda Ross, Davenia McFadden, and Verda Bridges star in the film, which received positive reviews from *The Washington Post* and *People* magazine.

STUDDARD, RUBEN. Studdard, dubbed the "velvet teddy bear" by **Gladys Knight**, won *American Idol* in 2003 and began to sing on numerous talk and variety series. One was *Christmas in Washington* in 2004.

STU ERWIN SHOW, THE *(ABC, 1950–1955).* **Willie Best** was the houseman for a dysfunctional family headed by a dysfunctional father, played by Stu Erwin. Erwin used his own name in the series. As a character, Best was slow moving and slow talking, and critics felt he was too negative a portrayal, much like Stepin Fetchit in films. Erwin was dissatisfied with his own role and had to fight to become less of a fool. *See also* SERIES WITH ONE BLACK SUPPORTING ACTOR/PERFORMER BEFORE 1980.

SUDIE AND SIMPSON *(LIF, September 11, 1990).* **Louis Gossett Jr.** played Simpson, a black man befriended by Sudie (Sara Gilbert), an adolescent girl who confronts racism and a secret.

SUGAR HILL TIMES *(CBS, 1949).* This one-hour variety series was live and hosted by Willie Bryant of the Apollo Theater. It aired three times a week, and **Timmie Rogers** and **Harry Belafonte** were regulars.

SUGAR RAY LEONARD FIGHTS. Television viewers watching ABC's *Wide World of Sports* on July 26, 1975, saw young Sugar Ray Leonard first in the North American Continental Boxing Championships. Announcer Keith Jackson called him "a young boxer to watch." Leonard defeated Willie Rodriquez in his first professional televised bout on May 14, 1977. On October 17, 1981, Leonard was the victor by a 14th-round technical knockout in the WBC/WBA Welterweight Championship Fight with Thomas Hearns. *See also* BOXING MATCHES ON TELEVISION.

SUGAR RUSH *(Food Network, 2005–).* Washington, D.C., baker Warren Brown hosted this series about the sweet things in life. He visited bakeries and eateries and prepared dishes.

SUMMER, CREE. Summer played Winfred "Freddy" Brooks on the sitcom *A Different World* (1988–1993) and Reese on the legal drama *Sweet Justice* (1994–1995). She provided voice-overs for many animated productions including Susie Carmichael in *Rugrats*, Penny in *Inspector Gadget*, and Cleo in *Clifford the Big Red Dog*. She was nominated for an Emmy Award for the latter in 2001.

SUMMER, DONNA. Recording artist Summer made numerous appearances on *The Midnight Special* from 1976 to 1980. She hosted her own special in 1980. She was one of the celebrities at *The 50th Presidential Inaugural Gala* held two days prior to the inauguration of President Ronald Reagan in 1985.

SUMMER OF MY GERMAN SOLDIER (*NBC, October 30, 1978*). **Esther Rolle** played a key role in this dramatic motion picture made for television and won an **Emmy Award** as Outstanding Supporting Actress in a Limited Series or Special in the 1978–1979 season. The two-hour film was the story of a teenage Jewish girl (Kristy McNichol) who, during World War II, falls in love with an escaped Nazi prisoner of war.

SUPREMES, THE. The Supremes made early appearances on *The Ed Sullivan Show* and *American Bandstand* and most variety series from the mid-1960s and into the 1970s. The group consisted first of **Diana Ross**, Mary Wilson, and Florence Ballard. When Ballard was dropped from the group, Cindy Birdsong joined the group. The name of the group became Diana Ross and The Supremes. Shortly thereafter, Ross left the group to be a solo performer. Some of the variety specials on which the group appeared were *Diana Ross and The Supremes and The Temptations on Broadway* in 1969, *The Bob Hope Special* in 1973, and *Kate Smith Presents Remembrances of Rock* in 1973.

SUPER BOWL HALFTIME SHOWS. Super Bowl games are as much about entertainment as about football. Several African-American entertainers have headlined the halftime shows. At Super Bowl II (1968), the famous Grambling University Marching Band entertained at halftime and performed the National Anthem. The celebrated Florida A& M Band performed halftime at both Super Bowl III (1969) and Super Bowl V (1971). By 1972, the halftime shows were not merely marching bands, and **Ella Fitzgerald** and other entertainers paid tribute to **Louis Armstrong** in Super Bowl VI. In 1975, **Duke Ellington** was the subject of the tribute by Mercer Ellington at Super Bowl IX; the Grambling Band made its third appearance. In 1982's Super Bowl XVI, there was a salute to the 1960s and Motown. In 1987's Super Bowl XXII, **Chubby Checker** entertained in a show with 88 grand pianos and the Rockettes. In 1993, **Michael Jackson** starred in his "Heal the World" anthem, which featured 3,500 children (that same year, **O. J. Simpson** tossed the coin to begin the game). In 1995, **Patti LaBelle** and others were featured in "Indiana Jones and the Temple of the Forbidden Eye" at Super Bowl XXIX. **Diana Ross** was back in 1996's Super Bowl XXX to celebrate 30 years of Super Bowls; the finale featured Ross being taken from the stadium in a helicopter. In 1997's Super Bowl XXXI, **James Brown** was featured. There was a tribute to Motown's 40th anniversary with Boyz II Men, **Smokey Robinson**, **Queen Latifah**, **Martha Reeves**, and **The Temptations** in 1998's Super Bowl XXXII. **Stevie Wonder** and Toni Braxton sang at Super Bowl XXXIV in 2000. **Janet Jackson** and Justin Timberlake were the headliners at 2004's Super Bowl XXXVIII. The performance, on February 1, 2004, concluded with Timberlake grabbing Jackson's leather bustier, revealing her right breast and a nipple-piercing shield. The incident was the subject of newscasts for several days. Timberlake called it a "wardrobe malfunction," and Jackson apologized. An estimated billion people saw it.

SUPER BOWL NATIONAL ANTHEM SINGERS. Since the Super Bowl began in 1967, the following African-American entertainers have performed the National Anthem: 1968, Grambling University Band; 1974, **Charlie Pride**; 1975, Grambling University Band; 1982, **Diana Ross**; 1986, **Wynton Marsalis**; 1990, **Aaron Neville**; 1991, **Whitney Houston**; 1994, **Natalie Cole** with the Atlanta University Chorus; 1996, **Vanessa L. Williams**; 1997, **Luther Vandross**; and 2004, **Beyonce Knowles**. In Super Bowl XXXV (2001), **Ray Charles** sang "America the Beautiful"; **Mary J. Blige** and Marc Anthony sang it in 2002.

SWANN, LYNN. A pro football Hall of Fame wide receiver, Swann joined ABC in 1976. His credits include numerous sports—horse racing, football, rugby, and basketball. These include segments of *Wide*

World of Sports, halftime and sidelines of *Monday Night Football*, and commentator on coverage of the U.S. Football League in 1983–1985. He also provided commentary for the bobsled competition for coverage of the 1988 Calgary Winter Olympics and for weightlifting during the 1984 Summer Olympics. He covered NCAA football in 1983. He was seen on numerous events on *ABC's Wide World of Sports* including the English Rugby League Cup Final, the travels of the Harlem Globetrotters in Hong Kong, and the Jeep Superstars. He hosted coverage from 1988 to 1991 of the Iditarod dogsled race from Alaska. In entertainment television, he hosted the same show, *To Tell the Truth*, in 1990.

S.W.A.T. (*ABC, 1975–1976*). In this police action drama, **Rod Perry** played Sgt. David "Deke" Kay, the second in command of the Special Weapons and Tactics Unit of the Los Angeles Police Department. The S.W.A.T. team was made up of Vietnam War veterans who used military tactics to fight tough, violent criminals the regular police force could not tackle.

SWEET JUSTICE (*NBC, 1994–1995*). **Cicely Tyson** starred in this legal drama series as Carrie Grace Battle, a longtime, highly respected civil rights attorney who fought not only for racial equity but also for women's rights and the rights of any other disenfranchised people. The story was set in the South, where young, white, female attorney Kate Delacroy (Melissa Gilbert) came home to practice law. She chose to work for Battle rather than her father's (Ronny Cox) conservative, prestigious firm. **Cree Summer** and **Michael Warren** had regular roles.

SWINGIN' WITH DUKE: LINCOLN CENTER JAZZ ORCHESTRA WITH SWING INTO SPRING (*CBS, April 10, 1959*). This one-hour musical special simply celebrated the year 1959 with entertainers **Ella Fitzgerald**, **Lionel Hampton**, Benny Goodman, Peggy Lee, William Curly, and Andre Previn.

SYKES, BRENDA. Popular in film and television in the 1970s, Sykes played a central character in the short-lived sitcom *Ozzie's Girls* (1973). She played Summer Johnson in the drama series *Executive Suite* (1976–1977).

SYKES, WANDA. Sykes (aka Wanda Sykes-Hall), before starring in the 2003 sitcom *Wanda at Large*, was a stand-up comedienne who did comedic comment on *Inside the NFL*. She was part of the team that won the **Emmy Award** for Outstanding Writing for a Variety or Music Program in 1999 for *The Chris Rock Show*. She had extensive writing credits. In the fall of 2004, her comedy series *Wanda Does It* made its debut.

SYLER, RENE. Syler joined CBS Network News after first working for a CBS-owned station in Dallas/Fort Worth. She began her position at the network as cohost of *The Early Show* in 2000.

SYLVESTER, HAROLD. In series television, Sylvester played Deputy Fairfax in *Walking Tall* (1981), Harry Dresden in *Mary* (1985–1986), Griff in *Married . . . With Children* (1987), and Col. John McGuire in *The Army Show* (1998) and a doctor in *City of Angels* (2000). His TV films include the following: *In the Deep Woods* (1992), *Love and Curses . . . And All That Jazz* (1991), *Line of Fire: The Morris Dees Story* (1991), *Double Your Pleasure* (1989), *Sister Margaret and the Saturday Night Ladies* (1987), *If Tomorrow Comes* (1986), *The Atlanta Child Murders* (1985), *Wheels* (1978), and *Richie Brockelman: The Missing 24 Hours* (1976). He is also a writer.

– T –

TALK SHOWS. African Americans wield a commanding presence when it comes to the television talk show genre. Media personality **Oprah Winfrey** led the charge, leveraging her talk show clout into various media ventures including a glossy magazine, boosting literacy and book sales through her on-air book club, acting, and producing made-for-television movies.

Other African-American talkers include **Bryant Gumbel**, **Montel Williams**, **Queen Latifah**, RuPaul, **Arsenio Hall**, **Starr Jones**, **Ananda Lewis**, **Tavis Smiley**, **Tempestt Bledsoe**, **Whoopi Goldberg**, **Tony Brown**, and **Iyanla Vanzant**. According to researcher Timberg, Hall was "the first African-American to become a star of late-night talk." Syndicated like *Oprah*, *The Arsenio Hall Show* showcased African-American culture and entertainers, including Spike Lee, **Eddie Murphy**, and Johnetta Cole, then president of Spelman, a historically black women's college in Georgia. Hall appealed to a younger audience than other late night talk shows. There was no sidekick or desk to sit behind like other talk show hosts, making the setting more intimate. *The Arsenio Hall Show* ended in 1993. Tavis Smiley premiered a new talk show, *Tavis Smiley*, on PBS in 2004.

African-American hosts steered talk shows in four of the major talk show subgenres: issues-oriented shows (*Tony Brown*); late night entertainment (*The Arsenio Hall Show*) marked by celebrity guests and curious supporting or second acts, such as animal tricks; daytime audience participation shows (*Oprah* and *Montel*) targeting women and designed to allow the host to mediate or facilitate discussion between audience members and experts or celebrities; and the early morning news/talk magazine hybrids, such as *The Today Show* and *Good Morning America*, mixing newsbreaks with celebrity interviews and general interest feature stories. Bryant Gumbel stands out as perhaps the best-known African American to work in this latter genre. He later hosted similar morning shows and an evening newsmagazine program for CBS. Talk show hosts control the flow of the show. The host is a link between viewers, the studio audience, and the on-camera experts and guests; manages the program; introduces guests; alerts viewers to commercial breaks; and leads discussions.

TAMU. The actress played Caroline Fuller in the made-for-television motion picture *Crisis at Central High* in 1981. She had a role in the 1979 TV film *And Baby Makes Six*.

TAPPIN' (*SYN, January 8, 1989*). Sammy Davis Jr. and **Gregory Hines** starred and hosted this one-hour documentary about the making of the feature film *Tap*, the film traces tap dancing through movie history. Guests were Gene Kelly, Buddy Briggs, Suzanne Douglas, and others.

TARKINGTON, ROCKNE. Tarkington was probably the only black guest star on the sitcom *The Andy Griffith Show*. In 1967, he played the neighborhood football coach, Flip Conroy, who took Opie away from his piano lessons, until it was revealed that Flip played piano too. He also played the veterinarian, Rao, on *Tarzan* (1966–1968).

TA-TANISHA. She played Pam, a student, in *Room 222* (1970–1972).

TATE, LARENZ. Tate played Redd Foxx's grandson, Curtis, in *The Royal Family* (1991–1992) and Andre Mosley in *South Central* (1994).

TAVIS SMILEY (*PBS, 2004–*). Smiley, the popular radio talk show host who was fired by **Black Entertainment Television** (BET), returned to television with his own series based on the West Coast. He was the first African American to host a five-night-a-week show on PBS. The show was designed to have three segments in one hour with the same basic format as his National Public Radio show and offered a mix of guests not usually seen on television. Actors, financial gurus, rapper-moguls, authors, and political celebrities were among the types of guests. Among the guests on during the first season were former President Bill Clinton, Prince, **Maya Angelou**, **Aretha Franklin**, **Ice-T**, Tom Cruise, Essie Mae Washington Williams, and Barak Obama. Smiley said the show challenges the audience to consider issues from new points of view and addresses overlooked issues. The show's audience was expected to be a "younger, more ethnically diverse audience than typically watches public TV," according to Smiley. When the series was renewed for 2005, PBS announced that *Tavis Smiley* had the highest percentage of African-American viewers than any other prime time or late night series on PBS. *See also* TALK SHOWS.

TAYLOR, BILLY. Jazz musician Taylor started narrating segments on music for *CBS Sunday Morning* in 1981. On his 25th anniversary with the series, CBS correspondent **Ed Bradley** said of Taylor that he "had a remarkable ear for young talent, recognizing many well before fame struck. He profiled 21-year-old **Wynton Marsalis**, 22-year old Harry Connick Jr., and a young Diana Krall."

TAYLOR, CLARICE. Taylor had an important role in the made-for-television motion picture *Beulah Land* in 1980. She played Anna Huxtable, mother/paternal grandmother, on *The Cosby Show* (1984–1992). She was Idella Landy in the TV version of the Broadway musical *Purlie* (1981). In series television, she was also Harriet on *Sesame Street* (1976–1990) and Nurse Bailey in the medical drama *Nurse* (1981).

TAYLOR, MESHACH. Taylor played Tony in the acclaimed sitcom *Buffalo Bill* (1983–1984); Anthony Bouvier, the designing man among the *Designing Women* (1986–1993); and Sheldon in the sitcom *Dave's World* (1993–1997).

TAYLOR, NATHANIEL. Taylor played the character Rollo on both *Sanford and Son* (1972–1977) and *Sanford* (1980–1981). He was Jim-Jam on *The Redd Foxx Show* (1977).

TAYLOR, PAUL. Taylor played Isaac Jenkins (1999–2003) in the daytime drama *As the World Turns*.

TAYLOR, REGINA. Taylor played Minniejean Brown, one of the black students who integrated an Arkansas High School amidst great controversy, in *Crisis at Central High* in 1981. She played Lilly Harper in the drama series *I'll Fly Away* (1991–1993) and Assistant U.S. Attorney Sandra Broome in the legal series *Feds* (1997). Taylor played Anita Hill in *Strange Justice*, a 1999 made-for-television movie. She played Cora Jenkins, the lead character, in the TV film *Cora Unashamed* in 2000.

TAYLOR, WALLY. Taylor played Curtis Vincent on the sitcom *Roc* (1992–1993).

TEACHER, TEACHER (*NBC, February 5, 1969*). This 90-minute drama was a *Hallmark Hall of Fame* production about three men experiencing difficult periods of their lives. **Ossie Davis** played Charles Carter, a handyman who actually wanted to be a commercial airline pilot but believed there were no opportunities. David McCallum played Hamilton Cade, an alcoholic who struggled to revive his career as a tutor. Billy Shulman played Freddie, a retarded kid whom Charles and Hamilton tried to reach. This production won the **Emmy Award** for Outstanding Dramatic program of 1968–1969.

TEDDY PENDERGRASS IN CONCERT (*HBO, September 11, 1982*). Singer **Teddy Pendergrass** entertained in a 60-minute concert.

TELEVISION PIONEERS. Some black performers made appearances on network variety series even before television became national in 1951 or shortly afterward. The following appeared on *The Toast of the Town* (later titled *The Ed Sullivan Show*) between 1949 and 1953: **Sarah Vaughn**, twice in 1949; **Sammy Davis Jr.**, as the youngest member of the Will Maston Trio, twice in 1951; **Billy Eckstine**, in 1949, 1951, 1952, and 1953; and **Cab Calloway**, in 1949 and 1951. **Pearl Bailey** was on *Toast of the Town* in 1949, three times in 1952; she was on *Your Show of Shows* twice in 1951. **Lena Horne** sang on *Your Show of Shows* in 1951 and 1953 and on *Toast of the Town* in 1951. **Ella Fitzgerald** sang on *Cavalcade of Stars* in 1950.

The following were mystery guests on the game show *What's My Line?* before 1955: Lena Horne (1953), Pearl Bailey (1955), and Sammy Davis Jr. (1955).

In drama, on episodes of anthology series, **P. Jay Sidney** played Cato in "The Plot to Kill General Washington" on *Hallmark Hall of Fame* in 1952; **Juano Hernandez** had a role in "Decision at Arrowsmith" on *Medallion Theatre* in 1953. **Bernie Hamilton**, **Juanita Moore**, and **Nick Stewart** were among the black actors who had roles as African natives in *Ramar of the Jungle* (1952–1954). Then, in 1955, a turning point and in that year alone, there were numerous roles for blacks in anthology series. Prime among them was **"A Man Is Ten Feet Tall"** on the *Philco Playhouse* starring **Sidney Poitier** and "Winner by Decision" starring **Harry Belafonte** and **Ethel Waters** on *General Electric Theater*. **Clarence Muse** was in "Casablanca" on *Warner Bros. Presents* in 1955; **Juanita Moore** had a role in "Walk Wide of Lions" on *Soldiers of Fortune* in 1955. Bernie Hamilton played Christy in "D.P." on *General Electric Theater* in the same year.

Also, the actors in the pioneering sitcoms must be remembered: **Alvin Childress, Spencer Williams Jr., Tim Moore, Johnny Lee, Ernestine Wade, Nick Stewart, Amanda Randolph** (also on *Make Room for Daddy*), **Lillian Randolph, Roy Glenn**, and **Jester Hairston** in *Amos 'n' Andy* (1951–1953); **Ethel Waters, Louise Beavers,**

Butterfly McQueen, **Ruby Dandridge**, Percy (Bud) Harris, Dooley Wilson, and Ernest Whitman in *Beulah* (1950–1953); and **Willie Best** in *The Stu Erwin Show* (1950–1955) and *My Little Margie* (1952–1955). In comedy/variety series, there was **Eddie "Rochester" Anderson** in *The Jack Benny Show* (1950–1965 and 1977). In musical variety, there was Willie Bryant, Harry Belafonte, and **Timmie Rogers** in *Sugar Hill Times* (1949) and **Hazel Scott** in *The Hazel Scott Show* (1950). *See also* ANTHOLOGY SERIES; SITCOMS; VARIETY SERIES; VARIETY SPECIALS.

TEMPERATURES RISING (*ABC, 1972–1974*). This sitcom (later called *The New Temperatures Rising*) had three different casts between September 1972 and August 1974 as the network tried to make the series successful. The only actor who starred in all three versions was **Cleavon Little** as Dr. Jerry Noland. The series was set in hospitals each time, but the characters and the story line changed each time. Little played an intern who was the hospital's resident bookie in all versions.

TEMPESTT (*SYN, 1995–1996*). **Tempestt Bledsoe**, formerly one of the kids on *The Cosby Show*, hosted this talk show at the age of 22. The subjects of conversation on the show ranged from serious to frivolous.

TEMPTATIONS, THE (singing group). The Temptations shared the spotlight with their former sister group in *Diana Ross and The Supremes and The Temptations on Broadway* in 1969. They also entertained in numerous variety specials—*It's What's Happening, Baby!* in 1965, *The Smokey Robinson Show* in 1970, *Good Vibrations from Central Park* in 1973, *Motown 25: Yesterday, Today, and Forever* in 1983, *Liberty Weekend: Closing Ceremonies* in 1986, *Motown Merry Christmas* in 1987, *The 4th of July Spectacular* in 1989, *Merv Griffin's New Year's Eve Special* in 1991, and *The Grand Opening of Euro Disney* in 1992. They also provided the voice-overs for *Garfield Cartoon—Garfield Gets a Life* in 1991. The group sang in the Super Bowl XXXIII tribute to 40 years of Motown in 1998 and on *Motown 45* (2004), marking the 45th anniversary of the company. Though the individuals in the group changed over the years because of deaths and other reasons, the group consistently continued to perform.

TEMPTATIONS, THE (TV miniseries) (*NBC, November 1–2, 1998*). This four-hour miniseries told the story of the original Motown singing group from the point of view of its sole surviving member, Otis Williams. The film focused on Otis (**Charles Malik Whitfield**), Melvin Franklin (D. B. Woodside), Eddie Kendricks (Terron Brooks), Paul Williams (Christian Payton), and David Ruffin (Leon). The story was told chronologically from when they were high school boys singing on street corners of Detroit in the 1950s, through the climb to the top of mainstream America's record charts, and through struggles of personal relationships, addictions to drugs and alcohol, and towering ego problems—their own and others. Along the way, the group amassed, at the time of the miniseries, 54 albums, 16 number one singles, a string of gold records, a 38-year history, and four tragic deaths. Despite the downside, it was also a story of bonding and love. The music was also an integral part of the production with songs like "Papa Was a Rolling Stone," "Ain't Too Proud to Beg," "My Girl," "Cloud Nine," "Just My Imagination," and numerous others. Fred Bronson in *Billboard* (November 7, 1998) said the production was "one of the finest rock-era biopics ever made. *The Temptations* shines in every aspect from casting (the five main leads are outstanding) to tech credits like costumes, hair, and makeup." Suzanne De Passe was an executive producer; Otis Williams was a coproducer. The miniseries not only received good reviews but also was a ratings victory. As 23 million viewers watched, it propelled NBC into first place for the week in the important November sweeps.

TENAFLY (*NBC, 1973–1974*). **James McEachin** starred in this detective drama as Los Angeles private eye Harry Tenafly. Tenafly did not have the look of the romance hero but rather an ordinary man whose job just happened to be investigating crimes. He was also a dedicated family man. Some critics said the character was ahead of its time. **Lillian Lehman** played his wife, Ruth; Paul Jackson played his son, Herb. **Lillian Randolph** and Bill Walker played contentious relatives. The series played every four weeks, alternating with other dramas in *The NBC Wednesday Movie,* and never found a loyal audience. The interactive Web site Super70s.com recently read, "James McEachin, now an author of mainstream and cop fiction, played Tenafly to the punch-the-clock, trudge-to-the-next witness, take the kids to school hilt."

TENSPEED AND BROWN SHOE (*ABC, January 27, 1980*). The TV film starred **Ben Vereen** as a streetwise, smooth-talking con artist E. L. "Tenspeed" Turner, who teamed up with demure stockbroker Lionel Whitney (Jeff Goldblum) to form a detective agency. Tenspeed called Whitney "Brown Shoe" because he wore a three-piece suit and brown shoes. This was the pilot for the series, which ran for about six months in 1980.

THAT'S MY MAMA (*ABC, 1974–1975*). **Clifton Davis** and **Theresa Merritt** starred in this sitcom. Davis was Clifton Curtis, and Merritt was his mother. Curtis ran a barbershop and liked being a bachelor and spending time with his pals, who worked in or gathered at the barbershop. His mother wanted him to settle down with a nice spouse as his sister Tracy (played first by **Lynne Moody** and then by **Joan Pringle**) had done. Tracy's stuffy spouse was Leonard (**Lisle Wilson**). Curtis's cronies were Earl, the mailman (played first by **Ed Bernard** and then by **Theodore Wilson**); Wildcat (**Jester Hairston**); Josh (DeForest Covan); and Junior (**Ted Lange**). Some critics complained that the characters were negative stereotypes. African-American historian Donald Bogle said that the mother came across as "the all-sacrificing, large, dowdy, warm-hearted mammy" and that the son "was something of a lively but emasculated male living in the standard black-female dominated home that television seems most comfortable with." The show survived its premiere season but was canceled early in the second season.

THAT'S SO RAVEN (*DIS, 2003–*). **Raven** (aka **Raven-Symone**), who played Cliff Huxtable's granddaughter on *The Cosby Show*, starred in this sitcom as teenager Raven Baxter, who was always getting into trouble and using disguises and other angles to solve the crises of the moment. She was either blessed or cursed with the power to see the future, and she used this power to solve the problems of strangers. Only her parents and closest friends were aware of her psychic ability. **Orlando Brown**, **T'Keyah Keymah**, Kyle Orlando Massey, **Rondell Sheridan**, Anneliese van der Pol, and Alex Welch made up the cast. Reviewer Laura Fries of *Variety* (January 17, 2003) said, "If there's a way to solve a problem sensibly, Raven heads straight for silly and turns left at outrageous. And as far as slapstick physical comedy goes, Raven, the actress, is up to the task. The laughs are geared to a less than sophisticated audience; for younger viewers, it's a nice escape devoid of innuendo and harsh reality." Orlando Brown sang part of the theme song.

THEA (*ABC, 1993–1994*). **Thea Vidale** starred in this sitcom as a super single mother who could handle her kids plus a full-time and a part-time job. Her kids were played by **Adam Jeffries**, **Jason Weaver**, Brandy Norwood (aka **Brandy**, her first series role), and Brenden Jefferson. **Yvette Wilson** played Thea's sister and **Cleavant Derricks** played her brother-in-law.

THEME MUSIC. Many African-American singers and composers have done theme music for television series. *The Jeffersons'* theme was written and sung by **Ja'Net DuBois**. **Quincy Jones** composed the themes for *Sanford and Son* and *In the Heat of the Night*. Jones and **Bill Cosby** wrote the theme for the 1969 series *The Bill Cosby Show*. Andre Crouch did the music for *Amen*. **Queen Latifah** and **Will Smith** performed raps that served as themes to their series *Living Single* and *The Fresh Prince of Bel-Air*, respectively. **Brandy** sang her theme for *Moesha*, **Nell Carter** for *Gimme a Break*, **Marla Gibbs** for *227*, and **Della Reese** for *Touched by an Angel*. Babyface Edmonds composed theme music for *Soul Food*. **Sammy Davis Jr.** sang the theme songs for *Baretta* and *Hell Town*. **Isaac Hayes** did the theme for *The Men*. Al Jarreau cowrote and sang the theme for *Moonlighting*. Solange Knowles sang the theme for *The Proud Family*. Heavy D & the Boys did the theme for *In Living Color*. Al Jarreau sang the theme for *Moonlighting*. **Orlando Brown**'s voice was heard on the theme song for *That's So Raven*. **Aretha Franklin** sang the theme for the later seasons of *A Different World*.

Questions sometime arise over why many black series feature the stars dancing in the opening sequences. Some of these shows are *The Cosby Show*, *Living Single*, *The Parkers*, *Soul Food*, and *Moesha*.

Even Judge Joe Brown danced in the opening of his 2004–2005 season. African-American producers simply say that it is only natural to dance when good music is playing.

THERE WAS ALWAYS SUN SHINING SOMEPLACE: LIFE IN THE NEGRO BASEBALL LEAGUES (PBS, September 7, 1983). The production centered on interviews with the men who played in the Negro leagues and also featured photographs and films of the old games. James Crutchfield, James Bell, and Ted Page—all of the Pittsburgh Crawfords—dominated the hour. The Crawfords' lineup also included Josh Gibson and Satchel Paige. The players spoke of their meager salaries, the long bus rides, and the problems of being black in a white man's game. However, as the title of the show indicates, the players also had a good time. **James Earl Jones** was the narrator.

THIGPEN, LYNNE. Primarily a stage actress, Thigpen (aka Lynn and Lyne) acted in *Hallmark Hall of Fame* presentations *Night Ride Home* and *The Boys Next Door*. She starred in the televised Broadway musical *When Hell Freezes Over, I'll Skate* in 1979. She was Ruth Stovall in the miniseries *Separate but Equal* in 1991. She played Aunt Flora Baxter in 1983 and Grace Keefer in 1994 on the daytime drama *All My Children*. Thigpen played Chief in the PBS children's program *Where in the World Is Carmen Sandiego?* and *Where in Time Is Carmen Sandiego?* She was also Ella Farmer, Manion's director of administrative services, on *The District* but died of a heart attack during the show's third season in 2003. She was 54.

THIS MAN STANDS ALONE (*NBC, May 30, 1979*). This 90-minute drama (also titled *Lawman without a Gun*) was a dramatization of a black civil rights activist who, after the assassination of Martin Luther King Jr., goes home to a small southern town and runs for office against a popular segregationist. The story was inspired by a real-life story, but when the film aired, there were charges that last-minute editing of the film by the network "emasculated" the production. **Louis Gossett Jr.** played Tom Haywood, **Mary Alice** was Minnie Haywood, **James McEachin** was Harris McIntyre, **Philip Michael Thomas** was Rufus, and **Helen Martin** was Mrs. Cartwright. *See also* BIOPICS.

THOMAS, CLARENCE. *See* CLARENCE THOMAS'S SUPREME COURT CONFIRMATION HEARINGS.

THOMAS, ERNEST. Thomas was Raj in *What's Happening!!* (1976–1979) and *What's Happening Now!!* (1985–1988). He played Kailuba in the miniseries *Roots* (1977).

THOMAS, PHILLIP MICHAEL. Thomas played the starring role of Detective Richardo Tubbs in *Miami Vice* from 1984 to 1989. He was host of *Motown Merry Christmas* in 1987. He also appeared in *Disney's Totally Minnie* in 1988 and *The Debbie Allen Special* in 1989. In made-for-television films, he had important roles in *Valentine* and *This Man Stands Alone*, both in 1979.

THOMAS, PIERRE. Thomas was CNN's Justice Department correspondent from 1997 to 2000. He joined ABC News later to cover the Justice Department and law enforcement issues primarily for *World News Tonight with Peter Jennings* but also for *Good Morning America*, *This Week*, *Nightline*, and ABC News special events.

THOMAS, SEAN PATRICK. Thomas played Detective Temple Page in the drama series *The District* (2000–2004).

THOMASON, MARSHA. Thomason played Nessa Holt in the drama series *Las Vegas* beginning in 2003.

THOMPSON, JOHN. An inductee in the Basketball Hall of Fame and former head coach at Georgetown University, Thompson joined Turner Sports as a National Basketball Association (NBA) analyst during the 1999–2000 season and returned for another season. He had served as analyst for Turner Sports' annual NBA draft coverage since 1997.

THOMPSON, WESLEY. Thompson played Wardell on the sitcom *He's the Mayor* (1986) and Vernon Morris in *Pursuit of Happiness* (1987–1988).

THORNWELL (*CBS, January 28, 1981*). Glynn Turman starred in this two-hour dramatic movie for television as James Thornwell, who claimed that the U.S. Army forced him to take mind-control drugs to get him to confess that he stole secret documents while stationed in France in 1961. The real Thornwell was awarded $625,000 by the U.S. Congress 20 years later and died a few years after that. The story was based on a 1979 *60 Minutes* segment. **Howard E. Rollins Jr.**, **Julius Harris**, **Debbi Morgan**, **Shirley Jo Finney**, **Al Fann**, **Roger Aaron Brown**, **Maidie Norman**, and Le Tari played key roles. *See also* BIOPICS.

THREE FOR TONIGHT (*CBS, June 22, 1955*). **Harry Belafonte**, along with dancers Marge and Gower Champion, performed numbers for which they are most remembered.

3 GIRLS 3 (*NBC, 1977*). This musical comedy was **Debbie Allen's** first television series. She and fellow stars Mimi Kennedy and Ellen Foley auditioned and were selected over hundreds of others because of their multitalents. All could sing, dance, and act, although each had a special talent. Allen's was dancing. Foley's was singing. Kennedy's was comedic acting (she also went on to numerous roles in series). In addition to performing, the show also explored their personal lives. Critics praised the show for being innovative, but ratings never climbed sufficiently to warrant more than the original order for four episodes.

THREE MO' TENORS IN CONCERT (*PBS, August 6, 2001*). Victor Trent Cook, Thomas Young, and Roderick Dixon, the three tenors, sang the songs of various composers and genres of music: opera, gospel, spirituals, **Cab Calloway**, and **Duke Ellington**. In 2005, the trio sang in a *Great Performers* concert on PBS with a more politically correct title, *Cook, Dixon, and Young in Concert.*

TILLMAN, SPENCER. After serving as host of *NFL Ticket* on CBS and being a reporter for the network's NCAA tournament coverage, Tillman joined CBS Sports as lead analyst for *College Football Today* in 1999.

TIMEX ALL-STAR JAZZ SHOW, THE (*NBC, 1957–1959*). There were four of these variety specials airing a few months apart in a little more than a year's time. All four were performances by jazz musicians, and the programs were sponsored by Timex watches. Each concert had some black musicians and singers; all four had **Louis Armstrong** and his trumpet. Show I aired December 30, 1957, and featured **Duke Ellington** and **Carmen MacRae**. Show II aired April 30, 1958, and featured **Lionel Hampton**. Show III aired November 10, 1958, and featured Hampton. Show IV aired January 7, 1959, and featured Ellington and **Dizzy Gillespie**.

TINA TURNER: BREAK EVERY RULE (*HBO, March 14, 1987*). Singer **Tina Turner** was host and star of this one-hour variety special, on which she sang songs from her album *Break Every Rule*. Her guests were Robert Cray and Max Headroom.

TINA TURNER IN CONCERT (*HBO, June 8, 1985*). Tina Turner was the headliner in this concert which originated from Birmingham Stadium in England. Her guests were Bryan Adams and David Bowie.

TINA TURNER: LIVE IN RIO (*HBO, January 16, 1988*). The concert originated from the Macarena Stadium in Rio de Janiero before a screaming audience of nearly 200,000 fans. Longtime Tina Turner fan Justin Schutz described the concert: "It was such a great performance. It had Samba dancers, glitter and fireworks and started with great footage of Tina walking around the beach and enjoying the city and coming into the stadium complex via motorcade. It was at the end of her really successful year-long Break Every Rule Tour, which had played to about four million over the course of 230 concerts. It was, at the time, the largest audience ever assembled to see a single performer and got Tina into the Guinness Book of World Records."

Turner sang, with a massive rock 'n' roll band in the background, "Private Dancer," "I Can't Stand the Rain," Better Be Good to Me," "What's Love Got to Do with It," and "Proud Mary."

TINA TURNER'S WILDEST DREAMS (*SHO, February 8, 1997*). This compilation of Turner's performances in the New Amsterdam Arena for three nights was part of her Wildest Dreams European Tour. The tour was 150 shows for three million fans.

TIRICO, MIKE. Tirico joined ESPN in 1991 and ABC Sports in 1991 and was play-by-play announcer for college football on both networks. At ESPN, his credits include contributing to ESPN *Sports-Center* and play-by-play announcing for NBC coverage. At ABC, he hosted ABC Sports' golf coverage and earned an **Emmy** nomination for his work. Later, he became studio host for ABC's National Basketball Association telecasts, including the finals.

TO DANCE WITH OLIVIA (*CBS, March 9, 1997*). Louis Gossett Jr. and **Lonette McKee** starred in the story of Daniel Stewart, a small-town lawyer who, after the death of his young son, struggled to find a meaningful life with his wife, Olivia.

TODAY AT 35 (*NBC, January 31, 1987*). *The Today Show* celebrated its 35th anniversary (it premiered on January 14, 1952) with **Bryant Gumbel** and Jane Pauley, then hosts of *The Today Show*, as host of the one-hour special. Also appearing were former hosts of the morning show and other news celebrities: Frank Blair, Tom Brokaw, John Chancellor, Hugh Downs, Betty Furness, Joe Garagiola, Jim Hartz, Jack Lescoulie, Edwin Newman, John Palmer, Willard Scott, Gene Shalit, and Barbara Walters.

TODAY AT 40 (*NBC, January 14, 1992*). Exactly 40 years after it premiered, *The Today Show* celebrated the anniversary with hosts **Bryant Gumbel** and Katie Couric. Many newsmen who had attended the 35th anniversary made appearances and were joined by Faith Daniels and Willard Scott.

TODAY SHOW, THE (*NBC, 1952– *). Bryant Gumbel was the first African-American broadcast journalist to cohost a nationally televised morning show when he took on this position in 1982 and resigned in 1997. In 1998, he said he believed *The Today Show* during his tenure did a decent, not a good, job of diversity. "Television's habit was that you would bring out someone of color whenever the issue was civil rights, whenever the issue was welfare, whenever the issue was a social program, whenever the issue was food stamps, whenever the issue was poverty. I wanted to make sure that we had people of color whenever the issue was economics, or foreign policy, or trade, or health, so that we stopped stamping things as 'black issues.'" He said his broadcast from Africa in 1992 was the trip of which he was most proud. "Over there, there are a million untapped stories because America ignores them. If two kids get hit by a truck in London, they do an hour special. If a bus turns over in Nairobi and one hundred black folks get killed, it's a line of agate type on the bottom of your television screen."

TODD, BEVERLY. Todd had a key role in the miniseries *Roots* in 1977 and in the TV films *The Jericho Mile* in 1979 and *Don't Look Back: The Story of Satchell Paige* in 1981. She was Felicia on *The Redd Foxx Show* in 1977.

TOLBERT, BERLINDA. Tolbert was Jenny Willis on the *The Jeffersons* (1975–1985) and had a role in the TV film *A Connecticut Yankee in King Arthur's Court* (1989).

TOM JOYNER SKY SHOW (*TV1, 2004–*). Joyner hosted, from local urban theaters across the United States, several two-hour specials featuring leading comedians (like Tommy Davidson and Kim Coles) and soul performers (like Al Green and Chaka Khan). These popular shows entertained live and radio audiences for years, then TV One brought the *Sky Show* to television.

TONEY, JAY STONE. Toney was a member of the gospel singers **Southernaires Quartet**; the group had a show in 1948.

TONIGHT SHOW WITH JAY LENO, THE (*NBC, 1992–*). The long-running talk-variety show took on the same format established by his predecessors but with his added comic style and his own writers. The first leader of Leno's studio band was **Branford Marsalis**. The second band leader, also black, was **Kevin Eubanks**.

TONIGHT SHOW WITH JOHNNY CARSON, THE (*NBC, 1962–1992*). Just as many entertainers got their big breaks in the 1950s and 1960s on *The Ed Sullivan Show*, after Sullivan the show to do was *The Tonight Show with Johnny Carson*. Carson was called "The Late Night King." Rising stars in television and film made their first television appearances as themselves to plug their projects. Recording artists boosted sales of their records. Comedians looked for a chance to be on the show as a real opportunity and a giant stride toward stardom. Carson's staff would observe comics at local mike nights at comedy clubs and invite the best to do monologues on the show. Comedians felt they had it made if, after their monologues, Carson invited them to join him on the couch to talk. **Flip Wilson** got his big break on Carson's show after **Redd Foxx** had appeared on the show and said, "There's a guy named Flip Wilson who's so funny it's scary." Carson invited him to the show, he eventually was guest host, and then he got his own specials and series. Comedian Byron Allen, now host and producer of *The Entertainer* and *Kickin' It*, was observed at mike night at The Comedy Store in Los Angeles. A teenager at the time, he was invited to the show and was subsequently hired to be one of the hosts of *Real People* (1979–1984).

TONIGHT WITH BELAFONTE (*CBS, December 10, 1959*). Harry Belafonte starred in this hour of variety. In addition to his Caribbean folk songs, he was joined by guests **Odetta**, Brownie McGhee, and Sonny Terry.

TONY BROWN'S JOURNAL (*PBS, 1970– *). This minority affairs show began as *Black Journal* in 1968 on PBS. Tony Brown was hired as host and executive producer in 1970. At first, it was a one-hour show that aired monthly, then Brown changed it to a half-hour weekly show in 1977, and it aired on commercial stations. He returned the show to PBS in 1982. The show always offers discussion on black issues.

TONY ORLANDO AND DAWN (*CBS, 1974–1976*). The variety show started as a summer replacement series for *The Sonny and Cher Comedy Hour*. The singing group had had big hits like "Tie a Yellow Ribbon, "Knock Three Times," and "Candida" in a period of about three years. The show returned in the regular season, and at one point the title of the show was changed to *The Tony Orlando and Dawn Rainbow Hour*. The show is significant in this volume because Dawn was black. **Telma Hopkins** and Joyce Vincent Wilson were Orlando's backup singers, but they participated in comedy skits and banter with the audience. The show was canceled in December 1976, and the group lasted only a few months longer. From this series, Hopkins launched a career as actress.

TOOTHPASTE MILLIONAIRE, THE (*ABC, November 27, 1974*). Young **Tierre Turner** starred in this *ABC Afterschool Special* as a 12-year-old boy who started a business making and selling toothpaste and finds himself coping with the challenges of government regulations and competition.

TOP SECRET (*NBC, June 4, 1978*). **Bill Cosby** and **Tracy Reed** starred in this two-hour made-for-television movie as a hip American agent and his beautiful associate who tried to recover stolen plutonium before it can be used by terrorists. Executive producer Sheldon Leonard also starred, as did **Gloria Foster**.

TOUCHED BY AN ANGEL (*CBS, 1994–2003*). Roma Downey (as Monica) and **Della Reese** (as Tess) starred in this drama series as two angels sent to earth to help people with their problems. When it aired, it was the most openly religious prime-time drama since *Life Is Worth Living* (1952–1957), when Bishop Fulton Sheen, a former radio star, offered weekly morality lessons. *Joan of Arcadia* followed as a religious drama in 2003. Tess was the senior, no-nonsense angel; Caryn James of the *Washington Post* (April 27, 1996), called her the series' "soul and greatest strength. She delivers unspeakable lines with sassy conviction." Reese, a Christian minister in real life, sang the theme song "Walk with You." **Paul Winfield** played Special Agent Angel Sam (1995–1999), who showed up occasionally to check things out. *See also* THEME MUSIC.

TOUGHEST MAN IN THE WORLD, THE (*CBS, November 7, 1984*). **Mr. T** (Lawrence Tero) starred in this made-for-television film as Bruise, an unschooled veteran who worked as a bouncer and spent his spare time in his center for at-risk youth. In order to keep the center going, he decided to compete for the title "Toughest Man in the World." The victory would provide him with enough money to run the center. However, he had to defeat the titleholder, who not only was physically strong but also had connections with powerful underworld figures who could keep him from winning and put his center out of business. **Lynne Moody** played Leslie. Mr. T rapped the theme "song." An online reviewer on IMDb.com said, "This is a movie that conveys a moralistic message but at the same time provides plenty of action and entertainment." Another online review on the Film Review site (http://filmreview.com) said, "I pity da fool that made this film?"

TOUSSAINT, LORRAINE. Toussaint starred as Rene Jackson in the drama series *Any Day Now* (1998–2002). She played Elaine Duchamps on the police drama series *Crossing Jordan* (2001–2003) and Dr. Mary Rocket in the sitcom *Where I Live* in 1993. She had key roles in the 1983 TV film *The Face of Rage* and the 1996 TV films *The Cherokee Kid* and *Nightjohn*. She played Philomena in "The Reunion" on **America's Dream** in 1995. She had a key role in the 1993 miniseries *Alex Haley's Queen*.

TOWERY, VECEPIA "VEE." Towery was the first black million-dollar winner on the reality television series *Survivor*. She participated in the fourth installment of the series: *Survivor: Marquesas* in the South Pacific.

TOWNES, JEFF. Townes (aka DJ Jazzy Jeff) played a recurring role on *Fresh Prince of Bel-Air* (1990–1996), appearing in 40 episodes.

TOWNSEND, ROBERT. The comedian and producer was one of the stars of *Uptown Comedy Express* in 1987. He starred in *Townsend Television*, a short-lived 1993 variety series. He starred in the sitcom *The Parent'hood* (1995–1999). Townsend was host of the musical variety series *Motown Live* (1998–1999). He had a key role in the TV film *Love Songs* in 1999 and directed one of the three segments.

TOWNSEND TELEVISION (*FOX, 1993*). **Robert Townsend** starred in this one-hour variety series. In addition to a stand-up act, Townsend also helped write and directed videotaped segments of the show. There were regulars who participated in sketches and performed musical numbers as well as guest stars. Tom Shales of the *Washington Post* (September 11, 1993) said that it had "in its favor a genial, upbeat, nonviolent attitude in contrast to much of the cruel and harsh comedy so popular on Fox." The series lasted two months.

TRACKERS, THE (*ABC, December 14, 1971*). **Sammy Davis Jr.** starred in this 90-minute western, an unsold pilot, as Zeke Smith, a strong-willed frontier scout in an uneasy alliance with Sam Paxton, a stubborn rancher (Ernest Borgnine), to find out who killed the latter's son. Davis was credited with writing the story with executive producer Aaron Spelling and also had credit as producer.

TRACY MORGAN SHOW, THE (*NBC, 2003–2004*). **Tracy Morgan** starred as Tracy Mitchell, a blue-collar business owner with a wife, Alicia (**Tamala Jones**), who was a full-time mother and two children: young teen Derrick (Marc John Jeffries) and his younger brother Jimmy (Bobbe' J. Thompson). Mitchell owned an auto garage where he must cope with bickering mechanics (John Witherspoon and **Dwight "Heavy D" Myers**).

TRAPPER JOHN (*CBS, 1979–1986*). **Brian Mitchell** (later known as Brian Stokes Mitchell) and **Madge Sinclair** became recognizable to television viewers on this medical drama series. Sinclair was Nurse Ernestine Shoop (1980–1986), scrub nurse to the chief of surgery, who was nicknamed Trapper John in *M*A*S*H*. This series was a spin-off of *M*A*S*H*. Mitchell was Dr. Justin Jackson, nicknamed Jackpot.

TRENT, LES. A reporter who joined the syndicated *Inside Edition* in 2000, Trent covered Princess Diana's funeral and the eruption of the volcano on the Caribbean island of Montserrat and spent five years as a correspondent on King World's *American Journal*.

TRIAL OF BERNHARD GOETZ , THE (*PBS, May 11, 1988*). This *American Playhouse* miniseries was based on 4,600 pages of transcripts of the trial of a white man, an electrical engineer, who, on December 22, 1984, shot four black youths on a New York City subway. In his confession, he said he thought they were about to rob him. Public opinion was divided, largely along racial lines, in that some considered him a folk hero for protecting himself, while others considered him a vigilante who took the law into his own hands. His gun was unlicensed. He was acquitted of all charges except criminal possession of a weapon. Peter Crombie played Goetz. **Larry B. Scott** played James Ramseur, one the boys shot by Goetz. The *New York Times* (May 11, 1988) said of Scott's performance, "Mr. Ramseur, searingly depicted by Larry B. Scott, comes on like an uncontrollable whirlwind, his contempt for . . . the defense lawyer expressed with unconcealed zest." *See also* HISTORICAL EVENTS DRAMATIZED.

TRIBUTE TO MARTIN LUTHER KING: A CELEBRATION OF LIFE, A (*SYN, January 15, 1984*). This two-hour special tribute show was intended to celebrate the life, memory, and legacy of Martin Luther King Jr. In addition to performances, numerous celebrities spoke about the late civil rights leader or told stories. *Variety* (January 18, 1984), in its review, said, "Of the speakers, Dick Gregory, **Robert Guillaume**, Patrick Duffy, and late arrival **Stevie Wonder** were the most effective. Performing kudos for the evening went to such acts as **Ray Charles**, Phyllis Hyman, **Patti LaBelle**, Joan Baez, and Michael Warren. . . . Perhaps the greatest tribute to King during the course of the evening was a recognition of the performers themselves and the contributions they've brought to society as Black Americans and as artists."

TROUBLE WITH FATHER, THE. *See* THE STU ERWIN SHOW.

TRUE COLORS (*FOX, 1990–1992*). **Frankie Faison** starred in this sitcom as a widowed dentist, Ron Freeman, who married a kindergarten teacher, Ellen (Stephanie Faracy). Ron had two teenage sons (**Claude Brooks** and **Adam Jeffries**), while Ellen had a teenage daughter (Brigid Conley Walsh). What made this different is that Ron was black and Ellen was white. This was groundbreaking in television sitcoms. Tom and Helen Willis (Franklin Cover and **Roxie Roker**) on *The Jeffersons* (1975–1985) were a mixed couple, but they were supporting characters, not the characters on which the show was built. For some angry viewers of *True Colors*, having a black man and a white woman married was too much to bear; they sent hate mail that was threatening enough for producers to call in the Federal Bureau of Investigation (FBI). Faracy said the FBI advised the cast on how to secure their lives. Reviewers, like David Nicholson of the *Washington Post* (July 28, 1991), had already written that most episodes were not concerned with race at all and that that showed that perhaps race no longer matters. Star Faison said he took the role because he thought it would be "a real breakthrough for television . . .

I thought it would be challenging and we would deal with issues— like *All in the Family.*" Instead, Faison said the show "eased" into the concept, making racial differences minor to the stories. Faison left after the first year, and **Cleavon Little** took the lead for the final year. *See also* INTERRACIAL ROMANCES/ RELATIONSHIPS.

TUCKER, CHRIS. Tucker hosted the *2002 NAACP Image Awards* and made appearances on numerous award and talk shows.

TURMAN, GLYNN. Turman was the teenage son, Lew, in the black family introduced in the final year (1968–1969) of the first primetime soap opera, *Peyton Place* (1964–1969). He was Theo in the TV film *Ceremonies in Dark Old Men* in 1975. He played Ike in *J.D.'s Revenge* in 1976 and Harry Brown Jr., the lead role, in *Minstrel Man* in 1977. Turman was Nate Person in the epic miniseries *Centennial* in 1978, played Raymond Franklin in *Attica* in 1980, and played James Thornwell in *Thornwell* in 1981. He portrayed the roles of Jesse in *Secrets of a Married Man* in 1984, Solomon in *Race to Freedom: The Underground Railroad* in 1994, Judge Roullard in *Someone Else's Child* in 1994, Coach Powell in *Rebound: The Legend of Earl "The Goat" Manigault* in 1996, Joyu in *Buffalo Soldiers* in 1997, T-Bone Lanier in *Freedom Song* in 2000, and Robert Aimes Sr. in *Fire & Ice* in 2001. He had a key role in *Carter's Army*, a 1970 made-for-television film. In series television, he was Col. Taylor on the sitcom *A Different World* from 1988 to 1993 and Secretary of State Larue Hawkes in the 1985 sitcom *Hail to the Chief*. Turman performed in comedy specials like *The Richard Pryor Special?* in 1977 and the *American Film Institute Comedy Special* in 1987.

TURNER BROADCASTING SYSTEM'S TRUMPET AWARDS. Beginning in 1993, each year, the Trumpet Awards honored African Americans and their accomplishments in diverse fields as entertainment, law, and politics. The ceremony is held each year in Atlanta. The 2001 ceremony celebrated **Leslie Uggams**, Carmen de Lavallade, **Geoffrey Holder**, **Willie Mays**, former Senator Edward Brooke, former Congresswoman Shirley Chisholm; **Ray Charles** received the Living Legend Award. The 2002 ceremony honored Andrew Young, **Cicely Tyson**, and Tom Joyner; **Sidney Poitier** received the Living Legend Award. The 2003 Awards honored **Destiny's Child,** **Spike Lee, Pam Grier,** Julius Erving, Vernon Jordan, **Ossie Davis,** and **Ruby Dee.** The American Hero Award went to Lt. Col. Marilyn Wills, who pulled victims from the fire following the September 11 terrorist attack on the Pentagon. **Quincy Jones, Maya Angelou, Gladys Knight,** and Johnnie Cochran were previously honored.

TURNER, DAIN. A child actor in the 1970s, Dain Turner played the youngest son in the 1978 telefilm *Love Is Not Enough* and went on to play the same role in the subsequent family drama series *Harris and Company* in 1979. Dain and **Tierre Turner** are brothers.

TURNER, TIERRE. A child actor in the 1970s, Turner starred in *The Toothpaste Millionaire* in 1974 and had a key role in *The Secret Life of T. K. Dearing* in 1975. He performed in the variety special *The Richard Pryor Special?* in 1977. He is the brother of Dain Turner.

TURNER, TINA. Tina Turner guest-starred in variety specials *Good Vibrations from Central Park* in 1971, *Ann-Margret Olsson* in 1975, *Van Dyke and Company* in 1975, *The Sounds of Summer* in 1978, *John Denver and the Ladies* in 1979, *Olivia Newton-John's Hollywood Nights* in 1980, *State Fair, U.S.A.* in 1981, *Rolling Stone Magazine: 20 Years of Rock and Roll* in 1987, *A Tribute to Elton John and Bernie Taupin* in 1991, and *The Grand Opening of Euro Disney* in 1992. She made numerous appearances on *The Midnight Special* in 1974–1979. She also hosted the variety specials *Tina Turner in Concert* in 1985, *Tina Turner: Break Every Rule* in 1987, *Tina Turner: Live in Rio* in 1988, and *Tina Turner's Wildest Dreams* in 1997. She was one of the divas in *Divas Live '99*.

TUSKEGEE AIRMEN, THE (*HBO, August 26, 1995*). The first squadron of African-American U.S. Army Air Corps combat fighter pilots in World War II, the "Fighting 99" trained at Tuskegee Institute in Alabama. When they began training, few if any in the army wanted them there. They had to prove they were stronger, tougher, smarter, and better fliers than most white pilots. The Tuskegee Airmen distinguished themselves and won medals for the all-black 332 Fighter Group but still had to do battle with American racism before they could battle Hitler. **Lawrence Fishburne** starred in this drama as Lt. Hannibal Lee, a law school graduate who trained with the Tuskegee Airmen and went into action in the skies of North Africa and Europe. Also starring were **Malcolm-Jamal Warner, Courtney B. Vance, Andre Braugher, Cuba Gooding Jr.**, John Lithgow, Christopher McDonald, Allen Payne, and Rosemary Murphy. Tuskegee airman Robert W. Williams, coexecutive producer, said, "We graduated 992 at Tuskegee, 445 of us went into combat, 66 died in combat, and of all of the missions the men flew bomber escort, they never lost a bomber." Most reviews were decidedly positive, similar to Ann Hodges of the *Houston Chronicle* (August 20, 1995), who said, "It has taken 43 years to make this remarkable story into this fine movie." David Bianculli of the New York *Daily News* (August 25, 1995) agreed with the quality of the film but said, "HBO could have done it better and should have done it longer." He felt the film should not have ended with the 332 Fighter Group heading for a key mission but should have dramatized that mission and followed the pilots home after the war where "battles of a different sort would continue to rage."

TV ONE. This cable network targeting African-American viewers was launched on January 19, 2004, Martin Luther King's Birthday. The network resulted from a joint venture between Alfred C. Liggins III and his mother, Catherine L. Hughes, chairperson and chief executive officer, respectively, of Radio One, Inc., and Comcast Corporation. At the time of the venture, Radio One was the largest broadcaster targeting African-American and urban listeners and the seventh-largest radio chain in the United States; Comcast was the number one cable operator. Also participating in the venture were Bear Stearns' Constellation ventures, Syndicated Communications, Pacesetter Capital Group, and Opportunity Capital Partners. Hughes admitted that Radio One is her dream, while TV One is her son's dream. Liggins said, "We have the opportunity to be in African-American media what Univision (UVN) has become in Hispanic media." In order to give **Black Entertainment Television** (BET) competition, Liggins planned to offer more adult-oriented programs.

In its first months, the network had the following original programs: *Living It Up with Patti LaBelle*, a look at the songstress and her life; *Gospel Challenge*, a reality program featuring a competition of gospel choirs and gospel groups; *The Gospel of Music with Jeff Majors*, a weekly gospel concert series starring recognized singers in the gospel realm; *Donna Richardson: Mind, Body, & Spirit*, a physical, nutritional, and spiritual fitness show; *American Legacy*, profiling African-American heroes and discoveries as featured in the magazine *American Legacy*; *Cowboys of Color*, a look at African-American, Hispanic, and Native American rodeo competitions; *TV One Access*, a look at African-American Hollywood celebrities; *Tom Joyner Sky Show*; specials hosted by Joyner, who brings entertainment into theaters around the country; *Get the Hook-Up*, a mating-type game with a studio audience; and others. The network also airs syndicated series and reruns of classic sitcoms and dramas of interest to black viewers. During the first season, reruns of *Good Times*, *227*, and *City of Angels* were broadcast. The second season brought reruns of *Boston Public* and *Martin* as well as new original series *Living with Soul*, *Makeover Manor*, and *G. Garvin*.

TV One plans continued expansion across the country in cities and communities with African-American populations. Its chief executive officer, Jonathan Rodgers, a veteran TV executive, said he planned to attract advertisers with more affluent viewers, aged 25 to 54, while BET's median age is 21.

TV ONE ACCESS (*TV1, 2004–*). Shaun Robinson hosted this monthly one-hour special as well as daily one-minute entertainment updates of news of black entertainers in Hollywood, including premieres, concerts, fashions, romance, and other issues. *Access Hollywood* was producer of the broadcasts.

24 (*FOX, 2001–*). This espionage drama series is significant in this volume only in that an African-American actor, **Dennis Haysbert**, plays the president of the United States, David Palmer. He was not the lead of the series (Keifer Sutherland was), but he was the reason for the actions of the other characters, namely, to protect the president. Said Haysbert to *Jet* (May 27, 2002), "I am gratified to have been chosen to shoulder this responsibility. We don't see characters like this on stage or TV. I want society to begin to see black people in a different light. I want the industry to see the versatility and complexity of the character." Each episode of this groundbreaking series covers one hour in a day; 24 episodes of the season cover a full day, midnight to midnight. **Penny Johnson Jerald** played Palmer's scheming wife, Sherry, but they were divorced. **Vicellous Shannon** played Keith Palmer (2001–2002).

TWILIGHT: LOS ANGELES—STAGE ON SCREEN (*PBS, April 29, 2001*). **Anna Deavere Smith** performed her one-woman play, adapted to film, in which she portrays people who participated in and people who saw the 1992 Los Angeles riots.

227 (*NBC, 1985–1990*). The sitcom **227** began as a Christine Houston stage play of the same title that played at **Marla Gibbs**'s Crossroad Academy, an inner-city theater in Los Angeles and starred Gibbs, **Hal Williams**, and **Regina King**, three of the regulars in the series. Actor/producer **Scoey Mitchlll** brought NBC President Brandon Tartikoff to see the play and eventually set the wheels in motion to get the series on the air. The premise was a blue-collar family living in the Addams-Morgan section of Washington, D.C. Mary Jenkins (Gibbs), her contractor husband Lester (Williams), and their teenage daughter Brenda (King) lived in one apartment of the apartment building with the address 227. Their landlord was Rose Holloway (**Alaina Reed**), who had a younger daughter, Tiffany (**Kia Goodwin**, who was only in the first season). Sexy Sandra Clark (**Jackee Harry**) was the primary subject of neighborhood gossip and was the series' breakout character. Nosy neighbor Pearl Shay (**Helen Martin**) was guardian to her grandson, Calvin (Curtis Baldwin), who was Brenda's puppy-love interest. Playwright Houston was hired as a member of the writing team, but she was later fired from her own creation. In subsequent seasons, others were added to the cast including the following: **Countess Vaughn** as 11-year-old Alexandra; Toukie Smith as Eva; **Paul Winfield** as Julian Barlow, who bought the building from Rose; Stoney Jackson as Travis, a limo driver; **Kevin Peter Hall**, Reed's real-life husband, as Warren; and the token white actor, Barry Sobel, as Dylan, who also lived at the 227 address.

TYLER, AISHA. Tyler played recurring roles on two series simultaneously in 2004. She was a lab technician on *CSI* and a data analyst on *24*. She was host of *The 5th Wheel*, a syndicated dating show in 2001, and host of *Talk Soup*, a comedy show (2001–2002). She was a rare black actress recurring on the sitcom *Friends* as Ross's romantic interest.

TYLER, WILLIE. Ventriloquist Willie Tyler and his dummy Lester guest-starred in variety specials *Lola* (1976) and *Sea World's All-Star Lone Star Celebration* (1988). They performed in the tribute *Dean Martin Celebrity Roast* of Ted Knight (1977), in the comedy special *Blockheads* (1982), and in the musical special *A Christmas Dream* (1984).

THE TYRA BANKS SHOW (*OXY, 2005–*). Model **Tyra Banks** hosted this daytime talk show targeting women.

TYSON (*HBO, April 29, 1995*). The story of Iron **Mike Tyson**, the youngest heavyweight champion in boxing history, this made-for-television movie starred acting newcomer **Michael Jai White** in the title role. The story followed him from his childhood in the poorest area of Brooklyn, where he was arrested 38 times by age 13, to fame and fortune as the heavyweight champion. Then his dream turned into a nightmare because of his own decisions and poor advice. The film also examined the people who influenced Iron Mike: promoter Don King (**Paul Winfield**), trainer/father figure Gus D'Amato (George C. Scott), managers Jim Jacobs and Bill Cayton (Tony LoBianco and James B. Sikking), actress Robin Givens (**Kristen Wilson**), and childhood buddy Rory Holloway (**Malcolm-Jamal Warner**). *See also* ATHLETES' BIOPICS.

TYSON, CECILY. Tyson had a regular role in *East Side/West Side* in 1963–1964 and was the first black woman with a regular role in a drama series. She had a secondary role in a made-for-television motion picture, *Marriage: Year One*, in 1971. She starred in *The Autobiography of Miss Jane Pittman* in 1974, *Just an Old Sweet Song* in 1976, *Wilma* in 1977, and *A Woman Called Moses* in 1978, and she played Coretta Scott King in *King* in 1978. She played Binta in the miniseries *Roots* in 1977. She had the female lead in *Benny's Place*, a 1982 TV film, and a key role in the miniseries *The Women of Brewster Place* in 1989 and the title roles in *The Marva Collins*

Story in 1981 and *Mama Flora's Family*, a 1998 miniseries. She starred in *Heat Wave* in 1990, *The Road to Galveston* in 1996, and *Ms. Scrooge* and *Riot* in 1997. She played a major role in the miniseries *Aftershock: Earthquake in New York* in 1999. Tyson played Leona in the made-for-television film *The Rosa Parks Story* in 2002. She won two **Emmy Awards** in 1974: one for Best Lead Actress in a Drama (portrayal of Miss Jane Pittman) and the other for Actress of the Year—Special. In specials, Tyson was a guest at the testimonial dinner *AFI Salute to James Cagney* in 1974. She guest-starred in retrospective specials like *CBS: On the Air* in 1978 and *The Kennedy Center Honors* in 1988.

TYSON, MIKE. The life of the heavyweight champion was the subject of the TV motion picture *Tyson* in 1995. *See also* MIKE TYSON FIGHTS.

– U –

UGGAMS, LESLIE. Uggams made her first national television appearances at the age of six on *Beulah*; she played Beulah's (**Ethel Waters's**) niece. At age eight, she was featured on *Paul Whiteman's TV Teen Club*. She appeared on *Arthur Godfrey's Talent Scouts* in 1952. Mitch Miller saw her, at 15, as a contestant on the musical game show *Name That Tune* and was impressed with her vocal talents. From 1961 to 1966, she was a regular on *Sing Along with Mitch*. She hosted a variety music special titled *Leslie* in 1968 and headlined *The Leslie Uggams Show*, a variety series, in 1969; both were short-lived. She was Kizzy in the popular miniseries *Roots* in 1977. She played Lillian Rogers Parks, the White House seamstress, in *Backstairs at the White House* in 1979. In 1982, she was one of three cohosts of *Small World*, a variety special spotlighting the talents and opinions of children.

A popular guest star on variety/music specials in the late 1960s and 1970s, Uggams did the following: *The Alan King Show* in 1969, *The Super Comedy Bowl 1* and *Swing Out, Sweet Land* in 1971, *Jack Lemmon in 'S Wonderful, 'S Marvelous, 'S Gershwin* in 1972, *The Henry Fonda Special* in 1973, *Perry Como's Spring in New Orleans* in 1976, *Sinatra and Friends and the Celebrity Challenge of the*

Sexes 2 in 1977, and *The Kraft 75th Anniversary Show* and *General Electric's All-Star Anniversary* in 1978. In the specials of the 1980s, she guest-starred in the following: *The NBC Family Christmas Party* in 1982, *Christmas in Washington* in 1983, *Night of 100 Stars* in 1985, *Placido Domingo   Stepping Out with the Ladies* in 1985, and *The Ice Capades with Jason Bateman and Alyssa Milano* in 1989. She had a key role in the television movie *Sizzle* in 1981. *See also* CHILD STARS WHO MAINTAINED SUCCESS AS ADULTS IN SHOW BUSINESS.

UMOJA: THE SPIRIT OF TOGETHERNESS (*PBS, August, 2004*). This lively celebratory special of song and dance was about the South African culture featuring South African entertainers, but much of the entertainment showed great connections with African-American culture. The intricate steps and powerful rhythms of the gumboot dancers predated the culture of "stepping" favored today by African-American college fraternities and sororities. Some gospel music from 1970s South Africa was influenced by American hymns that were adapted into African culture with unique style. *Pata Pata*, a U.S. hit from South African singer Miriam Makeba, was performed in a segment about Shebeen, an illegal drinking club during early apartheid days reminiscent of Prohibition in the United States. Other songs, dance, and narration were strictly African history and culture. Many of the performers were from disadvantaged communities, and their raw talent had been developed to make a world tour before taping this special, which was used for a PBS pledge drive.

UNDERWOOD, BLAIR. Underwood played Bobby on the daytime drama *One Life to Live* (1985–1986) and Terry Corsaro in the police drama series *Downtown* (1986–1987). He earned prime-time fame as young attorney Jonathan Rollins in the drama *L.A. Law* (1987–1994). He starred in the police drama series *High Incident* (1996–1997) and the short-lived but acclaimed medical drama series *City of Angels* (2000). In the fall of 2004, he began a starring role in the drama series *LAX*. He had key roles in the 1990 films *Murder in Mississippi* and *Heat Wave*, *Soul of the Game* (1996), and *Mama Flora's Family*, a 1998 miniseries. He had a key role in 1993's *Father and Son: Dangerous Relations* and was also associate producer.

UNDERGROUND RAILROAD (*A&E, 1998*). This instructional documentary hosted by **Alfre Woodard** centered on the Underground Railroad for the escape of slaves from the southern states before the Emancipation Proclamation. It had no rails and no trains. The travelers sought freedom from slavery and oppression, and they were helped by freed blacks and antislavery whites as they made the trek north. If they failed, they had to return to plantation life and even more mistreatment. The Underground Railroad ran for 200 years. The documentary chronicles the achievements of Harriet Tubman, Frederick Douglass, Harriet Beecher Stowe, and William Lloyd Garrison. Leading historians were interviewed. Dramatic re-creations of escapes and depictions of heroes were highlights. *See also* HISTORICAL EVENTS DRAMATIZED.

UNDER ONE ROOF (*CBS, 1995*). There have been several series titled *Under One Roof*. This one is the black-cast drama for which discerning black viewers had great hope for a successful drama about a black family.

It was supposed to work because **James Earl Jones**, considered by many to be the ultimate actor, was the star. Jones played Ben Langston, a widower, retired police officer, and owner of a Seattle duplex. He lived downstairs, and upstairs lived his son, Ron (**Joe Morton**), and Ron's wife, Maggie (**Vanessa Bell Calloway**). Ron owned a lumber and hardware store; Maggie was soon to graduate from college. They had two children: teenager Charlotte (**Essence Atkins**) and preteen Derrick (Ronald Joshua Scott). The Langstons were a loving family.

It was supposed to work because reviewers like Anne Hodges of the *Houston Chronicle* (March 14, 1995) said, "This fine drama is about an African-American family which makes [it] a near miracle for television. It's a welcome one-of-a-kind amid TV's overpopulation of black-family sitcoms with cartoon characters and insulting stereotypes." And Dorothy Rabinowitz of the *Wall Street Journal* (March 20, 1995) said, "It isn't every day that programs come along in which characters talk and act . . . as people in the real world might. Even less often—to put it mildly—does a program about a black family come along that can make such a claim." Matt Roush, then of Gannett (March 14, 1995), said the show was "gifted by director/

producer **Thomas Carter** [with a] no-weak-link cast led by Jones, Morton, and Calloway [which was] distinctive, intriguing, engaging." The series lasted one month. Jones told online writer Laurence Washington, "Most of *Under One Roof* was thrown together in a panic over one weekend. And in that panic, no one accounted for the fact that writers need time to understand the characters—so they can turn in good episodes. We had two out of six episodes that were well-written. The quality just wasn't enough. We had a great cast and concept." *See also* DRAMA SERIES; FAMILY SERIES.

UNFORGETTABLE, WITH LOVE: NATALIE COLE SINGS THE SONGS OF NAT KING COLE (*PBS, March 7, 1992*). **Natalie Cole**'s concert performance was a musical tribute to the songs of her father, **Nat "King" Cole**. A few months previously, Natalie had recorded the album *Unforgettable: With Love* featuring a number of her father's songs. The finale includes the digitally remastered song "Unforgettable," which she sings with her father as a duet.

UNFORGIVABLE BLACKNESS: THE RISE AND FALL OF JACK JOHNSON (*PBS, January 17–18, 2005*). This two-part documentary (part 1 was the "Rise," and part 2 was the "Fall") tells the story of Jack Johnson, the first African-American heavyweight champion of the world, whose dominance over his white opponents, particularly Jim Jeffries (nicknamed "The Great White Hope"), spurred furious debates and race riots in the early part of the 20th century. The production also tells the story of Johnson's determination to date white women and prostitutes at a time when black men were often lynched for less. This annoyed blacks as well as whites. Booker T. Washington was especially vocal in his disdain for the man, saying, "A man with muscle, minus brains, is a useless creature." Johnson was convicted of the interstate/international transportation of women for "prostitution, debauchery, or for any other immoral purpose" in 1920 and served a year in prison. Filmmaker Ken Burns said he was leading a campaign to earn a posthumous pardon for Johnson. Actor **Samuel L. Jackson** provided the voice of Johnson in colorful quotes. **Wynton Marsalis** composed the soundtrack. *See also* ATHLETES' BIOPICS.

UNION, GABRIELLE. Union played Clare in the TV film *Something the Lord Made* (2004). She played Keisha Hamilton in the drama *7th Heaven* (1996–1999).

UNITED NEGRO COLLEGE FUND TELETHON: AN EVENING OF STARS (*SYN, annually*). **Lou Rawls** is master of ceremonies for the national telethon airing annually in approximately 70 cities. Concerts of singers and musicians are featured. Other celebrities make guest appearances. The program also informs the viewing audience of how the United Negro College Fund (UNCF) provides opportunities to students who otherwise might be unable to get college educations. The local broadcasts, aired simultaneously with the national broadcast, feature community notables who answer phones and take pledges from viewers. Corporate representatives are featured making donations in hopes of encouraging other corporate grants. The fund-raiser has amassed more than $200 million for financial assistance to 39 member historically black colleges and universities. An estimated total of more than 300,000 students have benefited from the UNCF telethon. The telethon first aired in the mid-1970s. The 2004 telecast celebrated Rawls's 25th anniversary as host of the four-hour show.

UNIVERSOUL CIRCUS (*HBO, February 8, 1999*). The world's first African-American circus performed soulful superacrobatics and other circus acts as well as singing and dancing.

UNSTOPPABLE: A CONVERSATION WITH MELVIN VAN PEEBLES, GORDON PARKS AND OSSIE DAVIS (*Black Stars, February 13, 2005*). Van Peebles, Parks, and Davis, the first black men to direct Hollywood feature films, discussed issues, struggles, and triumphs of their careers. Younger directors—Julie Dash, Mario Van Peebles, Reginald Hudlin, and others—provided tributes to the trio.

UPN TRIBUTE TO MARTIN LUTHER KING JR. (*UPN, January 21, 2002*). Black-cast sitcoms on UPN broadcast special episodes to honor the Martin Luther King holiday. *The Hughleys* had an episode titled "I Have a Scheme," which dealt with young Michael Hughley

(Dee Jay Daniels) leading a futile neighborhood effort to rename a street after the civil rights leader. The story tackled the subject of tolerance but also made jokes about only streets in high-crime inner-city neighborhoods bearing the name of Dr. King. *The Parkers'* episode was "The Revolution" and centered on the professor (Dorien Wilson) teaching the students a history lesson about the importance of the King legacy by telling the story about how the black studies program at the college developed. *Girlfriends* presented "I Have a Dream House" about an effort to get an employer to recognize the King holiday. *The Los Angeles Sentinel* (January 23, 2002), an African-American newspaper, said that each of the three comedy shows "are routinely fresh and funny" but that only *The Hughleys* episode had "comedy and substance."

UPTOWN (*NBC, May 30, 1980*). This two-hour variety series, a tribute to the famed Apollo Theater, featured celebrities who played at the popular Harlem spot in their early careers. Featured were **Cab Calloway, Natalie Cole, Gladys Knight, Lou Rawls, Nipsey Russell**, Sandman Sims, **Ben Vereen**, and **Flip Wilson**.

UPTOWN COMEDY CLUB (*SYN, 1992–1994*). Taped from a Harlem nitery, comics performed stand-up acts and acted in comedy sketches. The cast was racially integrated, but most of the comics were black. They were the following: **Flex Alexander**, Ronda Fowler, Macio, Monteria Ivey, the team of Arceneaux & Mitchell, Debra Wilson (1992–1993), Corwin Moore (1992–1993), **Tracy Morgan** (1993–1994), and Little Rascal (1993–1994). The token white comics were Jim Breuer and Rob Magnotti.

UPTOWN COMEDY EXPRESS (*HBO, May 9, 1987*). Eddie Murphy was host of this comedy special, which was taped at **Nick Stewart**'s Ebony Showcase Theatre in Los Angeles. Featured were **Marsha Warfield, Robert Townsend, Arsenio Hall**, and **Chris Rock**.

U.S.A. MUSIC CHALLENGE, THE (*ABC, June 2, 1992*). Malcolm-Jamal Warner hosted this one-hour variety special in which musicians from all over the United States compete to win a recording contract.

– V –

VANCE, COURTNEY B. Vance had starring or key roles in the made-for-television films *Race for Freedom: The Underground Railroad* (1994), *The Piano Lesson* (1995), *Ambushed* (1998), and *Whitewash: The Clarence Brandley Story* (2002).

VANCE, DANITRA. Vance was a regular on *Saturday Night Live* (1985–1986) and the first African-American woman to do so. She starred in *The Colored Museum* in 1991. She was born in 1959 and died of breast cancer in 1994.

VANDROSS, LUTHER. Singer Luther Vandross was a guest on the special *The Patti Labelle Show* (1985), on *Motown on Showtime: Smokey Robinson* (1990), and also on *American Bandstand's 40th Anniversary Special* (1992). He headlined *Luther Vandross: In the Spotlight: "An Evening of Song"* (1994). He was one of the friends on *Vanessa Williams & Friends: Christmas in New York* (1996) and sang the National Anthem at Super Bowl XXXI in 1997. Vandross was a guest on the *Soul Train Christmas Starfest* (1998). Vandross died on July 1, 2005 after suffering a severe stroke in 2003. He was 54.

VANESSA WILLIAMS & FRIENDS: CHRISTMAS IN NEW YORK (*ABC, December 1, 1996*). Taped at Broadway's Shubert Theatre, singer Williams performed, and so did **Savion Glover**, **Luther Vandross**, and others in an hour of Christmas music.

VANGELIS MYTHODES; MUSIC FOR THE NASA MISSION: 2001 MARS ODYSSEY (*Bravo, November 25, 2001*). Sopranos **Kathleen Battle** and **Jessye Norman**, in a concert taped live from the Temple of Zeus in Athens, Greece, performed the epic choral symphony.

VAN PEEBLES, MARIO. Mario Van Peebles's first role was as a young boy in his father's film *Sweet Sweetback's Baadasss Song* in 1971. As an adult, he starred in *Sonny Spoon*, a 1988 detective drama. He played Luke, the oldest son, in *Mama Flora's Family*, a 1998 miniseries. He had key roles in the made-for-television films *Stompin' at the Savoy* in 1992, *Riot* in 1997, and *Sally Hemings: An American Scandal* in 2000. *See also* CHILD TV ACTORS WHO MAINTAINED SUCCESS AS ADULTS IN SHOW BUSINESS.

VAN PEEBLES, MELVIN. Van Peebles wrote the teleplay and the theme song for the 1976 drama *Just an Old Sweet Song*. He also sang the theme song with Ira Hawkins. He played Mel, the father of *Sonny Spoon*, the detective drama in which his real-life son, **Mario Van Peebles**, played the title role in 1988. He wrote the teleplay, wrote the theme song "Greased Lightning," and had a key role in the 1981 miniseries *The Sophisticated Gents*.

VANZANT, IYANLA. The self-help guru/author hosted the 2001 talk show *Iyanla*.

VARIETY SERIES. There were musical shows with black performers/ stars in the late 1940s and early 1950s. The *Southernaires Quartet* had a show on which the group sang on ABC as early as 1948. *Sugar Hill Times*, which aired irregularly in 1949, was also musical variety with **Harry Belafonte** and **Timmie Rogers**. It also was known as *Uptown Jubilee* and *Harlem Jubilee*. *The Hazel Scott Show*, in 1950, was a showcase for Miss Scott's voice. Then *The Nat "King" Cole Show* started in 1956 with Cole and singing guests.

The first 30 years of television had numerous variety series; *The Ed Sullivan Show* was the longest running. In addition to singers, there would be animal acts, ballet dancers, and impressionists—the word "variety" is meaningful.

In 1966, there was the first true variety series with a black star, *The Sammy Davis Jr. Show*, which lasted four months. Then CBS's *The Leslie Uggams Show* in 1969 included a running comedy sketch titled "Sugar Hill" and also lasted about four months. The first hit variety series with a black star was *The Flip Wilson Show* from 1970 to 1974.

None were successful after Wilson's show. *The Richard Pryor Show* lasted a month in 1977. *Redd Foxx*, in 1977, lasted four months. Several variety series were summer replacements series that did not find spots on the regular season's schedule. Some were the following: *The Marilyn McCoo and Billy Davis Show* (1977), *Ben Vereen Comin' at Ya* (1975), *3 Girls 3* (1977), and *The Gladys Knight and the Pips Show* (1975). *The Jacksons* survived the summer of 1976 and returned in 1977 but for only about three months.

In the new millennium, variety series are late night talk shows, award shows, stand-up comedy, and musical concerts—anything that does not have a reality format or dramatic story line. The term "variety' has a different meaning.

Cedric the Entertainer Presents, which premiered in 2002, was an effort to launch a true variety series with various kinds of acts; it was the highest-rated series among African-American viewers but number 94 among all viewers; it was canceled in 2003. **Wayne Brady** had a syndicated talk/variety show (2002–2004) that won an **Emmy Award** for Outstanding Daytime Talk Show, yet it suffered from poor ratings and was canceled after two seasons. *Chappelle's Show*, basically comedy with a musical act, was so innovative that it earned an Emmy nomination in 2004 and sold more DVDs than any other TV show ever. *See also* TELEVISION PIONEERS; VARIETY SPECIALS.

VARIETY SPECIALS. In the late 1940s and 1950s, there were a few black entertainers on variety specials. Bob Hope did 269 specials between 1950 and 1993. There were usually three guests on each special. **Pearl Bailey** was a guest on two 1956 Bob Hope specials, and there were no other black guests until 1965, when **Nancy Wilson** made an appearance. Then, beginning in 1968, there was a black act on nearly every Bob Hope special. Perry Como had 46 specials from 1963 to 1986. There were usually two or three guests on each special. There were only six blacks on the specials during all those years: **Ella Fitzgerald** in 1967, Nancy Wilson in 1967, **Flip Wilson** in 1970, **Jimmie Walker** in 1974, and **Charley Pride** in 1976. A special program celebrating the 25th anniversary of television aired in 1972. Twenty-five stars who had helped make television history appeared in the show. None of them was black. After the advent of cable television, variety specials became popular on Showtime, HBO, and others. These were, however, mostly concert shows or comedy shows, not true variety, and included comedy skits and acts like ventriloquists, magic, dance, and so on. True variety specials have not been popular since the 1980s. *See also* TELEVISION PIONEERS; VARIETY SERIES.

VAUGHN, COUNTESS Television viewers discovered Countess Vaughn (aka Countess Vaughn James) as a singer who won the junior vocalist competition and the overall junior championship on 1988's *Star Search* when she was nine years old. Her first regular role on a series was that of Alexandria, Rose's daughter, on the sitcom *227* in 1988–1989. After numerous guest-star roles, she was cast as Kim Parker in the sitcom *Moesha* in 1996. She won an NAACP Image Award for her *Moesha* role. Her character was spun off to form the series *The Parkers* in 1999. Countess Vaughn guest-starred in the variety special *Disneyland's All-Star Comedy Circus* in 1988. *See also* CHILD STARS WHO BECAME ADULT STARS.

VAUGHAN, PARIS. Vaughn had a key role in the 1990 TV film *Heat Wave* and played Leslie in the drama series *Knightwatch* (1988–1989). **Sarah Vaughan** was her mother.

VAUGHAN, SARAH. Vaughan sang on *Portrait of Nancy Wilson* in 1972 and on the jazz tribute special **Duke Ellington . . . We Love You Madly** and a Tony Bennett special in 1973. In 1981, she was one of the musical stars on *100 Years of America's Popular Music*. She won an **Emmy Award** for her performance on *Rhapsody and Song—A Tribute to George Gershwin* during the 1980–1981 season. In 1986, she graced the cast of *A Capitol Fourth*, a Fourth of July celebration originating from Washington, D.C. Sarah Vaughn was born in 1924 and died in 1990 of lung cancer.

VEGA$ (*ABC, 1978–1981*). **Greg Morris** added color to this detective drama series when he joined it in 1979 as Las Vegas Police Lt. David Nelson, who was instrumental in helping Dan Tanna (series star Robert Urich), the private eye, solve cases.

VELJOHNSON, REGINALD. Though he had quite a career before 1989, VelJohnson's face became recognizable in 1989 when he began a nine-year role as Carl Winslow on the sitcom *Family Matters*. His made-for-television motion picture credits include the following: *Doing Life* in 1986, *Quiet Victory: The Charlie Wedemeyer Story* in 1988, *Grass Roots* in 1992, *One of Her Own* in 1994, and *Deadly Pursuits* in 1996. He performed in the musical **When Hell Freezes Over, I'll Skate** in 1979.

VEREEN, BEN. Vereen's first television show after making his mark on Broadway was in the 1975 summer series **Ben Vereen . . . Comin' at Ya**. He played Chicken George, a starring role in the 1977 miniseries **Roots**. In 1978, he headlined his own special **Ben Vereen: Showcase for a Man of Many Talents** as well as **Ben Vereen—His Roots**, a one-man show. In 1980, he was one of several top celebrities who appeared in **Uptown**, the tribute to the Apollo Theater. That same year, he starred in the TV film **Tenspeed and Brown Shoe** and the subsequent series of the same title. He had a major role in *Ellis Island*, a made-for-television film in 1984. In other made-for-television films, he played the title role in **Louis Armstrong— Chicago Style** in 1976 and key roles in **The Jesse Owens Story** in 1984 and **Anne Rice's "The Feast of All Saints"** in 2001. He was a regular in the sitcom **Webster** (1984) playing Webster's uncle.

Vereen guest-starred in variety specials *Jubilee* in 1976, *The Stars Salute Israel* in 1978, *The Cheryl Ladd Special* in 1979, *The International All-Star Festival* in 1981, *Night of 100 Stars* in 1982, *A Salute to Lady Liberty* in 1984, *Lynda Carter: Body and Soul* in 1984, and *Here's TV Entertainment* and *The ABC All-Star Spectacular* in 1985. He also participated in the *All-Star Party for "Dutch" Reagan* in 1985. In addition, Vereen was in *The Magic of David Copperfield VIII . . . In China* in 1986, *George Burns' 95th Birthday Party* in 1991, the documentary *Walt Disney . . . One Man's Dream* in 1981, the TV special *The Secret World of the Very Young* in 1984, *Circus of the Stars* in 1989, and *The Chipmunks—Rockin' through the Decades* in 1990.

VERNON JOHNS STORY, THE (*ABC, January 15, 1994*). This television movie was based on the life of Vernon Johns, a controversial preacher who battled racism and became a leader in the civil rights movement. **James Earl Jones** played Rev. Johns. **Mary Alice** portrayed Altona. **Cissy Houston** was Rose. **Joe Seneca** was Deacon Wilkes. *See also* BIOPICS.

VH1 DIVAS (*VH1, April 18, 2004*). Gladys Knight, Patti LaBelle, Eve, Ashanti, Cyndi Lauper, Jessica Simpson, Deborah Harry, and others performed in this, the seventh annual charity concert. It aired live from the MGM Grand in Las Vegas. Videos of Usher, **Chaka Khan, Vanessa Williams, Mary J. Blige,** Alicia Keys, Britney Spears, and others were featured. **Tyra Banks** and the girls from *The Apprentice* made appearances. The event raised more than $300,000 for restoring music education programs to public schools.

VH1 DIVAS DUETS (*VH1, May 22, 2003*). Top female singers celebrated the hottest music of yesterday and today. **Queen Latifah** was the host with divas **Mary J. Blige, Beyonce, Chaka Kahn, Whitney Houston, Ashanti,** Jewel, and Lisa Marie Presley. A special diva tribute to **Stevie Wonder** was a highlight. There were performances by Bobby Brown, Aisha Taylor, Celine Dion, Shania Twain, The Isley Brothers, and Sharon Osbourne.

VH1 DIVAS LIVE 2001: THE ONE AND ONLY ARETHA FRANKLIN (*VH1, April 10, 2001*). Celebrated musical artists performed at Radio City Music Hall while spotlighting **Aretha Franklin.** Included were **Mary J. Blige** and **Janet Jackson.**

VH1 DIVAS 2000: A TRIBUTE TO DIANA ROSS (*VH1, April 11, 2000*). Divas **Donna Summer**, Mariah Carey, Faith Hill, and former **Supremes** paid tribute to **Diana Ross** at a concert from Madison Square Garden.

VIBE AWARDS (*UPN, 2003– , annually*). This award show was held to celebrate urban music and culture including hip-hop, rhythm and blues, and fashions. The show takes a look at the past year and the best in these areas. Contemporary musical performances and special celebrity appearances were included. Awards were determined by the editors of *VIBE* magazine.

VICTORY AT ENTEBBE (*ABC, December 13, 1976*). Julius Harris played Idi Amin, president of Uganda, in this two-hour film about the July 4, 1976, Israeli raid on the airport at Entebbe, Uganda. Harris replaced **Godfrey Cambridge**, who died during production. The film was shown in theaters outside the United States. *See also* RAID ON ENTEBBE; HISTORICAL EVENTS DRAMATIZED.

VIDALE, THEA. Vidale played the title role in the 1993–1994 sitcom *Thea*.

VIDEO MUSIC AWARDS. *See* MTV VIDEO MUSIC AWARDS.

VITTE, RAY. Vitte played Woody Henderson, in the TV series *Doc* (1975) and Mother in the TV film *Mother, Juggs, and Speed* (1978). He had key roles in the TV films *The Man in the Santa Claus Suit* (1979) and *Grambling's White Tiger* (1981). He was a regular in the adventure series *The Quest* in 1982. On February 20, 1983, police went to his apartment in Studio City, California, after receiving reports that he was shouting and chanting. They said Vitte "lunged at them" several times, and they tried to subdue him with tear gas and by striking him several times with a nightstick. They said the efforts had "no apparent effect," that Vitte ran toward a swimming pool, fell on the concrete, and slipped partly into the pool. He was handcuffed and carried to a police car where he "ceased breathing" and was pronounced dead on arrival at a hospital. There was never an explanation of why he was chanting or shouting, and there was great concern from those who knew him that it was just plain police brutality. Vitte was not a big man, so many felt that he could have been subdued without killing him.

VOICES FOR TV CHARACTERS. Bill Cosby was the first African American to make a success of cartoon voices when his was the voice of the character he created, Fat Albert, in the 1970s animated series *Fat Albert and the Cosby Kids*. Cosby's voice was also used for other characters in that series including Mudfoot, Mushmouth, and Bill. Cosby lent his voice again for the superhero *The Brown Hornet.*

Muhammad Ali played himself in the biographical cartoon *The Adventures of Muhammad Ali*. **Flip Wilson** played several voices in his biographical cartoon *Clerow Wilson and P.S.14*.

Eddie Murphy's voice was used for the lead character, housing project super Thurgood Orenthal Stubbs, in *The PJs*, a foamation series he created in 1998. **Ja'Net Dubois** also lent her voice to a character in *The PJs*, Ms. Avery, and she won an **Emmy Award** for the portrayal in 1999. **Loretta Devine**'s voice was used for the character Muriel, Thurgood's wife, in *The PJs*.

Isaac Hayes was the voice of Jerome "Chef" McElroy on *South Park*. **Cree Summer**'s voice was used for the character Susie Carmichael, the black girl in *The Rugrats*. **Kevin Clash**, a Jim Henson puppeteer, spoke for Elmo on *Sesame Street* for many years. He also provided the voices for Hoots, Natasha, and Kingston Livingston III. **Bill Bellamy** was the voice of the hip puppet Skeeter on *Cousin Skeeter*.

Kyla Pratt's voice was heard for the character Penny on *The Proud Family*, while **Cedric the Entertainer** won an NAACP Image Award for his voice work for Penny's Uncle Bobby. On the same series, **Tommy Davidson** was Oscar Proud, **Jo Marie Payton** was Suga Mama, **Karen Malina White** was Dijonay Jones, and **Paula Jai Parker** was Trudy Proud. There are numerous others.

– W –

WADE, ADAM. A veteran recording artist and singer, Wade was the first black host of a nationally televised game show when he headed *Musical Chairs* in 1975. Unfortunately, the show lasted only one season.

WADE, ERNESTINE. A talented vocalist and organist, Wade worked as a secretary in Hollywood before getting her first acting work—doing voice-overs for the Disney film *Song of the South*. In the 1940s, she auditioned for and landed the role of Sapphire, the Kingfish's wife, in the radio show *Amos 'n' Andy*. She continued the role when the show went to television and stayed with it until 1953, when it was canceled because of complaints by the National Association for the Advancement of Colored People and other civil rights groups that the show was full of "negative stereotypes of Black Americans." She played a few episodic series roles, and throughout the rest of her life, she argued that her portrayal of Sapphire had value and dignity and was not demeaning to black women. She described the character as a woman who loved her husband, stood by him through adversity, and was loyal to him. She said she scolded him only when he deserved it and that she was careful to tone down the black dialect in the scripts. She died in 1983 at the age of 76. *See also* HAIRSTON, JESTER; STEREOTYPES.

WALKER, ARNETIA. Walker starred in the sitcom *The Big House* (2004–) and had a regular role as Miss Ross, a teacher, in the first year (1999–2000) of the school drama *Popular*. She played Nurse Annie Roland in *Nurses* (1991–1994).

WALKER, JIMMIE. Walker earned television fame as J. J. Evans, the older son in the family featured on the sitcom *Good Times*. His character always spoke the catchphrase, "Dy-no-mite." He was also the star of the short-lived 1987–1988 sitcom *Bustin' Loose* based on the **Richard Pryor** film of the same name; he played Sonny Barnes. At one time, several celebrities destined for stardom—Jay Leno, David Letterman, and **Byron Allen**—were hired by him to write comedy material. After *Good Times*, he was popular on game shows including *The Match Game* and *The Hollywood Squares*. Walker guest-starred in TV specials *Battle of the Network Stars* in 1976 and *US against the World II* in 1978, *The Rowan and Martin Special* in 1973, *Cotton Club '75* in 1974, *Perry Como's Summer of '74* in 1974, *State Fair America* in 1977, *Cinderella at the Palace* in 1978, *General Electric's All-Star Anniversary* in 1978, and *The Osmond Brothers Special* in 1978. He also appeared on the *Dean Martin Celebrity Roast* of **Redd Foxx** in 1976, *The Mad, Mad, Mad, Mad World of the Super Bowl* in 1977, and *The Comedy Store's 20th Birthday* in 1992. He played key roles in the TV films *Murder Can Hurt You* (1980), *At Ease* (1983), and *B.A.D. Cats* (1980).

WALLACE, ROYCE. Wallace had key roles in the telefilms *Green Eyes* in 1977 and *To Find My Son* in 1980.

WANDA AT LARGE (*FOX, 2003*). Stand-up comedienne **Wanda Sykes** was a field correspondent on *Inside the NFL* offering a comedic aspect to the show. Then she starred in this sitcom and played a character, Wanda Hawkins, who was a comedic correspondent on a political talk show. **Phil Morris** played Bradley, the show's moderator. Dale Godboldo played Keith, Wanda's best friend and segment producer. Wanda Hawkins had two children—Barris, played by Robert Bailey Jr., and Holly, played by **Jurnee Smollet**. The show seemed to be a hit at first, but it was moved from Wednesday nights after *Bernie Mac* to Fridays, hit a ratings wall, and was canceled after eight episodes.

WANDA DOES IT (*CC, 2004*). **Wanda Sykes** was star of this partly scripted comedy show in which she attempted to do jobs outside show business. Wanda's attempts included repossessing a car and doing minor surgery. In one show, she sought pointers from a bordello madam and a prostitute and was selected by a john from a line of ladies of the night.

WARD, DOUGLAS TURNER. Ward played key roles in 1975's *Ceremonies in Dark Old Men* and 1989's *Women of Brewster Place*.

WARD, RICHARD. Ward played Pharoah in 1957's **"The Green Pastures."** In TV films, he played Blind Jordan in *The Sty of the Blind Pig* (1974), a police informant in *Contract on Cherry Street* (1977), and Ned in *Freeman* (1977). He was William Piper in the brief drama series *Beacon Hill* (1975). Ward was born in 1915 and died in 1979.

WARFIELD, MARLENE. Warfield played the third maid cast in the sitcom *Maude*, Victoria Butterfield, in 1977–1978. She had a role in *The Sophisticated Gents* in 1981 and *The Marva Collins Story*, also in 1981. *See also* DOMESTIC WORKERS IN THE 1970s.

WARFIELD, MARSHA. The comedienne played Roz in the sitcom *Night Court* from 1986 to 1992, Dr. Maxine Douglas in the sitcom *Empty Nest* (1993–1995), and Principal Dowling in *Smart Guy* (1997). In TV film, she had roles in *Doomsday Rock* (1997) and *The Marva Collins Story* (1981). In variety and specials, she was featured in *Uptown Comedy Express* in 1987, *The Soul Train Music Awards* (1987 and 1992), the *NAACP Image Awards* (1987 and 1988), *Motown Merry Christmas* (1987), *Stand Up America* (1987), *Truly Tasteless Jokes* (1987), and *A Party for Richard Pryor* (1991). She performed and wrote for *The Richard Pryor Show* (1977).

WARFIELD, WILLIAM. Warfield was the first black male singer to guest-star on a television variety series when he appeared on *The Ed Sullivan Show* in 1951. In 1957, he played "deLawd" in **"The Green Pastures."** Warfield died in 2002 from injuries from a fall.

WARNER BROTHERS PRESENTS: CASABLANCA. *See* CASABLANCA.

WARNER, MALCOLM-JAMAL. First recognized by television viewers as Theo in *The Cosby Show* (1984–1992), Warner guest-starred in TV specials *Andy Williams and the NBC Kids Search for Santa* in 1985, *Walt Disney World's 15th Birthday Celebration* in 1986, and *A Star Spangled Celebration* in 1987. He also hosted the variety specials *Disneyland's Summer Vacation Party* in 1986 and *The U.S.A. Musical Challenge* in 1992. Warner hosted the children's program *Kids Killing Kids/Kids Saving Kids* in 1994. He had a role in the after-school special *A Desperate Exit* (1986) and key roles in the TV films *The Father Clements Story* (1987) and *Tyson* (1995). He starred in the sitcoms *Here and Now* (1992–1993), *Malcolm and Eddie* (1996–2000), *Jeremiah* (2002–2003), and Listen Up (2004–). He also became a director. *See also* CHILD TV ACTORS/ PERFORMERS WHO MAINTAINED SUCCESS AS ADULTS IN SHOW BUSINESS.

WARREN, MICHAEL. Warren played Officer Bobby Hill on *Hill Street Blues* (1981–1987), Officer Willie Miller on *Paris* (1979–1980), Michael T-Dog Turner in *Sweet Justice* in 1995, and Ron Harris in *City of Angels* in 2000. He played Clark Coles in *Oprah Winfrey Presents: The Wedding* (1998). He had a key role in *Buffalo Soldiers* (1997).

WARWICK, DIONNE. Warwick hosted *The Dionne Warwick Special* in 1969, *Sisters in the Name of Love* in 1986, and *Dionne Warwick in London* in 1988. She guest-starred in numerous variety specials— *It's What's Happening, Baby!* in 1965, *Tin Pan Alley Today* in 1967, *Feliciano—Very Special* and *The Engelbert Humperdinck Special* in 1969, *Danny Thomas Looks at Yesterday, Today and Tomorrow* in 1970, *Everything You Always Wanted to Know about Jack Benny and Were Afraid to Ask* in 1971, *The Fifth Dimension Traveling Show* in 1971, *The Magical Music of Burt Bacharach* in 1972, *Dean Martin's Christmas in California* in 1975, *Celebration: The American Spirit* in 1976, *The Original Rompin' Stompin' Hot and Heavy, Cool and Groovy All-Star Jazz Show* in 1976, *The Stars and Stripes Show* in 1976, *The People's Command Performance* in 1977, *Variety '77: The Year in Entertainment* in 1978, *Barry Manilow—One Voice* in 1980, *Crystal* in 1980, *Sinatra: The First 40 Years* in 1980, *Debby Boone*

. . . *One Step Closer* in 1982, *I Love Liberty* in 1982, *All-Star Party for Frank Sinatra* and *George Burns Celebrates 80 Years in Show Business* in 1983, *The Kennedy Center Honors* and *Anne Murray's Winter Carnival from Quebec* in 1984, *American Bandstand's 33 1/3 Celebration* and *Here's TV Entertainment* in 1985, and *That's What Friends Are For* in 1990. She appeared in the TV special *Circus of the Stars* in 1986 and hosted *The Grammy Lifetime Achievement Awards* in 1987. In one of the early 1990s infomercials, Warwick pushed a psychic network.

WASHINGTON, DENZEL. The 2002 Academy Award winner played Wilma Rudolph's 18-year-old boyfriend, Robert Ethridge, in the made-for-television film *Wilma* in 1977. In 1979, he played Kirk in the miniseries *Flesh and Blood*, and in 1984, he had an important role in the telefilm *License to Kill*. From 1982 to 1988, he played a regular role, Dr. Phillip Chandler, in the medical drama series *St. Elsewhere*. *See also* MOVIE STARS WHOSE CAREERS BEGAN ON TV SERIES.

WASHINGTON, ISAIAH. Washington played Miles in the series *Soul Food* (2000–2004). Then he joined the cast of the drama *Grey's Anatomy* in midseason 2004–2005. He played a key role in the TV films *Mr. and Mrs. Loving* (1996) and *Dancing in September* (2001).

WASHINGTON, KENNETH. Washington joined the cast of *Hogan's Heroes* after **Ivan Dixon** departed. Washington played Sgt. Richard Baker (1970–1971).

WATERS, ETHEL. Waters was a singer and an actress who had a career that spanned film and stage before television. *The Ethel Waters Show*, in 1939, was an NBC experiment in television that is likely the first show ever televised and even more likely the first with an African-American star. Then, in 1950–1952, she played the title role in *Beulah*, the first of several actresses to play the role and resign from the role. She also guest-starred or had roles in dramatic series and in anthologies. In her early years, she sang sultry, torch songs, but during later years, she would sing only spirituals and said, "God's music is all that matters." In 1954, she was interviewed by Edward R. Murrow on the prestigious *Person to Person* from her modest home in New York. Then, in 1955, she said she worked only two months, and that was in summer stock at notoriously low salaries. So she had fallen on extreme hard times by 1957, when she appeared on the quiz show *Break the Bank* to earn money to pay back taxes. She answered questions in the category of music and won $10,000. One would think that such a versatile actress would have been financially secure, but that was not the case. In 1955, she starred with **Harry Belafonte** in *Winner by Decision*, a drama on *General Electric Theater*. Ethel Waters was born in 1896 and died in 1977 of heart disease. *See also* DOMESTIC WORKERS OF THE 1950s.

WATERS, MUDDY. Vintage footage of Waters performing was a highlight of *The Blues*, a seven-part series about the music genre in 2003.

WATKINS, JAMES. Watkins played Jerry Wallace, the pilot who flew the plane for and brought cases to *The Magician* (Bill Bixby), who was also a crime solver in the 1973–1974 drama series.

WATSON, JAMES. Watson (aka James A. Watson Jr.) was a member of the repertory company on *Love, American Style* from 1972 to 1974. He had a key role in the TV film *First You Cry* in 1978.

WATSON, VERNEE. Watson (aka Vernee Watson-Johnson) played Verna Jean in the sitcom *Welcome Back Kotter* (1975–1977), Lucille Banks in the sitcom *Carter Country* (1977–1979), and Denise in the sitcom *Foley Square* (1985–1986). She recurred as **Will Smith**'s mother on *Fresh Prince of Bel-Air*. She had a role in the TV film *Love's Savage Fury* in 1979. Hers was the voice of Danielle Craig in the sitcom *Baby Talk* (1991–1992).

WATTS, ANDRE. Pianist Watts narrated and performed *The Chamber Music Society of Lincoln Center 30th Anniversary Gala* in 1998.

WATTS, ROLANDA. Watts was a reporter for *Inside Edition* before she got her own talk show, *Rolanda*, in 1994. After the show ended, she guest-anchored *Extra* and *Talk Soup* and took on acting roles in drama, comedies, and commercials.

WATTSTAX 1973 (*PBS, September 2004*). This documentary about the black experience was filmed in 1973, but its circulation was limited. Part of the show was entertainment acts originating from the Los Angeles Coliseum. **Isaac Hayes** arrived in a stretch limousine in disguise, then performed his "Theme from Shaft." The **Rev. Jesse Jackson** did his poem "I Am Somebody." The Staple Singers, Luther Ingram, and others sang their hits. Featured was comedian **Richard Pryor** telling humorous stories. Also participating were **Ted Lange** (before his debut on *The Love Boat*) and **Raymond Allen** (before his role on *Sanford and Son*). Director Mel Stuart said he was the only white crew member, that all the cameramen and sound men were black. His insistence on having a black crew was unusual in 1973.

WAYANS BROS., THE (*WB, 1995–1999*). This sitcom was a production of the multitalented Wayans family. **Keenen Ivory Wayans** cocreated the series, and his younger brothers, **Shawn Wayans** and **Marlon Wayans**, starred as Shawn and Marlon Williams, brothers in their midtwenties who cohabited a brownstone in New York. They had very little in common. Shawn, the older of the two, aspired to be a successful businessman and ran a newsstand in the lobby of an office building. Marlon was a free spirit, taking life as it comes, who worked part time in the kitchen of his father's (Pops, played by **John Witherspoon**) diner. Marlon was always getting into tight spots that his brother and Pops had to resolve. Other characters included the following: Lisa (**Lela Rochon**), a college student whom Marlon wanted to marry when he became successful; Dee Baxter (**Anna Maria Horsford**), the no-nonsense security guard at the office building; and Monique Lattimore (**Paula Jai Parker**, 1995–1996), who worked in the gift shop and was the object of Shawn's affections. **Ja'net DuBois** played Grandma Ellington (1996–1998). Jermaine Hopkins played Dupree (1996–1998). Jill Tasker played Lou Malino (1995). Benny Quan played Benny (1995). Joanna Sanchez played Lupe (1995). **Phill Lewis** played T.C. (1995–1998).

WAYANS, DAMON. Television viewers first recognized Wayans as a featured performer on *Saturday Night Live* (1985–1986). He was writer and star of the show produced and hosted by his brother **Keenen Ivory Wayans**, *In Living Color* (1990–1994). He was particularly known for the running comedy skit "Men on Film" as half of a team of effeminate homosexual critics. Wayans's credits also include *Damon*, a 1988 sitcom in which he starred and was executive producer. He was creator and executive producer of *413 Hope Street*, a one-hour drama series (1997–1998). He was executive producer of *Waynehead*, a Saturday morning animated series featuring the voices of his siblings, Kim, Marlon, and Shawn Wayans. In 1991, he did a stand-up special for HBO called *Damon Wayans: The Last Stand?* He announced it as his last time doing stand-up, but it was not. In 1996, he did another stand-up comedy special titled *Damon Wayans: Still Standing*. He was one of several comedians who participated in *The Comedy Store's 20th Anniversary* in 1992. In 2001, he began his starring role in the sitcom *My Wife and Kids*; he was also cocreator and executive producer.

WAYANS, KEENEN IVORY. Wayans was creator, producer, and host of *In Living Color*, a comedy/variety series that ran from 1990 to 1994 and featured his siblings, Damon and Kim. He left the series after the second year because he was not satisfied with decisions the Fox network made about the direction of the series. He was a member of the cast of the 1983 drama series *For Love and Honor*, about U.S. Army paratroopers. He guest-starred in a variety special *Motown 30: What's Going On?* in 1990. Wayans was one of the creators on the sitcom *The Wayans Bros.* (1995–1999). He was host and executive producer of *The Keenen Ivory Wayans Show* (1997–1998) and was executive producer of the TV film *Hammer, Slammer, and Slade* (1990).

WAYANS, KIM. Wayans played a regular role on *In Living Color*, hosted by her brother **Keenen** and also starring her brother **Damon** and other family members. She also played Mrs. Walker in *Waynehead* in 1996, Allison in *A Different World* (1987–1988), and Tonia in *In the House* from 1996 to 1998.

WAYANS, MARLON. Wayans costarred with his brother **Shawn** in the sitcom *The Wayans Bros.* as Marlon Williams (1995–1999).

WAYANS, SHAWN. Wayans costarred with his brother **Marlon** in the sitcom *The Wayans Bros.* as Shawn Williams (1995–1999).

WAYNE BRADY SHOW, THE (*ABC, 2001–2002*). Comedian **Wayne Brady** hosted this variety series, which centered on improvisations. There was sketch comedy, musical performances, impersonations, and improvisation. Celebrity guest stars made appearances, and there was a stable of sketch performers and dancers.

WAYNE BRADY SHOW, THE (*SYN, 2002–2004*). Comedian **Wayne Brady** hosted this talk/variety series. Reminiscent of variety series of the 1970s, Brady sang himself and interviewed his guests who were often plugging their current projects. In 2003, the show won the **Emmy Award** for Outstanding Talk Show, and Brady won for Outstanding Talk Show Host.

WAYNEHEAD (*WB, 1996–1997*). A Saturday morning cartoon, this half-hour production was inspired by the childhood of **Damon Wayans**. Ten-year-old Damey Wayans and his family lived in lower Manhattan. When he had no money, which was usual, Damey made up for the situation through creativity. If he wanted a toy, he built it from junk he found in the neighborhood. Damey's family and friends were Monique, Shavonne, Tof, Blue, Tripod, and the three-legged dog. The Wayans siblings—Kim, Shawn, and Marlon—provided voices, but **Orlando Brown** provided the voice for Damey. Damon Wayans was executive producer.

WEATHERS, CARL. Known first as Apollo Creed in the *Rocky* feature films, Weathers starred in the TV series *In the Heat of the Night* (1993–1994) as Chief Hampton Forbes, in *Street Justice* (1991) as Sgt. Adams Beaudreaux, and in *Tour of Duty* (1989–1990) as Col. Brewster. In TV films, he had roles in *The Hostage Heart* (1977), *The Bermuda Depths* (1978), and *Dangerous Passion* (1990). Weathers was in the TV remake of *The Defiant Ones* in 1986. He played Roy Brown in *Assault on Devil's Island* (1997) and the same role on *Assault on Death Mountain* (1999).

WEAVER, JASON. Weaver played Marcus Henderson on *Smart Guy* (1997–1999) and Jerome in the sitcom *Thea* (1993–1994). He was Matthew Thomas on the short-lived series *Brewster Place* (1990).

WEBSTER (*ABC, 1983–1987*). This sitcom made its debut pre-*The Cosby Show*, a period during which television programming executives thought that series had to be racially integrated to be successful in the ratings. So when a show was developed for cute little **Emmanuel Lewis** of the Burger King commercials, it was not a difficult creative decision to make him a boy with white parents. *Diff'rent Strokes* had already been a hit built around another cute short black kid (Gary Coleman) with a white father. *Gimme a Break* had been built around Nell Carter as the mother figure to white kids, and it was a hit. Lewis was 12 but looked much younger, so he was seven in the series. His character, Webster Long, showed up at the doorstep of George and Katherine Papadapolis (Alex Karras and Susan Clark) after his parents had been killed in a car accident. George was friends with Webster's father and was his godfather. The scripts told sweet stories, the kind that make you cry. **Ben Vereen** entered the series in 1984 to play Webster's Uncle Philip, who wanted to get custody of him.

WEDDING, THE. *See* OPRAH WINFREY PRESENTS: THE WEDDING.

WELCOME BACK, KOTTER (*ABC, 1975–1979*). This sitcom centered on Brooklyn High School teacher Gabe Kotter (Gabriel Kaplan), who returned to the high school from which he graduated to teach the Sweathogs, a group of unruly remedial students. Among the Sweathogs were two black characters: Freddy "Boom Boom" Washington (**Lawrence Hilton-Jacobs**) and Verna Jean (**Vernee Watson**). Washington's catchphrase was "Hi there!" John Travolta's character, the cool Vinnie Barbarino, was the sensation of the series, so when he was absent to do films, there was a void. Also, even the Sweathogs couldn't stay in high school forever.

WELCOME HOME HEROES WITH WHITNEY HOUSTON (*HBO, March 31, 1991*). Promoted as her first-ever televised solo concert, **Whitney Houston** performed at the Naval Air Station in Virginia for veterans returning home from the war, Desert Storm, in the Persian Gulf. Songs included "I'm Your Baby Tonight," "All the Man That I Need," "I Wanna Dance with Somebody," and "The Star-

Spangled Banner." Houston was thrilled to do the live concert and said, "Because there were more troops than seats for the show, we invited 3,000 to the dress rehearsal Saturday night. The concert Sunday was probably the most memorable and rewarding of my career. What an audience! Army, Air Force, Navy, Marines, and the Coast Guard all so happy to be back home."

WELDON, ANN. Weldon played Mama Ritt Ross in *A Woman Called Moses* in 1978. She played a key role in the TV film *Sidney Shorr: A Girl's Best Friend* in 1981. She played Clair on the sitcom *9 to 5* (1982–1983) and Edna on the sitcom *One in a Million* (1980). She portrayed the character Charlaine on the sitcom *Roc* (1992–1993).

WELDON, CHARLES. Weldon played Shadrack Davis in *A Woman Called Moses* in 1978. He had a key role in the TV film *Another Woman's Child* in 1983.

WHAT'S HAPPENING!! (*ABC, 1976–1979*). In a sitcom somewhat derived from the feature film *Cooley High*, three teenage friends—Raj (**Ernest Thomas**), Rerun (**Fred Berry**), and Dwayne (**Haywood Nelson**)—grew up in Los Angeles. Raj was an aspiring writer, and the house he shared with his mother, Mama/Mrs. Thomas (**Mabel King**), and sister, Dee (**Danielle Spencer**), was the primary set. Another set was Rob's Diner, where the boys hung out and where Shirley (**Shirley Hemphill**) was the waitress. Raj and Dee's father (**Thalmus Rasulala**) appeared occasionally, but he was estranged from their mother. This was a sensitive point for longtime theater actress King, who insisted that one of the worst tragedies of television was black families without two parents, that fatherless homes did not make good role models. Though her character was a strong woman who represented what was morally right, she also was unhappy that her character was a maid. She often suggested script changes to eliminate references to Mama's job. She wanted her character to go to school and get a better job. King and most of the cast were also discontent about having their lines written to set up Dee for the punch lines. During the second season, Danielle Spencer was involved in an auto accident that killed her stepfather and left her seriously injured. She did return to the series sporting a broken arm (which was written into the story line). Also, in the second season, Thomas and Berry made demands for higher salaries; Berry even wanted an "MDD" (million dollar deal). They made about $3,000 per episode for 22 episodes. Needless to say, they did not get MDDs. Raj and Rerun graduated from high school and got their own apartment, and King's role was diminished. By the third season, King was dropped from the series, and Shirley moved into the Thomas house. Also, new characters were brought into the story. Despite beginning its third year as the 16th most popular series on television, the show was canceled before the end of its third year. Most of the cast members returned for the revival series *What's Happening Now!!* (1985–1988).

After that series ended, most of the actors were rarely to never seen in television or film. Danielle Spencer became a veterinarian and apparently dropped out of the Screen Actors Guild; otherwise, the current actress, Danielle Spencer, would be unable to use the name. Rasulala died of a heart attack in 1991; he was 52. Mabel King, suffering from diabetes, became a double amputee and died on November 9, 1999. Alone in her home, Shirley Hemphill died of kidney failure on December 10, 1999; she was 52. Berry, who had had a stroke, died on October 21, 2003; he was 52. *See also* RATINGS; WHAT'S HAPPENING NOW!!

WHAT'S HAPPENING NOW!! (*SYN, 1985–1988*). **Ernest Thomas** (Raj), **Fred Berry** (Rerun), **Haywood Nelson** (Dwayne), **Danielle Spencer** (Dee), and **Shirley Hemphill** (Shirley) from the original cast of *What's Happening!!* formed the basic cast of the revived sitcom in 1985. Raj was married to Nadine (**Anne-Marie Johnson**) and was trying to make a living as a writer. Raj and Nadine took in a foster child, Carolyn (**Reina King**), and the family lived in the same house Raj grew up in. Raj and Shirley also were partners in running the diner. Dwayne was a computer programmer, and Rerun was a used car salesman. Berry began to demand higher wages, maintaining that he was the center of the series. Berry's character was subsequently written out of the series. Added to the cast were **Martin Lawrence** as Maurice, a busboy at the diner, and Ken Segoes as Darryl, Maurice's buddy.

WHATTA YEAR . . . 1986 (*ABC, December 29, 1986*). **Quincy Jones, Ben E. King, Smokey Robinson,** and **O. J. Simpson** were in this variety special that looked back, in fun, at the songs, television shows, motion pictures, and personalities of 1986. Justine Bateman and Ron Reagan were hosts.

WHEN HELL FREEZES OVER, I'LL SKATE (*PBS, 1979*). This Broadway musical production, taped before an invited New York audience, celebrated the survival spirit of the African-American culture and experience with poetry and song. Some of the poems were set to original music by twin entertainers **Clinton Derricks-Carroll** and **Cleavant Derricks.** Producer Vinnette Carroll used the poetry and writings of Paul Lawrence Dunbar, Countee Cullen, Langston Hughes, Paula Giddings, Nikki Giovanni, Saundra Sharpe, and others. The poetry ranged from those of the era of slavery (Dunbar's "When Malindy Sings") to then-modern love poems and poems with black feminist themes. **Derricks, Derricks-Carroll, Lynne Thigpen, Reginald VelJohnson,** Brenda Braxton, Jeffrey Anderson-Gunter, Lynne Clifton-Allen, and Marilynn Winbush were the performers. *See also* BROADWAY PLAYS AND MUSICALS.

WHERE I LIVE (*ABC, 1993*). The sitcom starred **Doug E. Doug** as Douglas St. Martin, the leader of three buddies who hung out on a Harlem stoop and solved all of life's challenges. The other two were **Flex Alexander** as Reggie and Shaun Baker as Malcolm. Douglas's parents, played by Sullivan Walker and **Lorraine Toussaint,** showed up to bring the dreamers into reality. Yunoka Doyle, Jason Bose Smith, and Alma Yvonne also appeared. The series was praised for not having stereotypical characters.

WHITAKER, FORREST. Whitaker had a starring role in the TV film *Deacons for Defense* in 2003. He was in *Anne Rice's "The Feast of All Saints"* in 2001 and played a key role in the TV film *Witness Protection* in 1999 and in *Rebound: The Legend of Earl "The Goat" Manigault* in 1997.

WHITE, BRIAN J. White as Nigel was a regular in the series *Second Time Around*, which premiered in 2004. He had key roles in the series *Moesha* (1999) and *The Shield* (2002–2004). In TV films, he had a key role as Sweet Money in *Nancy Drew* (2002).

WHITE, JALEEL. White was Robert in the sitcom *Charlie & Co.* (1985), Cadet Nicholls in *Cadets* (1988), and Steve Urkel and Stefan Urquelle in *Family Matters* (1990–1998). He provided voice for the *Sonic The Hedgehog* game (1993, 1999) and was also the voice of Bladebeak in *Quest for Camelot* (1998). He played a role in the series *The Grown Ups* in 1999.

WHITE, KAREN MALINA. White played Charmaine in *A Different World* (1992–1993) and Nicolette in the sitcom *Malcolm and Eddie* (1996–2000). She was the voice of Dijonay Jones in the animated series *The Proud Family* (2001–).

WHITE LIE *(USA, September 25, 1991).* **Gregory Hines** starred as a New York mayor's savvy press secretary who goes back home to the South to bring the man who murdered his father 35 years before to justice.

WHITE MAMA *(CBS, March 5, 1980).* This two-hour telefilm was written especially for movie star Bette Davis, who earned an Emmy nomination for the role of Estelle Malone, a poverty-stricken woman who took in a streetwise black teenager (played by **Ernest J. Harden Jr.**) as a foster child to keep from going on welfare. **Virginia Capers** and **Ernie Hudson** were also in the cast.

WHITE, MICHAEL JAI. White played heavyweight champion **Mike Tyson** in the HBO film *Tyson* (1995) and had a key role in *Captive Heart: The James Mink Story* (1996). In 1999, he starred in the TV film *Mutiny*, based on events during World War II, and *Freedom Song* in 2000.

WHITE, PERSIA. White was one of the girlfriends (Lynn) in the sitcom *Girlfriends* (2000–). She had roles in the TV films *Operation Sandman* (2000) and *Suddenly* (1996). She played Kineisha "K.C." Burrell in *Another World* (1999).

WHITE, SLAPPY. Slappy White (née Melvin White) guest-starred in variety specials *The Redd Foxx Special* in 1978 and comedy tribute *Dean Martin Celebrity Roast of Redd Foxx* in 1976. He played Melvin, a recurring character on *Sanford and Son* (1972). White was born in 1921 and died in 1995.

WHITE SHADOW, THE (*CBS, 1978–1981*). This drama series was a racially integrated high school drama and centered on an inner-city basketball team with a white coach (played by Ken Howard) and his primarily black players. The stories dealt not only with winning games but also with the problems, pleasures, and hopes of the team members. Serious subjects such as drugs, racism, and sex were included in the story lines. The black players were Warren Coolidge (**Byron Stewart**), Morris Thorpe (**Kevin Hooks**), Curtis Jackson (**Eric Kilpatrick**), and Milton Reese (**Nathan Cook**). **Jason Bernard** was the principal in the pilot episode, but **Ed Bernard** played the series role. **Joan Pringle** was the vice principal. *See also* SERIES ABOUT SCHOOL LIFE.

WHITEWASH: THE CLARENCE BRANDLEY STORY (*SHO, April 21, 2002*). **Courtney Vance** starred in this true story of an innocent young black man charged with a crime solely because of his skin color. A strong legal team helps by fighting long-standing prejudices and racism.

WHITFIELD, CHARLES MALIK. Whitfield starred in the miniseries *The Temptations* as singer Otis Williams (1998). He also played James Mooney in the legal drama series *The Guardian* (2001–).

WHITFIELD, DONDRE T. Whitfield was introduced to television viewers as a youngster when he played Robert, boyfriend to one of the Huxtable daughters, on *The Cosby Show*. He had a role in the daytime drama *Another World* before joining the cast of the daytime drama *All My Children* in 1991, playing Terrence Frye, a role for which he earned three Emmy nominations and two nominations for the NAACP Image Award. From 1997 to 1999, he starred in the sitcom *Between Brothers*. He had a role in the *ABC Afterschool Special* "All That Glitters."

WHITFIELD, FREDRICKA. Whitfield's credits include serving CNN as news anchor for the weekend newscasts *CNN Saturday* and *CNN Sunday* and as correspondent for the network covering breaking news. In 2003, she covered Operation Iraqi Freedom. Before joining CNN, she was a news correspondent for *NBC Nightly News* and *The Today Show*.

WHITFIELD, LYNN. Whitfield was one of seven performers in the Broadway choreopoem *For Colored Girls Who Have Considered Suicide/When the Rainbow Is Enuf* in 1982. Whitfield performed in the drama special *Zora Is My Name* in 1990. She starred or had important roles in numerous made-for-television motion pictures including the following: *Johnnie Mae Gibson: F.B.I* and *The Women of Brewster Place*, both in 1989; *The Josephine Baker Story* in 1991, *Stompin' at the Savoy* in 1992; *Sophie and the Moonhanger* in 1996; *Oprah Winfrey Presents: The Wedding* in 1998; *Dangerous Evidence: The Lori Jackson Story*, *Deep in My Heart*, *Love Songs*, and *The Color of Courage*, all in 1999; and *Redemption* in 2004.

WHITNEY HOUSTON: THE CONCERT FOR A NEW SOUTH AFRICA (*HBO, November 12, 1994*). Whitney Houston performed in a live, sold-out performance of more than 70,000 fans in Johannesburg, South Africa.

WHITNEY HOUSTON: THIS IS MY LIFE (*ABC, May 6, 1992*). Whitney Houston shows highlights of her European tour with help from her mother, gospel singer Cissy Houston, and Kevin Costner, who starred with her in the film *The Bodyguard*. Whitney Houston, Cissy Houston, and John Houston were producers.

WHO KILLED MARTIN LUTHER KING? (*FOX, January 22, 1993*). This documentary examined the assassination of the civil rights leader Martin Luther King Jr. in Memphis in 1968. Laurence Fishburne hosted.

WHOOPI (*NBC, 2003–2004*). Whoopi Goldberg starred in this sitcom as Mavis Rae, a singer who once had a hit record. Realizing her diva days were over, Mavis used her earnings to buy a small hotel in

Manhattan. She ran the Lamont Hotel with an assortment of characters including her brother, Courtney, played by Wren T. Brown. The comedienne told *Jet* (October 27, 2003), which compared the series to the politically incorrect *All in the Family*, that "Mavis smokes, drinks straight out of the bottle, makes racist remarks, and challenges all kinds of stereotypes." The show was taped in Queens, New York. Goldberg was executive producer.

WHOOPI GOLDBERG—DIRECT FROM BROADWAY (*HBO, January 20, 1985*). **Whoopi Goldberg** went solo in this comedy concert with very explicit language.

WHOOPI GOLDBERG SHOW, THE (*SYN, 1992–1993*). **Whoopi Goldberg** was host of this talk show featuring interviews with show business and political celebrities. The show was seen five days a week and was critically acclaimed, though it fared poorly in the ratings. A reported 200 episodes were produced, but research indicates the series lasted only six months.

WIDE WORLD OF SPORTS (*ABC, 1961– *). This sports anthology series showcased various sports. Each show began with a montage of exciting sports film as the announcer, Jim McKay, said the catchphrase, "the thrill of victory and the agony of defeat." The **Muhammad Ali** fights with **Joe Frazier** and **George Foreman** were first aired on closed circuit pay-per-view but were rebroadcast the following Saturdays on this series. Ali would provide commentary during the fight and verbally box with Howard Cosell. The Ali bouts were great ratings earners. Another top ratings earner for this series was **The Harlem Globetrotters**. In recent years, *Wide World of Sports* has been the title for ABC's weekend sports programming.

WILCOX, RALPH. Wilcox played Raymond McKay in the sitcom *Big Eddie* (1975), Raymond St. Williams in the sitcom *Busting Loose* (1977), and Duke in the sitcom *One in a Million* (1980). In TV movies and miniseries, he had roles including the following: *White Lie* (1991), *Stompin' at the Savoy* (1992), *Simple Justice* (1993), *With Hostile Intent* (1995), *Deadly Pursuits* (1996), *Last Dance* (1996), *To Love, Honor, and Deceive* (1996); *Ruby Bridges* (1998), and *From the Earth to the Moon* (1998).

WILD WOMEN DON'T SING THE BLUES (*PBS, February 27, 1989*). This one-hour documentary profiled five lady blues legends who sang between 1910 and 1930: Ma Rainey, Bessie Smith, **Ethel Waters**, Alberta Hunter, and Ida Cox.

WILKINSON, LISA. Wilkinson played Nancy Grant on the daytime drama *All My Children* (1972–1982).

WILLIAMS, BILLY DEE. Williams starred in *Brian's Song* as Gale Sayers in 1971. He was a guest at the testimonial dinner *The American Film Institute Salutes Henry Fonda* in 1979. He hosted the documentary *Classic Creatures: Return of the Jedi* in 1983 and *Brown Sugar* in 1986. Williams also guest-starred in variety specials *Night of 100 Stars II* in 1985 and *Diana Ross . . . Red Hot Rhythm and Blues* in 1987. In TV films, he had starring or key roles in *Carter's Army* in 1970, *Truman Capote's "The Glass House"* in 1972, *Christmas Lilies of the Field* in 1979, and *The Jacksons: An American Dream* in 1992. He appeared in the tribute special *It's Black Entertainment* (1997) and *Motown 40: The Music Is Forever* (1998).

WILLIAMS, CLARENCE III. Williams played Linc, one of the three undercover cops, on *The Mod Squad* (1968–1973). He also had a role in the drama special *The Hero Who Couldn't Read* (1984). He played a key role in *Rebound: The Legend of Earl "The Goat" Manigault* (1996).

WILLIAMS, CRESS. Williams played Terrence ("Scooter") on the sitcom *Living Single* in 1994 and D'Shawn Hardell on *Beverly Hills 90210* (1993–1994).

WILLIAMS, DARNELL. Williams played Jesse Hubbard on the daytime drama *All My Children* from 1981 to 1988 and again in 1994. He won the **Emmy Award** for Outstanding Lead Actor in a Daytime Drama Series for the 1984–1985 and 1985–1986 seasons. When he won, he thanked everyone who "helped me get a bookend." He had three bookends because he had already won the statuette in 1982–1983 for Outstanding Actor in a Supporting Role in a Daytime Drama Series. Williams played dual roles in the *ABC Afterschool Special* "The Celebrity and the Arcade Kid."

WILLIAMS, DICK ANTHONY. Williams played Malcolm X in the miniseries *King* in 1978 and also in the *American Playhouse* production of *The Meeting* in 1989. Also in 1978, he played John Tubman in *A Woman Called Moses*. He was one of the gents in the 1981 miniseries *The Sophisticated Gents*. Williams had key roles in the following TV films: *Hollow Image* in 1979, *The Night the City Screamed* in 1980, *Brave New World* in 1980, *This Is Kate . . . Bennett* in 1982, *A Gun in the House* in 1982, *Sister, Sister* in 1982, and *Night Partner* in 1983. He was one of the main characters in the drama series *Homefront* (1991–1993).

WILLIAMS, GARY ANTHONY. Comedian Williams was a regular on the sketch comedy series *Blue Collar TV* beginning in 2004.

WILLIAMS, HAL. Williams had major roles in *Sanford and Son* (as the cop, Smitty) from 1972 to 1976, *227* (as Lester, husband to **Marla Gibbs**'s character) from 1985 to 1990, *The Sinbad Show* (as the grandfather) from 1993 to 1994, *On the Rocks* from 1975 to 1976, and *Private Benjamin* from 1981 to 1983. He had roles in the following TV films: *The Police Story* (1973), *Sidekicks* (1974), *Off the Wall* (1977), *Thou Shalt Not Commit Adultery* (1978), *The Sky Is Gray* (1980), *Don't Look Back: The Story of Satchel Paige* (1981), *T. J. Hooker* (1982), *All the Money in the World* (1983), *Percy and Thunder* (1993), *The West Side Waltz* (1995), and *The Cherokee Kid* (1996). He played Aleck Haley, one of Alex Haley's ancestors, in *Roots: The Next Generations* in 1979. He had roles in two *ABC Afterschool Specials*: "*Run, Don't Walk*" in 1981 and "*The Celebrity and the Arcade Kid*" in 1983.

WILLIAMS, JUAN. Williams joined Fox News in 1997 as a political contributor. He became a regular panelist on the public affairs program *Fox News Sunday*. He also anchors weekend daytime live coverage for Fox News. He wrote several television documentaries including *Politics—The New Black Power* and the nonfiction best-seller *Eyes on the Prize: America's Civil Rights Years, 1964–1965*.

WILLIAMS, KELLIE SHANYGNE. Also known as Kellie Williams, she was Laura Winslow on *Family Matters* (1989–1998), Katie in the TV film *After All* (1999), and Alice Adams in the series *What About Joan* (2001).

WILLIAMS, MALINDA. Williams played Bird in *Soul Food* (2000–2004). She starred in the miniseries *Laurel Avenue* in 1993 and played a key role in *Dancing in Washington*, a 2001 TV film.

WILLIAMS, MONTEL. An actor as well as a talk show host, Williams has hosted *Montel* since 1991 (it was also titled *The Montel Williams Show*), more longevity than any talk show hosted by an African-American male. In 1991, Williams was diagnosed with multiple sclerosis, and since then he has openly shared his struggles and used his position to inform the world about the debilitating disease in hopes of finding a cure. As an actor, he starred in the short-lived high school drama series *Matt Waters* in 1996 as a U.S. Navy retiree who becomes a science teacher. Williams himself was a former naval intelligence officer who counseled families of fellow officers and later became a motivational speaker. He has also guest-starred in drama series, like *Jag*.

WILLIAMS, SAMM-ART. He played Matt Henson in *Cook & Perry: The Race to the Pole*, a 1983 TV film. He had roles in the following TV films: *The Women of Brewster Place* (1989), *The Adventures of Huckleberry Finn* (1985), and *The Color of Friendship* (1981). Williams is also a writer and producer.

WILLIAMS, SPENCER, JR. Williams played Andy, the gullible pawn to the Kingfish, in *Amos 'n' Andy* (1951–1953). He was born in 1893 and died in 1969.

WILLIAMS, STEVEN. Williams starred as Russell Lincoln, the proprietor of the bar and grill, in the dramedy series *Lincs* (1998–2000).

WILLIAMS, TONYA LEE. Williams began her role as Olivia Barber Winters on the daytime drama *The Young and the Restless* in 1990. She also had a role in *A Very Brady Christmas*, a reunion special of the classic series *The Brady Bunch*; she played Cindy Brady's best friend.

WILLIAMS, VANESSA (actress). Williams played Maxine in the drama series *Soul Food* (2000–2004). Other series roles included

Heavy Gear: The Animated Series (2001), *Murder One* (1995), and *Melrose Place* (1992). In TV films, she had roles in *Playing with Fire* (2000) and *Incognito* (1999).

WILLIAMS, VANESSA L. (singer/actress). Miss America 1984, Williams had a starring role in the television film *Stompin' at the Savoy* in 1992. She cohosted *Carnegie Hall Salutes the Jazz Masters* (1994) and sang the National Anthem at Super Bowl XXX in 1996. She hosted the tribute special *It's Black Entertainment* in 1997. She starred in the TV movies *Courage to Love* and *Don Quixote* in 2000. Williams sang duets with Donny Osmond in the special *Donny Osmond: This Is the Moment* and joined Placido Domingo in Christmas music in *Our Favorite Things*, both in 2001. She sang in the *Christmas in Washington* special in 2004.

WILLIAMS, VICTOR. Williams played Deacon Palmer in the sitcom *The King of Queens* (1998–).

WILLIAMSON, FRED. Williamson played a recurring role in *Julia* as Diahann Carroll's love interest in 1969–1970. In TV films, he had key roles in *Carmen: A Hip Hopera* (2001), *Blackjack* (1998), *3 Days to a Kill* (1991), *Half Nelson* (1985), *Express to Terror* (1979), and the miniseries *Wheels* (1978).

WILLIAMSON, MYKELTI. He began his TV career as a dancer on *Soul Train*. He played Los Angeles Police Department detective Bobby Smith in *Boomtown* (2002–2003) and Deejay Cunningham in the police drama *Bay City Blues* (1983). He played a key role in the drama *Having Our Say* (1999) and the TV films *Soul of the Game* (1996), *Buffalo Soldiers* (1997), and *Holiday Heart* (2000).

WILMA (*NBC, December 19, 1977*). Olympic track star Wilma Rudolph was portrayed in this biopic starring **Shirley Jo Finney** in the title role. The TV film depicted Rudolph's childhood in Tennessee and her struggles to overcome polio. It builds to her success in the 1960 Olympics, where she won three gold medals. **Cicely Tyson** played Rudolph's encouraging mother. **Jason Bernard** played Coach Temple. **Joe Seneca** played Ed Rudolph. **Denzel Washington** played

18-year-old Robert Ethridge, Wilma's boyfriend. Finney said the film was a longtime dream for her and for Rudolph, who had been her track coach and friend for some time. The actress, dressed in an orange running suit with her hair cut like Rudolph's, showed up at producer Bud Greenspan's door for the audition. She said, "Hi. I'm Skeeter Rudolph." The producer, pleased at the resemblance, said, "You sure are." *See also* ATHLETES' BIOPICS.

WILSON, CAL. Wilson was a regular on *The Jerry Reed When You're Hot You're Hot Hour* (1972). He played several roles in sitcoms, including *Sanford and Son* and *Good Times*. He is also a writer.

WILSON, CHANDRA. Wilson played Claudia in the short-lived 2001 sitcom *Bob Patterson* and was part of the regular cast of the drama series *Grey's Anatomy* when it made its debut in the 2004–2005 season.

WILSON, DEMOND. Wilson's first television role was as a cherub in **"The Green Pastures"** on *Hallmark Hall of Fame* in 1957. He played a burglar in a 1971 episode of *All in the Family*, a role that helped him get cast in the costarring role of Lamont in *Sanford and Son* (1972–1977). Both shows were Norman Lear shows with the same casting heads. He starred in the sitcoms *Baby I'm Back* (1978) and *The New Odd Couple* (1982–1983). Wilson became a minister.

WILSON, DORIEN. Wilson played Professor Ogelvee in the sitcom *The Parkers* (1999–2004). He played a recurring role as Warrington Steele on *The Steve Harvey Show* (1997–2002). He also played Franklyn Goode in the **Sherman Hemsley** sitcom *Goode Behavior* (1996–1997), Terrence Winninham on *Sister, Sister* (1995–1996), and Eddie Charles on *Dream On* (1995).

WILSON, FLIP. In 1970, Wilson premiered *The Flip Wilson Show*, the first and, so far, only hit variety show starring a black performer. Wilson was a guest on numerous variety shows and specials beginning with *The Tonight Show Starring Johnny Carson*, where he got his break. Carson had him as a guest on the show several times; he even guest-hosted when Carson was on vacation. He also was a guest on *The Fifth Dimension Special: An Odyssey in the Cosmic Universe of Peter Max* in 1970.

Wilson hosted several one-hour specials of music and comedy following his retirement from his NBC variety series in 1974. They were the following: *Flip Wilson . . . Of Course* in October 1974, *The Flip Wilson Special* in December 1974, *The Flip Wilson Special* in February 1975, *The Flip Wilson Special* in May 1975, *Travels with Flip* in October 1975, and *The Flip Wilson Comedy Special* in November 1975. He also starred in one other series, *Charlie & Co.*, a 1986 sitcom costarring **Gladys Knight**. Wilson performed in the 1990 drama special *Zora Is My Name*.

Wilson guest-starred in TV specials *The Andy Williams Special* in 1971, *Cher* in 1975, *Pinocchio* in 1976, *Celebrity Challenge of the Sexes 2* in 1977, *Battle of the Network Stars* in 1984, and in a *Dean Martin Celebrity Roast* of Bob Hope in 1974. He made appearances in variety specials *Bing Crosby—Cooling It* in 1970, *The Many Moods of Perry Como* in 1970, *Jack Benny's First Farewell Show* in 1973, *Milton Berle's Mad Mad Mad World of Comedy* in 1975, *The Muhammad Ali Variety Special* in 1975, *Nadia—From Romania with Love* in 1976, *Bob Hope's Comedy Special* in 1976, *Us against the World—U.S. Team* in 1977, *The Stars Salute Israel at 30* in 1978, *A Tribute to "Mr. Television" Milton Berle* in 1978, *The Leif Garrett Special* in 1979, *Uptown* in 1980, and *The Suzanne Somers* Special in 1982. Wilson was born in 1933 and died in 1998 of liver cancer.

WILSON, KRISTEN. Wilson played Robin Givens in the 1995 TV film *Tyson*. She was Nicole Moore in *Matt Waters* (1996) and Kendall Truman in the drama series *The District* (2002).

WILSON, LISLE. Wilson played Leonard in the sitcom *That's My Mama* in 1974–1975.

WILSON, NANCY. Nancy Wilson hosted her own special *Portrait of Nancy Wilson* in 1972. She was a guest of several male hosts of specials including the following: a Bob Hope special in 1965, *Perry Como Springtime Show* in 1967, a **Bill Cosby** special in 1971, *Monsanto Presents Mancini* hosted by Henry Mancini in 1971, and *The Scoey Mitchlll Show* in 1972. She sang the theme song for the two-hour drama *Who Has Seen the Wind?* in 1965. She recurred on *The Sinbad Show* (1993–1994), playing the grandmother.

WILSON, TEDDY. Musician Wilson guest-starred in variety specials *The Ford 50th Anniversary Show* in 1953, *The Big Band and All That Jazz* in 1972, and *Benny Goodman: Let's Dance—A Musical Tribute* in 1986. Wilson was born in 1912 and died in 1986.

WILSON, THEODORE. Primarily a comedic actor, Wilson played High Strung in the short-lived sitcom *Roll Out* in 1973 and Earl, the mailman, in *That's My Mama* in 1974–1975. He played the lead in the sitcom *The Sanford Arms*, a spin-off of *Sanford and Son*, in 1977 and had a role on the short-lived *The Redd Foxx Show* the same year. He played a key role in the 1981 TV film *The Oklahoma City Dolls*. He was Ernie in the drama series *Crazy Like a Fox* (1984–1986) and Durwood M. Pinner in the sitcom *You Can't Take It with You* (1987–1988). Wilson was born in 1943 and died in 1991.

WILSON, YVETTE. Wilson played the role of Andell Wilkerson in *The Parkers* (2000–2004), a character she also played on *Moesha* for five seasons. She also played Lynnette in the sitcom *Thea* in 1993–1994. A stand-up comedian, she appeared on various comedy revue series.

WINBUSH, CAMILLE. Winbush played four-year-old Emma in the sitcom *Minor Adjustments* (1995–1996), Lynn Hamilton in the drama *7th Heaven* (1996–1999), and Vanessa in *The Bernie Mac Show* (2001–).

WINBUSH, TROY. Winbush played a medical investigator in the drama *Medical Investigation*, which premiered in 2004. Previously, he was Denny on *The Cosby Show* (1987–1991). In TV films, he had roles in *Gambler* (1988), *Luther's Choice* (1991), *Golden Years* (1991), *Heart of Fire* (1997), and *Mutiny* (1999).

WINFIELD, PAUL. Winfield acknowledges that his first break into television was as Paul Cameron, a love interest to Diahann Carroll's character in the sitcom *Julia* from 1968 to 1970. He was the Magic Mirror in *The Charmings*, a 1987–1988 sitcom based on the fairy tale of Snow White and Prince Charming. In 1989, he was Isaac Twine in the police drama *The Wiseguy*. He was Julian Barlow in the sitcom

227 (1989–1990). Winfield's numerous credits include made-for-television movies *It's Good to Be Alive* in 1974 and *Green Eyes* in 1977. In 1978, he played the title role in the miniseries *King*, a dramatization of the life and work of Martin Luther King Jr. In 1979, he played Dr. Horace Huguley in the miniseries *Roots: The Next Generations* and was nominated for an **Emmy Award**. In 1980, he had a key role in the TV film *Angel City*. He played Richard Wiggins in *The Sophisticated Gents* in 1981. He had a key role in *Sister, Sister* in 1982. Also in 1982, Winfield played Jonathan Henry in the Civil War miniseries *The Blue and the Grey*. He starred in *Go Tell It on the Mountain* in 1985. In 1989, he was Sam Michael in *The Women of Brewster Place*. In 1995, he played Don King in the TV film *Tyson* and starred in the TV film *White Dwarf*. He played Thurgood Marshall in the made-for-television movie *Strange Justice* in 1999. Winfield also made appearances in specials *With All Deliberate Speed* in 1976 and *The War between the Classes* in 1985. His voice was used in the special *The Wish That Changed Christmas* in 1991. He was narrator for the A&E documentary series *City Confidential* until his death of a heart attack in 2004.

WINFREY, OPRAH. Winfrey was the first African-American woman to host a successful daytime talk show and one of the most successful women in the entertainment industry. *The Oprah Winfrey Show* was syndicated in 1986. She formed Harpo Productions, a film and television production company, in 1988. In 2003, Harpo, with $314.5 million in sales, was listed as number 9 on the *Black Enterprise* list of the top 100 industrial/service companies. Winfrey, as chief executive officer, became the first female African-American billionaire.

She acted in and produced several feature films and made-for-television movies including *The Women of Brewster Place*, a 1989 miniseries; 1993's *There Are No Children Here* and *Oprah Winfrey Presents: Before Women Had Wings* in 1997; and *Tuesdays with Morrie* in 1999. Some of the films she produced aired under the umbrella title *Oprah Winfrey Presents*. In 2000, she joined with producers Tom Warner and Marcy Carsey and Nickelodeon founder Geraldine Laybourne to launch Oxygen Media LLC, which includes a women's cable network. Winfrey cohosted *Grammy Legends* in

1990 and hosted *Scared Silent* in 1992 on CBS, NBC, PBS, and ABC, a documentary about child abuse. Productions include her highly rated 90-minute interview of **Michael Jackson** in 1993. She has been honored with numerous awards and titles. Among them are the George Foster Peabody Individual Achievement Award in 1996, *TV Guide*'s Television Performer of the Year in 1997, Time's 100 Most Influential People of the 20th Century, and the International Radio and Television Society's Gold Medal Award. She and her show won numerous **Emmy Awards** and NAACP Image Awards. In 2002, she was honored with the Bob Hope Humanitarian Award at the Emmy Award telecast.

WINNER BY DECISION (*CBS, 1955*). This drama from the *General Electric Theater* anthology series starred **Ethel Waters** and **Harry Belafonte**. Waters played a strong, determined mother who wanted her son (Belafonte), a Golden Gloves boxer, to become a physician.

WINSTON, HATTIE. Winston played several characters on *The Electric Company* from 1973 to 1977. She had roles in daytime dramas *The Edge of Night* and *Port Charles*. She was a regular cast member on the medical drama *Nurse* from 1981 to 1982, on *Homefront* in 1991, and on *Becker* in 1998 and was a panelist on the game show *To Tell the Truth* in 2000. She had a key role in the telefilm *Hollow Image* in 1979 and also the TV films *Saving Grace, Common Ground*, and *The Dain Curse*.

WITHERSPOON, JOHN. Witherspoon was a regular on *The Richard Pryor Show* in 1977, *Townsend Television* in 1993, and *The Wayans Bros.* from 1995 to 1996. He played Spoon on *The Tracy Morgan Show* (2003).

WKRP IN CINCINNATI (*CBS, 1978–1982; SYN, 1991–1993*). This sitcom centered on the employees of a Cincinnati radio station that was changing its format from calm music for elderly listeners to "top 40" rock 'n' roll records for the youthful audience. There were two versions of this sitcom. The first began in 1978 with **Tim Reid** as a regular character, Gordon Sims, also known as Venus Flytrap, a hip-talking disk jockey. The show lasted for four years; then nine years later, another version aired. This time, the black character was Donovan Alderhold, the program manager played by **Mykelti Williamson** (1991–1993). The original series' time slot was changed 11 times, and fans said that ratings suffered because viewers could not find the show. Also, the series was an MTM production on CBS. Grant Tinker, the head of MTM, left the production company to be president of NBC, the competition. The second version was a hit in syndication. *See also* SERIES WITH ONE BLACK SUPPORTING ACTOR/PERFORMER BEFORE 1980.

WOMAN CALLED MOSES, A (*NBC, December 11–12, 1978*). Cicely Tyson starred in this historical drama, a miniseries centering on the life of former slave Harriet Tubman, who had escaped to freedom herself and returned to the South to lead numerous slaves over the Mason-Dixon Line through the Underground Railroad. Also starring were **Robert Hooks** as William Still, **Jason Bernard** as Daddy Ben Ross, **Judyann Elder** as Bernette Wilson, **Mae Mercer** as Aunt Juba, **Hari Rhodes** as Tazwell Robinson, **Charles Weldon** as Shadrack Davis, **Dick Anthony Williams** as John Tubman, **Marilyn Coleman** as Molly, **Ann Weldon** as Mama Ritt Ross, **Jean Renee Foster** as Young Harriet Tubman, and **James Bridges** as Young Shadrack Davis. Will Geer and James Sikking also starred. Lonne Elder III wrote the teleplay. Ike Jones was a producer. *See also* BIOPICS; HISTORICAL EVENTS DRAMATIZED.

WOMEN OF BREWSTER PLACE, THE (*ABC, March 19–20, 1989*). This miniseries, based on the Gloria Naylor novel, starred **Oprah Winfrey** and was produced by her Harpo Productions. She was executive producer. Also starring were **Mary Alice, Jackee, Lynn Whitfield, Barbara Montgomery, Phyllis Yvonne Stickney, Robin Givens, Olivia Cole, Lonette McKee, Paula Kelly, Cicely Tyson, Paul Winfield, Moses Gunn, and Douglas Turner Ward**. The story spanned several decades.

It opened with Mattie (Winfrey), who refused to reveal to her parents (Alice and Winfield) the name of her unborn child's father. She moved to Brewster Place, the home of Eva Turner (Montgomery), and after Eva died, she inherited the house. She lost the home after she used it as collateral for bond when her son got in trouble and jumped bail. The other characters had other stories about how they got to Brewster Place.

All the stories told of their fights against racism, poverty, and conflicts with black men. In fact, much of the criticism of the miniseries centered on negative images of black male characters. The National Association for the Advancement of Colored People (NAACP), realizing the negative male characters in Naylor's book, requested to see the script for the film before production began. Winfrey refused, but she did alter several roles to make them less objectionable. The producers said they cast actors in the male roles who would bring a sense of dignity and sensitivity to the characters, making them multidimensional. Still, African-American columnist Dorothy Gilliam of the *Washington Post* called the miniseries "one of the most stereotype-ridden polemics against black men ever seen on television."

WONDER, STEVIE. Wonder entertained on *The Smokey Robinson Show*, a 1970 special. He was one of the acts in *Motown 25: Yesterday, Today, and Forever* in 1983. In 1990, he was cohost of *Grammy Legends,* a tribute to recording artists who had won Grammy Awards. That same year, he was on the bill of *Motown 30: What's Going On* and *The Sammy Davis Jr. 60th Anniversary Celebration.* In 1991, he was one of the highlights of *Ray Charles: 50 Years of Music, Uh-Huh* and *A Party of Richard Pryor.* In 1995, Wonder was in *Soul Train's 25th Anniversary Hall of Fame Special.* He sang in Super Bowl XXXIII's tribute to 40 years of Motown in 1998. In 1996, he sang on *Celebrate the Dream: 50 Years of Ebony Magazine.* In 1999, Wonder was among the honorees on *The Kennedy Center Honors.* In 2002, he participated in *American Bandstand's 50th . . . A Celebration.* He sang duets on *VH1 Divas Duets* in 2003.

WOODARD, ALFRE. She was one of seven performers in the mounted Broadway choreopoem *For Colored Girls Who Have Considered Suicide/When the Rainbow Is Enuf* in 1982. That same year, she played a key role in the TV film *The Ambush Murders.* She had starring roles in *Mandela* in 1987 and *Race to Freedom: The Underground Railroad* in 1994. She played the female lead in 1995's *The Piano Lesson.* In 1997, she won the Golden Globe award for her starring role in the made-for-television film *Miss Evers' Boys.* She had key roles in made-for-television films including *Freedom Road* in 1979, *The Sophisticated Gents* in 1981, and *Funny Valentines* in 1999. In series television, she played Marcia, the secretary, in the detective drama *Tucker's Witch* (1982–1983), Rosalynn Dupree in the sitcom *Sara* (1985–1988), and Dr. Roxanne Turner in the medical drama *St. Elsewhere* (1985–1987). Woodard won the **Emmy Award** in 1984 and 1987 for guest-starring roles on *Hill Street Blues* and *L.A. Law*. In 1997, she won for Outstanding Lead Actress for her role in *Miss Evers' Boys*. She had a key role in the 2000 TV film *Holiday Heart*.

WOODARD, APRIL. A reporter for *Inside Edition*, Woodard was guest anchor on *The BET Nightly News* and a journalism expert on *BET Tonight with Ed Gordon*. She has done live reports for *Up to the Minute* on CBS, *The Today Show* on NBC, and CNN.

WOODARD, CHARLAYNE. Woodard (aka Charlaine Woodard) had the title role in the first black musical version of Cinderella, *Cindy*, in 1978. She was a member of the four-person musical ensemble of *Ain't Misbehavin'* in 1982. She had a key role in *Oprah Winfrey Presents: The Wedding* in 1998. She played Gail Devers in the *Run for the Dream: The Gail Devers Story* (1996). Woodard had a key role in the TV film *Lackawanna Blues* (2005). She had a recurring role on *Roseanne*.

WOODBINE, BOKEEM. Woodbine played the rapist who terrorized the hospital on the drama series *City of Angels* in 2000. He played Khalid X in the TV film *Jasper, Texas* (2003).

WOODBURY, GENE. Woodbury played a teenager charged with killing two women in 1963 Manhattan in *The Marcus-Nelson Murders*, a 1973 television movie. He had a role in *To Kill a Cop*, a 1978 television movie.

WOODSIDE, DAVID BRYAN. Woodside played Aaron Mosly in the dramatic series *Murder One* from 1996 to 1997 and the same role in *Murder One: Diary of a Serial Killer*, a 1997 miniseries that concluded the series. He also played bass singer Melvin Franklin in the TV film *The Temptations* in 1998.

WOODS, REN. Woods played Fanta in *Roots* in 1977.

WOOPS! (*NBC, 1992*). **Cleavant Derricks** starred in this short-lived darkly humored sitcom about the unlikely survivors of an accidental nuclear war. He played Dr. Frederick Ross, a pathologist who helped rebuild civilization.

WORLD OF LOVE, A (*CBS, December 22, 1970*). **Bill Cosby** hosted this variety special of Christmas music for children all over the world. Shirley MacLaine also hosted. **Harry Belafonte** was in the cast, as were Julie Andrews, Richard Burton, Florence Henderson, Audrey Hepburn, and Barbra Streisand.

WORLD OF MAGIC, THE (*NBC, December 26, 1975*). **Bill Cosby** hosted this special about magic and illusion starring magician Doug Henning. Gene Kelly and Julie Newmar were guests.

WORTHY, RICK. Worthy was a private eye in the drama series *Eyes*, which premiered in the 2004–2005 season. He was also Nathan Jackson in the western drama series *The Magnificent Seven: The Series* (1998–1999) and Rickey Latrell in the legal drama *Murder One* (1996–1997).

WRIGHT, JEFFREY. Wright played Martin Luther King Jr. in the TV film *Boycott* (2001). He won the **Emmy Award** in 2004 for Supporting Actor in a TV miniseries for various roles in *Angels in America*. One role was Belize, a nurse who, despite being revolted by Roy Cohn's politics, was forced to treat him. He was the only African-American actor to win the Emmy that year. He had won the Tony Award for the same role for the play on which the film was based. In 2005, he had a key role in the TV film *Lackawanna Blues*.

WRIGHT, SAMUEL. Wright played Officer Turk Adams in the 1980–1981 series police sitcom *Enos*. He had a key role in the TV movies *Hollow Image* (1979), *Brass* (1985), *The Gift of Amazing Grace* (1986), and *Strapped* (1993) and the miniseries *Queen* (1993). He had provided voices for characters in numerous productions including the voice of Sebastian in the 1989 and 2000 animated features as well as the 1992 television series *The Little Mermaid.*

– Y –

YANCY, EMILY. Yancy played Stella Byrd in the TV film *Jasper, Texas* in 2003. In other TV films, she had roles in *Second Chance* (1972), *Poor Devil* (1973), and *Heat Wave* (1990).

YEATES, ROY. Yeates was a member of the gospel singers *Southernaires Quartet*; the quartet had a musical series in 1948.

YOUNG LAWYERS, THE (*ABC, 1970–1971*). This drama series was about idealistic law students in Boston who provided legal aid to people who could not afford real lawyers. Pat, played by **Judy Pace**, was the black female in the group who understood the streets as well as the books. Lee J. Cobb was the star of the series, which lasted only one season. *See also* SERIES WITH ONE BLACK SUPPORTING ACTOR/PERFORMER BEFORE 1980.

YOUNG, LEE THOMPSON. Thompson starred in the children's series *The Famous Jett Jackson* beginning in 1998.

YOUNG, OTIS. Young was the first black actor to star in a western television series when he played a former slave turned bounty hunter in the series *The Outcasts* in 1968. He also played a role in *Palmerstown, USA*, a series derived from Alex Haley's life. In TV films, he had roles in *Valley of Mystery* (1967), *Columbo: Identity Crisis* (1975), and *Twin Detectives* (1976).

YOUNG, WILLIAM ALLEN. Young was the son, Jeff Jackson, of the character portrayed by **Muhammad Ali** in the made-for-television films *Freedom Road* in 1979 and *Women of San Quentin* in 1983. He had key roles in *The Atlanta Child Murders* miniseries in 1985 and *Johnnie Mae Gibson: FBI* in 1986. He played the Reverend in *My Past Is My Own* in 1989. The same year, he was Eugene in *The Women of Brewster Place*. He played Cliff Templeton in *Knot's*

Landing from 1992 to 1993. He was the father, Frank Mitchell, in the sitcom *Moesha* (1996–2000).

YOU'RE THE TOP (*CBS, October 6, 1956*). This was a one-hour variety special about the life and music of Cole Porter. **Dorothy Dandridge** made a rare television appearance. **Louis Armstrong** was also on the bill with George Chakiris, Bing Crosby, Peter Lind Hayes, Shirley Jones, and George Sanders.

– Z –

ZOOMAN (*SHO, March 19, 1995*). **Louis Gossett Jr.** and **Charles S. Dutton** starred in this TV film about a black family's emotional reaction when the young daughter was the victim of random violence. No one in the neighborhood was willing to come forward with clues to the identity of the killer; they didn't want to be involved. Gossett played Reuben Tate, the father of Jackie (Alyssa Ashley Nichols), the child who was in the line of fire when Zooman (Khalil Kain) aimed for an adversary. Cynthia Martells played the child's mother, Rachel Tate, and Hill Harper played Rachel's brother Victor, who tried to shame the neighbors into talking. The effort backfired. Also in the cast were **C. C. H. Pounder** as Ash, **Vondie Curtis-Hall** as Davis, and **Tommy Hollis** as Mr. Washington.

ZORA IS MY NAME (*PBS, February 14, 1990*). **Ruby Dee** produced and led a stellar cast in a stage presentation of the folk stories of Zora Neale Hurston. Among the actors dramatizing the tales were **Louis Gossett Jr.**, **Flip Wilson**, **Oscar Brown Jr.**, **Paula Kelly**, **Roger Mosley**, **Beah Richards**, Count Stovall, and **Lynn Whitfield**. Dee wrote the teleplay based on Hurston's semiautobiographical books, which stemmed from the Harlem Renaissance, her childhood in Florida, and her travels in the South in the 1930s. Neema Barnette directed.

Appendix A
Series Rankings and Ratings

Five series with black casts or black lead stars are listed in the top 100 series of all time. The listing (done by Tim Brooks and Earle Marsh) is based on the number of seasons the series aired and the ratings. The five are the following: number 13, *The Cosby Show*; number 27, *The Jeffersons*; number 37, *Sanford and Son*; number 44, *A Different World*; and number 90, *The Flip Wilson Show*. The black-cast series (or series with black stars) that ranked in the top 30 of all series by year were the following:

In 1951–1952, *Amos 'n' Andy* was number 13 with a 38.9 rating.

In 1952–1953, *Amos 'n' Andy* ranked number 25.

Between 1953 and 1966, there were no black-cast series or series with black leads in the top 30.

In 1966–1967, *I Spy ranked number 29 with a 20.2 rating.

In 1968–1969, *Julia* was ranked number 7 with a 24.6 rating, and *The Mod Squad was ranked number 28 with a 20.5 rating.

In 1969–1970, *The Bill Cosby Show* ranked number 11 with a 22.7 rating, *Julia* ranked number 28 with a 20.1 rating, and *The Mod Squad* ranked number 23 with a 20.8 rating.

In 1970–1971, *The Flip Wilson Show* ranked number 2 with a 27.9 rating, and *The Mod Squad* ranked number 11 with a 22.7 rating.

In 1971–1972, *The Flip Wilson Show* ranked number 2 with a 28.2 rating, *Sanford and Son* ranked number 6 with a 25.2 rating, *The Mod Squad* ranked number 21 with a 21.5 rating, and *Room 222* ranked number 28 with a 19.8 rating.

In 1972–1973, *Sanford and Son* ranked number 2 with a 27.6 rating, *The Flip Wilson Show* ranked number 12 with a 23.1 rating, and *The Rookies ranked number 23 with a 20.0 rating.

In 1973–1974, *Sanford and Son* was number 3 with a 27.5 rating, **Good Times** was number 17 with a 21.4 rating, and *The Rookies* was number 25 with a 20.3 rating.

In 1974–1975, *Sanford and Son* was number 2 with a 29.6 rating, **The Jeffersons** was number 4 with a 27.6 rating, and *Good Times* was number 7 with a 25.8 rating.

In 1975–1976, *Sanford and Son* was number 7 with a 24.4 rating, *The Jeffersons* was number 22 with a 21.5 rating, *Good Times* was number 24 with a 21.0 rating.

In 1976–1977, *The Jeffersons* was number 24 with a 21.0 rating, **What's Happening!!** was number 25 with a 20.9 rating, *Good Times* was number 26 with a 20.5 rating, and *Sanford and Son* was number 27 with a 20.3 rating.

In 1977–1978, there were no black-cast series or series with black leads in the top 30.

In 1978–1979, **Diff'rent Strokes** was number 27 with a 19.9 rating, and *What's Happening!!* shared number 28 with *Monday Night Football* and had a 19.8 rating.

In 1979–1980, *The Jeffersons* was number 8 with a 24.3 rating, **Benson** was number 23 with a 20.6 rating, and *Diff'rent Strokes* was number 26 with a 20.3 rating.

In 1980–1981, *The Jeffersons* was number 6 with a 23.5 rating, and *Diff'rent Strokes* was number 17, tied with *Fantasy Island* and *Trapper John M.D.*, and had a 20.7 rating.

In 1981–1982, *The Jeffersons* was number 3 with a 23.4 rating.

In 1982–1983, *The Jeffersons* was number 12 with a 20.0 rating.

In 1983–1984, *The Jeffersons* was number 12 with a 20.0 rating, and **Webster** was number 25, tied with four other series; all had a 17.2 rating.

In 1984–1985, **The Cosby Show** was number 3 with a 24.2 rating. Again *Webster* tied with two other series for number 25 and had a 17.0 rating.

In 1985–1986, *The Cosby Show* was number 1 with a 33.7 rating, 3.7 points higher than the number 2 show, *Family Ties*;* **Miami Vice** *was* number 9 with a 21.3 rating; and **227** was number 20 with a 18.8 rating.

In 1986–1987, *The Cosby Show* was number 1 with a 34.9 rating, **Amen** was number 13 with a 19.4 rating, *227* was number 14 with a 18.9

rating, and *Miami Vice* tied with *Knots Landing* for number 26 and had a 16.8 rating.

In 1987–1988, *The Cosby Show* was number 1 with a 27.8 rating; *A Different World*, the spin-off of *The Cosby Show*, was number 2 with a 25.0 rating; *Amen* was number 15 with a 17.5 rating; and *227* was number 27 with a 16.3 rating.

In 1988–1989, *The Cosby Show* was number 1 with a 25.6 rating, *A Different World* was number 3 with a 23.0 rating, and *Amen* was number 25 with a 16.2 rating.

In 1989–1990, *The Cosby Show* was number 1 with a 23.1 rating, and *A Different World* was number 4 with a 21.1 rating.

In 1990–1991, *A Different World*, at number 4 with a 17.5 rating, beat *The Cosby Show* at number 5 with a 17.1 rating. *Family Matters* was number 15 with a 15.8 rating.

In 1991–1992, all the black-cast series moved to the bottom half of the top 30. *A Different World* was number 17 with a 15.2 rating, *The Cosby Show* was number 16 with a 15.0 rating, *The Fresh Prince of Bel-Air* was number 22 with a 14.3 rating, and *Family Matters* was number 27 with a 13.5 rating.

In 1992–1993, *The Fresh Prince of Bel-Air* and *Hangin' with Mr. Cooper* were tied at number 16 with a 14.6 rating.

In 1993–1994, *The Fresh Prince of Bel-Air* was number 21, tied with *Dave's World* with a 13.7 rating, and *Family Matters* was number 30, tied with the *ABC Sunday Night Movie* with a rating of 12.6.

In 1994–1995, there were no black-cast series or series with black leading stars in the top 30.

In 1995–1996, there were no black-cast series or series with black leading stars in the top 30.

In 1996–1997, *Cosby* was number 21 with a 11.2 rating.

In 1997–1998, *Cosby* was number 25 with a 9.5 rating.

In 1998–1999, there were no black-cast series or series with black leads in the top 30.

In 1999–2000, there were no black-cast series or series with black leads in the top 30.

In 2000–2001, there were no black-cast series or series with black leads in the top 30.

In 2001–2002, there were no black-cast series or series with black leads in the top 30.

In 2002–2003, there were no black-cast series or series with black leads in the top 30.

In 2003–2004, there were no black-cast series or series with black leads in the top 30.

In 2004–2005, there were no black-cast series or series with black leads in the top 30.

*The series *I Spy*, *The Mod Squad*, *The Rookies*, and *Miami Vice* are listed because they had ensemble casts. The black actor in the series was as much of a star as the white actor(s) at a time in television history when that would be called unusual casting.

Appendix B
Emmy Award Winners

Winners listed are individual blacks, shows with black casts or stars, and shows with black themes who won the prime time Emmy Award presented by the Academy of Television Arts and Sciences. In the case of black-cast shows and black-themed shows, names of individuals (whose ethnicity is known by the author to be black) are in bold. The list does not include daytime or local Emmy Awards presented by the National Academy of Television Arts and Sciences.

1959–1960
Outstanding Performance in a Variety or Music Program or Series:
    Harry Belafonte, *Tonight with Belafonte*, *The Revlon Revue* (CBS)

1960–1965
No African-American winners.

1965–1966
Outstanding Actor in a Drama Series: **Bill Cosby**, *I Spy* (NBC)

1966–1967
Outstanding Actor in a Drama Series: **Bill Cosby**, *I Spy* (NBC)

1967–1968
Outstanding Actor in a Drama Series: **Bill Cosby**, *I Spy* (NBC)

1968–1969
Outstanding Music or Variety Program: *The Bill Cosby Special* (CBS)
Outstanding Coverage of Special Events (Programs): "Coverage of Martin Luther King Assassination and Aftermath," *CBS News Special Reports and Special Broadcasts* (CBS)

1969–1970
Outstanding New Series: *Room 222* (ABC)
Outstanding Magazine-Type Programming (Programs): *Black Journal* (NET)

1970–1971
Outstanding Variety Series—Music: *The Flip Wilson Show* (NBC)
Outstanding Writing in Variety or Music: Herbert Baker, Hal Goodman, Larry Klein, Bob Weiskopf, Bob Schiller, Norman Steinberg, **Flip Wilson**, *The Flip Wilson Show* (NBC)

1971–1972
Outstanding Program: *Brian's Song* (ABC)

1973–1974
Outstanding Special: *The Autobiography of Miss Jane Pittman* (CBS)
Outstanding Actress in a Drama: **Cicely Tyson**, *The Autobiography of Miss Jane Pittman* (CBS)
Actress of the Year—Special: **Cicely Tyson**, *The Autobiography of Miss Jane Pittman* (CBS)
Outstanding Writing in Variety or Music (Special): Herbert Sargent, Rosalyn Drexler, Lorne Michaels, **Richard Pryor**, Jim Rusk, James R. Stein, Robert Illes, Lily Tomlin, George Yanok, Jane Wagner, Rod Warren, Ann Elder, Karyl Geld (CBS)

1975–1976
No African-American winners.

1976–1977
Outstanding Limited Series: *Roots*, David L. Wolper, executive producer; Stan Margulies, producer (ABC)
Outstanding Actor for a Single Performance in a Drama or Comedy Series: **Louis Gossett Jr.**, *Roots* (ABC)
Outstanding Single Performance by a Supporting Actress in a Comedy or Drama Series: **Olivia Cole**, *Roots* (ABC)
Outstanding Directing in a Drama Series: David Greene, *Roots* (ABC)
Outstanding Writing in a Drama: Ernest Kinoy, William Blinn, *Roots* (ABC)

Outstanding Music Composition (Series): **Quincy Jones**, Gerald Fried, *Roots* (ABC)
Outstanding Film Editing (Drama Series): Neil Travis, *Roots* (ABC)
Outstanding Film Sound (Series): Larry Carow, Larry Neiman, Don Warner, Colin Mouat, George Fredrick, Dave Pettijohn, Paul Bruce Richardson, *Roots* (ABC)

1977–1978 (Presented September 17, 1978)
Outstanding Directing in a Comedy-Variety or Music Special: Dwight Hemion, *The Sentry Collection Presents Ben Vereen—His Roots*, March 2, 1978 (ABC)

1978–1979 (Presented September 9, 1979)
Outstanding Limited Series: *Roots: The Next Generations*, David L. Wolper, executive producer; Stan Margulies, producer (ABC)
Outstanding Supporting Actor in a Comedy-Variety or Music Series (for a Continuing or Single Performance in a Regular Series): **Robert Guillaume**, *Soap* (ABC)
Outstanding Individual Actress in a Limited Series or a Special: **Esther Rolle**, *Summer of My German Soldier*, October 30, 1978 (NBC)

1979–1980
No African-American winners.

1980–1981 (Presented September 13, 1981)
Outstanding Lead Actress in a Comedy Series: **Isabel Sanford**, *The Jeffersons* (CBS)
Outstanding Individual Achievement—Special Class: **Sarah Vaughan**, performer, *Rhapsody and Song—A Tribute to George Gershwin* (PBS)

1981–1982 (Presented September 19, 1982)
Outstanding Individual Achievement—Special Class: **Nell Carter**, performer, *Ain't Misbehavin'* (NBC)

1982–1983 (Presented September 25, 1983)
Outstanding Variety, Music, or Comedy Program: *Motown 25: Yesterday, Today, Forever*, Suzanne de Passe, executive producer; Don

Mischer and Buz Kohan, producers; Suzanne Coston, producer for Motown (NBC)
Outstanding Individual Performance in a Variety or Music Program: *Leontyne Price, Live from Lincoln Center* (PBS)

1983–1984 (Presented September 23, 1984)
Outstanding Supporting Actress in a Drama Series: **Alfre Woodard**, "Doris in Wonderland," *Hill Street Blues* (NBC)

1984–1985 (Presented September 22, 1985)
Outstanding Comedy Series: *The Cosby Show*, Marcy Carsey and Tom Werner, executive producers; Earl Pomerantz and Elliot Schoenman, co–executive producers; John Markus, supervising producer; Caryn Sneider, producer; **Earle Hyman**, Jerry Ross, and Michael Loman, coproducers (NBC)
Outstanding Variety, Music, or Comedy Program: *Motown Returns to the Apollo,* Suzanne de Passe, executive producer; Don Mischer, producer; Suzanne Coston and Michael Weisbarth; coproducers (NBC)
Outstanding Lead Actor in a Comedy Series: **Robert Guillaume**, *Benson* (ABC)

1985–1986 (Presented September 20, 1986)
Outstanding Individual Performance in a Variety or Music Program: **Whitney Houston**, *The 28th Annual Grammy Awards* (CBS)
Outstanding Guest Performance in a Comedy Series: **Roscoe Lee Browne**, *The Cosby Show* (NBC)
Outstanding Directing in a Drama Series (Single Episode): **Georg Stanford Brown**, "Parting Shots," *Cagney & Lacey* (CBS)

1986–1987 (Presented September 20, 1987)
Outstanding Supporting Actress in a Comedy Series: **Jackee Harry**, *227* (NBC)
Outstanding Guest Performer in a Drama Series: **Alfre Woodard**, *L.A. Law* (NBC)

1987–1988 (Presented August 28, 1988)
Outstanding Guest Performer in a Comedy Series: **Beah Richards**, *Frank's Place* (CBS)

1988–1989 (Presented September 17, 1989)
Outstanding Guest Actor in a Comedy Series: **Cleavon Little**, "Stand By Your Man," *Dear John* (NBC)

1989–1990 (Presented September 16, 1990)
Outstanding Variety, Music, or Comedy Program: *In Living Color*, **Keenen Ivory Wayans**, executive producer; Kevin S. Bright, supervising producer; Tamara Rawitt, producer; Michael Petok, coproducer (FOX)
Outstanding Variety, Music, or Comedy Special: *Sammy Davis Jr.'s 60th Anniversary Celebration*, George Schlatter, producer; Buz Kohan, Jeff Margolis, and Gary Necessary, coproducers (ABC)
Outstanding Directing in a Drama Series (Single Episode): **Thomas Carter**, "Promises to Keep," *Equal Justice* (ABC)

1990–1991 (Presented August 25, 1991)
Outstanding Drama/Comedy Special or Miniseries: *Separate but Equal*, George Stevens Jr. and Stan Margulies, executive producers (ABC)
Outstanding Lead Actor in a Drama Series: **James Earl Jones**, *Gabriel's Fire* (ABC)
Outstanding Lead Actress in a Miniseries or Special: **Lynn Whitfield**, *The Josephine Baker Story* (HBO)
Outstanding Actor in a Miniseries or Special: **James Earl Jones**, *Heat Wave* (TNT)
Outstanding Supporting Actress in a Drama Series: **Madge Sinclair**, *Gabriel's Fire* (ABC)
Outstanding Supporting Actress in a Miniseries or Special: **Ruby Dee**, "Decoration Day," *Hallmark Hall of Fame* (CBS)
Outstanding Directing in a Drama Series (Single Episode): **Thomas Carter**, "In Confidence," *Equal Justice* (ABC)

1991–1992 (Presented August 30, 1992)
Outstanding Directing in a Drama Series (Single Episode): **Eric Laneuville**, "All God's Children," *I'll Fly Away* (NBC)
Outstanding Individual Achievement in Classical Music/Dance Programming-Performing: Placido Domingo and **Kathleen Battle**, *The Metropolitan Opera Silver Anniversary Gala* (PBS)

1992–1993 (Presented September 19, 1993)
Outstanding Supporting Actress in a Drama Series: **Mary Alice,** *I'll Fly Away* (NBC)
Outstanding Guest Actor in a Drama Series: **Laurence Fishburne,** "The Box," *Tribeca* (FOX)

1993–1994 (Presented September 11, 1994)
Outstanding Supporting Actress in a Miniseries or Special: **Cicely Tyson,** *Oldest Living Confederate Widow Tells All* (CBS)

1994–1995 (Presented September 10, 1995)
Outstanding Guest Actor in a Drama Series: **Paul Winfield,** "Enemy Lines," *Picket Fences* (CBS)

1996–1997 (Presented September 14, 1997)
Outstanding Variety, Music, or Comedy Special: *Chris Rock: Bring on the Pain,* **Chris Rock,** Michael Rotenberg, and Sandy Chanley, executive producers; Tom Bull, producer (HBO)
Outstanding Made-for-Television Movie: *Miss Evers' Boys,* Robert Benedetti and **Laurence Fishburne,** executive producers; Kip Konwiser and Derek Kavanagh, producers; Peter Stelzer and Kern Konwiser, coproducers (HBO)
Outstanding Lead Actress in a Miniseries or Special: **Alfre Woodard,** *Miss Evers' Boys* (HBO)
Outstanding Writing in a Variety or Music Program: **Chris Rock,** writer, *Chris Rock: Bring the Pain* (HBO)
The President's Award: *Miss Evers' Boys* (HBO)

1997–1998 (Presented September 13, 1998)
Outstanding Made-for-Television Movie: *Don King: Only in America,* **Thomas Carter,** executive producer; David Blocker, producer (HBO)
Outstanding Lead Actor in a Drama Series: **Andre Braugher,** *Homicide: Life on the Street* (NBC)

1998–1999 (Presented September 12, 1999)
Outstanding Made-for-Television Movie: *A Lesson before Dying,* Ellen Krass, Joel Stillerman, and Ted Demme, executive producers; Robert Benedetti, producer (HBO)

Outstanding Voiceover Performance: **Ja'net DuBois** as Mrs. Avery, *The PJs* (FOX)

Outstanding Directing for a Drama Series (Single Episode): **Paris Barclay**, "Hearts and Souls," *N.Y.P.D. Blue* (ABC)

Outstanding Writing for a Variety or Music Program: Tom Agna, Vernon Chatman, Louis C.K., Lance Crouther, Gregory Greenberg, Ali Leroi, Steve O'Donnell, **Chris Rock**, Frank Sebastiano, Chuck Sklar, Jeff Stilson, **Wanda Sykes-Hall**, and Mike Upchurch, *The Chris Rock Show* (HBO)

1999–2000 (Presented September 10, 2000)

Outstanding Miniseries: *The Corner*, Robert F. Colesberry, David Mills, and David Simon, executive producers; Nina Kostroff Noble, producer (HBO)

Outstanding Made-for-Television Movie: *Oprah Winfrey Presents: Tuesdays with Morrie*, **Oprah Winfrey** and Kate Forte, executive producers; Jennifer Ogden, supervising producer (ABC)

Outstanding Children's Program: *The Color of Friendship*, Alan Sacks, executive producer; Christopher Morgan and **Kevin Hooks** producer; Carole Rosen, supervising producer; Amy Schatz, producer (HBO)

Outstanding Lead Actress in a Miniseries or Movie: **Halle Berry**, *Introducing Dorothy Dandridge* (HBO)

Outstanding Guest Actress in a Drama Series: **Beah Richards**, *The Practice* (ABC)

Outstanding Directing for a Miniseries, Movie, or Special: **Charles Dutton**, *The Corner* (HBO)

2000–2001 (Presented November 4, 2001)

Outstanding Voiceover Performance: **Ja'net DuBois** as Mrs. Avery, "Let's Get Ready to Rhumba," *The PJs* (WB)

2001–2002 (Presented September 22, 2002)

Outstanding Guest Actor in a Drama Series: **Charles S. Dutton**, *The Practice* (ABC)

2002–2003 (Presented September 24, 2003)

Outstanding Guest Actor in a Drama Series: **Charles S. Dutton**, *Without a Trace* (CBS)

Outstanding Guest Actress in a Drama Series: **Alfre Woodard,** *The Practice* (ABC)
Outstanding Individual Performance in a Variety or Music Program: **Wayne Brady,** *Whose Line Is It Anyway?*

2003–2004 (Presented September 19, 2004)
Outstanding Supporting Actor in a Miniseries or Movie: **Jeffrey Wright,** *Angels in America.*

Bibliography

INTRODUCTION

Much of the data in this dictionary are derived from personal experience and interviews. The following list of references includes additional sources used to develop the dictionary; it also includes sources not used but are probably valuable to researchers on similar topics.

Some of the most useful sources for this volume were both print and online sources. The website IMDb (Internet Movie Database) at www.imdb.com is extremely thorough in its listing of actors and their credits. Unlike similar sites, it distinguishes television from film, series roles from guest-starring roles, and names of characters. It even has credits of performers on television in the 1940s. The African American Registry and BlackFlix.com are also very helpful, as are others listed under "websites."

The Complete Dictionary of Prime Time Network and Cable TV Shows, by Tim Brooks and Earle Marsh (Random House), is very valuable among print sources. Its eighth edition was on the stands in 2003. It lists most prime-time series, the characters and the actors who played them, a description of the plot, the dates the series aired, and the authors' observations of the series. Alex Mc-Neil's *Total Television* (Penguin Books) is a similar book that also mentions specials. Both books list top-rated and award-winning shows.

Donald Bogle is the most published historian in African-American television and film. His book *Primetime Blues: African Americans on Network Television* was published (Farrar, Straus & Giroux) in 2001. In 2005, he published *Bright Boulevards, Bold Dreams: The Story of Black Hollywood* (One World/Ballantine); it centers on black Hollywood in the first half of the 20th century and examines the cohesiveness of social life that resulted from segregation and limited opportunities.

J. Fred MacDonald's *Black and White TV: African Americans in Television since 1948* is a noteworthy historical document with an extensive bibliography. Beretta Smith Shomade's *Shaded Lives: African-American Women and Television* (Rutgers University Press) published in 2002 tackled how women and race interconnect. Kristal Brent Zook's *Color by Fox: The Fox Network and the*

509

Revolution in Black Television (Oxford) is a 1999 published doctoral dissertation. Related is *The Historical Dictionary of African American Cinema* (Scarecrow Press) written by S. Torriano Berry and Venise T. Berry for 2006 publication.

James Haskins, who died in 2005, was probably the most prolific African-American biographer with dozens of life stories of famous blacks, some in entertainment. Among them are Richard Pryor, Lena Horne, Nat "King" Cole, Bill Robinson, Scatman Crothers, Lionel Hampton, Ella Fitzgerald, Stevie Wonder, Bill Cosby, Spike Lee, and many more. He has written books specifically for adults, young adults, and children.

Some libraries are great sources of information. The Schomburg Center for Research in Black Culture in Harlem is notable as far as African-American life is concerned, and it has also a library of photographs. Other libraries are sources of data about television and include some African-American data. Among them are the following: Museum of Television and Radio in Beverly Hills and in New York; UCLA Film and Television Archives; University of Southern California Cinema/Television Library; Annenberg Reserve Video Collection in the Annenberg School of Communication Library at the University of Pennsylvania; Television News Archive at Vanderbilt University; Library of American Broadcasting at the University of Maryland, Baltimore; University of Iowa's Library of Television and Film Studies; International Federation of Television Archives; and the Library of Congress in Washington, D.C.

CONTENTS

I. GENERAL

Adamo, Gregory. "Race and Production of Culture: African American Responses to Television Work." Ph.D. diss., Rutgers University, 2001.

Alan, Kage. "DVR Review/It's Black Entertainment." www.modamag.com, 1 November 2004.

Anderson, L. *Mammies No More: The Changing Image of Black Women on Stage and Screen*. Lanham, Md.: Rowman & Littlefield, 1997.

Atkin, David. "An Analysis of Television Series with Minority-Lead Characters." *Critical Studies in Mass Communication* 9 (1992): 31–49.

Bates, Karen Grigsby. "Where's the Color on Primetime TV?" *Los Angeles Times*, 19 September 1997, B9.

Bel Monte, Kathryn I. *African-American Heroes and Heroines: 150 True Stories of African American Heroism*. Hollywood, Fla.: Lifetime Books, 1998.

Berry, G. "Television and Afro-Americans: Past Legacy and Present Portrayals." In *Television and Social Behavior: Beyond Violence and Children*, edited by S. Withey and R. Abeles. Hillsdale, N.J.: Lawrence Erlbaum Associates, 1980.

Berry, Gordon L., and Claudia Mitchell-Kernan. *Television and the Socialization of the Minority Child*. New York: Academic Press, 1982.

Berry, S. Torriano, and Venise T. Berry. *Historical Dictionary of African-American Cinema*. Lanham, Md.: Scarecrow Press, 2006.

Berry, Venise T., and Carmen L. Manning-Miller, eds. *Mediated Messages and African-American Culture: Contemporary Issues*. Thousand Oaks, Calif.: Sage, 1996.

Bogle, Donald. *Blacks in American Films and Television: An Encyclopedia*. New York: Garland, 1988.

———. *Prime Time Blues: African Americans on Network Television*. New York: Farrar, Strauss & Giroux, 2001.

———. *Toms, Coons, Mulattoes, Mammies and Bucks: An Interpretative History of Blacks in American Films*. Rev. ed. New York: Continuum, 1990.

Boyd, Herb. "African-American Images on Television and Film." *Crisis* 102 (2, 1996): 2–25.

Bristor, Julia M., Renee Gravois Lee, and Michelle R. Hunt. "Race and Ideology: African-American Images in Television Advertising." *Journal of Public Policy and Marketing* 14 (1, 1995): 48–59.

Brooks, Tim, and Earle Marsh. *The Complete Directory to Prime Time Network and Cable Shows*. 8th ed. New York: Ballantine Books, 2003.

Chessher, Melissa. "Where Comedy Gets Crunked." *Southwest Airlines Spirit*, October 2003, 102–8.

Color Adjustment. Produced by Vivian Kleiman and directed by Marlon Riggs. 88 min. California Newsreel, 1991. Videocassette.

Comer, J. "The Importance of Television Images of Black Families." In *Black Families and the Medium of Television*, edited by A. W. Jackson. Ann Arbor: Bush Program in Child Development and Social, University of Michigan, 1982.

Cortes, Carlos E. *The Children Are Watching: How the Media Teach about Diversity*. New York: Teachers College Press, 2000.

Cosby, C. *Television's Imageable Influences: The Self-Perceptions of Young African Americans*. Lanham, Md.: University Press of America, 1994.

Cottle, Simon, ed. *Ethnic Minorities and the Media*. Buckingham, England: Open University Press, 2000.

Cummings, M. S. "The Changing Image of the Black Family." *Journal of Popular Culture* 22 (2, 1986): 75–85.

Dates, Jannette L. "Fly in the Buttermilk." In *Split Image: African Americans in the Mass Media*, 2nd ed., edited by J. L. Dates and W. Barlow. Washington, D.C.: Howard University Press, 1993.

Dates, Jannette L., and Carolyn Stroman. "Portrayals of Families of Color on Television." In *Television and the American Family*, edited by Jennings Bryant and J. Alison Bryant. Mahwah, N.J.: Lawrence Erlbaum Associates, 2001.

Dent, Gina, ed. *Black Popular Culture*. Seattle: Bay Press, 1992.

Dintrone, Charles V. *Television Program Master Index*. 2nd ed. Jefferson, N.C.: McFarland, 2003.

Doty, Alexander. *Making Things Perfectly Queer: Interpreting Mass Culture*. Minneapolis: University of Minnesota Press, 1993.

Entman, Robert, and Andrew Rojecki. *Black Image in the White Mind: Media and Race in America*. Chicago: University of Chicago Press, 2001.

Ethnic Notions. Produced by Marlon Riggs and directed by Marlon Riggs. 58 min. California Newsreel, 1986. Videocassette.

Fife, M. "Black Images in American TV: The First Two Decades." *The Black Scholar* 6 (1974): 7–15.

Freeman, Michael. "Change of Guard at 'Ananda.'" *Electronic Media*, 15 October 2001, 8.

Freeman, Mike. "KWP Confirms Les Brown Show." *Broadcasting*, 28 September 1992, 17.

Fries, Laura. "Soul Food." *Variety*, 26 June 2000, 28.

Ford, Thomas E. "Effects of Stereotypical Television Portrayals of African-Americans on Person Perception." *Social Psychological Quarterly* 60 (3, 1997): 266–75.

Garber, Marjorie. *Vested Interests: Cross Dressing and Cultural Anxiety*. New York: Routledge, 1992.

Gates, Henry Louis, Jr. "TV's Black World Turns—but Stays Unreal." *New York Times*, 12 November 1989, Arts and Leisure, 1, 40.

Goldberg, Bernard. *Arrogance: Rescuing America from the Media Elite*. New York: Warner Books, 2003.

Gray, Herman. "The Endless Slide of Difference: Critical Television Studies, Television and the Question of Race." *Critical Studies in Mass Communication* 10 (2, 1993): 190–97.

———. "Remembering Civil Rights: Television, Memory, and the 1960s." In *The Revolution Wasn't Televised: Sixties Television and Social Conflict*, edited by Gil Scott-Heron. New York: Routledge, 1997.

———. "Television, Black Americans and the American Dream." *Critical Studies in Mass Communication* 6 (1989): 376–87.

———. *Watching Race: Television and the Struggle for "Blackness."* Minneapolis: University of Minnesota Press, 1995.

Greenberg, B. S., and J. E. Brand. "Minorities and the Mass Media: 1970s to 1990s." In *Media Effects: Advances in Theory and Research*, edited by J. Bryant and D. Zillman. Norwood, N.J.: Ablex, 1994.

Greenberg, B. S., and K. Neuendorf. "Black Family Interactions on TV." In *Life on Television: Content Analysis of U.S. TV Drama*, edited by B. S. Greenberg. Norwood, N.J.: Ablex, 1993.

Haas, Nancy. "A TV Generation Is Seeing beyond Color." *New York Times*, 22 February 1998, sec. 2, p. 1.

Hill, R. B. *The Strengths of African American Families: Twenty-Five Years Later*. Lanham, Md.: University Press of America, 1998.

Kellner, Douglas. *Television and the Crisis of Democracy*. Boulder, Colo.: Westview Press, 1990.

Killens, John Oliver. "Our Struggle Is Not to Be White Men in Black Skin." *TV Guide*, 25–31 July 1970, 6–9.

Kim, Lahn Sung. "Maid in Color: The Figure of the Racialized Domestic in American Television." *Dissertation Abstracts International* 58 (12, 1997), 4484 (UMI No. 9818036).

Kolbert, Elizabeth. "From 'Beulah' to Oprah: The Evolution of Black Images on TV." *New York Times*, 15 January 1993, B4.

Lewis, Latif, Tamara Holmes, and Arletha Allen. "Up, Up, and Away: African American Women Business Owners on the Rise, Continue to Soar to the Top of the BE 100s." *Black Enterprise*, June 2003, 38.

Lichter, S. Robert, Linda S. Lichter, and Stanley Rothman. *Prime Time: How TV Portrays American Culture*. Washington, D.C.: Regnery, 1994.

MacDonald, J. Fred. *Blacks and White TV: Afro-Americans in Television since 1948*. Chicago: Nelson-Hall, 1990.

McDaniel, Diane. "Tuning In to Media Spectacles." Ph.D. diss., University of Southern California, 2001.

McKissack, F. "The Problem with Black TV." *The Progressive*, February 1997, 38–40.

McNeil, Alex. *Total Television*. New York: Penguin Books, 1991.

Merritt, B., and C. A. Stroman. "Black Family Imagery and Interactions on Television." *Journal of Black Studies* 23 (1993): 492–99.

Moret, Jim. "Def Comedy Jam Appeals to Blacks and Whites." www.lexis-nexis.com, 9 April 1992.

Navarro, M. "Trying to Get beyond the Role of the Maid." *New York Times*, 16 May 2002, E1.

Noble, Gil. *Black Is the Color of My TV Tube*. New York: Lyle Stuart, 1990.

Noble, Peter. *The Negro in Films*. London: British Yearbooks, 1949.

O'Connor, John J. "Blacks on TV: Scrambled Signals." *New York Times*, 27 October 1991, sec. 2, 1, 36.

"100 Most Memorable TV Moments." *TV Guide*, 4–10 December 2004, 31.

Peterson, April L. "Picking Up After the American Family: Domestic Work in the World of Television." Ph.D. diss., University of Washington, Seattle, Washington, 2005.

Poindexter, P. M., and C. N. Stroman. "Blacks and Television: A Review of the Research Literature." *Journal of Broadcasting* 25 (1981): 103–22.

Potter, Joan. *African American Firsts*. New York: Kensington, 2002.

"Pressure to Be Perfect." *People*, 26 July 2004, 74–75.

Romero, M. *Maid in the U.S.A.* New York: Routledge, 1992.

Ross, Karen. *Black and White Media: Black Images in Popular Film and Television*. Cambridge, Mass.: Polity Press, 1996.

Rudolph, Ileane. "African Americans Viewing Habits on the Rise." *TV Guide*, 26 March–2 April 1994, 36.

Sklar, Robert. *Prime-Time America: Life on and behind the Television Screen*. New York: Oxford University Press, 1980.

Smith, Beretta Eileen. "Shaded Lives: Objectification and Agency in the Television Representation of African American Women, 1980–94." Ph.D. diss, University of California, Los Angeles, 1997.

Smith, Jessie Carney. *Black Firsts*. 2nd ed. Detroit: Visible Ink, 2003.

Smith, Karen M. "Advertising Discourse and the Marketing of I'll Fly Away." In *Mediated Messages and African American Culture*, edited by Venice Berry and Carmen L. Manning-Miller. Thousand Oaks, Calif.: Sage, 1996.

Smith-Shomade, Beretta E. *Shaded Lives: African American Women and Television*. New Brunswick, N.J.: Rutgers University Press, 2002.

Spigner, Clarence. "Black Impressions: Television and Film Imagery." *Crisis* 101(1, 1994): 8–16.

Steenland, Sally. *Unequal Picture: Black, Hispanic, Asian, and Native American Characters on Television*. Washington, D.C.: National Commission on Working Women, 1989.

Taylor, Ella. *Primetime Families*. Berkeley: University of California Press, 1991.

Taylor, Gwendolyn C. "A Few in a Thousand: The Experiences of African-American Female General Managers of Broadcast Radio and Television Stations." Ph.D. diss., Ohio University, 1997.

Terrace, Vincent. *Television Specials*. Jefferson, N.C.: McFarland, 1995.

Torres, Sasha, ed. *Living Color: Race and Television in the United States.* Durham, N.C.: Duke University Press, 1998.

Turner, P. A. *Ceramic Uncles and Celluloid Mammies: Black Images and Their Influence on Culture.* New York: Anchor Books, 1994.

Waters, Harry F., and Janet Huck. "TV's New Racial Hue." *Newsweek*, 25 January 1988, 52–54.

Weigel, Russell H., Eleanor L. Kim, and Jill L. Frost. "Race Relations on Prime Time Reconsidered: Patterns of Continuity and Change." *Journal of Applied Social Psychology* 25(3, 1995): 223–36.

Wilkerson, Isabel. "Black Life on TV: Realism or Stereotypes?" *New York Times*, 15 August 1993, Arts and Leisure, 1.

Zook, Kristal B. "How I Became the Prince of a Town Called Bel Air: Nationalist Desire in Black Television." Ph.D. diss., University of California, Santa Cruz, 1994.

II. TELEVISION GENRES

Abernathy, Gloria E. "African Americans Relationships with Daytime Serials." Ph.D. diss., University of Wisconsin, Madison, 1992.

Andrejevic, Mark. *Reality TV: The Work of Being Watched.* Lanham, Md.: Rowman & Littlefield, 2004.

Bramlett-Solomon, Sharon, and Tricia M. Farwell. "Sex on the Soaps: An Analysis of Black, White and Interracial Couple Intimacy." In *Mediated Messages and African American Culture*, edited by Venice Berry and Carmen L. Manning-Miller. Thousand Oaks, Calif.: Sage, 1996.

Braxton, G. "Black and White TV: Though the Casts of Many Dramatic Series Represent a Racial Mix, Most Sitcoms Show Little Integration—A Fact That Has Some Observers Troubled." *Los Angeles Times*, 27 January 1991, F-1.

Coleman, R. R. M. *African American Viewers and the Black Situation Comedy: Situating Racial Humor.* New York: Garland, 1998.

Dickerson, Sandra A. "Is Sapphire Still Alive? The Image of Black Women in Situation Comedies in the 1990s." Ph.D. diss., Boston University, 1991.

Fine, M., and C. Anderson. "Dialectical Features of Black Characters in Situation Comedies on Television." *Phylon* 41 (1980): 396–409.

Foss, Michele S. "Let That Be Your Last Battlefield: Hegemony and the Construction of Bi-Raciality in Situation Comedy, Soap Opera and Science Fiction Television." Ph.D. diss., University of Florida, 2002.

Hochman, David. "The Color of Funny." *TV Guide*, 19–25 July 2003, 32–34.

Johnson, Michelle A. "Imagined Inequalities: Servants on American Television Situation Comedies, 1960–1980." *Dissertation Abstracts International* 56 (03, 1994), 1092 (UMI No. 9523833).

Lewis, Freda D. "Getting By: Race and Parasocial Interaction in a Television Situation Comedy." Ph.D. diss., University of Kentucky, 1994.

O'Connor, John J. "Veiling Black Rage in Broad Humor on TV." *New York Times*, 31 January 1991, C17.

Orbe, Mark P. "Constructions of Reality in MTV's 'The Real World': An Analysis of the Restrictive Coding of Black Masculinity." In *Critical Approaches to Television*, edited by Leah R. Vande Berg, Lawrence A. Wenner, and Bruce E. Gronbeck. Boston: Houghton Mifflin, 2004.

Pinckney, Darryl. "Step and Fetch It: The Darker Side of Sitcoms." *Vanity Fair* 46 (1, March 1983): 118–19, 256, 260, 264.

Pines, Jim. "Black Cops and Black Villains in Film and TV Crime Fiction." In *Crime and the Media: The Post-Modern Spectacle*, edited by David Kidd-Hewitt and Richard Osborne. London: Pluto, 1995.

Stephens, Rebecca L. "Socially Soothing Stories? Gender, Race, and Class in TLC's 'A Wedding Story' and 'A Baby Story.'" In *Understanding Reality Television*, edited by Su Holmes and Deborah Hermyn. London: Routledge, 2004.

Timberg, Bernard M. *Television Talk: A History of the TV Talk Show*. Austin: University of Texas Press, 2002.

Tyus, Jeffrey L. "Difference as the Norm: An Interpretive Study of the Audience for Black Sitcoms on the WB and UPN Networks." Ph.D. diss., Ohio University, 1999.

Zook, Kristal Brent. "Serious in Seattle: *Under One Roof* Breaks Prime Time's Ban on Black Drama." *L.A. Weekly*, 17 March 1995, 39–40.

III. TELEVISION PROGRAMS

American Bandstand: The Rock 'n' Roll Years, 1956–1962. Vol. 1. AMI Specials, 2003.

Arneson, Erik. "Homicide: Life on the Streets." www.mysterynet.com, 15 July 2004.

Bennetts, Leslie. "James Baldwin Reflects on 'Go Tell It' PBS Film." *New York Times*, 10 January 1985, C17.

———. "TV Film by Parks Looks at Slavery." *New York Times*, 11 February 1985, C18.

Bobo, Jacqueline, and E. Seiter. "Black Feminism and Media Criticism: The Women of Brewster Place." *Screen* 32 (1991): 3.

Cannon, Sherry L. "A Study of Viewer Response to the Television Presentation, Roots." Master's thesis, North Texas State University, 1977.

Collier, Aldore. "Guillaume Series Features an Interracial Romance." *Jet*, 21 November, 1988, 60.

———. "'The Robert Guillaume Show' Features Interracial Romance and a Nosey Dad Whose Humor Adds Sparkle to New TV Series." *Jet*, 24 April 1989, 58–60.

Cripps, Thomas. "Amos 'n' Andy and the Debate over American Racial Integration." In *American History/American Television: Interpreting the Video Past*, edited by John E. O'Connor. New York: Ungar, 1983.

Ely, Melvin Patrick. *The Adventures of Amos 'n' Andy: A Social History of an American Phenomenon*. New York: Free Press, 1991.

"'Family Matters' TV's Longest-Running Black Show." *Jet*, 2 June 1997, 58–61.

Fox, Ted. *Showtime at the Apollo*. Rhinebeck, N.Y.: Mill Road Enterprises, 2003.

Garfinkle, Perry. "Frank's Place: The Restaurant as Life Stage." *New York Times*, 17 February 1988, C1.

Kelly, Venita Ann. "Revealing the Universal through the Specific in 'A Different World': An Interpretive Approach to a Television Depiction of African-American Culture and Communication Patterns." Ph.D. diss., University of Kansas, 1995.

Orbe, Mark P. "Constructions of Reality in MTV's 'The Real World': An Analysis of the Restrictive Coding of Black Masculinity." In *Critical Approaches to Television*, edited by Leah R. Vande Berg, Lawrence A. Wenner, and Bruce E. Gronbeck. Boston: Houghton Mifflin, 2004.

"Reid Faults Time Changes, Shifts for 'Frank's Place' Drop; And Invites Gripes," *Jet*, 25 April 1988, 58.

Schulman, Norma M. "The House That Black Built: Television Stand-Up Comedy as Minor Discourse. *Journal of Popular Film and Television* 3 (fall 1994): 108–15.

———. "Laughing across the Color Line: In Living Color." *Journal of Popular Film and Television* 1 (spring 1992): 2–8.

Shales, Tom, and James Edward Miller. *Live from New York: An Uncensored History of "Saturday Night Live."* Boston: Little, Brown, 2002.

Smith, Karen M. "Advertising Discourse and the Marketing of I'll Fly Away." In *Mediated Messages and African American Culture*, edited by Venise Berry and Carmen Manning-Miller. Thousand Oaks, Calif.: Sage, 1996.

IV. TELEVISION NEWS

Broh, C. Anthony. *A Horse of a Different Color: Television's Treatment of Jesse Jackson's 1984 Presidential Campaign*. Washington, D.C.: Joint Center for Political Studies, 1987.

Dixon, Travis L. "Over-Representation and Under-Representation of African-American and Latino Lawbreakers on Television News." Ph.D. diss., University of California, Santa Barbara, 1998.

Entman, Robert. "Blacks in the News: Television, Modern Racism, and Cultural Change." *Journalism Quarterly* 69 (1991) :41–61.

———. "Modern Racism and the Images of Blacks in Local Television News." *Critical Studies in Mass Communications* 7 (December 1990): 4

———. "Representation and Reality in the Portrayal of Blacks on Network Television News." *Journalism Quarterly* 71 (1994): 9–20.

Entman, Robert M., and Andrew Rojecki, eds. *The Black Image in the White Media: Media and Race in America.* Chicago: University of Chicago Press, 2000.

O'Connor, John J. "Little Rock, 1957: 'Crisis at Central High.'" *New York Times,* 4 February 1981, C22.

Rada, James A. "Effects of Television News Portrayals of African Americans: The Consequent Altruism of Viewers." Ph.D. diss., University of Georgia, 1997.

Stone, Vernon. "Women Gain, Minorities Lose in TV News." In *Facing Difference: Race, Gender and Mass Media,* edited by Shirley Biagi and Marilyn Kern-Foxworth. Thousand Oaks, Calif.: Pine Forge Press, 1997.

Wood, Jennifer F. "House Negro versus Field Negro: The Inscribed Image of Race in Television News Representations of African-American Identity." In *Say It Loud! African-American Audiences, Media and Identity,* edited by Robin Means Coleman. New York: Routledge, 2002.

V. TELEVISION NETWORKS

Auletta, Ken. *Three Blind Mice: How the TV Networks Lost Their Way.* New York: Random House, 1991.

Banks, Jack. *Monopoly Television: MTV's Quest to Control the Music.* Boulder, Colo.: Westview Press, 1996.

Battaglio, Stephen. "Black Viewers Warm Up to Casting on WB, UPN." *Hollywood Reporter,* 7 March, 1996, 6.

———. "Fox Net Keeps Its Edge with Black Households. *Hollywood Reporter,* 21 March 1995, 4.

———. "Young Nets in the Hood: UPN, WB Wooing Blacks." *Hollywood Reporter,* 17–19 May 1996, 1.

Braxton, Greg. "Has NBC Given Up on Black Shows?" *Los Angeles Times,* 16 June 1993, F1.

Carter, Bill. "Two Upstart Networks Courting Black Viewers." *New York Times,* 7 October 1996, C11.

Denisoff, R. Serge. *Inside MTV*. New Brunswick, N.J.: Transaction Books, 1988.

Freeman, Mike. "Ratings Block Minority Syndicators." *Broadcasting and Cable*, 27 September 1993, 30–31.

Grossberg, Josh. "Method Man Raps Fox." www.eonline.com, 21 June 2004.

Jones, F. "The Black Audience and the BET Channel." *Journal of Broadcasting and Electronic Media* 34 (1990): 477–86.

Jones, Joyce. "BETing on Black." *Black Enterprise*, January 2001, 48.

Longino, Bill. "Big Four Beef Up Minority Roles, Changing the Face of Network TV." *Charlotte Observer*, 30 July 1997, E6.

Reed, Ishmael. "Tuning Out Network Bias." *New York Times*, 9 April 1991, op-ed.

Shales, Tom. "Beyond 'Benson,' Black-Oriented Channel from a Cable Pioneer." *Washington Post*, 30 November 1979, C1.

Siegel, Ed. "The Networks Go Ethnic." *Boston Globe*, 16 September 1989, Living/Arts, 7, 14.

Sterngold, James. "A Racial Divide Widens on Network TV." *New York Times*, 29 December 1998, A1.

Tait, Alice A., and John T. Barber. "Black Entertainment Television: Breaking New Ground and Accepting New Responsibilities." In *Mediated Messages and African-American Culture*, edited by Venise Berry and Carmen L. Manning-Miller. Thousand Oaks, Calif.: Sage, 1996.

Tyus, Jeffrey L. "Difference as the Norm: An Interpretive Study of the Audience for Black Sitcoms on the WB and UPN Network." Ph.D. diss., University of California, Santa Cruz, 1994.

Zook, Kristal Brent. *Color by Fox*. New York: Oxford University Press, 1999.

VI. PERSONALITIES

"Actor Ray Vitte Dies after Battling Police." *The Globe and Mail*, 22 February 1983, 20.

Aquirre, Holly. "Celebrities Online: Byron Allen Takes His Show on the Web." www.looksmart.com, 15 July 2002.

Browne, Margretta. "Interview: John Amos, The First Dad of Black Life Telling It Like It Is." www.blackfilm.com, 6 December 2004.

Farley, C. J. "Queen of All Media." *Time*, 5 October 1998, 82–85.

Finder, Chuck. "Picking Gumbel CBS' Super Call." *Pittsburgh Post-Gazette*, 29 January 2001, D5.

Fretts, Bruce. "What! Dave Chappelle Is What!?" *TV Guide*, 8–14 August 2004, 20–26.

Gabrielli, Betty. "Avery Brooks: The Man behind the Mask." *Alumni Magazine* (Oberlin College), summer 1997, www.oberlin.edu/alummag.

Gillespie, Dizzy, and Al Fraser. *To Bop or Not to Bop: Memoirs of Dizzy Gillespie*. Garden City, N.Y.: Doubleday.

Guillaume, Robert, with David Ritz. *Guillaume: A Life*. Columbia: University of Missouri Press, 2002.

Haag, Laurie L. "Oprah Winfrey: The Construction of Intimacy in the Talk Show Setting." *Journal of Popular Culture* 26(4, 1993): 115.

Harris, Joanne. "Catching Up with Kevin Hooks." *American Visions*, June–July 1998, 36.

Haskins, Jim. *Richard Pryor: A Man and His Madness*. New York: Beaufort Books, 1984.

Hauser, Thomas. *Muhammad Ali: His Life and Times*. New York: Simon & Schuster, 1991.

Hawkins, Walter L. *African American Biographies 2: Profiles of 332 Current Men and Women*. Jefferson, N.C.: McFarland, 1994.

Hiestand, Michael. "Scott Uses What He Can to His Advantage." *USA Today*, 16 February 1998, 2C.

Jackson, Carlton. *Hattie: The Life of Hattie McDaniel*. Lanham, Md.: Madison Books, 1990.

"J.J. Jackson: The Pioneering Veejay Gave Millions Even More Reason to Want Their MTV." *People Weekly*, 5 April 2004, 74.

Jones, Quincy. *The Autobiography of Quincy Jones*. New York: Random House, 2001.

Kanter, Hal. *So Far, So Funny: My Life in Show Business*. Jefferson, N.C.: McFarland, 1999.

Kaufman, Joanne. "Blair Underwood Sheds His L.A. Law Chic to Play Slain Civil Rights Activist James Chaney." *People Weekly*, 5 February 1990, 51–52.

King, Norman. *Everybody Loves Oprah: Her Remarkable Life Story*. New York: William Morrow, 1987.

Linden, Amy. "Queen Latifah: From Here to Royalty." *The Source*, August 1998, 154–60.

McClaurin-Allen, Irma. "Working: The Black Actress in the Twentieth Century Interview with Rosalind Cash." *Contributions in Black Studies: A Journal of African and Afro-American Studies* 8 (1987): 67–77.

Nichols, Nichelle. *Beyond Uhuru: Star Trek and Other Memories*. New York: Putnam's, 1994.

Poitier, Sidney. *The Measure of a Man: A Spiritual Autobiography*. San Francisco: HarperCollins, 2001.

Reid, Tim. "A Tale of Two Cultures: An Actor-Producer's Perspective during Black History Month." *Los Angeles Times*, 20–26 February 1994, TV Times, 1, 5.

Sellers, P. "The Business of Being Oprah: She Talked Her Way to the Top of Her Own Media Empire and Amassed a $1 Billion Fortune." *Fortune*, 1 April 2002, 50–64.

Sharkey, Betsy. "Doing the Woo with Ru." *Mediaweek*, 30 September 1996, 14.

Simon, George T. "Mahalia Jackson." In *Simon Says: The Sights and Sounds of the Swing Era, 1935–1955*. New York: Galahad Books, 1971.

Simonelli, Rocco. "Short Takes: Muhammad Ali." *Films in Review*, July/August 1996, 57.

Sinclair, A. "Martin Lawrence Blasted by Charles Dutton." *Amsterdam News*, 30 April 1994, 3.

"Smith, Whitten Feud over 'Fresh Prince' Exit." *Jet*, 30 August 1993, 59.

Smith, Yvonne. "Ntozake Shange: A 'Colored Girl' Considers Success." *Essence*, February 1982, 12.

Washington, Laurence. "Celebrity Interviews: James Earl Jones." www.Black flix.com/interviews, 11 August 2004.

"Where Are They Now? The Fresh Prince of Bel Air, 1990–1996." *People Weekly*, 26 June 2000, 84–88.

"Whitten Riled by Recent Firing from NBC-TV's 'Fresh Prince of Bel Air,'" *Jet*, 9 August 1993, 17.

Wilson Mary. *Dreamgirl: My Life as a Supreme*. New York: St. Martin's Press, 1986.

Wolff, Daniel. *You Send Me: The Life and Times of Sam Cooke*. New York: Quill/William Morrow, 1995.

VII. BILL COSBY AND *THE COSBY SHOW*

Budd, Mike, and Clay Steinman. "White Racism and The Cosby Show." *Jump Cut* 37 (1992): 12–14.

Christon, Lawrence. "The World According to Cos." *Los Angeles Times*, 10 December 1989, Calendar, 6, 45–47.

Cosby, William H., Jr. "50 Years of Blacks on TV." *Ebony* 51 (1, 1995): 215–17.

Downing, John. "'The Cosby Show' and American Racial Discourse." In *Discourse and Discrimination*, edited by Geneva Smitherman-Donaldson and T. van Dijk. Detroit: Wayne State University Press, 1988.

Dyson, Michael. "Bill Cosby and the Politics of Race." In *Get It Together: Reading about African-American Life*, edited by Akua Duku Anokye and Jacqueline Brice-French, pp. 237–43. New York: Longman, 2002.

Fuller, Linda K. *The Cosby Show: Audiences, Impact, and Implication.* Westport, Conn.: Greenwood, 1992.

Hartsough, Denise. "'The Cosby Show' in Historical Context: Explaining Its Appeal to Middle Class Women." Paper presented to the Ohio University Film Conference, Athens, 1989.

Inniss, Leslie B., and Joe R. Feagin. "'The Cosby Show': The View from the Black Middle Class." *Journal of Black Studies* 25 (1995): 692–711.

Jhally, Sut, and Justin Lewis. *Enlightened Racism: The Cosby Show, Audiences, and the Myth of the American Dream.* Boulder, Colo.: Westview Press, 1992.

McCain, Nia. "The Significance of Cosby." *Boston Globe*, 20 February 1986, Living Arts, 69–70.

Miller, Mark Crispin. "Cosby Knows Best." In *Boxed In: The Culture of TV*, edited by Mark Crispin Miller. Evanston, Ill.: Northwestern University Press, 1988.

Normant, Lynn. "The Cosby Show: The Real Life Drama behind Hit TV Show about a Black Family." *Ebony*, April 1985, 27–34.

Real, Michael. "Bill Cosby and Reading Ethnicity." In *Television Criticism: Approaches and Applications*, edited by Leah R. Vande Berg and Lawrence A. Wenner. London: Longman, 1991.

Smith, Ronald L. *Cosby.* New York: St. Martin's Press, 1986.

———. *Cosby: The Life of a Comedy Legend.* Amherst, N.Y.: Prometheus Books, 1997.

VIII. RACE

Bodroghkozy, Aniko. "'Is This What You Mean by Color TV?' Race, Gender, and Contested Meanings in NBC's *Julia*." In *Private Screenings: Television and the Female Consumer*, edited by Lynn Spigel and Denise Mann. Minneapolis: University of Minnesota Press, 1992.

Braxton, Greg. "Jackson Calls TV Racist, Urges Action." *Los Angeles Times*, 26 July 1994, B1.

Buckley, Gail Lumet. "When a Kiss Is Not Just a Kiss." *New York Times*, 31 March 1991, sec. 2, 1.

Cuklanz, Lisa M. *Race on Prime Time: Television, Masculinity, and Sexual Violence.* Philadelphia: University of Pennsylvania Press, 2000.

Deggans, Eric. "TV Reality Not Often Spoken of Race." *St. Petersburg Times*, 22 October 2004, 1E.

Gray, Herman. *Watching Race: Television and the Struggle for "Blackness."* Minneapolis: University of Minnesota Press, 1995.

Lambert, Pam. "What's Wrong with This Picture? Exclusion of Minorities Has Become a Way of Life in Hollywood." *People*, 18 March 1996, 41–52.

Lovell, Glenn. "Kissing in Color in Hollywood. Love Is Mostly a Segregated Thing." *Pittsburgh Post-Gazette*, 12 September 1994, C1.

O'Connor, John J. "Blacks' Vague Prime-Time Future." *New York Times*, 20 May 1996, C14.

———. "The Historic Challenge to Segregation." *New York Times*, 5 April 1991, C24.

"Profiling African Americans on TV (Past and Present)." *New York Beacon*, 13 March 2002, 29.

Stroman, C. A., B. D. Merritt, and P. W. Matabane. "Twenty Years after Kerner: The Portrayal of African Americans on Prime-Time Television." *Howard Journal of Communication* 2 (1989–1990): 44–56.

"TV's Ethnic Kissing Game." *Sun Reporter*, 20 September 1969, 4.

Zook, Kristal Brent. "Blackout: Charles Dutton Talks about Fox's Great Black Purge of '94." *Village Voice*, 28 June 1994, 51–54.

IX. WEBSITES

ABC Family Channel: www.abcfamily.go.com
African American Registry: www.aaregistry.com
Africana: The Gateway to the Black World: www.africana.com/articles
Afro Centric News Network: www.afrocentricnews.com
AllWatchers.com: www.allwatchers.com
American Broadcasting Company: www.abc.com
Arts and Entertainment Channel: www.aetv.com/tv
Black Entertainment Television: www.bet.com
BlackFlix.com: www.blackflix.com
Cable News Network: www.cnn.com
Children's Television Workshop: www.ctw.org
Columbia Broadcasting System: www.cbs.com
Comedy Central: www.comedycentral.com
Court Television: www.courtTV.com
DVD Talk: www.dvdtalk.com
DVD Town: www.dvdtown.com
Disney Channel: www.Disney.go.com
ESPN: www.espn.com
Film Review: http://filmreview.com

Fox Broadcasting: www.fox.com
Fox Sports Net: www.foxsports.com
Home Box Office: www.hbo.com
Internet Movie Database: www.imdb.com
Lexis Nexis: lexis-nexis.com
Lifetime: www.lifetimeTV.com
Looksmart: www.dvdlooksmart.com
MTV: www.mtv.com
Museum of Broadcast Communications: www.museum.tv/archives
National Broadcasting Company: www.nbc.com
Nick at Nite: www.nick-at-nite.com
Nickelodeon: www.nick.com
Oxygen Network: www.oxygen.com
Pop Matters: www.popmatters.com
ProQuest: www.proquest.umi.com
Public Broadcasting: www.pbs.org
Showtime: www.sho.com
TV Land: www.tvland.com
TV One Cable Network: www.tv-one.tv
TV Party: www.tvparty.com
TV Tome: www.tvtome.com
Turner Broadcasting: www.tbs.com
Turner Network Television: www.tnt.tv
UPN: www.upn.com
USA Network: www.usanetwork.com
VH1: www.vh1.com
WOUB Radio & Television: www.woub.org/tv
Warner Bros. Television: www.TheWB.com
Writers Guild of America: www.wga.org

About the Author

Kathleen Fearn-Banks, a tenured associate professor, joined the faculty of the School of Communications, University of Washington (Seattle) in 1990 after more than 25 years in the communications profession. In addition to being a feature writer at the *Los Angeles Times* and a news writer, producer, and reporter for a Los Angeles network affiliated television station, she also headed, for more than 20 years, nationwide publicity campaigns for NBC Television Network series, specials, and movies.

She was also vice president of development and public relations for the Neighbors of Watts, an entertainment industry nonprofit that raised funds for day care centers in underprivileged areas of Los Angeles.

In addition to her work in academia, Fearn-Banks counsels companies and organizations on crisis prevention and crisis communications and helps them develop crisis communications plans. In January 1999, she was elected "PR Professional of the Year" by the Seattle branch of the Public Relations Society of America (PRSA).

She is author of *Crisis Communications: A Casebook Approach* published first in 1996 by Lawrence Erlbaum Associates, Inc., and now in its second edition (2002). A third edition will be published in 2006. The book is popular as a business as well as a university text and is used in more than 50 colleges and universities. She is coeditor, with Anthony Chan, of *People to People: An Introduction to Mass Communications* published in 1997 by American Heritage Publishing, a division of Forbes, Inc.

In 2005, she was editor of a special crisis communications issue of the *Journal of Promotion Management*. She has written several articles for *Emmy Magazine*, the official magazine of the Academy of Television

Arts and Sciences, as well as articles for numerous other magazines, journals, and newspapers and several book chapters.

She was educated at Wayne State University, UCLA, and the University of Southern California. She is a Golden Lifetime member of Delta Sigma Theta Sorority, Inc., and a member of the Writers Guild of America.

ABOUT THE COVER ARTIST

Beverly Thomas has shared her artistic talents as a musician and educator for many years. She received a M.A. in organ performance from the University of Michigan, and after teaching music and serving as department head of fine arts and foreign language at Detroit's Mumford High School, she retired as principal of the award-winning Renaissance High School, also in Detroit.

A lifelong artist for her own relaxation and personal satisfaction, she traveled from 1988 through 1992 with her husband, African-American Episcopal Church Bishop Robert Thomas Jr., throughout South Africa. The experience greatly motivated her work as a serious artist. Thomas's expressive paintings have been exhibited in the United States, Canada, South Africa, and Namibia. She excels in painting on canvas with oils and acrylics and exciting pastel creations on paper. Her Limited Edition Collection Plate depicting the Isaiah 11:6 scripture trumpeting "peace" was introduced during her 1996 Louisville, Kentucky, art exhibition. Portions of all her art sales are donated to her special A.M.E. Church scholarships funds. Her work has been exhibited in galleries, as well as by several organizations, churches, and universities. She is a Golden Lifetime member of Delta Sigma Theta Sorority, Inc.